DRINK

A Social History
of America

Also by Andrew Barr

Wine Snobbery: An Insider's Guide to the Booze Business
Wine Snobbery: An Exposé
Pinot Noir
Drink: An Informal Social History

DRINK

A Social History of America

ANDREW BARR

CARROLL & GRAF PUBLISHERS, INC.
NEW YORK

First Carroll & Graf cloth edition 1999
First Carroll & Graf trade paperback edition 2000

Carroll & Graf Publishers, Inc.
19 West 21st Street
New York, NY 10010-6805

Library of Congress Cataloging-in-Publication data is available.
ISBN: 0-7867-0743-7

Manufactured in the United States of America

To Izzy and Melvin, for always being there

Acknowledgments

I should like to thank Ruth Barr, Elizabeth Board, Kent Carroll, Joseph Dorton, Peter Duff, Marcus Grant, Nigel Higgins, Elizabeth Holmgren, Peter Mitchell, Clive Morrick, Chris Morris, Harold Mulford, Carolyn Panzer, John Reed, Ann Rittenberg, Johanna Ryan, Mary J. Ryan, and Susan Wilkie for helping me beyond the call of duty.

Contents

Preface

I t is not generally appreciated how extreme American attitudes about alcohol appear from the other side of the Atlantic. There are not, in Britain, large areas of the country where the sale of alcoholic drinks is forbidden, even in the very places where they are made; preachers in Britain from the pulpit do not condemn the consumption of alcoholic beverages; police officers do not raid private houses because they have been informed that teenagers are drinking in them; pregnant women are not directed to abstain and charged with "fetal abuse" and incarcerated if they are thought to have flagrantly disobeyed this instruction; people who drink too much are not told that they are suffering from a disease that requires treatment and that even after they have been treated they will never be able to drink again, even in moderation. In its view of liquor, America is out of step with the rest of the Western world.

Yet the consumption of alcoholic drink has played a major role in American history. For colonists, it served to assert independence; for warring states, to affirm local diversity or national unity; for democrats, equality; for immigrants, identity; for women, emancipation; for the wealthy, status; for the country as a whole, civilization.

It is the ambition of this book to explain this dichotomy, the tendency to swing from one extreme to another, from prohibition to licence, from abstinence to revelry, from condemnation to celebration.

Drink: A Social History of America also has a wider purpose: to look at American culture through the prism of alcohol, to try to understand the history of the United States through its attitudes to liquor and its changing tastes in drink. For this reason, the approach is thematic rather than narrative: Each chapter deals with a specific topic, such as the different attitudes to drink and drugs, discrimination between male and female drinkers, and the distinction made by doctors and legislators between fermented drinks such as wine and distilled spirits. *Drink* is social history. Politics, economics, and technology are all considered, but in respect to the motivations of those involved.

Drink is history, but it is also polemic: It uses historical evidence to question the wisdom of prohibiting drink to children and to drivers and of banning drugs, and it encourages the development of healthier patterns of eating and drinking. While some of the opinions expressed may give pleasure, others may cause offense. In this respect, *Drink* follows the model established by its predecessor, *Wine Snobbery,* which was described by one reviewer as "a book to hurl against the floor but which bounces back, demanding your attention."

Andrew Barr
London
October 1998

DRINK

A Social History
of America

A MORAL AND PHYSICAL THERMOMETER.

A scale of the progress of Temperance and Intemperance.—Liquors with effects in their usual order.

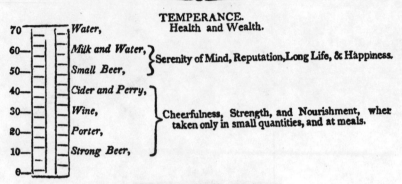

TEMPERANCE.
Health and Wealth.

70 — Water,	
60 — Milk and Water,	} Serenity of Mind, Reputation, Long Life, & Happiness.
50 — Small Beer,	
40 — Cider and Perry,	
30 — Wine,	} Cheerfulness, Strength, and Nourishment, when taken only in small quantities, and at meals.
20 — Porter,	
10 — Strong Beer,	
0 —	

INTEMPERANCE.

	VICES.	DISEASES.	PUNISHMENTS.
0			
10 — Punch,	Idleness, Gaming,	Sickness,	Debt.
20 — Toddy and Egg Rum,	peevishness,	Tremors of the hands in the morning, puking,	Jail.
30 — Grog—Brandy and Water,	quarrelling Fighting,	bloatedness, Inflamed eyes, red nose	Black eyes, and Rags,
40 — Flip and Shrub,	Horse-Racing,	and face, Sore and swelled legs,	Hospital or Poor house.
50 — Bitters infused in Spirits and Cordials.	Lying and Swearing,	jaundice, Pains in the hands, burn-	Bridewell.
60 — Drams of Gin, Brandy, and Rum, in the morning,	Stealing & Swindling,	ing in the hands, and feet Dropsy, Epilepsy,	State prison
70 — The same morning and ning. The same during day & night,	Perjury, Burglary, Murder,	Melancholy, palsy, appo-plexy, Madness, Despair,	do. for Life. Gallows.

Drink and Drugs

When Columbus and his followers arrived in America, they found its inhabitants indulging in witchcraft. At least that was how the God-fearing Europeans interpreted the Amerindian[1] religious ceremony in which a shaman entered into a trance in order to communicate with the spirit world and bring back information for his tribe. The shaman did not usually enter into his trance spontaneously, but drank infusions made from hallucinogenic plants or smoked the leaves of the plant that later became known to the Europeans as tobacco. Once in the spirit world, the shaman spoke in tongues: He appeared to be possessed, and described what he saw in a voice that was not his own. This was recognized by the Eur-

---

[1] In this book the terms "Indian" and "Amerindian" have been used in preference to "Native American." Those people who insist on employing the latter term have succeeded, under the guise of political correctness, in replacing one misnomer for another. The description "Native American" properly applies to anyone who was born in the United States. It was frequently used in the nineteenth century to distinguish Americans of European extraction who were born in the country from more recent immigrants. Amerindians themselves generally do not object to being described as "Indians," although they prefer a reference to the specific tribe from which they come.

opeans as diabolic possession, and they took care not to investigate the matter any further.

If its role in helping shamans to enter another world had been the only purpose for which Amerindians had smoked tobacco, then it would probably never have been adopted by Europeans. But tobacco was also employed in America as a cure for the diseased persons on whose behalf the shaman had embarked on his spiritual travels. This the Europeans could understand—that tobacco could be used as a medicine. The men who traveled to the New World believed that they would find remedies for all sorts of diseases among its flora, even a panacea that would cure all of them. From the succor that it gave to the Indians, there seemed every prospect that tobacco was the plant for which they had been looking. In his *Joyful News out of the New Found World,* the Spanish physician Nicholas Monardes claimed that the Indians took tobacco to treat colds; pains in the chest, stomach, and joints; kidney stones; toothache; chilblains; worms and sores; and that it enabled them to keep going when tired and to do without food or drink for days on end.

By interesting themselves in the medical but not shamanic aspects of tobacco smoking, European travelers were divorcing the cure from its context. This led to a debate back in the Old World between those who regarded tobacco as a miraculous new medicine—a gift from God—and those who thought it was the opposite, an instrument of the devil, who had given it to the Indians in order to produce deceptive hallucinations. The opponents of tobacco found it hard to understand how civilized people should have been so quick to adopt a custom from mere "savages."[2] King James I of England (King James VI of Scotland), who imagined himself as something of an intellectual, published anonymously a pamphlet entitled *A Counterblast to Tobacco* in which he wondered why good English people should want to imitate "the barbarous and beastly manners of the wild, godless, and slavish Indians," and described smoking as "a custom loathsome to the eye, hateful to the nose, dangerous to the lungs, and in the black stinking fume thereof nearest resembling the horrible Stygian smoke of the pit that is bottomless."

James was especially concerned because his subjects had converted

---

[2]When the pipe emerged as a symbol of British sophistication in the nineteenth century, scholars tried to demonstrate that it had not originated among Amerindians after all but had an honorable pedigree in an Old World civilization.

from smoking tobacco as medicine to indulging in the practice for pleasure. In the same year as he published his pamphlet, he ordered that the import duty on tobacco be raised by 4,000 percent, on the grounds that "whereas tobacco . . . was used and taken by the better sort . . . only as a physic to preserve health, [it] is now at this day, through evil custom and the toleration thereof, excessively taken by a number of riotous and disordered persons of mean and base condition, who, contrary to the use which persons of good calling and quality make thereof, do spend most of their time in that idle vanity." James believed that by raising the duty on tobacco to a prohibitively high level he would put a stop to recreational smoking, and restrict consumption to medicinal purposes. It did not work. People smuggled tobacco into England, evading customs duty. So James reduced the tax (although not to its original level) and farmed out the right to collect it to one of his favorites, in return for a large annual fee. Distributors and retailers took to stretching their stocks of tobacco with the ground-up leaves of other plants, forcing James to introduce a system of inspection, thus establishing himself as the guardian of the purity of a drug that, a few years earlier, he had tried to suppress.

The English experience was repeated across the rest of northern Europe. In the first half of the seventeenth century, most northern European countries had adopted laws forbidding trading in tobacco or smoking it or both; in most cases the penalties were relatively small fines, but Russia tried more severe measures, prescribing at various times whippings, slit noses, torture, deportation to Siberia, and death. These restrictions all proved ineffective. Instead, the English experience was repeated: Prohibition of tobacco did not work, so why not legalize it and tax it instead? By the end of the seventeenth century, tobacco was legal throughout Europe.

In colonial America, tobacco assumed even greater economic importance. The settlement of Virginia would probably have failed had it not been for the cultivation of tobacco. Most of the people who emigrated there from Europe in the first quarter of the seventeenth century either died of summer fever or starved to death in the winter. The first successful tobacco crop was grown in 1612 by John Rolfe, now better remembered as the husband of Pocahontas. Within a generation, Virginians had become wealthy on their new produce; and the revenue from this colony, along with money raised from taxes on tobacco at home, ensured that the English king abandoned all complaints about smoking. People were less concerned about arguing that tobacco was the devil's doing once they realized how much money they could make from it.

Why, it might be wondered, had tobacco become so popular a drug in Europe that it had defeated all attempts to ban it, and had been responsible for the success of the Virginia colony? Its opponents believed it had won favor for similar reasons as alcohol. Both were believed to have medical properties if used in moderation but to be dangerous if enjoyed to excess.[3] As in the case of alcoholic drinks, it was all too easy to overindulge in tobacco as "a point of good fellowship." Excessive consumption of tobacco was regarded as a form of gluttony, and a "branch of the sin of drunkenness."

Although tobacco helped Indian shamans to travel in their imaginings to another world, Europeans found that it helped them to bear the world in which they actually lived. Nicotine, the principal drug in tobacco, exerts a biphasic effect. Different doses act differently. A small dose (a short puff) excites the smoker, while a large one (a long drag) calms him down. Both of these effects—stimulation and sedation— were ones that Europeans found helpful in coping with the outside world.[4]

The contrasting purposes for which Europeans and Amerindians used tobacco were exemplified by the different strains of the plant they developed. As well as the English in Virginia, other European nations established tobacco industries in their American colonies: the French in the West Indies, the Spanish in Venezuela, the Portuguese in Brazil. Because European settlers in North America would not smoke Indian tobacco, the tobacco that had been produced in European colonies in the Americas for export to Europe was reexported to North America for consumption by Europeans in those areas where they had first encountered Indians smoking it. European explorers and traders also brought tobacco with them when they traveled to America, to give to the natives. Although the Amerindians had their own supply, protocol

---

[3]The medical uses of alcohol are discussed in Chapter 4.

[4]Alcohol exerts a similar biphasic action, which has conventionally been attributed to psychological factors. It is said that alcohol is a depressant, which in small doses disinhibits people by suppressing feelings of anxiety and insecurity, making them more lively and sociable; larger doses depress them. Current research, however, suggests that there may also be chemical factors in the stimulating effects of alcohol: that it releases endogenous opioids, or that the body anticipates its depressive effects by raising its own level of arousal. The way that people learn how to respond to alcohol is discussed later in this chapter and in Chapter 3.

dictated that a pipe ceremony and gifts of tobacco preceded barter exchange. But the Indians would not smoke Virginia tobacco, so the English and French, who produced large quantities of cheap tobacco in their American colonies, were obliged to import tobacco from Brazil to give to Amerindians who produced plenty of tobacco themselves.

Europeans did not like Indian tobacco, nor Indians Virginia tobacco, because they were different. Whereas the Indians had deliberately, over successive generations, developed strains of tobacco with the highest nicotine content and the greatest hallucinatory powers, European planters took care to produce tobacco with a lower nicotine content. They had no interest in using tobacco to enter a trance, but as a means of obtaining mildly stimulating and tranquilizing effects.

In addition to tobacco, European settlers and traders brought gifts for Indians of which the latter had no knowledge.[5] The first recorded consumption of alcohol by Indians occurred in 1609, when an expedition led by the English navigator Henry Hudson encountered some Indians on an island in the bay of New York. The account of this meeting that had been handed down among the Indians themselves was written down two centuries later by a Moravian missionary named John Heckewelder, who had been told the story by a Delaware he knew and trusted. According to this account, some Indians who were out fishing noticed at a great distance a large object floating on the water, of a kind they had never before seen. They returned to the shore and told the other members of their tribe. Together they hurried back out to sea. They all saw the object but could not agree what it was. Some said that it was an uncommonly large fish or animal, others that it was a big house floating on the sea. They decided they had better send messengers to warn the other Indian tribes in the neighborhood. The chiefs and warriors of these tribes came to look for themselves. Collectively they concluded that the object was a large house in which the manitou—the Supreme Being—was coming to see them. They instructed their shamans to interpret this visitation, but the shamans were unable to tell them what it meant. They could see, however, as the house approached, that it was full of human beings, of a different color from the Indians, and strangely clothed, and that one of them was dressed entirely in red, who must surely be the manitou himself.

---

[5]Some Indian tribes did know mildly alcoholic fermented drinks but none knew spirits. Indian drinks are discussed in the next chapter.

In time, the house stopped, and a canoe came onshore with the man in red clothes and some others in it. The manitou greeted the Indians in a language they did not understand, and his servants poured an unknown substance from a bottle into a cup. He drank the contents of the cup, then ordered it to be refilled and handed it to the chief standing next to him. The chief smelled it but did not drink the contents before passing it round the other chiefs, who did the same. It was about to be returned to the manitou without anyone having drunk it, when one warrior started to harangue the assembly on the impropriety of so doing. Surely this might cause offense to the manitou, provoking him to bring down his wrath on all of them? It was for the good of the Indian nation as a whole that the contents should be drunk and, if no one else would do it, then the warrior would do so himself, whatever the consequences might be, for it was better that one man should die than a whole nation be destroyed. The warrior took the cup, bade farewell to the rest of the Indians, and drank the contents. He soon began to stagger, and then fell onto the ground. His companions thought he had died. In fact, he had fallen asleep. When he awoke, he jumped up and declared that he had enjoyed the most delicious sensations and had never felt so happy as after he had drunk the cup. He asked for more, and was given it; the rest of the Indians followed his example, and they all became drunk.

As a result, says Heckewelder, the Delaware called the place "the island where we all got drunk"—in their own language, *Manahach-tanienk,* later corrupted to "Manhattan." Unfortunately for this tale, it is now generally believed that the name "Manhattan" means "island of the hills." And it is more likely that the story condensed into one incident the general reaction of the Indians to alcohol than accurately relates the events that occurred at the first meeting with Hudson's expedition—although it is clear, from Hudson's own account, that some of the Indian chiefs he met did try both wine and spirits, and did get drunk.

The Indians assumed that alcoholic drinks served the same purpose as hallucinogenic plants and tobacco, and treated them in the same way. They imagined that they were possessed of magical powers, which would be made available to the drinker only if he consumed them in sufficient quantity to fall entirely under their influence. The Indians therefore drank spirits, not by the shot, but by the bottle. According to the first English-language description of New York, written sixty years after Hudson's expedition, the local Indian tribesmen "are great lovers of strong drink, yet they do not care for drinking unless they have enough to make themselves drunk; and if there be so many in their company that there is not sufficient to make them all drunk, they usually select so many out of their company, proportionable to the quantity of drink, and the rest must be spectators. And if any one chance to be drunk before he hath finished his proportion (which is ordinarily a quart of brandy, rum or strong waters[6]) the rest will pour the rest of his part down his throat."

European immigrants took advantage of the Indian propensity to drink alcohol to the point of insensibility in order to persuade them, while in a drunken state, to part with their lands and goods. At the signing of the Treaty of Easton in 1758, in which the Indians gave up claims to huge tracts of land, the colonial negotiators kept them supplied from beginning to end with as much as they could drink. As Governor George Thomas of Pennsylvania had observed a few years earlier, "Our traders . . . take advantage of their inordinate appetite for it to cheat them out of their skins and their wampum[7], which is their money, and often to debauch their wives into the bargain. Is it to be wondered at, then, if when they recover from the drunken fit, they should take severe revenges?"[8]

Although the Europeans who traveled to America in the seventeenth and eighteenth centuries responded differently to alcohol and tobacco from the Indian tribes they found there, their ancestors had behaved very much like the Indians. In prehistoric times Europe, like North America, had been populated by tribes whose recreation and rituals centered around the smoking of narcotic drugs rather than the consumption of alcoholic drinks. Europeans converted from a smoking to a drinking culture as a result of the spread of agriculture beyond its origins in the Near and Middle East. Shamanism survived in America long after it had died out in Europe because Amerindian societies were essentially hunter-gatherers, and prowess in hunting was believed to be based on the supernatural powers with which shamans were supposed to be able to communicate. European societies had lost this aspect of their culture when they had become agricultural.

It is possible that some wine was made from wild grapes by preag-

---

[6]Any other kind of distilled liquor.
[7]Bead belts.
[8]Not all Indian tribes had a problem with handling alcohol.

ricultural hunter-gatherer communities in Europe or the Near or Middle East, since the ability of grapes to ferment and to turn into wine must originally have been discovered by accident. But the systematic production of wine on a sufficient scale for it to become a staple of the diet would have been impossible before the development of agriculture. It is believed that this transition—from wild vines to cultivated ones as part of the development of an agricultural society—took place sometime in the fifth millennium B.C.

Cultivated vines produce wine of better quality and flavor and higher alcohol content than wild ones. They do, however, require a long-term investment, as they take several years to produce their best crops. They have to be tended throughout the season, and the wine made from them has to be watched carefully during fermentation and storage. A settled agricultural society is far better suited to the production of wine than a mobile hunter-gatherer one.

In time, the production of wine came to serve as a marker of a sophisticated agricultural society. This provides the most likely explanation of why Muslims—the followers of the prophet Mohammed—were forbidden to drink alcohol. This prohibition was supposedly imposed following an incident that occurred while the prophet's disciples were drinking together after a dinner in Medina. One of his Meccan followers began to recite an uncomplimentary poem about the tribe of Medina, whereupon one of his Medinite followers picked up a bone from the table and hit the Meccan on the head. Although the wound was not serious, the incident caused Mohammed such concern that he asked Allah how he could prevent it from happening again. Allah replied, "Believers, wine and games of chance, idols and divining arrows are abominations devised by Satan. Avoid them, so that you may prosper. Satan seeks to stir up enmity and hatred among you by means of wine and gambling, and to keep you from the remembrance of Allah and from your prayers."

Like most legends, this story simplifies a deeper truth. By the time of the prophet (the seventh century A.D.) wine had been the traditional inebriant of Near Eastern cultures for thousands of years. But now the balance of power in the region was being transferred from the sophisticated vine-growing agricultural societies of the river valleys and the Mediterranean coast to the desert tribes, who followed the prophet. These tribes expressed their cultural values by replacing wheeled vehicles with camels, by substituting chairs and tables with cushions and brass trays on folding wooden frames, and by prohibiting the eating of pork and the drinking of wine. They condemned wine because of its symbolic importance to the people they had conquered, who had incorporated it into their religious rituals. Wine was consumed in the central ceremony of the Christian faith as a symbol of Christ's blood, which he had offered to his disciples at the Last Supper.[9] It served as a cultural marker for Christianity. The prophet Mohammed forbade his followers to drink wine in order to distinguish his faith from the Christian one.

Just as Muslims rejected wine because of its association with a rival creed, so the Christian Church proscribed the narcotic drugs used ceremonially by the older, pagan religions. A monotheistic, statist faith such as Christianity was put in danger by shamanistic rituals, because the information brought back from the spirit world might not agree with official teaching and could well be subversive. Between the fourth and eighth centuries A.D., kings and chiefs across Europe converted to Christianity, and replaced shamans as advisers and leaders of sacred ceremony with Christian priests. The mass of the population soon followed. Because they were already used to worshiping a multitude of gods, they readily accepted the Christian God as part of their pantheon. But then they found that the Church insisted that they give up all their old religions. The disparate mixture of cults to which they had been devoted could not make common cause against the new monotheistic faith, so disappeared.[10]

Some historians have attempted to argue that the populace retained its pagan beliefs for several centuries, until the Christian Church finally lost its patience and suppressed them by force, in the witch burnings of the Middle Ages. There is no evidence for this. It is possible that medieval witches employed some vestiges of old pagan and shamanistic practices, but this is different from saying that they were surviving practitioners of a pre-Christian religion. This said, the Church burned witches because they represented competition in the same way as the

---

[9] The role of wine in Christian ritual is discussed in the Conclusion.

[10] A thousand years later, Indian tribes in North America were also compelled by the Christian Church to abandon their shamanistic rituals. The peyote ceremony, which was imported into the United States from Mexico in the late nineteenth century by the Kiowa and Comanche, is not shamanism but a type of Christianity in which the ingestion of the hallucinogenic peyote cactus enables the worshiper to communicate directly with God, without the medium of a priest. This ceremony is an invented, sanitized tradition, comparable to the Scottish kilt, the Welsh eisteddfod, and the lavish ceremonial of the English monarchy.

old pagan religions. Just as, during the Dark Ages, the Church had regarded the shamanic practices of pagan religions as the work of the devil, so, too, during the Middle Ages, did it consider satanic any practices that incorporated shamanistic elements or relied on visions induced by hallucinogenic drugs.

It is a matter of dispute among historians whether witchcraft did incorporate some residual elements of earlier shamanistic practices. Relatively little is known about what the witches themselves thought and did, because history is written by the victors and the witches were the victims. The activities of European witches did resemble the rituals of the shamans of other cultures. The one thing that most people know today about them is that they sat on broomsticks and flew through the air. The ability to fly has been, and remains today, an attribute of shamans in many societies; it is symbolized by the birdlike costumes of Siberian shamans. Of course, the shamans do not actually fly; flight serves as a metaphor for their ability to travel from the material to the spiritual world.

The witches did not really fly either. But they imagined that they did, having excited their imagination by rubbing their bodies with hallucinogenic plants such as henbane, mandrake, and belladonna (deadly nightshade). The purpose of the broomstick was probably suggestive: It influenced the effect of the drugs, encouraging the witch to believe that she was flying through the air to a "sabbath," where she would participate in orgiastic encounters with demons.[11]

As far as the Church was concerned, however, witches performed real magic, a manifestation of the power the devil had given them in exchange for their loyalty. Whereas Catholic churches had their own forms of ritual to compete with witchcraft, the new Protestant churches that emerged in the sixteenth century had abandoned most of the Catholic ceremonies and had no magic of their own to offer the populace.

Witchcraft posed a particular problem for the Protestant churches in New England, an area that in the opinion of ministers had belonged to the devil until God sent the English along. The Indians belonged to the devil, and their shamanistic rituals were the devil's work. At the

---

[11]The term "sabbath" was taken from Judaism, then regarded, like witchcraft, as a form of anti-Christianity. Despite the modern popular belief that witches were female, they could also be male, but the vast majority of those accused of witchcraft were women, because they were less well able to defend themselves.

Salem witch trials in 1692, people who said they had seen the devil insisted that he looked just like an Indian.

The Salem trials were the last gasp of the witch craze. From the beginning of the eighteenth century, the tendency to attribute the inexplicable to the work of malevolent forces was swept away by the new ideas of the Enlightenment and the development of a belief in natural explanations for apparently supernatural phenomena.

At the same time, the sort of hallucinogenic plants to which the witches had been attracted came to be put to a different use. Just as European travelers to America had ignored the use of tobacco in shamanic rituals by Amerindians but adopted it for medical purposes, so, too, they treated purely as medicines a number of other plants that were possessed of powerful hallucinogenic potential. This was especially true of opium, which was regarded by doctors in the eighteenth and nineteenth centuries as a panacea.[12] In America, as in Europe, opium was used to dull pain, induce sleep, control insanity, alleviate coughing, stop diarrhea, and to treat a wide range of communicable diseases, including malaria, smallpox, syphilis, and tuberculosis. Benjamin Franklin regularly took laudanum (a solution of opium in wine) in order to alleviate the pain of kidney stones during the last few years of his life. When Alexander Hamilton was shot in a duel with his rival, Aaron Burr, and lay dying with a bullet in his spine, it was for the laudanum bottle that his physician reached to assuage his suffering.

At first sight the argument that Europeans and Americans of European stock were not interested in the hallucinogenic potential of opium but only its analgesic power would appear to be contradicted by those celebrated literary works in which the hallucinogenic properties of opium were made all too clear. In his *Confessions of an Opium-Eater,* published in 1822, Thomas De Quincey publicized the vision-inducing potential of the drug; Samuel Taylor Coleridge was inspired by opium when he wrote his most famous poem, *Kubla Khan.* But they did not use opium for its pleasurable effects; they took it for medical reasons. De Quincey took opium to counteract stomach pains and to ward off tuberculosis, of which he thought he was beginning to show symptoms. Coleridge took opium for toothache; in 1797, when he wrote *Kubla*

---

[12]The difference between tobacco and opiates is that the use of tobacco as a medicine was quickly forgotten, whereas it was the use of opiates for nonmedical purposes that was largely ignored.

Khan, he was using it to mitigate the pain of dysentery as well as to free his mind from financial worries. Other writers of this period, too, took opium not so much to encourage literary creativity as to treat the illnesses or the anxiety that threatened to stifle it. Charles Dickens turned to opium after suffering both psychologically and physically on his reading tour of America, and wrote about the drug's effects in 1870 in his unfinished novel *The Mystery of Edwin Drood.*

The one American writer of this period who subsequently became famous for taking opium was Edgar Allan Poe. Or, rather, the legend has developed that Poe was an opium addict. Certainly there are passages in his letters that can be read as describing addiction or withdrawal symptoms, and his writings contain numerous references to opium. But there is no evidence that he was addicted to it. Poe, who was an alcoholic, took opium only occasionally, and for the same reason as other people—as an all-purpose painkiller.

Poe, like Franklin and Hamilton before him, would most likely have taken his opium dissolved in a solution of alcohol. In the second half of the nineteenth century, however, the method of administration changed. The hypodermic syringe was introduced for injecting morphine, an opium derivative. Injection produced stronger and quicker results, with fewer side effects. But it also tended to lead to addiction, especially when used to treat chronic ailments. This created a major problem in the South, where morphine was employed to treat endemic diseases such as malaria and diarrhea, as well as the lingering trauma of the Civil War. Throughout the country, people took morphine to alleviate pain and found that even after the pain had gone, they were unable to abandon the drug. Eugene O'Neill, whose mother had suffered in this manner, later dramatized the experience in *Long Day's Journey into Night.*

Another cause of the growing use of opiates in the second half of the nineteenth century was the increasing popular disapproval of alcohol, which led to prohibition in a number of states.[13] Popular hostility to the recreational use of alcoholic drinks encouraged many people to use opium instead, especially among the upper classes, who wished to dissociate themselves from the lower-class connotations of liquor and drunkenness. It was also suggested that the older members of the community were more inclined to take drugs, while younger

---

[13]Aspects of state prohibition in the nineteenth century are mentioned in Chapters 3, 4, and 5.

people drank alcohol (an inversion of present-day preferences). The American delegation reported to the International Opium Commission in Shanghai in 1909 that in some American states "there has been an enormous growth of the morphine habit, especially in rural communities where the sterility in social life has driven the elderly members of the communities to this habit. A large percentage of this class have become addicted to the morphine habit largely as a result of sincere objection to the use of alcohol in any of its forms."[14]

Of course, saying that people sought release in opiates because they did not feel that they could be seen drinking alcohol is not the same thing as saying that given a straight choice between the two, they would still have preferred the opiates. It is also likely that some of the men who favored opium over alcohol did so because it was harder to detect, rather than because they regarded it as less disreputable. "The gentleman who would not be seen in a bar-room, however respectable, or who would not purchase liquor and use it at home, lest the odor might be detected upon his person, procures his supply of morphia and has it in pocket ready for instantaneous use," observed the *Catholic World* in 1881. "It is odorless and occupies but little space . . . He zealously guards his secret from his nearest friend—for popular wisdom has branded as a disgrace that which he regards as a misfortune."

In the later years of the nineteenth century, attitudes began to change, and opium started to attract a greater degree of disapproval than alcohol. The spread of opium dens in the Chinese sectors of American cities led people to associate the drug with the poverty, strangeness, and unsanitary living conditions of these areas. From this it was deduced that the use of opium had contributed to the decline of China from its former splendors and to its torpor in the face of Western expansion.

The spread of opium dens also encouraged the idea that the drug was disreputable. The dens were patronized only by the Chinese and by members of the underworld. No ordinary white person would have chosen to go to an opium den because the recreational use of the drug automatically designated the user as a member of a deviant subculture.

Up to this point, comparisons by doctors of alcohol and opiates had tended to favor the latter. As a Dr. J. R. Black explained in an article entitled "Advantages of Substituting the Morphia Habit for the In-

---

[14]Many women also chose opiates in preference to alcohol for the same reason, as discussed in Chapter 3.

curably Alcoholic," morphine "is less inimical to healthy life than alcohol . . . [it] calms in place of exciting the baser passions, and hence is less productive of acts of violence and crime; in short . . . the use of morphine in place of alcohol is but a choice of evils, and by far the lesser."[15] Opiates seemed more respectable than alcohol because they did not lead to violence. On the other hand, they were more debilitating. They enslaved the user. It was said that "It is not the man who eats opium, but it is opium that eats the man." People who used opiates were less productive; they were a drag on society. This helps explain why, after a flirtation with opiates in the second half of the nineteenth century, respectable people generally came to the conclusion that they preferred to take alcohol. They did not want to take a drug that made its user passive and introspective when it was an American characteristic to prize liveliness and sociability. The qualities that were most appreciated in American society—action, aggression, competition—were represented by alcohol, not by opiates.

By the beginning of the twentieth century, opium was much less useful as a medicine than previously. New drugs had been developed that fulfilled the same functions with less risk. Instead of taking opium as an analgesic, it was now possible to take aspirin; in place of opium as a sedative, barbiturates were available. There was no longer any need for general over-the-counter sales of opium in pharmacies. Apart from a few people who were widely regarded as deviants, there was no constituency to argue in favor of the recreational use of opiates. Opium derivatives such as morphine and heroin were now understood to be addictive. The consumption of heroin had come to be associated with violent behavior by unemployed youths in the cities. It seemed obvious that the use of these drugs for anything other than strictly medical purposes should be banned. Modern drug controls on opiates, as well as coca and its derivative cocaine, were introduced in 1914.

These restrictions were soon followed by a ban on alcohol. During national Prohibition between 1920 and 1933, the trade in alcohol, like that in drugs, was limited to medical purposes, and its manufacture and sale for recreational purposes was illegal. The different attitudes that the majority of Americans now held toward alcohol and drugs were amply demonstrated during this period, when there was no reason to choose one over the other on grounds of legality.

---

[15]Even as late as the 1930s and early 1940s older physicians in Kentucky were converting alcoholics to morphine.

Alcohol consumption did decrease during Prohibition, by about one third, but not because of any general desire to respect the law that banned it. Consumption fell because the illicit nature of the trade in alcohol caused the price to increase markedly.[16] Prohibition did not stop people from drinking if they wanted and could afford to do so. Even the highest in the land disregarded the embargo. The president, Warren Harding, might have shrunk away from having alcoholic drinks served openly at official dinners, but he made sure that cocktails were offered in the upstairs hall outside his room before them.

Some people feared that the introduction of Prohibition would cause people to turn to drugs, but there is no evidence that this happened. In 1929, during the debate in Congress on a bill that proposed tougher penalties for bootleggers, Senator James A. Reed of Missouri, the leader of the pro-alcohol faction, stated it as a fact that drug addiction had increased during Prohibition. Well, he would, wouldn't he?[17]

Contemporaries were all too ready to assume that people started taking drugs as a result of the ban on alcohol, and historians have been all too eager to follow them. There is no evidence, however, that drug use increased during Prohibition. The number of opiate addicts had been in decline since the end of the nineteenth century, and, although the smoking of marijuana became more common in the 1920s, this was directly attributable to increased immigration from Mexico.

This said, the prohibition of drugs proved no more effective than the prohibition of alcohol. By the 1930s the public had withdrawn its support for alcohol Prohibition, which was repealed. Yet, if anything, the public increased its support for the prohibition of drugs. Whereas alcohol was drunk by a substantial proportion of the population and by all classes, opiate use was now thought to be concentrated in a small criminal subculture.

Between the late nineteenth century and the 1960s, only an insignificant fraction of the American population indulged in the recrea-

---

[16]In the first years of Prohibition consumption had fallen still further, to one third of its previous level, because it took the illegal trade some time to organize itself.
[17]The comment made in a British court by Mandy Rice-Davies in 1963 when told that Lord Astor had denied any impropriety in his relationship with her. Astor had introduced Rice-Davies and her friend Christine Keeler to the minister of war, John Profumo. Keeler had embarked on an affair with Profumo, who was married, while at the same time sleeping with the Russian naval attaché. The story was later portrayed in the film *Scandal*.

tional use of drugs. This practice was considered aberrant by the majority of Americans because it was largely restricted to outsiders: Chinese and Mexicans, gamblers and prostitutes, and later jazz musicians and hippies. During this period, the use of drugs was a symbol of deviancy. People who were regarded as disreputable by the rest of society even went so far as to assert their status by deliberately taking drugs. Most of the criminals who took drugs committed their crimes before they started using them.

It is true that in the last two generations a substantial proportion of young middle-class people have begun to take drugs for recreational purposes. But this does not mean that the practice has ceased to be considered aberrant. Young people take drugs precisely because these are thought bad by their parents and other authority figures. Drug taking is a means of rebelling against the prevailing values of American society.

In the 1960s and 1970s young people began to take drugs for a variety of reasons: They wanted to demonstrate their rejection of the world they were meant to inherit and to focus on their own individual pleasure at the expense of their perceived social duty. Because drug taking was a symbolically deviant act, many people were indiscriminate in the substances they consumed, and would move freely from one to another ("polypharmacy"). This said, the most popular drug of the period was marijuana, which was considered less dangerous than chemicals, and benefited from familiarity with cigarette smoking.[18] It also achieved the desired effect. The National Commission on Marijuana and Drug Abuse reported in 1972 that "use of the drug is linked with idleness, lack of motivation, hedonism, and sexual promiscuity. Many see the drug as fostering a counterculture that conflicts with basic moral precepts as well as with the operating functions of our society. The 'dropping out' or rejection of the established value system is viewed with alarm. Marijuana becomes more than a drug; it becomes a symbol of the rejection of cherished values."

Many of the young people who took up marijuana in this period were explicitly reacting against their parents' increased consumption of alcohol. Between 1960 and 1980 the quantity of spirits and beer drunk in the United States each year doubled, and the amount of wine

---

[18]Moves to legalize marijuana are discussed in Chapter 5. Some hippies believed that these were part of a conspiracy to deprive them of their pleasure in rebelling against the law.

trebled. Just as, during Prohibition, young people drank alcohol as a mark of rebellion against the laws that associated the consumption of alcohol with illegality and vice,[19] so in the 1960s and 1970s they smoked marihuana as a symbol of defiance because alcohol had cemented its place as the legal drug of respectable society.[20]

The differences between the effects of alcohol and marijuana are obvious to anyone who compares them. The anthropologist G. M. Carstairs spent 1951 living in a large village in the state of Rajasthan in northern India. The ruling caste, the Rajputs, were fighting men with certain prerogatives, notably the right to eat meat and drink alcohol, the latter in the form of a spirit called *daru*. They were taught to put great stress on individual bravery in the face of danger. This danger was seldom met, but every young Rajput lived with the anxiety that he might not prove adequate to the occasion when it finally came. He was therefore inclined to assuage his worries in the convivial relaxation of a drinking party.

The members of the other top caste group in the village, the Brahmans, denounced the use of *daru,* which they said was inimical to the religious life. "The result of eating meat and drinking liquor," declared one of them, "is that you get filled with passion and rage, and then the spirit of God flies out from you." The Brahmans were often intoxicated, but with *bhang,* an infusion of marijuana leaves and stems, which they believed enhanced the spiritual life. They said that this gave good *bhakti,* a devotional act that consisted in emptying the mind of all worldly distractions and thinking only of God. The Rajputs did not condemn *bhang* as fiercely as the Brahmans denounced *daru,* but, as one of them pointed out, *bhang* "makes you quite useless, unable to do anything. *Daru* isn't like that, you may be drunk but you can still carry on."

Carstairs suggested that Westerners should be compared to the Rajputs, since they, too, were committed to a life of action, were brought up to regard individual achievement as important, and found the ex-

---

[19]This is discussed in Chapter 5.
[20]Taking drugs is a normal manifestation of rebellion by teenagers and young adults—something that the parents of today's children seem to have forgotten. A poll in 1987 found that 46 percent of Americans aged between 18 and 44 had taken drugs, but that 94 percent of parents would disapprove if their own children experimented with them. The generation that said yes to drugs now tells its children to just say no.

perience of surrendering their powers of volition (through marijuana) to be threatening and distasteful.[21]

Just as, in the early years of the twentieth century, respectable Americans generally came to the conclusion that they preferred alcohol to opium because they associated the former with action and aggression and the latter with passivity and introspection, so, too, in the second half of the century, they have tended to prefer alcohol to marijuana because they feel more in control when they drink. It has often been said that Americans as a nation tend to be overly concerned about remaining in control.

Many others do not drink at all. Approximately one third of Americans (according to opinion polls) abstain from alcohol, fearing that this, too, will cause them to lose control. They believe that alcohol is an addictive drug, just like heroin and cocaine. It cannot be consumed in moderation. Only if you do not drink can you be sure of being safe. One drink, and you risk becoming an alcoholic. This notion has been encouraged by health campaigners. The former surgeon general, Dr. C. Everett Koop, has written in his memoirs that "alcohol is a toxic, potentially addictive drug." Betty Ford, in a rare appearance in Washington, D.C., in 1991, criticized the Bush administration for ignoring alcohol in its "war on drugs," pointing out that alcohol was "the number one drug of addiction in this country."

An addictive drug is one that creates dependency in the user, who comes to rely on that drug to improve or maintain his sense of mental or physical well-being. This reliance amounts to a compulsion, and if the person tries to do without the drug he has to confront not only these feelings of compulsion but also withdrawal symptoms, which cause him sufficient discomfort to induce him to return to the drug. It is hard to see how alcohol can be described as an addictive drug when the vast majority of people who use it suffer neither from feelings of

---

[21]There are drugs that help people to work, notably cocaine. Robert Louis Stevenson wrote *The Strange Case of Dr. Jekyll and Mr. Hyde* in three days and three nights in the autumn of 1885; following criticism by his wife he burned the manuscript, and then rewrote it in three days and nights. It has been suggested that cocaine gave Stevenson, who was sick, the energy to write so much so fast, and that the personality changes that can be caused by cocaine may help to explain the plot of the novel. Confusion about the effects of different drugs is encouraged by misuse of the term "narcotic," which properly means "benumbing" and should not be applied to stimulants such as cocaine.

compulsion nor from symptoms of withdrawal. Even the minority of drinkers who abuse alcohol—those classified as alcoholics—often fail to develop withdrawal symptoms; even those who do suffer from withdrawal symptoms (such as hand tremors) are able to resist the supposed compulsion to drink while suffering from them. Alcohol can hardly be a very addictive drug when even alcoholics do not experience feelings of compulsion when they try to do without the substance on which they supposedly depend.

Alcohol is certainly a drug, which is a substance that affects the body in some way, but it is a less addictive one than caffeine. According to a report in the *Journal of the American Medical Association* for October 1994, researchers at Johns Hopkins University have found that the caffeine in coffee, tea, and cola produces the full range of characteristics associated with classic psychoactive dependence, including persistent, unsuccessful attempts to reduce consumption; continued use despite side effects such as sleeplessness, anxiety, and gastrointestinal problems; tolerance, that is the need for ever-higher doses to achieve the same effect; as well as withdrawal symptoms, in the form of headaches, lethargy, and depression when use is stopped.

Do the health campaigners who describe alcohol as an addictive drug really believe what they say? or are they making their statements for propaganda purposes? By associating alcohol with drugs, they have persuaded both the government and the public to take alcohol-related problems seriously. The psychiatrist Morris Chafetz became involved in alcohol problems because, as a Jew in Massachusetts in the 1950s, few hospital staff jobs were available to him. Other psychiatrists were not interested in alcoholics at the time, so this was one area where he was able to find employment. In 1971 he was appointed the first director of the National Institute on Alcohol Abuse and Alcoholism. It was his job to see to it that alcohol-related problems were taken seriously, so he started calling alcohol a drug.

It has also suited antidrug campaigners to make the connection with alcohol. In order to sustain the idea that America is suffering from a drug crisis that demands greater investment in antidrug agencies and harsher antidrug laws, campaigners have lumped together all substances that can conceivably be called drugs. This enables them to exaggerate the number of people who are dependent on drugs or are suffering from drug-related problems. It also permits them to shift attention from one drug to another without having to answer awkward questions about the extent to which they have manufactured stories about particular "drug crises" in order to gain money and exposure.[22]

Not only do many people abstain from alcohol because they have been told that it is an addictive drug, but others who have drunk it to excess at some point in their lives are convinced that they must henceforth abstain altogether because they have been infected with the disease of alcoholism. They believe that the ingestion of alcohol biochemically triggers an irresistible craving for the substance, and that if they take a single drink they will be set inexorably on a downward course.

It is generally imagined that the concept of alcoholism as a disease was invented by Alcoholics Anonymous. This is not the case. The idea that alcoholism was an illness rather than a failure of the will had been widespread among the medical community in the nineteenth century. But it was not communicated to the general public. Instead, people were told by temperance campaigners that habitual drunkenness was a moral failing. These campaigners would hardly have promulgated the disease theory of alcoholism, as it contradicted the message they wanted to spread: that alcohol and the people who made and sold it were evil, and that its manufacture and trade should be banned.

The population at large came to hear that alcoholism was a disease only following the creation of Alcoholics Anonymous in 1935. The founders of AA, William Wilson and Dr. Robert Smith, adopted the disease theory because it helped them to persuade potential recruits that they were indeed "powerless over alcohol." They publicized the idea through a group they helped set up, the National Council for Education on Alcohol (NCEA),[23] which devoted itself to communicating to the public the "momentous discovery" that alcoholism was a sickness. In the late 1940s and 1950s, a large number of articles in mass-circulation magazines presented the statement that "alcoholism is a disease" as an established fact. Whereas public opinion surveys in the late 1940s found only one fifth of interviewees willing to agree that

---

[22]Although health and antidrug campaigners still seek to promote the idea that alcohol is a drug, government agencies, having taken in the late 1980s and early 1990s to referring to "alcohol and other drugs," have now retreated from this position and come to accept the evidence in favor of the health benefits of moderate drinking. The official term for excessive drinking and drug taking is no longer "drug addiction" but "substance abuse." The "drug war" is discussed in Chapter 5 and the health benefits of moderate drinking in Chapter 4.

[23]Now the NCADD, the National Council on Alcoholism and Drug Dependence.

an alcoholic was sick and that alcoholism was an illness, by the early 1960s nearly two thirds of respondents accepted these propositions. As a result of the publicity given to the disease concept by the NCEA, membership in AA soared.

The disease concept was widely accepted not only by members of the public but also by professionals working with alcohol and alcohol problems. The drinks industry looked favorably upon a theory that did not blame it for the harm caused by drink, as Prohibition had done. The disease concept was also accepted by doctors, because they thought it would encourage hospitals to accept alcoholic patients. In the first half of the twentieth century, general hospitals had normally refused to admit habitual drunkards for treatment on the grounds that they were uncooperative, especially when it came to paying their bills. The hospitals changed their attitude once they accepted that alcoholism was a disease rather than a bad habit. Doctors also believed that by calling alcoholism a disease they would make it easier for alcoholics to seek treatment. It is likely that fewer people by far would have been prepared to admit to being alcoholics if they had also to admit that they were not suffering from a disease but merely from a failure of personality.

The benefits of treating alcoholism as a disease can be demonstrated by the example of the military, which has never accepted the idea and regards the abuse of alcohol as willful misconduct. Within the armed forces the consumption of alcoholic beverages is officially regarded as "a personal choice that makes everyone personally responsible for their [sic] conduct." Although military personnel are officially encouraged to seek assistance for alcohol or drug problems, they rarely do so for fear that disciplinary action would be taken against them. Yet there is more abuse of alcohol among the armed forces than in the general population, enough to damage their effectiveness in combat. In 1980, more than one in six military personnel reported having experienced serious consequences in work performance, health, or social relationships as a result of heavy drinking during the previous year. If the armed forces were prepared to adopt the disease theory of alcoholism, more of their members would be prepared to seek treatment.

The disease theory might seem helpful, but there is no evidence that treating alcoholics on this basis helps them to break the habit. The few scientifically reliable studies that have been carried out show that attending AA works no better than no treatment at all. It is true that drinkers who persist in AA remain abstinent. But this does not mean that it is AA that keeps them so. Drinkers remain in AA only if they are able to remain reasonably abstinent and to accept the AA way of life. The vast majority of heavy drinkers never try AA, and most who do join drop out.

It has even been suggested that attending AA is less effective than allowing the abusive drinker to get over his problem on his own. Those who join AA are told that they can never drink again. This prohibition encourages many AA members to switch their fixation from alcohol to cigarettes, coffee, and high-calorie desserts without dealing with the underlying problem that led to the abusive drinking in the first place.

Nor is it necessary for alcoholics to give up drinking for life, as AA and other proponents of the disease theory insist. This view, which prevails in America, has found little favor in Europe, where a great deal of effort is put into teaching alcoholics how to drink responsibly. Books that argue in favor of controlled drinking therapy (teaching alcoholics how to drink in moderation) are quickly knocked down in America; no treatment center in the country pursues this as its official policy. In Britain, three quarters of alcohol treatment units offer it. Research conducted by psychologists in Britain has shown that hospitalized alcoholics who believe that alcoholism is a disease are more likely to drink excessively after having a single drink than those who do not subscribe to the disease theory. The belief that alcoholism is a disease makes it hard for recovering alcoholics to develop a pattern of moderate drinking.

Telling alcoholics that they can never drink again produces the same unhealthy consequences as national Prohibition in the 1920s and the prohibition of alcoholic drink to young people today. This approach makes it more likely that people will develop the habit of alternating sobriety with occasional lapses into binges, rather than learning how to drink in a controlled and civilized manner.[24] As Stanton Peele, a leading expert on addiction and a staunch opponent of the disease theory, has argued, "The devaluation of moderate drinking as a treatment goal, and a social norm, is dangerous . . . When we promote the belief that many people cannot taste alcohol without catastrophic results, we may be fulfilling our own prophecy."

The disease theory is unhelpful, and it is wrong. The idea gained acceptance without any serious examination. Alcoholism does not dis-

---

[24]The unintended consequences of prohibitions are discussed in Chapter 5, and binge drinking in the Conclusion.

play specific symptoms, follow a particular course, or respond to treatment in the same way as infectious diseases. It lacks a pathogen, an agent that causes the disease. Some people have argued that the alcohol itself is a pathogen, just like, say, the tuberculosis bacillus. How so? Most people are not caused any problems by alcohol. Are we supposed to accept that they have somehow developed immunity to it?

Only a minority of the people who are supposed to know professionally about disease—doctors—believe that alcoholism is one. According to two opinion polls carried out in the early 1980s, 79 percent of the general population believed that alcohol was a disease, but only 21 percent of doctors did so. Doctors have adopted the disease theory largely for policy reasons, in order to get alcoholics into treatment, not because they believe in it.

The disease theory can be compared to the emperor's new clothes. It suits people to believe it, so they believe it, even though it isn't really there. Rather than accepting blindly that alcoholism is a disease, it makes more sense to follow the observation of the medical theorist Thomas Szasz that "the misuse of alcohol, whatever the reason for it, is no more an illness than is the misuse of any other product of human inventiveness, from language to nuclear energy."

The disease concept of alcoholism is destroyed by its own internal contradiction. Any alcoholic who seeks treatment is told that by drinking alcohol he sets off an irrepressible desire for the substance and that he must therefore agree as a condition of his treatment to abstain from drinking. Yet if he does as he is told and abstains during treatment, he is disproving the theory that alcoholism is a disease that causes an inability to abstain from drinking.

The disease concept of alcoholism is based on the idea that the alcoholic loses all control over his drinking. This is untrue. Scientific research shows that the amount alcoholics drink depends on the benefits they think they receive from alcohol and the effort they have to make to obtain it. They don't just go on drinking until they pass out. In this respect, alcohol differs from drugs: It is not a case of taking a single dose in order to obtain the desired effect, but of taking a whole sequence of doses in order to achieve a whole range of effects. Conscious choice comes into it at every stage.[25]

---

[25]Because alcohol gives the user a greater degree of control than do drugs, many people take it in preference to tranquilizers to treat stress or depression. Unlike Prozac, which must be taken in a prescribed amount and requires several days to

The disease theory has also been debunked by placebo tests. In one such test in the 1970s, psychologists at the University of Wisconsin selected sixty-four people, of whom half were social drinkers and half had been diagnosed as alcoholics. Some were given alcohol in the form of vodka and tonic, and told that they were being given alcohol, while others were given alcohol but told that they were being given a placebo, plain tonic water. Still others were given a placebo but told that they were being given alcohol, while a fourth group received a placebo and were told as much. According to the disease theory of alcoholism, any time that an alcoholic takes a drink he will be seized by an irresistible craving and will be unable to stop, while an alcoholic who is deprived of drink will suffer from painful withdrawal symptoms, such as the "shakes." Yet, in this test, one of the men who had been expecting to receive alcohol but had been given tonic water began acting in an intoxicated manner, whereas several of the men who had been told that they would be drinking tonic water but were actually drinking alcohol continued to suffer from withdrawal symptoms, even after consuming the equivalent of double vodkas. This and other tests indicate that someone's reaction to alcohol, far from being biochemically determined, depends on how he expects it to affect him.

To a substantial extent, the way in which we respond to alcohol is a learned behavior, a psychological rather than a chemical reaction.[26] Indian tribes in the colonial period believed that alcohol had magical powers, and that drunkenness was a sacred state; a man was not responsible for the acts he committed while drunk. Tribal leaders, who normally punished violent actions with great strictness, exonerated those who had behaved violently when intoxicated. Many Indians took advantage of this state of affairs. As one French missionary in Montreal pointed out, "It is a somewhat common custom amongst them when they have enemies to get drunk and afterwards go and break their heads or stab them to death, so as to be able to say afterwards that they committed the wicked act when they were not in their senses." It was also suggested that some Indians feigned drunkenness in order to be able to attack others and avoid the consequences.

---

achieve its effect, alcohol acts quickly and can be taken when the person thinks he needs it; since it is dose respondent, it can be taken in the quantity he thinks he needs. This is not a recommendation, but it is often done.

[26] The same is also true of many drugs, such as tobacco—which Europeans interpreted very differently from Amerindians.

As these Indians had realized, it is not alcohol that causes men to become violent, but rather the belief that it will have this effect. The alcohol was not in itself any more responsible for their behavior than it is today for husbands who beat wives or young men who commit crimes of violence. Indeed, one researcher at Brown University discovered that just like Indians in the past, many prisoners had been stone-cold sober when they committed their crimes but had told the judge that they had been drunk, in the hope of obtaining a lighter sentence.

There is no doubt that spousal abuse is linked with abuse of alcohol. But this does not mean that husbands are induced by the consumption of alcohol to beat their wives, nor that they would necessarily refrain if they remained sober. If husbands drink before beating their wives, it is partly because this is expected of them. Society associates alcohol with violence, so they do too. The statistical connection between drunkenness and wife beating exists principally because households predisposed to violence are also predisposed to abuse of alcohol, as well as the abuse of drugs and many other social problems. In one test, blood samples were taken from a group of men who had been arrested for assaulting their wives. According to verbal reports, half of them had been drinking excessively at the time. Yet the results showed that fewer than one in five had sufficient alcohol in their bloodstream to be regarded as unfit to drive. According to sociology professors Richard Gelles and Murray Straus, leading experts on the subject, "Drinking (or claiming to be drunk) provides the perfect excuse for instances of domestic violence. 'I didn't know what I was doing when I was drunk' is the most frequently heard excuse by those who counsel violent families. When women claim their husbands are like 'Dr. Jekyll and Mr. Hyde,' they are actually providing the excuse their husbands need to justify their violent behavior. In the end, violent parents and partners learn that if they do not want to be held responsible for their violence, they should drink and hit, or at least say they were drunk."

In these circumstances, it is hardly surprising that alcohol has been accused of causing so many ills in American history. No scapegoat could be more convenient than one that relies for its effect on the expectation of the drinker, and that can therefore be blamed for almost any social problem one might want to choose.

The disease theory of alcoholism is not merely wrong, but harmful. If alcoholism is a disease, then it needs to be treated, but many people who are infected with it do not recognize the fact. Hence the concept of "denial": that denying you are suffering from the disease of alcoholism is one manifestation of the illness.

Denial is based on the reasonable notion that people do not realize they are relying on mood modifiers (such as alcohol) in order to remedy their bad feelings about their failure to cope with their lives. But this is very different from saying that denial is part of the disease of alcoholism: that it results from seeking solace in drink. In fact, denial is a precondition for such behavior. People who try to hide from reality are the sort who become alcoholics; it is not alcohol that causes them to avoid the truth. Denial is not caused by the disease of alcoholism; it is denial of reality that causes people to become alcoholics.

Although the concept of denial is misconceived, it leads to people being forced into treatment on the grounds that the denial is part of their disease and they have to be treated for their own good. Many of the people who attend AA meetings and associated treatments for alcoholism have been coerced into doing so. Some are threatened by their employers with dismissal unless they undergo AA-style therapy; others have been convicted by the courts of driving under the influence of alcohol and agree to undergo treatment as an alternative to more severe penalties, such as losing their license.

Having been coerced into therapy, people who attend AA meetings find they are forced to participate in a religious ritual, redolent of fundamentalist revivalist Christianity. "God" and a "higher power" are mentioned in six of the twelve steps of AA, which arose out of the Oxford Group, an early-twentieth-century evangelical movement that sought to return to the ways of primitive Christianity, including surrender to a higher power as a means of changing one's life. Many people are shocked to discover this aspect of AA therapy. As one woman, who had been convicted of driving under the influence, wrote in her diary about the treatment she felt pressured into entering as an alternative to having her license suspended for a year, "I keep reminding myself that this is America. I find it unconscionable that the criminal justice system has the power to coerce American citizens to accept ideas that are anathema to them. It is as if I were a citizen of a totalitarian regime being punished for political dissent." Most so-called alcoholism treatment in America is not medical treatment, it is brainwashing.

The disease theory of alcoholism also corrupts the wider community because it panders to a common psychological inadequacy: the tendency to blame one's problems on an external cause rather than to accept that they arise from an inability effectively to deal with the outside world.[27]

In 1976, Jules Masserman, a former president of the American Psychiatric Association, stated that "addiction to drink is a 'disease' only in the sense that excessive eating, sleeping, smoking, wandering, or lechery can be so classified." This was intended as a reductio ad absurdum to ridicule the notion that a behavior could be regarded as an illness. But within a few years disease treatments were developed not only for all the things Masserman had listed but for much else as well.

The disease of alcoholism is primarily defined by a loss of control over one's drinking. Loss of control is a subjective experience. It might just as well be applied to shopping. Certainly people can feel out of control of their spending. If alcoholism is a disease, so, too, is shopaholism. So, too, according to this criterion, are over- and undereating, anxiety and depression, obsessive-compulsive disorder, and even intimate relationships. The claim is commonly made that some women are biologically driven repeatedly to form inappropriate and destructive relationships; men (including presidents of the United States) are more often said to be addicted to sex. With "love addiction" and "sex addiction" we have arrived at a ridiculous situation in which the problems of conducting everyday relationships are described as a disease. People never have the chance to develop; they are never given the opportunity to grow up.[28]

So widely has it become accepted that we can abrogate personal responsibility for our actions by claiming that we are suffering from a disease that defendants charged with murder, rape, and robbery have used, and sometimes succeeded with the defense that they had been overcome by a compulsion beyond their control. As Peele points out, "These defenses seem to describe a completely self-gratifying uni-

---

[27] This "victim culture" has created an absurd state of affairs in which people who confess to having allowed alcohol or drugs to impair their professional and personal lives are shown sympathy, while others who have been strong enough to carry on in spite of their habit are condemned.

[28] The concept of behavior as a disease represents the abandonment of responsibility for one's own life in a similar way to "repressed memory syndrome." People go to therapists and are encouraged by them to "discover" that the root cause of their lack of fulfillment lies in childhood sexual abuse. They are attracted to this idea because it places them at the center of their own world, just as they were when they were children. But in most cases there is no evidence that the abuse ever happened, and it certainly does not help the "victims" to come to terms with their own lives.

verse. . . . The hallmark of a civilized society is that people learn to restrain their impulses in line with the needs of their communities, neighbors, and families."

Today we blame our own failings on an external compulsion, which we call a "disease." In medieval Europe, and in early modern America, the specter of witches was summoned for the same purpose. The Salem witch trials of 1692 centered on young girls who suffered from fits in which they seemed to lose control over their words and actions: They uttered blasphemies; they interrupted church meetings; they refused to pray. The girls claimed to be tormented by witches, or, rather, devils whom Satan had delegated to take on the likeness of witches. The girls' irreligious behavior while under diabolical influence suggests that they were using the latter as an excuse for improper conduct. During the previous winter, several of the girls who later became possessed had experimented with divination. They must have realized this was illicit. By claiming to have been possessed, they were able to shift responsibility for their wickedness to demons within them. Adults were inclined to believe that the devil was at work, and to accuse their neighbors of witchcraft, as it offered an explanation of their recent suffering as a result of raids by Indians (whom in any case they linked with witchcraft and the devil on account of their mysterious shamanistic rituals). Psychologically, it is difficult to accept that one has suffered as a random act of chance. It is easier to attribute responsibility to someone or something else. The modern habit of blaming our wrongdoings on some power beyond our control, which we call a disease, is no different from the pre-modern habit of blaming it on witches.

The Royalist Club

CHAPTER 1

The Americanization of European Taste

A t the time the first English immigrants arrived on the eastern seaboard of North America, the Indians who then occupied the country drank very little alcohol. It is not true (as is often supposed) that they had no alcoholic drinks, but not all tribes made them, and the ones they did produce were low in alcohol. They preferred in the winter to brew tea from sassafras and wild mint, and in the summer to make a refreshing drink from sumac berries called sumacade.

The lack of fermented drinks on the eastern seaboard of America posed a major problem for those arriving from Europe, who were not accustomed to drinking water, which they considered unsafe. They followed the teaching of the sixteenth-century dietitian Andrew Boorde that "water is not wholesome solely by itself for an Englishman. . . . If any man do use to drink water with wine, let it be purely strained, and then [boil] it; and after it be cold, let him put it to his wine."[1]

Even when water was not contaminated, it was scorned by the English because it was free. People drank water only if they could not afford to buy ale. "Would you believe it," wrote César de Saussure, a Swiss visitor to England in the 1720s, "though water is to be had in abundance in London, and of fairly good quality, absolutely none is

---

[1]The use of wine (and spirits) to decontaminate water is discussed in Chapter 4.

drunk? In this country . . . beer . . . is what everybody drinks when thirsty."

The settlers who arrived in America in the early seventeenth century had to make do with water, however. The farther down the East Coast they settled, the warmer the climate, and the more likely the water to be contaminated with pathogenic bacteria. The first contingent of permanent settlers arrived in Virginia in 1607. Six years later, according to a letter of appraisal written by a Spaniard to his government, "There are about three hundred men there, more or less; and the majority sick and badly treated, because they have nothing but bread of maize, with fish; nor do they drink anything but water—all of which is contrary to the nature of the English—on which account they all wish to return and would have done so if they had been at liberty." A decade later a young English settler named Richard Ffrethorne wrote home to his parents to lament that "I am in a most heavy case . . . I have nothing to comfort me, nor is there nothing to be gotten here but sickness and death." He complained that whereas back in England people grew fat and healthy on strong beer, in Virginia they had to make do with water, which weakened those who drank it.

The settlers could not bring supplies of beer with them from England, because it took up valuable space in the cramped ships and it did not always arrive in drinkable form. The governor and council of Virginia complained more than once about "stinking beer" that had killed passengers and settlers alike.

In theory the colonists could have made their own beer. In England this was normally brewed from barley but it could also be made from other kinds of grain, including maize, which the Indians cultivated. As early as 1585, members of the first, abortive settlement on Roanoke Island (off the coast of what is now North Carolina) managed to brew satisfactory beer from Indian maize. Moreover, the colonists of the early seventeenth century planted barley. So why did it take another generation to produce enough beer to fulfill the demands of the settlers?

In part, the answer is to be found in a proposal sent in 1620 to the Virginia Company back in London by a Mr. Russell for making "artificial wine" by boiling up sassafras and licorice together in water. Russell made great claims for the medicinal and keeping qualities of his product, which he said was necessary because "There is in Virginia . . . three thousand people and the greatest want they complain of is good drink." Wine was too expensive, and barley had mostly to be imported from England. Even if more barley was grown in the colony, "it were hard in that country, being so hot, to make malt[2] of it, or if they had malt to make good beer." The obstacle was the climate. Not until the introduction of artificial refrigeration two and a half centuries later was a solution found to the problem of producing beer in the warm and humid conditions of the American South.

In the light of the experience of the settlers in Virginia, it is hardly surprising that in 1619, when the Pilgrims were mulling over the possibility of emigrating to America, one of the first doubts they raised was that "the change of air, diet, and drinking of water would infect their bodies with sore sicknesses and grievous diseases."[3] When they did eventually reach America, they were not intending to land at Cape Cod, but farther south; they had to settle on the Massachusetts coast because the supply of beer was running short. The sailors who had brought the Pilgrims over hastened them ashore and made them drink water because they wanted to keep the remaining beer to themselves— believing, apart from anything else, that it helped to prevent scurvy.

The Pilgrims might not have wanted to settle as far north as they did, but, as a result, they found water of much better quality than the Virginia settlers had been compelled to consume. According to William Bradford, who became the governor of the colony, they found the first water they drank "as pleasant to them as wine or beer had been in foretimes." This was hardly surprising, because they were suffering greatly from thirst. They would have preferred beer, but they were generally prepared to put up with water. Forced to drink water through lack of choice, they found that it was not as bad as they had imagined. In the opinion of one of their number, William Wood, "It is thought there can be no better water in the world, yet dare I not prefer it before good beer, as some have done, but any man will choose it before bad beer. . . . Those that drink it be as healthful, fresh, and lusty as they that drink beer."[4] By the 1630s, however, the colonists

---

[2]Malting is the process of steeping, germinating, and drying the grain in order partially to convert the starches into sugars so that they are able to ferment.
[3]At least they were fortunate in their choice of ship. The *Mayflower* had been involved in the wine trade, sailing from London to Bordeaux, so its hold was relatively "sweet" and free from disease. The voyage to America, which lasted just under eight weeks, proved healthier than many: "only" five out of 149 on board died.
[4]In 1629 the minister Higginson of Salem commented that "whereas my stomach could [previously] only digest and did require such drink as was both strong and

had begun to brew some beer, made from malted barley shipped from England.

By this time, too, the health of the Virginia settlers had much improved. With the introduction of a more regular supply of beer, wine, and cider, the high death rate among the colonists, which would have rendered the settlement impossible to sustain in the long term, fell dramatically. It was not just a more sensible choice of drinks that explained the better health of the colonists: They also reduced their consumption of oysters and clams during the summer, when these were more likely to be contaminated with harmful bacteria. The Virginians themselves did not realize why they were healthier and believed that the change should be attributed to an improvement in the climate as a result of forest clearance.

Once the colonists had found better things to drink, they abandoned water precisely because they associated it with the privations of the early days. Roger Clap, who emigrated to New England as part of the Great Migration of 1630, later recalled in his *Memoirs* that "in the beginning many were in great straits for want of provision. . . . In those days God did cause his people . . . to be contented with mean things. It was not accounted a strange thing in those days to drink water."

By the eighteenth century, Americans were able to do as they would have done in England, and refuse to drink water on the grounds that it might well be unhealthy and was fit only for those who could not afford to drink anything better. Soon after the revolution, Filippo Mazzei, a recent immigrant from Italy,[5] attended a large dinner party where he "asked for a glass of water. I perceived some confusion among the servants, and the water did not arrive. The host, next whom I sat, whispered in my ear, asking with a smile if I could not drink something else, because the unexpected request for a glass of water had upset the entire household and they did not know what they were about."

Ordinary Americans of the colonial period did not, however, become beer drinkers, as they might have had they remained in England. Instead, they became great guzzlers of rum.[6] By the end of the seven-

---

[mature], I can and ofttimes do drink New England water very well." Higginson died soon after making this observation.

[5]Mazzei had come to America with the intention of growing vines, and had been given land by Thomas Jefferson near his estate at Monticello in Virginia for that purpose.

[6]An abbreviation of "rumbullion," itself a term of unknown origin, perhaps an

teenth century, according to the visiting English writer Edward Ward, rum was "adored by the American English. . . .'Tis held as the comforter of their souls, the preserver of their bodies, the remover of their cares, and promoter of their mirth; and is a sovereign remedy against the grumbling of the guts, a kibe-heel[7] or a wounded conscience, which are three epidemical distempers that afflict the country."

Rum had originated as a by-product of sugar production on the island of Barbados, an uninhabited island in the West Indies that had been claimed by the English in 1625. Originally the settlers who arrived on Barbados had tried to grow tobacco, in response to the high prices that were already being obtained by Virginia tobacco in England. Unfortunately, Barbados tobacco was not very good. Even the planters preferred to import tobacco from Virginia for their own use. Next they tried cotton, and then indigo, but these did not succeed either. The Barbadian economy found a firm footing only when the planters turned to growing sugar cane in the mid-1640s.

The Portuguese had long been producing sugar in their colony of Brazil, and had also been distilling a spirit from the juice of the sugar cane. But it was the British in Barbados who discovered how to produce rum from molasses, the sludge left over from the process of refining the sugar. Economically, this proved a leap forward. In the 1640s, British planters in Barbados had been growing their sugar cane solely for distillation, but they soon discovered that they could eat their sugar and drink their rum as well. By the 1650s they had become the richest men in the New World.

Much of the molasses was not distilled in Barbados itself but exported to New England for distillation there. The first commercial distillery was opened in Boston in 1700, followed by others throughout New England. Rum became a staple of the economy, with substantial exports, principally to Africa.

It has since become a popular notion that rum played a role in a "triangular trade," in which molasses was exported from the Caribbean to New England, rum from there to Africa, and then slaves back to the West Indies, all in the same boat. In fact, the existence of such a trade should largely be regarded as mythical: New England merchants played only a minor role in the slave trade. The idea of a tri-

---

old English country slang word that attempted to produce an onomatopoeic imitation of the noise that the drink seemed to set off in the head of the drinker.
[7]A chilblain.

angular trade has taken hold because it panders to the popular concept of hypocritical, self-righteous Puritans who prayed for their own souls while trafficking in the bodies of others.[8]

The popularity of rum in colonial America in fact owed much less to economic motives—the so-called "triangular trade"—than to climate and convenience.

Rum became popular in colonial America for much the same reason as beer in England. Workingmen in England consumed a lot of beer because they believed it gave them strength. Benjamin Franklin traveled to London at the age of eighteen in 1724, and soon found employment at a printing house. At first he worked at the press, alongside fifty other workmen. He drank only water,[9] and was called the "water American" by the others, who were "great guzzlers of beer . . . My companion at the press drank every day a pint before breakfast, a pint at breakfast with his bread and cheese, a pint between breakfast and dinner, a pint at dinner, a pint in the afternoon about six o'clock, and another when he had done his day's work"; in all, six pints a day of "strong beer."[10]

But in much of America—in the South, in country districts, and especially on the western frontier—beer was not readily available. John Melish, an Englishman who made two lengthy visits to America on business at the beginning of the nineteenth century, observed that "there is unquestionably too much spirituous liquors drank in the newly settled parts of America, but a very good reason can be assigned for it. The labor of clearing the land is rugged and severe, and the summer heats are sometimes so great that it would be dangerous to drink cold water. . . . Where the country is entirely new, there are no apples, and consequently no cider. [Beer] will not keep, spirituous liq-

---

[8]It was petty-minded New England historians of the late nineteenth century who, by allowing provincial animosities to overcome their historical judgment, established the historical commonplace that New England merchants had played a key role in the introduction of slaves to America. When, in 1886, a Massachusetts historian delivered a paper to the American Antiquarian Society claiming that Rhode Island had been more deeply involved in the slave trade than Massachusetts, a Rhode Island historian responded by delivering another paper in which he said that Massachusetts had been much more guilty than Rhode Island. They magnified the evidence to shame each other and as a result succeeded in shaming New England as a whole.

[9]Franklin became quite a drinker himself later in life, and even went so far on one occasion as to suggest that God had given humanity an elbow positioned just as it was—rather than lower or higher—for the sole purpose of making it possible to raise glasses of wine conveniently to the mouth.

[10]The nutritional value of beer is discussed in Chapter 4.

uors are soon prepared and are in fact the only beverage to which settlers have access. . . ." As the interior parts of America were developed, he believed, apple trees would be planted to make cider and barley malted to make beer, and drinking habits would gradually become more temperate.[11]

The distinction between the drinking habits of English workers, who consumed beer, and American laborers, who preferred spirits, reflected the relative sizes and population of the two countries. In England, a lot of people lived close together, so it made economic sense to brew beer, which had to be served directly from cask in a pub and did not keep well. In America, which was much larger and more sparsely populated, beer could be provided only in a few large towns.

American laborers tried claiming that drinking spirits helped them to do their work better than beer would have. They argued that they could bring in the harvest only if they were permitted frequent recourse to liquor. They were wrong. "Let it not be said," wrote the Philadelphia physician Benjamin Rush, that "ardent spirits have become necessary from habit in harvest and in other seasons of uncommon and arduous labor. The habit is a bad one, and may easy be broken." There were, he explained, many other "pleasant and wholesome liquors" that would refresh and revive tired workers more effectively than rum, such as wine made from native fruits or water sharpened with vinegar and sweetened with molasses. Were farmers to give these to their laborers instead of spirits, "their grain and hay will be gathered into their barns in less time and in better condition . . . and a hundred disagreeable scenes from sickness, contention, and accidents will be avoided." Rush's advice was not heeded, however. The custom of spirit drinking was too well established for people to change their habits.

As the Englishman Melish had suggested, Americans of this period believed it was healthier to consume tepid alcoholic drinks in hot weather than to refresh themselves with cold water. "During hot weather thirst is so widespread and irresistible in all American cities that several persons die each year from drinking cold pump water when hot," wrote Médéric-Louis-Elie Moreau de Saint Méry, a Frenchman living in Philadelphia at the end of the eighteenth century.[12]

---

[11]The reason they did not is explained in the Conclusion.
[12]Moreau de Saint Méry was a Creole—a Frenchman born in the West Indies—who had traveled to France and played a part in the revolution but been forced

"Printed handbills are distributed each summer to warn people of these dangers. Strangers especially are warned either to drink grog or to add a little wine or some other spirituous liquor to their water. People are urged to throw cold water on the faces of those suffering from water drinking, and bleeding is also suggested. Sometimes notices are placed on the pumps with the words: 'Death to him who drinks quickly.' But all these teachings are ignored."

When the Scotsman James Flint landed at New York in the summer of 1818, he was informed that eleven people had recently died in the city as a result of drinking cold water, several of them strangers who had only just arrived. He was advised that water should not be drunk straight from the well but should be allowed to stand for a few minutes, and that it should be taken in small mouthfuls, which should be warmed in the mouth for two or three seconds before swallowing.[13]

Among the newcomers who suffered as a result of their inability to resist the temptation of cool water in warm weather was an English emigrant named Joseph Pickering, who had arrived in Baltimore at the end of 1824, and encountered the hot climate of the United States for the first time in May of the following year. He wrote in his diary that "on drinking a little cold water this morning, it struck a chill over me; a fit of ague[14] came on, and afterwards a strong fever, which forced me to bed." His experience did little to dissuade him, however, for a few weeks later he "drank most delicious water at one of the city springs. . . . Water is the general drink here for quenching thirst, and no one that has never been out of our cool climate can conceive its delicious taste in a hot one."

Today we unthinkingly consume large quantities of cold water in hot weather and find it hard to conceive of anyone preferring to drink tepid spirits in such conditions. People made the latter choice in the past, however, because of contemporary perceptions of physiology. It was believed that when someone sweated in hot weather, not only did

---

to flee the guillotine in 1793. Fearing that it would not be safe to go home to the West Indies, he spent a few years in exile in Philadelphia before returning to France in 1798.

[13]This "cold water" of which people were told to be so wary was not really cold: It had not been chilled in any way but simply drawn from a street pump. Any harm it caused should probably be attributed to contamination with pathogenic bacteria rather than to its temperature. For the development of water purification systems in the nineteenth century, see Chapter 4.

[14]Shivering.

this conduct heat from the inside of the body to the outside, but it left the inner parts, and especially the stomach, in need of warmth and fortification. Doctors recommended that after sweating, people should warm up their stomachs by drinking distilled spirits.[15]

"Certainly strong drinks are very requisite, where so much heat is," wrote Richard Ligon in his account of life on Barbados in the mid-seventeenth century. "The spirits being exhausted with much sweating, the inner parts are left cold and faint, and shall need comforting and reviving." Because the science of the day taught that liquor was essential in hot weather, it was taken by everyone, and even given to slaves. Ligon stated that a dram or two of rum was "a great comfort and refreshing" to laborers who had been sweating in the sun for ten hours at a stretch.

A comfort, but hardly of benefit. Hard liquor acted as a diuretic on the constitutions of people who needed to rehydrate their bodies after sweating in hot weather. Visiting South Carolina soon after the American Revolution, the German doctor Johann Schoepf[16] observed the harmful consequences of the "prevalent misconception that a free use of [fermented and spirituous drinks] in warm weather prevents debility and cools the body. . . . [South] Carolina would be for many a toper a loved country; it is the doctrine here that during the warm months one should think and work little, and drink much. . . . Men therefore die frequently in the bloom of their years and leave behind for others young and rich widows. Most of them hasten their death by the incautious use of spirituous drinks, in which they seek refreshment and fortification against the relaxing effect of the hot climate."

Just as the dangers of drinking cold water in hot weather were thought to be greatest among newcomers to the country, so, too, the potential for harm of excessive alcohol consumption in hot weather was considered to be largest among recent immigrants.

Georgia was the last part of the East Coast to be colonized. The founder of the colony, the philanthropist and politician James Oglethorpe, accompanied the first settlers on their voyage across the Atlantic in the winter of 1732–33. They arrived in America unused to the climate, and the remedy to which they all too readily turned was quick

---

[15]They also advised people to eat chili peppers.
[16]Schoepf had served as chief surgeon to the troops from Ansbach (in what is now Bavaria) who fought in America during the Revolutionary War, then set off traveling around the country once a truce was established in 1783.

to take its toll. By the summer, people were already dying from the effects (it was believed) of drinking too much rum. Oglethorpe considered that the prosperity of the new colony depended on the industry of young men and women. He could not afford to have their strength sapped by excessive devotion to spirits—as appeared already to be happening back in England. Dr. Stephen Hales, one of the London-based trustees of the new colony, warned in a pamphlet entitled *A Friendly Admonition to the Drinkers of Brandy and Other Distilled Spirituous Liquors* that many English people were so weakened by an excessive reliance on spirits "that they have neither will nor power to labour for an honest livelihood; which is a principal reason of the great increase of the poor in this nation, as also the much greater number of robberies. . . ." One of the motives behind the settlement of Georgia had been to found a new colony where the sort of people who had suffered as a result of their own or other people's excessive consumption of spirits in England could start a new life. So Oglethorpe returned to England and had a bill passed through Parliament that prohibited the sale of rum in Georgia.

This prohibition did not work. The settlers knew perfectly well that the rum they were not allowed to buy in Georgia could readily be obtained on the other side of the Savannah River, in South Carolina. Oglethorpe did his best to see to it that one South Carolina alehouse was closed down after fourteen workmen had drowned rowing there and back. But boats from South Carolina continued to sail to Savannah laden with spirits. Magistrates in Savannah stopped some of these boats and staved in their kegs, leading to a good deal of hostility between the two colonies. And the drinking went on.

The consequences were much as Oglethorpe and Hales had feared. In February 1735–36[17] Oglethorpe went to see how work on the new Tybee lighthouse was progressing, only to find that nothing had been built except the foundations. He berated the foreman, who replied that "the chief reason of his delay arose from his men's not working; that rum was so cheap in Carolina, from whence they easily got it, that one

---

[17] Dates between January 1 and March 25 before 1752 often appear in this double form, as the year was then generally (but not universally) considered to begin on the latter rather than the former date. The modern style of January 1 was not firmly established in Britain and its colonies until 1752. February 1735–36 refers to the end of 1735 according to the old style but to the beginning of 1736 according to the new one.

day's pay would make them drunk for a week, and then they neither minded him nor anything else."

The prohibition ceased to be enforced from 1742 onward, and was eventually repealed in 1749. It failed partly because of a shortage of available alternatives.

Oglethorpe tried to persuade the colonists to drink beer instead of rum. In the early years of the colony, however, there were no means for brewing, and barley was reluctant to grow in the climate. So the beer had to be imported—which raised the price, and meant that supplies were sporadic, to say the least. The secretary of the colony, William Stephens, wrote in his journal about a sloop just in from New York in October 1738, "having plenty of well-brewed beer aboard, which at this season of the year was much wished for by most people; more went without any than the few who could find money to buy, and the public stores had none."

Oglethorpe also wanted to encourage wine production in the new colony. Had he not, after all, already established a vineyard in the much less suitable climate of England, at his own estate at Westbrook in Surrey? Did not this produce a "wine like Rhenish," which apparently satisfied the sophisticated tastes of Oglethorpe's social circle?

Vine cuttings from various sources were sent to the colonists in Georgia as soon as they arrived in 1733. But they failed to grow satisfactorily in the swampy soil. Wine was made, but only from the native American vines that grew wild all around—which did not produce wine of the finest quality. In September 1740 Stephens left Savannah for Frederica[18] on St. Simon Island, where Oglethorpe was lying ill of fever, bringing with him a large stone bottle containing native wine. Oglethorpe tasted it in front of Stephens and pronounced it to be "something of the nature of a small French white wine, with agreeable flavour." But Major James Carteret, who had also been present on this occasion, later told the trustees that he had tasted the wine too, and found it "sad stuff, and bitter, rather the juice of the stalk than of the grape." As Sir John Mordaunt (admittedly no friend to the trustees) had said in a debate on the future of the colony in the English Parliament earlier the same year, he wished the colonists good luck with their efforts at growing vines, "but if they were to drink no liquor

---

[18]This town no longer exists.

except wine of their own making they would be the soberest people under the sun."[19]

Instead of their own wine, therefore, those Georgian colonists who could afford it drank the same wine as their neighbors in Carolina and Virginia—imported from Madeira, a Portuguese-owned island 400 miles off the coast of West Africa.

It is easy to understand why ships bound for America from Europe should have stopped on their way at Madeira. It was a matter of winds. The prevailing winds made it difficult to cross the North Atlantic in a westerly direction. It was easier to sail down the coast of Portugal and then pick up the northeasterly trade winds just south of Madeira. These would carry a ship straight to Charleston or Savannah. And since the prevailing winds on the North American coast are southerly, the ship could run up to the northern ports from there.

It is also easy to understand why Madeira should have become popular in the West Indies and America in the late seventeenth and early eighteenth centuries, as it withstood the rigors of the voyage and the extremes of temperature better than other wines. The young sugar planter Christopher Jeaffreson wrote to his cousin in London from the island of St. Kitts in the West Indies that "There is no commodity better in these parts than Madeira wines. They are so generally and so plentifully drunk, being the only strong drink that is natural here, except brandy and rum, which are too hot."[20] Not only was Madeira less likely than other wines to go off in the warm climate, but it managed to remain refreshing, thanks to its relatively high level of acidity. As Hugh Jones wrote in his account of the habits of the Virginians in the early eighteenth century, the most popular wine in the colony was Madeira, "which moderately drank is fittest to cheer the fainting spirits in the heat of summer, and to warm the chilled blood in the bitter colds of winter, and seems most peculiarly adapted for this climate."

It is less easy to understand why Madeira retained its popularity in America, and especially in the South, after the middle of the eighteenth century, when it began to be fortified by the addition of brandy. This

---

[19]The failure of vine growing in the other colonies is covered in the Conclusion.
[20]"Hot" could mean "alcoholic" but more likely refers to the old humoral system of medicine, according to which diseases were caused by a lack of balance within the body. Brandy and rum, Jeaffreson believed, provoked an imbalance.

change occurred partly as a consequence of disturbed sea conditions around Gibraltar, which prevented ships bound for America from calling at Madeira; merchants on the island distilled some of the excess stocks that had built up in order to preserve the rest of the wine while waiting for ships to arrive. When normal trading resumed, Madeira had changed its character and become a fortified wine. The wine merchant Andrew Newton complained from Virginia that men who had hitherto drunk two bottles every day now made do with one.

Although it was much more alcoholic than before, Madeira succeeded in retaining its popularity as a result of the accidental discovery that it was now not merely sufficiently robust to travel to America but was actually improved thereby. It was found that the wine tasted better after pitching and rolling across the tropics in the hull of a ship. British connoisseurs started to insist that their barrels of Madeira should be loaded on ships bound for the West or East Indies, to be treated as ballast on board and to be returned with the ship to Europe. Wine merchants soon began to experiment with means of replicating the conditions of a ship's hold. In the 1830s the English journalist Cyrus Redding suggested in his *History and Description of Modern Wines* that "The expense of a voyage to the East Indies is superfluous, as motion and heat will do it in any climate. . . . A pipe of Madeira has been attached to the beam of a steam engine, in the engine house, where the temperature is always high and the motion continual, and in a year it could not be known from the choicest East India."

Madeira was also improved by the conditions in which it was necessarily stored on the southeastern seaboard of America. The high level of the water table in Charleston and Savannah rendered the construction of cellars impossible; instead of being kept underneath houses at a cool, constant temperature, Madeira was placed in attics and thus exposed to the heat of summer and cool of winter. In conditions in which other wines would have turned to vinegar, Madeira matured to an even greater level of quality than could have been achieved by carrying it across the tropics. So successful was this method of storage that it came to be used in those parts of America where the construction of cellars was possible. Captain Thomas Hamilton, an English officer and gentleman who visited New York at the beginning of the 1830s, and dined in the best society, recorded that "I have never drunk any Madeira in Europe at all equalling what I have frequently met in the United States." As a result, he added, "The gentlemen in America pique themselves on[21] their discrimination in wine, in a degree which is not common in England."

Although now a fortified wine, Madeira could still be turned into a refreshing beverage by adding water, sugar, and nutmeg or other spices in order to produce a long drink called "sangaree."[22] Gottlieb Mittelberger, a German organist who emigrated briefly to Upper Providence in Pennsylvania in the middle of the eighteenth century, did not enjoy the climate, complaining that "during the summer it is so often so hot and, so to speak, airless, that one comes close to suffocation." What he did enjoy was drinking sangaree, for which he specified a ratio of two parts water to one of wine. In his opinion, it was "even more delicious to drink" than the most popular mixed drink of the period—rum punch.

Although based on West Indian molasses, rum punch was in fact a legacy of the English colonial experience in another hot climate, that of India.

At much the same time as they planted settlements in America, the English were beginning to establish trading posts on the Indian subcontinent. Here they encountered not only a climate that posed similar problems to that of the American South but also a more sophisticated indigenous civilization, which already had developed its own form of alcoholic drinks. One of these was punch, which supposedly had existed for some 1,500 years. The name is derived from the Hindi word for five *(panch)*, the number of the ingredients: alcohol, sugar, citrus juice, water, and spices. The alcohol in question was a local spirit called arrack, usually distilled from the fermented sap of palm trees. It was not very pleasant to drink on its own and therefore needed to be mixed into a punch in order to render it palatable.[23]

Punch was consumed in substantial quantities by European expatriates in India during the seventeenth century. It was then introduced to England by merchants who traded with the Indian subcontinent, and soon became popular. According to César de Saussure, "A light punch

---

[21]Take pride in.
[22]By the nineteenth century, sangarees were being made with all kinds of wine, but most often port or sherry. Today unfortified table wine is generally used, with the addition of slices of fruit. It has reverted to its original Spanish name, sangria.
[23]Like bootleg spirits during Prohibition. See later in this chapter.

in summer time is a most acceptable and refreshing drink, and slakes thirst much more efficaciously than wine would."[24]

Saussure cited a recipe that included not only arrack from the East Indies but also brandy from France and rum from the West Indies. These might all have been available in England, but in America French brandy could be hard to find and East Indian arrack was virtually unobtainable. Rum, on the other hand, was widely available and cheap. It therefore made sense, when mixing punch in America, to forget about the arrack and brandy and concentrate on the rum. In Pennsylvania in the 1750s, punch was made from one part rum to three parts water, plus sugar and lemon juice. It probably helped to slake the thirst in hot weather even better than César de Saussure's recipe.

Punch was only one of various mixed drinks made with rum in the eighteenth century, although it must be said that a variety of names often concealed indistinguishable recipes. Punch was usually served cold, but sometimes warmed with a red-hot iron in cold weather. Sling, which (like punch) was made from rum, water, sugar, and sometimes lemon, was usually but not always cold. Toddy, made from rum and hot water and sweetening, was evidently hot. So was flip. To make this, a mug was filled about two thirds of the way to the top with strong beer, sweetened with sugar or molasses, and flavored with rum. In some taverns, a mixture of eggs and cream was also added. A red-hot stirrer was then thrust into the flip, making it bubble and foam, and giving it a burnt and bitter taste, which the drinkers of the period apparently appreciated.

Rum was a versatile spirit, being equally well suited to mixing with water and fruit juice, to make a refreshing long summer drink, and to warming with sugar and spices, to make a fortifying winter one.[25] This versatility helps to explain why it was so much more popular than beer in the changeable American climate. It also kept well, whereas, especially in warm weather, beer turned sour quite rapidly. Rum suited the extreme climate of the New England and Middle Atlantic colonies, which were, by European standards, very hot in summer and very cold

---

[24]Saussure meant "light" in flavor rather than in alcohol: His own recipe for punch contained just as much arrack as it did spring water.

[25]In the nineteenth century the celebrated bartender Jerry Thomas (see later in this chapter) refused to serve a Tom and Jerry, a hot eggnog of his own devising, until after the first snowfall. In support of his principles, he smashed a punch bowl containing the mixture which he found in a rival establishment in September.

in winter. Mittelberger's complaints about the Pennsylvanian climate were not limited to the summer heat. He did not like the winter either, finding that it was "marked by frequent penetrating cold spells which come so suddenly that human beings as well as the cattle and the birds in the air are in danger of freezing to death."

In the South, the need for a refreshing drink was even greater. It was found in the mint julep, which was based not on rum but on imported brandy or domestically produced whiskey.[26] It was made by putting mint leaves and sugar at the bottom of a tumbler, filling it one third of the way with liquor and then topping up the tumbler with crushed ice. "With the thermometer at 100 degrees," wrote the visiting English novelist Frederick Marryat, the mint julep is "one of the most delightful and insinuating potions that ever was invented."

Its original purpose appears to have been medicinal. Mint had long been used in Europe to treat all kinds of ailments (although nobody there had thought of sweetening the medicine by making it the basis of an alcoholic drink). There was also a tradition of adding local herbs or berries to whiskey in Ireland and Scotland. During the eighteenth century, it became common to add bitters, so called because they were extracted from bitter-tasting roots or herbs, to alcoholic drinks. The Scottish and Scotch-Irish who settled the back country of the southern colonies made great use of the combination of spirits and bitters, as it was believed that the bitters helped ward off tropical diseases. Mint was regarded as having the same effect.

The English journalist William Howard Russell visited the South to report on the Civil War for the London *Times*. When staying at a plantation near New Orleans, he was awoken by a slave offering him a mint julep—an offering he regarded, at that time of day, as something of an "ordeal." As he warned his readers: "In the early morning a stranger in a Southern planter's house may expect the offer of a glassful of brandy, sugar and [mint] beneath an island of ice—an obligatory panacea for all the evils of the climate."

The mint julep uniquely combined medicinal virtue with the intoxicating effects of alcohol and the capacity for refreshment. In the later years of the nineteenth century, however, it fell out of popularity as a

---

[26]Almost always whiskey after the Civil War left the South impoverished and unable to afford expensive imported spirits. The history of whiskey is covered in Chapter 6.

result of the growth of temperance sentiment, and it was all but killed off by Prohibition. It was not revived afterward because it was regarded as redolent of the Old South, which was popularly reviled as backward, hierarchical, and racist. Mint juleps are drunk today principally at the Kentucky Derby, as a deliberate nostalgic gesture.

Nevertheless, the mint julep lives on in popular culture through its descendant, the cocktail. The term "sling" has already been mentioned in connection with the various mixed drinks made with rum in the eighteenth century. It was simply a mixture of rum, water, and sugar. If bitters were added to a sling, this was known—at least from the beginning of the nineteenth century—as a cocktail.[27]

The first known reference to the word "cocktail" comes from a magazine called *The Balance and Colombian Repository,* published in Hudson, New York, in 1806. A reader having written to ask what a cocktail might be, he is informed by the editor that it is "a stimulating liquor, composed of spirits of any kind, sugar, water, and bitters—it is vulgarly called a bittered sling and is supposed to be an excellent engineering potion, inasmuch as it renders the heart stout and bold at the same time as it fuddles the head."

For the first half-century or so of its existence, therefore, a cocktail was specifically a sling to which bitters had been added, and which was intended to provide the same stimulant or prophylactic effect as a mint julep. The celebrated bartender Jerry Thomas, who published the first guide to mixed drinks in 1862, gave a number of recipes for cocktails, each of them containing bitters. The cocktail, he noted, "is a modern invention, and is generally used on fishing and other sporting parties, though some patients insist that it is good in the morning as a tonic." At this time the cocktail was either drunk in the morning as an "eye-opener" or was bottled for trips into the country; it was not generally sold over the bar as a refreshment. Not until the end of the nineteenth century did "cocktail" develop its modern meaning as a generic term for all kinds of mixed drinks, which might be consumed on all kinds of occasions, for any reason whatsoever.[28]

---

[27] No one knows how the name "cocktail" originated, although a great deal of time and timber has been wasted on discussing various theories, most recently in William Grimes's *Straight Up or On the Rocks.*

[28] There are those who would still limit its use. David Embury, whose *Fine Art of Mixing Drinks,* published half a century ago, remains the seminal work on the subject, insisted that the term "cocktail" should properly be used only for a short

During national Prohibition, the range of drinks encompassed under the name "cocktail" served a different if no less practical purpose. The number and variety of cocktails reached their apogee in the 1920s because of the necessity of devising mixtures in which the bad taste of bootleg spirits would be obscured.

Johnny Brooks, who worked as a bartender during Prohibition, later wrote an account of his experiences, *My Thirty-five Years Behind Bars,* in which he boasted of the number of mixed drinks he had invented. He was especially proud of the Cubanola, which he devised for a customer who came into his bar and ordered a Bacardi cocktail, a simple mixture of rum, lime (or lemon) juice, and grenadine. "The bootleg Bacardi we had wasn't the real stuff," Brooks recorded, "and it was raw. I decided to doctor it up a bit." By adding not only grenadine and lemon juice but also orange juice, pineapple juice, and egg white, Brooks succeeded in tempering the rawness of his bootleg rum.

A few of the cocktails introduced during Prohibition did outlast the ban on the trade in spirits and have come to be regarded as classics. One such is the Jack Rose, a mixture of apple brandy, grenadine, and lemon or lime juice, which was supposedly named after the New York gangster of that name. The majority of the cocktails invented during Prohibition, however, have gone the way of Brooks's Cubanola, which disappeared from the repertoire of bartenders once legitimate rum again became available. The swiftest to disappear were the thick, sweet "alcoholic milk shakes" that cannot possibly have been intended to serve any legitimate purpose other than disguising the poor quality of the spirits with which they were made. One of the very few to have survived is the Alexander, then based on gin (the most commonly available bootleg spirit[29]), to which crème de cacao and cream were added. It has persisted in a different form, having been found to taste a little less sickly if made with brandy. Most other, similar cocktails disappeared after Prohibition was repealed. "A general return to reason has done away with most of the exotic drinks," observed the author of *The Gun Club Drink Book.* "A real cocktail is short and snappy."

Soon after Repeal, Patrick Gavin Duffy, who had worked as a bartender before Prohibition, published a guide to the mixing of cocktails

---

drink, comprising one or more spirits and a modifying agent such as vermouth or bitters.

[29]Gin was much quicker and easier to counterfeit—by adding oil of juniper to diluted alcohol—than rum, brandy, or whiskey. Vodka was then unknown.

in which he did not shrink back from expressing his opinion of the innovations of the 1920s. "Although we include in this collection many of the cocktail creations of those hectic days," he wrote, "we caution barkeepers and others against adopting some of them for general use. They are published here as a matter of record and as a mirror in which future Americans may see the follies which the enactment of the Eighteenth Amendment[30] produced."

After Prohibition, the dry martini[31] became the classic American cocktail. The lead was taken by Franklin D. Roosevelt, who became president in 1933, the year of Repeal, and who, it has been suggested, may have mixed the first legal martini. According to Lowell Edmunds, the most scholarly of several authors who have written on the history and ritual of the martini, "such was Roosevelt's use of the White House, such was his dramatization of the presidency, that he gave the cocktail hour, and the martini rite in particular, an official sanction. He was the chief priest celebrating before the whole nation the same rite that each citizen would imitate in his private devotions."[32]

The rise of the martini was directly linked to the end of Prohibition. It made sense that people should turn to a simple cocktail in reaction against the extravagant concoctions in which the poor quality of bootleg spirits had been concealed. Also, many wealthy people had been able to avoid these mixtures because they had laid down a large supply of spirits before the traffic was banned. During Prohibition they continued to have access to the good-quality gin on which a dry martini—made from a lot of gin and a little vermouth—depended. As a result, the martini acquired status. No wonder it became so popular once Prohibition was repealed, and properly distilled gin was made legally available once more.

In particular, the martini suited the demands of those people who climbed into the upper-middle classes in the 1940s and 1950s. The man who had "arrived" needed a drink that was appropriate to his new position, and found it in the martini. This helps to explain the cult of dryness: the obsession with mixing a martini with as much gin

---

[30]The Amendment to the Constitution by which national Prohibition was introduced.

[31]The origin of the name has never been established.

[32]Roosevelt's martinis were notoriously bad—notwithstanding the polite comment of Joseph Stalin, who, after drinking one at the Teheran conference in 1943, pronounced it good although "cold on the stomach." Roosevelt added too much vermouth to his martinis, and sometimes fruit juice.

and as little vermouth as possible, which led in the 1950s to the invention of the vermouth atomizer, which blew a fine mist of vermouth over the martini glass, and in the 1960s to "martini stones," marbles that were soaked in vermouth and then placed in the gin. Doing one's best to eliminate all but the merest hint of vermouth from a cocktail comprised solely of gin and vermouth might seem pointless, since the result is little more than neat gin. But the purpose is symbolic: the production of a cocktail that is as pure as possible. This had always been the point of the martini. Ernest Hemingway published *A Farewell to Arms* in 1929, during Prohibition. When the hero of the book, Frederic Henry, joined his lover, Catherine Barkley, at a hotel bar on Lake Maggiore in northern Italy to eat sandwiches and drink martinis, he commented, "I had never tasted anything so cool and clean. They made me feel civilized."

For all the excesses of the Prohibition period and the excessive minimalism of the dry martini, the history of the cocktail serves as a testament to American inventiveness. It appeared in a response to a climate that required the development of new kinds of drinks and among a people who were not restricted by reverence for tradition and who were led by a democratic desire to produce drinks that could be enjoyed by all, rather than restricted to the sophisticated palates of the upper classes. When Marryat visited America in the 1830s, he was greatly impressed by "the pleasantness, amenity, and variety of the potations." In New York for Independence Day in 1837 he was amazed to see the whole length of Broadway lined with booths "loaded with porter, ale, cider, mead, brandy, wine, ginger-beer, pop, soda-water, whisky, rum, punch, gin slings, cocktails, mint juleps, besides many other compounds, to name which nothing but the luxuriance of American English could invent a word."

No such inventiveness was evident across the Atlantic in Britain. America in the nineteenth and early twentieth centuries regarded itself as a new country in which experiments were not merely possible but necessary. This experimentation extended from the organization of society—such as Prohibition, which came to be known as the "noble experiment"—to what people were prepared to eat and drink. In Britain, most people regarded social experimentation with horror. Here the idea of drinking anything before dinner was regarded as barbaric. Marryat complained that during his time in the States he was compelled to drink much more than he would otherwise have wanted, in order to be sociable, "yet still I gave most serious offence . . . because

I would not drink ... before dinner, which is a general custom in the States. . . . This refusal on my part . . . was eventually the occasion of much disturbance and of great animosity towards me."[33] Thomas Grattan, the British consul in Massachusetts in the 1840s, said that he did his best to taste "some of the beverages technically called 'drinks'," but did not progress much further than the mint julep, which he found "detestable. . . . The bad taste, in giving vulgar names to their articles of food or refreshment, is an obvious defect in American manners, and certainly unpleasing to a foreign ear." In the 1860s the authors of a British book entirely devoted to mixed drinks expressed their disapproval of the "sensation drinks which have lately travelled across the Atlantic" and their "gratification at the slight success which 'Pick-me-up,' 'Corpse-reviver,' 'Chain-lightning' and the like have had in this country."

The English did not start drinking cocktails—or anything before dinner—until more than half a century later, after the First World War. The war led not only to social change in what had been a rigidly conservative society, but also to a new receptiveness to the tastes of the Americans alongside whom British soldiers had fought in the trenches and who had played such a significant part in winning victory. There were also a large number of Americans who came to live in London after the war had ended. They were now accepted into polite society, and they brought the cocktail along with them. At the beginning of the Second World War, Robert Graves, already famous for his historical novels about the Roman emperor Claudius, coauthored a social history of the previous generation in Britain in which he observed that after the First World War the British had "gladly welcomed gay American fashions in dress, music, dancing and fun, having temporarily lost their own inventive power." The British even accepted cocktails, which went directly against upper-class tradition, the chief ingredients being gin, which was considered to be a lower-class drink, and vermouth, which was regarded as "dangerously Parisian."

---

[33] Having arrived in America as a celebrity, Marryat left it as a notoriety, having, in the course of his visit, been threatened by a lynch mob, watched his books burned in public bonfires, and on at least two occasions, seen himself hung in effigy by crowds—not because of his reluctance to drink before dinner but because of his political opinions. (He had publicly condemned a rebellion in Canada that most Americans had supported.)

Quite apart from their innate conservatism and reluctance to drink anything before dinner, English people who first encountered American cocktails in the middle of the nineteenth century found them colder than anything they had drunk before. The principal ingredient of the mint julep was not so much mint or whiskey (or brandy) but ice; the same was true of the other popular mixed drink of the period, the sherry cobbler, made by pouring sherry and sugar syrup or a sweet liqueur over ice, with a twist of lemon, and sipped through a straw.

Few if any Englishmen, and certainly no Englishwomen, were prepared to suck a drink through a straw, an act that ran directly counter to Victorian notions of propriety. In an age when people took pains to avoid openly showing pleasure in food and drink,[34] it imbued the process of drinking with too much dangerous sensuality.

It was not just that drinking ice cold cocktails through a straw offended British ideas of behavior, but also that ice in Britain was a rare commodity. As a result, the consumption of ice cold drinks in Victorian Britain was limited largely to the upper classes—as indeed it had been in most countries in the past.

The cooling of drinks in warm weather with snow and ice that has been stored in icehouses has a long history, going back to the construction of the first recorded icehouses in Mesopotamia almost four thousand years ago. The theory seemed simple: Snow was brought down from the mountains in winter, pits were dug and lined with straw, the snow was packed into them, and branches placed on the top. The technology may not have been complex, but it was an expensive business, transporting snow and storing it until the summer (by which time a substantial proportion would have melted). Cost alone restricted the availability of ice to the better-off.

Even then ice tended to be used in the most efficient manner, being dropped directly into drinks rather than placed around them. This process not only diluted the drinks in question but could also spoil them, since the cleanliness of the ice (and especially the straw in which it was packed) could not be guaranteed. Yet it was regarded as an act of great extravagance; when this custom was introduced from Italy into France

---

[34]The poet Robert Browning, a man so fastidious that he would not go out-of-doors without putting on a pair of gloves, and so ignorant of matters sexual that he included the word "twat" in his poem *Pippa Passes* in the mistaken belief that it referred to an item of nun's attire, regarded eating and drinking as such private acts that he could not bear anyone to see him indulging in them.

toward the end of the sixteenth century by King Henry III and his court, it was regarded as an example of their effeminate ways and indulgence in every kind of luxury.[35]

In Britain at this period ice was virtually unobtainable, as there was nowhere to store it. Icehouses had been introduced into the country by the Romans, but had been allowed to fall into ruin during the Middle Ages. They were reintroduced into Britain from the Continent in the second half of the seventeenth century, "as the mode in some parts of France and Italy and other hot countries, for to cool wines and other drinks for the summer season." The reintroduction of icehouses in Britain was merely one aspect of a general indulgence in opulence on the French model that accompanied the restoration of the monarchy after a period of austere parliamentary government. As King Charles II, himself a trendsetter in these matters, complained to Parliament, "The whole nation seemed to him to be corrupted in their excess of living."

By the middle of the eighteenth century, icehouses were also being built in America. Unlike Britain, America, with its cold winters and hot summers, had both a large supply of ice available in winter and a great need of it in summer.[36] Even so, and despite the apparent simplicity of the technology involved, pioneers of American icehouse construction ran into difficulties. George Washington laid up a store of ice in a well in his cellar on his Mount Vernon estate during the winter of 1784–75, but when he came to use it at the beginning of June he found that "there was not the smallest particle remaining." During the following winter he had a well-insulated icehouse constructed, and from then on enjoyed a reliable supply of ice in summer.

By the end of the century, many farmhouses in the northern states had their own icehouses. It was also possible to buy ice in the cities of the South, brought down by ships (and, in the interior of the country, flatboats) from lakes in the North. It did not come cheap, however. Northern farmers might be able to collect their own ice for free, and to store it for no more than the cost of the construction and maintenance of an icehouse, but in cities it was available only to the wealthy. Ice was expensive because it had to be laboriously hacked by hand and was then inefficiently stored until time of use. In the mid-1820s the

---

[35]Including the use of forks for eating. Why, people wondered, could the king not use his fingers like everyone else?

[36]Before they had access to ice in summer, people diverted streams into stone buildings near their homes, where they kept wine, milk, and other drinks.

invention of a new kind of above-ground icehouse reduced wastage from the 60 percent that had been the norm in underground houses to less than 8 percent. At the same time, a horse-driven ice cutter was introduced. Even though transportation costs remained high, these improvements caused the price of ice in New Orleans to fall from 12½ cents for one pound in 1819 to between 50 cents and $3 for one hundred pounds in 1847.[37]

It became possible for city dwellers to buy and keep ice for their domestic consumption in a refrigerator (or, rather, icebox, since it was then cooled with ice rather than by chemical means). This had been invented at the beginning of the century by Thomas Moore, a Maryland farmer and the son of a cabinet maker, in order to keep his dairy produce fresh. It was a wooden box enclosed in a larger one, the gap in between filled with charcoal for insulation, and a tin holder for ice fixed at the top. In 1838 it was commented in the *New York Mirror* that although "it is but a few years since it came into use, [the icebox] . . . is now justly considered as much an article of necessity as a carpet or dining table." Admittedly, householders relied upon a daily delivery from the iceman, as the box would not normally preserve a lump of ice weighing five or six pounds for longer than twenty-four hours. And, the insulation being fairly primitive, moisture tended to gather within the wall, corroding the metal lining and promoting the growth of bacteria. Nevertheless, it was thanks to the introduction of the icebox, wrote the *Mirror,* that "joints of meat are kept good for several days, wine is cooled, butter is hardened, milk saved from 'turning,' and a supply of ice kept always on hand for the more direct use of the table."

The author of an article in *De Bow's Review* in 1855 regarded the popularity of ice in America as a mark of its democratic spirit. As in government, so, too, in luxuries such as ice "we are democratic and popular. The great mass of the people . . . in America can and do enjoy these creature comforts of existence daily, which are, in European nations, the Sabbath wonder of the humbler domestic circles. . . . The use of ice is esteemed a rare blessing [in Europe], and like all good things beyond the water is adopted by the aristocracies. Dietetically, the poorer, and even middle classes, know nothing of ice. It is confined to the wine cellars of the rich, and the cooling pantries of first-class confectioneries. . . . In America the use of ice is as widely extended

---

[37] In the early nineteenth century the purchasing power of a dollar was between ten and twenty times as great as it is today.

among the people as the heat is, and with a very trifling individual cost. We use it for seven or eight months of the year—all the year in the South; and even in New York there are numbers of families who ice their Croton[38] throughout the winter. . . . Ice is an American institution—the use of it an American luxury—the abuse of it an American failing."

In America, where ice was cheap and widely available, it was used unthinkingly by the majority of the population, to chill water, milk, wine, and mixed drinks such as mint juleps and sherry cobblers. In Britain, where it was expensive, ice was used self-consciously, to show off. A certain amount was produced domestically, skimmed from rivers and streams, but this was insufficiently clean to be placed directly in a glass of wine or punch. Ice found favor among the British middle and upper classes only if it had been imported in a pure state from America.

This transatlantic ice trade began in the 1840s. A number of shipping merchants banded together to construct a series of icehouses on Wenham Lake, six miles north of Salem, Massachusetts. These houses were made of timber, and well insulated. With the use of specially constructed railway cars, and careful preparation of ships' holds insulated with sawdust, straw, wood shavings, tarpaulins, and boards, ice could be transported over remarkable distances. The first cargo of Wenham Lake ice arrived in England in the summer of 1844, and the English branch of the company opened its main office in the center of London the next year. Henry Coleman, a native of Salem who was visiting England at the time, recorded in a letter home that a block of ice about eighteen inches square and twelve inches thick was displayed in the window. "The Londoners look upon it with amazement," he wrote. "I am told they sometimes go into the shop, after gazing through the window, and put their hands on it, to be sure that it is not glass."

In 1845 Queen Victoria and Prince Albert expressed their admiration of its "purity and cleanliness" and directed that a supply of Wenham Lake ice should be always available to them thereafter. The *Liverpool Times* reported that Wenham Lake ice had become an essential element at all the better establishments in London, claiming that "a particle dropped in a beaker of claret instantly reduces the temperature of the beverage without in the least deteriorating its quality, a result wholly

---

[38] Water brought by aqueduct from the Croton River upstate. See Chapter 4.

unobtainable by the substitution of English ice."[39] The nouveaux riches took to flaunting their wealth by putting enough ice in their wine to chill it to a point of insensibility. Even wine connoisseurs insisted on icing their Bordeaux. As George Saintsbury later recorded in his *Notes on a Cellar Book,* the middle of the nineteenth century was an "Ice Age" of claret-drinking, "a barbarous time" when people used "marsupial claret jugs with a pouch for ice."[40]

One drink into which the British did not put ice was tea. This is ironical, considering that iced tea is supposed to have been invented by an Englishman.[41] According to tradition, an Englishman named Richard Blechynden had come over to try to promote tea from India at the St. Louis World's Fair in 1904. Unfortunately, he had not realized quite how hot midwestern summers could be. No one was interested in trying his hot tea. As a desperate measure, he crammed ice cubes into a glass, poured tea over them, and eureka! iced tea was born.

Like most such legends, this story seeks to encapsulate a gradual development in a single incident.[42] It is not in fact known when or where iced tea was invented, although it does seem probable that it emerged out of the hot "Russian" tea that became very popular at women's high teas in the mid and late nineteenth century. This was served in glasses, with lemon but without milk.

Despite its present-day reputation as *the* quintessential southern drink, there is no evidence that iced tea was invented in the South. It was already being drunk in northern cities at the beginning of the 1870s. Mary Stuart Smith did assert in her *Virginia Cookery Book* in 1885 that "the use of tea as a cooling drink originated in Virginia, and is well-nigh universal there as soon as warm weather begins," but there is good reason to believe that local patriotism had clouded her judgment. Iced tea could not have been "universal" when it was available

---

[39]By 1850, however, less and less ice was being cut from Lake Wenham and the American market was requiring more and more of it. The Wenham Lake Ice Company, therefore, took to harvesting ice for English consumption in Norway, from Lake Oppegaard, ten miles south of Oslo—taking care, for trading purposes, to rename their new Norwegian source "Lake Wenham."

[40]Ever since the Middle Ages the British have called red Bordeaux "claret," in reference to its original pale red color (*clairet* in French).

[41]The pre-revolutionary taste for hot tea and the conversion to coffee are discussed in Chapter 6.

[42]Compare the story of the first Indian encounter with alcohol in the Introduction and Geoffrey of Monmouth's account of the origins of toasting in the Conclusion.

only to those families who could afford ice. As was observed by the author of a survey of the post–Civil-War South, "In these hot climates, cold tea lemonade iced, is declared by the few who have tried it to be more fragrant and refreshing than the most liberal libations of soda-water or other effervescing liquids." It would appear that from the end of the war onward, well-to-do southerners drank iced tea. Harriet Sikes, born in 1906 into a wealthy North Carolina family, remembered in 1995 drinking iced tea all year round. Ordinary people drank iced tea only rarely. Puckette Wooten, who was born in Virginia in 1924 and grew up during the Depression, remembers iced tea as a treat that was available only on Sundays, after the iceman had come. In the South before the Second World War, iced tea remained largely an urban beverage, because only a small minority of the people who lived in the countryside purchased ice. According to one survey in the 1930s, very few small farmers and less than one third of even the wealthiest farming families in the rural South drank iced tea. Its consumption spread generally from urban into rural areas only after the Second World War, along with the refrigerator.

It had taken, in all, a century for people living in the rural South to achieve the easy access to refrigeration that was enjoyed by people living in cities and by their counterparts in the North. Although artificial forms of refrigeration had been known as early as the 1850s and had widely been employed in industry toward the end of the nineteenth century,[43] it was not until the second decade of the twentieth century that refrigerators were mass produced on a domestic scale. The delay can be attributed to the difficulty of reducing large machinery to domestic scale, and to economic factors. It was possible to achieve economies of scale only if a lot of people bought domestic refrigerators. When they were first introduced, in 1916–17, they cost $900 each (the equivalent of more than $10,000 today). As more people purchased them, the price fell, and more people could afford to buy them. By 1940, when there were over three million refrigerators in the country, the price had fallen to $154. During the next decade they reached into every corner of the nation, including the rural South.

With the introduction of the refrigerator, iced tea finally became the staple drink of the rural South. But it did not reach Britain, where only a minority of people had access to domestic refrigeration until after the Second World War. Even as recently as the end of the 1960s, little

---

[43]Most extensively in the brewing industry, for which see later in this chapter.

more than half the British population possessed a refrigerator. Even today, when virtually everyone in the country has a refrigerator, iced tea remains a rarity. Many British people retain the old colonial notion that it is healthier to drink something warming than a cold drink in hot weather. Hot tea, whatever the weather, whatever the time of day, remains the national beverage.

In America, not only is almost all the tea drunk in the South iced, but so is 80 percent of all the tea consumed in the country. Admittedly, much of the iced tea drunk elsewhere in America is an ersatz version, sold in a soft-drink can and with little if any tea flavor, but in the South, even in fast food restaurants, iced tea is made from bags containing real tea leaves. The South also has its own tea garden, the Charleston Tea Plantation on Wadmalaw Island in South Carolina, which produces a light tea with little astringency that is especially suitable for making iced.[44]

Thus, iced tea is not only a quintessentially southern drink, but also a fundamentally American one. Like the cocktail, its history demonstrates the American genius for transforming drinks that have been popular in Europe into a form that suits the American climate and American tastes. The great advantage of tea is that the leaf is dried at the point of production, making it cheap and easy to transport and unlikely to spoil. It can also be made from water that is contaminated with pathogenic bacteria, because the water is boiled as part of the tea-making process.[45] But—British preconceptions aside—a hot drink, made from boiled water, is not really ideal in a hot climate. With the benefit of hindsight, this might seem obvious, but it took the American spirit of inventiveness to cool it down and make a refreshing summer drink.

In America today, it is no longer just the consumable that is cooled but also the consumer. The installation of air-conditioning for the purposes of comfort rather than for the better functioning of machinery began in the 1920s, initially in theaters. During the 1930s it was extended to shops, restaurants, and the like. Not until the 1960s, how-

---

[44]Sold under the brand name American Classic. The estate is open to visitors on the first Saturday of each month during the harvest season.

[45]Now that piped water supplies are safe to drink, it is better to make iced tea by steeping leaves in cold water in the refrigerator overnight, rather than from hot tea. Not only is it less astringent but it does not turn cloudy, as hot tea does when it is cooled—necessitating the addition of a slice of lemon to clarify it.

ever, was air-conditioning commonly introduced into homes and automobiles. The belated spread of air-conditioning into private lives cannot be explained by the cost alone but principally by the fact that it took some years for the perception to be established that it was worthwhile.[46] Attitudes to air-conditioning in America at the beginning of the 1960s can be compared to Britain today. In the last few years, air-conditioning has generally been installed in theaters, shops, and offices, but air-conditioned automobiles are only just beginning to become popular, and air-conditioning in private homes remains rare. It simply does not occur to people to invest in this particular aspect of their own comfort. In America since the beginning of the 1960s air-conditioning has spread to such an extent that three quarters of new homes come equipped with air-conditioning, as do 90 percent of new cars. Without air-conditioning, it is unlikely that middle-class whites and blacks whose families left the South for northern cities during the first half of the twentieth century would have returned in the 1980s and 1990s as they have.

The doubts that Americans had expressed about air-conditioning before the 1960s, and are felt by many British people today, were enunciated in 1992 by the British anthropologist Gwyn Prins in an article in the academic journal *Energy and Buildings* in which he argued that "physical addiction to air-conditioned air is the most pervasive and least noticed epidemic in modern America." He pointed out that his experience of living in Zambia in sub-Saharan Africa had taught him that people could perfectly well live in a hot climate without air-conditioning; it was simply a matter of adjusting one's lifestyle. And the human body has a very efficient cooling mechanism of its own, in the form of sweat.

If Americans were addicted to air-conditioning, he argued, it was for cultural reasons. They wished to dissociate themselves from the poor blacks who sweated in hot weather in the South, and from the poor whites who had once labored in sweatshops in the cities of the North. They wished to remind themselves that they were no longer living in the Depression. Air-conditioning, Prins said, "exuberantly expresses

---

[46]A primitive form of air-conditioning had been employed last century. Mrs. Maury, an Englishwoman who visited America in 1845 in the hope that a change of climate and culture would help her recovery from a nervous breakdown, "found it a most refreshing practice to place several jugs of iced water in my bedroom during the great heats: the atmosphere became perceptibly cooled."

the achievement of the American dream. . . . We shiver, therefore we are. . . . We shall be cool, our plates shall overflow, and gas shall be $1 a gallon. Amen."

Prins's article was greeted with outrage by the American academics who were given the opportunity to reply in the same issue of the journal. He was accused of indulging in an "anti-American diatribe," an "ethnocentric attack on U.S. culture," and a "farrago of non sequiturs." Ruth Cowan of the State University of New York in Stony Brook pointed out, "Prins doesn't lead the tropical life in Zambia anymore, but the leisured life of a scholar in that ivoriest of ivory towers, Cambridge."

This was a typical British-American confrontation. If Prins was being condescending, then his critics were overreacting. By referring to the cultural significance of air-conditioning for many Americans rather than prosaically stating that it made life much more pleasant if one cooled one's home and car in hot weather, Prins was making a valid point. By indulging in air-conditioning, many people are, at least subconsciously, distancing themselves from the primitive and brutal life of the frontier and the insecurity and discomfort experienced by immigrants in the big cities. They have never really freed themselves from their fear of poverty and hunger and continue to overreact to them. They are trying to live down a collective folk memory.

And Prins's argument could be extended to apply to the popular taste for cold drinks. Now that air-conditioning is so common—and often so fierce that people put on jackets or sweaters when they go indoors in summer—the preparation of ice cold drinks in hot weather is no longer really necessary. There is no need to add so much ice to a glass of water as to hurt the teeth of the drinker, nor to numb the taste of a good whiskey that has taken years of careful maturation and a great deal of skillful blending by filling up the glass with ice. As the Soviet leader Nikita Khrushchev said to President Richard Nixon in 1969 on being given a glass of I. W. Harper bourbon, "This is a very good whiskey, but you Americans spoil it. You put more ice in there than whiskey."[47]

---

[47] This attitude achieves its reductio ad absurdum in the form of the pseudo-science of cryonics. A few people have spent $100,000 or more on having their corpses deep frozen immediately after death, in the hope that doctors in the future will be able to bring them back to life. The process has been discredited by conventional cryobiologists (who freeze sperm and the like), who point to the extensive cell damage associated both with death and with the freezing process. Arthur

If this habit persists, it is for more than just practical reasons. Surely, it is a relic of a reaction to the harsh life and deprivations encountered by those who emigrated to America, and settled its frontier, to whom refreshing drinks in summer were a luxury?

Surely, it is a relic of the days of the mint julep and sherry cobbler, before the introduction of artificial means of refrigeration, when packing one's drink with ice was the only way that it could effectively be cooled?

In today's air-conditioned world, there is no need any longer to serve beer at the freezing point of water, so cold that it clouds the glass with condensation. Unfortunately, after more than a century producing beer in a style that enables it to be served as cold as possible, it is too late. By focusing exclusively on its refreshing qualities, American brewers have ended up by making a beer that—by European standards—tastes of nothing at all. If it were served any warmer, its absence of flavor would be evident. At 32 degrees Fahrenheit, it does not really matter.

Beer drinkers who lament the blandness of most American beer have only themselves (and their predecessors) to blame. They asked for a beer that was light and refreshing and that is what the brewers gave them. It is no good trying to blame the brewers for producing a style of beer with little taste that needed to be served at a low temperature, and then foisting it upon their customers. Such an accusation simply cannot be supported by the history of American beer production.

In the colonial period, the same kind of beer was drunk in America as in Britain. Some of it was imported from Britain, some of it was brewed in America. But wherever it was produced, it was the same dark, nutritious beer that ideally suited the damp climate of England. It was less well suited to the much drier climate of New England, although it could certainly be sustaining on a cold winter's day. But it was wholly inappropriate for drinking in the summer, or at almost any time of year in the much warmer climate of the southern colonies. The Swedish pastor Israel Acrelius described the beer brewed in Pennsylvania in the 1750s as "brown, thick and unpalatable."[48] No wonder people preferred rum.

Rowe of the New York University School of Medicine compares it to "believing you can turn a hamburger back into a cow."

[48]For better opinions of the beer brewed in Philadelphia later in the century, see the Conclusion.

Beer was made in this style in the seventeenth and eighteenth centuries partly because consumers back in Britain enjoyed the taste, and partly because of technological limitations. A dark, strong beer with a lot of bitter-tasting hops could safely be brewed in large quantities without being spoiled if the temperature in the fermentation vat rose too high. A paler, more delicate beer would not survive the experience. Then, at the end of the eighteenth century, British brewers introduced an early form of temperature control by placing lengths of coiled copper piping in the fermentation vat and circulating cold water through them. This device (the attemperator) made it possible to brew a pale ale in large quantities. Brewers began to convert to a lighter style of beer—to make the forerunner of the pale, thirst-quenching ale that is known in Britain today as "bitter."

American brewers did not have attemperators, and remained stuck with their old-fashioned beer. Not only were they smaller than their British counterparts and therefore less well able to afford expensive equipment but also technologically less advanced. In this respect, they reflected the post-revolutionary economy as a whole. Whereas Britain was the world's most advanced country, America lagged behind in both economy and technology. This was partly because the new republic had to focus its energies on providing itself with a basic infrastructure before it could start thinking about spending money on industrial development. But it was also because Britain had made it that way. Britain had sought to run America as a colonial economy that concentrated on exporting raw materials to the mother country.

During the course of the nineteenth century the relative economic positions of Britain and America were exchanged. By the middle of the century the American industrial revolution had caught up with and was beginning to pass the British one. At precisely this time a new style of beer, paler in color, lighter in taste, and better suited to the American climate, was introduced by immigrants from Germany.

It is believed that German-style lager was brewed in America for the first time in 1840, in a small brewery in the rear of a house in Philadelphia owned by John Wagner, who had worked as a brewer in Bavaria before emigrating to America, carrying with him a sample of lager yeast. Wagner did not, however, brew beer commercially in America, but simply as a treat for friends from the old country. It was not until the 1850s, after the settlement of well over a million immigrants from Germany, that German-type lager began to replace English-style beers.

Although the immigrants provided a reliable customer base for the new kind of beer, this was not the main reason lager became so popular. Between 1840 and the end of the 1850s the appearance if not the taste of the lager that was drunk in Europe had changed dramatically. The lager that Wagner brewed in 1840 would have been a dark, slightly cloudy beer, no lighter in color than the paler beers that had become popular in Britain. The lager that proved such a success in America less than a generation later was a bright, golden beer.

Although it is popularly imagined that the term "lager" indicates a light-colored beer, this is not necessarily the case. *Lager* is a German word meaning "a store"; it refers to the method, discovered in Germany in the fifteenth century, of preventing beer from spoiling in summer by storing it at a low temperature, in caves packed with ice.[49]

The technique for producing a bright, light beer was invented just after Wagner had brewed the first German-style lager in America. One of the great advances of the industrial revolution, it occurred principally as a result of the conversion from coal to steam by breweries in Pilsen in what is now the Czech Republic.[50] By converting from a direct to an indirect source of heat, the brewers were able to dry the malted barley from which they made their beer without causing it to overheat and turn dark. Because the barley remained light in color, the brewers could use it to produce a pale beer. In homage to its origin in Pilsen, this style of lager has been known ever since as Pilsner (or Pils).

The old-fashioned, pale brown, slightly cloudy lager had been popular only in a small area of central Europe. But the new clear, golden Pilsner spread rapidly across almost the whole of the Continent, its journey speeded by another great advance of the industrial revolution, the railway. Having conquered most of Europe, it traveled across the North Sea to Scotland (but not to England or Wales or Ireland). It also crossed the Atlantic to America. The yeasts needed to ferment lager had already been brought to America by old-style German brewers such as Wagner; once the malting process had been modified, it was simple enough to produce the new-style Pilsner beer. This lager came to dominate American beer production during the second half of the nineteenth century.

---

[49]This type of beer is also described as having been "bottom-fermented," as the yeast gradually settled to the bottom rather than having to be skimmed off the top.

[50]It was then joined with what is now Germany in the Austro-Hungarian Empire.

Or, rather, the dominance was achieved by an American variant of the Pilsner style. Whereas in Europe lager had been made entirely from malted barley, in America other grains were introduced, such as rice and corn. By the end of the century the Pabst brewery in Milwaukee was making what it called Pilsner beer from a mixture of one part corn meal to two parts malt. It still made pure malt beers, largely for its German-born customers, but these were more expensive than the Pilsner and accounted for only one tenth of the total production.

The majority of other lager brewers followed Pabst in using corn, although there were some, notably Anheuser-Busch, who preferred rice. Anheuser-Busch continues to use rice today in its production of Budweiser—a beer named in homage to the town of Budweis,[51] which had developed a similar style of golden beer to that of Pilsen, eighty miles away. Anheuser-Busch is proud of its use of rice, which it insists contributes to the "snappiness" of the beverage.

"Snappy," of course, is a euphemism for a beer that can be drunk quickly without bothering the taste buds too much on the way down. The manner in which American brewers have succeeded in removing most of the flavor from Pilsner lager has been much criticized by beer connoisseurs—and deservedly so—but the fact remains that the style was changed in response to demands from consumers. There is plenty of documentary evidence to support this, such as correspondence in 1880 from Pabst's manager in Chicago to Fred Pabst in Milwaukee asking for "a paler, purer beer . . . our reputation in Chicago will certainly suffer if we don't get a different beer."

The reason American consumers chose a blander beer than was enjoyed in Europe has much challenged beer historians. In his history of Pabst, written half a century ago, Thomas Cochran suggested that

---

[51]The coexistence of American and Czech beers called "Budweiser" has caused a great deal of confusion. For years Anheuser-Busch and the Czech Budweiser brewery have been fighting court battles all over the world in order to determine who owns the right to the "Budweiser" trademark. In some countries (such as the United States) the right belongs to Anheuser-Busch, in others (including much of Europe) it belongs to the Czech brewery. Britain is an open market where both companies are allowed to use the name. Since the Velvet Revolution of 1989 in which the people of the Czech Republic overthrew their Soviet-backed communist government, Anheuser-Busch has been trying to solve the problem once and for all by buying the Czech Budweiser brewery, but it has been rebuffed. There is little resemblance any longer between the two Budweiser beers. Josef Tolar, head brewer at the Czech Budweiser brewery, has described the American version as "soda water with a dash of color."

"Americans wanted a lighter, drier beer than was made in Europe . . . due partly to the hot summer climate of the United States, and to the desire to drink rapidly." He does not explain, however, why Americans should have wanted to drink their beer more rapidly than was the practice among Germans in Germany, or indeed among German settlers in America—although there is no doubt that native Americans in the second half of the nineteenth century generally spent much less time eating, drinking, and socializing than their German-born counterparts.[52]

It would also make sense that Americans should have chosen a lighter lager than beer drinkers in Europe because they preferred colder drinks, having better access to ice. Whereas American-style lager is served at a temperature that suits its absence of taste, traditional Pilsner, with its much higher content of bitter-tasting hops as well as malted barley, not only loses its flavor if served too cold but can also appear excessively bitter.

Refrigeration has played a major part in the popularization of lager in America. The process of lager production requires that the beer be fermented as well as stored at a low temperature. Both in Europe and in mid-nineteenth-century America, lager was produced during the winter and then stored for the summer months. But this meant that the brewer had to predict how much lager he was likely to sell in any given summer. Too much unsold beer, and he would lose money. Too little, and his customers would be disappointed. By the mid-1860s, according to a spokesman for the chamber of commerce in Cincinnati, "so necessary has the article become in the estimation of the masses, as a beverage, that a scarcity of lager is regarded in a similar light with a dearth of corn; and from the fondness displayed for it, and the rush made to those beer shops where a fresh keg of lager has been tapped, the conclusion seems natural that a large number of citizens would dispense with their bread rather than their beer."

As long as the brewing industry relied on supplies of natural ice, lager could be brewed only in the winter months—and then only where there was a sufficiently large supply of natural ice to keep the beer cool while it was maturing over the spring and summer. It was feasible to make and store lager in the cities of the Northeast and the Midwest, where a great deal of ice was created during the freezing cold winters,

---

[52]The speed of American eating is discussed in the next chapter, and the lack of socializing in the Conclusion.

but not in the South. Yet it was in the hot and humid climate of the South that a refreshing beer was most needed.

These problems were solved by the development of artificial refrigeration, which enabled lager to be made anywhere in the country, at any time of year. This technology developed out of the discovery that certain gases permit themselves to be liquefied under pressure, absorbing heat, thus producing cold when allowed to expand. The importance of this discovery for the brewing industry is demonstrated by the fact that brewing was the first activity in the northern states to use mechanical refrigeration extensively, from the 1870s onward; by the last decade of the century nearly every brewery was equipped with refrigerating machines.

Indeed, so important was mechanical refrigeration to the brewing industry, and so important were its brewery customers to the refrigeration industry, that the two businesses developed in tandem. Brewers willingly experimented with all kinds of refrigerating devices, often losing batches of beer when a new machine went wrong. But, in the long run, it was worth it. Apart from being able to brew all year round and in the South, maturation periods were reduced because the cold produced mechanically was more reliable and more intense than the kind provided by natural ice. Beer became cheaper to make, and even lighter and blander in taste.

As the history of refrigeration demonstrates, America, having been a technologically backward country at the end of the eighteenth century, had become an advanced one a hundred years later. Whereas breweries had once lacked the cooling equipment to produce English-style bitter, now, thanks to mechanical refrigeration, they were able to produce German-style lager on demand.

Britain was no longer, relatively speaking, as technologically advanced at the end of the nineteenth century as it had been a hundred years earlier. Breweries had not generally installed refrigerating equipment, which helps to explain why they did not make much lager. British breweries started manufacturing lager on a significant scale only in the 1960s, and British drinkers did not acquire a taste for it until the 1970s. Only in the last few years has the consumption of lager passed that of bitter and other beers. In part, the milder climate explains why British breweries have been relatively slow to adopt refrigeration, and why British beer drinkers have taken so long to start drinking lager. But there is also the fact that bitter was considered to be refreshing beer. Contrary to popular belief, bitter was (and is) neither warm nor flat but is served at cellar temperature (between 50 and 55 degrees Fahrenheit) and with a gentle degree of carbonation. It is reasonable to wonder whether American beer drinkers would have taken so readily to a version of German lager if they had been able to drink bitter instead of the heavier and darker ales that preceded it. Certainly many Americans of British stock, well into the twentieth century, retained ideological objections to what they regarded as an alien beer that had been brought into their country by aliens.[53]

Now, of course, it is too late for Americans to start drinking bitter. The microbreweries and brew pubs[54] that have opened all over the country in recent years may profess to produce English-style bitter but, for the most part, they do not.

The brew pubs certainly play on tradition in marketing their product. Many of them decorate their premises with historic photographs to demonstrate that however recently they may have opened, they are established in a community with a long tradition of local brewing. They imply that they make beer the way it used to be made. According to Mark Garvey, an architect who designs brew pubs in Portland, Oregon, they attract people who are looking to escape the "air-conditioned-mall mentality" of modern America, who have experienced "a yearning for simpler times and [for] a place that felt real to people, where they could maybe sweat a little and rediscover humanity."

Many American brew pubs more closely resemble English pubs, which express a lively sense of community, than American bars. But the beers they offer are neither accurate reproductions of contemporary British beers, nor authentic revivals of historic American ones, because they are dominated by the modern American taste for ice cold beer. They may be reacting to the mentality that has brought about the air-conditioned mall, but they cannot escape from it.

The reason bitter and other traditional English beers, such as porter and stout, are served at cellar temperature is not that the English have eccentrically retained a taste for warm beer but that the beer undergoes a process of "conditioning" in the pub cellar. This is a secondary fer-

---

[53]Aliens come from another country, not another planet. Popular hostility toward German-Americans on the grounds that they were aliens is discussed in Chapter 6.

[54]A microbrewery is a small brewery, although not necessarily as small as its name suggests; a brew pub is a pub that brews its own beer for sale on the premises but not elsewhere.

mentation, which produces complex yeasty flavors and creates a small amount of carbon dioxide gas. If the cellar is too cold, the yeasts will not be able to work properly, and the beer will be flat. The ideal temperature for this process of "cask-conditioning" is between 50 and 55 degrees Fahrenheit. This is therefore the temperature at which English beers have traditionally been drunk.

Managing the conditioning of beer in cask has always been regarded as part of the art of cellarmanship that has been handed down from one generation of publican to another. After the Second World War, however, many of the men who left the armed forces bought pubs without first learning how to look after beer. This led to a decline in the quality of cask-conditioned beer. Then, in the 1960s, England was belatedly overtaken by a spirit of modernization and a belief in the virtues of "progress." The major brewers abandoned traditional cask beer in favor of the "keg" or "brewery-conditioned" version. This was filtered and pasteurized to prevent any secondary fermentation from taking place and then artificially carbonated to replicate the natural conditioning that would have been produced by secondary fermentation in the pub cellar.

Because keg beer did not need to ferment for a second time, it could be served much colder than the traditional cask version. The colder it was kept, the more gas was retained in the beer, and the fizzier it tasted. The greater degree of carbonation and colder serving temperature masked its comparative lack of flavor. To a palate accustomed to cask-conditioned beer, keg beer was a poor substitute. The conversion of the major breweries to keg beer led to a rebellion by the massed ranks of beer drinkers. They founded the Campaign for Real Ale (CAMRA), which by lobbying vociferously succeeded first in dissuading smaller regional breweries from following the major companies into converting to keg beer and then in persuading the major companies to restore cask-conditioned beer in many of the pubs from which it had previously been removed. CAMRA, which has 40,000 members, including a number of Members of Parliament, continues today to campaign enthusiastically on behalf of traditional cask-conditioned beers.

In the light of the history of English beer in the last half-century, it is ironic that supposedly quality-oriented brew pubs in the United States have set store by the production of keg beer. A few establishments, principally on the West Coast, do serve English-style cask-conditioned beer, but elsewhere in the country they are rare. Brew pubs are prevented from serving cask-conditioned beer by the prevailing American taste for cold, fizzy beer. As Steve Deptula, the owner of the Park Slope brew pub in Brooklyn, points out, "New Yorkers aren't ready for cask-conditioned beer. They'd say it was warm and flat." Park Slope, like most American brew pubs, serves its beers at a little over 40 degrees Fahrenheit, midway between the temperature of traditional English beers and that of mainstream American ones. And even then, Deptula says, customers often complain that they are too warm.

Whereas low temperatures may be appropriate for mainstream American lager, they do no favors for the beers brewed by microbreweries and brew pubs, which are supposed to distinguish themselves by their superior flavor. In order to make sure they can be tasted through all that cold and fizz, they are often brewed with exaggerated hop and malt flavors; beers as delicate and subtle as the best English bitters would simply not be noticed. As a result, many American microbrewery and brew-pub beers end up as pastiches of traditional English beers. To that extent, they resemble the relationship between California wines and their French exemplars.

Whereas the flavor of beer depends largely upon the manner in which the malt has been treated and the process by which it is turned into beer, that of wine is principally determined not only by the variety of grapes from which it is made and the manner in which they are transformed into wine but also by the climate in which they have been grown. Ninety percent of the wines produced in the United States come from California, the equivalent of two billion standard-sized bottles a year. The California wine industry was established as a result of the Gold Rush of 1849, which brought a large number of immigrants into the state, many of whom soon discovered that wine production offered them a more secure livelihood than panning for gold.[55] Indeed, they made so much money from wine that gold fever was followed by vine fever, and people emigrated to the state to grow grapes. In 1862 it was predicted in the French viticultural journal *Revue Viticole* that California was the one American region "capable of entering competition with the wines of Europe . . . in the distant future." By the later years of the century, a number of fine California wines were doing precisely that. At the Paris Exposition of 1889, the most famous of these wines,

---

[55]The planting of the first vineyards in California by Franciscan missionaries in the late eighteenth century is discussed in the Conclusion.

from the Inglenook vineyard in the Napa Valley, were given a special award for their "excellence and purity." "It means that France, our greatest rival," trumpeted the *San Francisco Merchant and Viticulturalist,* "has declared to the world that the products of California's vintages rank with those of her own."[56]

The climate of California was both better and worse than that of France. Better, because it was usually warmer and so the grapes could be relied upon to ripen perfectly; worse, because the warmth posed new problems when it came to turning the grapes into wine. The warmer climate meant that the grapes were gathered earlier than in France, before the summer heat had altogether declined. This meant that they came into the winery hotter than they would have in France, and had to be fermented in hotter conditions. As a result, the fermentation was liable to rise to a higher temperature. If grapes are fermented at too high a temperature—90 degrees Fahrenheit or above— the yeasts that transform the sugar in the grapes into alcohol may well become exhausted, so that the fermentation stops and the wine tastes sweet and unbalanced. There is also the danger that undesirable microorganisms will get to work on the unfermented sugars, causing the wine to spoil. Even if the yeasts continue working, fermenting grapes at a high temperature tends to produce wines with a "cooked" character and relatively little fruit flavor.

These problems plagued the California wine industry in the late nineteenth century. According to George Husmann, a leading vine grower of the period, winemakers in California "have suffered more from improper and interrupted fermentation than from all other causes."

So why, then, did they not use refrigeration, like their counterparts in the brewing industry? The technique of cooling fermenting grape juice by running cold water through a coil in the vat was recommended by some wine scientists, but there is no evidence of its having been used. Even the most ambitious wineries appear to have been happy to rely upon their relatively cool cellars to control their fermentations for them. No winery was more ambitious than Inglenook, owned by a Finnish sea captain named Gustav Niebaum, who had made a fortune in the Alaskan fur trade in the 1860s and 1870s. Niebaum had wanted to spend his money on building a ship, but his wife did not share his love of the sea, so he bought a vineyard instead. With the ambition of

---

[56]The difficulties encountered by California wineries in marketing their produce in America are discussed in Chapter 6.

making the finest possible wines regardless of expense, he imported and planted the best vine varieties from Europe and built a three-story Gothic-style winery out of stone. With the back of the winery built into the rock and huge double doors at the front of the cellar, the temperature inside was kept to about 60 degrees Fahrenheit year-round. This may well have helped to control the temperature of the wine during fermentation, but it did not guarantee it as a cooling mechanism would have. His great-nephew, John Daniel, Jr., who revived the winery thirty years after Niebaum's death, at the end of the 1930s, had many problems with fermentation temperatures.[57]

Niebaum was obsessive about the cleanliness of his winery. Machinery, vats, and floors all had to be scrubbed with soda after use. Niebaum toured his winery wearing white gloves, which he ran along the working surfaces; his workers were punished if the gloves became soiled.[58] So why did Niebaum not use cooling equipment? It might be that he considered the possibility and rejected it. Maybe he was reluctant to place a metal coil inside his wooden fermentation vats because he feared it might taint the wine. This fear had already led to the abandonment of the technique in Australia.

It is also possible that Niebaum, like other winemakers, may have been opposed to cooling equipment for emotional reasons. Vine growers in Europe had been making fine wines for hundreds of years without the benefit of temperature-control techniques, so it did not appear to be part of the ethos of their profession. Brewers might have had all the latest equipment, but then they were working in a factory; wine producers, who had to labor long and hard in their vineyards before they could harvest the grapes from which they would make their wine, believed that they were following an agricultural ethos rather than an industrial one. They regarded their wines as the natural products of their soil rather than the man-made products of their toil. Winemakers shrank away from installing temperature-control equipment because it seemed to them to be cheating. When the celebrated Russian-born winemaker André Tchelistcheff brought cooling machinery into Califor-

---

[57] The winery (but not the Inglenook brand name) is now owned by the film director Francis Ford Coppola, and is open to the public. It is situated on Highway 29 in Rutherford in the Napa Valley.

[58] Niebaum also made brandy, but, having been offended one day by the manner in which a revenue agent inspected his distillery, ordered it to be torn down the following morning.

nia at the end of the 1930s, it was regarded as a matter for secrecy and the refrigerators were placed out of sight.[59]

Tchelistcheff had been born into the Russian aristocracy and had fought against the Bolsheviks in the Russian Revolution. Afterward, his family traveled westward across Europe, ending up in France, where he found a job in the wine business. There he encountered Georges de Latour, returned temporarily from California, where he had emigrated in the late nineteenth century after his vineyard in France had been destroyed by disease. Latour had planted vines in the Napa Valley, at a location he called Beaulieu ("beautiful place") and managed to keep his winery active during Prohibition by producing sacramental wine for the Church. As a result, his estate was in a much better condition than that of his rivals (including Inglenook, which had been closed) when Prohibition ended in 1933. Now he needed a new winemaker, and had gone to France to find one. He was introduced to Tchelistcheff, whom he persuaded to emigrate to California in 1938.

When he arrived at Beaulieu, Tchelistcheff was appalled by the primitive conditions at what was then one of the most advanced California wineries. In interviews later in his life he remembered how he was "amazed" to encounter "such an obsolete system of wine-making" in "the most technically progressive country." The open fermentation vats released clouds of carbon dioxide gas that intoxicated birds and caused them to fall into the wine. In one tank of sauvigon blanc a rat swam contentedly. And there were vinegar flies in the wine. "What the hell are you doing?" Tchelistcheff asked the cellar man. "Oh, young man, you don't know what's good," he replied. "This wine is so excellent that all the flies go to it. It doesn't do any damage." Tchelistcheff sought succor from Dr. Maynard Amerine, head of the winemaking school of the University of California at Davis. "You've got to be patient," Amerine told him. "We just started. We used to make wonderful wine, but we've been destroyed by Prohibition."

The antidrink campaign of the early twentieth century had halted the development of the California wine industry, and the subsequent imposition of Prohibition had closed it down.[60] As a result, a whole era of technical process had passed by the industry. The winemaking

---

[59]Tchelistcheff might also have wanted to conceal his expensive new equipment from his employers, with whom he continually battled about money.

[60]It killed off wine drinking as well as winemaking: See Chapter 2. The various causes of the antidrink campaign are discussed in Chapters 3, 5, and 6.

technology of the 1930s had not merely failed to advance but had actually retreated from that of half a century earlier. It required fresh talent from Europe to enable American winemakers to catch up.

By the 1960s American wine technology had not only caught up with that of Europe but had overtaken it. Thus, the history of American winemaking in the twentieth century can be compared to the development in the preceding century of the American brewing industry, which had lagged far behind that of Britain in the first half of the century but passed it in the second.

Just as in the brewing industry, the belated but enthusiastic application of modern technology proved revolutionary. Those few wineries that had adopted temperature control in the 1940s[61] had used it in order to ensure that the fermentation temperature did not rise to a dangerously high level. In the 1950s and 1960s, electricity became much cheaper, as did stainless steel. Wineries now started using a more efficient system of temperature control. Instead of circulating cold water in stainless steel pipes within wooden fermentation vats, they had tanks constructed entirely out of stainless steel, with double walls between which a coolant could be circulated. These enabled them not only to prevent the fermentation temperature from rising too high but to maintain it at artificially cool levels, in the case of white wines at only about 50 to 60 degrees Fahrenheit. This new "cold fermentation" produced a much fresher, fruitier wine. It is no coincidence that the introduction of this technique by wineries in California was followed in the 1970s by a wine boom among the public. People who had previously drunk cocktails now rejected them in favor of the new, more refreshing style of white wine.[62]

Just as the brewers used their technological expertise to produce an increasingly tasteless style of lager, so, too, did many American wineries take cold fermentation too far. They used it to produce wines that were fresh and fruity but lacked distinguishing characteristics. Like the brewers, they employed refrigeration in order to counteract the consequences of their climate: to try to make light, clean European-style white wines. In the 1970s and 1980s many winemakers made the mistake of focusing on the application of modern technology and failed

---

[61]André Tchelistcheff at Beaulieu, John Daniel Jr. at Inglenook, Robert and Peter Mondavi, Ernest and Julio Gallo, and possibly one or two others.
[62]The wine boom is discussed in the next chapter.

to allow the naturally full, ripe flavor of California grapes to come through into their wines.

In the last decade or so, winemakers have come to understand the importance of expressing their warmer climate in the taste of their produce, because they have been shown that this serves their financial interest. In 1986 the influential wine writer Robert Parker suggested in his newsletter *The Wine Advocate* that sales of California wines had declined because "many California vintners were in search of more finesse and elegance in their wines and became convinced (or should I say confused) that bland, innocuous, technically perfect, and squeaky-clean wines that had . . . perfect acidity and just the right amount of alcohol, but little flavor, would somehow be considered more elegant and satisfying than wines with dynamic and distinctive regional characters and personalities. . . . It was this image of wine as a boring, bland, standardized product akin to a beer or liquor that in the long run has hurt California wine sales in the 1980s more than the strong dollar and the succession of high-quality wine crops from France, Germany, Italy, and Spain." Today most California wines successfully combine the fresh fruit flavors obtained by a carefully controlled fermentation with the naturally ripe flavors of grapes grown in a warm climate. And the wineries are hard pressed to keep up with demand.

Not only does the climate mean that California wines are bigger and fuller than French ones, but this suits the taste of Americans. Even fine French wines are specifically produced in specially ripened and full-bodied versions in order to satisfy the taste of American consumers. Importers of red and white burgundies have persuaded producers to mature their wines in new oak casks. Maturation in new oak produces wines that are tremendously appealing in their youth. It gives them not only a toasty, spicy character and a taste of vanilla but actual sweetness—unfermentable sugar is extracted from the oak by the solvent action of alcohol. Also, because the pores of new casks are more open than old ones, there is more exchange between the wine inside and the air outside, with the result that the wine is oxygenated to a greater extent and develops more rapidly. Wines that have been matured in new casks taste rounder, more fruity, and more opulent in their youth than ones matured in older casks (although they do not taste better when mature).

The preference of wine drinkers for the big, ripe wines produced in

California, and for bigger and riper versions of the wines normally produced in France, can be linked with American ideas of democratization and accessibility. These preferences arise from a belief that anyone can enjoy good wine: It is not necessary to be a connoisseur to do so. These attitudes are personified by Robert Parker, who became the most influential wine writer in America (and indeed the world) because he represents the typical American wine lover. He did not train in the wine trade but came to the subject as a consumer and started writing about it because he felt that wine drinkers had been given a lot of bad advice. Parker's approach is to deconstruct the most complex of wine regions by reducing them to the taste and quality of the wines, and ultimately to a score out of 100. This produces a distorted view of the wines on which he comments, but that does not bother his fans. It does, however, bother British wine critics, who have generally trained in the wine trade and have frequently taken Parker to task for his failure to appreciate the subtleties of some of the wines and the intricacies of some of the wine regions on which he passes judgment. Notoriously, he prefers ripe, rich accessible wines to more reserved and subtle ones—but so, too, do most of the readers for whom he writes.

There is nothing new about this American preference for fuller, bigger wines. The most popular wine in the eighteenth century was robust and frequently fortified Madeira. Again, in the late nineteenth century, Husmann identified "a growing taste and increasing demand among the American public for full-flavored, heavy wines." Americans of this period generally shrunk away from light, Bordeaux-style "clarets," believing that the natural acidity in the wine would promote acidity of the stomach. According to the journalist Frona Wait, "They really look with aversion upon any claret of a tart nature, call it undrinkable, and claim it disagrees with them."

The English in the late nineteenth century, on the other hand, became crazy about claret. This had to do with social snobbery. The working classes, who had previously drunk beer, took to serving port or sherry from a decanter to their friends because (it was said at the time) "they look upon it as a more genteel thing than drinking a glass of beer." The middle classes, who had previously drunk port and sherry, were now obliged to distinguish themselves from the working classes by adopting claret. While the English turned to lighter wines because they considered them more sophisticated, Americans stuck with heavier wines because they liked the taste. Even today many English wine drinkers reject California wines as crude versions of French originals.[63]

The socially motivated differences between English and American taste in wine can be compared to their contrasting attitudes to cocktails, invented and popularized in America as democratic drinks that could be enjoyed by all, and only belatedly accepted by more conservative drinkers on the other side of the Atlantic. It is no coincidence that the English took to cocktails only after the First World War, during a period of new and rapid social change, as part of their own process of democratization. Like cocktails, California wine represents an original, enduring, and democratic response to the different climatic and cultural conditions that European settlers found in the New World.

[63]See Chapter 6.

CHAPTER 2

"Stranger, You'll Take Hash"

Before the Revolutionary War, most Americans accepted the indoctrination of their English masters and regarded the French with hostility and their cookery with contempt. After thcy had won their freedom, those who visited France found that they had been misinformed. As one of the revolutionaries, John Adams, reported home from France, where he had been sent on a diplomatic mission on behalf of the new republic, "The cookery and manner of living here, which you know Americans were taught by their former absurd masters to dislike, is [sic] more agreeable to me than you can imagine."

In 1781 Elkanah Watson, a native of Massachusetts who was then living in France, published an article in which he contrasted French and American manners, to the benefit of the former. He pointed out that he had been "taught at an English school, from infancy, that the French people eat frogs, make soup from old bones, and are a half-starved nation; that politeness in France is formed by ceremony, and the grimaces of the monkey." Yet in fact, "in no country does genuine politeness . . . so generally predominate as in France, while in no land does there prevail so much gloom, formality, and awkwardness as in England, where we have derived our tone."

Those Americans who stayed at home took rather longer to free themselves of the notions that had been instilled in them by colonial propagandists. When, after the revolution, the new nation entered into an alliance with France, and the first French squadron arrived at Boston, a gentleman by the name of Nathaniel Tracy held a great feast for the admiral and officers of the fleet. In order to demonstrate the refinement of his hospitality, he had the swamps of Cambridge searched for green frogs, which were served whole in the soup at a formal dinner—and was mightily offended when his guests became convulsed with laughter.

Many of the French who came to America after the revolution were less than impressed by what they found there. The mission of the Comte de Moustier to the States in 1787 did not prove a success, as Moustier upset the Americans with his snobbery, while he was offended by what he regarded as their vulgarity. After returning to the comfort of Paris, he declared that "the society of New York is not sociable, the provisions of America are not good, the climate is very damp, the wines are abominable, and the people are excessively indolent."

Similar problems were encountered by other French aristocrats who were forced to flee to America after the French had revolted in their turn in 1789. Charles Maurice de Talleyrand-Périgord, the son of a count, who was exiled to America in 1794, did not enjoy his sojourn in a country which he said boasted "thirty-two religions and only one dish," and was greatly relieved to be able to return to France two years later.[1] Not only were the aristocrats exiled from France as a result of its revolution but also many of the people who had worked for them, notably their chefs. Arriving in America with no visible means of support, they capitalized on their culinary skills. Many went to New Orleans, which was at the time a distinctively French city (the only one in the country, although then under Spanish control). Finding a market that already appreciated their skills, they opened a number of restaurants and rapidly established a reputation for culinary excellence for their adopted city that it retains to this day.[2]

---

[1] Back in France he forged a successful career as a statesman, serving both Napoleon and the royal family who were eventually restored in his stead.

[2] At some point during the nineteenth century the cuisine in New Orleans restaurants was transformed from its French origins into today's unique hybridized style, which incorporates Spanish, Italian, African, and Amerindian as well as French elements. This "Creole" cuisine had become very popular by the 1880s, but it is not known whether restaurants before the Civil War had offered more traditional French dishes.

The first French immigrant to establish a restaurant in New England was Jean-Baptiste Julien, who opened Julien's Restorator in Boston in 1794. As the name of his establishment indicates, the French word "restaurant" had not yet entered the English language; before this time such places had been called "cook shops." Soups had not previously been appreciated by Americans (having been among those aspects of French culture that they had been taught by the English to dislike), but Julien established such a great reputation for his soups among Bostonian diners that he acquired the nickname "the Prince of Soups."

On the whole, however, French immigrants who opened restaurants in the northern states found it harder to attract customers than they had in Louisiana. But at least they managed to introduce Americans to ice cream. Another French exile, the celebrated gastro-philosopher Brillat-Savarin, later described in his *Physiologie du Goût* ("Physiology of Taste") how "women in particular found so novel a taste irresistible, and nothing could be more amusing than the little grimaces they made while eating [the ices]. They were utterly at a loss to conceive how a substance could be kept so cold in a temperature of 90 degrees." French immigrants also contributed to the increased popularity of ice in this period as a means of cooling wines, punches, and lemonades.

How far, it might be wondered, did French influence in the late eighteenth and early nineteenth centuries affect American taste in wine? Hitherto, the majority of American wine drinkers had entertained a firm preference for the fortified wine produced on the Portuguese island of Madeira.[3] "Most of the wine which is drunk here [in New York] and in the other colonies," reported the visiting Swedish economist Pehr Kalm, "is brought from the isle of Madeira and is very strong and fiery." People who liked Madeira drank a lot of it. John Rutledge, a prominent lawyer in Charleston, South Carolina, who later became the state's first governor after the revolution, was accustomed to drink two *quart* bottles of Madeira a day, a habit in which he took a good deal of pride. Rutledge accepted that one bottle a day might be sufficient when a man dined with his family, but insisted that if he was entertaining guests, he should drink two bottles at least.

Rutledge did keep some Bordeaux in his cellar, should visitors prefer it. But relatively little French wine was drunk in America before the revolution. Whereas Madeira was imported directly into America,

---

[3]The origin of this taste, and the high quality of the Madeira that was drunk in colonial times, have already been described in the previous chapter.

French wines might legally be brought into the colony only if they had first been landed in Britain and British customs duty paid. Furthermore, Britain was often at war with France at this period, and the importation of French wines was banned. They could be obtained in America from smugglers, but they were hard to find and expensive.[4]

The American Revolution opened the American market to the French wine industry. Unfortunately, unscrupulous traders took advantage of the new situation in order to export poor quality wine from Bordeaux to the United States, which created a bad reputation for French wines in general. Within a few years, however, the French Revolution had deprived the leading wine estates of their principal customers, the free-spending aristocrats who were now forced to leave the country (or this world). As a result, an increasing quantity of good-quality French wines began to arrive in the United States. This produced a glut on the market, which forced down the price.

By the early nineteenth century, French wines were being imported into America in substantial quantities. Eventually, even the inhabitants of Boston took to them. According to Frederick Marryat, the Bostonians were "so wedded . . . to their old customs" that it was not until about 1830 that they started drinking French wines in preference to Madeira (and port). The reason for their conservatism, he explained, was that they "consider themselves, and pride themselves, on being peculiarly English; while, on the contrary, the majority of Americans deny that they are English." At the beginning of the Civil War, according to the anonymous author of *The Perfect Gentleman,* a guide to correct social behavior, Bordeaux had become "a great favorite in this country, in hot weather especially. . . . It is light, agreeable, gently exhilarating, and a great quencher of thirst."

By this time, sales of Madeira were in decline, the consequence of the devastation of the island's vineyards by the oïdium fungus. "Madeira is a delightful wine, if we could only ever get any of it," lamented the author of *The Perfect Gentleman.* "Let no happy enthusiast deceive himself with the delusive bliss that he is drinking pure Madeira. So destructive has been the disease of the vine in Madeira for many years that such an event as any of its charming wine reaching this country is not to be hoped for." Just as the wine drinkers of the eighteenth century had preferred Madeira to Bordeaux not so much for reasons of taste as

---

[4]See Chapter 6 for American resistance to the attempt by the British government to impose an excise duty on wines imported from Madeira.

because Madeira better withstood transport across the Atlantic and storage in extreme climatic conditions and because Bordeaux was expensive and hard to obtain, so, too, the eventual victory of Bordeaux over Madeira should not be attributed to any general acceptance of French culture but to the difficulty of obtaining Madeira.

The new preference for Bordeaux had little do with any notion that it complemented food better than Madeira. Although we nowadays regard Madeira as a wine best suited to drinking after meals, diners in the eighteenth century were not so dogmatic. A number of people did drink Madeira with their food, especially in hot climates, where other wines were not available. Those who dined in taverns in Jamaica in the West Indies were given a pint of Madeira to wash down their food. And British colonists in India frequently watered down their Madeira for drinking with meals in a proportion of one part Madeira to three parts water.

This practice of diluting wine with water had a long history, going back to ancient Greece. It was common in France in the eighteenth and nineteenth centuries and is still done in many parts of France today. Although inappropriate for wines of good quality, the addition of water reduces wines with a high alcohol content to a strength more appropriate to drinking with food.

In early colonial and republican America it often made good sense to add water to Madeira, not only to lower its alcohol content but also to dilute its taste. Henry Wansey, an English clothier who visited the States in 1794, was served Madeira and often port at the inns at which he dined. In Boston he stayed at a lodging house where "each man had his pint of Madeira before him" at dinner as part of his full board. At New Brunswick "the port wine was so bad as not to be drinkable, the Madeira so hot and fiery that we were obliged to mix water with it to make it palatable." He repeated the experience at Jamaica on Long Island.

When people drank high-quality Madeira, on the other hand, they waited until they had finished eating, so that they could give the wines their full attention. The same was true of the majority of those people who transferred their allegiance to French wines. In the late eighteenth and early nineteenth centuries, Americans continued to follow the English and colonial tradition of drinking beer or cider with their meals, and wine afterward.[5] This was true even of the most famous American

---

[5]There were exceptions, notably in Louisiana, which had been settled by the French

wine connoisseur, Thomas Jefferson, draftsman of the Declaration of Independence and third president of the United States.

As far as is known, Jefferson had enjoyed the same taste in wine as other American gentlemen before he was sent on a mission to France in 1784 at the age of forty-one. Up to that point, it is reasonable to assume, he would have drunk mostly Madeira. Soon after he arrived in Paris, Jefferson was introduced to the finest of French wines by his fellow Americans Benjamin Franklin and John Adams when he dined at their homes, just outside the city. Although Franklin and Adams were both enthusiastic consumers of French wines, Jefferson took his interest much further than they: He appears to have been bitten by the wine bug and to have developed an obsession with the subject in the same manner as generations of Americans who have encountered French culture since his time. Not only did Jefferson drink fine French wines when in Paris but he took the trouble to spend the spring of 1787 traveling around the vineyards of Burgundy, the Rhône Valley, and Bordeaux, and the next spring visiting the Rhine Valley in Germany, Alsace, and Champagne. These travels gave him an intimate knowledge of the wines. He learned when in Bordeaux, for example, that only by purchasing directly from the vineyard owners could he avoid the blending with other wines as practiced by the merchants, and this was how he subsequently obtained his supplies.

Jefferson put his knowledge of the wines to practical use on his return to the States when the French Revolution broke out in the summer of 1789, and not just in buying wine for his own cellar. He advised on their purchases of wines both the presidents who preceded him in the office, George Washington and John Adams, as well as the two who succeeded him, James Madison and James Monroe, all of them his personal friends.[6]

---

and continued to exhibit the influence of French taste long after its incorporation into the United States at the beginning of the nineteenth century. When the journalist Frederick Law Olmstead visited Louisiana in 1853, he found that Bordeaux was the usual drink at dinner. At the hotel in which he stayed and in the steamboats on which he traveled, bottles of this wine were placed upon the table at meals, for the free use of the guests.

[6]Recently some of the wines that were supposedly purchased by Jefferson have resurfaced in auction rooms, where they have sold for very high prices, notably a bottle of what was claimed to have been a Château Lafite 1787, which was bought by the publisher Malcolm Forbes in 1985 for $156,450. Forbes put it in his museum in New York, under spotlights—which caused the cork to dry out and fall into the wine. Another bottle, supposedly containing the same vintage of Château

Jefferson married his love of French wine with a taste for French cuisine. After his election as president in 1801, he hired a French chef, whom he had found in Philadelphia, to cook in the White House. Jefferson devoted an enormous amount of time, effort, and money to entertaining guests during his presidency. In one single year he spent $6,500 on provisions and groceries, and another $2,800 on wines. And this when a laborer earned a dollar a day, enough to buy him a gallon of ordinary wine. Even the wines from the top châteaux in Bordeaux cost no more than sixty cents a bottle if they were bought directly from the estates, which was what Jefferson did. During his eight years as president, Jefferson purchased in total more than 20,000 bottles of wine from Europe.

Despite his love of French food and French wine, both in the White House when president and at Monticello after he retired, Jefferson continued to serve his wines in the American rather than the French manner: after rather than during meals. He chose light French wines in preference to fortified ones such as Madeira as much because he thought they were healthier as because he preferred their taste. "I am anxious to introduce here these fine wines in place of the alcoholic wines of Spain and Portugal," he wrote. "The delicacy and innocence of these wines will change the habit from the coarse and inebriating hitherto only known here."

Jefferson's preference for French food and wine provoked criticism from Americans who were proud of never having crossed the Atlantic. Patrick Henry attempted while on the stump to smear him for having brought back from France an effete taste for French gastronomy and for having in consequence "abjured his native victuals." According to the journalist and antislavery campaigner Thurlow Weed, writing in his memoirs about New York in 1815, there was at that time "a general prejudice against French cooking." And no wonder, when it remained associated in the public mind with snobs such as the Comte de Moustier, who had insisted on bringing his own chef along to dinner

---

Margaux, was offered for sale by the New York wine retailer William Sokolin for $519,750. In April 1989 he took the bottle to the Four Seasons restaurant in order to show it to the present owners of the winery, who were attending a dinner sponsored by their American importers, but knocked it against a serving trolley, causing the glass to break and the wine to spill out on the carpet. It remains a matter of dispute whether these or any of the other "Jefferson wines" that have reappeared should be regarded as genuine.

at the home of John Adams. The company had been repelled not only by his presumption but also by a dish his chef produced for their delectation, comprising game birds perfumed with truffles. As Jefferson had told Marie Antoinette when she had asked him how the people of America could manage without an aristocracy of their own, "Your Majesty, the influence of your own is so powerful that it is the general impression that we can do without them."[7]

When French-style cuisine was introduced to New Yorkers by the Delmonicos in the 1820s and 1830s, it divided the generations in much the same way as Charles Darwin's anthropological writings later in the century. The Delmonicos were not in fact French but two Italian-speaking brothers from Switzerland who began by opening a wine shop, and then a café in which they originally sold only wines, cakes, and ices, but which became so popular that it developed into a restaurant offering fine French cuisine. It appealed to "Knickerbocker youths who were on the lookout for something new," as one of their number, Abram Dayton, later explained in his memoirs. Dayton and his friends "at once acknowledged the superiority of the French and Italian cuisine as expounded and set forth by Delmonico"; they were, he wrote, "converts from the plain roasted and boiled doctrine to the new rich gravy faith." They had, however, to keep their visits to Delmonico's secret from their families, "for, if detected, we were certain . . . to be soundly berated in the first place for our foolish extravagance, and secondly pitied for our lack of taste for giving preference to 'such vile greasy compounds' which we were assured would destroy our stomachs; while if we dared to mention the cool, refreshing *vin ordinaire,* that delightful beverage was denounced as a miserable substitute for vinegar." Nevertheless, the restaurant proved such a success that further members of the Delmonico family were brought over from Switzerland to establish other, newer, bigger, smarter branches, while rivals opened up imitations up and down the eastern seaboard.

By the 1840s top hotels, too, were offering French cuisine, produced by chefs who had either come north from New Orleans or who had traveled across the Atlantic from France, attracted by the promise of high wages. But the mass of the population remained hostile to French

---

[7]Jefferson himself preferred the simpler *cuisine bourgeoise* to the fancy haute cuisine; what he admired about the French "pleasures of the table" was that "with good taste they unite temperance." One of his favorite dishes was macaroni (what we today would call spaghetti), then very fashionable in France.

food, partly because it incorporated ingredients that most people found distasteful, such as garlic and offal, but principally because it seemed too fancy. As Jefferson Williamson suggested in his history of the American hotel, published in 1930, "The French chef introduced culinary frills to America. . . . But the average American preferred simplicity. For many years the public attitude toward *la cuisine française* was somewhat like that of today toward Chinese cookery—it was all right to eat it once in a while, as a sort of lark, but as a steady diet it was out of the question."

Like Chinese food in the twentieth century, it may well be that the principal reason French cuisine acquired such a bad reputation in America was that people attempted to reproduce it without really having much idea about what they were doing. Thomas Grattan, who spent seven years in the early 1840s as British consul in Massachusetts, condemned the "odious attempts at *la cuisine française,*" as a result of which, he said, the cooking in hotels was generally "detestable; in private houses, very indifferent. . . . You hear of French cooks very often, but you see little of French cookery. Every broken-down barber, or disappointed dancing master, sets up as a cook. . . . In a word, the science of the table is in the earliest stages of infancy in the United States."

This was a period, it should be understood, when restaurants in the booming cow towns and mining camps of the West used menu cards copied directly from those of Delmonico's. Any correspondence in the food that they served was, however, accidental. In his novel *The Virginian,* Owen Wister related the story of a traveler who saw *vol-au-vent* on a bill of fare in Texas and ordered some. The proprietor pulled out his six-shooter and told him, "Stranger, you'll take hash."

This clash of cultures came to a head in the presidential campaign of 1840. It began with a sneering article by a Democratic journalist from Baltimore, who expressed the opinion that if the Whig candidate, William Henry Harrison, were offered a pension of $2,000 and a barrel of hard cider,[8] he would prefer to retire to a log cabin with the cider rather than enter the White House.

---

[8]American usage, which distinguishes alcoholic "hard cider" from nonalcoholic "cider," is at odds with the rest of the world here. All cider is, strictly speaking, "hard," in the sense of being alcoholic; it derives from the Hebrew *shekar,* meaning "strong drink." If unfermented apple juice is intended, then the proper term is not "cider" but "apple juice."

It made sense to the Democrats to try to portray Harrison as a simple frontiersman, ill equipped for the leadership of a great nation. He had fought on the frontier; part of his home at North Bend, Ohio, had once been a log cabin; and it was said that cider rather than wine was served at his table (as would not, indeed, have been unusual for the time).

As a smear, however, it failed. It played into the Whigs' hands. They eagerly took up the "log cabin and hard cider" tag, carrying miniature log cabins in their processions and serving cider at their political meetings. They portrayed Harrison as a war hero[9] and man of the people, who worked hard on his farm and lived simply on "raw beef without salt," in contrast to his opponent, the Democrat Martin Van Buren, who indulged in the dangerously sybaritic luxuries of strawberries, raspberries, celery, and cauliflower. A campaign song ran:

> Let Van from his coolers of silver drink wine,
> And lounge on his cushioned settee;
> Our man on his buckeye bench can recline,
> Content with hard cider is he.

This was largely the opposite of the truth. Van Buren, who was up for reelection, was hardly the spoiled child of luxury but had been born in humble circumstances, one of the five children of a small farmer and tavern keeper. Far from indulging excessively in foreign luxuries during his presidency, as was alleged, he had lived as modestly as was consistent with the dignity of his office. And Harrison was not the plain man of the people, but an aristocrat from Virginia. Certainly, part of his home had once been a log cabin, but only one *wing* of it. But the campaign worked. Harrison won.[10]

Ever since this campaign, politicians have been careful to manifest public disdain for fancy food and wine, especially during elections, as Waverley Root and Richard de Rochemont point out in their history of eating in America; modern high-priced fund-raising dinners have everything to do with finance and nothing to do with food. "Gastro-

---

[9]Harrison had famously won a battle against the Indians at Tippecanoe, near the present Lafayette, Indiana, in 1811; hence his campaign slogan "Tippecanoe and Tyler too," Tyler being his running mate.

[10]Unfortunately, living in a log cabin on cider and raw beef did not prove as healthy as the Whigs had portrayed it, for Harrison died only a month after he assumed the presidency, at the age of sixty-eight.

nomic know-nothingism," they add, "constitutes a special case of that anti-intellectualism that crops up so disconcertingly often in the United States, an extension of the yokel's distrust of anyone better educated, better mannered, or even merely cleaner than himself."

As was shown by the result of the log-cabin-and-hard-cider campaign, not only did a taste for French food and wine clash with long-established American tradition that many still held dear, it was associated with the sort of snobbery and ostentation that was regarded by the great majority of the population as undemocratic and therefore un-American. Many Americans regarded not only French food but also French ways of dining as antidemocratic. Americans may have been inclined to favor the French because they, too, had undergone a revolution in which they had overthrown their masters, but most of the French chefs who came to America were part of the aristocratic tendency that had been dispossessed. Harrison won his presidential campaign because his propagandists succeeded in touching a popular nerve. By attacking Van Buren's taste for French food and his hiring of a French chef for the White House, they were able to implant the idea that he had aristocratic inclinations and may even have been a closet monarchist.

Nor is there any doubt that part of the appeal of smart French restaurants such as Delmonico's lay in the encouragement that they gave to such socially divisive attitudes as snobbery and deference. The banker Samuel Ward, one of the great nineteenth-century American gastronomes, first dined at Delmonico's as a student. "I remember entering the café with something of awe," he recalled. "The dim, religious light soothed the eye, its tranquil atmosphere the ear . . . I was struck by the prompt and deferential attendance, unlike the democratic nonchalance of [the New York 'ordinaries' of the period]."

Delmonico's introduced New Yorkers not only to the quasi-aristocratic delights of fine French food and service, but also to the associated practice of excluding from a public dining establishment those people who were regarded by the management as being socially unsuitable. After all, there was not room for everyone, so the Delmonicos and their staff had to use their discretion in deciding whom they were prepared to seat and serve and whom they were to ignore. Many of those whom they chose to reject were members of the new moneyed classes who swamped New York society in the middle of the nineteenth century, pushing aside the old Knickerbocker aristocracy. Social snobbery was the only weapon the aristocrats had left.

Delmonico's had the black list. Anyone who offended other diners was put on this list, and employees were forbidden to serve him. Black-listed persons were permitted to enter the restaurant, seat themselves at table, and order. But the orders were never filled. After politely taking the order, the waiter disappeared. After a tiresome interval the customer would summon the headwaiter, who would promise to "see about it." The headwaiter, too, would disappear, and presumably the customer would take the hint and leave.

Another aspect of French dining habits that many people considered undemocratic was the introduction of the à la carte service of meals in hotel restaurants. In colonial times it had been the practice for inns to serve meals to all their guests together at long tables at fixed hours, and to charge them an all-inclusive daily price. The first hotels in the early nineteenth century had simply continued this custom. The entire meal was placed on the tables at once, and the guests helped themselves.

In the 1830s, however, the larger eastern hotels brought some degree of order by dividing their meals into courses. Next, some of the larger hotels discarded the fixed courses in favor of menus from which each guest ordered separately. Still, however, guests paid a fixed price for bed and board, regardless of the amount of food they ordered, or indeed whether they ate their meals or not. This system, known as the American plan, was challenged by the importation from France of the European plan, according to which the guests ate the food they wanted when they wanted and paid for that.

The social significance of this alternative system was brought to the attention of the American public as a result of the opening of the New York Hotel in New York in 1844. S. Baptiste Monnot, who had full charge of the kitchen and dining room, announced that the hotel would serve its meals à la carte, with food cooked to order, rather than offering its guests a preselected table d'hôte. This led to a storm of criticism from the New York newspapers, who suggested that by offering different people the opportunity to eat different foods at different prices, Monnot was threatening the very foundations of the republic. Monnot also announced that the New York Hotel would make a speciality of serving diners their meals in private rooms, rather than compelling them to eat communally in vast public dining rooms, as had been the custom hitherto. The poet and journalist Nat P. Willis, writing in the New York *Weekly Mirror,* argued that this proposal directly contradicted American ideals of democracy, and engendered the spread of dangerously aristocratic habits. "There are some very republican advantages in our present system of hotels," he added, "which the country is not yet ready to forego. Tell a country lady in these times that when she comes to New York she must eat and pass the evening in a room by herself, and she would rather stay at home.... Dining with two hundred well-dressed people, and sitting in full dress in a splendid drawing room with plenty of company, is the charm of going to the city.... The public table is the tangible republic—the only thing palpable and agreeable that we have to show, in common life, as republican."

Outside the large eastern cities, the European plan spread only gradually. Not until the 1870s did more than a small number of hotels offer à la carte service to their guests. After that, it become more common for hotels to offer their guests a choice of either plan, although the fixed-price American plan remained standard outside the big cities. And it survives today in the form of fixed-price, all-you-can-eat meals in mass market chain restaurants such as Denny's and Shoney's.

Diners persevered with the American plan because it appeared to them to offer better value for money—even though it led to a great deal of food being thrown away. "The thing which . . . strikes me most disagreeably in the American hotel dining room is the sight of the tremendous waste of food that goes on at every meal," commented the French author Léon Paul Blouet, who made a lecture tour of the United States in 1887. "There are rarely fewer than fifty different dishes on the menu at dinner time. Every day and at every meal you may see people order three or four times as much of this food as they could under any circumstances eat, and, picking at and spoiling one dish after another, send the bulk away uneaten."

The tendency of customers to insist on being served a great deal of food, relatively little of which they actually intended to eat, did not encourage chefs to excel in the quality of their cuisine. Emily Faithfull, who made three visits to the States in the 1870s and early 1880s, referred to the preference for "quantity rather than quality. A sagacious black waiter once remarked to me when travelling through Alabama, 'What people want here is a good square meal; they are not particular about what they eat, if only they have a lot of things placed in front of them.'"

Not only did customers order huge quantities but everything was brought to them at the same time. Even when the food was good, it was ruined by this method of service. "The cooks in hotels are always

French and one would be able to eat in a supportable way were it not for the American custom of serving meals, which spoils them," suggested Paul de Rousiers, a visiting French sociologist. "Their custom is to set everything ordered . . . on the table at once, forming a circle of small plates, where the meats grow cold." Into these small plates the typical diner "plunges his fork at random . . . , fishes out something from the confused heap, or makes the most formidably seasoned mixtures of a thousand different ingredients, after which he imagines that he has dined. . . . French cooks protest against these barbarous customs, whereby the results of their skill are spoiled."

The popular insistence on being served large quantities of food all at once, giving a forcible impression of plenty, would suggest that the privations suffered by western pioneers still weighed heavily in the popular mind. Certainly those Americans who opened up the western frontier in the late eighteenth and early nineteenth century had encountered great difficulty in obtaining anything decent, or even anything at all to eat. As Prince Maximilian of Wied discovered on a visit to Jefferson City, Missouri, it was impossible to "obtain any provisions except salt pork, biscuits and whiskey." A shortage of fresh items, combined with erratic food supplies, led to odd combinations. A Swedish visitor to the Alabama frontier was served a three-course dinner that began with pickled pigs' feet, advanced to bacon and molasses, and concluded with a main course of milk and black bread soaked in whiskey.

On the frontier there were no ovens for baking, which encouraged the cooks to fry both their corn cakes and their salt pork in butter or lard. Fried foods became the American gastronomic speciality, and have remained so ever since. Even visitors from England, hardly a country noted for its gastronomy, were shocked by the greasiness of American food. The celebrated novelist Anthony Trollope, who visited the States in the early 1860s, found mealtimes at hotels to be "periods of disagreeable duty . . . [your meat] is brought to you in horrid little oval dishes, and swims in grease. . . . A beef steak is not a beef steak unless a quarter of a pound of butter be added to it."

The defects of American gastronomy in the nineteenth century cannot simply be explained away by reference to a shortage of supplies. French peasants had managed for centuries to produce excellent food from very meager resources, using parts of animals that Americans would not have been willing to touch. It would be more reasonable to attribute the poverty of American cooking at this period to an excess of supplies than to a shortage of them. There was so much good food available that there was very little incentive to make the best of it. As James Fenimore Cooper observed in *The American Democrat,* "The Americans are the grossest feeders of any civilized nation. . . . Their food is heavy, coarse, ill prepared, and indigestible. . . . There is not, perhaps on the face of the globe, the same number of people among whom the good things of the earth are so much abused, or ignorantly wasted, as among the people of the United States."

Considering the poor quality of the food, it is hardly surprising that people ate it so rapidly. James Boardman, an Englishman who spent from 1829 to 1831 in the States, described how gentlemen at hotels in New York "take their meals in one great public room, where from fifty to a hundred persons regularly sit down at the same table. Numbers who do not sleep in the hotels eat at such places, and assemble a few minutes before the appointed hours, in either the bar or coffee room. The moment the bell is rung, and the dining-room doors are thrown open, there is a simultaneous rush to the chairs, and in an instant all the knives and forks are in full operation. . . . The despatch at meals, particularly among the mercantile class, is almost incredible to those who have not witnessed it—five to ten minutes sufficing for breakfast, not much more than twice that time for dinner. . . . Each person leaves the table as soon as the business of eating is finished, without regard to his neighbour's proceedings. Englishmen are always the last, do what they will; for however little I ate I always found myself quite unable to keep pace at meals with Americans."

Boardman was wise not to try to keep up. "Several persons have died in New York lately by being choked with edibles at their meals," commented the Washington *National Intelligencer* in November 1836. "This is the result of the *bolting system,* which is so generally adopted among our people. We wonder that disasters of this kind are not more frequent than they are. A practice so pernicious and so detrimental to health as quick eating—to say nothing of its positive danger—does not exist in the country. At the table d'hôte of an inn, where great numbers convene together, the practice of bolting would seem to be done by steam, and those who perform it jaw-moving automata."

At this period, the speed of eating was clearly encouraged by the service of all the food at the same time, and the necessity of grabbing whatever one wanted oneself, but the introduction of courses and ordering from menus did little to slow down what was by then a well-established custom.

It is possible that the haste in which people ate their meals can be explained by the poor quality of much of the food—although equally one of the reasons it was unappetizing was that people ate it so rapidly. Another cause of the speed of eating, like the unpalatable food, was the great wealth of supplies. Abundance bred indifference: There was so much food available that people could not be bothered to devote any time to appreciating it.

The rapid eaters themselves tended to refer to the requirements of business. "The habits of life are those of an exclusively working people," wrote Michel Chevalier, a Frenchman who spent two years studying the workings of social and political life in the States in the mid-1830s. "From the moment he gets up, the American is at his work, and he is engaged in it till the hour of sleep. Pleasure is never permitted to interrupt his business. . . . Even meal time is not for him a period of relaxation, in which his wearied mind seeks repose in the bosom of his friends; it is only a disagreeable interruption of business, an interruption to which he yields because it cannot be avoided but which he abridges as much as possible."

But people ate rapidly whether they had to go back to work or not. The English temperance campaigner and social reformer James Silk Buckingham, traveling with his family around the States, found that even when taking the waters at Saratoga Springs the guests at the larger hotels spent an average of ten minutes over their breakfast, and fifteen over their dinner. "In the busy cities," he commented, "the reason assigned for this haste is the keen pursuit of business, and the eager desire to get to the counting house or store; but here, with the entire day before them, and nothing whatever to do, they eat with just the same haste as at other places. . . . People eat as if they were afraid that their plates were about to be snatched from them before they had done. . . . In nine cases out of ten, persons do not remain in their chairs to finish the meal, short as it is, but rise with the last mouthful still unswallowed, and dispose of it gradually, as they walk along."[11]

It would appear that the speed of eating should be attributed not to a specific need to return to work, but to the generally accelerated pace of life in a huge new country, ripe for exploitation, which promised

---

[11]Buckingham and his family spent four years traveling in the States, despite their frequently expressed dislike of the food, "though not at all fastidious in our taste, or difficult to please in this respect, preferring always the plain and simple in food, as well as drink."

untold wealth as a reward for enterprise and dynamism, and in which social mobility made anything possible.

The food that the majority of people ate, and the manner in which they ate it, hardly encouraged the consumption of wine of any kind. The monotony of a diet based on salt meat and corn bread and the national preference for fried and oily foods found their liquid complement, not in wine, but in whiskey. Fried corn cakes, salt pork, and whiskey were all made from the same raw material, since the pigs had been fed on corn and the whiskey distilled from it. And only whiskey was strong enough to cut through all that grease, and sweet enough to neutralize the excessive saltiness of the pork. Whiskey broke the monotony of a corn- and pork-based diet and, in a country where food supplies were sometimes erratic, it could provide a substantial part of an American's daily requirement of calories. Furthermore, it was believed that spirits such as whiskey aided digestion, and Americans who wolfed down fried, starchy foods certainly needed help in digesting them.

Not only did the speed at which people ate their meals encourage the use of whiskey rather than wine to wash them down, but it led them to obtain that assistance in the bar after meals rather than at table while eating. The Scottish minister David Macrae, who visited the States in 1867–87, found that the main difference between American and British drinking habits was that Americans drank much less at home—whether with meals or before or after them—but much more in bars. "This practice," he pointed out, "is not confined to the poorer classes. I was surprised to see a class of men 'liquoring up' at these bars who, in our country, would no more be seen entering a public house than they would be seen entering a house of ill fame."

Because people ate quickly, they did not generally drink wine with their meals but "liquored up" afterward; on the other hand, it is possible to argue that one of the reasons they ate quickly may have been that they did not generally drink wine with their meals but preferred to spend their free time drinking spirits in the bar. Witnessing the rapid consumption of dinner by his fellow guests at the New York hotel in which he was staying in the early 1830s, Thomas Hamilton suggested that "an American is by no means a convivial being. He seems to consider eating and drinking as necessary tasks, which he is anxious to discharge as quickly as possible. I was at first disposed to attribute this singularity to the claims of business. . . . But this theory was soon relinquished, for I could not but observe that many of the most expeditious bolters of dinner spent several hours afterwards in smoking and lounging at the bar."

The habit of drinking spirits at the bar may have had as much to do with the relative cost of different drinks as with the speed of eating: Whereas wine at table was expensive, drinks at a bar were not, which obviously encouraged the choice of the latter over the former. The wealthy might have been willing to drink wine, and able to pay for it, but the majority of the population neither wanted nor could afford to do so.

Changes in the practice of innkeepers also contributed to people leaving the dining table early in order to drink at the bar. In many places in the early nineteenth century, spirits had been placed on the table during dinner for people to help themselves.[12] By the 1850s most hoteliers had abandoned this generous practice, partly, one suspects, because they realized that this reduced the money they might make from selling spirits at the bar afterward. The cost of the American plan, no more than $1.50 or $2 a day in the best hotels before the Civil War, and from $2 to $5 a day afterward, was regarded by European visitors as incomprehensibly low. Given the amount of food that was wasted with this system, it would not have been possible for the hoteliers to make money on their meals; they depended for their profits on the sale of drinks. Since people did not take wine with their meals, it was in the economic interest of hoteliers to encourage their customers to eat rapidly and go off to the bar afterward.

The other reason hoteliers gave up placing spirits on the table for free was the growing influence of the temperance movement, which disinclined people from drinking any alcoholic beverages with their meals. At dinner in the large hotels "there were seldom seen more than one or two bottles of wine," commented the publisher William Chambers in his account of his visit to the States in 1853. "Nor did any exciting beverage seem desirable. A goblet of pure water, with ice, was placed for the use of every guest; and in indulging in this simple potation, I felt how little is done in England to promote habits of sobriety by furnishing water, attractive alike for its brilliant purity and coolness."[13]

---

[12]The cheapness of spirits at this period is discussed in Chapter 4.

[13]This is still true today of restaurants in Britain, which do not generally place water on the table for the free use of their customers. Waiters can often be per-

Yet the influence of the temperance movement did not, in the nineteenth century, stop people from drinking after dinner in bars; it may even have encouraged it. An English lawyer, Evelyn Fanshawe, spent eight months in the United States investigating drinking habits in 1892–93. He found that outside the eastern cities, there was often no one drinking wine or beer with dinner in the dining rooms of the hotels in which he stayed. Yet the bars were often busy at all hours of the day. The reason, he suggested, was that even people who themselves drank alcohol deferred to the widespread feeling that "there is something sinful or disreputable about the use of intoxicating liquor" and "would be ashamed to be seen with a glass of beer at their dinner and prefer to go to the bar, where they are not so likely to be seen."

Thus, one of the principal effects of the influence of the temperance movement on dining in restaurants and hotels was to encourage people to drink spirits in the bar rather than wine with their meals. This was unfortunate, given that the temperance movement had originally been directed at persuading people to give up spirits for healthier drinks such as wine.[14] It certainly helped people to resist any temptation they might have felt to drink wine with their meals. The English journalist George Augustus Sala, on a visit to the States in 1879–80, found that "in the hotels, from the grandest to the humblest, iced water, and nothing but iced water, is the almost invariable rule at meal times. . . . After a while a foreigner accustomed to drink a little wine . . . with his lunch or dinner ceases for very shame to ask for anything to drink of a fermented nature."

Any desire that people might have felt to drink wine with their meals in restaurants had always been tempered by the price. In the first half of the century, when brandy and water had been placed on the table for free, Bordeaux could usually be had for $1 a bottle, but good-quality Bordeaux cost $2, as did a bottle of sherry or Madeira—as much as was charged for bed and three square meals in even the very best class of hotel. Because of the high cost of wine, people did not get in the habit of drinking it, which meant that when they did choose to drink wine, they did not know anything about it, enabling hoteliers

---

suaded to bring a glass of tap water to the table, usually without ice, but only after they have done their best to persuade the customer to buy a bottle of exorbitantly priced mineral water instead. For more on iced water, and the encouragement it gave to the temperance movement, see Chapter 4.
[14]See Chapter 4 for this as well.

to fob off on them poor wines at high prices, which disinclined them from trying wines again. Alfred Bunn, an Englishman who spent some time in the country in the early 1850s, was shocked by the poor quality of the wine in hotel restaurants. "It is an undoubted fact," he wrote, "that some of the vilest rubbish, called wine, is vended at nearly all the hotels throughout the Union, and that Americans, as well as the visitors to their country, pay a most exorbitant price for the villainous compounds they imbibe." Bunn referred (at second hand) to the confession by the landlord of an apparently very respectable establishment in Philadelphia that he bought his wine at 75 cents a *gallon* before selling it on to his customers for between $2 and $5 a bottle. Furthermore, it was all the same wine. The landlord insisted, however, that his customers had demanded that he offer a range of wines at different prices. He recounted how, on the previous day, a customer had ordered a bottle of Madeira, drunk a glass of it, and pronounced it "damned bad wine." When he asked the price, the landlord told him that it was $2—to which the customer replied, "Oh, that accounts for it. Landlord, I've been used to drink good wine, and I can't drink bad wine. Send me a bottle of your five-dollar wine." The landlord took the wine away, poured it into another decanter, and brought it back to the customer. "Ah!" he said on tasting it. "This is wine fit for a gentleman to drink!"

Thus, to the charge that he marked up the price of his wines to an excessive extent, the landlord answered that "if I was only to charge fifty cents for a bottle of my wine, nobody would drink it."

People might have acquired a taste for wine by drinking it at home. Certainly it was not so ridiculously expensive when bought in bulk for one's own consumption. But if people were not in the habit of drinking wines, if they did not experiment by trying the occasional bottle when they went out to dine in restaurants and hotels, then they would hardly have bought wine in bulk, at what were still pretty high prices, for home consumption. In private houses, as in hotels and restaurants, it was rare to find wine on the table. "You rarely see at the American dinner table any other beverage than water," commented George Towle, the American consul at Bradford in Yorkshire. "Wine is very expensive, and it is only once in a while that it appears on the tables even of the rich. . . . Sherry, port, claret, Madeira, and champagne are rare luxuries, and only appear on festive occasions, or in the houses of epicures and wealthy foreigners."

The principal exception to the rule that wine was not drunk with meals was to be found on those occasions on which guests were being entertained. Hosts often sought to overwhelm them with the number and variety and expense of the wines, rather than with their quality or their suitability for drinking with the food with which they were served. The author of *The Perfect Gentleman* warned that this behavior was not becoming of a person of good taste. "The producing of a great variety of wines at a quiet visiting dinner party looks like an ostentatious display, and is not usually practiced by gentlemen in this country," he wrote. "It is but a vulgar notion which associates expense with gentility." A profusion of wine at a dinner party in a private house confirmed that the hosts were not accustomed to drinking wine at their family table.

People did not generally drink wine with their meals, not just because of the cost but because it had never become part of their culture. The Briton James Stuart, who spent three years traveling in the States between 1828 and 1831, found that his American friends were in the habit of taking small quantities of spirits and water on regular occasions throughout the day, "according to the general custom of the country." Yet they professed themselves "surprised, and often shocked, when they find foreigners sitting for some hours at dinner, and partaking liberally, as we do, of wine, while eating and afterwards, according to what I consider our more convivial and more agreeable habits."

The English in the eighteenth and early nineteenth centuries had preferred port just as their American counterparts had favored Madeira, and had treated it in the same way, as an after-dinner drink. During the course of the nineteenth century, however, the English middle classes abandoned their taste for strong, sweet wines and got into the habit of drinking light, unfortified wines with their meals, especially Bordeaux—despite their continuing hatred of France and all things French. They did so in order to distinguish themselves from the working classes, many of whom were now drinking port, and because the duty on French wines had been reduced. They were also persuaded to change their tastes as a result of traveling on the continent of Europe and finding out what people ate and drank over there. Americans did visit the Continent, too, but not in the same numbers. It took them much longer to get there, and cost them much more. The introduction of steamships after the Civil War reduced the journey time but did not bring down the price to a level that many people could afford. Most Americans stayed at home, stuck to their old ways, and never acquired a taste for light wines. As the British visitor Emily Faithfull pointed out in the 1880s, "The light wines, which with us have supplanted the fiery sherries and full-bodied ports of our ancestors, are only used by Americans whose tastes have been cultivated by foreign travel; they would not be appreciated by the general palate. . . . Fine cellars of wines are to be found in the houses of millionaires, but otherwise they are rare in the States and not to be met with, as in England, in the more ordinary households."

The journalist Frona Wait explained in her account of the California wine industry that "the American proper is not a wine-drinker. . . . He does not make wine a part of his food, the same as tea or coffee, but treats it as a foreign substance, to be used only for its exhilarating effects. He thinks of wine as a tipple and . . . much prefers something a little stronger, and unless his taste has been properly educated nearly always selects a sweet wine when he indulges in such an extravagance."

Or a fizzy one. Just as when people served wine at dinner parties in private houses they sought to impress their guests by offering an ostentatious profusion when one or two would have done, so when people did order wine in restaurants, they usually chose only the most ostentatious, in the form of champagne. Thomas Nichols, an American living in England,[15] told his new neighbors, "An American, who means to do the thing handsomely, takes champagne. No other wine is worth his drinking." Champagne was so much "the king of wines at the convivial board in the United States," added the author of *The Perfect Gentleman,* "that when 'a bottle of wine' is proposed it is understood to be champagne, unless some other name is expressly given."

We might balk today at serving champagne other than with a first course, or maybe a dessert, but in the nineteenth century it was considered correct to drink it with the course with which the roast meat was served. At a banquet given for General U.S. Grant at the Peabody Hotel in Memphis in 1880, Château d'Yquem was served with baked salmon, followed by Roederer champagne with filet of beef and then Mumm champagne with broiled spring chicken on toast. This penchant for drinking champagne with the entrée should not be regarded as an example of the bad taste of our predecessors. Champagne tasted

---

[15] Nichols, born in New Hampshire in 1815, had lived in many parts of the United States but, having refused to fight in the Civil War, fled to England. In 1864, principally for reasons of nostalgia, he published in London an account of his life in America.

different from the version we have today: It was made from lower-yielding vines and generally contained a higher proportion of the black grape Pinot Noir; it was a fuller-bodied wine, better able to stand up to food. This said, the majority of the people who drank champagne in restaurants in the past were quite careless about the food it accompanied. Champagne was the best, so that was what they wanted. As the manager of one of the branches of Delmonico's complained in 1910, fine dining was being corrupted by a fondness for "beginning with cocktails and drinking champagne pretty much all through dinner."

So great was the demand in the United States for champagne, so limited was the area of France that could supply the genuine version, and so small was the knowledge of wines of the majority of the people who demanded it that most of the so-called champagne that was drunk in the States was not really champagne at all. "The quantity of champagne drunk is enormous, and would absorb all the vintage of France, were it not that many hundred thousand bottles are consumed more than are imported," Marryat explained. "The small state of New Jersey has the credit of supplying the American champagne, which is said to be concocted out of turnip juice, mixed with brandy and honey. It is a pleasant and harmless drink, a very good imitation. . . ." The author of *The Perfect Gentleman* was less generous about the domestic product, warning of "that fatal poison which is manufactured in such immense quantities in this country out of cider and cheap Rhine wine, and almost invariably served up as champagne at public dinners."

Most people, it appears, were not bothered by the genuineness of what they were drinking, as long as it was fizzy and other people noticed that they appeared to be wealthy enough to afford to drink champagne. It is no coincidence that *coupe* ("cup") glasses were introduced at this period, for the more ostentatious service of champagne. These wide, flat glasses were hardly suitable for the appreciation of champagne, as they made it all but impossible to enjoy the bouquet, and the bubbles tended to disappear more rapidly than they would have done from an ordinary wineglass. But the use of *coupe* glasses did demonstrably mark out the person who was using them as someone who had ordered champagne.[16]

---

[16]The tulip glasses that tend to be used instead for champagne today do show off the bubbles much better, but are not ideal for smelling champagne and are certainly no less ostentatious than the *coupes* of old.

Champagne was the perfect instrument of the conspicuous consumption in which the moneyed class indulged at this period. This new class had emerged as a result of the great growth in wealth in America after the Civil War. This prosperity was divided so inequitably that by 1890 one percent of the population possessed half the nation's wealth. The new rich sought to distinguish themselves from those above whom they believed they had risen in the social order by acquiring as many goods as possible, and by demonstrating their ownership and consumption of these goods in the most public manner. Hence the term "conspicuous consumption" (which was coined by the sociologist Thorstein Veblen in his famous book *The Theory of the Leisure Class*).

One means by which the members of the new moneyed class sought to demonstrate their assumed superiority was by eating as much as they could, and by putting on weight to show that they had done so. Fat was sexy in the late nineteenth century; indeed, fashionable clothing emphasized the size of busts and bottoms rather than the reverse, as it does today. The feminine ideal was represented by the two-hundred-pound actress Lillian Russell, whose enormous appetite was almost as legendary as her beauty.

But in a country where food was abundant, it was not enough simply to eat a lot in order to consume conspicuously; it was necessary to favor a different kind of food from ordinary people. The moneyed class therefore took with great enthusiasm to French haute cuisine, distinguishing themselves by the requirement that their food be prepared in an elaborately French manner, described with obscure French code words, and eaten in a ritualistically French way. Whereas in the 1860s and early 1870s the menus in smart hotels had mostly been written in English, with American dishes, by the late 1870s they had converted to French terms and dishes. This change occurred even in boom towns in gold-mining areas. When miners struck it rich, or believed they were going to, they celebrated their entry into the moneyed class by consuming French cuisine. By the mid-1870s there were fine French restaurants in towns such as Tombstone, Arizona. Whereas an enjoyment of French haute cuisine had previously been regarded as un-American, and people who indulged in it had been condemned as snobs, it now acquired a new, classless status. The ability to appreciate fine French food was now regarded as a mark of wealth, which was (theoretically) accessible to all, and therefore freed it from the aristocratic connotations that had previously attracted hostility.

Sometimes it even tasted good as well. This was especially true of

Delmonico's, for which many Americans made great claims. "It is better and more sumptuous, New Yorkers say, than the best restaurant in Paris," reported one French visitor—"and it's true." Unfortunately, much of the food served at Delmonico's went unappreciated by the people who could afford to eat there. Indeed, Paul de Rousiers suggested that the opulence of meals given by New York millionaires at Delmonico's demonstrated their lack of interest in and knowledge of what they were eating and drinking. "Such extravagances are disgusting to European tastes," he wrote, "but they cost many dollars and do not need the complex and educated taste of a gourmet of high standing to value them at their worth, so they suit rich Yankees wonderfully well." Many of the other expensive French restaurants of the period were more remarkable for the showiness of their food than for its sophistication. As John Mariani has suggested in his history of American restaurants, *America Eats Out*, the food in the smart restaurants of the late nineteenth century must "at the very least . . . have resembled the kind of overly elaborate cooking and presentation done to this day in casino hotels in Las Vegas and Atlantic City, but, as in those two cities, the sophistication level of free-spending customers might well have favored ostentation over delicacy of taste."

The new rich not only sought to demonstrate their wealth by holding extravagant dinners in restaurants but also by giving lavish dinner parties in their own homes. Any old millionaire could afford to pay for a one-off party in a restaurant, but you really had to be wealthy to own a large enough home, with a full-time French chef and a sufficient number of servants to entertain a large number of guests at dinner on a regular basis.

Now that dinner parties had become the focus for entertaining guests, the manner of serving the meal changed as a consequence. The practice of placing different dishes on the table at the same time, from which diners might serve themselves, was replaced by the modern form of service, then called *service à la russe* ("Russian service")[17] according to which food was presented to the guests already arranged on individual plates. This system became popular in America in the 1870s

---

[17]So called because it had supposedly been introduced into France by the Russian ambassador early in the century; it had first appeared in America in the late 1830s but had been regarded by many at the time as an unnecessarily pretentious French innovation.

because it drew attention to the quality and sophistication of the individual dishes.

The adoption of the *service à la russe* helped the members of the moneyed class to use the conspicuous consumption of fine French food as a means of differentiating themselves from their perceived lessers. The size of the middle class expanded tremendously during the last two decades of the nineteenth century; its members developed a new self-consciousness, with social aspirations to match. They sought to emulate the new styles in dining that had swept the moneyed class. Middle-class dinners became formal affairs that were intended to impress guests with the magnificence of the home and the meal. But the middle class failed to fulfill its social ambitions because it could not afford the number and quality of servants necessary to serve a succession of delicately presented courses, as was the fashion among the wealthy. For a while it tried what was called "modified *service à la russe,*" in which the servants served some dishes from the sideboard while the host carved the roasts onto the diners' individual plates. But often the host knew no better how to carve than his servants. The eventual solution was to give up trying to emulate the style of dining of the moneyed class, and to follow the arguments of a new generation of home economists and pseudo-scientists who were telling people to eat more simply. Then came the First World War, with its patriotic message that food should be conserved rather than squandered. French haute cuisine fell out of fashion. It was then killed off by Prohibition.

The introduction of Prohibition in 1920 was not intended to compel the closure of restaurants across America. But that was its effect. Now that people could no longer legally drink wine with their meals in public restaurants, there did not seem to be much point in going out to the sort of smart establishment that had previously prided itself on offering the whole French experience of combining fine food and fine wine. "Many things have been said about Prohibition," wrote the British journalist Collinson Owen, who visited the States in the late 1920s, "but not sufficient attention has been paid, I think, to this wholesale assassination of the charm and pleasure of dining. Throughout that vast country practically every restaurant is a sepulchre, however richly gilded, a fraud, a sham. Of what use is all this surging and clamant prosperity of which we hear so much, if one of the simplest, easiest and profoundest pleasures of civilised existence is ruthlessly suppressed?"

Prohibition had destroyed American gastronomy, wrote Julian Street in the *Saturday Evening Post* in 1931. Not only was it impossible to cook many of the finer French dishes without wine, or to enjoy them without appropriate accompanying wines, but (he claimed) the great prewar hotels and restaurants had relied on bars for most of their profits, charging modestly for rooms and serving generous portions of food made from first-class ingredients at below cost to attract customers who would also order high-margin wines and spirits. Deprived of this income, many fine hotels and restaurants were forced to close. In New York, the latter included both Delmonico's and its great rival, Sherry's. Those that managed to remain open were forced to economize in their kitchens, turning to second-rate meals and smaller portions.

Now that alcoholic drinks could not legally be obtained in restaurants, many people took to dining instead in speakeasies, where they could get a drink. On the whole the patrons of speakeasies drank cocktails before (or after) dinner rather than wine with them, but it would be wrong to imagine that wine was not available in speakeasies, or at least in the better class of them. A survey of New York speakeasies published in *Harper's Monthly Magazine* in 1932 cited a place called Jerry's, where it was perfectly possible to drink Chablis with sole followed by burgundy with partridge. And the food, apparently, was excellent. "As a matter of fact it's good in most of the better speakeasies. That's why, in New York at any rate, the hotels are losing money on their restaurants. Speakeasies have run away with the cream of the dinner trade, not only because they serve drinks but because they serve more palatable food."

These comments are confirmed by Mary Agnes Hamilton, a former Member of the British Parliament for the Labour Party, who visited the States in 1931–32. "The places of the sort to which I was taken in New York were elegant, quiet, agreeable restaurants, in which the food was as good as the drink," she wrote. "The speakeasy of good class is killing the other restaurants in New York. . . . Indeed, if a man asks a woman out to lunch she is disappointed if she is taken anywhere else."

If people did not go out to speakeasies, or could not afford the extortionate prices that were charged in the better kinds of them, then they could always hold or attend a dinner party in a private home, where a householder might provide drinks without fear of being raided by the police. Although a few states had individually banned the possession of liquor in the home, in most of the country there was nothing, even in theory, to stop hosts from serving drinks to their guests. (Where and how they had obtained those drinks was a different matter.) As a result, Prohibition helped popularize dinner parties. Indeed, it was suggested at the time that Prohibition had "saved" dinner parties—even if the latter happened to be "dry"—because it provided a subject that interested almost everyone and about which nearly all guests had something interesting to say.

Prohibition did not, however, give nearly as much encouragement to dinner parties as it did to cocktail parties.[18] People who continued to eat out in restaurants, or who went to public functions at which the law had necessarily to be observed, could not drink wine in a leisurely manner with their meals. But they were usually offered opportunities to drink cocktails before they sat down to eat, however rapidly or surreptitiously they might have to down them. There already existed a long-established tradition of drinking water with one's meal rather than wine, and taking spirits in the bar afterward. Now Prohibition introduced an element of compulsion where previously there had been only habit and preference. Even those wealthy sophisticates who had enjoyed wine with their meals were now forced, at least on public occasions, to give up the practice and to concentrate their drinking into brief periods before and afterward.[19] Sir Charles Igglesden, who visited the United States in 1928 as guest of the Carnegie Trust for Universal Peace, cited the example of "a public dinner where only iced water or mineral water is provided. But a few minutes before the repast you are ushered into a private room and offered cocktails. In those few minutes I have seen men swallow four or five cocktails, drinking against time, as it were. They feel that for the whole evening their only beverage will be water and hence their panicky feeling to make hay while the sun shines."

People who had previously drunk wine in restaurants but were now compelled, if they wanted to drink anything at all, to choose spirits

---

[18] The impetus that was given by Prohibition to the development of cocktails, largely because of the necessity of devising mixtures in which the bad taste of bootleg spirits would be obscured, has already been discussed in the previous chapter.

[19] Just as the temperance movement in the nineteenth century had encouraged people to drink spirits in bars rather than wine with their meals, so Prohibition, the culmination of that movement, persuaded people to give up drinking wine altogether and turn to spirits instead. All this of a campaign that once sought to turn people away from spirits toward wine. See Chapter 4.

instead took their new habits home with them. They were still permitted to drink wine with their meals at home, but few of them did. Wine was hard to obtain. Bootleggers focused their efforts, quite naturally, on trading in alcoholic drinks in the form in which they were most concentrated and most profitable, as spirits rather than in the relatively dilute form of wine or beer.[20] The only people who continued to drink imported wines with their meals throughout Prohibition were those who were so fabulously rich as to have been able to afford not only to have bought enough wine beforehand to keep them going for thirteen years, and a cellar large enough to hold it, but also armed guards to protect their stocks from raids by bootleggers.[21]

People could also drink cocktails in speakeasies, but these charged a lot for drinks, and were often raided by the police. It was cheaper and easier to attend a cocktail party in someone's home. "Cocktail parties have become the line of least resistance in entertaining," wrote Alice-Leone Moats in *No Nice Girl Swears*. "All you need is a case of synthetic gin and a tin of anchovy paste. The greater the number of guests, the smaller and more airless the room, the stronger the gin, the more successful the party. But if you give one, you must be prepared to have your friends on your hands until two in the morning, as they will invariably forget their dinner engagements and stay on until the last shakerful is emptied." This new fashion for holding and attending cocktail parties was given further impetus by the Depression, when many people no longer had the means to invite their friends and acquaintances to dinner. In any case, they now lived in smaller homes and could not afford so many servants, so they would not have been able to entertain many people to dinner even if they could have afforded it. Cocktail parties remained the most popular form of private entertainment for many years afterward, because they were relatively

---

[20] They can be compared to drug dealers today who prefer to sell their clients more concentrated heroin rather than more bulky marijuana. People who go to dealers in search of marijuana often find themselves cajoled into trying heroin instead. Thus, by making marijuana illegal, the government has encouraged the trade in heroin. See Chapter 5.

[21] In *The Cup of Fury* Upton Sinclair described how his uncle, John Randolph Bland, "a practical man [who] recognized the oncoming of Prohibition before the legislation actually became part of our Constitution," spent $6,000 (the equivalent of more than $50,000 today) on filling the cellar of his Maryland mansion with enough liquor to keep him going for many years. Unfortunately, when Bland moved back to his town house in Baltimore for the winter, thieves broke in "and carried off every case of his treasures."

inexpensive and could be written off against tax if business colleagues were invited.

Not only did Prohibition contribute significantly to the abandonment of the habit of drinking wine with food both in restaurants and in the home, but opposition to this custom had been one of the motives behind the campaign that led to Prohibition. The pattern of immigration into America had changed significantly between the middle and the end of the nineteenth century. Whereas the majority of immigrants had previously come from northern Europe—from Britain, Ireland, Germany, and Scandinavia—now they came from farther south and east, from Italy and Greece and the Austro-Hungarian and Russian empires. The vast majority of the fifteen million immigrants America received between 1890 and the outbreak of the First World War in Europe in 1914 came from eastern Europe and the countries surrounding the Mediterranean.

These newcomers brought with them very different cultural values from their predecessors. Fearing that their own customs and beliefs were being threatened, older immigrants and native-born Americans now began to campaign for restrictions on immigration in order to prevent the "problem" from growing worse. As the question was put at the end of the nineteenth century by the Immigration Restriction League, did Americans want their country "to be peopled by British, German, and Scandinavian stock, historically free, energetic, progressive, or by Slav, Latin, and Asiatic races, historically downtrodden, atavistic, and stagnant?" Restrictions on immigration were introduced at the same time as Prohibition, in the 1920s.

Many native-born Americans believed that the Latin habit of taking leisurely meals, accompanied by wine, was symptomatic of their sloth and inability to contribute to the culture of a nation whose inhabitants demonstrated their dynamism and commitment to work and to bettering themselves by taking as little time as possible over their meals. It was also widely believed by those in authority that the immigrants would not be able to free themselves of their old-country attitudes toward work, society, and politics until they abandoned their old-country ways of living and eating. Hence the attack on drinking wine with food. "The American does not think it is necessary to drink with his meals," explained the English expatriate Maurice Low at the beginning of the twentieth century. "It is a foreign and extravagant fashion that he does not encourage."

This helps to explain why Prohibition was regarded as such an important measure by those who campaigned for it in the early twentieth century. It was not seen as an isolated issue, but as a totem of a wider cultural conflict. The imposition of Prohibition, claimed its supporters, formed part of the defence of the American way of life. Speaking to a Women's Christian Temperance Union national convention in 1928, its president Ella Boole declared, "This is the United States of America, my country, and I love it. . . . It is all I have. . . . As my forefathers worked and struggled to build it, so I will work and struggle to maintain it unsoiled by foreign influences, uncontaminated by vicious mind poison. . . . Its people are my people, . . . its enemies are my enemies, and its enemies shall not prevail."

On the other side of the cultural divide, recent arrivals from Italy thought the idea of prohibition so ridiculous that they could not see anything wrong in breaking this new law. One young Italian immigrant wrote to his parents back in Tuscany in the spring of 1918, referring to the progress of prohibitory legislation as "something incredible. . . . It seems very probable that within two or three years drinking a glass of wine will be a federal offence. Can you imagine a law more stupid? . . . I have discussed this matter with several of my business associates, and we have agreed that prohibition will offer an opportunity to make some easy money." He thought so little of the prohibitory law that he was prepared even to tell his parents that he intended to become a bootlegger—which he did.

In 1927 social workers in various parts of the United States contributed reports to a study on whether Prohibition was working. From Cleveland it was reported that "at first the Italian groups thought Prohibition affected only whiskey-drinkers . . . and went ahead with their wine, many times quite openly." In Buffalo it was said that "our Italian people have no conviction that they are doing anything morally wrong in making and drinking their native wines. They cannot understand why Prohibition was adopted. Generally speaking, they feel that it is an evidence of fanaticism, and while they are obliged in certain ways to conform to the law, they have no special scruples against violating it." In New York, before Prohibition, Italian-Americans bought [wine] "as they bought bread in this new America, as a matter of convenience. Now they make it as they would make bread if the bread shops were closed."[22]

This hardly endeared them to those native-born Americans who had

---

[22]Home winemaking during Prohibition is discussed in Chapter 4.

imagined that Prohibition would teach the immigrants to abandon their old habits. As Andrew Sinclair puts it in his history of Prohibition, "The spectacle of immigrants making and drinking their wine drove the drys to paroxysms of fury, so that they recommended the deportation of alien violators of the Volstead Act." A bill to this effect passed the House of Representatives in 1922 by a wide margin, but was killed by Senate indifference.

The demand from Italian- (and Greek-) Americans for grapes from which to make their own wine provided a lifeline for vine growers in California, who were able to stay in business during Prohibition by shipping grapes to Chicago and the East Coast for sale. The variety of grape that looked best in the market, traveled best, and made the deepest-colored, strongest-flavored wine was the hitherto obscure alicante bouschet, which had been developed in France in the late nineteenth century as a coloring grape to grow alongside the productive but pale-colored varieties that dominated the vineyards of the south of the country. Although it was hardly reputed for the quality of the wine that it produced, alicante bouschet offered the advantage of being so strongly colored that it could be passed through several pressings and still produce a passable red wine. By adding sugar and water to later pressings, a home winemaker (or a bootlegger) could produce 600 or 700 gallons of wine from a ton of grapes compared with the normal 150. As a result, alicante bouschet, which was hardly known in California before Prohibition, dominated all vineyard plantings in the 1920s. Unfortunately, this meant that California wineries did not have access to an adequate supply of decent grapes after Prohibition was repealed in 1933, and were therefore in no position to resume the production of fine wine. Even as late as 1961, more than a generation after Repeal, only 0.5 percent of the vineyard area of California was planted in cabernet sauvignon and only 0.1 percent in chardonnay.

In 1941 the journalists Frank Schoonmaker and Tom Marvel published a book on American wines in which they chronicled the progress (such as it was) of California wine since Prohibition and sought to persuade consumers to renew their interest in their native produce. As they pointed out, "There was almost no sound and well-aged wine on hand in this country at the time of Repeal. Instead of frankly admitting that this was the state of affairs, California's wine industry decided to brazen the thing out, and no more ridiculous, dishonest, and disastrous policy was ever adopted by a major industry. Wines that were poor, unsound, artificially 'aged,' artificially flavored, misrepresented, and mislabeled, became the rule rather than the exception on the American market. It is to our everlasting credit that we recognized these for the frauds they were and turned instead to cocktails and highballs."

Sound and well-aged European wines had become available again after Prohibition had ended, but only a relatively small proportion of the population could afford to spend any money on such luxuries during the Depression, and many of them were unsure when and how to drink the wines of which they had been deprived for twenty years (shipments having effectively ceased in 1914, when the First World War broke out in Europe). According to C.R.V. Thompson, the American correspondent of the London *Daily Express,* when Prohibition was repealed "New Yorkers had no taste for the finer wines that were now available to them. They didn't even know whether to order white or red wine with chicken,[23] and so most of the restaurants found it wise to print wine suggestions alongside their lists of entrées."

This lack of knowledge about what to drink and when to drink it led to unfortunate consequences at private dinner parties. Although it had been possible to find good French table wines, for a price, in the most sophisticated speakeasies during Prohibition, the types of wine that had been most readily available had been sparkling and sweet fortified wine. By Repeal, four times as much sweet as dry wine was being sold. People were washing down their food with sweet wines that had been intended for drinking after meals (or else at the end of them). Abdullah Simon, wine buyer for Chateau & Estates, the fine-wine section of the Seagram empire, remembers going to dinner in a smart apartment in New York in 1944 and finding Château d'Yquem, the most prestigious of all sweet white wines, served with roast beef.

The effects of Prohibition on wine-drinking habits lasted for many years. The first great post-Prohibition restaurant, Le Pavillon in New York, opened in 1941. Its owner Henri Soulé not only served French haute cuisine but had a superb cellar, including 161 champagnes in 56 vintages. Yet he was compelled, much to his distress, to watch people drink whiskey throughout their meals. His most celebrated customer, John F. Kennedy, often ordered milk. This was served in a silver bucket, like champagne, and cost $2 a bottle.

Although it is sometimes suggested that many Americans took up wine drinking because of their experience in Europe during the Second

---

[23]Either would have done.

World War, there is little evidence of this. According to Simon, Americans who fought in Europe did not drink wine but brandy. Simon served in the army from 1944 to 1946 and never saw a bottle of wine during that period. Ten years after the war had ended, a cross-section of the public was asked by market researchers whether they thought wine was a drink for Americans. Ninety percent said no. Then they were asked, if it was not a drink for Americans, then whom did they think it was for? They replied that wine was for rich people, or for foreigners, or for drunken bums—but not for Americans.

Only after people began to travel voluntarily to Europe did they start to bring a taste for wine back home with them, just as Thomas Jefferson had done in the eighteenth and the English in the nineteenth century. This happened in the 1960s, when the commercial introduction of jet planes made it quicker and cheaper to fly to Europe. Many of the people who now traveled to Europe drank wine there, took the labels off bottles, brought them back, and looked for the wines in America. Not until 1968, however, did sales of table wine pass those of sweet, fortified wine. The United States did not really start to become a wine-drinking country—to enjoy a wine boom—until the 1970s.

There is no doubt that in the last thirty years the popularity and consumption of wine have grown enormously. Market research carried out in 1990 on behalf of the *Wine Spectator* magazine (of which more than 100,000 copies are sold bimonthly) found that 42 percent of adult Americans drink wine. And the proportion of wine drinkers in the main wine-drinking areas on the East and West coasts must be much greater than this, because the 42-percent figure includes the vast majority of the population in great areas of the Midwest who drink only beer and spirits as well as all those people in the Bible Belt who do not drink at all, or at least do not admit publicly to doing so.[24]

The popularity of wine today is demonstrated by the development of vineyards in virtually every state of the Union (including such unlikely places as Indiana, Kentucky, Tennessee, Alabama, Arkansas, Oklahoma, Kansas, Wisconsin, Minnesota, Montana, Idaho, Utah, Colorado, Arizona, New Mexico, and Texas), and the commercialization of vine growing in California to such an extent that wine tourism has become a substantial industry in its own right.

---

[24]Attitudes to drinking in the Bible Belt are discussed in Chapter 5 and in the Conclusion.

Not only are more and more people drinking and making wine, American consumers are exerting a significant effect on wine production and prices in Europe. The development of specially ripened and full-bodied burgundies in order to satisfy the taste of American consumers has been mentioned in the previous chapter. The marketing of the top wines of Bordeaux is also profoundly affected by American demand, since approximately one third of all the exports of the most prestigious châteaux are sent to the United States.

At the same time as the habit of drinking wine, once regarded as the exclusive province of immigrants from southern and eastern Europe, has become popular in America, so have the types of food which these people were previously criticised for eating.[25] At the beginning of the twentieth century public health workers condemned traditional immigrant peasant dishes as unhealthy because they combined different types of food and therefore required a greater amount of energy to digest. And they denounced the strong seasonings—garlic, herbs, and spices—that gave some flavor to bland but cheap foods on the supposed grounds that they overworked the digestive process and stimulated cravings for alcohol.

Ironically, Prohibition played its part in encouraging white Anglo-Saxon Protestants to develop a taste for more "exotic" kinds of food. Italian restaurants in Italian areas of New York (Little Italy and Greenwich Village) first became popular among non–Italian Americans in the 1920s precisely because the restaurateurs regarded Prohibition as a joke and served their homemade wine (often camouflaged in coffee cups) to their customers. The customers came for the wine and began to develop a taste for the food. At the same time, the restrictions on immigration encouraged the Italians to become more Americanized because there was no longer a sufficient number of new arrivals to keep them purely European in their tastes. This led to the development of a hybrid Italian-American taste in food. Spaghetti and tomato sauce became a characteristically American dish—except that it was made with ketchup rather than canned or fresh tomatoes, no garlic was used, and the pasta was cooked until soft.

This said, it took the majority of the population just as long to develop a taste for foreign foods as it did to begin to indulge in the

---

[25]The modern belief in the health benefits of a "Mediterranean diet" are discussed in the Conclusion.

foreign habit of drinking wine. As in the case of wine, it is commonly believed that the assimilation of European tastes in food began with the Second World War—that the experience of the millions of Americans who fought overseas during the war contributed significantly to the broadening of American tastes; as with wine, there is no evidence of this happening. The troops did not have any opportunity to eat local foods in the areas through which they marched and in which they fought. The only effect on their preferences came as a result of their all being served the same food in their mess halls: The war caused Americans to abandon their regional and class differences and adopt an all-American taste.[26]

As with wine, many people began to interest themselves in foreign foods as a result of holidaying in Europe in the 1960s. The discovery by tourists that restaurants in France offered simple bourgeois cuisine as well as the pretentious version served in smart French restaurants in America did a great deal to popularize French food (and wine).

It would be difficult, however, to attribute the growth in popularity of Chinese food in America in the 1950s and 1960s, of Japanese food in the 1970s and 1980s, and of "fusion food" (combining elements of several Asian cuisines) in the 1990s to foreign travel, when relatively few Americans have visited these parts of the world. The historian Harvey Levenstein argues in his history of American eating habits, *Paradox of Plenty,* that while travel to specific countries played only a small part in the growth of interest in specific types of ethnic food, "it did stimulate a growing cosmopolitanism, which made people receptive to foreign foods in general. . . . The United States had become the center of an impressive, worldwide, informal empire. As in Rome at the peak of its influence, a certain amount of distinction rubbed off on those whose tables manifested the cosmopolitan nature of the empire."

This would help to explain the popularity of fusion food today. This cuisine, which originated in California in the 1980s, combines several different cultures in a single dish. Diners at Eos in San Francisco, named after the Greek goddess of the dawn (which rises in the east), might find pasta stir-fried with coconut and curry, shrimp cakes served with ginger aïoli, and blackened catfish alongside lemongrass risotto.

---

[26]It has been suggested that American troops fighting in Italy brought home with them a taste for pizza. But pizza was not yet generally available in Italy. It was a Neapolitan speciality that was popularized by Italian immigrants in America in the 1950s.

As will be all too readily evident, fusion food can rapidly descend into what its critics have taken pleasure in describing as "confusion cooking." In 1996, for example, the restaurant at the Beverly Prescott Hotel in Los Angeles made the error of allowing S. Irene Virbila, the restaurant critic of the *Los Angeles Times,* to order its Thai Dyed Shrimp Pizza, made from "bready dough smeared with achingly sweet Thai barbecue sauce and topped with slivered vegetables, rosy shrimp, and crispy wonton noodles . . . more weirdly awful than whimsical."

Far be it from an Englishman to criticize American food, but the present-day fashion for fusion cuisine appears perfectly to demonstrate both the virtues and the failings of the American character when it comes to food: enthusiasm for novelty and a willingness for experimentation, combined with a tendency to take a good idea to such extremes that it loses its original value. Similar ideas are influencing cooks elsewhere in the world, including Australia (and even Britain), but they are not taken to quite such excess.

One could argue, indeed, that the excesses of modern fusion cuisine simply perpetuate an American tradition of mixing all kinds of different foods on the same plate. In the nineteenth century the practice of serving different kinds of food at the same time encouraged many Americans to "mix things together with the strangest incongruity imaginable" (according to the account of Fanny Trollope, mother of the novelist Anthony, who lived for some years in Cincinnati at the end of the 1820s).

But there is more to it than that. One feature that distinguishes some of the great cuisines of the world—French, Indian, and Chinese—is their ability to combine different ingredients in a single dish so as to create a whole that is greater than the sum of its parts. In the case of fusion cuisine, the opposite is true. Different ingredients are brought together in such a manner that the flavor of each of them remains distinctive and individual, so that each can enjoy its fifteen seconds of fame on the palate of the person who is eating them.

"People need to be shaken up," explains John Sedlar, chef at Bikini in Santa Monica in California. "I love to jar their perceptions of what food can be."

Not surprisingly, many people find great difficulty in matching wines with this new style of food. French wines that were designed to harmonize with classically integrated French cuisine find themselves at odds with the jarring of flavors within fusion cooking, and are often swamped by them. California wines, which are mostly based on French grape varieties and French techniques, with some adjustments to suit local growing conditions and local tastes,[27] do not make ideal partners either, although their greater degree of fruitiness enables them to withstand the experience rather better. Some styles of California wine can work quite well, notably those that are not based on French originals— such as wines made from newly imported Italian grape varieties and especially that great Californian original zinfandel, made from an Italian variety that is believed to have been imported to the United States in the early nineteenth century (and accounted for the majority of the fine wines produced in California before Prohibition). But the whole affair becomes quite an effort. Diners simply do not know which wines to drink with fusion food; they cannot follow the rules that they have learned so carefully, such as that white wine goes best with fish or that Bordeaux or cabernet sauvignon combines well with lamb. No wonder many of them give up and make do with water instead.

Others ignore any attempt to match what they are drinking with what they are eating, and stick with what they know they like. The wines that most people prefer are chardonnay and cabernet sauvignon, which remain the most popular types of wine in restaurants, accounting between them for roughly half of all the wines consumed. Yet the dryness and astringency of cabernet sauvignon and the sweet oakiness of chardonnay marry very ill with modern fusion and ethnic cuisines. Chardonnay in particular matches most foods pretty badly. The vast majority of the chardonnay drunk in the United States is produced in California, and much of that comes in a crowd-pleasing style that blends ripe fruit with sweet oak and some residual sugar so that the wine tastes richer and more rounded. The popular preference for this exaggerated style of chardonnay is demonstrated by the history of the Vintner's Reserve from Kendall-Jackson, which had become by 1996 the best-selling chardonnay in terms of value in the country, with sales of nearly twenty million bottles a year. This wine became popular in the 1982 vintage, when the grapes would not finish their fermentation, leaving a certain amount of residual sugar, which Jed Steele, the consultant winemaker, tried to balance by maturing the wine in a greater amount of French oak than in the past. The public liked the result, so the winery stuck to the style in subsequent vintages.[28] Jed Steele later

---

[27] These adjustments are discussed in Chapter 1.
[28] When Steele left the winery in 1991 to set up in business on his own, Jess Jackson, the owner of Kendall-Jackson, successfully sued him for misappropriating

justified the practice of making a slightly sweet chardonnay on the grounds that "the first duty of wine is to taste good." Well, not with food, it doesn't.

On the whole, it would seem that most people order whatever they want to drink when they dine out in restaurants, regardless of whether it complements the food or of any recommendation they might have been given. This is what the wine trade magazine *Wine & Spirits* found in 1996 when it asked restaurateurs whether their customers were prepared to take advice on what wines to choose with their food, as part of the magazine's annual survey of drinking habits in restaurants across America. Most people who ordered seafood chose chardonnay to drink with it regardless of the alternatives that were put to them; very few diners were prepared to follow the suggestion that they might prefer to drink, say, pinot noir. "I think the disparity exists," suggested the magazine's editor, Joshua Greene, "because there are a lot of people in the restaurant business and a lot of journalists who feel they should be helping people put food and beverages together in an interesting way. But it's perceived as more precious and fussy than anything else."

Maybe people would be more prepared to take the advice of sommeliers in restaurants, would be more willing to experiment, and would be less defensive in the face of a challenging menu and extensive wine list if restaurateurs charged less for their wines. It does not appear that a great deal has changed in the attitude of the majority of restaurateurs to the pricing of their wines in the century and a half since Alfred Bunn was told about the Philadelphia landlord who justified selling wine to his customers for between ten and twenty-five times as much as it had cost him to buy on the grounds that if he were to charge a reasonable price, nobody would drink it. On one occasion in the 1980s, Frank Prial, the wine correspondent of the *New York Times,* was lunching with a wine importer in a neighborhood restaurant where the house white—which the restaurateur bought from the importer—cost $13. The importer told Prial that he sold it to the restaurateur for $2. Prial asked the restaurateur why he marked up the price by so large a margin. "Listen," was the reply, "I get a high-class clientèle here. They'd be insulted if I charged them less."

Prial sought out the views on this practice of Alan Lewis, director of the Windows of the World restaurant at the World Trade Center,

---

the recipe of the Vintner's Reserve Chardonnay on the grounds that it was a "trade secret."

famous for its extensive (and reasonably priced) wine list. Lewis explained that earlier in his career, when manager of the Forum of the Twelve Caesars in the Rockefeller Center, he had tried adding a wine to the list at only $6. "I didn't sell a bottle. I raised it to $12 and it became a hit." As Lewis explained, many of his customers were unsure of themselves when confronted with a wine list in a smart restaurant. "They prefer to play it safe and go by the price when they are uneasy," he said. "So they come in somewhere in the middle." And there were others, he added, who insisted on coming in rather higher up the list than that. "Expense account customers will never order from the low end of the list. They don't want to appear cheap."

Perhaps the ultimate example of this latter category was provided by Nelson Durante when he spent $6,500 on a bottle of 1925 Brunello di Montalcino from Biondi-Santi in Ristorante Dieci in New York. As he told the *Wine Spectator,* which was researching a story about people who had spent very large sums of money on buying wine in restaurants, he had been trying to sell a communications business—for tens of millions of dollars—and had promised himself that if he succeeded, he would buy the most expensive bottle of wine he could find. "Every sip I took of the wine, I remembered the bottom line of the contract," he explained.

Since consumers appear to judge wines on price, it may seem a little harsh to blame restaurateurs for charging as much for their wines as they can get. They take advantage of their customers' ignorance about wine in order to offload their food costs onto their wines. As a result, people who drink wine in restaurants, and especially people who drink expensive wines, end up subsidizing those of their fellow diners who simply drink water with their meal. Although they mark up the cost of raw ingredients by 250 percent, restaurants in fact make little money on food. Their customers would simply not be willing to pay the sort of prices that would cover not only food costs (and wastage) but also labor costs (both cooking and serving), the expense of equipment, electricity, rent, taxes, and the restaurateur's profit margin. Therefore the profit margin is transferred to wine. The standard markup on wine is much the same as that on food. But the service of wine involves restaurants in little expense beyond a few breakages, so they make a huge profit.

It is not as if the service of wine in the majority of restaurants greatly enhances the wines that they sell so expensively. In most restaurants red wines are served much too warm and white wines much too cold.

It is well known that red wines should be served at room temperature (what the French call *chambré*) but this refers to the temperature of rooms in English and French houses in the nineteenth century, which were heated with open coal and wood fires, not to the much warmer temperature of modern centrally heated American homes and restaurants. Most red wines taste best at about 65 degrees Fahrenheit; any higher and too much alcohol evaporates and overwhelms the bouquet. The flavor of low-tannin, fruit-driven styles of red wine, such as most pinot noirs, is enhanced by being served a little cooler, at about 60 degrees Fahrenheit. Yet in many restaurants red wines are kept in or near the heat of the kitchen and are served positively warm. And it requires a good deal of both courage and confidence on the part of a customer to insist that the waiter bring him an ice bucket in order to cool down his red wine. White wines, on the other hand, should be served thoroughly chilled only if they are essentially tasteless and are intended as simple refreshers. The flavor of fine white wines is best enjoyed at a cool cellar temperature, say 50 degrees Fahrenheit. But most restaurants serve them straight from the refrigerator. And the more pretentious establishments insist on keeping them out of the diner's reach, in ice buckets, where their temperature continues to fall, rather than placing them on the table, where they can warm up gently to the right temperature for drinking.

Another common fault is the insistence of staff on repeatedly filling glasses to the brim, thus preventing diners who actually know something about wine from swirling it around in order to enjoy its bouquet. This practice is compounded in many restaurants by the unnecessarily small size and inferior quality of the glasses. And then there is the refusal of waiters, whether they know anything about wine or not, to replace bottles of wine that a customer has tasted and found to be corked, oxidized, or otherwise defective, on the supposed grounds that "it is meant to taste like that." People who work in the wine business during the day frequently find themselves fighting battles with restaurant staff in the evenings on precisely this issue. And if professional wine tasters encounter great difficulty in persuading waiters to accept that they have good reason to complain, what hope is there for ordinary mortals who do not have the same degree of confidence in their ability to determine whether a bottle of wine is in good condition or not?

In 1991 the *Wine Spectator* asked a random selection of one thousand of its subscribers what they thought about wine service in restaurants. Sixty-five percent of those who replied rated the service as less than satisfactory, and only nine percent considered it to be good or excellent. A reader from St. Louis, Missouri, wrote to say that "we don't eat out as often as we'd like because wine lists are so bad here. None of the staff ever knows anything. We often share wines we've ordered with the staff because they've never tasted them."

These defects are only partially mitigated by the increasingly popular custom of serving a range of wines by the glass, a practice in which restaurants in the United States far excel their counterparts in Britain and Europe, and that enables consumers to experiment with wines that they might not otherwise take the risk to try. Today more than half the restaurant sales of such a prestigious wine as Opus One are by the glass. On the other hand, buying wine by the glass in a restaurant is, relatively speaking, even more expensive than doing so by the bottle; the average price, according to the *Wine & Spirits* survey, is more than $6 a glass.

And most of the wines people buy by the glass in restaurants are not the sort of interesting or unusual or expensive wines they would not normally try, but basic chardonnays or cabernet sauvignons. The popularity of wines by the glass in restaurants (now accounting, according to the *Wine & Spirits* survey, for more than one third of all restaurant wine sales) should be explained principally by the unwillingness of customers to order as much as a whole bottle. The practice of serving a range of wines by the glass originated as a result of the growth in neotemperance sentiment during the 1980s, and because of the publicity given to the dangers of drinking and driving and the increasingly severe penalties imposed for so doing. Thus, drinking habits in restaurants today do not differ significantly from those of the nineteenth century, when most people drank iced water with their meals, and only a few people were so bold and so extravagant as to order a bottle of wine. Today, even in the smartest restaurants, even on Friday evenings and on weekends, it is common to see nothing more alcoholic than a bottle of sparkling mineral water on many tables, leavened by the occasional glass of wine.

Just as they chose to do a hundred years ago, and were forced to do during Prohibition, most people would apparently prefer to drink cocktails before a meal than wine with them. For this reason, much of the wine boom of the last generation should be regarded as illusory. In 1985 Frank Prial wrote an article in the *New York Times* in which he declared that "we have never been and are not now a wine-drinking nation, and the jury is still out on whether we will ever be." He explained that the switch from sweet "dessert" to dry "table" wine in the 1960s and 1970s was not really a conversion to table wine, since it never occurred to most Americans to combine wine with meals. Instead, they thought of wine as a refresher or a cocktail; as a result, it was usually white. The so-called wine boom was actually a boom in drinking white wine as an apéritif.

In the 1970s and 1980s many people chose white wine in preference to a cocktail because it was more fashionable, because it was lower in calories, and because they thought it was better for their health. Many of them have now returned to cocktails because that is what they prefer.[29] "A whole generation has become bored reciting, 'I'll just have a glass of white wine,' and then having something set in front of them that tastes foul and has no kick," explains Ed Moose, proprietor of Moose's Restaurant in San Francisco.

The revival of the cocktail has coincided with a rise in the consumption of red wines in restaurants. This should not necessarily be interpreted, however, as indicating that an increasing number of people are realizing not only that a cocktail gives a bigger kick than a glass of white wine but also that red wine generally goes better with food than white. It is true that there has recently been a great increase in the popularity of merlot in restaurants, up to the level of cabernet sauvignon. It also happens that merlots often make rather less unsatisfactory partners for fusion and various types of ethnic and regional American food than do cabernet sauvignons. But the reason for the popularity of merlot in restaurants has less to do with its suitability for drinking with currently fashionable styles of food than with the development of the popular notion that it is softer and suppler and less tannic than cabernet sauvignon, in other words, tastes less like a red wine.[30] It is also easier to pronounce.

It would be naïve to attribute the relative growth in popularity of red wines in restaurants to their tendency to marry better with food than white. The majority of people who have taken up drinking red wines have been inspired to do so because they think they are good for their health. This idea was implanted by a report in 1991 on the

---

[29]The current cocktail revival is discussed in the Conclusion.

[30]Many consumers are disabused of this notion only after they have tasted a number of merlots and discover that they are mostly no more than a thinner version of the same kind of wine as cabernet sauvignon.

widely watched and influential television program *60 Minutes* about the "French paradox," the fact that the French suffer much less from heart disease than the Americans or British, despite their relatively unhealthy lifestyles. The program suggested that the explanation for the paradox lay in the widespread consumption in France of red wine. Popular belief in the virtues of red wine has subsequently been encouraged by scientific research that has identified certain substances in the skins of black grapes, from which red wine is made, which might help to prevent heart disease.[31] As a result of the publicity given to these findings, sales of red wine have increased dramatically. In the six years following the *60 Minutes* program, according to the annual survey published by *Wine & Spirits*, red wines increased from 38 to 52 percent of the wines sold; by 1997, in other words, sales of red wines in restaurants in America had surpassed those of white.

The fact that many diners in restaurants have converted from chardonnay to cabernet sauvignon and merlot should not necessarily be interpreted as a decisive stage in the development of America as a wine-drinking country. In May 1996 the Smithsonian Institution sponsored a two-day seminar on American wine called "Red, White, and American." Among the speakers was Warren Belasco, chairman of the American studies department at the University of Maryland, who said that "I'm not sure that I see Americans becoming really significant wine drinkers. . . . Wine has a central place in cultures based on very long, leisurely meals and pedestrian transportation. And that's probably not the future in America unless we experience a major economic and environmental collapse."

On the whole, restaurants are the only places where people spend time over their meals and thus have a proper chance to drink wine. In their own homes, people are increasingly turning to rapidly cooked "convenience" foods, and appear largely to have abandoned the habit of communal family dining in favor of individual "refueling" whenever the tank appears to be running low.[32] This has been made possible principally by the introduction of the microwave oven, which has turned each member of the family into his own personal chef. So ut-

---

[31]See Chapter 4 for both the *60 Minutes* program and the subsequent research.

[32]This is unfortunate, as it may well be that the principal explanation of the "French paradox" lies not so much in the wine itself as the fact that it is drunk during the course of a leisurely family meal, a process that cannot adequately be replicated by the clinical administration of one glass of red wine per day.

terly have microwave ovens transformed American eating habits that it has been suggested by Mona Doyle, president of Consumer Network in Philadelphia, which advises the food industry on consumer habits, that the microwave "has changed our perceptions of time, much as telephones changed them at the turn of the century." As a result, "even fast food restaurants [do] not seem fast, because at home you don't have to wait in line."

Nor do these microwaved meals take very long to eat. How could they, when they are cooked to suit individual demands for the immediate satisfaction of hunger, and when microwaved food turns cold so much quicker than dishes that have been cooked conventionally on a stove or under a grill or in an oven?

Sometimes, of course, people still eat together. Or, rather, they eat at the same time. They do not necessarily talk to each other, or socialize, or share the experience over a glass of wine. According to a market research survey conducted in 1989, only one in three Americans typically dined at home with other people and engaged in conversation during meals without other distractions. Two thirds watched television, read, worked, or did something else while eating.

The average family dinner does not last very long. In this respect, little has changed in the century and a half since Thomas Grattan, the British consul in Massachusetts, pointed out that in America "eating and drinking *en famille* is a mere operation of appetite, without any social feeling connected with it; and the more quickly and least expensively it can be performed, the better."

Most people eat rapidly at home, and rapidly when they go out. They naturally incline toward establishments serving fast food, where they are not required to bother with such time-consuming niceties as cutlery or crockery or glassware, and nobody expects them to sit down in order to eat. People eat just as rapidly in the fast food restaurants of the late twentieth century as they did in the inns and taverns and ordinaries of the nineteenth. It remains an American characteristic to bolt one's food—to eat several snacks a day rather than two or three main meals; to eat on the hoof, in the streets; to graze, in other words. It has even been suggested that at the end of the twentieth century people have abandoned "grazing" (picking at different foods all day long) for "refueling" at a pit stop, where they inject food into their mouths before making a rapid departure.

None of these habits is conducive to the enjoyment of wine with one's meal. Fast food restaurants do not even serve alcoholic drinks, partly because this might encourage their customers to spend too long on the premises, thus damaging the profitability of the business, which depends on achieving as rapid a turnover as possible.[33]

By eliminating the social conventions of more formal restaurants, fast food establishments satisfy not only the popular desire for convenience but also the popular obsession with democracy. It is a fundamental part of national mythology to imagine that the United States is a classless society, where everyone indulged in the same food and drink or at least the same food and drink are available to all. Fast food is considered to be democratic in nature. It can be ordered without a knowledge of arcane restaurant ritual or obscure foreign food terms. Most people can afford to order as much of it as they want to eat, and they are at liberty to consume it as quickly as they might want. It satisfies a continuing popular preference for quantity over quality, and convenience over comfort. The enjoyment of elaborate meals accompanied by fine wines, on the other hand, is regarded by many people as elitist and therefore un-American. Popular attitudes toward fancy foreign dining have not changed significantly since it was suggested, a century and a half ago, that the introduction by the New York Hotel of à la carte meals and private dining threatened the ideological foundations of the American republic. To show interest in such matters is to associate oneself with the decadence of the old-world order—those European elites which the founders of modern America abandoned several centuries ago, in order to create a new and fairer society.

Popular attitudes to the enjoyment of food and drink thus hark back to the first Puritan immigrants from England. The Puritans were not "puritan" in the sense in which that word is now used. They did not object to pleasure per se—merely to those activities that interfered with their effort to fashion their own version of civilization. If they objected to overindulgence in food and drink, it was because this wasted time that could have been devoted to helping to conquer the wilderness. Even today many people avoid lingering over their meals because they prefer it to be thought that they are spending their time working to create a better country.

The survival of peculiarly American eating habits, like the prevailing American taste for ice cold drinks and the collective "addiction" to

---

[33]Branches of McDonald's in several countries on the continent of Europe do offer beer in their "restaurants" because otherwise parents would be less willing to take their children to them than they already are.

air-conditioning,[34] demonstrate the continuing influence on American culture of the privations suffered by the first European settlers of New England, by the pioneers who opened up the western frontier, and by the immigrants who tried to build a new life for themselves in the nineteenth century amid the squalor of the rapidly growing cities. Americans have not become a nation of wine drinkers because they do not want to spend the money, and they do not want to spend the time.

---

[34]These have been discussed in Chapter 1.

CHAPTER 3

Drink and Sex

Another explanation offered by foreign visitors in the nineteenth century to explain the peculiar American habit of dining with great rapidity in public restaurants, not pausing to drink wine with one's meals but rushing to the bar afterward, reflected a chivalrous view of social behavior. "I have sometimes thought," suggested the English journalist George Sala following his visit in 1879–80, "that this excessive temperance at meal times is due to the wonderful courtesy shown by Americans towards the fair sex. As the ladies are, as a rule, total abstainers, and look on our drinking customs with sheer horror, it may be that an American gentleman thinks it ungallant to drink anything stronger than water in a lady's company."

It was a new phenomenon that women were allowed to dine in public restaurants at all. Before the second half of the nineteenth century, women had not accompanied their husbands and male friends when the men went out to eat.

The restaurant had developed in late-eighteenth-century Paris as an institution specifically designed to cater to men away from home. Although it had originated just before the French Revolution, it received its main impetus from the revolution itself, which led to the arrival in Paris of large numbers of deputies from the provinces, who lodged in boardinghouses and needed somewhere to go out to eat; the new source of customers encouraged the former chefs of aristocratic house-holds to set themselves up in business in restaurants. Other chefs, scared for their lives because of their association with their former aristocratic masters, fled abroad and opened restaurants in the countries where they settled, including America. For the first half century or so of their existence in America, restaurants catered exclusively to a male clientele.

Women started to patronize restaurants only as a result of a change in eating hours. Before the Civil War, women had not needed to eat in public, since they had plenty of time for shopping and paying calls on their friends and acquaintances between breakfast and the dinner they took at home in the middle or at the end of the afternoon. From the 1870s onward, however, dinner parties became the focus for entertaining guests, and the dinner hour moved to the evening. A new meal was introduced to fill the gap between breakfast and dinner, called lunch.[1] Women who went to town and were not prepared to fast until evening needed to find somewhere to eat lunch. But they had never gone into restaurants because they had not needed to. Restaurants had been patronized only by men, as a result of which they had acquired an air of male exclusivity, which someone was going to have to be brave enough to break.

In the 1860s fashionable ladies who came to New York to look at the latest clothes usually made do with a pastry snatched from a baker which, according to their favorite publication, *Madame Demorest's Mirror of Fashions,* "some ladies eat against their judgment from a dislike to enter a public restaurant." It was therefore an audacious step when a number of the city's most prominent women formed the Sorosis Club and proposed lunch meetings. They had some trouble finding a restaurant that would accommodate them. Eventually, they persuaded Delmonico's to make available a second-floor room, and the first meeting took place on April 20, 1868. This caused a scandal. Some of the members were compelled to resign under pressure from their husbands, and the whole idea of a club for women was ridiculed. The editor of one of the leading New York dailies prophesied its early death, insisting that no female society other than a sewing circle could last. But the Sorosis Club survived and prospered. The idea of women lunching in a restaurant became by stages fashionable and then re-

---

[1] Probably a corruption of "lump," as it was originally taken in the form of a lump of bread and cheese.

spectable. By the 1890s Delmonico's was allowing women to have dinner in the evening as well, and this too became a respectable activity.

By this time, in Britain it had become the height of fashion for women to dine out in the restaurants that had opened in a number of London hotels, notably the Savoy. This was managed by César Ritz, the most famous hotelier of his time, and its restaurant run by Auguste Escoffier, the most celebrated chef. Escoffier developed a simpler and lighter style of restaurant food, which suited women much better than the gargantuan meals that had previously been presented to the men who had dined out without the benefit of female company.[2] In the first half of the nineteenth century, explained Ritz's widow Marie-Louise, ladies "were not supposed to possess palates any more than they were supposed to have legs. When Escoffier and Ritz began their careers together, the tempo of life was increasing and even more important than that, perhaps, was the fact that the epoch of the 'New Woman' had begun. Women were beginning in the Eighties to demand equal rights with men—even in such matters as food! They were beginning to assert their right to appear in public places with men, and to share some of their worldly pleasures. When Ritz decorated and furnished his hotels he always considered *first* the requirements and taste of ladies, and Escoffier was the first great chef to esteem their taste in food or cater for it." Early in the twentieth century Escoffier introduced his regime into America, at the Knickerbocker and Ritz-Carlton hotels in New York and the Grand Hotel in Philadelphia.

Women had now won the freedom to dine in restaurants, but this was pretty much all they could do if they went out with a man for the evening. A man could entertain a respectable woman only by taking her to dinner, the theater, and then supper; dancing remained out of the question. So restaurants became a focus for social display. As Escoffier explained in the preface to his *Guide to Modern Cookery*, the new hotel restaurants had become fashionable because they "allow of observing and of being observed [and] are eminently adapted to the exhibiting of magnificent dresses." Their customers, he added, "only had eyes for one another."

---

[2]The description "nouvelle cuisine" was occasionally applied to the new style of food introduced by Escoffier, but when it was revived in the 1960s it was applied to a generation of chefs who rebelled against his teachings.

Why had women been required to go to such lengths to assert their right to eat in restaurants? Why would their presence in them as late as 1860 have been regarded as "fast, if not disreputable," in the words of the English writer Clement Scott, describing how conventions had changed during the last forty years of the nineteenth century? As Scott explained, in 1860 "women were kept almost wholly in the background . . . and were universally treated by men with immense respect. . . . In nothing has life so changed in forty years as in the social relations between men and women. In 1860 women were idols and goddesses, now they are good fellows and chums."

One explanation of the historic exclusion of women from public restaurants was offered more than half a century ago by Jefferson Williamson in his history of the American hotel, still the standard work on hotel dining in the nineteenth century. Williamson explained that not only did women not eat in restaurants, but even when they stayed in hotels they were provided with separate dining rooms from male guests. This, he suggested, was a survival of the Puritan custom of dividing the sexes at worship and at social events.

It is true that in many (though not all) hotels, men and women were allocated separate dining rooms, known as the "men's ordinary" and the "ladies ordinary." But the sexes were not necessarily separated. Men were allowed into the ladies' ordinaries as long as they were related to or invited by them. It is also true that in Puritan New England, men and women sat separately in church and entered the meeting house by separate doors. The sexes were divided in this way in order to demonstrate that women were regarded as subordinate. But it is hard to see how ritual behavior in colonial New England can explain dining customs in republican America—especially since, in the colonial period, the sexes had associated with each other quite closely in other areas of their life. Men and women danced together at parties, and (contrary to popular belief about Puritan society) courted each other quite freely. Women even dined alongside male travelers in taverns. Puritan tradition cannot explain the origin of the practice of serving men and women separately in hotel restaurants.

Nor can Puritan custom account for the early-nineteenth-century practice of inviting only men to dinner parties and not their wives. The mistress of the house sat at the table with her husband, surrounded by their invited male guests. Conversation could often be limited, and the manners displayed were not always the best. According to Fanny Trollope, "Mixed dinner parties of ladies and gentlemen are very rare, which is a great defect in the society, not only as depriving them of the most social and hospitable manner of meeting, but as leading of frequent dinner parties of gentlemen without ladies, which certainly does not conduce to refinement."

Even when the sexes dined at the same table, they did not necessarily associate. Elkanah Watson, who lived in France from 1779 to 1782, reported how he was "enraptured by the ease and freedom exhibited in the table intercourse. . . . At the table, the ladies and gentlemen were mingled together, and joined in cheerful conversation, each selecting the delicacies of various courses and drinking of delicious light wines. . . ." This behavior he contrasted with the custom in England and America, where "instead of the ladies mingling in the arrangement at the table, as in France, they are clustered around the lady of the house, at one extremity, as if seeking her protection. The effect of this usage is to withdraw the ladies from the conversation of the social board, and to throw around them a studied reserve and chilling constraint. The ladies of France take the lead in social intercourse, and talk upon every subject, whether they understand it or not."

In America in the eighteenth and early nineteenth centuries, even when the sexes dined together the ladies withdrew after they had finished eating, leaving their menfolk at table to drink Madeira.[3] This was a British custom (except that in Britain men drank port after dinner rather than Madeira). People dined in the early afternoon and rarely felt the need to bother themselves with business afterward. So they sat around for hours, drinking. According to the author of *The American Chesterfield,* a guide to social etiquette written by a Philadelphia lawyer in the 1820s, "Habit having made a pint of wine after dinner almost a necessity to the man who eats freely, which is not the case with women; and as their sitting and drinking with men would be unseemly, it is customary . . . for the ladies to retire, and leave the men to themselves." The manners of the men were inclined to deteriorate as they went on drinking without the civilizing effect of female company. The Marquis de Barbé-Marbois, secretary to the French legation during the Revolutionary War, found it difficult to get used to seeing the women leave the table. "We were told," he wrote, "that it is part of the strictness of the customs of these people, who have thought it desirable to send away the women at the time when the

---

[3]The popularity of Madeira has been described in Chapter 1.

men, excited by liquors or by wine, might forget the respect which is due to them." Once the women had left, the men drank toasts, discussed politics, and told dirty stories.

While the men remained at table drinking Madeira, the women sat in the drawing room drinking tea. This nonalcoholic beverage symbolized female culture in colonial America. Women's lives were permeated with tea. Pehr Kalm, traveling around America in the middle of the eighteenth century, found tea drinking almost universal among the women, however lowly their station, whereas the men "care very little for tea, and a bowl of punch is much more agreeable to them." While women drank tea in the morning, afternoon, and evening, their menfolk joined them only for the afternoon tea party, a ceremony in which the status of the mistress of the household was reinforced. By pouring tea for the men of her family, she symbolized her role as the manager of the household and the provider within it of physical sustenance, moral support, and good health. In the tea ritual, women served while men deferred. For the latter to ignore the ceremony or perform their part incorrectly was a major breach of etiquette. When, in 1731, some of the young ladies of New York issued a complaint against the young men who they believed were not paying them due attention, they took care to include in their statement "That the said ladies are great admirers of tea, to the utter confusion of the distressed petitioners, who are altogether unacquainted with the ceremony which usually pass [sic] at the tea table, which ignorance of theirs makes them appear excessively awkward and ridiculous."

The significance of the tea ritual was emphasized by the expense, not only of the china teapot and teacups and silver teaspoons but also of the tea. One pound cost as much as a gallon of New England rum, or a half gallon of Madeira. The money that was spent on tea drinking occasioned protests from old-fashioned citizens who remained attached to a less ostentatious mode of living. In 1734 one New Yorker complained that "our luxury consists more in an expense of what is imported from foreign parts than what is of our own growth manufactories; I am credibly informed that tea and china ware cost the province, yearly, near the sum of £10,000; and people that are least able to go to the expense must have their tea though their families want bread. Nay, I am told, they often pawn their rings and plate to gratify themselves in that piece of extravagance."

Tea performed such an important role in the lives of American women that they continued to drink it even after it had been tainted during the revolution as a symbol of British oppression.[4] They did not abandon their after-dinner tea for coffee until the middle of the nineteenth century, when they also abandoned their practice of withdrawing from the dining table at the end of the meal, leaving the men sitting at the table drinking Madeira. This particular improvement occurred first in England, following the accession to the throne in 1837 of Queen Victoria, who required gentlemen to join her in the drawing room shortly after the ladies had left the dining room. This influenced a similar change in the United States, where members of society wished to see themselves as practicing the same civilized, modern manners as their counterparts on the other side of the Atlantic, and rejected what they regarded as antiquated or provincial behavior. Women no longer left the men after dinner, and the old custom by which women had been excluded altogether from dinner parties in some households disappeared.

At the same time, a change in taste in wine favored the communal consumption of coffee. It was thought appropriate to drink coffee after a meal only if light, unfortified wines had been consumed during it. Since the men in most well-to-do American households had been in the habit of finishing their meals with Madeira, coffee had been deemed unsuitable. As Thomas McMullen explained in his *Handbook of Wines,* "The system adopted, in imitation of the French custom, of taking strong coffee after wine, though so very agreeable, is injurious if the wines taken during the meal have been port, sherry, or Madeira, but not so if those of a lighter quality have been drunk." In the middle of the century Madeira became increasingly hard to obtain following the devastation of the vineyards by disease, and the drinking of Bordeaux with meals became more popular; so, too, did the consumption of coffee after them. "Formerly," explained a writer in the *Illustrated Manners Book* in 1855, "when ladies were supposed to be deficient in intellect, and gentlemen were truly deficient in decency, as soon as the dinner was over, and the gentlemen were ready for drinking, talking, smoking, and vile stories, and viler songs, the lady of the house gave the signal, the ladies rose, the gentlemen also, someone opened the door, and the ladies retired to the drawing room while the gentlemen enjoyed their own peculiar pleasures." Since that time manners had changed. "Now that ladies can talk quite as well on most subjects as

---

[4]Women did, however, boycott tea temporarily in the 1760s and 1770s on patriotic grounds. The part played by tea in the revolution is discussed in Chapter 6.

their lords, and that gentlemen think it well to be decent in their own society, ladies remain at the dinner table, take champagne very prudently, if at all; coffee is served last and at the dinner table; and all retire together to the music, conversation, or the flirtations of the drawing room."

The sexes were no longer separated at meals. Instead of placing all the men at one end of the table, and all the women at the other, the practice was introduced of seating men and women at table alternately (the procedure that prevails at dinner parties today). The reason for the change, according to the author of *The American Chesterfield,* was "for the better convenience of a lady's being attended to, and served by the gentleman next to her." Not only did men and women now drink together, it was the job of each male diner to see to it that the lady sitting next to him was provided with wine. A woman was not supposed to ask for wine herself: The man beside her would ask whether she wanted some wine, and either served her himself, or summoned one of the servants. The woman would be expected to select a wine appropriate to her "delicate" nature, a "lady's wine" such as still or sparkling champagne or Moselle. Out of politeness the man would also take some of this wine himself, and they would bow to each other before drinking.[5]

The greater intercourse between the sexes at meals that developed during the nineteenth century did more to impose female habits on men than the other way around. The more time that women spent at the dinner table with men, the less the latter drank. Hence Sala's comment attributing the temperate habits of the late nineteenth century to "the wonderful courtesy shown by Americans towards the fair sex." Hence also the tendency of men to leave the company of women with whom they had dined in a hotel or restaurant in order to drink in the bar. "The men have a curious habit of flocking to the bar-room immediately after dinner to imbibe the stimulant that preference or custom or the fear of their wives has deprived them of during the meal," explained James Fullarton Muirhead, the author of *Baedeker's Handbook to the United States.*

By the time Sala and Muirhead made their observations, many women had given up drinking altogether. Previously, it had been regarded as bad manners to refuse an offer of wine; now it became acceptable. Many hostesses even refused to make wine available at all.

---

[5]Drinking rituals are covered in the Conclusion.

A precedent was established by "Lemonade Lucy," the wife of President Rutherford B. Hayes; after her husband's election in 1877 she decreed that no alcoholic beverages were to be served in the White House.[6] "Society has at last reached the point," wrote The Christian Herald a few years later, "where it is not considered a breach of good form to serve a dinner without wine. . . . The hostess who simply does not offer wine to any guest under any circumstances is using her influence effectively and courageously in the cause of temperance in support of Christian principles."

The extent of female abstemiousness should not be exaggerated, however. Although women were supposed to drink only in moderation, to show a preference for the wines that best suited their supposedly fragile constitutions, and to avoid spirits, they could get drunk when they wanted.

Many women became accustomed to the regular consumption of a substantial quantity of alcohol through the ingestion of pseudo-medicinal compounds that were supposed to help sustain their delicate constitutions, in the form of cordials, "stomach elixirs," and other patent medicines. The English phrenologist George Combe, traveling in the United States in 1839, was informed by a lady who was "extensively acquainted" in both Boston and New York, that "she knew some American ladies who indulge in as much as three glasses of wine after dinner and then, by means of lavender and cordials, support a state of artificial excitement during the remainder of the evening." The female consumption of cordials and patent medicines created something of a minor scandal at the beginning of the twentieth century, when Edward Bok, of the Ladies' Home Journal, wrote to fifty members of the Women's Christian Temperance Union and found that three quarters of them were using highly alcoholic patent medicines. Popular remedies of the period included Parker's Tonic, labeled "purely vegetable" and "recommended for inebriates," which was found on analysis to be 42 percent alcohol by volume, as strong as whiskey; Hoofland's German Bitters, "entirely vegetable, and free from alcoholic stimulant," 26 percent alcohol; Kaufmann's Sulphur Bitters, which claimed on its label that it contained no alcohol although analysis revealed its alcohol content to be 26 percent (and its sulphur content to be zero); Whiskol, supposedly "a non-intoxicating stimulant, whiskey

---

[6]In 1880 Hayes was not renominated as the Republican candidate, partly because of the controversy caused by his wife's temperance activities.

without its sting," in fact 28 percent alcohol; Colden's Liquid Beef Tonic, "recommended for treatment of alcohol habit," 27 percent alcohol. The recommended dosage of these medicines varied from one teaspoon to one wineglass, to be taken between one and four times a day and "increased as needed." The most famous patent medicine, Lydia Pinkham's Vegetable Compound, which was marketed as a "remedy for female complaints," contained between 18 and 20 percent alcohol, about the same as port or sherry. No wonder it inspired its devotees to break into song:

> Let's drink the drink the drink
> To Lillie the Pink the Pink the Pink
> The savior of the human race,
> For she invented a medicinal compound
> Efficacious in every case.[7]

Other women were more resourceful. A reporter for the Canadian Women's Christian Temperance Union newspaper, seeing a woman buy a large quantity of eau de cologne in a drugstore, asked the salesman whether the customer was going to have a perfumed bath. No, the salesman replied, she was going to get drunk. "You never heard of cologne drunkards?" he asked. "That woman is . . . one of the worst of them. . . . She buys from one to two dozen of those long slim bottles . . . every week, and she takes it entirely herself . . . on lumps of sugar."

Many women also achieved intoxication without resorting to alcohol. "As a rule, women take opiates and men alcohol, both seeking the same pleasurable results," one doctor observed in 1891. "A woman is very degraded before she will consent to display drunkenness to mankind, whereas she can obtain equally if not more pleasurable feelings with opiates, and not disgrace herself before the world." Several surveys of opiate use in the late nineteenth and early twentieth century found that approximately two thirds of users were women. Many women preferred to eat opium than drink alcohol because they could

---

[7]Another popular patent medicine of the period was a nonalcoholic product that had been developed in 1886 as "a valuable brain tonic and a cure for all nervous afflictions—sick headache, neuralgia, hysteria, melancholy, etc." Marketed under the name of Coca-Cola, its active principle was cocaine. The Coca-Cola Company removed cocaine from the beverage in 1903 and has since sought to deny that it ever contained this substance.

do the former in private, while the latter was generally done in public.[8] Also, a woman who took drugs did not smell of them afterward, unlike one who drank alcohol. It was not regarded as ladylike to have alcohol on one's breath.

Drugs were also considered by many people to be the height of fashion at a time when alcohol was falling out of it. A Colorado physician suggested in 1880 that drug taking was "the growing and fashionable vice among the rich—especially the fashionable women who, in the giddy round of evanescent pleasure, must have a stimulant. Whiskey and champagne are painful in their after-effects rather than pleasant. Beer is vulgar. . . ." It was especially smart to take the drug of one's choice by the up-to-date method of hypodermic medication. As one dealer in medical instruments commented in 1882, "People have discovered that [syringes] are not only of great service in the alleviation of extreme pain, but that they afford a convenient sort of respectable intoxication." By "respectable" he meant "nonalcoholic." The hypodermic kit was preferred to the decanter in many respectable homes.

While a number of middle-class women preferred to take drugs rather than alcohol, many respectable working-class women were perfectly happy to consume alcoholic drinks as long as they were able to do so in the privacy of their own (or other people's) homes.[9] In the Irish immigrant community, women operated as the providers as well as the consumers of alcoholic drinks in kitchen grog shops, unlicensed drinking places that were known in Ireland as "shebeens." Back in the old country, the keeping of a shebeen had been a "recognized resource of widows"; in America, Irish immigrant women continued to insist on their right to make a living from selling liquor, despite the failure of the local laws to recognize it. They sold alcoholic drinks at all hours to friends and neighbors of both sexes. As was commented in a study of Boston's South End in the 1890s, the "liquor habit . . . is practically

---

[8]Opium eating by women in the nineteenth century can be compared to the use of tranquilizers by women in the more recent past: Both habits have enabled women to cope with a society that has put more pressure on women than on men to conform to conventions, yet has offered them fewer outlets for anxiety and frustration.

[9]The distinction that existed in America in the nineteenth century between what was regarded as appropriate behavior for women in public and in private can be compared to contemporary attitudes in Islamic countries, where women are expected to wear the veil in public yet privately dress in the latest Western fashions.

universal among both men and women."[10]So much did women drink
in their homes that researchers estimated that women comprised between one in ten and one in three of problem drinkers. Although
women were generally regarded as the greatest supporters of Prohibition, one antialcohol campaigner chastised mothers "who won't vote
for Prohibition because you want to have beer on your own tables in
your own homes."

Respectable working-class women may not have gone to drink in
saloons, but they did enter them, by a side door, in order to buy beer
to drink at home.[11] This was known as "rushing the growler." The
"growler" was the bucket or other container which the woman
"rushed" to the saloon to be filled and then "rushed" back home to
drink. A growler of beer was a bargain, for the saloon keeper was
expected to fill the container to the brim and charge only ten cents (the
price of a pint), regardless of the dimensions of the vessel. Though
some women drank alone in their tenement flats, others sought the
company of female neighbors. "With the women," said one New
Yorker, "it was a constant parade of beer kettles from early morning
until late at night." Many young women in New York also participated
with men in "can rackets": informal outdoor drinking parties, held
anywhere they could find, up on rooftops or down in alleyways.

Respectable working-class women were prepared to drink in private,
even in the company of men, but they were not prepared to enter the
public drinking place, where men held sway. The saloon was the anti-
home, where men went to escape from their homes and their wives, to
take "time out" from their responsibilities. As Leslie Fielder put it in
Love and Death in the American Novel, the saloon "was a refuge for
escaping males nearly as archetypal as the wilderness and the sea."[12]

Nineteenth-century saloons were male institutions in which respectable women would have felt uncomfortable, confronted with pictures
of naked women on the walls.[13] The naked women made the point not

---

[10]By this time most of the customers of shebeens were women, the men having
left to drink in the saloons, for which see later in this chapter.

[11]Sometimes they would send their children to the saloon to fetch the beer for
them.

[12]The social activity in saloons is discussed in the Conclusion.

[13]The most famous painting of nude women in this period was Adolphe William
Bouguereau's *Nymphs and Satyr,* which hung in the bar of the Hoffman House,
then celebrated as a social center for the rich and famous, on Broadway in New
York.

only that saloons existed to offer men the sort of entertainment they could not obtain at home, but that the sort of women who entered saloons did not mind removing their clothes if they were offered enough money to make it worth their while.

Prostitutes had always touted for business in places where people congregated to drink and socialize, but by the end of the nineteenth century the connection between prostitution and the saloons had been formalized in many of the big cities into a symbiotic relationship in which prostitutes made a good living from commissions on the sale of drinks (quite apart from the money they charged their clients afterward). In one survey of prostitution in Chicago, investigators employed by the Vice Commission visited 445 saloons and were solicited on 236 occasions. They were encouraged to buy pint bottles of beer for themselves and "cocktails" (consisting of colored water and a cherry) for the women who solicited them, for which the women were paid a 20 percent commission. The Vice Commission calculated that each prostitute would have earned at least $3 a day from these liquor commissions alone, more than three times what she would have expected to gain in the ordinary course of employment (and the equivalent of about $50 today). As the Vice Commission pointed out in its report, *The Social Evil in Chicago,* the money that women could earn as saloon prostitutes explained why so many entered the business. "Many of the women who frequent the saloons at the beginning are not professional prostitutes," the report explained. "They are weak morally with a strong desire for drink. They learn that generous men are there who willingly buy them drinks. Gradually these women find that they are able to earn commissions from the saloon management on drinks. Thus their visits become more frequent until they gradually drift into a life of professional prostitution for the extra money."

No wonder, in this period, respectable young women crossed streets or even took detours of several blocks in order to avoid walking past the entrances to saloons.

A few women insisted on asserting their right to drink in saloons, and to avail themselves of the "free lunch," by which the saloons sought to encourage custom in the middle of the day by allowing anyone who paid five cents for a drink to help himself from a buffet without further charge. One afternoon in 1905, a young woman worker in a commercial laundry in New York collapsed "with nausea and exhaustion." Her middle-aged colleague, Mrs. Mooney, said this had happened because of "them rotten cold lunches you girls eat" and urged them to try the free lunch at the nearby Devlin's saloon. The following day, Mooney, along with Dorothy Richardson (who recorded the story for posterity) and four others went into the back room of Devlin's. "The room was filled with working men drinking beer and smoking at the little round tables, and when they saw us each man jumped up and, grabbing his glass, went out into the barroom," Richardson wrote. Mrs. Mooney explained to her coworkers that "it's a proper hotel you're in, and it's decent working men that comes here, and they knows a lady when they see her, and they up and goes." They ordered "six beers with the trimmins!" the latter apparently including bowls of soup. Richardson declared that "I instantly determined never again to blame a working man or woman for dining in a saloon in preference to the more respectable and godly dairy-lunch room. We all ate ravenously, and I, who never before could endure the sight or smell of beer, found myself draining my 'schooner' as eagerly as Mrs. Mooney herself." Soon they became regular patrons.

Saloon keepers tried to satisfy respectable female customers such as these laundry workers by constructing separate "wine rooms," where they could drink without being bothered by the lewd paintings or the prostitutes, and without bothering the men who had gone to the saloon to escape from their wives. But because they were private, these wine rooms attracted the very prostitutes they had been intended to exclude. It appeared that the only way of cracking down on prostitution was to prevent women from going into saloons at all. In Boston in 1904 a new chairman was appointed to the police board, Judge William Henry Harrison Emmons. After investigating the city's lowlife for himself and interviewing those who worked within it, Emmons issued an order banning women from all places serving liquor other than hotels. The "Emmons rule" never became law, and soon proved unenforceable. The owners of large restaurants applied political pressure and gained exemptions. Faced with growing criticism from newspapers, Emmons withdrew the rule. Although it had remained in effect for only a few months, the Emmons rule lent credence to the popular view that women could not drink in public without being considered prostitutes.

It was certainly believed by many men that any woman who entered a saloon was in the business of selling sexual favors. Saloons in Denver capitalized on this assumption in order to taunt female reformers. Members of the Women's Christian Temperance Union stationed themselves at saloon doors to record who entered, how long they stayed, and their condition when they left. Some bars retaliated by posting their own guards at the window to watch the saloon watchers. If the lady tried to enter, customers chanted in unison, "Whore!"

But how much truth was there in the belief that women who went into saloons were looking for customers? It was in the interests of those who campaigned against drink and the saloons to suggest that the latter fostered prostitution. Certainly prostitutes worked in saloons. But to suggest that the saloon promoted prostitution, and that the closure of the former would somehow serve to suppress the latter, was patently absurd. Prostitutes approached men in a wide variety of meeting places: cafés, dance halls, theaters, cinemas, lake steamers, and public parks. Throw the prostitutes out of the saloon, and they simply plied their trade elsewhere. When Emmons tried to ban women from saloons in Boston in 1904, the prostitutes moved into massage parlors, bookstores, and other places without liquor licenses, or established themselves in even greater number in cheap hotels.

Nevertheless, so closely were saloons associated in the popular mind with prostitution that efforts were made not only to exclude female customers but also to prevent women from working in them. The English lawyer Evelyn Fanshawe, after traveling all over the United States at the beginning of the 1890s, concluded that barmaids were "an object rarely, perhaps never, seen in America," pointing out that in some states the employment of women in saloons was prohibited by law.

There is no doubt that the presence of attractive barmaids and waitresses served to entice vulnerable youths, as well as weak old men into saloons—as they had always done. Accounts of travelers in the eighteenth century frequently rated the attractiveness of waitresses in their diaries along with the quality of food and atmosphere. Perhaps the most charming to survive from this period is the *Itinerarium* of Dr. Alexander Hamilton, a doctor from Annapolis, Maryland, who traveled to Maine and back again in the summer of 1744, a total of 1,624 miles on a journey "intended only for health and recreation." Dr. Hamilton may have enjoyed a reputation in Maryland society as a gentleman of great courtesy and charm, but in his diary he rarely missed an opportunity to describe the women who served him in the taverns where he ate and lodged. "There were three buxom girls who served us at supper," he wrote of Flatt's Tavern in Huntingdon, Long Island. "One was an Indian girl named Phoebe, the other two were Lucrezia and Betty, but Betty was the top beauty of the three." At the Whitehall public house outside Newport, Rhode Island, Hamilton "drank punch and tea and had the company of a handsome girl," the publican's daughter. "She was the most unaffected and best behaved country girl ever I met with," he commented. "Her modesty had nothing of the prude in it nor had her frolicsome freeness any dash of impudence." At least Hamilton showed greater discretion in his dealings with serving women than did Mr. Parker, a gentleman who accompanied him on the stretch of his journey northward from New York to Boston. Hamilton records that when they dined together at the Pettit Tavern in Hempstead, Long Island, "There was a pretty girl here with whom Parker was mightily taken and would fain have stayed that night. This girl had intermitting fevers. Parker pretended to be a doctor and swore he could cure her if she would submit to his directions. With difficulty we persuaded Parker to mount horse."

Given this kind of precedent, it is not surprising that in the nineteenth century, legislators sought to prevent young girls from being molested by the like of Mr. Parker by forbidding their employment in saloons. According to Emily Faithfull, who made three visits to America in order to investigate the progress of women's rights, "The one employment from which Americans turn their faces in righteous horror is that of the barmaid. They consider it a degrading position, and cannot understand how English people reconcile with their professions of Christianity the barbarous practice of exposing women to the atmosphere of a liquor bar at a railway station, where they must often run the gauntlet of the insolent attentions of the 'half-intoxicated masher,' endure vulgar familiarity, and overhear low conversation. It is indeed an objectionable occupation for women, though I have heard of barmaids who knew how to make even that office dignified and respectable." Thus, laws were imposed against the employment of barmaids not only as an antivice measure but also in order to ensure that respectable young women were not exposed to the unsuitable atmosphere of saloons.[14]

As is indicated by the gulf between the opinions expressed by Alexander Hamilton and those divulged to Emily Faithfull, it was not just the drinking place that had changed between the eighteenth and the late nineteenth century, but also attitudes toward women and their place in the world.

The Puritans were not puritanical about sex. Far from being a taboo

---

[14]The English had found that the presence of women in bars, serving drinks to customers, in fact made the customers behave in a more civilized manner than they otherwise would.

subject in seventeenth-century Massachusetts, copulation was discussed so openly that Puritan writings required heavy editing before they were thought fit to print even in the mid-twentieth century. The Puritans never encouraged sexual asceticism, nor valued chastity in the Catholic sense. They believed that an intimate sexual bond between husbands and wives was an important and even a necessary part of marriage. Certainly they condemned sex outside marriage, even when it involved a young man and woman who were engaged to each other; and adultery was a capital crime, for which people were occasionally hanged. These rules were obeyed. Bastardy and prenuptial pregnancy were very rare. It would be wrong, however, to conclude that this sexual discipline was achieved by self-denial. Instead, it was assumed that if healthy adult men and women met alone together, they would probably engage in sexual relations. Therefore, married men and women were generally forbidden to meet privately with others of the opposite sex, unless they were related. Unmarried people were carefully watched by the community, and offenders were publicly denounced.[15]

In the colonial period, when Hamilton was commenting with such enthusiasm on the appearance and behavior of the women who served him in taverns, it was accepted that women had sexual feelings, just like men. The traditional Western European view still held that women, like Eve the temptress, embodied carnal desire. By the middle of the nineteenth century, however, attitudes had changed to such an extent that most people would have agreed with the statement by the British physician William Acton (who was widely read in America) that "the majority of women (happily for them) are not very much troubled with sexual feeling of any kind." Sexual desires, it was now believed, were the mark of a prostitute. As the New York physician William Sanger explained in his *History of Prostitution,* "The full force of sexual desire is seldom known to a virtuous woman."

The principal influence in changing attitudes toward female sexuality had been evangelical Protestant reformers, who believed that the best means of achieving a religious regeneration lay in appealing to women, who were generally more pious than men, and who were in a position to inspire not only their husbands but also the next generation. In the early nineteenth century, evangelical reformers successfully trans-

---

[15]The Puritans also banned sex on the Sabbath. At New London in 1670, a courting couple were brought to trial merely for "sitting together on the Lord's Day under an apple tree."

formed the popular view of women from sexual beings into moral ones, who elevated "passionlessness" into a virtue and who provided the source of spiritual renewal.

It was now considered that respectable women should indulge in sexual relations only for the purpose of procreation within marriage. As Walter Lippmann later explained in his *Preface to Morals,* the main conventions of sex in the nineteenth century were first that a woman "must not encourage or display any amorous inclinations except where there was practical certainty that the young man's intentions were serious; second, that when she was married to the young man she submitted to his embraces only because the Lord had somehow failed to contrive a less vile method of perpetuating the species. . . . The whole system was organized on the premise that procreation was the woman's only sanction for sexual intercourse."[16]

Clearly, if women did not have sexual feelings, then it was unwise for them to drink, or to be in places where men were drinking, since it was well understood that alcohol weakened their ability to resist advances from men.

This heightened perception of female delicacy not only helps to explain why they did not go to public drinking places,[17] and why middle-class women now shrank away from drinking even in private, but may also help to explain why they should have voluntarily avoided the public eating place. "Eating is so entirely a sensual, animal gratification," stated one etiquette manual, "that unless it is conducted with much delicacy, it becomes unpleasant to others." Guests at polite dinner parties avoided commenting on the food before them, even to praise it. "It does not become a man, possessed of an intellect and a moral nature, to spend his time talking about the feeling of his body," explained Timothy Howard, professor of English literature at the University of Notre Dame in Indiana and author of *Excelsior, or Essays on Politeness.* "It is said that man was made a little lower than the angels, but these food-talkers seem to have been made a little higher than the beasts."

---

[16]Female prudery at this period also extended to medical examination. "I am proud to say that in this country generally," commented Professor Meigs of the Jefferson Medical College in Philadelphia, "women prefer to suffer the extremity of danger and pain rather than waive those scruples of delicacy which prevent their maladies from being fully explored. I say it is evidence of a fine morality in our society."

[17]Women had patronized taverns in colonial times, when attitudes were different.

These rules were applied with special rigor to women, who were not supposed to eat food in indelicately large quantities, or to consume anything too spicy, which might leave its smell on their breath. The author of *The American Chesterfield* explained that "as eating a great deal is deemed indelicate in a lady (for her character should be rather divine than sensual), it will be ill manners to help her to a large slice of meat at once, or fill her plate too full." In the early nineteenth century some women even ate with their gloves on, although in time it became accepted practice for them to remove their gloves once they were seated at table. Even then, the rules of polite dining required that the food was touched as little as possible. That is why a waiter would wrap a napkin around his thumb when serving so that his hands never actually touched the surface of the plate; that also helps to explain why dining *à la russe* became fashionable, as it served to minimize the carving of meat in the presence of guests, the passing of dishes at table, and the sight of leftovers.

In these circumstances, it is hardly surprising that women should have avoided eating in places where they would be exposing themselves to strangers. Etiquette manuals warned against eating in genuinely public places, whether on the street, in a place of amusement, or in a railroad coach.[18] To many women, dining in a restaurant seemed equally unthinkable.

The new concept of women as sexless but spiritual beings gained acceptance partly because it gave them moral superiority over men, who were relegated to a lower status because of their supposedly more frequent need for sex. Women accepted the denial of their own sexuality as the price of enhancing their position within the family. In the eighteenth century they had been allowed to entertain sexual desires but had been regarded as second-class citizens within their own homes, little more than domestic functionaries. With the industrial revolution and the development of the market economy, an increasing number of men went out of the house to work, to negotiate for their family in the outside world. They left their wives at home to manage the household. This led to the establishment of what historians have termed "separate sexual spheres." Men worked in public, and women ran the

---

[18]In Britain even today respectable young ladies are taught that it is bad manners to eat in the street or on public transportation.

home. Men provided the drive and the energy; women provided the moral and spiritual framework.

In order to protect their private sphere of the home and family, wives tried to prevent their husbands from drinking. They began their campaigns in frontier settlements on the western side of the Appalachian Mountains in the early nineteenth century. Life on the frontier could be uncomfortable and even frightening for women who were isolated on their farms with their children; they naturally resented the saloons where their husbands frittered away their time and money. They began to campaign against alcohol in an attempt to enforce the male social role as provider and protector of the family. These concerns and campaigns soon spread to the eastern cities. When Margaret Davis married a New York merchant "of high standing in life," she had (as she later explained) "every prospect of future prosperity and happiness." At first he proved "a kind husband and affectionate father." Within a few years, however, drinking had turned him into "a terror to those whom it was his duty to protect," whom he subjected to privations "better imagined than described." After his death Mrs. Davis became a temperance lecturer, telling her own story in the hope that it would make other women aware of their impotence when confronted with a drunken husband.

One possible resource was a sex strike. In the 1840s groups of married women formed associations to demand that their husbands pledge themselves to abstain from alcoholic drinks, on pain of withdrawal of conjugal favors. Nubile young women also banded together to agree that "we will promise marriage to no young man who is in the habit of tippling, for we are assured his wife will come to want and his children go barefoot." Embargoes such as these may well have exerted some effect in small towns and rural communities, where people knew each other, but they can hardly have had any impact in the relative anonymity of the big cities.

Pressure from women, together with the efforts of male temperance campaigners, did help to reduce the popularity of alcoholic drinks in the 1830s and 1840s. But then came the Irish and the Germans. Millions of immigrants poured into the United States in the 1840s, few of whom shared the temperate habits that had recently been acquired by many native-born Americans. How would it be possible to persuade these heavy-drinking immigrants to subscribe to the temperance cause? As is well known, the Irish came to America principally because their potato crops failed; the Germans came not so much because they had taken part in unsuccessful political uprisings (as is popularly believed) but because they, too, had suffered from agricultural failures. The vast majority of Irish and German immigrants were untutored farmers of a kind who could hardly be expected to respond to intellectual appeals to restrict their drinking—even if they could understand them, which many of the German immigrants could not.

As it now appeared impossible to turn America dry through persuasion (known as "moral suasion"), temperance campaigners began to argue in favor of compulsion as the only means of ensuring that the immigrants abandoned their old-country drinking practices and adopted the highest moral standards of their new home. As a result, prohibition was imposed in several states, beginning in Maine in 1851, and known everywhere it was introduced as "the Maine Law."

Female campaigners who had previously played an active part in efforts to persuade Americans voluntarily to abandon alcoholic drinks now found themselves excluded from the temperance movement: They could not vote for prohibitory legislation because they were not enfranchised. Having been removed from the legal process, they resorted to extra-legal methods. Soon after the end of the Civil War a reader wrote to the *New York Tribune* to say that the war of women against whiskey had already commenced in Perrysville, Ohio. He told how women had opposed the opening of a saloon in the town and how, when the proprietor refused to sell out to them, the women smashed all his liquor supplies. The letter concluded with the prophecy that "the people in this part of Ohio honestly think the next war in this country will be between women and whiskey; and though there may not be much blood shed, you may rest assured rum will flow freely in the gutter. As the women here have taken the matter in hand once before, we claim to have fought the Bunker Hill of the new Revolution."

The most famous attacks on saloons were carried out by Carry Nation in Kansas at the beginning of the twentieth century, with the aid of a hatchet. At first she acted alone, but her righteous violence inspired others, and soon there were mobs smashing up saloons in Topeka and Wichita; people were getting beaten and shots were being fired. "What if a few people do get killed?" wrote one woman campaigner to a Women's Christian Temperance Union journal. "I'm tired of this sentimental gush about 'stopping before it comes to bloodshed.' I, for one, hope a thousand more of them will be smashed in Kansas before she stops." As Nation explained in her autobiography, she had tried to persuade men to stop drinking and the saloons to cease selling alcohol, but they had refused to listen.[19] "Moral suasion!" she cried. "If there's anything that's weak and worse than useless, it's this moral suasion. I despise it. These hell traps of Kansas have fattened for twenty years on moral suasion." Nation, like many of those who followed her example in smashing up the saloons, came from a respectable background. She resorted to "hatchetation" because she perceived that the saloon, and everything that went on inside, posed a threat to the private sphere of the home and family. "We hear 'A woman's place is at home,' " she wrote. "That is true, but what and where is home? Not the walls of a house. Not furniture, food, or clothes. Home is where the heart is, where our loved ones are. If my son is in a drinking place, my place is there. If my daughter . . . is in trouble, my place is there. That woman would be selfish or cowardly who would refuse to leave her home to relieve suffering or trouble. . . . Women now are forced to go out and save the home."

Women took to smashing up the saloons because, according to an article in *Scribner's* magazine, "For years and years, and weary, suffering years, multiplied into decades, have the women of America waited to see the traffic destroyed which annually sends 60,000 of their sons, brothers, fathers, and husbands into the drunkard's grave. They have been impoverished, disgraced, tortured in mind and body, beaten, murdered. Under the influence of maddening liquors the hands that were pledged to provide for and protect them, have withdrawn from them the means of life, or smitten them in the dust. Sons whom they have nursed upon their bosoms with tenderest love and countless prayers, have grown into beasts of whom they are afraid, or have sunk into helpless and pitiful slavery. They have been compelled to bear children to men whose habits had unfitted them for parentage—children not only tainted by disease, but endowed with debased appetites. They have seen themselves and their precious families thrust into social degradation and cut off forever from all desirable life by the vice of men they loved. What the women of this country have suffered from drunkenness, no mind, however sympathetic, can measure, and no pen, however graphic, can describe. It has been the unfathomable black gulf into which the infatuated multitudes of men have thrown their fortunes, their health, and their industry, and out of which have come only—in fire and stench—dishonor, disease, crime, misery, despair,

---

[19]Nor could she agitate for prohibition, because that was already in force. The saloons to which she objected were illegal ones.

and death. It is the abomination of abominations, the curse of curses, the hell of hells!"

The alternative was for women to agitate to be given the right to vote, so that they could legislate to prevent men from spending money on alcoholic drink. The length of time it took for the prohibitionist movement to achieve its ends—a gap of sixty-nine years between the introduction of state prohibition in Maine in 1851 and the imposition of national Prohibition in 1920—can partly be explained by the amount of time and energy expended on obtaining for women the right to vote. In this respect the female suffrage campaign can be regarded as an interlude between the early temperance campaigns and their final resolution.

The resistance they encountered in their efforts to persuade men to give up liquor led many women to conclude that they should be allowed to vote. The Women's Christian Temperance Union, which attracted a huge number of female members during the last two decades of the nineteenth century, was primarily concerned with stopping men from drinking. But it favored anything that might help to further this cause—including women's suffrage. A number of its members reported having experiences analogous to religious conversion, in which they realized that it was their duty as Christian women to demand the vote—even though they personally found the idea abhorrent.

Jack London voted for female suffrage in California in 1911 so that the women could then vote to deprive him of liquor. "I voted that women might vote, because I knew that they . . . would vote John Barleycorn out of existence and back into the historical limbo of our vanished customs of savagery," he wrote in his account of his experiences with alcohol, *John Barleycorn*. "The women are the true conservators of the race. The men are the wastrels, the adventure-lovers, and gamblers, and in the end it is by their women that they are saved. . . . There has never been a day when the women have not resented man's use of alcohol, though they have never had the power to give weight to their resentment. The moment women get the vote in any community, the first thing they proceed to do is close the saloons. In a thousand generations to come, men of themselves will not close the saloons. As well expect the morphine victims to legislate the sale of morphine out of existence."

The women's antidrink movement contributed significantly to the women's pro-vote movement. It would be wrong to suggest that the latter would not have happened without the former. But it is unlikely that woman suffrage would have gained as much support as it did, or have been achieved as soon as it was, had it not been for the women's temperance campaign.

It was therefore no coincidence that national Prohibition and female suffrage were both introduced in the same year, 1920 (as the Eighteenth and Nineteenth Amendments to the Constitution, respectively). Ironically, the introduction of votes for women, for which so many female temperance workers had campaigned, caused many women to abandon their support for Prohibition. As one writer on feminism had warned a few years earlier, once women had the vote they would "drink, smoke, bet, swear, gamble, just as men do. Whether they like it or not, does not matter; men do these things, therefore women must, to show that they are as good as men."

Women declared their newfound freedom in the 1920s in many ways. They drank alcohol and smoked cigarettes. They painted their faces with cosmetics and wore short skirts, causing President Murphy of the University of Florida to complain that "the low-cut gowns, the rolled hose, and short skirts are born of the devil and his angels, and are carrying the present and future generations to chaos and destruction." In several states legislators introduced bills to forbid the new form of female dress.

Women also started dancing with men, cheek to cheek. The *Catholic Telegraph* of Cincinnati complained that "The music is sensuous, the embracing of partners—the female only half dressed—is absolutely indecent; and the motions—they are such as may not be described, with any respect for propriety, in a family newspaper." Whereas previously a woman had not even been supposed to kiss a man until her husband came along, now otherwise respectable young ladies got into the habit of retiring from dances to darkened rooms or parked cars in order to indulge in petting or necking. Women were no longer prepared to subscribe to the notion that they must remain virgins until they were married. In many places the authorities tried to stay the tide of moral change by law, by making it illegal for a man and a women to have sex in the town unless they were married to each other.

The consumption of alcohol was a central feature of the new manners. Female drinking gained a great deal of encouragement from Prohibition, which, by closing down the saloons and preventing law-abiding restaurants from serving wine, brought drinking out of the public and into the private sphere. Everywhere, it seemed, people were holding cocktail parties. "Life, in the hours between the closing of the desk and the summons to dinner, in most large cities and for most of those in easy circumstances, seems to be but one cocktail party after another," reported the Washington correspondent of the London *Times*. "There can be little doubt that the number of women, members of that class which should be the social and political backbone of the country, who have admitted the cocktail and 'highball' to personal favour, and who are undismayed by what they see around them, is larger than it was. 'You know, I hardly ever touched anything at all before Prohibition came in,' is a phrase all too often on the lips of women to permit a denial of its truth or a closing of the eyes to its significance. The taking of a drink became an adventure, and when time dulled the zest of the adventure, the habit of the beverage had taken its place as an incentive."

Not only did women start drinking in private homes, they also went out to speakeasies. In the old-time, legal saloon women customers had either been prostitutes or had been treated as though they were, but illegal speakeasies catered without prejudice to both sexes. In New York the speakeasies were attended by "whole platoons of women and girls, among the latter debutantes of this year, last year, and the year after next," explained the author of an article about the phenomenon in *Harper's Monthly Magazine*. "When I was a boy, girls of their upbringing weren't allowed to move a step without chaperones or personal maids, and a spoonful of eggnog on New Year's Day was the extent of their drinking. Now they stand up at the bar and order whiskey sours like seasoned cannoneers." However bad the old saloons had been, commented the author Heywood Broun, at least the men who drank in them did not have to fight their way through a crowd of schoolgirls to reach the bar.

Alcohol also served as a catalyst for other elements of female liberation. Because Prohibition was in force, people had to do their drinking in private; therefore, when dances were held in hotels, the custom grew up of hiring rooms where drinks could be served in privacy to guests of both sexes, who lounged on the beds. A gin flask did not have to be passed around for very long in a hotel bedroom during a dance before the room began to be used for one of the purposes for which it had been originally intended.

The importance of the introduction of Prohibition and of votes for women should not be exaggerated; these were not the only causes of female liberation. It has been argued that the most important factor was the growing independence of women from the drudgery of housekeeping, because people were moving into smaller houses or apartments, and because machines were introduced to make housework much easier. Many women, whose lives had previously been dominated by cooking and cleaning, now found time on their hands; some took jobs, which gave them a feeling of economic independence and enabled them to move into apartments of their own.

Still, it was the part played by Prohibition in engendering what was regarded by many older people as moral decay among the nation's youth that inspired an influential women's campaign to have it repealed. The Women's Organization for National Prohibition Reform was set up by Pauline Sabin, a wealthy socialite with an impeccable political pedigree. Her grandfather (Julius Sterling Morton) had been secretary of agriculture under Grover Cleveland, and her father (Paul Morton) had been secretary of the navy under Theodore Roosevelt. Sabin herself had been prominent in presidential campaigns on behalf of the Republican nominees in the 1920s. At this time she had favored Prohibition because she believed it would help her two sons. "I thought a world without liquor would be a beautiful world," she later explained. But she altered her opinion for various reasons, including a maternal one. As she wrote in an article in *Outlook* entitled "I Change My Mind on Prohibition," mothers had believed that Prohibition would eliminate the temptation of drinking from their children's lives, but found instead that "children are growing up with a total lack of respect for the Constitution and for the law." Again, in 1930 she commented that "many of our members are young mothers—too young to remember the old saloon. But they are working for repeal because they don't want their babies to grow up in the hip-flask, speakeasy atmosphere that has polluted their own youth." The campaigns of Sabin's group showed that what were regarded as female concerns—the stability of family life and the proper upbringing of children, the motivations that had led women's groups to agitate for Prohibition—now persuaded a large group of women that Prohibition had to be repealed.

How large a group, it is not known for sure. Supposedly, at its peak, the Women's Organization for National Prohibition Reform had one and a half million members. But then, it has been the custom throughout history to exaggerate the size of the membership of mass, voluntary societies, not least because such claims are hard to verify or contradict.[20] It would not be surprising if the leadership of the group had

---

[20]One of the most exaggerated claims was made for the temperance campaigns of

exaggerated the number of its members, not so much for the sake of self-aggrandizement as to contradict the generally held belief that women, who had played such a large part in the passage of Prohibition, were wedded to its continuance. The Women's Organization for National Prohibition Reform dissipated much of the credibility that the support of the Women's Christian Temperance Union had brought to Prohibition. It played a major part in ensuring that Prohibition was repealed. If it has not subsequently received the credit it deserved, if its role has largely been forgotten, then that is because people were more interested at the time in looking forward to the New Deal.

Also, the social consequences of Prohibition did not influence the government as directly as its economic effects. Proponents of Prohibition had claimed that it would benefit the country economically: that expenditure would be diverted from alcoholic drink to dry goods, leading to increased production, more jobs, and higher wages. This claim appeared to have been borne out by the prosperity of the 1920s, but was exploded by the Depression, which began at the end of the decade.[21] The Depression forced the government to look for new sources of income; since liquor taxes had provided between thirty and forty percent of its revenues at the beginning of the century, the solution was obvious. Prohibition was abandoned in 1933—the only instance in American history in which an amendment to the Constitution has been repealed.[22]

Ironically, the Depression, which led to the repeal of Prohibition, also caused many women to abandon the alcoholic drinks they had taken up when Prohibition was in force. The Depression compelled many women to leave the workplace and return home, and encouraged a revival of traditional, family-centered values, with less tolerance of "deviant" behavior in women. Women did not stop drinking altogether, but they did so less often and less openly than during Prohibition. In 1938 the *Ladies' Home Journal* conducted a nationwide survey of drinking attitudes among women and found that the majority would not teach their daughters to drink, although most did not object

---

"Father" Toby Mathew in Ireland in the late 1830s and 1840s, when he is supposed to have persuaded between five and six million people—three quarters of the population—to forswear alcoholic drink.

[21]In fact, the claim was never correct. Although less liquor was drunk during Prohibition, it cost more; the amount of money spent on it was much the same.

[22]The prohibition of tobacco in Europe in the seventeenth century had also been repealed for economic reasons, as described in the Introduction.

to alcohol use by their sons. More than half thought it was wrong for women to drink at all, while two thirds believed that women should not be seen imbibing in public.

Attitudes changed again after the Second World War, when women won more independence. According to Gallup polls, from 1939 to 1978 the proportion of women in the United States who drank alcohol jumped from 45 to 66 percent, while the number of men who drank rose more modestly from 70 to 77 percent. During this period, women who had not previously consumed alcohol were enabled to acquire a taste for it by the development and marketing of drinks specifically designed to appeal to palates unaccustomed to the harshness of whiskey or acidity of wine or bitterness of beer: clear-colored, neutral-flavored spirits such as vodka and white rum in which the flavor of the alcohol could be masked by the addition of fruit juice or cola; sweet-tasting fruit-flavored pop wines and coolers made from a mixture of alcohol, fruit juice, and sparkling water; easy-drinking, slightly sweet Lambrusco and white zinfandel.

In the last generation, attitudes toward drinking by women have changed again. A long period of licence has come to an end. The transformation in the popular perception of female drinking was encapsulated by an incident in 1991 at the Red Robin Restaurant in Tukwila, a suburb of Seattle, when a young woman ordered a raspberry daiquiri to drink with her meal, only to be refused and berated by two members of the waiting staff. The customer complained to the assistant manager, who fired the waiters on the grounds that it was not their job to harangue customers about their drinking habits. This incident stimulated a great deal of discussion throughout the country, with many commentators supporting the waiters, who had, after all, believed they were acting from the best of motives in reminding the customer of the official advice that women should not drink any alcohol while they were pregnant—as the customer obviously was.

There is nothing new about this concern for the dangers of drinking during pregnancy.[23] The social devastation caused by excessive con-

---

[23]It has been suggested that alcohol was forbidden to pregnant women in biblical times, on the basis of a passage in the Book of Judges in which an angel appears to Samson's mother and informs her that although she has been barren up to then, she will conceive a son, who will begin to deliver Israel from the hands of the Philistines. "Now therefore beware," he tells her, "and drink not wine nor strong drink." The angel made this instruction, however, because Samson had been cho-

sumption of spirits in England in the first half of the eighteenth century has already been mentioned as underlying the abortive attempt by James Oglethorpe to prohibit the consumption of rum in early colonial Georgia. The problem was worst in London, where women tried to anaesthetize themselves against the poor living conditions caused by urbanization and industrialization. The magistrates reported to Parliament that "With regard to the female sex, we find the contagion has spread among them, and that to a degree hardly possible to be conceived. Unhappy mothers habituate themselves to these distilled liquors, whose children are born weak and sickly, and often look old and shrivelled as though they had numbered many years; others, again, give [gin] daily to their children, whilst young, and learn them, even before they can [walk], to taste and approve of this great and certain destroyer."

Similar concerns about the effect of maternal drinking on children were expressed by physicians and temperance campaigners in America in the eighteenth and nineteenth centuries. Physicians believed in the inheritance of acquired characteristics and thought that the condition of the parents at the time of conception could determine the child's constitution. In his *Temperance Manual,* the campaigner Justin Edwards listed numerous cases of damaged offspring resulting from parental drinking. "Facts abundantly show," he claimed, "that the children of mothers who drank alcohol are more likely than others to become drunkards, and in various ways to suffer. Often they are not so large and healthy as other children. They have less keenness and strength of eyesight, less firmness and quietness of nerves, less capability of great bodily and mental achievement, and less power to withstand the attacks of disease or the vicissitudes of climates and seasons."

The effect of maternal drinking on offspring was widely discussed in America in the nineteenth and early twentieth centuries. It was then forgotten partly as a result of Prohibition: The ban on the trade in alcohol led many doctors and researchers to assume (however unwisely) that expectant mothers no longer drank. When they returned to the subject in the 1940s, they dismissed the idea that the consump-

---

sen to become a Nazirite, that is someone who dedicated himself to God; and two of the rules that applied to Nazirites were that they were not allowed to drink wine and that they were forbidden to cut their hair. Far from advising pregnant women to abstain, the Talmud actually recommended that they drink wine in order to ensure the birth of healthy, strong, and good-looking children.

tion of alcohol by pregnant women could have any effect on their offspring, suggesting that this claim had been made in the past only because doctors needed to have a reason to tell women not to drink. "The belief that intoxication at the time of procreation might cause damage to the child . . . has maintained itself up to present times," stated the biometrician[24] Elvin Morton Jellinek in a distillation of scientific research into alcohol that he published in 1942. "On the basis of present knowledge, however, it may be dismissed. . . . The fact is that no acceptable evidence has ever been offered to show that acute alcoholic intoxication has any effect whatsoever on the human germ, or has any influence on altering heredity, or is the cause of any abnormality in the child." If drunken parents were more likely to produce damaged children, he argued, this should not be attributed directly to the alcohol but to the poor nutrition of the alcoholic mother and the bad influence of the alcoholic home.

Medical interest in the effect of maternal drinking on offspring was revived at the beginning of the 1970s, when an investigation into alcoholism among Amerindians suggested that a number of children born to alcoholic mothers suffered from comparable defects, for which the researchers coined the term "fetal alcohol syndrome." This stimulated a great deal of research into the effect of maternal drinking, which appeared to point to the conclusion that not only heavy but also moderate drinking by mothers could cause harm to their unborn children. In 1981 the surgeon general published advice that women who were pregnant or who were considering pregnancy should not drink any alcoholic beverages on the grounds that significantly decreased birth weight had been observed among children of some women who consumed on average as little as two drinks per day during pregnancy. During the course of the 1980s several major cities introduced laws requiring bars and liquor stores to display notices warning that women should not drink alcohol at all during pregnancy. In 1988 Congress passed the Omnibus Drugs Act, which required all containers of alcoholic beverages to carry the warning that "according to the surgeon general, women should not drink alcoholic beverages during pregnancy because of the risk of birth defects."

It was just such a warning label, peeled from a beer bottle, that one of the waiters at the Red Robin Restaurant brought to the pregnant customer in place of the daiquiri she had ordered, with the comment

---

[24]Someone who applies statistical methods to biology.

that "this is just in case you didn't know." So why was the customer so offended to be reminded of official government health advice? And why did the incident spark such heated national debate?

As the customer later explained, "I had been very careful throughout the whole pregnancy, and I thought it would be safe to have just this one drink, which I ordered with dinner. . . . I've always made a point to read everything I could find about alcohol and pregnancy. I felt guilty enough as it was for ordering the drink." She said she was offended when the waiter placed the warning label on the table, because "they tried to make me feel like a child abuser or something, and they were just plain rude."

In this case, the effect of the official advice that women should not drink during pregnancy was to make one young woman feel anxious and guilty, and to lead two waiters to upset and offend her when she ordered a drink. And for no reason. Not only did the woman in question give birth to a healthy baby boy, there is no evidence in the scientific literature to suggest that she would have endangered her child by drinking a daiquiri.

When the surgeon general issued his advice in 1981, he was relying on a report published in the *American Journal of Public Health* that had found significantly decreased birth weight among children born to women who consumed two or more drinks a day during pregnancy. What the surgeon general had apparently failed to appreciate was that this report did not discriminate between women who drank only two drinks a day and those who drank more. This paper did not demonstrate that there was a correlation between babies with low birth weights and mothers who drank only two drinks a day. All the babies with lower birth weights could perfectly well have come from mothers who drank much more than two drinks a day.

Furthermore, in passing the 1988 act, Congress was relying on hearings it held in which the key witness was Dr. Kenneth Jones, one of the physicians who had first identified and named the syndrome in 1973. He told Al Gore, the chairman of the subcommittee, that "we see [the fetal alcohol syndrome] in alarming percentage of moderately drinking women"; that a woman who considered herself a moderate drinker but drank a couple of glasses of wine when she came home from work and another with dinner, had an 11 percent chance of conceiving a baby with fetal alcohol syndrome. Al Gore replied, "That is really astounding."

The problem with the 11 percent figure cited by Dr. Jones is that it, too, grouped together women who drank moderately and women who drank to excess. It derived from research in which damage to infants was related to women's average consumption over a week. This research made no distinction between women who consumed one or two drinks each day and women who consumed between seven and fourteen drinks in a single session once a week. To say that 11 percent of women who consumed an average of between seven and fourteen drinks a week produced babies who were in some way affected adversely by the alcohol is quite different from saying that it was the women who consumed one or two drinks each day who had the damaged babies. It is perfectly possible that all the damaged infants came from mothers who were binge drinkers.[25]

Indeed, it is quite likely. It is not possible to substantiate an assertion that moderate drinking during pregnancy increases the risk of birth defects. This is generally acknowledged by doctors in Great Britain. One authoritative study carried out at Dundee University in Scotland of 592 children born in 1985 and 1986 concluded that there was no risk whatsoever associated with the consumption of one drink or so a day and that there was only a significant risk of fetal damage among women who took an average of five drinks a day or more. The findings of this study were backed up in 1997 by the British Royal College of Obstetricians when it issued its first guidelines on drinking in pregnancy, in which it said that there was no evidence that women who consumed up to two drinks a day risked causing damage to their unborn children. It would be surprising if moderate drinking did produce fetal damage, given that in many European countries women continue to drink when pregnant without producing increased numbers of affected children.

Reporting in the *Wine Spectator* the results of the Dundee University study, the world's leading female wine writer Jancis Robinson commented, "I honestly believe that at some point over the next ten or twenty years . . . all women will come to realize that during the 1980s they were victims of an enormous confidence trick. . . . Why have we all accepted the official line on alcohol and pregnancy, now shown to be absurdly overrepressive, so meekly? Presumably it is partly because pregnant women represent a minority over whom the rest of the world likes to assume dominion anyway."

---

[25]For more on the harmful consequences of binge drinking, see Chapter 5 and the Conclusion.

Yet American doctors still tell pregnant women that they should not drink alcohol at all. They justify persisting in this advice on the grounds that there is no proof that light drinking is not dangerous. This may sound contradictory, but apparently it makes sense to members of the medical profession. No absolutely safe level of drinking has been established, therefore (doctors say) the only way that a pregnant women can be sure that she will cause no harm to her fetus is by avoiding drinking altogether. This attitude demonstrates the extent to which many medical experts are divorced from the real world in which moderate alcohol consumption plays a major role in social interaction, the reduction of tension, and the enjoyment of meals.[26] If women should not be allowed to drink alcohol when pregnant because no safe level of consumption has been established, then logically they should also be prevented from taking part in other human activities for which no safe level has been established, such as driving on the road or breathing city air.

The principal effect of warnings about fetal alcohol syndrome has been to frighten the women who are most likely to listen to experts but are least likely to produce unhealthy children. Instead of being able to calm their nerves with the occasional drink during pregnancy, these women are caused extra stress if they do so, not least because they are likely to be berated by others. There are instances of women telephoning pregnancy advice hotlines in a frantic state because they have inadvertently eaten salad with a wine vinegar dressing. It might reasonably be argued that a fetus runs a greater danger of being harmed if its mother suffers from stress or guilt because she continues to consume alcohol during pregnancy in the face of official medical advice than if the mother were allowed to drink moderately without being told that she ought to worry about it.

On the other hand, women who are most in need of advice and assistance, who run the greatest risk of having children born with fetal alcohol syndrome, who come from the poorest and worst-educated and worst-fed and worst-housed sectors of society, have paid little attention to well-meaning advice from the surgeon general that they really ought to abstain from drinking while pregnant.

The solution? States have called in their pregnancy police.

In Laramie, Wyoming, at the beginning of 1990, a twenty-nine-year-old woman named Diane Pfannensteil, who was four months pregnant,

---

[26]The social benefits of moderate drinking are discussed in the Conclusion.

went to the police for protection after being beaten by her husband. The police smelled alcohol on her breath and had her blood-alcohol level tested. It came out at 0.1 percent, the standard used to determine drunk drivers. So she was arrested and charged with felony child abuse. When the case came to court, however, it was dismissed by the judge on the grounds that the state had failed to produce probable cause that the fetus had indeed been injured.

On March 16, 1996, Deborah Zimmerman, a thirty-five-year-old waitress from Racine, Wisconsin, who had a history of alcohol problems, and had once spent some time in prison for killing a man by driving while drunk, went out and got drunk on cocktails, although nine months pregnant. A few hours later she gave birth to a baby girl in hospital, after having fought against the doctors, who had been trying to deliver the child by an emergency C-section, screaming, "If you don't keep me here, I'm just going to go home and keep drinking and drinking and drink myself to death. And I'm going to kill this thing because I don't want it anyways." The child was born with signs of fetal alcohol syndrome, including a blood-alcohol level twice the legal limit for drivers. Racine County assistant district attorney Joan Korb charged Ms. Zimmerman with attempted homicide, explaining that it was time to "start holding women accountable for the harm they do their unborn children."

What an extraordinary way to treat a severely distressed alcoholic mother who had already survived one abusive marriage and who had been raped several times in her life, the last occasion when she was pregnant. Ms. Zimmerman was in need of help, not of prison. What possible benefit could there have been to the state in prosecuting her? Was this supposed to help to stop other alcoholic women from drinking heavily during pregnancy? Did it not occur to anyone that apart from the further and unnecessary distress it would cause to Ms. Zimmerman and her child, it would dissuade other women in a similar situation from seeking help?

In 1998 South Dakota became the first state to introduce legislation to make drinking while pregnant a form of child abuse. It gave judges the power to determine whether an expectant mother is drinking to excess and to confine her in a detoxification center for the rest of her term. Senator Barb Everist, who sponsored the legislation, explained that fetal alcohol syndrome is "totally preventable." Maybe so, but not by the course she has chosen. Relative to its economic wealth, the United States suffers from a significantly elevated rate of infant mortality compared with those European countries where mothers regularly drink alcohol in moderation during pregnancy. And yet the states are spending time and money prosecuting mothers for "fetal abuse" when they could be reducing infant mortality by improving prenatal care. It is not alcohol that is the root cause of fetal alcohol syndrome, but the poverty and malnutrition with which alcoholism is all too often associated. By condemning mothers who drink, the states are treating the symptoms but ignoring the disease.

Another effect of prosecuting women who drink or take drugs during pregnancy is to elevate the rights of the fetus above those of the mother. In an article entitled "Fetal Neglect: Pregnant Women as Ambulatory Chalices" the medico-legal writer George J. Annas has posed the question "Does it make any sense to decree that the pregnant woman must, in effect, live for her fetus? . . . Favoring the fetus radically devalues the pregnant woman, and treats her like an inert incubator, or as a culture medium for the fetus. This view makes women unequal citizens, since only they can have children, and relegates them to performing one main function: childbearing."

Those who seek to elevate the rights of the unborn child over those of the pregnant woman should be aware of the historical precedents for their actions. In eighteenth-century London, campaigners who complained about the effects of maternal alcohol consumption were not concerned so much for the sake of the children as for the country as a whole. It was believed at this period that the health of a nation depended on the strength and number of its workers, soldiers, and sailors. Many of the temperance campaigners who expressed concern about the consequences of mothers drinking simply wanted their children to live healthily into their twenties so that they could die a little less prematurely on behalf of their country. American physicians were also more concerned about the race as a whole than about the welfare of individual mothers and children. They subscribed to the moralistic view that the sin of intemperate parents could be visited on their children to several generations. This argument was propounded in 1826 by the Massachusetts clergyman Lyman Beecher in his *Six Sermons on the Nature, Occasions, Signs, Evils and Remedy of Intemperance*. "The free and universal use of intoxicating liquors for a few centuries," he pronounced, "cannot fail to bring down our race from the majestic, athletic forms of our Fathers, to the similitude of a despicable and puny race of men."

By the early twentieth century, the idea that heavy-drinking mothers produced children who were less useful to their country became intertwined with the then fashionable "science" of eugenics. The idea spread that alcohol was a "race poison" transmitted by parents to their children. Drunkards, it was believed, should not be allowed to have children. Laws were introduced in a number of states to provide for their compulsory sterilization.

Antidrink campaigners suggested that were alcohol to be prohibited, the American race would be strengthened, and that the need for such a measure was urgent, because the national stock was already degenerating as a result of the immigration of wine-drinking Italians, Greeks, and European Jews. The census of 1910 found that there were thirteen million immigrants in the country. "By continuing the alcoholization of the immigrant," wrote the campaigner Emma Transeau, "we are bringing ourselves dangerously near the time when the question will be not what America will do for the immigrant but what the immigrant will do for America." Such racist, eugenicist sentiments played a major part in the passage of the vote to introduce national Prohibition. In the opinion of the leading teetotal politician William Jennings Bryan, "We are going to have purer blood as the poison of alcohol becomes eliminated. We are going to have a stronger race because of Prohibition." While the trade in alcohol was forbidden, many people were poisoned and thousands died as a result of drinking poorly distilled moonshine or industrial alcohol that had been deliberately contaminated in an attempt to prevent people from drinking it as a beverage. This, according to some campaigners, was simply the price that had to be paid for the improvement of the race. "It is not the individual poisoning which constitutes the chief menace of alcohol," argued Clarence True Wilson and Deets Pickett, respectively the general secretary and the research secretary of the Board of Temperance, Prohibition, and Public Morals of the Methodist Episcopal Church. "It is the chronic and racial poisoning which strikes at the root of future generations and lowers the level of citizenship. Better hundreds sent to their graves by wood alcohol which they were under no compulsion to drink rather than millions cut short of their full possibilities by alcohol which perhaps they themselves never drank at all."

One historical example of the refusal of alcohol to women does not fit into a pattern of elevating concern for the fetus and for future generations of men over the interests of the mother who bears the child. In the early days of classical Rome, alcohol was forbidden to all married women, whether they were of childbearing age or not. This prohibition was imposed because it was believed that women who drank wine were more likely to commit adultery. Romulus, the legendary founder of the city, supposedly introduced a law imposing the death penalty for women who committed adultery or drank wine, "as being the gravest offences women could be guilty of, since he looked upon adultery as the source of reckless folly, and drunkenness as the source of adultery," explained Dionysius of Halicarnassus (writing in the first century B.C.). "Both these offences continued for a long time to be punished by the Romans with merciless severity," he added. Valerius Maximus (writing in the first century A.D.) told of the fate of one Roman matron whose husband caught her in the wine cellar: "Egnatius Metellus . . . beat his wife to death because she had drunk some wine; and this murder, far from leading to his being denounced, was not even blamed. People considered that her exemplary punishment had properly expiated her offence against the laws of sobriety, for every woman who drinks wine immoderately closes her heart to every virtue and opens it to every vice." Since wine was forbidden to women whether they were capable of bearing children or not, the principal motive cannot have been to prevent children being born out of wedlock. Women were refused wine because it was believed that this would lead them to lose control of their sexuality, or rather to express it to its fullest. Women were forbidden wine as an instrument of male control.

By later Roman times, this prohibition had fallen into abeyance, and women drank quite freely. The same was true in medieval Europe. The ancient Roman disapproval of female drinking was revived in England in the sixteenth and seventeenth centuries, when moralists began to use the weight of the classical authorities in an attempt to enforce temperance on women. In a sermon in 1608, Thomas Thompson drew the attention of his congregation to "an ancient Roman Law by which it was enacted that neither servant, maid, nor freewoman, neither matron nor virgin should drink wine, lest they should fall headlong into some dishonest action: Because the next degree of intemperance to the excess of wine is unlawful lust and filthy venery." The old disapproval of female drinking was revived because the authorities were concerned by disorderly conduct by women, including scolds who publicly abused family members or neighbors, single women who refused to enter service, wives who bullied or even beat their husbands, and suspected witches. The Church and the state both wanted to reinforce the patriarchal model of the family, in which the husband and father exerted absolute control over his wife and children. Condemning women who drank too much helped to put them in what was regarded as their place. It ensured that women would not trespass on the alehouse, which men regarded as their own territory.

A few women did visit public drinking places in England and America in the seventeenth and eighteenth centuries, but they were not allowed to drink as much as the men; they were expected to remain sober. For a woman to drink in public became an act of defiance against the social order—even when she was living in a climate in which it was thought necessary to drink alcoholic beverages for the sake of one's health.[27] A Scottish woman, Janet Schaw, visiting Antigua in the West Indies in 1774, reported of dinner at her lodgings that "the young ladies drank nothing but lime juice and water. They told me it was all the women drank in general. Our good landlady strongly advised us not to follow so bad an example—that Madeira and water would do nobody harm, and that it was owing to their method of living that they were such spiritless and indolent creatures. The ladies smiling replied that the men indeed said so, but it was custom and everybody did it in spite of the advices they were daily getting. What a tyrant is custom in every part of the world! The poor women, whose spirits must be worn out by heat and constant perspiration, require no doubt some restorative, yet as it is not the custom, they will faint under it rather than transgress this ideal law. I will however follow our good landlady's advice, and as I was resolved to show I was to be a rebel to a custom that did not appear founded on reason, I pledged her in a bumper of the best Madeira I ever tasted."

Hostility to drinking by women reached its climax in the nineteenth century, when respectable women were frowned upon if they drank more than small amounts of "ladies' wines," and when they avoided saloons, because women who went into them were regarded as whores. Although whores did ply their trade in saloons, the connection between saloons and whoring was as much a matter of image as of reality. Freedom with drink was associated with freedom with one's body: Whores drank, and heavy-drinking women were whores. "That woman should herself be guilty of the bestiality of drunkenness," commented Governor Gipps of New South Wales in Australia, "but this indeed could hardly be, for ere it can arrive, the creature is unsexed, the soft and endearing name of woman shall no longer be applied to

---

[27]This belief is discussed in Chapter 1.

her; call her fiend-fury-Hecate or invent some new term of insult in the language to designate a thing so fallen, and so vile. There is nothing in the whole catalogue of crime so thoroughly revolting as drunkenness in a woman, there is no object of disgust or horror that offends the sight of God or man so entirely loathsome as a drunken woman."

Although no one would now resort to such language, this male disapproval of female drunkenness survives today. It can be argued (and is by many feminists) that men are frightened by disinhibited sexuality in women, brought on by drinking, because it threatens existing power relationships between the sexes. "The restriction of women's sexual freedom is one of the key means by which men have traditionally exerted control over women," writes Marian Sandmaier in a book about women's drinking problems. "Man's need to control woman's sexuality in order to ensure his exclusive possession of her is so intense that even the threat of losing that control often activates male fear and consequent outrage. Thus the problem-drinking woman, whose usual clamps on her sexuality may in fact be somewhat loosened by alcohol, is denounced as a 'whore' even before the facts of her sex life are known."

Alcohol causes women to lose control over their sexuality partly for physiological reasons: The alcohol increases the level of the male sex hormone testosterone in the female body. But biochemistry alone cannot explain the dramatic effect of alcohol on many women's sexual activity. As was described many centuries ago in the Talmud (in a manner that would not now be considered acceptable), "One glass of wine is becoming to a woman, two are somewhat degrading, and if she has three glasses she solicits coitus, but if she has four, she solicits even an ass in the street and forgets all decency."[28] Women behave differently after drinking because they expect and are expected to do so. Many women believe that the consumption of alcohol permits them to behave in a way they might want to do when sober but feel they cannot. Given the readiness with which people have used alcohol as a scapegoat for misbehavior, drinking becomes an excuse to avoid being brought to account for one's actions.

A world in which female drunkenness is condemned because it is

---

[28]The effect of alcohol on men is a little different, as was explained by the porter in Shakespeare's *Macbeth*: "Drink, Sir, is a great provoker of three things, . . . nose-painting, sleep and urine. Lechery, Sir, it provokes and unprovokes: It provokes the desire, but it takes away the performance."

believed to lead to uncontrolled sexual behavior, and in which women often act irresponsibly after drinking because they imagine it absolves them of responsibility for their own behavior, suits many men well. As generations of men have discovered to their advantage, it is easier to persuade a woman to indulge in sexual activity if she has first been plied with alcohol. In a survey of 520 students at a college in the Pacific Northwest in 1974, 70 percent of male drinkers said that they had used alcohol in order to make women more sexually responsive, and 73 percent of men and women reported that alcohol either sometimes or always increased their sexual activity.

Many manufacturers advertise their wares by linking them with sex, but alcohol producers have more reason than most to do so. Much of the tequila sold in America is consumed by men in their twenties in raucous Mexican-style restaurants and bars that play loud rock music. Many of these young men believe that by knocking back shot glasses of tequila they will achieve the confidence they need to seduce members of the opposite sex, and hope that by purchasing tequila-based cocktails (such as margaritas) for young women whom they find attractive they will increase their chances of persuading these women to submit to their advances. It is therefore not surprising that tequila companies have marketed their product by referring to its usefulness as a tool of seduction. The American distributor of one brand of tequila, Two Fingers, used to feature an attractive woman in its advertisements with the slogan "Two Fingers Is All It Takes." In the last few years the bottling and marketing of the brand have been taken over by a bourbon distillery, which has decided to persevere with the same theme, launching a campaign in which it proclaims "Just Think What You Can Do with Two Fingers."

"*The three-Martini lunch looks good.*"

CHAPTER 4

"No Nation Is Drunken
Where Wine Is Cheap"

A mong the hundreds of thousands of Italians who emigrated to America in the early years of the twentieth
century was a young man named Giuseppe Gallo. A
native of the vine-growing region of Piemonte in
northwest Italy, Giuseppe (or Joe, as he came to be
known in America) naturally entered the wine business in California.
Like the majority of other Italian Americans, he did not see how there
could possibly be anything wrong with selling wine, and entertained
few moral qualms about continuing to do so after Prohibition was
introduced and the wine business outlawed. At least he managed to
escape punishment for his bootlegging activities—unlike his brother
Mike, who was less discreet, who was arrested more than once and
who eventually spent a month in prison.[1]

As well as dealing illegally in wine during Prohibition, Joe Gallo
produced his own grapes for sale to his neighbors and shipped grapes
to Chicago for sale to dealers, who then sold them on to home winemakers. In these latter activities he was assisted by his two sons, Ernest
and Julio—who later achieved fame as the founders of the largest and
most successful wine business in America. Considering that bootleg-

---

[1] It is not known whether Joe's connection with the criminal underworld as a result
of his bootlegging contributed to his killing his wife and then himself in 1933.

ging was illegal, it is not surprising that Ernest and Julio Gallo subsequently denied not only that they were involved in this business
during Prohibition, but also that their father was. But there is no doubt
that they had worked for their father during this period and that they
had helped him in his grape-shipping business. Nor was there anything
to prevent them from doing so. Unlike the sale of wine, the sale of
grapes to people who then turned them into wine in their own homes
remained legal during Prohibition.[2]

The Gallos' grape-shipping business was legal because the law that
regulated national Prohibition—the Volstead Act—permitted the production of wine at home for one's own use. Section 29 of the act
provided that the penalties imposed for contravention of the act "shall
not apply to a person for manufacturing nonintoxicating cider and
fruit juices exclusively for use in his home." This was interpreted as
meaning that people could make wine and cider at home for their own
use. On the face of it, it might seem implausible that anyone could
have interpreted "nonintoxicating fruit juices" as meaning wine, especially since the act had already defined any drink that contained
more than 0.5 percent alcohol as "intoxicating." But the courts held
that the term "nonintoxicating" as applied to homemade wine and
cider must have meant something different from what it meant elsewhere in the act, on the grounds that otherwise Section 29 would have
been meaningless. It was left for juries to determine what precisely was
meant by "nonintoxicating" in Section 29 on those occasions when
they were called to determine whether someone who had made wine
or cider for domestic consumption was guilty of a breach of the Volstead Act.

The wording of Section 29 was not meaningless, but it was confus-
ing, and deliberately so. It had been intended to reconcile the interests
of those farmers who had always made their own cider with the insistence of ardent prohibitionists that all alcoholic drinks should be forbidden. Hence the insertion of the term "nonintoxicating" to apply to
drinks that were undoubtedly capable of intoxication.

Section 29 had not, however, been intended to permit Americans of
Italian and Greek birth to make wine for their own consumption. Or,
rather, those prohibitionists who had countenanced the permission to

---

[2]The grape-shipping business also attracted the interest of bootleggers, who bought
many of the grapes themselves to turn into wine, which they then sold illegally.
Ernest Gallo later told how he had delivered grapes to Al Capone.

make cider did not realize that the production of wine would also be allowed. Had the intention been to exempt fermented drinks, then homemade beer would have been permitted, but this was forbidden, as it was still regarded largely as a foreign drink made by German-born Americans for German-born Americans.[3] Cider was different, being the traditional beverage of certain of the rural, Protestant native-born American groups that had been chiefly responsible for the introduction of Prohibition. Apparently these people thought they could be trusted to go on making their own drink but that foreign-born Americans could not be trusted to continue producing theirs.

Once the Volstead Act had been passed, prohibitionists tried to argue that Section 29 did not permit the manufacture of homemade wine, but the Supreme Court held that it did. After much deliberation, it concluded that no human law could prevent fruit juices from fermenting spontaneously, as it was their natural inclination to do.

Whether or not this loophole in the Volstead Act had been intended, it was much exploited during Prohibition, when the consumption of wine in America probably rose by two thirds. The Bureau of Prohibition calculated that by 1930 more than 100 million gallons of wine were being made in private homes each year.[4]

Not only was it legal to make wine and cider at home, it was legal to serve them to one's guests. Many a host might have imagined that by serving wine at a dinner party, he was indulging in the thrill of covert law-breaking, and making a gesture against what he considered a ridiculous law, but in fact he was not doing anything illegal.

Although many campaigners may have wanted to prevent other people from drinking altogether, this was never the main purpose of Prohibition, which was directed at the trade in alcoholic drinks, at the abuses associated with saloons,[5] and at distilled spirits, and only peripherally, if at all, at the consumption of fermented beverages in the privacy of one's own home.

In distinguishing wine from spirits, the prohibitionists of the early twentieth century were perpetuating the attitudes of their predecessors.

---

[3]See Chapter 6.

[4]As well as fresh grapes, grape juice in kegs and packages of pressed grapes called "wine bricks" were sold to home winemakers, along with a yeast pill and a printed warning not to use it, "because if you do, this will turn into wine, which would be illegal."

[5]See Chapter 6 for details of these abuses.

When James Oglethorpe founded Georgia in 1733, he attempted to prevent the colonists from drinking rum and to persuade them to drink wine or beer instead. Unfortunately, beer was scarce in the new colony, while Oglethorpe's efforts to encourage the cultivation of vineyards did not meet with success.[6]

Maybe, with persistence, wine production might eventually have been established in Georgia, but those who sought to develop the infant colony had more important things on their mind. Successful wine production required a long-term investment in land and labor, and the latter was in short supply because Oglethorpe had banned slavery. In 1738 a number of the settlers wrote a letter to the trustees of the colony back in London, pleading for the repeal on the ban on Negro slaves, stating that "we do not in the least doubt but that in time silk and wine may be produced here . . . but since the cultivation of land with white servants only cannot raise provisions for our families . . . it is likewise impossible to carry on these manufactures."

Similar problems confounded efforts to establish wine industries in other colonies.[7] The comments of the German doctor Johann Schoepf about the harmful effects of the excessive consumption of spirits in South Carolina in the late eighteenth century have already been cited. "From the first, much wine has been drank in America, and much money has gone out for it to foreign states," he wrote. "The reason why vineyards have not been set and vine culture taken up by the farmer generally is the great labour which the tending of the vines requires, and the time that must go by before there is a profit. The American farmer has grown accustomed, after little and easy work, to have in his hand immediate or yearly gains; his wheat and his cattle do this for him; whereas a vineyard, from its first establishment, hardly yields a fair profit in six to seven years."

Whereas economic factors opposed the cultivation of vines, they en-

---

[6] These are discussed in Chapter 1.

[7] It might have been expected that the French would achieve more success in their American territories such as Louisiana (under French control from 1682 to 1762, when it was transferred to Spain, and from 1800 to 1803, when it was ceded to the United States), but the French government had no desire to see the development of an industry in its colonies that competed against one of its own. It banned the cultivation of vines in Louisiana, and did its best to prevent vine growers and winemakers from accepting the offers of English colonists to come over and help them establish a wine industry. For the failure of vine growing in other English colonies, see the Conclusion.

couraged the distillation of spirits. In colonial times, the favorite drink was rum, distilled from imported molasses. These could be purchased from European colonies in the West Indies at a very low price, being merely a by-product of the process of sugar refining. The molasses were often imported surreptitiously from non-British colonies, without payment of excise duties to the British government.[8]

After the Revolutionary War, the new federal government needed to raise revenue to pay the debts of the states, which it had agreed to underwrite. Many federalists favored imposing an excise duty on spirits. Alexander Hamilton argued in favor of such a measure, on the grounds that "if it should tend to diminish the consumption of [that article], such an effect would be equally favorable to the agriculture, to the economy, to the morals, and to the health of the society."

In 1789 Hamilton was appointed secretary of the treasury. A tax was imposed on imported molasses. Hamilton also proposed an excise duty on spirits distilled from domestic crops. This proposal was debated in the House of Representatives in January 1791. Georgia Representative James Jackson condemned it as "odious, unequal, unpopular, oppressive." He pointed out that the South had neither cider nor beer—beverages that would escape taxation. The excise, he warned, would "deprive the mass of the people of almost the only luxury they enjoy, that of distilled spirits. . . . I plainly perceive the time will come when a shirt shall not be washed without an excise." But northern representatives generally favored the measure, arguing that distillers in country districts in the South and West who made whiskey from locally grown cereals should not be favored over distillers in the northern cities who produced rum from imported molasses. The proposal was carried.

The excise proved difficult and unprofitable to collect. In many states, distillers put up passive resistance. In some, they actively opposed the tax. An attempt by excise officers to levy the duty on distillers in western Pennsylvania provoked the area into open rebellion against the authority of the federal government, which had to call up the militia and conduct an action against its own citizens. Even after this uprising had been suppressed,[9] the tax remained difficult, even

---

[8]The development of the rum industry has been discussed in Chapter 1; the attempt by the British government to force American rum distillers to pay taxes on imported molasses is covered in Chapter 6.
[9]This rebellion is discussed in Chapter 6.

impossible to collect. In order to offset the shortfall, the government had to raise import duties, which meant that the excise on domestic spirits was no longer necessary, and in 1802 it was repealed.

From this point (with the exception of a brief period after the War of 1812, when excise duties were imposed to help pay for the cost of the war) no taxes were levied on domestically produced spirits until 1862, when the Civil War made it necessary to look for every possible source of revenue. The absence of taxation ensured that spirits remained cheap, and popular. Most of the men who went into taverns paid six cents or so for a glass of spirits: A decanter full of spirits and an empty tumbler were set before them, and they were allowed to pour as much alcohol into the tumbler as they chose, mixing it with as much or as little water as they wanted. In some bars, six cents bought them half a pint of spirits.

Wine, on the other hand, cost a dollar or two a bottle in a restaurant. Admittedly, the high price of wine in restaurants had more to do with the greed of restaurateurs and hoteliers than with the cost of the wine itself, but, even when purchased from a merchant for drinking at home, imported wine cost $1 per gallon, between three and four times as much as domestically produced whiskey or rum (although only between one third and one quarter as strong). Under the circumstances, it is hardly surprising that per capita consumption of spirits in the early nineteenth century ranged between four and five gallons per person, compared with an average consumption of only one fifth of a gallon of wine.

Attempts to establish a domestic wine industry having hitherto met with failure, politicians began to argue that the duties on imported wine should be lowered in order to encourage Americans to reduce their dependence on cheap, domestically produced spirits. Among their number was Thomas Jefferson, who had been trying to produce drinkable wine from his Monticello estate in Virginia since the 1770s. When, in 1818, the federal government proposed lowering taxes on imported wines in order to encourage temperance, the seventy-five-year-old Jefferson wrote approvingly of the measure. "It is an error," he observed, "to view a tax on [wine] as merely a tax on the rich. It is a prohibition of its use to the middling class of our citizens, and a condemnation of them to the poison of whiskey, which is desolating their houses. No nation is drunken, where wine is cheap; and none sober, where the dearness of wine substitutes ardent spirits as the common beverage. It is, in truth, the only antidote to the bane of whiskey. Fix but the duty at the rate of other merchandise, and we can drink wine here as cheap as we do grog; and who will not prefer it? Its extended use will carry health and comfort to a much enlarged circle. Everyone in easy circumstances (as the bulk of our citizens are) will prefer it to the poison to which they are now driven by their government."

While some suggested that a reduction in the price of imported wine would lure Americans away from distilled spirits, others (particularly farmers) argued in favor of a reduction of tariffs on imported wine because they hoped this would lead to decreased tariffs internationally, encouraging overseas trade and increasing the export of American foodstuffs to wine-producing areas. In 1829 Congress duly reduced wine duties from an average of 50 cents to an average of 30 cents a gallon.

The reduction did not, however, achieve the result that had been intended. Wine consumption increased only marginally, from two- to three tenths of a gallon per person per year. And many of the new wine drinkers were simply whiskey drinkers who had discovered that they could now get drunk cheaply on fortified wine. Merchants found it profitable to mix wine with whiskey to create a product containing 20 to 30 percent alcohol. Sometimes they also cut this concoction with water in order to increase their profits. Fortification, watering, and adulteration were so common that it was estimated that Americans drank five times as much "Madeira" as was imported. As Benjamin Waterhouse warned in his *Cautions to Young Persons Concerning Health,* many of the cheap wines available in America were "a vile mixture of deleterious articles, justly ranked among the remote causes of our nervous disorders, palsies, and apoplexies."

Maybe, if Americans had taken to drinking unfortified table wines, temperance campaigners would not have turned against wine as well as spirits, but even those people who could have afforded to drink the more expensive unadulterated wines preferred ones that had been fortified with brandy. For all the growing popularity of Bordeaux during the first half of the nineteenth century, the favorite American wine remained Maderia.[10]

It was well known that Madeira had been fortified in order to preserve it during transport and maturation. But it was not known quite how strong the fortification made it. Nor was it realized that unfortified wines also contained alcohol. Many upper-class opponents of

---

[10]See Chapter 2.

whiskey had favored wine precisely because they believed it to be free of alcohol, a chemical that a number of physicians and scientists regarded as a poison. Alcohol, they thought, was produced only by distillation and not by fermentation. Although a person could obviously become drunk on fermented beverages, wine (like beer and cider) was believed to contain only the constituent elements of alcohol, not alcohol itself.

It therefore came as an unpleasant surprise to many wine drinkers when the chemist William Brande succeeded in measuring the amount of alcohol in fermented drinks and not only proved that wine contained a higher percentage of alcohol than cider or beer, but also showed that more than one fifth of the volume of Madeira was made up of alcohol. Publishing the results of Brande's investigations, Justin Edwards, the corresponding secretary of the American Temperance Society, pointed out that "the man who drinks wine, drinks alcohol, as really as the man who drinks distilled liquor; and if he drink his wine clear, and his distilled liquor mixed with water, he may drink quite as much alcohol in one case as in the other."

Brande's statistics gave support to those temperance campaigners who argued against the consumption of wine on moral grounds. In 1835 Justin Edwards received a letter from Elisha Taylor, a temperance campaigner in New York State, who told him that "[I] have become acquainted with the history of a large number of moderate and immoderate drinkers of alcoholic beverages, from the light champagnes to fourth proof brandies. I have watched the reformation of some dozens of inebriates, and have been compelled to witness the relapse of many who had 'run well' for a time. And I say, without any fear of contradiction by anyone who has paid attention to the subject, that the greatest obstacle to the reformation of drunkards is the habitual use of wine, beer, cider, and cordials, by the respectable members of the community. And in very many, I believe in most cases, intemperate habits are formed, the love of alcoholic drinks induced, by the habitual use of these 'lighter beverages.' "

It appeared to be hypocritical to insist that the poor should give up their whiskey while allowing the rich to continue to drink their wine. Ebenezer S. Thomas, a well-known journalist in Charleston, South Carolina, criticized the gentlemen who formed a temperance society in that city in 1829 on the grounds that he knew most of them to be as fond of their Madeira as the workingmen were attached to their whiskey, and that they therefore "should not be so ready to deprive the laboring man of his drink. . . . We have a vast number of persons in the United States who, from their excess of patriotism, and having little to do, hit upon various modes of making themselves conspicuous, and the one of all others in which they appear to succeed the best is in minding everybody's business but their own."

Some Madeira-drinking temperance campaigners went so far as to introduce laws to prevent workingmen from drinking their whiskey, while making no commensurate sacrifice themselves whatsoever. In 1838 the Massachusetts legislature passed the Fifteen-Gallon Law, which prohibited the sale of spirits in quantities of less than fifteen gallons (except for medicinal purposes), but applied no such restriction to wine. In one democratically minded newspaper, the *Springfield Republican,* this was criticized for being "virtually a denial of equal rights."

Not only could the upper classes continue to drink their wine unhindered, but, if they wanted to buy spirits, they could easily afford to do so in bulk, unlike their humbler brethren. Yet the supporters of the law argued that if a group of workingmen pooled their money, they could buy fifteen gallons, and if together they could not raise as much as they needed, then surely their meager funds could be better spent? "Oppress the poor by closing the dram shop?" exclaimed one such pundit. "The dram shop oppresses the poor!"

The Fifteen-Gallon Law survived for only two years before it was repealed. In the following decade, more and more reformers came to the conclusion that the wine-drinking upper classes simply had to set an example by renouncing their own drink. When in the 1850s a number of states introduced local prohibition by means of what was known as the "Maine Law," the sale and manufacture of all alcoholic beverages was prohibited (an exception being made for medicinal purposes).

Even the Maine Law, however, did not bear down equally upon the wine-drinking rich and the whiskey-drinking poor. There was nothing to prevent the inhabitants of Maine Law states from importing drinks for their own consumption from neighboring states in which their manufacture and sale remained legal. Obviously this loophole much better suited those wealthy people who could afford to import wine from out of state in substantial quantity than poorer people who had been accustomed to buy their whiskey by the glassful or, at most, by the bottle. William Baxter, a Scottish politician who visited the States in 1853–54, recorded that he "met several persons who advocated and voted for [the Maine Law] because it would shut up a number of low tippling shops, while their own claret and Madeira would not be interfered with."

An exemption was also allowed for cider. This was done for the sake of the farmers, who otherwise were generally among the most enthusiastic supporters of prohibition, but who wished to continue not only to drink their own cider but also to sell it to people who wanted to use it to make vinegar or for cooking. The exemption for cider applied only if it was to be used for these reasons; the law forbade its sale "as a beverage or for tippling purposes." But farmers who sold cider were not required to ask their customers whether they intended to use it only in the manner in which the law prescribed.

Furthermore, in some states in which it had been introduced in the 1850s (though not in Maine itself) the Maine Law was amended to exempt wine and beer, as well as cider.[11] In Michigan, for example, permission was introduced for the sale of "beer and wine of domestic manufacture." This amendment was not made on ethical but on political grounds, in order to win the votes of the German-born population of the state.[12] It was thus condemned by the Rev. J. S. Smart in his *Funeral Sermon of the Maine Law:* "It is a pity that a few drunken Germans should be allowed thus to rule the thousands of American-born citizens in our state. Here, to secure the votes of a few foreigners to a party, we have imposed upon us the legal reopening of thousands of dens of drunkenness in the form of 'Dutch wine halls' and 'lager beer saloons.' But the legislature felt that something must be done to appease the virtuous American population of the state, and so the traffic in intoxicating liquors by Americans, that is, selling such liquors as Americans are accustomed to drink, was prohibited. Then it has come to this, has it? that foreigners, in this country, are free even to licentiousness, and their very vices are legalized, while our own native-born citizens must be kept under wholesome restraints! What greater insult could be offered to the native citizens of a state than is contained in

---

[11]Only a limited form of prohibition was introduced in the 1850s in Texas, Pennsylvania, and Ohio. Texas and Pennsylvania banned sales of alcoholic beverages in quantities less than one quart, while in Ohio the sale of spirits for consumption on the premises was prohibited.

[12]In Iowa, too, prohibition was amended to allow the manufacture and sale of wine and beer in order to win the German vote. The sale of spirits remained contraband, but they were readily obtained under the cover of the permission to sell wine and beer, so full prohibition was reintroduced in 1884.

that law? Foreigners, forsooth, may sell intoxicating liquors and get drunk after their fashion; but American-born citizens may not, unless indeed the Americans consent to humble themselves to these foreigners, so as to adopt their habits and get drunk on wine and lager beer. I ask if any man who would vote for such a law ever deserves a place of public trust from the hands of the American people again."

While a number of states experimented with various forms of prohibition during the second half of the nineteenth century, social reformers continued to argue that wine drinking promoted temperance and that efforts should be made to encourage the development of a domestic wine industry.

"By the concerted action of the people and the government we can become, as a nation, as distinguished for sobriety as we are now for intemperance," wrote the veteran journalist and antislavery campaigner Thurlow Weed. "By the acquisition of new territory we can become as extensively a grape-growing country as France or Switzerland. Let California, Kansas, and other states with soils adapted to grape culture turn their industries in that direction, and the practical remedy for intemperance will soon be reached. When the grape is produced in sufficient quantities to furnish cheap wine as a beverage for all classes, it will be within the scope and duty of Congress to perfect a reform that will emancipate our people from the horrors, and our nation from the reproach of intemperance. Congressional laws effectually prohibiting the adulteration of whiskey and other alcoholic drinks should be enacted. . . . If the time, labor, money, and talent that have been since 1820 devoted to well-meant but utterly fruitless efforts in favor of prohibition had been united in favor of the measures here briefly outlined, the curse of intemperance would have been removed from our borders. Light and palatable wine would have been substituted for inebriating and poisonous alcoholic liquors."

Weed wrote these comments in about 1870, just as the wine industry in California was being established and wine production was beginning to increase. By the end of the century the price of wine in California had fallen to a level at which the mass of the population could afford to drink wine instead of whiskey. "Wine has become so cheap in California," wrote the vine grower George Husmann, "that any family may, by purchasing it in five-gallon kegs, have good, sound light wine at a cost of 25 cents per gallon, delivered to their door. This is cheaper than tea or coffee, and should be kept in the house as a daily table beverage with the meals, for lemonades, etc. . . . Pure light wine as a general beverage is one of the most effective promoters of temperance that can be found, and the nations with whom it is in common use are the most sober and temperate."

Since they considered their product to be a temperate beverage, winemakers believed that they would be able to exempt themselves from the provisions of a national prohibition. In California in 1917 a bill was put forward to the state legislature proposing the abolition of the saloon and the prohibition of spirits but the continued sale of beer and wine under 14 percent alcohol in hotels and restaurants and the sale of fortified sweet wine up to 21 percent alcohol for consumption in the home. The Women's Christian Temperance Union and most "dry" (i.e., prohibitionist) state senators campaigned for the passage of this bill; it passed the senate, but was defeated in the assembly. In the opinion of many temperance campaigners, the wine industry had weakened its demands for special treatment by insisting that fortified sweet wines be given the same consideration as unfortified dry ones.

The brewers, too, believed in the early twentieth century that they would be able to exempt themselves from prohibitory laws. Since the Civil War, beer consumption had increased sixfold, while sales of spirits had fallen by half. The reason, according to the *Western Brewer*, was that "whiskey makes a man ugly and corrodes his stomach. . . . Beer, on the other hand, mellows him, links him with the universal brotherhood, superintends a physical and moral serenity, and makes him a friend to his kind." In Chicago, beer was described as "the almost universal beverage of the working people" and it was said that many people fed beer to their children as others did milk. "You can depend on the beer, but you can't tell about the milk you get down here," one man explained.

When the distillers asked the brewers to join their campaign for state regulation—as a counter to the threat of prohibition—the brewers refused on the grounds that "the beer business has nothing in common with the whiskey business. Quite the contrary. Their interests are apart and, under present conditions, antagonistic." The brewers believed that an increasing number of people would come to regard beer as a desirable temperance beverage compared with whiskey. They opposed state regulation because they thought that if the government did not interfere, beer would replace whiskey. The distillers, on the other hand, imagined that regulation would protect them: It would prevent abuses by saloons, while income from license fees would ensure the support of government officials and of many taxpayers.

Before 1913, beer sales steadily increased. While support for prohibition was strongest in rural areas, the market for beer was almost entirely urban, and the proportion of Americans living in cities was growing steadily. In 1907 the president of the United States Brewers' Association told its forty-seventh convention that "legislation of an unfavorable character has been undertaken by the legislatures of many states and notwithstanding the sales of beer have increased wonderfully. . . . We are justified in concluding the correctness of our old contention that beer will always be kept off the list of proscribed articles of diet."

After America joined the First World War, the Food Control Bill was introduced. During the debates on this bill (in 1917), attempts were made by dry campaigners to shape it so as to introduce national prohibition, by means of amendments that would have made it illegal to use any food materials in the manufacture of alcoholic beverages. This led some of the "wet" (i.e., antiprohibitionist) senators to threaten to filibuster the bill out of Congress. President Wilson asked the leaders of the prohibitionist faction to withdraw some of their demands so that the bill could go through in time for the fall harvest. So the beer and wine amendments were taken out of the bill but the spirits amendments remained. The bill as passed provided for the complete cessation of spirits production as of September 1917, while the president was given discretion to limit or prohibit the manufacture of beer and wine as he thought fit. In December he exercised this discretion by reducing the maximum permitted strength of beer to 2.75 percent alcohol by weight (the equivalent of 3.5 percent by volume).[13]

When Prohibition was introduced after the war, the brewers argued that the 2.75 percent beer that had been allowed during the conflict should continue to be permitted on the grounds that it did not constitute an "intoxicating beverage." In putting forward this argument, they were relying on the wording of the Eighteenth Amendment to the Constitution, by which Congress had introduced Prohibition. This amendment prohibited the manufacture, sale, and transportation within the United States of "intoxicating liquors." The meaning of "intoxicating" was not specified—quite deliberately. Despite protests from their more

---

[13]The strength of beer had previously varied from 5 to 7.5 percent alcohol by volume. Modern beers are mostly 5 percent.

radical supporters, the leaders of the prohibitionist campaign in Congress had accepted "intoxicating" rather than "alcoholic" in the wording of the amendment because they knew that otherwise it would have appeared too severely repressive to achieve ratification from a three-quarters majority of the states (as was required before the amendment could come into force).[14]

Hitherto in American legal practice, "intoxicating" had meant two different things. Federal and state liquor laws, designed primarily for tax purposes, generally classified any beverage containing more than 0.5 percent alcohol as intoxicating. Courts, on the other hand, defined intoxication in terms of the individual's ability to exercise basic self-control. By the first definition, all fermented beverages, including 2.75 percent beer, were intoxicating, by the second some of them, arguably, were not.

Many of the lawmakers who voted for the Prohibition amendment assumed that the matter of defining what was in fact "intoxicating" would be a matter for subsequent judicial interpretation, to be revised as society itself changed—in much the same way as the matter of defining what was "unreasonable" in searches and seizures or what was "freedom" of speech or of the press. These lawmakers were no less shocked than the brewers when in the Volstead Act—the enabling legislation that specified what was and what was not permitted during national Prohibition and which imposed penalties for breach of its provisions—the first of the two definitions of "intoxicating" was applied, and the manufacture and sale of all beverages over 0.5 percent alcohol by volume was prohibited.

The brewers continued to insist that the 2.75 percent beer that had been available during the war did not cause drunkenness, and therefore should not be called "intoxicating," arguing that in order to get drunk on it, one would have to consume more liquid than the human system could take. Jacob Ruppert, the owner of both a major New York brewery and the New York Yankees, challenged the ban on "war beer" in the federal courts. For this case, which was appealed up to the Supreme Court, several scientific experts prepared affidavits that 2.75 percent beer was not intoxicating. On the other side, Wayne Wheeler, attorney for the prohibitionist Anti-Saloon League, argued that it was necessary

---

[14]For the same reason, the prohibitionists in Congress had voted down the effort of Senator Thomas W. Hardwick of Georgia to add the words "use" and "purchase" to the amendment.

to interpret "intoxicating" on the strict lines set down by the Volstead Act for the sake of law enforcement. If the courts insisted on prohibiting only beverages that could actually be proved to have produced intoxication in the people who drank them, then there would be a whole mass of complex litigation about the properties and effects of different beverages and the police would have to analyze every beverage they seized to determine whether or not it was illegal. The Supreme Court accepted Wheeler's argument and upheld the Volstead Act definition of intoxicating beverages.

Legally, therefore, the only kind of beer that could be produced during Prohibition was "near beer," made by going through the brewing process and then removing nearly all the alcohol from the end product.[15]

Nevertheless, efforts continued to have the Volstead Act modified to permit the manufacture and sale of beer and light wine. Such a modification, it was argued, remained consistent with an interest in temperance, not least because it would lead people away from the illicit distilled spirits found mainly in speakeasies and toward less potent beverages that would legally be consumed at home. The leaders of the principal antiprohibition campaign group, the Association Against the Prohibition Amendment, emphasized that they favored temperance and were "unalterably opposed to the saloon." The association's letterhead bore the slogan "Beers and Light Wines NOW, but no Saloons EVER."

For this approach they enjoyed considerable popular support. In 1922 the *Literary Digest* conducted the first large-scale opinion survey on national Prohibition. Of more than 900,000 ballots returned, 38.6 percent favored enforcement of existing laws, 20.6 percent favored repeal of the Eighteenth Amendment, and 40.8 percent favored modifying the Volstead Act to allow light wines and beer. Among the factory workers who responded to the survey, 62 percent favored such modification.

Workers' representatives had from the beginning expressed great hostility toward the inclusion of beer in the prohibitory laws. Samuel Gompers, the leader of the American Federation of Labor, argued that prohibition was a class law against the beer of the workingman, pointing out that the middle classes had been given time to stock up their

---

[15]This encouraged gangsters to buy breweries and make near beer but send out the alcohol that had been removed at the same time as the near beer, so that the seller could spike the liquid back to its original condition.

cellars with wine before Prohibition came into effect, whereas "the workers who have no cellars and have not the opportunity of gratifying a normal even though temporary rational desire learn to hate their fortunate fellow citizens more bitterly and uncompromisingly." In 1919 Gompers warned the House Judiciary Committee that the abolition of beer was oppressive legislation that would lead to a rise of bolshevism and radicalism in America. Gompers's complaints were given substance by the fact that the home manufacture of wine continued to be permitted during Prohibition, whereas the brewing of beer for private consumption was forbidden.

Throughout Prohibition, the American Federation of Labor campaigned together with the Association Against the Prohibition Amendment to have the Volstead Act modified to permit 2.75 percent beer. In 1926 their arguments were considered by a subcommittee of the Senate Committee on the Judiciary. The federation's vice president, Matthew Woll, reported that there was great resentment against the Volstead Act's definition of intoxicants. Workers, he said, regarded the definition as "unsound, illogical, and in contravention of the intent and spirit of the Eighteenth Amendment," and they thought that a beverage of 2.75 percent alcohol content was not an intoxicant but "merely a stimulant." This opinion gained unexpected support from General Lincoln B. Andrews, the assistant secretary of the treasury, who admitted his personal belief that modifying the Volstead Act to allow the sale of light beers, not to be consumed in saloons, would aid in promoting temperance and eliminating the illicit liquor traffic.[16] Nevertheless, the Senate subcommittee endorsed the existing prohibitory laws, stating that the demands of the American Federation of Labor and the Association Against the Prohibition Amendment ran "contrary to the spirit and intent of the Eighteenth Amendment."

Following this decision, the Union Labor *Advocate* observed that "The chances for a modification of the Volstead Act are about as hopeful as the making of a summer resort out of the Sahara Desert." Within a few years, however, a majority of members of Congress had changed

---

[16]This suggestion, which led to Andrews's resignation as the government's chief prohibition enforcement officer, can be compared to an argument that has recently been advanced by some law officers, notably in Britain, that modifying the anti-drug laws to permit the cultivation and sale of marijuana, which is relatively mild and arguably nonaddictive, would help reduce the trade in illicit drugs. The issue of drug legalization is discussed in the next chapter.

their minds, for fear of what the workers might do if they were not given back their beer.

On being elected to the presidency in 1928, Herbert Hoover had appointed a commission under former attorney general George Wickersham to investigate the administration of criminal justice. This commission was informed by Matthew Woll that workers were losing faith in the government's willingness to help them, and that Prohibition exacerbated their mistrust of the authorities. By 1931, when the commission produced its report, the resentment had become serious. With the coming of the Depression, it seemed that the stability of American society was being threatened by an outbreak of lawlessness among the newly enlarged underclass. With more than fifteen million men out of work, riots and revolts were becoming common—as was the use of armed forces to control hungry and angry men and women. The upper classes were scared, and were prepared to believe those who told them that Prohibition made the problem worse. In 1930 Representative Robert Clancy of Cleveland warned the House Judiciary Committee that "this is a rather dangerous time, with the people in the cities, which hold sixty percent of the population of this country, in great discontent because of Prohibition and also in great discontent because of the unemployment situation."

It was suggested that legalizing beer would make workers feel better about the government and take their minds off their troubles. "Beer would have a decidedly soothing tendency on the present-day mental attitude of the workingmen," said Mr. McPurdy, another of the leaders of the American Federation of Labor. "It would do a great deal to change their mental attitude on economic conditions."[17] Former Michigan governor Fred Green went so far as to argue that the survival of the American government depended on the immediate repeal of Prohibition.

The ruling classes now needed a scientist to justify their change of heart over allowing the workers beer, and found him in Yandell Henderson, professor of applied physiology at Yale. Henderson, who had become an expert on "volatile poisons" as a result of his work on the effect of noxious gases on respiration, considered that alcohol was a "volatile poison" in much the same way as, say, carbon monoxide, of

---

[17] In 1982 the Reagan administration and in 1993 the Clinton administration considered increasing beer taxes but dropped the idea because beer was still perceived as the workingman's drink and they did not want to alienate workers.

which everyone now inhaled a certain amount but did not generally pose a danger because it was not intoxicating in small quantities. By this criterion, Henderson believed, beer, drunk in the manner in which it was normally consumed, was not intoxicating.

In December 1932 a bill was put to Congress "to provide revenue by the taxation of certain nonintoxicating liquor." The bill sought to modify the definition of "intoxicating" in the Volstead Act in order to permit the manufacture and sale of beer of up to 3.2 percent alcohol by weight (the equivalent of four percent by volume) in those states that did not have their own prohibition laws. Henderson, having been invited to give evidence on this bill to the House Ways and Means Committee, expressed the opinion that whereas whiskey was a narcotic that should be regulated in the same way as cocaine or opium, beer, "drunk as beer is generally drunk," was "virtually nonintoxicating." This opinion provided the basis for the legalization of 3.2 percent beer in the spring of 1933, eight months before the Eighteenth Amendment was repealed.

On April 7 the inhabitants of twenty-one states cheered the arrival of legal though rather weak beer. "Everywhere one went, in hotels, restaurants, clubs, homes, and even in some speakeasies, people were drinking the new beer and smiling," the New York Times reported the next morning. "As fast as the breweries[18] could load kegs and cases onto trucks and distribute them throughout the city, the beer drinkers consumed it. . . . New York certainly drank it fast—and why not? as was frequently remarked. Wasn't it nonintoxicating? Some people drank plenty of it during the day, but there was no apparent drunkenness. Everything went off quietly, with no disorder or trouble." Across the country, brewers sold between one and one and a half million barrels of beer in the first twenty-four hours. In many places, supplies were exhausted by early afternoon. Yet arrests for drunkenness actually dropped, and most of those who were taken into custody had been drinking something stronger than the 3.2 percent beer.

A week after beer was legalized, Jacob Ruppert told the Boston Herald that "Prohibition has accomplished one good among its many evils. Out of it has come legislation . . . that recognizes the distinction between mild malt beverages, such as 3.2 beer, and distilled spirits. The separation has at last been brought about by the sober sense of the

---

[18]These had kept operating during Prohibition by making malt syrup, malt extract, and ice cream, as well as near beer.

people themselves, and the foundation has thus been laid for true national temperance."

The largely beneficial consequences of the legalization of 3.2 percent beer provided a model for the liquor laws that were passed after Prohibition was repealed. The principles of the laws that were introduced in almost every state were laid out in the Rockefeller Report, sponsored by John D. Rockefeller Jr., and written primarily by his senior adviser Raymond Fosdick. In this report, which was issued in press releases to newspapers and magazines over several weeks in the fall of 1933 before being released in book form under the title *Toward Liquor Control*, Fosdick and his coauthor, Albert Scott, suggested that the states should treat beer that contained no more than 3.2 per alcohol by weight "as a nonintoxicating beverage. While this line may not be drawn with strict scientific accuracy, it has been popularly accepted as a result of the Act of Congress of March 22, 1933, permitting the sale of 3.2 percent beer. Since that date the nation has been a laboratory in which a remarkable experiment has been tried. During this time such beer was sold, even in populous centers like New York City, with little restraint. For some weeks it was obtainable like ice cream at any soda fountain. It has been drunk in enormous quantities. Yet the testimony is almost unanimous that there has been no increase in drunkenness, no disorder, no resort to illicit hard liquor. The evidence, as we have found it, is all the other way. Bootleggers have lost part of their patronage; in some places arrests for drunkenness have positively declined. The continued, unrestricted sale of beer having an alcoholic content of not more than 3.2 percent is clearly the part of wisdom. Such beer should be obtainable by the bottle, for off-premises consumption, practically without limitation. Its sale should be allowed by grocery stores, drugstores, delicatessen and general stores, and indeed by any merchant who so desires. . . . The sale of beer by the glass, with or without meals, should be permitted in restaurants, hotels, beer gardens, clubs, and indeed in any reputable establishment."

Fosdick and Scott also recommended that naturally fermented wines should be sold by the bottle for home consumption just as freely as 3.2 percent beer. The sale of wine for consumption on the premises, they argued, should be permitted only as part of the service of a meal in a "bona fide" restaurant or private club.

On the other hand, Fosdick and Scott recommended that the sale for home consumption of spirits, fortified wines, and "heavier" beers above 3.2 percent alcohol by weight should be restricted severely. They suggested that each state should take over as a public monopoly the retail sale of these more dangerous beverages, in order to eliminate the profit motive from the business. Retailers would not be tempted to try to persuade their customers to buy a greater quantity of liquor than might be wise or healthy, because they would not personally benefit thereby.[19]

In recommending the establishment of these public monopolies, Fosdick and Scott referred to the Swedish and Canadian examples. Whereas prohibition had been introduced in Russia, Norway, Finland, and Iceland in the early twentieth century along lines similar to the United States, in Sweden an alternative to prohibition had been introduced in the form of rationing of spirits. Whereas beer up to 3.2 percent alcohol by weight could be sold in any quantity in "beer cafés" and restaurants by the glass or under a grocer's license by the bottle, spirits could be obtained only from a state-controlled store by presentation of a ration book. The size of the ration varied according to the age of the applicant, but in general terms it was given only to married men, who were permitted to purchase anything from one to four liters of spirits a month on behalf of their families. Before a ration book could be issued, the applicant had to make a statement to the authorities about the amount of entertaining that he did and about his financial status. The authorities supplemented this with their own information about the applicant's personal, family, and financial history. In many cases officials made home inspections before deciding whether or not to issue a ration book, and what size of ration to allow. The ration was set according to the financial situation of the applicant. If he paid a lot in taxes, he would be allowed the maximum ration. If not, not. Ration books were often canceled or rations reduced on grounds of unemployment or low income, and no one who was in receipt of public relief was allowed a ration book. A man who spent in excess of his income or of the dictates of sobriety was at first cautioned. If this proved inadequate, the ration book might be given to

---

[19] The irony of a report sponsored by a Rockefeller warning about the dangers of the profit motive in business was not lost on contemporary observers. A state-controlled "dispensary system" had operated in South Carolina at the turn of the century but the salaries of the dispensing agents had been linked to the amount of liquor sold. The system had been condemned because it failed to reduce drunkenness and because it was regarded as too socialist for its time.

his wife. As a last resort, it would be canceled—as it would if he permitted his ration to be used by others.[20]

In Canada, prohibition had been introduced on a federal basis during the First World War, but after peace was restored the issue of the control of alcoholic drinks had devolved to the provinces. In Québec, which had been the last and least willing of the provinces to introduce wartime prohibition, the sale of beer, wine, and cider was allowed from 1919 onward, but spirits continued to be prohibited.[21] In British Columbia, a system was set up in 1921 to restrict the sale of spirits to state-controlled stores, on similar lines to Sweden. The other provinces all voted to reintroduce prohibition at the beginning of the 1920s. This soon encountered resistance, however, from moderation leagues, comprising gentlemen of immense respectability, who argued that the prohibitory laws should be repealed because they were un-British and "Yankee," and who suggested that the other provincial governments should follow the lead of British Columbia and take over the sale of alcoholic beverages themselves. At the same time, the other provinces could only watch jealously as Québec enjoyed a boom in tourism and its government raised millions of dollars from taxes on and licenses for the sale of alcoholic drinks. By the end of the decade, all the provinces that had reintroduced prohibition had now repealed it (with the exception of Prince Edward Island, where it remained in force until 1948). The provincial governments adopted similar regulations to British Columbia, with state control of the sale of spirits and the introduction of ration books to limit the amount that a person might purchase (although the allowances were considerably more generous than across the Atlantic in Sweden). Referenda were also held as to whether the sale of beer by the glass in "taverns" or "beer parlours" should be permitted: Alberta, British Columbia, and Manitoba (at the second attempt) voted in favor; Ontario and Saskatchewan against.

---

[20]People could exceed their ration only by drinking spirits by the glass in restaurants, where men were allowed to order up to 15 centiliters (the equivalent of about four present-day standard drinks) of spirits with meals but women only half as much. The retail sale of wine, like that of spirits, was limited to state stores, but there was no set restriction of the amount of wine that a man might purchase (although details of what he bought were recorded in his ration book). A person dining in a restaurant was not limited to the amount of light or sparkling wine that he might order, but was permitted to drink no more than a quarter-bottle of fortified wine with his meal (as an alternative to spirits).

[21]Québec later introduced the sale of spirits through state-controlled stores, like the other provinces.

The Swedish and Canadian systems provided a template for the alcohol control laws that were introduced in the various American states in the mid-1930s. Of the forty states that legalized the traffic in liquor,[22] fifteen created public monopolies for the sale of spirits through state-controlled "package stores."[23] It can hardly have been coincidental that more than half of these—Washington, Idaho, Montana, Michigan, Ohio, Pennsylvania, Vermont, and Maine—shared borders with Canada and were therefore in a good position to observe its example.

Most of these state governments did shrink away, however, from introducing ration books on the Canadian or Swedish model. An exception was Iowa, where anyone who wished to purchase a beverage stronger than 3.2 percent beer was required to obtain a liquor permit from the state, renewable annually for a fee of one dollar. Once equipped with his permit, the citizen might enter a state-owned liquor store, fill out an order form, and present this, together with his permit and the appropriate quantity of cash, to the clerk behind the counter. The clerk recorded the purchase in the customer's permit before handing him the goods. If he considered that the permit was being used too often, the clerk could refuse to fill the order. These liquor permits remained in use until 1963. By then it had become something of a premarital custom in the state for parents to demand to see the permits of their children's suitors.

While Iowa limited the sale of wine and beer over 3.2 percent as well as spirits to state stores, in a number of the other monopoly states these lighter forms of alcoholic drink could also be purchased for home consumption from privately owned outlets. Beer, in particular, was made widely available in grocery stores. This represented a significant change from the situation that had existed before Prohibition, when the saloon had been the place where people had gone both to drink liquor and to purchase it for consumption at home.

---

[22]Some of the states voted to retain prohibition, at least of spirits. Whereas by 1940 "nonintoxicating" (3.2 percent) beer was available everywhere, Kansas, Mississippi, and Oklahoma continued to prohibit the sale of spirits. Mississippi did not repeal its state prohibition law until 1966. In many states, moreover, "local option" provisions were introduced to allow individual counties to vote to retain prohibition, either of all kinds of drink or of spirits only. As late as 1973, one in six of all the counties in the United States still prohibited the sale of spirits.

[23]The term "package store" was invented by Fosdick and Scott, who referred in *Toward Liquor Control* to the introduction of state-owned retail stores for the sale of alcoholic beverages "by package only."

The laws applying to the sale of drink for consumption on the premises also distinguished, after Repeal, between spirits on the one hand and beer and wine on the other. In fifteen states the sale of spirits "by the drink" remained prohibited; in a number of others, spirits sales were permitted only in bona fide restaurants, with laws specifying a minimum number of food-preparation workers and square feet of kitchen space. At the same time, a new class of license for the consumption of beer (and in some places wine) was established, comparable to the Swedish "beer cafés" and the Canadian "taverns" and "beer parlours," which was liberally issued to restaurants and cafeterias. This, too, represented a major change from pre-Prohibition practice, when the saloon had sold all kinds of drink to anyone who wanted them.

In Oklahoma the sale of 3.2 percent beer was legalized in 1933 but the prohibition of spirits (and wine, although this had never been widely consumed in the state) remained in force for another quarter century. Then, in 1959, prohibition was repealed and replaced by what was known as the "bottle law," which made it possible for alcoholic drinks stronger than 3.2 percent beer to be obtained from a state-licensed package store—and from nowhere else. The sale of spirits by the drink remained prohibited. Someone who wanted to consume a beverage stronger than 3.2 percent beer in a public place had to buy a bottle in a package store and then take it himself to a private "bottle club" of which he was already a member. The club was allowed to serve the member with liquor, but only from his own bottle. This restriction was so ridiculous that it was regularly ignored: In many places, a stranger who walked into a "private club" immediately became a member and was served with a drink whether he had brought a bottle with him or not. By the early 1980s, hotels, restaurants, and cocktail lounges, at least in the cities, were selling liquor by the drink openly and with virtual impunity. Even then there were sporadic attempts at enforcement, notably during a convention of professional female bowlers in Tulsa in 1983—an experience that led the participants to vow never to come to the state again. In 1985 the majority of counties in the state, including the metropolitan areas of Tulsa and Oklahoma City, voted to legalize the sale of liquor by the drink.

In Utah, as in Oklahoma, the sale of 3.2 percent beer was legalized in 1933 but the prohibition of spirits remained in force for many years. Not until 1969 was the sale of spirits by the drink legalized in Utah, and then only in the form of minibottles, which the customer had to buy individually from special state liquor stores that were situated inside restaurants. The customer had to get up from the table, walk over to the liquor store, buy the minibottle, carry it back to the table, and mix it himself. And he was not allowed to do even this unless he ordered a meal at the same time. Not until 1990 was Utah state law changed in order to allow bartenders in restaurants to pour and mix drinks (provided that these did not contain more than one ounce of spirits).

Even today in Utah, bars technically remain prohibited: Spirits may be consumed by the drink only in a restaurant, where food must account for more than 70 percent of the bill, or in a private club (although the restrictions on membership of private clubs are laxly enforced). On the other hand, beer up to 3.2 percent alcohol by weight is available in supermarkets.

In South Carolina, too, the sale of spirits in bars continues to be prohibited, even in such popular holiday areas as Myrtle Beach and Charleston. Bars are permitted to sell beer and unfortified wine, but spirits may be sold by the drink only in restaurants, which are defined as places that are primarily in the business of the setting and preparing of meals. This said, there is no legal definition of "primarily," and it is easy enough for an establishment to evade the regulation by keeping a range of food in a freezer but not actually going out of its way to serve it.

In South Carolina, moreover, even today, spirits may be sold by the drink in restaurants solely from the kind of minibottles that are normally encountered only on airplanes—and which must, by law, be opened in view of the customer in order to demonstrate that no trickery is taking place. Full-sized bottles of spirits may be purchased only for off-premises consumption from package stores, which are easily distinguishable because the exterior is marked by one or more large red spots.[24] Apart from these red spots, a liquor store is also permitted

---

[24]There are various possible explanations for the origin of these spots; one of the more plausible is that they are supposed to represent the sun, because until recently they were permitted to open only from sunrise to sunset. Before minibottles were introduced in 1973, anyone who wished to consume spirits by the drink had been obliged to buy a full bottle from a package store, where it was placed in a brown bag for him to carry into a restaurant. This "brown-bagging" was widely condemned because it led people to drink more than they would otherwise have done, in order to avoid taking home partly filled bottles. The sale of spirits by the drink was then restricted to minibottles in an attempt to placate prohibitionists, who believed that serving people from smaller containers would ensure that they drank less. At the time similar laws existed in several other states, but they soon aban-

to carry a sign with the words "package store," the owner's name and license number, and the opening hours, but no other advertising whatsoever. It may not display any bottles in the front window, nor place any signs within the store that are visible from outside. It is permitted to sell wine as well as spirits, but not beer or any other goods.

Similar restrictions on the sale of spirits apply in the majority of states in the union. In thirty-one of the fifty states, spirits may be bought only from state-controlled or state-licensed liquor stores. Yet, in many of these states, beer and wine may be sold alongside food in supermarkets. The legal distinction between beer and wine on the one hand, and spirits on the other, survives to this day.[25]

There also remains an economic distinction between distilled spirits and fermented drinks such as beer and wine because spirits are required to bear higher levels of taxation at both state and federal level. Whereas federal excise duties on beer and wine were not increased between 1951 and 1989, spirits taxes were raised on several occasions because it was believed appropriate for beverages with a higher alcohol content to bear a heavier tax burden and because it was thought that people who drank spirits were wealthier and therefore better able to bear the expense.

Until very recently, distillers have been shy about campaigning to reverse what they have naturally come to regard as discrimination. This appears to have been partly because they have been concerned to develop their reputation as responsible corporate citizens. Certainly this was true of the distillery giant Seagram, which originated in Canada, and which established its fortune during Prohibition by supplying American bootleggers with spirits that had legally been distilled in Canada. In 1936 Seagram paid the United States government $1.5 million in a negotiated settlement of the claims against the company from prohibition violations.

After Prohibition was repealed, most distillers sought to market aggressive-tasting young, unblended bourbon and rye. But Seagram

---

doned them on the grounds that far from reducing consumption, the minibottles led many people to consume stiffer drinks than they would otherwise have done. In South Carolina, the only state to retain such a law, a minibottle contains 1.7 ounces (50 centiliters)of liquor; some bars elsewhere pour less than this in a single shot, others more: See the "equivalency argument" later in this chapter.

[25] The restrictions that apply to spirits also generally apply to wine that has been fortified with spirits; the less restrictive controls placed on the sale of wine apply in most cases only to unfortified table wines.

blended young American-distilled whiskey with mature Canadian stock to produce a "lighter" taste that rapidly became popular. Its Five Crown blend rapidly became the best-selling whiskey in the country. By the autumn of 1934 Five Crown whiskey was selling so well that Seagram launched a series of newspaper advertisements that were apparently designed to reduce its consumption. "We Who Make Whiskey Say: Drink Moderately" was the headline. "The real enjoyment which whiskey can add to the pleasure of gracious living is possible only to the man who drinks good whiskey and drinks moderately," read the copy. "The House of Seagram does not want a dollar that should be spent for the necessities of life." In response to these advertisements, 150,000 congratulatory letters and telegrams arrived at Seagram's head office, sent by wets and drys alike.

Seagram did not confront what it regarded as discrimination in the taxation, distribution, and marketing of its products for another half-century, until 1984, when its American liquor division was taken over by Edgar Bronfman Jr., grandson of the company's legendary founder, Sam Bronfman. A young man in his late twenties, Bronfman immediately moved to change his company's policy on controversial issues. It now began to lobby at both state and federal level to alter discriminatory legislation. "We're coming out of the closet," Bronfman said. "We will now direct our own destiny." In changing its policy, Seagram was responding to a decline in spirits consumption since the end of the 1970s (the consequence of changing tastes, health concerns, and tougher drink-driving laws). After lengthy internal discussions, the company came up with the notion of "equivalency": the fact that a twelve-ounce can of beer and a five-ounce glass of wine contain just as much alcohol as one and a quarter ounces of spirits, which it said was the quantity typically consumed in a mixed drink.[26] According to a Gallup survey carried out for the industry, only 27 percent of those polled knew that the three drinks were equivalent, while 52 percent thought that the spirits had the highest alcohol content.

---

[26]After winemakers counterattacked with the argument that Seagram's description of a "typical" cocktail's alcohol content understated the distiller's own recommended dose by at least a quarter of an ounce, Seagram increased the amount of spirits in its equivalency argument from 1¼ to 1½ ounces. In fact, many bars, especially in cities, offer a "free pour," in which the barman pours out just as much liquor for the customer as he considers appropriate. In one survey of bars in Atlanta the average amount of alcohol in a drink was found to be 1.97 ounces.

Seagram wanted to run a television advertising campaign to promote its equivalency message that "a drink is a drink is a drink." Spirits companies had never been formally been banned from advertising their products on television, although they had agreed on a voluntary ban as long ago as 1948. The three television networks refused to air Seagram's advertisements. Bronfman accused them of "contributing to the problem of public misinformation, rather than joining in the solution by broadcasting the facts."

It was another decade before Seagram was able to advertise its products on television. By this time the consumption of spirits had fallen by 40 percent from its peak in 1979, and it appeared likely that the decline would continue, as the older consumers of spirits died off and relatively few young people took their place. According to a 1994 Gallup opinion poll, only 10 percent of young people between eighteen and twenty-nine said they preferred spirits, while 69 percent said they would rather have beer. Spirits companies were desperate to advertise on television in order to attract young consumers. So Seagram tried again. Once more the broadcast networks refused to air Seagram's advertisements for spirits—but they could do nothing to prevent their affiliates from broadcasting liquor advertisements during their local programs, nor did their policy have any bearing on nonnetwork radio and television outlets. In June 1996 Seagram finally ended the industry's voluntary ban on spirits advertising by running advertisements for Crown Royal Canadian Whisky on a NBC-affiliated station in Corpus Christi, Texas.

President Clinton criticized Seagram's action in his weekly radio address to the nation on June 15. "For half a century," he said, "liquor companies have voluntarily kept their ads off the air for the simple reason that it was the right thing to do. So I was disappointed this week when a major company announced that it would break the ban and put liquor ads on TV, exposing our children to liquor before they know how to handle it or can legally do so.[27] After voluntarily staying away from this for fifty years, being good corporate citizens, companies are now considering changing plans. I ask the companies to get back to the ban. Pull these ads. We appreciate your good corporate citizenship, and our parents need it to continue."

Ignoring the president's pleas, in early November the rest of the

---

[27]A classic Clinton tactic: to claim his policy is the right one because the welfare of children supposedly depends upon it.

distillers joined Seagram in abandoning their formal allegiance to the ban. "We have been studying the issue for more than four years, and we found through focus groups that most people didn't know there's no federal law against liquor advertising," explained Marc Sherman, the assistant director for public issues at the Distilled Spirits Council of the United States. "Our members felt this voluntary ban was giving credence to critics who say that liquor is worse than beer or wine. In reality, all alcohol is equal."

Members of the brewing industry have expressed concern at the distillers' decision to start advertising on television because they fear that it will draw more attention to the issue of alcohol advertising in general and might set off a regulatory backlash that could affect beer and wine advertisements. And they have ridiculed the equivalency argument that lies behind the distillers' decision. "If you want to compare," says Jeff Becker, a vice president of the Beer Institute, "have someone drink twelve ounces of liquor, someone drink twelve ounces of wine, and someone else drink twelve ounces of beer. See who can walk out." This may seem facile, but spirits, being much stronger, do affect people in a different manner from relatively weak wine and much weaker beer. Certainly, if spirits are diluted to one quarter of their original strength by the addition of one or more mixers and ice, then they will affect the drinker in more or less the same way as wine, but many spirits are consumed in a much more concentrated form, such as martinis, and even when people consume long drinks with lots of ice they usually finish them before much of the ice has melted and diluted the drink.

To suggest that spirits are equivalent to wine or beer because an average serving contains the same amount of alcohol is tantamount to suggesting that a novel by Tom Clancy is equivalent to the New Testament because they contain a similar number of words. "We strongly reject the erroneous premise that equates beer, wine, and distilled spirits as simply quantitative versions of 'alcohol'," argues John De Luca, president of the Wine Institute of California. "Common usage tells us all drinks are not the same. Wine goes with different foods and enhances different tastes than beer and distilled spirits. It also contains a rich complexity of antioxidants and natural compounds. Wine's culture and tradition as a mealtime complement to a wide range of foods are grounded in many civilizations over thousands of years. Its usage and place in society have emerged over time and custom and represent a special heritage to many people. Our beverages are not 'equivalent,' so we cannot accept any notion of an 'equivalent' or 'common' code of advertising standards."

As De Luca suggests, wine has long been regarded as nutritious in those cultures that have been accustomed to consuming it on a regular basis. In France in the nineteenth and early twentieth century it was generally believed that wine gave one strength and was essential for heavy manual labor, so that those in the building trades vowed that they could not work without it. It was also thought that workers needed to drink wine in order to quench their thirst. Dr. E. Mauriac, a professor on the Bordeaux medical faculty, advocated in 1901 a daily consumption of two liters of wine for an adult male. These attitudes persisted for many years. According to market research conducted in 1948, it was believed by 95 percent of the population that wine was useful for men who were engaged in heavy labor, as well as by 85 percent that wine was generally good for the health, and by 79 percent that it was nourishing. As recently as the 1960s the wine industry was distributing blotters to schools stating that a liter (a little over a U.S. quart) of wine had a nutritive value equivalent to 30 ounces of milk, 13 ounces of bread, 20 ounces of meat, or five eggs.[28]

The same is true of beer in those countries in which it has traditionally been consumed. In the early eighteenth century, Benjamin Franklin's companion at the printing press in London justified his daily consumption of six pints of strong beer on the grounds that it was necessary if he was to be strong at his work.[29] A hundred years later, the passage of legislation to deregulate the sale of beer in Britain was underpinned by the belief that it would lead workingmen to convert from gin to beer. "They [will] have good beer instead of bad spirits," said Henry Brougham, a future chancellor of the exchequer, in the debate on the bill in Parliament. "To the poor the beer [is] next to a necessity of life."

The fact that beer was considered to play a fundamental part in people's diets placed a major obstacle in the way of teetotal campaigners in the second quarter of the nineteenth century. Early teetotalers, like pioneer vegetarians, were thought to be throwing away their lives as surely as professional boxers, urban bicyclists, or promiscuous male homosexuals today. In Warrington in the north of England the Tem-

---

[28]This quantity of wine would have contributed about 600 calories of energy.
[29]See Chapter 1.

perance Society regarded beer so highly that when, in 1830, an ex-drunkard asked for a teetotal pledge to sign, one had to be drawn up especially for him, and a friend tried physically to prevent him, calling out, "Thee mustn't, Richard, thee'll die."

These beliefs were not without foundation. It was calculated in Britain just after the Second World War that the energy value of a pint of fairly weak beer (3 percent alcohol by volume, 25 percent weaker than the 3.2 percent by weight beer that was legalized in America in 1933) was about 200 calories, and that a single pint provided between 10 and 20 percent of a man's daily requirement of riboflavin, nicotinic acid, calcium, and phosphorous. Using this calculation, it is possible to obtain a rough idea of the amount of their daily calorific requirements that people obtained from beer in the past. Franklin's companion at the printing press drank six pints of strong beer per day, which would have given him 1,500 calories. A worker in a heavy, well-paid job like coal heaving reportedly consumed as much as a gallon[30] of beer per day, giving him 2,000 calories. Not only did beer provide manual laborers with energy and vitamins as well as alleviate the monotony of their diets, it freed them from having to obtain their calories by eating a quantity of bread that would have been so large as to be indigestible.

Maybe the temperance movement in America would not have grown as strong as it did had workers been accustomed, as were their British counterparts, to sustain themselves with beer rather than to seek to do so with spirits. In the second half of the eighteenth century, the social reformer Anthony Benezet, a Quaker from Philadelphia, argued against the prevailing belief that spirits provided necessary sustenance to workers during the harvest, suggesting that they would do much better to drink beer. Writing during the American Revolution, Benezet argued that the ending of British rule would prove pointless unless Americans also rid themselves of spirits and slavery. In his opinion, a republic of free men had no place for the servitude of men either to other men or to spirits. "The unhappy dram-drinkers are so absolutely bound in slavery to these infernal spirits," he wrote, "that they seem to have lost the power of delivering themselves from this worst of bondage."[31]

---

[30] These are British pints and gallons, which are 25 percent larger than the American version.

[31] For the belief of workers that spirits helped to sustain their labors, see Chapter 1.

One hundred and fifty years later, labor leaders used similar arguments in support of their contention that the Volstead Act should be modified to permit 2.75 percent beer. In 1924 Samuel Gompers told the House Judiciary Committee that the law should be changed to allow the beer drinker to have his stimulant, palatable to the taste, that had the "nutritive value of a food and could be taken as part of a meal." Some brewers even went so far in their propaganda as to call their product "liquid bread." After beer was legalized in the 1930s, however, the American brewers stopped making claims about the food value of their product, having realized that many women were now concerned about controlling their weight and would not drink something they thought would make them fatter.

Whereas wine and beer had historically been regarded as nutritious beverages, spirits had originally been intended only as medicines.[32] Certainly this was how they were used in Europe in the Middle Ages. Given the limitations of medieval medical knowledge, it is easy to understand why doctors in this period should have regarded spirits as valuable. It was demonstrated by practical observation that they gave the people who drank them a feeling of warmth; as far as medieval doctors were concerned, this made them the ideal medicine for people who were suffering from fevers and other cold diseases. Spirits were also prescribed as prophylactics against and treatment for the plague. It is possible that the use of spirits spread across the continent of Europe largely as a consequence of the plague pandemic known as the Black Death that devastated the region in the fourteenth century, killing as many as twenty-five million people, or a quarter of the entire population.

Spirits were also applied externally to old people in an attempt to warm them. According to one, perhaps legendary account, such a treatment was applied to the ailing King Charles II of Navarre (then a separate kingdom comprising parts of what are now southern France and northern Spain) in 1386–87. On the advice of his doctors, he was wrapped in pieces of cloth that had been soaked in spirits; these were then sewn together in order to provide him with complete protection. One night, the servant whose job it was to stitch the cloth together,

---

For the view that the freedom to drink was fundamental to American liberty, see the Conclusion.

[32]It is not known for sure when spirits were invented, but the best evidence points to early medieval Europe.

instead of breaking off the end of the thread when he had finished, tried to burn it off with a candle. The thread caught fire; this spread to the cloth, which burst into flame. Nothing could be done to put out the fire; the king cried out continually and suffered from the most terrible agonies as he was burned to death. It appears that his demise was little mourned by those who survived him: Charles II is known to posterity as Charles the Bad.

There was also a philosophical basis to the medieval belief in the medical efficacy of spirits. The process of distillation was thought to release the finer essence of the subject distilled—its spirit—and the alchemists, who were trying to relate chemistry to a philosophic world system, believed that distilling would help them to discover the elixir of life, which would render men immortal. This appeared to be confirmed by the fact that spirits kept substances such as meat from rotting; it seemed reasonable to deduce from this that they could also keep human flesh from corruption and thus ensure long life on earth. As Michael (Puff von) Schrick claimed in the 1450s, "Anyone who drinks half a spoon of brandy every morning will never be ill; . . . when someone is dying and a little brandy is poured into his mouth, he will speak before he dies."

The prevailing belief in the medical efficacy of spirits led monks, who had a long tradition of preparing herbal remedies, to seek to preserve them for longerand supposedly to add to their powers—by distillation. In order to counteract the bitterness of the resulting product, they added sugar or honey to produce cordials or liqueurs, some of which survive more or less unchanged today. For example, Benedictine was first devised by Don Bernardo Vincelli at the Benedictine Abbey of Fécamp in Normandy in France in about 1510, using a combination of the wild plants and herbs that grew in profusion on the seaside cliffs and spices from the East[33] in order to produce an elixir that was supposed to combat the diseases that were prevalent in the countryside around the monastery. Today, in Europe and America, Benedictine is taken as a digestive, which may perhaps be regarded as a degradation of its original medicinal status; in the Far East, however, it continues to be taken by workers in tin mines, who spend long periods knee-deep in water and believe that Benedictine helps them to counteract rheumatism and other muscular problems.

---

[33]Spices were considered to have medicinal powers because it was believed that diseases were caused by miasmas (bad odors), which the spices would counteract.

The medicinal uses of spirits, and the belief that a cordial could be devised that would prove efficacious in the treatment of all diseases, were given further impetus by the discovery of the Americas, which provided a host of plants that were unknown in Europe. The celebrated explorer Sir Walter Raleigh, who had sponsored the settlement of the first English colony on Roanoke Island in 1585, traveled ten years later to Guyana on the north coast of South America in the hope of discovering the source of the fabled gold of El Dorado. He returned from his voyage without gold but with many new plants, among which he hoped he might find the ingredients that had been lacking in previous attempts to produce the elixir of life. He did not, however, find the time to devote himself to chemical experiments until he was forcibly confined in the Tower of London by the new king James I in 1603. During his imprisonment, Raleigh was allowed to set up a small laboratory in which he concocted a "great cordial" by macerating forty roots, seeds, and herbs in spirit, distilling the result, and then adding powdered bezoar stones (formed in the stomachs of animals), pearls, coral, deer's horn, amber, musk, antimony, and sugar. The queen, Anne of Denmark, and the heir to the throne, Prince Henry, were supporters of Raleigh's, and did their best to secure his release. The queen was convinced that the "great cordial" had saved her life in a serious illness, and the prince took a particular interest in Raleigh's experiments. When, in 1612, the prince was taken severely ill, Raleigh sent him some of the cordial, reportedly with the message that it would cure him providing he had not been poisoned. Such a comment was hardly likely to endear Raleigh to the king, since it was rumored that the king himself had poisoned his son, having grown jealous of his popularity. Henry died, in any case, and Raleigh was eventually executed in 1618.

Among the plants that were regarded at this period as possessing medicinal virtues was juniper, a diuretic that was recommended in the treatment of diseases of the kidneys, liver, and heart. Juniper berries also offered the advantage that they improved the flavor of spirits that had been produced from poor-quality raw materials. In the sixteenth century they began to be used by Dutch apothecaries in order to enliven the dull taste of spirits that had been distilled from rye. In the seventeenth century the use of this new medicine—"juniper water"—spread to England; in 1663 the celebrated diarist Samuel Pepys recorded having been advised by his doctor to take it for his health.

Before long this medicine was being abused by much of the population, especially in London, who took it, not for their health, but in order to get drunk. Its name changed to "geneva," after the Dutch word for juniper (*jenever*), which became corrupted to "gin." Still, doctors persevered in their belief that it was a medicine and not a beverage. In his *Essay of Health and Long Life,* published in 1724, the physician George Cheyne insisted that "strong liquors were never designed for common use"; he pointed out that they had always been sold in the past alongside other medicines in apothecaries' shops, and had been prescribed by doctors in the same way as other medicines, "to refresh the weary, to strengthen the weak, to give courage to the faint-hearted, and to raise the low-spirited." It was no less reasonable, he said, for a man to drink a draft of spirits for his amusement than it was to see him sit down to a dish of Sir Walter Raleigh's cordial.

One of the reasons gin caused so many problems among working-class men and women in London in the early eighteenth century was that they did not know how to handle beverage alcohol in so concentrated a form; until this time spirits had been regarded almost exclusively as medicines, and if people had wanted to get drunk, they had done so on wine or beer. Those who knocked back gin were overcome by the experience in a comparable manner to the American Indians who were given spirits by white traders at much the same time.[34] "Brandy has killed most of the Indians," wrote Pehr Kalm. "This liquor was entirely unknown to them before the Europeans came hither; but after they had tasted it, they could never get enough of it. A man can hardly have a greater desire of a thing that the Indians have of brandy. I have heard them say that to die by drinking brandy was a desirable and honorable death; and indeed 'tis no very uncommon thing to kill themselves by drinking this liquor to excess."

Unlike the native-born Indians, most European settlers in North America restricted their consumption of distilled spirits to medicinal purposes, at least at first. In hot weather in the West Indies and the southern colonies of America, and in cold weather in the northern colonies, European settlers drank spirits in the belief that these would help to protect them against the extremes of the climate. In cold weather they drank spirits because they gave them a feeling of warmth.[35] In hot weather they thought that spirits warmed their bodies

---

[34]This is covered in the Introduction.
[35]In fact, drinking spirits when exposed to cold is dangerous, as it adds to the

after sweating: They believed that sweat conducted heat from the inside to the outside of their bodies, leaving the inner parts in need of warmth and fortification.[36]

By the late eighteenth century, however, doctors were beginning to question the soundness of these beliefs. The Philadelphia physician Benjamin Rush argued that contrary to the claim that spirits were necessary in hot weather, "experience proves that they increase, instead of lessening, the effects of heat upon the body, and thereby dispose to diseases of all kinds. . . . As well we might throw oil into a house, the roof of which was on fire, in order to prevent the flames from extending to its inside, as pour ardent spirits into the stomach, to lessen the effects of a hot sun upon the skin."

Nevertheless, southerners continued to drink spirits mixed with herbs or roots on the grounds that these "bitters" served as a necessary prophylactic against the fevers of the region. The most famous of these compounds was the mint julep, which was defined in the 1806 edition of *Webster's Dictionary* as "a kind of liquid medicine." Rush and other doctors criticized the popular reliance on bitters, arguing that the intermittent fevers to which the inhabitants of the South were prone would be better prevented by taking quinine, and that the use of spirits for medicinal purposes led all too easily to their abuse.[37]

As civilization advanced, the medical administration of alcohol fell into decline and spirits were replaced in many cases by the progressive practice of bloodletting with leeches. The early nineteenth century saw a fashion for "heroic" medicine: a dependence on drastic remedies and drugs that produced violent reactions in the body. Bloodletting was frequently performed in cases of fever or inflammation because doctors believed that a patient benefited from any treatment that produced a significant change in his or her condition, and the leeches relaxed and apparently cooled restless patients. Emetics and cathartics, which cleaned out the system, were also popular—at least among doctors.

By the 1840s, however, heroic medicine was in decline. Doctors now began to doubt the benefits of bloodletting and purging, and replaced the lancet with the brandy bottle. Alcohol had long been considered to be a stimulant, and therefore useful if a doctor wanted to invigorate

---

risk of hypothermia by increasing the flow of blood through the skin and thus lowering the temperature of a greater volume of blood.

[36]This is discussed in Chapter 1.

[37]The mint julep and the abuse of spirits are discussed in Chapter 1.

a debilitated patient. Now, however, alcohol came to be regarded by many physicians as a panacea for all acute diseases. Physicians "brandied" patients suffering from conditions as diverse as pneumonia, typhus, and rheumatic fever. Prescriptions of as much as three pints of brandy a day, administered for between several days and a month or more, were not uncommon. In order to explain away the change in their practice, physicians argued that they had been forced to alter their methods because disease had changed: Previously it had overstimulated its victims, who had therefore to be calmed by bloodletting and similar treatments, but now it weakened them, so they needed to be stimulated with alcohol.

The most influential proponent of "alcoholic therapeutics" in the middle of the nineteenth century was Robert Bentley Todd, a medical professor at King's College, London. Todd believed that diseases could be cured only by natural processes and not by any drug or treatment. However, the administration of alcohol could assist these processes, sustaining the patient until nature provided a cure. Unfortunately, Todd killed himself with an overdose of his own medicine in 1860. Even so, the treatment he had pioneered was given the next year to the British prince consort, Albert, the husband of Queen Victoria, after he fell ill from what was believed to be typhoid. Albert did not recover either; and it was suggested in some quarters that the administration of large quantities of brandy had contributed to his death.

In America during the Civil War, when they were repeatedly hampered by a shortage of other medicines, doctors often used alcohol instead. They administered it in frequent doses, usually in the form of punch or eggnog made from brandy or whiskey, but sometimes undiluted. One sixteen-year-old soldier in a St. Louis hospital was apparently "kept alive" by 36 ounces of brandy a day. In a Virginia hospital one patient was given 48 ounces of eggnog (as well as two or three bottles of porter) every day for several weeks; another got a half-pint of egg and brandy every two hours; a third was to have as much of this mixture as he could take.

Long after the war had ended, spirits continued to be used very widely in medical practice, in order to treat all kinds of disease. They were also given to people who had been involved in accidents, especially if they were suffering from shock—the origin of the practice, much described in contemporary literature, of giving brandy to people who had fainted. And they were administered in vast quantities in cases of snakebite. It was believed that alcohol sought out the venom from snakebites and neutralized it. So antagonistic were these two substances thought to be that neither could exhibit its characteristic effects until it had gained superiority over the other. It was therefore imagined that a person could not become drunk until he had consumed more alcohol than was necessary to neutralize the venom in his system. During the second half of the nineteenth century, when the popularity of this treatment reached its apogee, the standard neutralizing dose was reckoned by most American physicians to be a quart of hundred-proof whiskey, to be downed within ten or twelve hours. However, in 1888 the Medical Register reported a case so critical that the patient had been required to consume four quarts of apple brandy in four hours. One must wonder how many of the people who supposedly died from snakebites were in fact killed by the enormous doses of alcohol that had been administered in an attempt to counteract them.

It might have been expected that the rise of the temperance movement would have led to a decrease in the use of alcoholic beverages as medicines, but in fact the opposite appears to have happened—for the reason that alcoholic beverages disappeared from everyday consumption.

In the first decades of the nineteenth century, many people had thought whiskey as essential a part of their diets as bread. Not only were bottles of it placed on tables at mealtimes, but the practice of stopping work to take a glass of whiskey at eleven in the morning and again at four in the afternoon was regarded as "absolutely indispensable to man and boy." In 1830 one journalist observed, in reference to the custom of drinking a glass of whiskey or other spirits before breakfast, that "so conducive to health was this nostrum esteemed that no sex, and scarcely any age, were deemed exempt from its application."

It was also believed that spirits were essential as a beverage, or as an ingredient of a beverage, because water was not safe to drink unless spirits were added in order to purify it. When James Oglethorpe had attempted to prohibit rum in the newly settled province of Georgia, there were those who opposed his measure from the beginning. In the summer of 1734 Thomas Penn, the proprietor of Pennsylvania, wrote to Oglethorpe to say that rum added to water, especially during the American summertime, was absolutely indispensable. And in 1738, one hundred and seventeen inhabitants of Savannah sent a petition to the board of trustees opposing the prohibition of rum on the grounds that "the experience of all the inhabitants of America will prove the necessity of qualifying water with some spirit (and it is very certain that no province in America yields water that such qualification is more necessary to than Carolina and Georgia)."

By the latter part of the eighteenth century, wiser counsels, who insisted that the harmful elements in bad water could not be tempered by the addition of spirits, began to be heard. Benezet argued against "the prevailing opinion, even with persons of reputation, that what they term a modest quantity of rum mixed with water is the best and safest liquor that can be drunk. . . . Where water is met with, as is sometimes the case, which is scarce fit to drink, it's vain to think to remove the noxious qualities by mixing it with spirit, for though bad water may be made more palatable by mixing spirit with it, yet all the bad qualities of the water will remain, to which will only be superadded the bad qualities of the spirit."[38]

Nevertheless, people continued to add spirits to water, if only to mask its unpleasant taste. "The [South] Carolinians have been accused of great intemperance in drinking," wrote the Scottish inventor Peter Neilson, who spent much of the 1820s in the United States on business. "This assertion has most probably arisen from the very general use of spirits to correct the bad qualities of the water. The inhabitants in general keep within the bounds of moderation."

This problem did not afflict only the South. "There is not perhaps in the Union a city more destitute of the blessing of good water than New York," wrote the satirist Asa Greene. "The town pumps are conveniently situated at the corners of the streets, everywhere throughout the city, so that no person who is athirst need perish for want of water. . . . If he stands in need of physic at the same time, the pump will furnish that also." The quality of the water, he explained, afforded "an excuse to many persons for continuing the excessive use of strong drink. The water is now so bad, they plead, that it is absolutely necessary to qualify it with a drop of ardent spirits to render it potable.

---

[38]Spirits were effective in sterilizing bad water only if so large a quantity was added to the water as to produce a beverage that contained just as much spirits as water. Wine would have done better, because the skins of the grapes contained compounds that killed bacteria, and which were made more potent by fermentation. The fact that water could be made safe to drink by adding wine had been known for centuries: It had been central to the organization of the campaigns of the Persian armies that conquered much of Asia in the sixth century B.C. and of the Roman armies that conquered large areas of Europe in the first century A.D. But this was rarely done in America outside the vine-growing districts.

But a single drop will not suffice, and many drops, even a full stream, are added to the glass." Neilson told the story of "a very worthy merchant who lived many years in New York, and being on a visit to the southern states was asked what kind of water they had in New York. He paused for a moment, and then candidly replied, 'Really, upon my soul, I cannot pretend to decide, as I never to my recollection tasted water in New York unmixed.' "

Some means of supplying decent water to the city was urgently required. But this requirement took a long time to be fulfilled. The first project to construct a city reservoir, to be supplied with water forced up from a well by a steam engine, was begun in 1774, but was prevented from progressing by the Revolutionary War. Many subsequent proposals in the later years of the eighteenth and early years of the nineteenth century failed for one reason or another. Finally, in 1832, it was decided to use water from the Croton River upstate. This was such a massive engineering project, requiring the construction of an aqueduct to carry water forty miles into the city, that it took a further ten years to complete. The new reservoir finally opened in 1842. At once residents began to switch from spirits to water. "Nothing is talked of or thought of in New York but Croton water," wrote Philip Hone, a former mayor of the city, in his diary, recording the ceremony to celebrate its opening. "It is astonishing how popular the introduction of water is among all classes of our citizens, and how cheerfully they acquiesce in the enormous expense which will burden them and their posterity with taxes to the latest generation. Water! Water! is the universal note which is sounded through every part of the city, and infuses joy and exultation into the masses." Two years later, on July 4, the teetotal mayor James Harper sought to counter the tradition of drinking spirits on holidays by placing a large basin of iced Croton water in the city hall park.

It appears that the provision of clean-tasting Croton water helped to disabuse the citizens of New York of the hitherto prevalent belief that spirits should be added to cold water not only in order to purify it but also in order to counteract the dangers posed to the human system by drinking cold water when hot.[39]

Peter Neilson explained the philosophy that had prevailed in the 1820s. "In summer, the excessive heat causes a very copious perspiration, which must be counteracted by some means or other," he wrote

---

[39] This is discussed in Chapter 1.

in his recollections of the time he had spent in the United States. "The incautious use of simple cold water having often produced very fatal effects, it must therefore be mixed with some spirit to prevent these effects. Ale and beer, although consumed in great quantities, are said to create bile in hot weather. The [medical] faculty during the prevalence of the yellow fever in New York in 1822 actually recommended brandy and water as the safest beverage for their fellow citizens; and, Heaven knows, they stood in little need of the hint."

At the end of the 1820s the first temperance societies were established, and the number of people who died after drinking cold water in hot weather increased. James Stuart, a British traveler who spent the summer of 1830 in the neighborhood of New York, attributed the rise in deaths to the fact that many laborers had recently joined the temperance societies and had therefore stopped adding spirits to their water. "In a country where laborers and mechanics cannot fail to be exceedingly overheated when at work," he wrote, "they cannot, I suspect, quench their thirst with any safety without mixing a small quantity of spirits with the liquid which they drink."

Nevertheless, the development of means of providing even colder water from the 1830s onward, as a result of the introduction of mechanized ice collection and eventually of the mechanical production of ice,[40] appears to have given encouragement to water drinking and thus afforded considerable support to the temperance movement. Isabella Bird, a young Englishwoman who visited the States in the summer of 1854 for the sake of her health, was delighted to find that water was "provided in abundance in the cars, the hotels, the waiting rooms, the steamers and even the stores, in crystal jugs or stone filters, and is always iced. This may either be the result or the cause of the temperance of the people." Campaigners would never have succeeded in persuading so many Americans to turn away from spirits had it not become possible for people to refresh themselves with iced water instead.

By this time it must have become obvious that it had not been the temperature of the pump water that had caused the deaths of a number of people who had drunk it in the first half of the century. But it does not appear to have been appreciated that the deaths must have occurred as a result of the contamination of water in hot weather by pathogenic bacteria. Although water had now become much more pop-

---

[40] These are discussed in Chapter 1.

ular, it had not become any safer to drink. Why, one might wonder, was it not filtered in order to eliminate the bacteria? The effectiveness of this treatment had long been known. The Chinese had for thousands of years used alum as a coagulant in muddy water in order to accelerate clarification; the filtration of water through charcoal was recommended in Sanskrit medical literature four thousand years ago. Writing at the time of the American Revolution, Benezet had suggested that people could purify their drinking water by filtering it through sand rather than by adding spirits. It was one thing, however, for individual householders to fill cisterns with sand or charcoal and filter water through it for their personal use, and quite another for cities to establish slow sand filters to treat the municipal supply. The latter was an expensive process in which cities were not prepared to invest until scientists had demonstrated the pervasiveness of water-borne disease. When cholera had first arrived in Britain from India in 1831, doctors had originally suggested that it was caused by an air-borne poison produced by the putrefaction of bodies or rotting vegetables. Temperance campaigners had claimed that it was caused by drunkenness. Eventually, researches into the epidemic of 1848–49 showed that the disease was water-borne, and legislation was introduced in Britain to require the filtration of water supplied by the cities for domestic use.

Nothing, however, was done in the United States to treat public water supplies until after the Civil War. The citizens of St. Louis had been accustomed to draw their water from the Mississippi, which was so muddy that it had to be allowed to stand before drinking, and the sediment often filled one quarter of the container. In 1866 the city authorities sent James P. Kirkwood to Europe to find out what could be done. He suggested treatments based on the best European practice, but these were inappropriate for American conditions: The water in most European cities was much clearer than the turbid water of their American counterparts such as St. Louis. A first attempt to purify a municipal water supply was made at Poughkeepsie, New York, where a plant was built in 1872 in accordance with Kirkwood's plans, but this and other efforts proved unsuccessful. So people went on drinking dirty water. On his lecture tour to America in 1887 Léon Paul Blouët recorded that "the Americans drink little else but water at table, and one cannot help wondering how it is that the filter seems to be an almost unknown institution in the land. Leave your glass untouched on the table, and in a few moments, a thick sediment of mud and sand will be visible at the bottom of it."

Eventually, a sense of urgency was added to American experiments with water purification after bacteriologists demonstrated that typhoid, like cholera, was a water-borne disease, and serious outbreaks occurred at Plymouth, Pennsylvania, and at Lowell and Lawrence, Massachusetts. The first sand filter was finally installed at Lawrence in 1893. Even so, at the end of the nineteenth century fewer than two million people, only six percent of the American population, enjoyed the benefits of filtered water supplies.

By this time spirits had largely disappeared from the daily diet.[41] They were no longer regarded as normal, everyday items of consumption but rather as specially powerful and potentially dangerous substances. As a result, their use as medicines increased. Now that many people no longer regarded spirits as beverages, doctors were considerably more enthusiastic about prescribing them as medicines.

Sometimes too enthusiastic. In his *History of Drink* James Samuelson accused the medical profession of promoting drunkenness by "too freely prescribing alcohol as a remedy for bodily ailments," claiming that "the downfall of many a man or woman has dated from the first dose prescribed by a heedless or mercenary physician." Doctors who prescribed alcohol for their patients found that many of those who were instructed to take it while they were sick continued voluntarily with the treatment after they had recovered. One antidrink campaigner cited the case of a man advised to take brandy as a prophylactic against cholera who had followed this advice so enthusiastically that in six months he had delirium tremens.[42]

John Beck, a medical professor at New York State University, considered in his lectures whether, because of the abuse of alcohol, it was ever justifiable for a physician to prescribe it in the practice of his profession. He acknowledged that many doctors believed it was perfectly possible to get along without administering alcohol. Beck himself was on one occasion asked by a temperance campaigner to sign a document stating that alcoholic stimulants were never necessary in the treatment of disease, but refused. In his opinion, the question of whether doctors could get along without alcoholic stimulants was "not

---

[41]Spirits were still drunk in hotel bars, as described in Chapter 2, but rarely in the home.
[42]The prescription of morphine caused similar problems, as has been described in the Introduction.

worth discussing. We might as well ask, Could we get along without opium or quinine?"

Not until the end of the century did attitudes begin to change, as beliefs about the benefits of alcohol were debunked by scientific research. Hitherto, it had been widely believed that alcohol was a food: Scientific investigation had shown that like ordinary foods, it was burned or oxidized in the body and liberated heat and energy. But researchers at the end of the nineteenth and beginning of the twentieth century found that alcohol depressed muscular activity. Contrary to popular belief, alcohol did not enable a person to do more work, nor did it stimulate a tired person to new exertions. Instead, after initially strengthening the muscles, it soon paralyzed the nerves controlling the muscles and seriously diminished a person's capacity to do physical work. One investigator concluded: "Both science and the experience of life have exploded the pernicious theory that alcohol gives any persistent increase of muscular power. The disappearance of this universal error will greatly reduce the consumption of alcohol among laboring men. It is well understood by all who control armies or large bodies of men engaged in physical labor, that alcohol and effective work are incompatible."[43]

Scientific investigation did confirm the results of earlier experiments that alcohol, like other foods, was oxidized in the body. But alcohol had always been regarded as only a partial food, since it could not build or repair tissues, could not be stored in the body for future use, and injured the body when consumed in excessive quantities. Some authorities, indeed, insisted that alcohol was not properly to be classified as a food at all. A few scientists, including several of the most prominent European physiologists, went further and declared that alcohol was not only not a food but was a narcotic poison.

Physicians now began to abandon the prescription of alcohol as a stimulant and as a therapeutic in the treatment of disease. The amount used in hospitals steadily declined. By 1915 doctors had so generally reduced the employment of alcohol in medical practice that the com-

---

[43]Nevertheless, marathon runners in the Olympic Games in the early twentieth century sought to sustain themselves with alcohol. In London in 1908 the Italian Dorando Pietri was famously disqualified after entering the stadium first but collapsing and having to be helped over the finishing line; he might have managed to finish of his own accord had he not spent the race gargling a mixture of red wine and strychnine.

mittee in charge of the United States Pharmacopoeia—the official list of nationally approved drugs—voted to remove whiskey and brandy from the list. In 1917 the House of Delegates of the American Medical Association (AMA) passed a resolution stating, "whereas we believe that the use of alcohol as a beverage is detrimental to the human economy, and whereas its use in therapeutics, as a tonic or a stimulant or as a food, has no scientific basis, therefore be it resolved that the American Medical Association opposes the use of alcohol as a beverage, and be it further resolved that the use of alcohol as a therapeutic agent should be discouraged." This resolution was influential in ensuring the passage of national Prohibition.

At first sight, this decision would appear to have reflected a consensus of the most progressive members of the medical profession. It did not. It was adopted principally as a result of pressure from the National Women's Temperance Union, which had written to the AMA House of Delegates requesting "a warning against alcoholic liquor." The precise wording of the resolution was much debated, and a compromise was reached. Hence the rather weak statement at the end that "the use of alcohol as a therapeutic agent should be *discouraged*."

Nor should it be surprising that the wording of the resolution provoked much debate, because the medical community remained divided on the usefulness of alcohol. At the time when the convention was held at which the resolution was passed, many doctors were still using alcohol as an aid to digestion and a means of stimulating the heart. During the very week that the AMA was considering its decision, the prominent clinician Dr. Beverly Robinson asserted in an interview with the *New York Times* that there were conditions that "absolutely demand the use of alcohol as a prominent part of medicine."[44]

Many doctors believed that spirits helped in the treatment of pneumonia, the complication that often made influenza fatal. Many patients were given alcohol during the great influenza epidemic of 1918–19, and it was subsequently claimed that the administration of alcohol had

---

[44]The resolution was also bad medicine because it mixed scientific with policy considerations. To say that alcohol should not be used as a beverage and that its use in therapeutics should be discouraged was social choice, not scientific necessity. Even if scientists considered the use of alcohol as a beverage to be harmful, the public might have wanted to use it for the pleasure it brought; even if the therapeutic value of alcohol was unproven, the public might have wanted to take advantage of the chance that it had some value (as in the case of "complementary medicine" today).

saved a considerable number of lives. It was suggested that in coming out publicly against the therapeutic use of alcohol, the AMA had deliberately ignored the part played by spirits in treating pneumonia because the Eighteenth Amendment had not yet been approved by the Supreme Court and the AMA might lose its fight for Prohibition if it admitted the truth.

The Volstead Act by which Prohibition was administered did not prohibit the prescription of liquor as medicine, but it did place tight restrictions on it. No more than one pint of spirits might be prescribed for a patient within a ten-day period.[45]

At the beginning of 1922 the *Journal of the American Medical Association* published the results of a poll to which more than 20 percent of the doctors in the country had replied. In response to the question whether they thought whiskey was a necessary therapeutic agent, 51 percent of respondents had said yes and 49 percent had said no.[46] Following this referendum, in 1922 the AMA House of Delegates passed another resolution calling for the relaxation of the prohibition laws, arguing that the use of alcohol for therapy should not "be determined by legal or arbitrary dictum."

Because so many physicians continued to prescribe whiskey and brandy, reliable standards for these liquors were deemed necessary, and the tenth revision of the United States Pharmacopoeia, which came into effect from the beginning of 1926, therefore included whiskey and brandy once again. This was a severe defeat for the drys, because it left them open to the charge that Prohibition laid a tax on the sick by requiring them to get a costly doctor's prescription in order to obtain necessary medicine, an argument that was often employed by wets. It especially applied to ailments such as colds and asthma, which were easily recognized and were usually treated at home. Whiskey was recommended in scientific journals for the treatment of asthma, and many doctors thought alcohol helped treat colds.[47]

---

[45]This restriction failed to prevent bootleggers from exploiting the exemption for medicinal alcohol from the prohibitory laws. The celebrated bootlegger George Remus bought chains of drugstores so that he might legitimately order truckloads of liquor, which he would then hijack during transit.

[46]Thirty-two percent thought wine and 26 percent thought beer necessary.

[47]Doctors at the Common Cold Research Unit near Salisbury, England, have recently confirmed that people who drink up to three shots of spirits a day (or the equivalent amount of wine or beer) are less susceptible to colds than abstainers.

*   *   *

Even more embarrassing for antialcohol campaigners was the evidence that now began to be presented to demonstrate that moderate drinkers lived longer than abstainers.

In the first half of the nineteenth century, the belief in the health-giving properties of alcohol had been so strong that life insurance companies had discriminated against abstainers in the belief that they did not live as long as drinkers. When, in 1840, Robert Warner, a young Quaker, applied to a London insurance company to take out a policy on his life, he was told that as a teetotaler he would have to pay an additional premium. Convinced of the fallacy of this view, he organized his own company, the United Kingdom and General Provident Institution, to insure fellow abstainers.

During the following half century, scientific opinion converted from praising alcohol as a food to condemning it as a poison. As a result, life insurance companies not only ceased to discriminate against total abstainers but now refused to insure heavy drinkers, or else charged them a much higher premium.

At this point, further evidence was produced to suggest that even the moderate used of liquor materially shortened life. In 1892 Professor Emil Kraepelin of the universities of Heidelberg and Munich demonstrated in laboratory experiments that alcohol, instead of stimulating the brain and nervous system, acted as an anaesthetic or narcotic. This finding was especially significant because Kraepelin had used very small quantities of alcohol, usually about one ounce diluted with water— less than the amount consumed by most moderate drinkers at meal-times. There had never been any question about the harm caused by large doses of alcohol, but it now appeared that even small quantities depressed the brain and nervous system. As a result, scientists stopped drinking alcohol. The English brain surgeon Sir Victor Horsley, the world's first neurosurgeon, stated that "the practical argument for total abstinence is based on the irrefutable proofs derived from physiological investigation. . . . From a scientific standpoint, therefore, the contention which we have so often had put before us by our friends, that small doses of alcohol, such as people take at meals, have practically no deleterious effect, cannot be maintained. . . . We can only come to one conclusion, that from a scientific standpoint total abstinence must

---

Some asthmatics are affected adversely by alcohol; others breathe more easily after drinking a glass or two.

be our course if we are to follow the plain teaching of truth and common sense."

This scientific research seemed to be confirmed by statistical investigation of the records of life insurance companies. The United Kingdom and General Provident Institution had originally insured only abstainers, but once it was well established, it accepted moderate drinkers as well (although it continued to refuse heavy drinkers). An examination of its records from 1866 to 1910 showed that the drinkers suffered from death rate 37 percent higher than the abstainers. After this and other investigations were published, British life insurance companies began to favor total abstainers by charging them lower premiums.

In America in 1908 forty-three life insurance companies investigated the records of two million policy holders over the previous forty-three years in order to find out whether they were running a greater risk when insuring moderate or heavy drinkers. They found that even moderate drinkers—people who took two glasses of beer a day or a glass of whiskey or the equivalent—suffered from a death rate 18 percent higher than the average among insured lives in general, and that people who drank more than this (but not so much as to have been considered unacceptable insurance risks) had a death rate 86 percent above the average. Thus, according to actuarial statistics, life appeared to be materially shortened even by the consumption of a moderate quantity of alcohol.

"There is a widespread popular opinion that life insurance companies have 'proved' that even the most moderate use of alcohol definitely and measurably shortens human life," wrote the statistician Raymond Pearl in 1917. "In common, as I suppose, with most persons who have made no special personal investigation of the original literature on the subject, I have supposed this statement to be true. . . . My curiosity was aroused to examine critically the actuarial evidence. The results were somewhat astonishing. The evidence on which the current statements are based would not be accepted by anyone trained in the critical valuation of statistical and biological evidence as 'proving' anything." The records of life insurance companies, Pearl pointed out, did not present a reliable picture of the drinking habits of the people they had insured, because the only point at which they asked people about their drinking habits was when they took out the insurance. No record was kept of whether people had changed their habits at some point before they took out the insurance, nor of whether they made such a change at any stage after the insurance had begun. Furthermore, people who insured their lives knew perfectly well that the companies with whom they took out their policies discriminated to a certain extent against heavy drinkers, but did not know at what level of drinking this discrimination began. So they naturally tended to underestimate their consumption of alcohol.

Having concluded that the records of life insurance companies were of no value when it came to judging whether abstainers lived for a longer or shorter time than moderate drinkers, Pearl set to collecting his own statistics that would help him to make such an assessment. By now a professor at the Johns Hopkins University in Baltimore, he employed trained field workers to conduct interviews with more than two thousand working-class people in the city in order to find out their personal histories.[48] Dividing them into the three classes of abstainers, moderate drinkers, and heavy drinkers, he found that on average the moderate drinkers lived longer than the abstainers (and a lot longer than the heavy drinkers). Cautiously, taking into account the possible errors, Pearl was not prepared to conclude that this proved that moderate drinkers lived longer than abstainers but merely that it disproved the currently held belief that abstainers lived longer than moderate drinkers.

Pearl published his findings in a book entitled *Alcohol and Longevity* in 1926. An academic statistician and biometrician, Pearl held no brief for the antiprohibitionist lobby, he simply wished to add to scientific knowledge in his area of professional expertise. But he could not prevent his work from becoming a weapon in the battle between those ardent prohibitionists who argued that the laws against the trade in alcoholic drink should be better enforced and those who believed that Prohibition had been proved a failure and should at least be modified if not repealed. Reviewing Pearl's book in *The American Mercury*, H. L. Mencken, an enthusiastic opponent of Prohibition, wrote that prohibitionists would have great difficulty in dismissing Pearl's evidence, and would therefore have to resort to their conventional slanders: that Pearl had been bought by the Whiskey Trust, that much of the money needed to buy him had come from the bolsheviks, and that he was therefore "a trashy and dubious fellow."

---

[48]These histories were originally collected in order to investigate tuberculosis, but included information about alcohol use, as it was believed that this might be of significance in the development of TB.

But Mencken did not know statisticians. It is easy enough for some-one who has a certain amount of statistical knowledge to debunk the work of a rival in the eyes of lay readers by claiming that its use of statistics cannot be relied upon, as this refers to a subject of which most laymen have no knowledge and on which they are happy to defer to the supposed expertise of those people who they imagine understand the subject better than they. A debunking of this nature also brings the benefit of reinforcing the perception that laymen will never understand statistics and should therefore desist in the future from daring to cri-ticise or interfere in any way with the work of statisticians. "I do not hesitate to say that it is one of the most confused books I ever read," wrote one of Pearl's rivals in the *International Review Against Alco-holism*. "It is often hardly possible to make out what statistical method the author has been following and his description of the material is particularly vague, whereas, on the other hand, his assertions are very forcibly expressed. . . . Professor Pearl has not yet succeeded in con-vincing his critics, and until his book has been most carefully and thor-oughly recast it cannot claim to be looked upon as a trustworthy scientific contribution to the serious problems of alcoholism."

Mencken believed that Pearl's book showed that the prohibitionists were "not only fools but also liars" and that it would "greatly advance the fatal illness of Prohibition." In the event, very little use was made of Pearl's book by campaigners for the repeal of Prohibition, because (contrary to what was stated in the *International Review Against Al-coholism*) he had been shy about expressing any assertions, and be-cause the statistics he had used were genuinely difficult to understand (although in fact clearly expressed). In any case, those who campaigned for repeal were more interested in arguing that moderate alcohol con-sumption did not intoxicate or cause other harm to the drinker in the short term than in suggesting that it might enable people to live a little longer. By the time Prohibition was repealed, it appeared that Pearl's detractors had succeeded in their aims, and his findings had been for-gotten.

Pearl's arguments were kept alive on the other side of the Atlantic. Most French people had been shocked by the passage of Prohibition, which they not only considered ridiculous but also believed ran counter to accepted scientific wisdom. Medical journals that undertook surveys of the opinions of general practitioners in France in the 1920s and 1930s received replies that noted a marked increase in the consumption of wine, which was generally regarded as a healthy sign; indeed, doctors in the Southwest extolled the health of peasants who drank five or more liters (well over a gallon) of wine a day. An association called the Medical Friends of Wines of France was established, under the leadership of Adolphe Portmann, a senator from the Gironde (which included the vine-growing region of Bordeaux) and an ear, nose, and throat specialist. Not only did the Friends extol the medicinal virtues of wine at their meetings, these were on occasions followed by applied research: After one congress in Bordeaux, members adjourned for a two-day visit to the major vineyards of the region, including Château Margaux and Château d'Yquem.

Although it was believed by many French health professionals that people who drank wine lived longer than those who did not, proof for this belief was lacking. In *The Black Horse of the Apocalypse,* an attack on Prohibition in America, Célestin Cambiare was able to contest the claim by antialcohol campaigners that abstinence prolonged life only by pointing to the longevity of many wine-drinking Frenchmen. Citing examples such as Marshal Foch, who led the French army to victory in the First World War at the age of sixty-six, he stated that "many Frenchman reach a very old age, and keep their mental faculties and vigor up to the end. At the age when men of other nations are generally incapacitated for any kind of work, many Frenchmen . . . are still very active."

The proof to support Cambiare's argument began to emerge only after the Second World War, and at first not in France, but in its neighbor, Italy. Here it had been widely believed by doctors that the regular consumption of wine helped to prevent heart disease—a belief that was given support by the discovery that certain plant compounds, which lowered the formation of blood cholesterol in animals, were present in wine. Then, at the beginning of the 1960s, a study was made of the habits of eighty people convalescing from heart attacks in Rome. It was found that thirteen of them were abstainers—an unusually high proportion in a country where wine drinking was a part of everyday life—and that twenty-five of the others had significantly decreased their consumption of wine in the period preceding their heart attack. The researcher, Claudia Balboni, made the point that "an intensive study of the drinking habits in coronary cases is urgently required."

At the same time, a comparison was being conducted in the United States between the death rate in the town of Roseto, Pennsylvania, where the vast majority of the population were of Italian origin and retained their Italian dietary habits, and mortality in five other communities, of German, Welsh, and mixed ethnic groups. It was found that a far smaller proportion of the population of Roseto than of the other towns had died from heart disease, even though they consumed many more calories and much more fat than the majority of Americans. They also drank vastly more wine. The researchers shrank back, however, from concluding that the low death rate from heart disease was directly related to the high consumption of wine. "The reason for the relatively salubrious condition of the Rosetans is not clear at the present moment," they observed. "Whether or not their . . . way of life contributes to their good health is still to be determined."

It was not until the 1970s that American medical researchers felt confident enough even to suggest that there might be a causal correlation between alcohol consumption and a reduced risk of heart disease. Arthur Klatsky, having trawled through the computerized medical records of 120,000 patients in the Kaiser-Permanente Medical Center in Oakland, California, in an attempt to find factors that affected the risk of heart disease, discovered that those who consumed alcohol in moderation were less likely to suffer heart attacks than nondrinkers. After examining the possible causes of this relationship, Klatsky suggested, a little guardedly, that "although the finding of a statistically significant negative association between use of alcohol and a first [heart attack] cannot at this time be interpreted as proof of the protective effect of alcohol on the coronary vessels, this happy possibility does exist."

Before long, other studies began to appear in support of Klatsky's findings. In 1981 the results were published in *The Lancet* of a ten-year study of 1,422 male government employees in London, which found that proportionately fewer of the moderate drinkers among the sample had died from heart disease than of either the nondrinkers or the heavy drinkers. The researchers offered a plausible explanation for their findings: They suggested that the protective effect of alcohol could be explained by the fact that it increased the level in the blood of "good" cholesterol (HDL, high-density lipoprotein), a substance that moves around the arteries retrieving and eliminating "bad" cholesterol (LDL, low-density lipoprotein), which would otherwise clog them up.

These studies were not alone. But nothing was done to spread the news among the general public, for several reasons. In the first case, the fact that several studies showed the existence of an inverse relationship between moderate alcohol consumption and heart disease, even if they offered reasons to account for it, did not prove that there was anything more than a statistical, as opposed to causal connection: These studies did not necessarily lead to the conclusion that it was the moderate drinking itself that did people good. It was suggested in some quarters that any apparent beneficial effect of moderate alcohol consumption on the state of the heart might be explained by the phenomenon of "competing risk": that is, people who drank alcohol regularly would be more inclined to die from heart attacks if the alcohol did not cause them to die prematurely from other causes. Furthermore, it was argued by Gerald Shaper, professor of clinical epidemiology at the Royal Free Hospital in London, that many of the people who were classified in studies as nondrinkers included a large number who had stopped drinking because of ill health. Having given up alcohol, they were included among the nondrinkers; because many of them were predisposed to heart disease, they caused the death rate among nondrinkers to be inflated.

On the surface, Shaper's argument appeared persuasive. But it suffered from a crucial flaw. If the higher mortality rate for teetotalers were to be explained, as Shaper suggested, by the fact that this group contained a large number of unhealthy ex-drinkers with a predisposition to heart disease, then it should also have included a disproportionate number of people at risk from other diseases that were known to be caused by excessive alcohol consumption, such as cirrhosis. But it did not. An increase in death from these diseases was to be found only in those consuming large amounts of alcohol daily, and not among nondrinkers.

If doctors chose generally to follow the arguments of detractors such as Shaper rather than to accept the ever-increasing body of research that indicated a connection between moderate alcohol consumption and a reduced risk of heart disease, it was because they considered it impolitic to show alcohol in a good light. As Arthur Klatsky pointed out at the beginning of the 1990s, "consideration of the harmful effects [of alcohol] almost completely dominates discussions in scientific and medical meetings, even when . . . consider[ing] light to moderate drinking."

"It seems that in medicine two different sets of criteria apply for accepting or rejecting evidence," suggested the Czech toxicologist Peter Skrabanek, an outspoken opponent of preventive medicine, in his book *The Death of Humane Medicine and the Rise of Coercive Healthism* in 1994. "If there is the slightest hint that something pleasurable may do harm, such evidence is immediately accepted, inflated, and disseminated. . . . If, however, such pleasurable activity is shown to be beneficial in any respect, such evidence must be suppressed, ridiculed, or dismissed."

Doctors shrank away from publicizing the beneficial effects of moderate drinking partly because they subscribed (at least publicly) to the belief that people who had suffered from problems as a result of their drinking should abstain from alcohol for the rest of their lives and were disinclined to offer them any opportunity for backsliding.[49] As Neil Stone, chairman of the nutrition committee of the American Heart Association, explained, "Wine can't be recommended as a public health measure because of those who can't control their drinking."

Doctors were also unwilling to publicize the beneficial effects of moderate drinking because they feared that this might lead people who did not drink alcohol to start doing so, and might encourage people who drank alcohol only occasionally to take up the habit on a more regular basis. The consequence of this would be to increase the amount of alcohol consumed in the country as a whole. This might not be a problem were not the medical profession wedded to a statistical theory (known as the Ledermann hypothesis after the French statistician who formulated it in the 1950s) that stated that any increase in per capita alcohol consumption would automatically lead to an increase in alcohol-related harm. If more people became drinkers, doctors feared, the amount of alcohol-related problems in the country would increase.

To a layman, the Ledermann hypothesis seems absurd. The harm caused by alcohol depends more on the context in which it is drunk than on the bare quantities consumed. Someone who drinks half a bottle of spirits on a Saturday night but nothing during the week is likely to cause more harm to himself and others than another person who consumes the equivalent quantity of alcohol over the course of a week, spread out in the form of a quarter-bottle of wine each day with meals. Yet, if the first person converts from drinking his half-bottle of spirits in a binge to sipping wine with food on a regular basis but consumes slightly more overall, say a third of a bottle of wine a day, then, according to Ledermann, he will be contributing to an increase in alcohol-related problems in his society.

Why, then, has the Ledermann hypothesis been adopted? For reasons of convenience. It appears to provide scientific justification for telling people to cut down on their drinking. Once it is accepted that

---

[49]This is discussed in the Introduction.

an increase in per capita alcohol consumption leads to a corresponding increase in alcohol-related harm, then it is logical (if no more sensible) to accept that if everyone reduces his alcohol consumption, the amount of alcohol-related problems will decrease accordingly. On the basis of the Ledermann hypothesis, the World Health Organization (WHO) declared in 1985 a policy of reducing alcohol consumption internationally by twenty-five percent by the year 2000. In pursuit of this policy, the WHO has gone out of its way to talk down the scientific evidence associating moderate alcohol consumption with a reduced risk of heart disease. In the fall of 1994 it held a press conference in Geneva and issued a press release entitled "Moderate Drinking: Serious Warning by WHO Specialists" in which it stated that "there is no minimum threshold below which alcohol can be consumed without any risk. This is how Hans Emblad, director of the WHO program of substance abuse, has reacted to a campaign which for some time has been trying to give the impression that moderate alcohol consumption could be good for health. According to this WHO specialist, the message should be instead: 'The less you drink, the better.' "

The WHO policy of reducing alcohol consumption has been adopted by the American government. A report called *Healthy People 2000*, published by the Department of Health and Human Services in 1990, declared that it was the goal of the government to reduce alcohol consumption by Americans over the age of fourteen from the equivalent of 2.54 gallons of pure alcohol per person in 1987 to 2 gallons by 2000.

At the same time, in pursuit of the belief that even moderate drinkers contributed to the overall level of alcohol-related harm, the Center for Substance Abuse Prevention, a government agency working to counter alcohol abuse, instructed its staff that they should always refer to "alcohol, tobacco, and other drugs" in order that people should realize that in the case of alcohol, just like illicit drugs, there was no such thing as responsible moderate consumption. The center also informed those private campaigning groups to which it distributed federal funds that they should not use the term "responsible use" in any written materials about alcohol on the grounds that alcohol cannot be used responsibly because "there is a risk associated with all use."

Thus, in the professional opinion of both doctors and government agencies, publicity should not be given to the benefits of moderate alcohol consumption on the grounds that even moderate drinkers should be encouraged to reduce the amount they drink so that the overall level of consumption in the country can be reduced. Yet these experts also believe that publicity should not be given to the benefits of drinking in moderation for fear that this would encourage people in remission from the supposed disease of alcoholism to take up drinking again, which would lead them down a slippery slope to their doom. Illogical, Captain. If you believe that alcoholism is a problem for which society in general is responsible, then you cannot also regard alcoholism as a disease that affects individuals. If you endorse the first of these beliefs, you cannot logically subscribe to the other, and vice versa.

Agencies that campaign against alcohol-related problems also claim that they are continuing to increase. Yet alcohol consumption in the United States has been in decline since the beginning of the 1980s: Between 1980 and 1994 per capita consumption fell by twenty percent. According to the philosophy to which the agencies subscribe, there is supposed to be a direct correlation between average alcohol consumption and alcohol-related harm, and any increase in per capita consumption necessarily leads to an increase in alcohol-related problems. So why do they not also say that a reduction in average consumption has led to a reduction in alcohol-related harm? Do they subscribe to the Ledermann hypothesis only when it is convenient to their campaigns? In rejecting their own philosophy they are not only illogical but also perverse.

At least the government agencies and departments have been clear about one thing: that they should discourage the dissemination of the good news about the benefits of moderate drinking to the general public.[50] In 1990, by which time a great deal of research pointing to the benefits of moderate alcohol consumption had been published in medical journals, the third edition of the official *Dietary Guidelines for Americans,* produced by a joint committee of the Department of Agriculture and the Department of Health and Human Services, stated that the alcohol in wine, beer, and spirits "has no net health benefit"

---

[50] They have been doing so since as early as 1972, when the Harvard epidemiologist Carl Seltzer examined data from an extensive study of heart disease in Framingham, Massachusetts, and found that moderate drinkers were less likely to suffer than abstainers. But the National Institutes of Health, which funded the research, refused to allow Seltzer to publish a paper on the results. An official stated that "an article which openly invites the encouragement of undertaking drinking with the implication of prevention of coronary heart disease would be scientifically misleading and socially undesirable in view of the major health problem of alcoholism that already exists in the country."

and that it "has physiologic drug effects and is harmful when consumed in excess." This advice was significant because the guidelines were used by the government to plan federal food programs and by private industry to dispense information about nutrition.

Also in 1990, the Bureau of Alcohol, Tobacco and Firearms (BATF), the branch of the Treasury Department that oversees the alcohol beverage industry,[51] rejected a request by the California-based wine importer Kermit Lynch to include on the label on a bottle of 1988 white Bordeaux a quotation from Thomas Jefferson that "wine from long habit has become an indispensable for my health." Tom Busey, head of the product compliance branch of the BATF, said that he was merely complying with a federal statute prohibiting "curative and therapeutic claims" on labels. "There are plenty of forums to promote the scientific beliefs, personal beliefs, and philosophical beliefs that wine is helpful, but a label is not the place to do it," Busey explained. Lynch responded that "the federal government has decided that Thomas Jefferson's words are too dangerous. They have decided that we can't read what Thomas Jefferson has to say about wine [because] we might think that Thomas Jefferson was right."

Early the next year, the Robert Mondavi Winery was ordered by the BATF to remove from the labels on its bottles the statement that "wine has been with us since the beginning of civilization. It is the temperate, civilized, sacred, romantic mealtime beverage recommended in the Bible. Wine has been praised for centuries by statesmen, philosophers, poets, and scholars. Wine in moderation is an integral part of our culture, heritage, and the gracious way of life." The BATF was concerned that the information that Mondavi had printed on its labels was "neither accurate nor specific," offered no details about the identity and quality of the product, and tended to "create a misleading impression." Yet Mondavi had decided to produce a statement about the cultural benefits of wine drinking because the government had been disseminating misleading information about alcoholic drinks, had introduced a law requiring all bottles to carry a statement warning that "women should not drink alcoholic beverages during pregnancy because of the risk of birth defects," and that the "consumption of alcohol beverages impairs your ability to drive a car or operate ma-

---

[51]The fact that alcohol is governed by the same department as controls the use of firearms is often cited by foreigners as a demonstration of the wrongheadedness of official American attitudes to the use of alcohol.

chinery and may cause health problems," and had done its best to keep information about the health benefits of moderate consumption out of the public sphere. In this case Mondavi fought back, and a compromise was reached in which Mondavi removed from its label the statement that wine was recommended in the Bible,[52] and changed the phrase "Wine in moderation is part of our culture" to "Wine in moderation is part of our family's culture."

Despite the best efforts of doctors and the government, information about the health benefits of moderate drinking was finally brought into the public sphere at the end of 1991—and in the most conspicuous manner possible. Food writers and nutritionists had been giving increasing prominence to the benefits of a Mediterranean diet, by which they meant the diet high in bread or pasta, vegetables, fruit, and fish and low in saturated animal fats that was consumed in the countries surrounding the Mediterranean, including Greece, Italy and the South of France. The Mediterranean diet also involved lingering over meals instead of bolting down one's food in the American manner.[53] The leisurely pace of eating was encouraged by the habit of drinking wine with both lunch and dinner; on the other hand, very few spirits were consumed and there was hardly any drinking outside meals.

In those countries where people consumed a Mediterranean diet, the death rates from heart disease were generally much lower than in America or Britain or other predominately Anglo-Saxon countries. This was true even if people also ate a lot of foods that were not supposed to be good for them, as in many parts of France, where diets tended to be high in animal fats. The benefits of drinking wine during leisurely meals applied even if in other ways people behaved in a manner that might have been expected to increase their risk of contracting heart disease, such as smoking cigarettes or doing very little exercise. This apparent contradiction of people who did lots of things that were supposed to be bad for their health yet suffered less from heart disease than Americans (or Britons) came to be known as the "French paradox."

Morley Safer, one of the reporters on *60 Minutes* and a long-term

---

[52]Although it was: See the Conclusion.
[53]The speed of American dining is discussed in Chapter 2. Interest in the Mediterranean diet in America began in 1975 when Ancel and Margaret Keys, two doctors from Minnesota, published a best-selling book called *How to Eat Well and Stay Well the Mediterranean Way.*

wine connoisseur and lover of French food and culture, came across an article about the French paradox, and decided that the story would be worth covering, not least because it would enable him to spend some time in Lyons, the gastronomic capital of France. The program, which was watched by 21.8 million households, aired on November 17, 1991. Safer was filmed traveling to Lyons to interview Serge Renaud, director of the French National Institute of Health and Medical Research, who had spent fifteen years investigating the French paradox. Safer pointed out that the death rate from heart disease in America was one of the highest in the world, with about one million deaths every year, and that a middle-aged American man was three times as likely to die from a heart attack as a middle-aged Frenchman. Renaud explained that the principal reason French people suffered so much less from heart problems than Americans was that the French regularly drank moderate amounts of alcohol with their meals, in the form of a few glasses of wine. He said that no other drug was so efficient in preventing heart disease as a moderate intake of alcohol, which reduced the risk of contracting the illness by up to fifty percent.

Not surprisingly, a number of American liquor companies were keen to promote their products by repeating what had been reported in the program. But the government continued to try to prevent them from doing so. When the Leeward Winery in Ventura, California, published a synopsis of the story in its spring 1992 newsletter, it was ordered by the BATF to remove the newsletter from circulation on the grounds that it constituted an advertisement, and advertisements for alcoholic beverages were allowed to refer to their possible health benefits only if they also presented their possible harmful effects. The information in the newsletter might have been factual, but as far as the BATF was concerned, it was misleading.

The same year, the BATF refused to allow a group of California wineries to distribute to wine shops a summary of an article that had appeared in *Alcohol Abuse,* the official publication of the National Institute on Alcohol Abuse and Alcoholism, acknowledging the evidence that moderate drinking decreased the risk of death from heart disease. The wineries responded by threatening the BATF with legal action for forbidding them to use information that was already in the public domain. The BATF backed down and gave its permission for liquor companies to disseminate the article in question, but insisted that they publish the full text and not merely a summary.

Not until 1995, in the fourth edition of the official *Dietary Guide-*

lines for Americans, did the government at long last acknowledge publicly the health benefits of moderate alcohol consumption of which scientists had been aware for a generation. The statement in the 1990 edition that "drinking has no net health benefit" was changed to "moderate drinking is associated with a lower risk for coronary heart disease in some individuals"; the statement in the 1990 edition that "consumption is not recommended" was altered to "alcoholic beverages have been used to enhance the enjoyment of meals by many societies throughout human history," and the statement in the 1990 edition that alcohol "has physiologic drug effects" was removed. Dr. Marion Nestle, chairman of the Department of Nutrition and Food Studies at New York University and a member of the advisory committee that drew up the guidelines, later stated that she thought that they had been conservative in their wording—they included a long list of the diseases associated with higher levels of alcohol consumption—and therefore the committee had not expected the guidelines to make news.

But make news they did. The *New York Times* ran a major article entitled "In an About-Face, U.S. Says Alcohol Has Health Benefits," which quoted the comments made by Dr. Philip Lee, assistant secretary of health, at a news conference announcing the new guidelines, that "there was a significant bias in the past against drinking. To move from antialcohol to health benefits is a big change." Even the London *Daily Telegraph* carried a news story about the changes, which began: "The land of Prohibition and Alcoholics Anonymous has finally bowed to the ancient wisdom of Europe: A daily tipple is both a pleasure and an aid to good health."

Now that the government had referred to the health benefits of moderate alcohol consumption in an official publication intended for public consumption, the wine industry's representative body, the Wine Institute, applied to the BATF for a general permission to add a message to the label of wine bottles stating, "To learn about the health benefits of moderate wine consumption, write for the federal government's *Dietary Guidelines for Americans.*" On reviewing this proposal, the BATF responded that "benefits" should be changed to "effects," but once this change had been made appeared to be disposed to allowing the label. In the spring of 1998, however, Strom Thurmond, the ancient Republican senator from South Carolina, wrote to the treasury secretary, Robert Rubin, to insist that the BATF should be instructed to withhold its permission for the label. The fact that the bureau had even contemplated allowing it, Thurmond added, had caused him to consider introducing legislation to deprive the bureau of its authority over health-related issues. "He is going to do whatever he can to stop any changes to the wine labels that implies alcohol is good for you," explained Thurmond's spokesman, John De Crosta. "The only change he would approve of is making the language in the warnings more explicit. . . . It's just wrong to suggest that there is something to be gained from [drinking wine]." Despite all the research that had been published about the health benefits of moderate alcohol consumption, despite the official acceptance of this research by the government, it appeared that wine producers were still not allowed to tell the public.

By this time, however, a lot of people had made up their own minds. The 60 Minutes program on the French paradox had exerted a dramatic effect on the drinking habits of the nation at large. Although Serge Renaud had stated in the program that it was alcohol that was beneficial, and that it was simply the French habit to consume this alcohol in the form of wine, Morley Safer did add a voice-over stating: "There has been for years the belief by doctors in many countries that alcohol, in particular red wine, reduces the risk of heart disease." Most people who saw the program appear to have interpreted it as recommending specifically that they should drink red wine, because it unleashed something of a red wine mania. Wine retailers and restaurateurs reported that people were buying red wine who had never tried it before in their lives. In Pennsylvania, the state liquor control board recorded a 97 percent increase in sales of red wine in the week following the broadcast. And this was not a nine days' wonder. In the year following the broadcast, sales of red wine—which had been in decline in the 1980s—increased by 39 percent. Before the 60 Minutes program, red wine had accounted for only 15 percent of supermarket wine sales. Three and a half years later it accounted for 26 percent. When wine had first become popular in the 1970s, most people had taken up drinking white wine because they were looking for a refreshing chilled beverage that they could consume in place of a cocktail or beer.[54] But by 1996, largely because of the impetus that had been given to the sales of red wine by the 60 Minutes program on the French paradox, it was being suggested by some in the industry that red wine sales had overtaken those of white. Whereas in the 1980s Californian

---

[54]The "wine boom" is discussed in Chapter 2.

wineries had been turning their black grapes into white zinfandel because they were unable to sell a sufficient quantity of red wine, now they were importing red wine in bulk from Europe for blending with their own or for sale under subsidiary labels in order to make up for a shortfall in their production.

In the autumn of 1995 the Competitive Enterprise Institute, a libertarian campaign group, carried out a poll into public knowledge about the health benefits of alcohol. Forty-two percent of respondents said they believed that moderate alcohol consumption reduced the risk of contracting heart disease, against thirty-eight percent who said they did not. Those who said they believed alcohol was beneficial were then asked to which types of alcohol they thought this benefit applied. Twenty-three percent said all types of alcohol; twenty-seven percent said wine only; twenty-one percent said only red wine.

Yet the first scientific evidence to suggest that wine is more beneficial than other forms of alcohol was not published until the year in which the Competitive Enterprise Institute conducted its poll, four years after the *60 Minutes* program. In the late 1970s researchers at the Institute of Preventive Medicine in Copenhagen[55] had asked 13,285 people aged between thirty and seventy living in the city whether they drank wine, beer, or spirits, how much of them they drank, and how often. They then followed all the interviewees for the next twelve years, during which time 2,229 died, a little more than half from diseases of the circulatory system. The researchers found that people who drank between three and five glasses of wine a day were not only much less likely than anyone else to die from heart disease but also only half as likely to die from any cause as people who did not drink wine; that people who drank between three and five twelve-ounce bottles of beer a day were less likely to die from heart disease than those who did not drink beer, but were neither more nor less likely to die from all causes than non–beer drinkers; that people who drank between three and five units of spirits a day were more likely to die both from heart disease and from all causes. In their report, which was published in the *British Medical Journal* in 1995, they pointed out that in the fifteen years

---

[55]Denmark, the researchers pointed out in their report, was a particularly appropriate country in which to conduct such a study, since Danes consume all three types of drink in more or less comparable quantities—and many drink all three—unlike the inhabitants of other countries, who tend to favor one kind over another (such as the French, who prefer wine).

preceding publication, deaths from heart attacks in Denmark had declined by about 30 percent, while overall alcohol consumption had remained stable. At the same time, the amount of alcohol drunk in the form of wine had increased from 17 to 30 percent of the total, which they suggested might have contributed to the decline in deaths from heart disease.

The Copenhagen researchers could not be sure why certain kinds of alcohol should offer better protection against disease than others, but they had plenty of ideas. They suggested that beer as well as wine helps protect against heart disease partly because the alcohol increases the amount of high-density lipoprotein ("good" cholesterol) in the blood—as had been suggested by the authors of the survey published in *The Lancet* back in 1981—and partly because the alcohol helps to flush away the platelets, the smallest of the blood cells, which are thought to contribute to heart disease because they cling to fatty deposits, clogging the arteries. They suggested that wine protected against heart disease better than beer because it was more effective at flushing away the platelets. They also suggested that there were various substances present in wine that helped to protect not only against heart disease but also against various forms of cancer. They concluded that "the biological mechanism behind the different effects of the three types of drink needs further research."

Although the Copenhagen researchers did not attempt to distinguish between the effects of red and white wine, their results were given a good deal of attention by Morley Safer when he reported again on the French paradox for *60 Minutes* in November 1995, four years after his original report. Once again Safer stated that red wine was best.

In the last few years researchers have begun to produce evidence to show why red wine might offer better protection against heart disease than white (or beer or spirits). The basic difference between red and white wine is that red wine is made from black grapes, and white wine from white ones. There are, however, some white wines that are made from black grapes, notably champagne, a great deal of which is manufactured from the black grapes Pinot Noir and Pinot Meunier. Champagne is a white wine not because of the color of the grapes from which it is made but because, after the grapes have been pressed in order to extract their juice, the juice is drained away from the skins before fermentation begins. Red wines are red not just because they are made from black grapes but because they are vinified by fermenting the juice of the grapes in contact with the skins. The skins contain the substances that give the wines their color and flavor. These substances, of which the best known are tannins, which give red wines their characteristic astringency, and anthocyanins, which give them their color, are known to winemakers as phenolic compounds.

To medical researchers, these phenolic compounds are known as flavonoids, and they are of interest for quite different reasons. They can help to counter the damage caused by free radicals—wandering, imperfect atoms with a unpaired electron, which search continually for another cell to which the lonely electron can become attached. Once attached, the atom becomes whole but the defect is handed along: The free radical has set up a chain reaction, and the instability spreads. Low-density lipoprotein is one of the targets of these free radicals. On their own, particles of low-density lipoprotein are fairly benign; it is only after being altered by contact with free radicals that they turn into dangerous and aggressive cells capable of penetrating and injuring the smooth walls of arteries.

The process by which free radicals convert otherwise benign substances into potentially harmful ones is known as oxidation. It has therefore been the concern of medical researchers to identify substances in the diet that inhibit this oxidation process. First they found that vitamins C and E were beneficial; recently they have suggested that the flavonoids in many fruits and vegetables may be even better. Best of all, it has now been discovered, are the flavonoids in red wine.[56] When members of the Free Radical Research Group at Guy's and St. Thomas's Hospitals in London compared the total antioxidant activity of various fruit juices with that of red wine, they found levels in the latter between four and eight times as high. Grape juice was the same level as other fruit juices, as was white wine. Furthermore, the fact that the flavonoids in wines are dissolved in alcohol probably makes them more easily absorbable than the flavonoids in fruits and vegetables.

Not only are red wines higher in flavonoids that white ones, some red wines are higher in flavonoids than others. Evidently, if flavonoids are extracted as a result of skin contact during fermentation, then red wines that are fermented in contact with their skins for a longer time will have a greater concentration of flavonoids. So, too, will red wines that are fermented at higher temperatures, which aid extraction. Therefore, red wines from the cooler regions of Europe will tend gen-

---

[56]The same compounds as make it possible to use wine to sterilize contaminated water.

erally to have higher levels of flavonoids than those produced in warmer regions of America and Australia, because in order to extract their color grapes grown in cooler climates need to be fermented for longer in contact with their skins than riper grapes from warmer climates. European wines also tend to be produced in a more traditional style, with higher fermentation temperatures and greater extraction of tannins.

Also, different flavonoids respond to different climatic conditions. One of them, resveratrol, is a natural fungicide produced automatically by grapevines when they are threatened by mold. It is therefore present in much greater concentrations in the skins of grapes that have grown in mild, damp climates, where mold is often a problem, such as Burgundy. Since the resveratrol content of a wine declines during barrel aging and maturation, the highest resveratrol content is to be found in a simple Bourgogne Rouge that has been vinified so as to be drunk young, rather than in a more prestigious, oak-aged red burgundy that needs to be matured to allow its flavors to develop and its tannins to soften. Among American wines, those produced in the relatively humid climate of the Finger Lakes in New York State have a higher resveratrol content than others.

Another flavonoid, quercetin, is found in highest concentrations in grape varieties that have grown under a hot sun. Unlike resveratrol, quercetin does not disappear as the wine ages.

It has also been found that both resveratrol and quercetin have anticarcinogenic properties—at least in mice. Whether these flavonoids can protect against cancer in humans as effectively as they do against cancer in mice is not yet known.[57]

That is the problem of the current state of scientific research—the gap that lies between the results of experiments and what happens in real life. It has been demonstrated by some researchers that wine offers better protection against heart disease and other forms of illness than other types of alcoholic drink, but it is not known for certain why that

---

[57] It is also possible that the antioxidants in wine might help reduce the risk of breast cancer in women, although research on the relationship between alcohol and breast cancer is both contradictory and controversial. Except at low levels of consumption, there appears to be a statistical association between alcohol intake and an increased incidence of breast cancer, but there is nothing to point to a causal connection, and it seems most likely that further research will show that this association can be explained by other factors that are linked with both alcohol consumption and an increased risk of breast cancer, such as weight and diet.

should be. Contrary to popular belief, it has not been demonstrated that red wine offers better protection in this respect than white, but, if it were someday to be shown that red wine is best, the compounds have been identified that might help to explain why. But it is not yet known whether these potentially beneficial compounds in red wine are capable of being utilized by the body. Just because something happens inside a test tube does not mean that the same thing will occur inside a person.

It may well be that people who prefer wine suffer less from heart disease and other health problems than people who drink mostly beer or spirits because they lead a healthier life in other respects, with a better diet and more exercise, as well as being generally better educated and wealthier. Furthermore, wine is normally consumed in a healthier manner than beer or spirits. Few people drink wine in binges; it tends to be drunk slowly, often as part of a meal. This is important, because there is evidence to show that—quite apart from the potential dangers of binge drinking—many of the benefits of alcohol consumption are lost if it is not consumed on a regular basis. Thus wine may be more salutary than beer and spirits simply because it is consumed regularly and slowly during meals rather than irregularly and at uncertain speed on its own. It gives the body a gradual protective dose of alcohol at the same time as its drinker is ingesting potentially dangerous saturated fats. Here lies the explanation of the French paradox: the capacity of wine to mitigate the effects of fatty food.

The benefits of wine drinking cannot be condensed into a pill (as some companies have attempted to do, with the development of dietary supplements made from the skins of black grapes). As John De Luca of the Wine Institute has pointed out, it is wrong to equate beer, wine, and spirits as no more than differently diluted versions of alcohol that should be treated in the same way by the government, because wine has always been treated differently by people who drink it. As Mondavi insisted on stating on its labels, the practice of drinking wine with meals dates back many hundreds of years; it has long been a part of civilized living and Western culture.[58] If drinking wine helps people to live longer, it is not just or even principally because of the manner it affects certain substances in the blood but because it enables the people who drink it to enjoy life more. The most important medicinal benefits

---

[58]There is a lot more about the social and cultural aspects of wine drinking in the Conclusion.

of wine lie in its potential to reduce stress and to make people feel happier. Evidently it is difficult for doctors, who rely on the results of scientific analysis, and are concerned to maintain their professional mystique, to accept that the ingestion of wine in moderate quantities improves the health of their patients for the simple reason that it gives them pleasure. Nevertheless, the use of wine as a medicine cannot be distinguished from its use as a beverage because wine is most effective as a medicine when it is taken as a beverage.

The Proyect Family, Dope Fiends

CHAPTER 5

The Failure of Controls

The one thing everybody knows about Prohibition is that it did not work. It had been intended to stigmatize the consumption of alcoholic drink within polite society; yet it encouraged a lot of respectable women to take up drinking who had not done so before.[1] "We can't suppress an ironical snicker," wrote Alice-Leone Moats, "when we think that all [the prohibitionists] succeeded in doing was transporting women from the drawing room into the speakeasy."

Prohibition also made drinking popular among young people, who were attracted to liquor by the extra thrill they could obtain from breaking the law. "People whose youth did not coincide with the Twenties never had our reverence for strong drink," wrote A. J. Liebling, who was born in 1904. "Older men knew liquor before it became the symbol of a sacred cause. Kids who began drinking after 1933 took it as a matter of course. For us it was a self-righteous pleasure. . . . [By] drinking, we proved to ourselves our freedom as individuals and flouted Congress. . . . It was the only period when a fellow could be smug and slopped concurrently."

By making it necessary to obtain liquor illegally, at a price that had been vastly inflated by the expenses involved in smuggling and paying

---

[1]This is discussed in Chapter 3.

kickbacks to law enforcement officers, Prohibition made drinking fashionable—not merely a mark of rebellion against the law but a sign of conspicuous consumption as well. This process was encouraged by the new medium of the movies, which portrayed violation of the Volstead Act as an essential element of sophisticated living. One survey in 1930 found that three out of four films referred in some way to liquor; whereas the hero drank in two out of five films and even the heroine in one out of five, the villain did so in only one film out of ten. People aspired to the behavior they saw in movies, so they drank alcohol.

As the consumption of alcohol became associated with wealth and cosmopolitan manners, it lost its old cultural links with immigrants and the working class.[2] Many working-class people were forced to give up drinking during Prohibition—not because they respected the law but because they could not afford the money. Even when purchased in wholesale quantities direct from a bootlegger, liquor cost several times as much as it had done before Prohibition. The prices were further inflated by the owners of speakeasies, who had to write off one third of their running costs as "protection money" paid to law enforcement officers. In Chicago the charge for a whiskey highball increased fivefold, from 15 to 75 cents. There were many in the city who regarded the price, rather than the purchase, as a crime. No wonder the speakeasies drew most of their customers from the middle and upper classes.

As the customers changed, so did the type of alcohol that people drank. In a period when consumers were less concerned with the qualities of alcoholic drinks than with their effect, bootleggers concentrated on the transportation of alcohol in its most concentrated and potent form—that of spirits. Before Prohibition, sales of beer had been rising and sales of spirits falling. Back in 1840, before lager was introduced and beer started on its long rise to popularity, spirits had accounted for 80 percent of the alcohol consumed in America and beer for only 5 percent. By 1880, sales of beer had increased to such an extent that it accounted for roughly the same proportion of overall alcohol consumption—45 to 47 percent—as spirits. By the time Prohibition was introduced, beer had long passed spirits and accounted for 55 percent of sales, compared with 37 percent for spirits. Ten years later, however, spirits accounted for 75 percent of all the alcohol drunk and beer for only 15 percent. During Prohibition, the consumption of beer declined by roughly 90 percent, while that of spirits—despite the dramatic rise

---

[2]These links are discussed in the Conclusion.

in price—slightly increased.[3] No wonder Heywood Broun described the Volstead Act (by which Prohibition was introduced) as a bill to discourage the drinking of good beer in favor of indifferent gin.

In this respect, Prohibition not only failed to work but achieved precisely the opposite of what had been intended. Following more than a century of temperance campaigns that had sought to persuade people to abandon spirits for healthier drinks such as wine and beer, the passage of national Prohibition saw to it that those people who continued to drink consumed mostly spirits.[4] When William Randolph Hearst, initially a supporter of Prohibition, changed his mind and came out for repeal in 1929, he explained that "I am against Prohibition because it has set the cause of temperance back twenty years; because it has substituted an ineffective campaign of force for an effective campaign of education; because it has replaced comparatively uninjurious light wines and beers with the worst kind of hard liquor and bad liquor; because it has increased drinking not only among men but has extended drinking to women and even children."

Prohibition proved counterproductive not only because it encouraged beer drinkers to convert to spirits (as well as destroying much of the wine culture that then existed) but also because it made drinking synonymous with drunkenness. People did not go to speakeasies in order to socialize with the bartender or their fellow customers, but to get drunk. The same was true of people who drank liquor in private homes. "No longer is drinking an art with Americans," commented Moats; "once they drank for the taste, but now they drink only for the effect. The more quick and fatal the liquor, the better they like it. They are either on the wagon or else. There was once a time when a man who got drunk in a lady's drawing room was never invited to that house again. If he showed the same lack of control in another home, he ran the risk of having every door closed to him. Now a hostess who insists that all her guests remain sober would find that she was giving parties to a chosen few, and very dull ones at that. She

---

[3]The exceptions were New Jersey and Illinois; the former through tradition and the latter through the organizational efficiency of Al Capone remained beer areas.
[4]Admittedly Prohibition also led to an increase in wine consumption, but most of that was homemade; with the enforced closure of restaurants that had sold good-quality imported and California wine, the only people who continued to drink fine wines during Prohibition were those who had been able to afford to lay in a stock before it came into force. See Chapter 2.

takes it for granted that the majority of her guests will be wavering before the evening is over."

The government could do nothing about it. The chief source of bootleg spirits was moonshine, distilled in remote and largely mountainous areas, which the government did not have the manpower to patrol. In 1925 agents for the Prohibition Enforcement Bureau seized 172,537 stills but, for every still captured, nine continued to operate. Nor did the government have the resources to police the Canadian border. It was impossible, people said, to keep liquor from dripping through a dotted line. Although it is not known how much liquor was smuggled into the United States, the liquor revenues of the Canadian government increased four times during Prohibition, while the consumption of spirits by the Canadian population almost halved. Prohibition therefore proved a blessing for the state-controlled alcohol monopolies of the Canadian provinces. As Ring Lardner put it, "Prohibition has sure been a godsend in a whole lot of ways. It has given lucrative employment to a great many men that did not have nothing before, only their courage. It has cemented the friendship between the U.S. and Canada. It has given gals and women a new interest in life and something to talk about besides hair and children. And it has made our govt appreciate the enormous extent of our coast line and tough it would be to defend same vs invasion."

At least the government could do something to prevent spirits that had legally been distilled in the United States for industrial production from being diverted by bootleggers, who diluted them, added color and flavoring, and sold them as "whiskey" or "gin." The government ordered that this industrial alcohol be laced with methanol (wood alcohol), a poison that could blind and kill, in order to dissuade people from drinking it. Those who persisted in drinking the poisoned alcohol would have to take the consequences. Journalists accused the Prohibition Bureau of conspiring to murder American citizens, because it knew that at least one gallon of industrial alcohol in ten would be diverted into the human stomach. In a series of articles in *The New York World,* Robert Barry compared the work of the Prohibition Bureau with that of the celebrated Italian Renaissance family of poisoners, the Borgias; unlike the bureau, he wrote, the Borgias had murdered only individuals rather than indulging in "collective slaughter," and "never could be accused of preparing venomous doses for the purposes of reform."

By this time, industrial alcohol was killing several thousand people each year.[5] At the end of 1926 the *New York Times* reported that the percentage of methanol to be used in denaturing industrial alcohol was to be doubled from the beginning of the new year. Supposedly, by making its odor more offensive, this would enable it to be detected more easily by drinkers. The newspaper commented that "it is apparently the belief of officials that the new formula will be no more dangerous than the one it supplants and will be far more unpalatable." It also cited the opinion of Wayne B. Wheeler, general counsel of the Anti-Saloon League, that "the government is under no obligation to furnish the people with alcohol that is drinkable when the Constitution prohibits it. The person who drinks this industrial alcohol is a deliberate suicide." Yet, as the article pointed out, someone who bought industrial alcohol was not even guilty of breaking the law, as the purchase (as opposed to the sale) of alcohol was not forbidden by Prohibition. Senator Edward I. Edwards of New Jersey issued a statement that the deliberate poisoning of industrial alcohol was "legalized murder, and the government is an accessory to the crime. Poisoning of industrial alcohol by the government cannot be justified on moral, economic, or spiritual grounds when an unpalatable, non-poisonous substance will serve the same purpose."[6]

A less harmful means of enforcing the prohibitory law was to try to prevent drinkers from getting hold of the industrial alcohol by cracking down on bootleggers. The Volstead Act had provided that people who traded in alcohol might be imprisoned for up to six months or fined $1,000. In 1929 this was supplemented by the Jones Act, which imposed a maximum penalty of five years in jail *and* a fine of $10,000, even for first offenders. This also made any liquor offense a felony; according to the federal criminal code, anyone who

---

[5]The worst of the drinks to appear during Prohibition may well have been "jake," a highly alcoholic extract of Jamaica ginger with methanol, which paralyzed drinkers in the arms and legs. Victims of "jake paralysis" walked with a goose step, as they could not control their feet. This drink was dispensed by drugstores for the treatment of stomach disorders at the cost of 50 cents for a two-ounce bottle. But it was purchased by drinkers, who mixed it with ginger ale or soda pop. In 1930 the Prohibition Bureau estimated that jake had paralyzed more than 15,000 people.

[6]Not that moonshine was much better. Distillers accelerated production by dumping chunks of carbide into their fermenters, which heated the mash but left a toxic residue. Other adulterants included sulphuric acid. Francis Pridemore, a former whiskey maker in the West Virginia hills, suggested that a skull and crossbones should be placed over the label of every bottle of whiskey made in his home region.

knew that a felony had been committed but failed to report it was by this failure himself committing a felony. This new law created a national outcry, and precipitated Hearst's change of sides. He described the Jones Act as "the most menacing piece of repressive legislation that has stained the statute books of this republic since the Alien and Sedition laws."

And still it did not work. However stiff the penalty that might be imposed on a bootlegger, it was necessary to convict him first. So many bootleggers were arrested and brought to court that they rapidly overloaded the system. The courts introduced "bargain days," when the backlog of cases was cleared by pleas of guilty from the defendants, in return for small fines or short jail sentences. Nine out of ten convictions under the Volstead Act were obtained on these "bargain days." Even if a bootlegger did come up for trial before a jury, he was likely to be acquitted—whatever the evidence might be. On one occasion, in Los Angeles, the jury was itself put on trial (to determine whether its members should be suspended from further duty) after it had drunk the evidence in a liquor case. The jurors sought to argue in their defense that they had merely been sampling the evidence—a pint of spirits— in order to determine whether it was of alcoholic content and thus constituted a violation of the law. They determined that it was, and that it did. Unfortunately, the evidence having disappeared, the person who had been accused of bootlegging, a hotel clerk named George Beven, had to be acquitted.

At the end of the 1920s public competitions were announced for the best suggestion as to how Prohibition could be made more effective, with prizes for the winners. Entrants proposed that bootleggers should be imprisoned in bottle-shaped cages in public squares, or made to swallow two ounces of castor oil, or forced to go to church every Sunday, or required to wear red trousers and—if caught without them—put in prison, or have indelible crimson dye sprayed on their noses. Clearly, members of the public had no better idea than the government of how Prohibition might be made to work.

The government, moreover, ought to have known in advance that Prohibition would be impossible to enforce, because previous prohibitory measures had failed.

The first such measure—a ban on spirits—had been introduced by Oglethorpe in Georgia two centuries earlier. It had led the settlers of the new colony to obtain their rum from the other side of the Savannah

River, in South Carolina; the prohibition was soon abandoned.[7] After this, no state introduced prohibition for a century. Then, in 1838, the Massachusetts legislature passed the Fifteen-Gallon Law, which forbade the sale of spirits in quantities of less than fifteen gallons. This law, too, was evaded easily enough. Writing after the Civil War, a elderly teetotal congregational clergyman described from memory the principal means by which the Fifteen-Gallon Law had been circumvented, known as "striped pig":

"At a general muster a man erected a tent, near the muster field, upon which was painted the notice that a striped pig might be seen within for the small fee of six-and-a-fourth cents, a silver coin then in general use. Curiosity influenced a few persons to enter the tent, in which was exhibited a common pig with stripes of paint drawn upon its body. In another part of the tent there was another 'critter' on exhibition, which proved to be the great attraction of the showman. It was New England rum in decanters, with sugar and water near them. Persons who paid their entrance fee looked at the pig, and were treated without extra charge. This show acquired great popularity. It was visited by the multitude, who loved the 'critter,' and certain individuals, it was said, went in to see the sight several times, and declared that it was truly worth seeing. The success of this evasion rendered it popular, and caused it to be very generally adopted. Men sold articles of small value for more than they were worth, and gave their customers intoxicating drinks without charge."

Not only was the Fifteen-Gallon Law evaded in this way, but more open violations often passed unpunished. Enforcement depended on informers, who were dissuaded from appearing as witnesses in court by violent treatment such as tarring and feathering. Far from contributing to the public good, the law made violence more common. Previously, rowdies opposed to the cause of temperance had limited themselves to acts of vandalism against property owned by temperance campaigners. But during the two years that the Fifteen-Gallon Law was in force, physical assaults and mob demonstrations became common.

Even though the Fifteen-Gallon Law had led to an increase in public disorder, prohibitory Maine laws were introduced in several states in the early 1850s in the belief that they would cause disorder to diminish. As temperance propagandists pointed out, not only did many people act violently when drunk, but drunkenness engendered sloth and dis-

---

[7] This is discussed in Chapter 1.

solution, which in turn encouraged a life of crime. It was claimed in Ohio in the 1840s that two thirds of all the crimes committed in the state were the product of intemperance, and that if liquor could be eliminated, there would be little further need for the courts or the jails. People were ready to believe such claims because they regularly read accounts in the daily newspapers of assaults and other crimes committed by those who were either intoxicated or known to be heavy drinkers.[8]

As might have been predicted, the Maine Law, far from reducing the level of alcohol-related disorder, served to increase it by introducing a new form of violent resistance to the law itself. This played a major role in discrediting prohibition, for Neal Dow—the mayor of Portland and the prime mover of the Maine Law—had claimed that the measure would eliminate violence and crime from the community. Moderates lost faith in the law once they discovered that enforcement produced more disorder than it eliminated. One widely publicized incident occurred in Portland in 1855. Under the Maine Law, municipalities established agencies to sell liquor for medical or industrial uses. As mayor of Portland, Dow made the technical error of ordering its initial stock of liquor from out of state in his own name. His political foes made capital out of his mistake. Dow corrected it. But it was too late. Rumors spread suggesting that Dow stood to profit from the liquor that the agency was going to sell. On the night of June 2, 1855, an angry mob assembled at the liquor agency and started stoning it. They demanded that the liquor Dow had purchased be destroyed and that he be arrested for violation of his own law. Dow, always quick to look to force in defense of morality, assembled the local militia. Some of the rioters broke into the agency; he ordered his troops to fire. Seven rioters were wounded and one killed. Efforts to hold Dow criminally responsible for the rioter's death came to nothing. But the affair did a lot of harm to the prohibitionist cause. Within a year the governor of the state, a supporter of the Maine Law, was defeated in his campaign for reelection; the state legislature revised the law to allow innkeepers to sell liquor by the drink and a limited number of retailers to sell alcoholic beverages for home use; no further states adopted Maine laws for themselves.[9]

---

[8] The same is true today, when we readily blame alcoholic drink for social problems of which it is in fact a symptom rather than a cause; this is discussed in the Introduction.

[9] Despite the tendency of the Maine laws to engender rather than reduce the level

It is not surprising that Dow resorted to violence, as he was under pressure to ensure that the Maine Law was properly enforced within the city of Portland, which he had made the focus of international attention. But even with occasional recourse to force, Dow failed to achieve his avowed aim. Soon after prohibition was introduced, a number of attractions similar to the Massachusetts striped pig were established, and attained a comparable degree of popularity. Alternatively, a citizen of Portland in search of a drink could pay a set fee for admission to a room in the wall of which a wheel revolved and produced a glass of rum. Or he could pay a storekeeper three or five cents for a soft drink and have some liquor thrown in free. Or he could walk down a back alleyway in search of one of the original bootleggers: a peripatetic salesman who carried a flask or two of liquor in the leg of his boot.

In 1871 the English writer Justin McCarthy published a report on a visit to Portland, in which he described at length the open evasion of the Maine Law. McCarthy saw that "anybody who wanted drink could go and have it whenever and almost wherever he pleased." He spoke to the current mayor of Portland, Mr. Kingsbury, who told him that "he is in favor of the principle of repression, and he thinks that the present repressive law is about as good as could well be devised. But he frankly admitted that he could never make up his mind as to whether there is less drinking in Portland under the repressive law than there would be without it. He was for several years the judge of the very cases to which the law applies. He began as an ardent repressionist, and was convinced that the law could be made a reality but for a lack of zeal on the part of the executive. But he owned . . . that experience had changed his views on that head. He had done his very best to enforce the law, but he was not now convinced that he had really diminished by one the number of grogshops in Portland."

Having traveled widely in the state, McCarthy concluded that "the repression of liquor-selling is possible and does exist in small villages

---

of alcohol-related violence, prohibitionists continued to claim that most crime was caused by drink and that if they could only get rid of the drink they would also get rid of the crime. If necessary, they supported their arguments with bald lies. In Kansas, where prohibition had been introduced in 1881, it was claimed at the end of the decade that this had led to a dramatic diminution of crime. In truth, Kansas had more prisoners in its penitentiary and county jails in proportion to its population in 1890 than it had had in 1880, and a higher ratio of prisoners to population than neighboring states where prohibition was not in force.

under peculiarly favourable circumstances [but] hitherto it has proved a failure in all towns which swell beyond the dimensions of a village. Where it is least needed it is practicable; where it is much needed it is impracticable." People who would naturally have been inclined to give up drinking without the assistance of a prohibitory law did not object to its passage because it did not affect them, while people who wanted to be allowed to continue drinking and therefore opposed prohibition found no difficulty in evading it. Ergo, prohibition was pointless.

Thomas Nichols, exiled to England during the Civil War, explained to his new audience that the Maine Law "failed of its intended effect because it went utterly beyond the bounds of constitutional legislation. It not only failed to answer the end proposed—it undoubtedly increased the evil of drinking and drunkenness. When the retailing of liquor was prohibited, men bought by wholesale; the express companies were loaded down with orders for kegs of liquor brought from other states. A thousand devices of smuggling were resorted to; people had no respect for a law which they looked upon as an unconstitutional violation of personal rights. They openly defied or secretly nullified it. In a few months it became a huge joke and a dead letter. The temperance reform, by moral suasion, did great good everywhere, and especially in the small villages and rural districts. The Maine Law increased the consumption of liquor and hurt the cause of temperance."

At the beginning of the 1890s, the English lawyer Evelyn Fanshawe investigated the workings of prohibition in the seven states that retained it, the consequences of prohibition in the ten states that had tried but abandoned it, and the operation of various forms of alcohol control laws elsewhere in the country. He interviewed a large number of people of all persuasions. Some told him that they thought prohibition had "greatly diminished the whole volume of drinking" and had led to "a marked improvement in the circumstances of workingmen and their families." Others told him differently. One parish clergyman, an advocate of temperance but not prohibition, who had lived in three different states in which the trade in alcohol was banned, told Fanshawe that "he had always noticed that system to be accompanied by an increase of home drinking and an increased tendency among young men to take to liquor. . . . It was, he said, a general rule, rather than an exception, that a stock of liquor came into houses where none had previously been kept."

In Georgia, under a "local option" law, the city of Atlanta had voted to go dry in 1885 and had remained so for two years. This had led to the development of an extensive "jug" trade. "Men in business, clerks, and others," Fanshawe was informed, "drank to an unprecedented extent, having bottles of whiskey open in their houses and offices, with which they regaled themselves and their friends, and much drunkenness resulted among men who before had not been at all in the habit of drinking. Some, it is said, fell into the habit, through a mere spirit of opposition to a law which sought to coerce them."

But then, it was suggested, the Maine Law was never really intended to work—or, rather, it did not particularly matter whether it did so or not. In the face of immigration from heavy-drinking Irish and Germans, the Maine Law served to validate the values of native-born Americans in much the same way as laws against adultery and dueling that were then passing through most state legislatures. Its job was to teach people how to behave, not necessarily to compel them to do so. Many of the citizens of Maine to whom McCarthy had spoken about the workings of prohibition "frankly admitted that the law was virtually inoperative [yet] still wished to have it retained. They were in favor of it partly as a protest against the vice of drunkenness, just as in some of the American states I have heard men applaud the penalties against simple fornication." And Fanshawe was told by William Sprague, a former governor of Rhode Island and chief of police at Narrangansett, that prohibition in the state (where it had been introduced in 1886) "may be compared to the elective franchise accorded the late slave; inoperative, but a powerful menace to the unbalanced mental structure."

Fanshawe was not so sure about the wisdom of this approach. "One point often urged for legal prohibition," he acknowledged, "is its influence as an educator of the young in the direction of a sentiment that total abstinence as a personal habit is right, and that the use of intoxicating liquor in any form or quantity as a beverage is wrong. . . . Upon this question of the educational bearing of prohibition, it must be said that much weight is attached by its opponents to the demoralising effects of a law which treats as a crime what many do not regard as wrong; which is often scandalously disregarded; and the transgressors of which, even when their offence is proven in court, in many cases cannot be convicted and punished. Such a law, it is urged, breeds contempt for all law. As things now are, it certainly is not a very uncommon thing to hear young men discussing the comparative ease or difficulty of obtaining beer and whiskey in different parts of the state, and the various methods adopted for evading the law, in a way that supplies arguments to those who hold that the educational influence of prohibition is not universally beneficial."

Much the same was true for national Prohibition. To a certain extent, it did not matter whether it worked or not. It was principally intended to be symbolic—to demonstrate to a recent influx of heavy-drinking immigrants from southern and eastern Europe the right way of living in American society, to assert the primacy of the principles of the white Anglo-Saxon Protestant family, among which the consumption of alcoholic drinks had no part to play.

Like the Maine Law, however, Prohibition, far from training the population to accept that alcoholic drink was a bad thing and should be abandoned, largely served to teach them that laws did not need to be obeyed.

William S. Kenyon, one of the members of the Wickersham Commission that investigated the enforcement of Prohibition, expressed his concern that the disregard for the prohibitory laws, so flagrantly demonstrated by those who ought to have been the leaders of society, offered a very bad example to the rest of the population. "It has been frankly stated before our commission that many of these people of great wealth and prominence will not obey the prohibition laws, do not intend to, and boast of the fact that they will not," he explained. "If that is to be the standard of law observance, our government will fail. The forger and the bank robber, the highwayman and the embezzler, do not believe in laws that restrain them. There is no more reason why what is termed the 'upper crust' of society should choose the laws they will obey than the same privilege should be extended to the 'under crust.' "

The Wickersham Commission reported in the middle of the Depression, when millions of men found themselves out of work, and the ruling classes had begun to fear that law and order might well collapse altogether. Prohibition, it now appeared, was not merely a joke, but a dangerous one. After all, it was not such a long journey from refusing to obey the prohibitory laws to rebelling against the rule of law in general. No wonder efforts were made to placate the workers by giving them back their 3.2 percent beer.[10]

John D. Rockefeller Jr. had been a lifelong teetotaler and a long-term supporter of Prohibition. Together with his father, he had con-

---

[10]This is discussed in the previous chapter.

tributed the best part of a million dollars to the work of the prohibitionist Anti-Saloon League. But then, in the summer of 1932, Rockefeller made the dramatic announcement that he had changed his mind and now believed that Prohibition should be repealed. As he explained, when the Eighteenth Amendment that introduced Prohibition had been passed, he had "earnestly hoped" that it would be supported by public opinion. But this had turned out not to be the case. Instead, what had happened was that "a vast army of lawbreakers has been recruited and financed on a colossal scale; that many of our best citizens, piqued at what they regarded as an infringement of their private rights, have openly and unabashedly disregarded the Eighteenth Amendment; that as an inevitable result respect for all law has greatly lessened; that crime has increased to an unprecedented degree." Although he believed that Prohibition had brought some benefits to society, as had been promised by those who had campaigned for its introduction, Rockefeller expressed the "profound conviction" that these benefits "are more than outweighed by the evils that have developed and flourished since its adoption, evils which unless promptly checked are likely to lead to conditions unspeakably worse than those which prevailed before."

Rockefeller's very public change of heart played a major part in hardening both public and political opinion against Prohibition, and in leading to the passage of Repeal in the following year. In his introduction to the report that laid out the framework for the alcohol control laws that were to replace Prohibition, he emphasized the importance of establishing laws that would be obeyed. "Rightly," he wrote, "the first objective is the abolition of lawlessness. Any program offered in lieu of the Eighteenth Amendment must make that its chief aim, even if—and I weigh carefully what I say—the immediate result is temporarily away from temperance."

Whereas Prohibition had been established on the principle that laws should first be passed that set out an ideal model for public behavior and then efforts should be made to persuade people to obey them, post-Repeal alcohol control laws followed a different premise—almost as though it were first determined what degree of control the public would be prepared to accept and then a system was established that would prove acceptable. It was argued in some quarters that the control of the consumption of drink had effectively been abandoned for the sake of the higher cause of maintaining social order. The Rockefeller Report was reviewed by one moderate prohibitionist under the title "Fitting the Law to the Lawless," with the observation that "the guiding principle in the report is the desire to construct a system which will be satisfactory to the people who want to buy and drink liquor. . . . I find in all its pages not one glimmer of hope that anyone will obey, or ought to be expected to obey any law that does not tell him to do what he was going to do anyway."

This proved something of an exaggeration, however. National Prohibition might have been repealed, but this did not mean that every adult American could legally buy alcoholic beverages within his own locality. The principal effect of Repeal was to replace federal authority over the sale of drink by controls at a more local level. Not only was the management of the sale of drink assigned to the states, in the majority of states it was devolved even further, to the counties. A system of "local option" was introduced which allowed the inhabitants of individual counties to vote on whether they wanted to allow the sale of drink within their locality. Many counties voted to go wet. Others, especially in the South, and most especially in the rural counties where antialcohol sentiment remained strongest, decided to stay dry.

Several states, moreover, retained their own form of prohibition after the federal prohibitory laws were repealed. Fifteen states continued to proscribe the sale of spirits "by the drink" in bars and restaurants. Three states banned altogether the sale of anything stronger than "nonintoxicating" 3.2 percent beer: Kansas, where the prohibition of spirits for home consumption was repealed in 1948 but the sale of liquor by the drink in bars remained forbidden until 1987; Oklahoma, where prohibition of package sales remained in force until 1959, after which the sale of liquor by the drink continued to be banned until 1985; and Mississippi, where all sales remained forbidden until 1966.

As the experience of state prohibition in Mississippi amply demonstrates, the hypocrisy with which national Prohibition was associated did not die with Repeal. The fact that the trade in alcoholic beverages remained illegal in Mississippi did not prevent anyone who wanted a drink from obtaining one. In 1944 the state legislature passed an act that enabled it to levy a ten percent tax on the sale of "any tangible property whatsoever, the sale or distribution of which is prohibited by law," the express purpose of this measure being "to discourage black markets." In fact, it achieved precisely the opposite. It enabled the bootleggers to go about their business without much fear of prosecution or other encumbrance, as long as they paid a tax to the state. It enabled the government to raise extra revenue, which rose from half a million dollars in the year in which the act came into effect to $4.5 million dollars in the last year before prohibition was repealed, twenty years later. It enabled those who supported the maintenance of prohibition to rest comfortable in the conviction that it remained in force. And it enabled people who wanted to buy liquor to do so more cheaply and more conveniently than their counterparts in states where the trade was legal. "Where else can you get your fifth and your tank filled up at the same time without even getting out of the car?" wondered one contented citizen. "And that ain't all. I can buy anything you name cheaper than you can up north or even in Louisiana, where our stuff comes from. Our boys don't need any fine store, advertising, and the likes o' that. They might have to help out the sheriff now and then, but he's got a small family and don't need too much. So a po' man here don't have to drink rotgut that might ruin his health and make him dependent on the county. He can afford a bottle of stamped whiskey."

This system survived until 1966, when, at the beginning of February, Governor Paul B. Johnson told the Mississippi legislature that it could not go on having its cake and eating it for any longer. "It is now high time for someone to stand boldly in the front door and talk plainly, sensibly, and honestly about whiskey, prohibition, black-market taxes, payola, and all the other many-colored hues that make up Mississippi's illegal aurora borealis of prohibition," he declared. The state, he added, "without a shadow of a doubt is the laughingstock of the nation as far as its so-called prohibition farce is concerned. This fact does us no good in other areas, such as economic development, tourism, or any other field of endeavor."

Three days after Johnson made his stand, sheriff's officers raided the Junior League Carnival Ball at the Jackson Country Club—attended by the governor and many of the state's leading citizens—and removed $10,000 worth of champagne and other "exotic wines and liquors." When this case came before the Hinds County Court in April, the judge ruled that by systematically taxing and regulating the trade in illegal liquor the state had already effectively repealed prohibition, adding that to have ruled otherwise would have meant that "this court would have to bury its head in the hypocritical sands of the past." Within a few weeks the state House of Representatives passed a bill to repeal prohibition. This was signed by the governor on May 21. Prohibition was replaced by local option, and the right of wholesaling was reserved to the state. The first counties voted to legalize the sales of liquor in

July. The Mississippi Baptist Convention asked each of its member churches to do all they could within their county to oppose moves to legalize the sales of liquor, and set aside July 31 as a day of prayer. By the middle of August, however, 28 of the state's 82 counties had already voted to go wet—more than in Kentucky, and many more than in Tennessee, although these two states were where much of the liquor drunk in Mississippi had been (and continued to be) produced. The director of the new Alcohol Beverage Control authority stated that bootleggers who had previously operated openly and paid their taxes to the government would mostly be granted licences to retail liquor, but that bootleggers who had operated in secret and had not paid their black-market taxes like good citizens would be barred.

Although, after 1966, no state continued to prohibit the sale of alcohol altogether, in ten states—Virginia, West Virginia, North Carolina, South Carolina, Tennessee, Arkansas, Texas, and Utah as well as Kansas and Oklahoma—the sale of spirits by the drink in bars remained forbidden. Moreover, the effect of local option ensured that most of the South remained dry. In all, fifteen states still had some dry counties, and nearly one quarter of the counties in the United States banned the sale of spirits within their locality.

This did not, of course, mean that the sale of spirits was prevented, much less their consumption. "Local option does not accomplish its avowed purpose, which is to create prohibition in a limited area," explained Randolph W. Childs in *Making Repeal Work*. "The man who lives in a dry community can get a drink either by going to a neighboring community or patronizing a bootlegger. . . . The practical effect of stopping the sale of alcoholic beverages in a community is that drinking is done behind closed doors, free from public observation and police control. The 'dive' supplants the licensed drinking establishment."

Local option also encouraged the illicit production of homemade spirits. Far from declining after the repeal of Prohibition, in some areas moonshining increased, because producers were no longer competing with untaxed spirits smuggled by land from Canada or by sea from the West Indies and Europe but with spirits on which taxes had been paid to the state. In the 1950s it was estimated that 70 million gallons of moonshine were being distilled each year in the backwoods of the South, one fifth of the spirits produced in the country. This illicit liquor often tasted unpleasant and could be harmful. Habitual moonshine drinkers sometimes went blind as a result of the toxic chemicals they had ingested. But this appeared not to have discouraged people from drinking it.[11]

" 'Dry' as the South may be in some spots," wrote the distinguished foreign correspondent John Gunther, "it is also the hardest-drinking region I have ever seen in the world, and the area with the worst drinking habits by far. There are no bars permitted in most cities; hence, people drink by the private bottle, and, as always, hypocrisy begets disorderly behavior. Never in Port Said, Shanghai, or Marseilles have I seen the kind of drinking that goes on in Atlanta, Houston, or Memphis every Saturday night—with officers in uniform vomiting in hotel lobbies, seventeen-year-old girls screaming with hysteria in public elevators, men and women of the country-club category being carried bodily off the dance floor by disinterested waiters. . . .

"Everywhere I went in the South I asked why it was so dry, legally speaking, and I got a considerable variety of answers. One was that Southerners fear outbursts of drunkenness by Negroes. Surely what this means is that they also fear outbursts of drunkenness by themselves. . . . The South contains a great number of profoundly schizoid people; the whole region is a land of paranoia, full of the mentally sick; most Southerners feel a deep necessity to hate something, if necessary even themselves. Their hatred (= fear) of alcohol is partly a reflection of bad conscience: the South feels that liquor will release is own most dangerous inhibitions. The Negro problem is inextricably involved; so is the sexual problem. A Southerner will, perhaps without expressing it consciously or concretely, work out an equation something like the following: 'We are not going to give up the Negro; therefore we must give up something else. We will not give up fundamentalism, sex, white supremacy or slavery; so we give up rationality instead.' "[12]

---

[11]The production of moonshine, although much reduced, continues today. Distillers in Franklin County, Virginia, the self-proclaimed "moonshine capital of the world," make about 750,000 gallons a year. Even in those places where whiskey can legally be purchased it is cheaper to buy the illicit version: At about $20 a gallon, the price of moonshine is less than the state and federal taxes levied on a gallon of legitimately distilled liquor.

[12]The fear that black men, stimulated by alcohol, would attack white women, had played in major part in the introduction of prohibition in the South. As Congressman Hobson from Alabama explained when speaking in the House of Representatives in 1914 on his resolution for a prohibition amendment to the Constitution, "Liquor will actually make a brute out of the Negro, causing him to commit unnatural crimes. The effect is the same on the white man, though the white man being further evolved it takes a longer time to reduce him to the same level."

Even the most prejudiced Yankee would have difficulty in arguing that the South remains filled with "schizoid" and "paranoid" people today. Nevertheless, these contradictory aspects of the southern character help to explain the continuing prevalence of local option in the region. Many God-fearing inhabitants of the Bible Belt[13] appear not to see a contradiction in personally consuming alcohol while continuing to support the maintenance of legal prohibition in their locality. For them there exists a clear distinction between the private consumption of alcohol and its public display.

The state with the greatest number of dry counties today is Kentucky, where of 121 counties 75 are totally dry and a further 24 prohibit the sale of spirits but allow wine and beer. There are, however, no restrictions on drinking in private and a person can keep as much stock in his home as he wants or can afford. Individual counties frequently hold referenda on whether to change from dry to wet, or vice versa. It is not necessarily wise, however, to be the person who proposes holding a referendum in a dry county on whether it should go wet. According to Jimmy Russell, distiller of Wild Turkey bourbon, "Whoever called for a wet vote used to be regarded as a leper. Preachers would get up and name you in front of their congregation. You were just an evil person trying to force liquor down the throats of little children."

Logically, one might say that liquor is more likely to be poured down children's throats in a dry county than in a wet one. After all, in dry counties the sale of alcohol is forbidden, so there are no laws setting a minimum age at which people can drink; it is wet counties, rather than dry ones, that impose a minimum drinking age of twenty-one.[14] But that is not how those people who insist that the counties in which they live should remain dry see it. A few years ago a vote was held on whether Mercer County should go wet, and the voters decided that it should remain dry. Bud Denman, the manager of the Beaumont Inn

---

There is some evidence of white people supporting prohibition in the South because they believed this would keep liquor away from blacks while at the same time provide a way for white people to obtain it. One of the motives behind the establishment of a state liquor monopoly in Alabama after Repeal was to prevent blacks from purchasing alcoholic beverages, since the liquor store officers would simply refuse to serve them.

[13]Religious attitudes to alcoholic drink are discussed in the Conclusion.

[14]The same applies to restrictions on the sale of alcohol on Sunday. It is often said in the South that the only real difference between a dry and a wet county is that in a dry county you can get a drink on a Sunday. For a critique of the minimum drinking age, see later in this chapter.

country house hotel told how "I had a friend who had three little girls. He used to go off and buy liquor by the case. When the vote came up I said, 'Charley, you can't vote against it.' But he did. He said, 'I'd rather raise my girls in a dry county.' "

The prevalence of dry counties in Kentucky is especially ironical considering the economic importance to the state of bourbon production.[15] Distilleries in Kentucky employ 6,500 people, and bourbon is the state's leading export, worth even more than tobacco. But it is illegal to buy bourbon in the counties in which they are produced: They all prohibit spirits. A person who takes the trouble to visit a bourbon distillery cannot end his tour by tasting the product or buying some bottles to take home, even though they are tantalizingly displayed by the cash register and the tour includes glossy videos of bourbon being poured into tumblers over ice.

For more than sixty years after the repeal of national Prohibition, the same was true in neighboring Tennessee, where the most famous American whiskey, Jack Daniel's, is distilled, as well as the less well known George Dickel brand. Jack Daniel's did spend a number of years trying to obtain permission to sell its product at the distillery but did not achieve any success until the early 1990s, when its efforts were supplemented by those of United Distillers, the new owners of George Dickel. Eventually, heavy lobbying in the state legislature by the two distilleries won the passage of a bill to permit them to sell to visitors special commemorative bottles that were not available elsewhere.[16] These went on sale at the beginning of 1995. The distilleries did not, however, press for visitors to be allowed to sample their products, because they knew that such a measure would never be passed and because they were concerned that someone who tried a sample and was then involved in an automobile accident might sue the distillery. Chris Morris of United Distillers believes that it would help in the marketing of George Dickel if it were allowed to give visitors samples to taste but "the people who come through understand the climate we live in—they laugh about it."

In 1997 Roger Brashears, the promotions manager of Jack Daniel's, was asked by a journalist working for the London *Independent*, who

---

[15]The history of bourbon is discussed in the next chapter.

[16]Even then, a further vote had to be taken in Moore County, in which Jack Daniel's was situated. This was not necessary in the city of Tullahoma, the home of George Dickel, as it had already voted to allow the sale of spirits.

had expressed her amazement at the number of dry counties in Tennessee, whether anyone drank at all in the state. "Yes, ma'am," he replied. "It's just that we don't do it in front of each other."[17]

The hypocrisy that was encouraged by national Prohibition, and which continues in the South, survives today in the rest of the country in the form of partial prohibition to people under the age of twenty-one.

In colonial and republican America, the consumption of alcohol by children had not been regarded as problematic. Many parents taught their children to drink at a very young age, even as babies. As soon as a toddler was old enough to sip from a cup, he would be given the sugary residue from the bottom of a glass of spirits. Parents intended this early exposure to alcohol to accustom their offspring to the taste of liquor, to encourage them to accept the idea of drinking small amounts, and thus to protect them from becoming drunkards.

Also, drinking by children was regarded as a manifestation of the independent spirit that was an essential concomitant of liberty and equality. "One of the greatest evils of a republican form of government is a loss of that subordination in society which is essentially necessary to render a country agreeable to foreigners," wrote Charles William Janson, an Englishman who emigrated to America toward the end of the eighteenth century but did not enjoy his time there and eventually returned home. "The meaning of liberty and equality, in the opinion of the vulgar, consists in impudent freedom, and uncontrolled licentiousness; while boys assume the air of fully-grown coxcombs. This is not to be wondered at, where most parents make it a principle never to check those ungovernable passions which are born with us, or to correct the growing vices of their children. Often I have, with horror, seen boys, whose dress indicated wealthy parents, intoxicated, shouting and swearing in the public streets."[18]

Some restrictions on drinking by children were included in temperance legislation in the second half of the nineteenth century, but only to prevent their being exploited by liquor sellers; in many states children continued to be permitted to enter saloons provided they were accom-

---

[17] In one survey in 1986 in Tucson, Arizona, 85 percent of people questioned by market researchers told them that they did not drink beer. But an examination of the city's garbage cans found that 75 percent had beer cans in them.

[18] American children are still generally considered today by European visitors to be laxly brought up—except in respect to the consumption of alcohol.

panied by their parents, and there was nothing to stop them from drinking at home, if their parents allowed them to do so. As one North Carolina court explained, the purpose of the statute limiting sales of alcohol to minors was "not to prevent . . . minors from having . . . intoxicants for proper purposes at proper times, but to prevent dealers from supplying them."

In this period the liquor dealers were the criminals, and children were their innocent victims. So different from attitudes today. The transformation in the perception of drinking by young people can be demonstrated by the progress of legislation in California. This state passed its first law concerning youthful drinking in 1872, banning the sale or gift of alcohol to children under sixteen for consumption on the premises, but exempting parents who gave alcohol to their children. In 1891 legislation was passed that raised the age to eighteen and deleted the parental exemption. In 1903 all visits to saloons by people under eighteen were banned, thus preventing minors from buying alcohol even for consumption off the premises. Then came national Prohibition, which lasted from 1920 to 1933. In 1935 a law was passed making it a misdemeanor to sell or give alcohol to anyone under twenty-one, with the exception of parents. In 1937 the parental exemption was deleted and minors themselves were made guilty of a misdemeanor if they purchased or consumed alcohol in a bar. In 1951 minors became subject to prosecution for possessing alcohol in public places. In 1956 the state constitution was amended to forbid the sale or gift of alcohol to anyone under twenty-one, and to prohibit anyone under twenty-one from purchasing an alcoholic beverage or entering and remaining on licensed premises without lawful business. At the same time, a constitutional clause that prohibited the sale of wine and spirits in bars was repealed. Here, the drinking-age issue was used as a smoke screen for the real purpose of the vote on the constitutional amendment—the legalization of the consumption by adults of liquor by the drink.

Thus, the motivations behind the continuing prohibition on drinking by children since the repeal of Prohibition have been very different from those of the temperance reformers who campaigned to have Prohibition introduced. The sociologist Mike Males has argued in *The Scapegoat Generation* that young people have been made responsible for the problems of American society. "The political failure of Prohibition meant that American adults would increasingly focus justifications for alcohol policy less on the perils of drunkenness and more on the tenuous concept that adults can drink properly but youths cannot or should not," he explains. "The foundations of today's anti–teen-drinking crusade are not logic, science, teenage safety, or responsibility with alcohol—none of which is has furthered—but the needs of the modern adult."

Until the late 1960s a minimum drinking age of twenty-one applied in almost all states. However, the Vietnam War proved a major catalyst for social change, and transformed attitudes toward young people. It began to appear hypocritical to both voters and legislators that men who were deemed old enough to fight and die in Vietnam—where the average age of serving personnel was nineteen—should be regarded as too young to drink, and too young to vote. The voting age was lowered nationally to eighteen and approximately half the states lowered the minimum drinking age to either eighteen or nineteen. When the war ended in 1973, legislators and older voters decided that they could no longer be accused of hypocrisy and the movement to lower the drinking age in the remaining states came to a halt. Within a few years it was going back up again. In 1971 a new federal agency had been established to deal with alcohol-related problems, the National Institute on Alcohol Abuse and Alcoholism (NIAAA). This agency needed to create publicity for its activities in order to ensure that it was given the money necessary for survival. It picked on teenage drinking. In 1973 the NIAAA commissioned a survey on teenage alcohol abuse, the results of which were widely reported. A *Time* cover story quoted Morris Chafetz, the director of the institute, as saying that "youths are moving from a wide range of other drugs to the most devastating drug—the one most widely misused of all, alcohol." The following year NBC broadcast a two-hour TV special entitled *Sarah T—Portrait of a Teenage Acoholic*. As a consequence of the interest it succeeded in generating in the subject, the NIAAA announced in 1977 the development of a five-year $83-million National Teenage Alcohol Education Program.

In the same year an exhaustive study of academic research into teenage drinking was carried out on behalf of the NIAAA. After reviewing some 1,100 documents, the authors concluded that there was no evidence of increased teenage drinking, nor of a growing problem as a result of teenage drinking. Nevertheless, Ernest Noble, who had succeeded Chafetz as the director of the institute, testified to Senate committees that "we have a devastating problem with alcohol among youth in our country. . . . We feel that the problem . . . is of epidemic proportion"; and that "every indication points to the conclusion that the teenagers in our country are not only drinking more, but that they are drinking earlier and experiencing more problems with alcohol."

Since these statements ran contrary to the evidence that his own researchers had collected, it is clear that Noble was thinking at least as much about the needs of the NIAAA as about the needs of teenagers. The NIAAA was a young agency, which had to compete for funds with older, better established agencies at a time when the federal budget for alcohol problems was much lower than for drug abuse or for mental health. By focusing on the emotionally charged topic of teenage drinking and claiming that this was a growing problem that urgently required an injection of funds, the NIAAA obtained the money it wanted.

The suggestion that teenage drinking was a growing problem that might partly be remedied by raising the minimum drinking age back to twenty-one received support from many health professionals and especially from members of the increasingly prominent discipline of sociology. Hitherto doctors had regarded alcohol-related problems largely in terms of a supposed disease called alcoholism whose victims were known as alcoholics,[19] but now sociologists pointed out that alcohol caused quite a lot of problems, not only among alcoholics but also among people who consumed large amounts of drink in a social context, and among people who drank much less than alcoholics did. In effect, sociologists challenged the medical ownership of alcohol-related problems by arguing that it was more of a social than medical problem, and therefore one over which they ought to be able to exert control.

They found support for their beliefs in an obscure statistical theory known as the Ledermann hypothesis,[20] which stated that there was a direct connection between the level of alcohol consumption in any given society and the amount of alcohol-related harm. They promoted this theory, extending it into the argument that if the average level of consumption can be reduced, then so can the amount of harm. One apparently simple means of reducing consumption would be to remove young people between eighteen and twenty-one from the equation by forbidding them from drinking. Sociologists therefore favored an increase in the minimum drinking age.

The public remained unaware of the Ledermann hypothesis and con-

---

[19] This is discussed in the Introduction.
[20] This is discussed in the previous chapter.

tinued to believe that alcoholism was a disease that affected individuals. They were unaffected by the palace coup carried out by sociologists and gave only marginal consideration to the activities of the NIAAA. But they did pay a great deal of attention to drink-driving[21] once it had been forced upon them.

The publicity that was now given to drink-driving, it must be said, had nothing to do with a perceived increase in alcohol-related accidents among young people, or among people in general, but arose from one person's conviction that the problem of drink-driving was not being dealt with seriously enough.

In May 1980, thirteen-year-old Cari Lightner was killed by a hit-and-run driver while walking along a bicycle path in Fair Oaks, California, a suburb of Sacramento. The driver was later found to be intoxicated. He was on probation for previous drink-driving convictions and had been let out on bail for another hit-and-run offense a few days before hitting Lightner. Cari's mother, Candy, was shocked to discover the leniency with which he had been handled. She asked legislators to pass tougher laws, but they did not listen. She had previously shown no interest in politics. But now she became a lobbyist. She held press conferences, testified before legislative committees, and organized what was to become Mothers Against Drunk Drivers (MADD).

MADD was incorporated as a nonprofit organization in August 1980. It attracted an enormous amount of publicity and by billing itself as a victims' rights organization—"the voice of the victim"—managed to obtain a great deal of money through direct mail solicitations. Lightner became preoccupied with maximizing media attention to what she called the "dirty little secret" of drink-driving, claiming that 250,000 American lives had been lost in alcohol-related car accidents in the preceding decade, that a million crippling or serious injuries resulted from similar accidents every year, and that drink-driving was the leading cause of death for sixteen- to twenty-four-year-olds.

One of her demands was that the minimum drinking age should be established nationally at twenty-one. This was just one of several

---

[21]In this book the British term "drink-driving" has been preferred to the American "drunk driving." The latter is an emotionally charged term that implies that everyone convicted of drinking and driving is drunk, which is true only insofar as the drink-driving laws define a person who has broken them as being ipso facto drunk. Whether that person really is incapable of driving a motor vehicle is a completely different matter.

changes she called for; others included mandatory prison sentences for repeat offenders and bans on happy hours in bars. Nevertheless, as the NIAAA had already found, teenage drinking was an emotionally charged issue and one that was guaranteed to attract media attention—which was exactly what Lightner needed. She appeared on many television shows and was interviewed in hundreds of newspaper and magazine articles. And she lobbied the government. Under pressure from Lightner and other members of MADD, in 1982 President Reagan appointed a presidential commission on drink-driving. This recommended that a national minimum drinking age of twenty-one should be established. The federal government did not, however, possess the constitutional authority to pass a minimum drinking age. This authority lay with the individual states. The federal government therefore sought to force the states to raise the minimum drinking age to twenty-one by roundabout means. Legislation was introduced to require the secretary of transportation to withhold federal highway construction funds from states that failed to introduce a minimum drinking age of twenty-one. Initially, the president opposed this measure, since he believed in the devolution of central authority, whereas the bill allowed the federal government to impinge on state's rights. But he was persuaded to change his mind largely because of the testimony of MADD in support of the bill, which convinced his advisers that it had been made into a "sleeping giant" of an "apple-pie issue" that he could not afford to oppose.

The president signed the National Minimum Drinking Age Act in the summer of 1984. Under this act, a proportion of federal highway funds would be withheld from states that had failed to introduce a minimum drinking age of twenty-one by fall 1986. A senior White House official said after the signing ceremony that it was not clear that the new law would compel states to raise their drinking ages, adding that some states, such as Florida, were resisting change because they considered it unfair to allow residents to vote and serve in the armed services at the age of eighteen but not to drink in public. In New York, where the minimum drinking age was nineteen, John J. Marchi, a Republican state senator for Staten Island and head of the powerful state Senate Finance Committee, described the new law as a "little prohibition."

At the time that the new act was passed, twenty-three states had a minimum drinking age of twenty-one, and a further nine states as well as the District of Columbia restricted sales of spirits but not beer and wine to people aged twenty-one and over. Most of the remaining states, including New York and Florida, were persuaded by the threatened loss of federal funds to raise their minimum drinking age to twenty-one within the prescribed two-year time period.

By early 1987, however, six states were still resisting what they regarded as a federal impingement upon their rights. South Dakota was fighting the National Minimum Drinking Age Act in the courts, arguing that it was unconstitutional because it ran counter to the Twenty-First Amendment to the Constitution by which Prohibition had been repealed and control over drink sales had devolved to the states. "People still want to have some independence and to be able to control their own destiny," explained Craig Eichstadt, an assistant attorney general in the state. But South Dakota was going to raise the age to twenty-one if it lost its court challenge, because it needed the federal highway funds. As Governor George Mickelson had explained, it would succumb to the federal "blackmail."

In June 1987 the Supreme Court rejected the argument of South Dakota and upheld the act. South Dakota raised its minimum drinking age to twenty-one, as did the other resistant states. Wyoming held out on its own from July 1987 to March 1988, but its isolation caused legislators in the state to grow concerned that it was becoming a destination for young drinkers; reports from state highway patrols indicated that officers were having increasing problems with nineteen- and twenty-year-olds coming in from other states to drink. Eventually, Wyoming, too, succumbed.

This did not mean, however, that resistance by individual states to a federally imposed minimum drinking age had ended. Indeed, rebellion against the national minimum drinking age has served as a convenient totem for states to demonstrate that they retain the right to govern their own affairs. Louisiana had been among the states that had introduced a minimum drinking age of twenty-one in 1985 without any great enthusiasm and principally as a result of "blackmail" by the federal government. As it had raised its minimum drinking age only under duress, the state government was not much concerned about the existence of a loophole: Although it was illegal for anyone under twenty-one to buy liquor, it remained perfectly legal for a bartender to sell it to him. As a result, alcoholic drinks effectively remained available to young people aged eighteen and over. Neither the federal government nor campaigning groups such as MADD were pleased by this loophole, and they placed increasing pressure on the Louisiana government to close it. Eventually, in 1995, the state criminalized the sale of alcoholic drinks to underage drinkers. But this law was immediately challenged by bar owners as well as those young people who now found alcoholic drinks denied to them. They claimed that the new law violated a clause in the state constitution that stated that no law will "arbitrarily, capriciously or unreasonably discriminate against a person" on account of his age. Before the state government could pass such a law, they argued, it needed to exhaust other, less discriminatory methods of addressing alcohol problems, such as increased public education and tax credits for bars and restaurants that supported designated-driver programs. In March 1996, by a 4-to-3 vote, the Louisiana Supreme Court agreed. It overturned both the 1995 law criminalizing the sale of drinks to people under twenty-one and the 1985 law criminalizing the purchase. Justice Catherine Kimball said that the continued existence of a legal minimum drinking age of twenty-one would "create a situation where eighteen- to twenty-year-olds are accorded the responsibilities and obligations of an adult, but are treated as though they are still children when it comes to the purchase and public consumption of alcoholic beverages." The justices added that the state had failed to prove that imposing a minimum drinking age of twenty-one "substantially furthers the important governmental objectives of improving highway safety."

This made the federal government very angry. It pointed out to the state that it stood to lose over $17 million annually in highway support if it failed fully to enforce the minimum drinking age standard, as well as reminding officials that Louisiana ranked well above the national average for every reported category of accidents and deaths involving motor vehicles, alcohol, and teenagers. The state government responded by asking its Supreme Court to rehear the case. In July the Louisiana Supreme Court voted by 5 to 2 to reinstate the law. This time a majority of the justices decided that prohibiting alcohol to people under twenty-one did not amount to unconstitutional age discrimination. It was now definitely illegal for eighteen-, nineteen-, and twenty-year-olds to buy or even possess alcohol—although they were graciously allowed to drink at home or when accompanied by their parents.

Many other states have proved no more willing to comply with federal diktat than Louisiana. There are loopholes all over the country. In 1991 the surgeon general, Antonia C. Novello, declared publicly that the minimum drinking age standard was "largely a myth" because state laws enacted to enforce it were "riddled with loopholes, laxity and lip service." Although the National Minimum Drinking Age Act of 1984 had required all states to set their minimum ages for both purchase and possession of alcoholic drinks at twenty-one, it had, she said, allowed for exceptions, which the states had in their turn widened into "huge loopholes." For example, the federal law provided that possession of alcoholic beverages by minors might be allowed under certain conditions; as a result, minors in thirty-eight states were allowed to possess alcoholic beverages in private homes or in private clubs or when accompanied by a parent, spouse, or guardian over the age of twenty-one. Novello did acknowledge that it would be "too prohibitionist" to enforce laws against underage drinking in private homes, but pointed out that this made it hard for the police to prevent the keg parties that had become popular among teenagers in many middle-class and affluent suburban communities.

At these parties, the entertainment is focused on the consumption of one or more kegs of beer. In an attempt to prevent them from taking place, some states have introduced "keg laws," which forbid the purchaser of a keg from allowing anyone under the age of twenty-one to consume its contents. When an adult buys a keg in these states, he is required to register his name and address with the seller, so that, if the police do find underage people drinking from the keg, they can trace its ownership and charge the owner with furnishing alcohol to a minor. One unintended consequence of this measure has been to encourage teenagers to switch from kegs to cans, which are much easier to conceal.

Moreover, in order to enforce keg laws and break up teenage drinking parties, the state police are required to trample upon the constitutional rights of property owners by gaining entry to private homes without an invitation. In the autumn of 1993 an eleven-officer task force was set up by the police in Montgomery County in Maryland (which covers the suburbs of Washington, D.C.) in order to crack down on teenage keg parties. With as much publicity as they could muster, they raided a number of homes, gave the teenagers citations, and set up checkpoints to give teenagers driving home from the parties Breathalyse tests. Several defense lawyers raised questions about the appropriateness of this action. Victor Crawford, a veteran lawyer in Montgomery, told the *Washington Post* that the police "feel that because someone is under twenty-one, they can leave the Constitution at the doorstep." Even some police officers expressed their doubts.

Walter Bader, president of the local police union, said he was worried that the department was "compromising people's rights. The problem of teenage drinking definitely should be attacked, but I have questions about barging into people's homes and confiscating beer and pouring it down sinks. If you came to my house and did that, you'd have a problem."

As one teenager pointed out to a *Washington Post* reporter who attended a raid on a party in Glenmont, "It's ridiculous. You're not going to stop it. Alcohol is just too easy to get. I mean, it's a waste of time. There are child molesters and mass murderers out there for them to go after."

But the raids went on. Among the teenagers who encountered the police at one such party in the autumn of 1995 was Sarah Gore, the sixteen-year-old daughter of Vice President Al Gore. In this case, the Montgomery task force had been alerted to the fact that teenagers were drinking at a party in Chevy Chase by a telephone call from a neighbor; there were no complaints about loud noise or any other kind of trouble. Sarah Gore was found in an automobile outside the party, holding an open can of beer, and was given a citation, as were eleven others. Yet the owners of the property had done their best to prevent children from drinking on the premises: they were home at the time, and had hired a guard to check for alcohol at the door. Teenagers were not found with alcohol inside the house but on the front lawn and in the backyard, as well as in automobiles.

Despite the best efforts of legislators and law enforcement officials, teenage drinking continues. According to an annual survey of drug and alcohol use by schoolchildren across the country conducted by social scientists at the University of Michigan and sponsored by the National Institute on Drug Abuse, a quarter of eighth-graders, 40 percent of tenth-graders, and more than half of high school seniors drink alcohol at least once a month. A law intended to prevent teenagers from drinking does not achieve its ends when teenagers not only continue to drink but do so in unsupervised situations. Instead of being allowed to drink at a party in a private home under adult supervision, children who choose to drink have to do so outside the party sitting in automobiles. In the summer in the outer suburbs, many teenagers attend "field parties," which are held in remote woods and meadows where they do not have to worry about possible damage to a parent's house and where they can consume alcohol without the same risk of being caught by the police. How, one might wonder, do they travel to and from these field parties? Might it not be wiser if they were allowed to drink at home under parental control rather than drink in an unsupervised setting and then drive home afterward?

When it comes to college students and their contemporaries—the age group that in many states was allowed to buy and drink alcohol during the 1970s and early 1980s—the law has proven even less effective, and its consequences have been even more counterproductive. Alcohol consumption is much more widespread among college students than among high school seniors. Surveys consistently find that 90 percent of students have tried alcohol and 75 percent of them consume alcoholic beverages on a regular basis. Of course, they are not allowed to drink on campus—that would be illegal. So they drink off campus instead. In order to travel off campus to drink, they often drive. As a result, a law that was imposed with the explicit purpose of preventing people under the age of twenty-one from drinking and driving appears to have achieved precisely the opposite. No wonder Thomas Petri, a Republican representative from Wisconsin, suggested in 1995 that the minimum drinking age should be lowered to nineteen. "I don't think having a twenty-one-year-old drinking age has eliminated underage drinking on college campuses," he explained. "It's just moved student drinking from supervised premises to keg parties at home."

The law that forbids people under the age of twenty-one from drinking does not merely fail to prevent them from doing so but encourages them to drink in an unhealthy manner. Lynn Zimmer, professor of sociology at Queen's College in New York City, suggests that forbidding alcohol to students has made them obsessed with it. They now plan entire weekends around how to get hold of alcohol, how to get into bars, and how to hide their drinks. "We really force young people to drink in situations where essentially nothing else is going on," she explains. "They can't go to a dance club and consume alcohol there. They can't go out to dinner in a restaurant and consume alcohol. So we're more and more pushing their alcohol consumption into these very isolated events in which that's the primary thing that's taking place. And that's the kind of situation that is conducive to heavy drinking, game drinking, macho drinking."

The minimum drinking age standard of twenty-one has produced a generation of young people who drink only to get drunk. They do not indulge in relaxed social drinking because that is something from which they are excluded by law. Instead, they drink until they throw up or pass out.

It would not be so bad if schools and colleges were able to explain to students how they might be able to drink more moderately and responsibly. But they cannot. They are allowed only to teach them that they should not drink. The Drug-Free Schools and Campuses Act requires all institutions of higher education to inform students about the health risks associated with the use of alcohol and illicit drugs, about treatment programs that are available to people who misuse them, and about the laws that forbid them from taking them at all. If a college fails to provide this information, it runs the risk of losing its federal funding. But it also risks being deprived of funds if it teaches students under the age of twenty-one how they might avoid the health risks associated with excessive or irresponsible alcohol consumption by drinking more moderately. If it did this, it could be regarded as giving its implicit consent to law breaking by the students in its charge.

This might appear an absurd state of affairs, but groups that campaign against the harmful effects of the misuse of alcohol appear to have no problems with it. As Katherine Prescott, the national president of MADD, stated in 1995, since drinking among young people has been outlawed, it would be quite wrong to advise them to drink wisely. "I don't think we should operate under the idea that they're going to do what they shouldn't do, therefore we should show them how to do it," she explained. Although many of today's campaigners against alcohol-related problems express themselves offended by attempts by members of the liquor industry to describe them as "neo-prohibitionists," it would be hard to think of a more truly neo-prohibitionist sentiment than this particular observation. Does Mrs. Prescott really believe that young people who break a law that they regard as discriminatory have only themselves to blame if they suffer as a result? This attitude is not so very different from that of the drys who supported the adulteration of industrial alcohol with poisonous methanol during Prohibition, even though they knew that people would drink the contaminated alcohol and die from it, on the grounds that these people were to blame for their own deaths. It takes a strange kind of morality to believe that if young people die after drinking alcohol, it is their own fault, because they were breaking the law, and that nothing should be done to try to stop them from killing themselves as a result of drinking immoderately or irresponsibly. After five Virginia college students died in alcohol-related accidents in one five-week stretch in the fall of 1997—two from falls and three in car crashes—Richard Cullen, the state attorney general, decided that enough was enough and it was time to consider whether it might not be wiser to lower the minimum drinking age. Cullen said that although he himself was inclined to oppose any reduction, he sympathized with those college officials who believed that lowering the minimum drinking age would encourage young people who drank to do so on campus under supervision rather than off campus and beyond any control.

At the same time, Peter Coors, the chief executive officer of Coors Brewing, the third-largest brewery in the country, argued that young people simply had to be informed of the dangers of excessive or unhealthy drinking. "We shouldn't be preaching 'Don't drink,' " he said. "We should be preaching responsible drinking. . . . Maybe the answer is lowering the drinking age so that kids learn to be responsible about drinking at a younger age. I'm not an advocate of trying to get people to drink, but kids are drinking now anyway. All we've done is criminalize them. What I'd like to see this country do is to have a situation where kids could learn to drink responsibly over time, but there should be zero tolerance for aberrant behavior associated with alcohol." Rather than respond to his arguments, Coors's opponents appear to have jumped to the conclusion that he was simply trying to increase the population to whom he might legitimately sell his product. In a joint press release, Advocates for Highway and Auto Safety and Mothers Against Drunk Driving rejected Coors's suggestion as "the single worst and most dangerous idea of the year." Laurie Leiber, the director of the Center on Alcohol Advertising, retorted that "I will ask Peter Coors to teach my kids to drink right after I ask Evel Knievel to teach them how to drive. . . . With Coors and other beer makers teaching their distorted version of responsibility our best hope for reducing the tragedy of youth drinking is to delay initiation as long as possible."

The United States has the strictest youth-drinking laws in Western civilization. In Portugal a person of any age may walk into a bar and order a drink. In France, Spain, and Italy the minimum purchase age is sixteen. In Germany and the Netherlands it is sixteen for beer and wine and eighteen for spirits. In Britain people have to be eighteen to buy alcoholic drinks from an off license (package store) or in a pub, but only sixteen to buy beer or cider in a pub to drink with a meal. And these are minimum purchase ages, not minimum drinking ages. Many countries allow minors to be given alcoholic drinks by their parents in public places such as restaurants, and only two "advanced" countries place restrictions on the minimum age at which young people may drink alcohol at home: Britain, which imposes a minimum legal drinking age of five, and the United States, which sets a minimum drinking age standard of twenty-one.

The United States is out of step with its counterparts. Other countries do not prohibit parents from introducing their children to the responsible consumption of alcohol by giving them small quantities of wine or beer to drink at home; other countries do not devote police resources to raiding private parties on the grounds that they have reason to suspect that they will find nineteen- and twenty-year-olds enjoying themselves consuming alcoholic drinks.

Yet, despite its strict laws, there are more alcohol-related problems among young people in the United States than in other industrialized Western countries. Of course, supporters of the twenty-one-year-old standard would argue that the extent of the problems justifies the severity of the laws. But might it not be the other way around? Might it not be that the strict laws exacerbate the problems? The exclusion of young people from bars until they have reached the age of twenty-one encourages them to imagine that there is something exciting about these places—to give them the appeal of forbidden fruit. If they were allowed to go into them, they might be able to see what ordinary places they really are. England and Wales have recently moved in the opposite direction from the United States and introduced legislation to permit children to go into pubs. Before 1995, children under fourteen were allowed only into separate "family rooms" or pub gardens, not the main bar area. Since then pubs have been able to apply for "children's certificates," which permit them to accommodate children of any age in a pub before nine P.M. provided they are accompanied by an adult. As the then Conservative home secretary Kenneth Clarke explained when he first announced the measure (at a press conference in a pub near Westminster Cathedral), allowing children into pubs would give them a more civilized introduction to alcohol than they might otherwise have. The new certificates, he said, "will enable children to see people drinking sensibly and perhaps stop them becoming lager louts[22] when they are allowed out on their own."

In the United States, increasing the minimum drinking age has made drinking habits more dangerous. In 1989 Henry Wechsler, a social psychologist at Harvard University's School of Public Health, investigated the drinking behavior of 1,669 freshmen at fourteen Massachusetts colleges, which he compared with a similar survey of more than

---

[22]Young men who drink too much lager and then become loutish.

7,000 students at 34 colleges across New England that he had conducted twelve years earlier.[23] In Massachusetts the minimum drinking age had been eighteen in 1977 but was raised to twenty in 1979 and to twenty-one in 1985. According to Wechsler's surveys, the proportion of students who got drunk between one and three times in a month had increased between 1977 and 1989 from 25 to 41 percent of the men and from 14 to 37 percent of the women, and the proportion who said they habitually drank in order to get drunk had risen from 20 to 40 percent of the men and from 10 to 34 percent of the women.[24] Whereas the number of frequent heavy drinkers among college freshmen remained essentially the same at 30 to 31 percent of the men and 13 to 14 percent of the women, the amount of abstainers increased markedly, while the frequent light drinkers virtually disappeared.[25] "What appears to be happening," Wechsler explained, "is the disappearance of light drinking on the college campus. Persons who drink more often than weekly are almost exclusively binge drinkers."

Young people today do not merely persist in drinking in contravention of the law, they do not just drink surreptitiously rather than in sociable surroundings, but a substantial proportion do so in rapid spurts, in the form of "binges." A more recent and more wide-ranging survey of drinking among college students carried out by Wechsler and his researchers, based on the behavior of a sample 17,592 students at 140 colleges and universities in forty states and the District of Columbia, found that 44 percent had engaged in binge drinking—defined for men as consuming five drinks in a row and for women four—in the two weeks prior to the survey. More than 80 percent of these binge drinkers reported having had a hangover since the beginning of the school year; half of them said that they had done something that they had later regretted; 40 percent reported having forgotten where they were or what they did; 30 percent admitted to having engaged in unplanned sexual activity, and 16 percent to not having used protection when they had sex; 31 percent said that they had argued with friends; 16 percent had damaged property; the same proportion had been hurt or injured. And these problems were much more prevalent among fre-

---

[23]Eight of the colleges surveyed in 1989 had been included in the 1977 research.
[24]These figures are not precisely comparable, as they relate all classes in 1977 to freshmen in 1989. The authors suggest that they may therefore underestimate the extent to which drinking has increased, on the grounds that students tend to drink more in the later stages of their college careers.
[25]Neither "frequent heavy drinker" nor "frequent light drinker" is defined.

quent binge drinkers—defined as people who had binged three or more times in the two weeks preceding the survey. About half the binge drinkers, or about one in five students overall, fell into this category. As many as 70 percent of these frequent binge drinkers cited wanting to get drunk as an important reason for drinking.

"Underage drinking and binge drinking, as shown in the 1995 study by the Harvard School of Public Health, are epidemic among our university and college students," observed Roderic Park, chancellor of the University of Colorado at Boulder. "Too often our response has been denial or piecemeal approaches to what has become an accepted cultural phenomenon among the young. . . . There is no educational requirement prior to legal alcohol purchase, such as knowledge of legal limitations and liabilities, the facts of alcohol-related crime statistics, or the role of alcohol in transmission of sexually transmitted diseases. Consumption of alcoholic beverages is a human activity largely left to trial and error, often with uncivil and sometimes tragic results." A better course, Park suggested, lay in inculcating a sense of responsibility among young people through a program of education and monitoring. He proposed that with parental permission, an underage person might apply for a "learner's permit" to allow the use of alcohol under monitored conditions, similar to a learner's driving permit. "One prerequisite for receiving the card would be taking a course on the expectations of responsible use of alcohol, what constitutes acceptable and unacceptable conduct, and the consequences of alcohol abuse. We have similar, clearly defined expectations for receiving a driver's license: Why not have the same for alcohol consumption? . . . I have always believed that people become responsible by giving them responsibility. I am convinced that federal legislation allowing states to experiment within certain guidelines and with careful monitoring would lead us to more civil, productive, and effective citizenship for our sons and daughters."

State government officials responded that Park's proposal sent a poor message to teenagers, and that it could place them at greater risk of damaging their health as well as of injuring other people in traffic accidents. Nevertheless, in the autumn of 1997 the Democratic representative from Boulder, Ron Tupa, announced that he was going to put forward a bill in the state legislature based on Park's proposals. He proposed that eighteen-year-olds should be allowed to purchase a "provisional drinking license," which would permit them to drink 3.2 percent beer as long as they did not drink and drive. If they were caught drinking and driving, not only would the permit immediately be revoked, but also their driver's license. This, he said, would make it the toughest drink-driving penalty in the state for any age group. As he explained when he announced his proposals, "The current drinking age is based more on politics and emotion rather than common sense or reason. It isn't fair, it isn't followed. It's failed in the past. It was called Prohibition. And it's impossible to enforce." To this suggestion, state treasurer Bill Owens, who as a legislator had sponsored the law that raised the minimum drinking age to twenty-one ten years earlier, responded that it was a "bad idea which would cost lives."

As Park suggested, there is a comparison to be made with the provisional licenses given to young people when they are learning to drive. You don't just let a child drive a car when he has reached sixteen—he has to be given instruction and guidance. Drink, like an automobile, can be dangerous when misused. So why are young people not taught how to use it? Maybe a "provisional drinking license" would be impractical. But at least Park's and Tupa's proposals represent a serious effort to encourage young people to learn how to drink responsibly and to establish minimum drinking age laws that might actually work.

So why have they been so summarily rejected? Might it be that the people who support the current laws do not really care whether they work or not? Just like the prohibition of alcoholic drink to the whole of the population during the 1920s, the laws are intended primarily to be symbolic: to demonstrate to young people how they ought to conduct themselves rather than actually to compel them to behave in that manner. According to Christine Lubininski, director of the Public Affairs Office of the National Commission on Alcoholism, the minimum drinking age standard sends "a message that as a nation we believe that drinking is not a healthy or appropriate activity for teenagers."

The problem with imposing symbolic laws that are not really intended to work is that they serve to engender disrespect for law in general. This is what happened during national Prohibition three quarters of a century ago; this is what is happening with young people today. The only difference is that in the present case, lack of respect is propagated in precisely that age group in which developing respect for law is most important.

Today's students are not merely told not to drink, but that for them there is no difference between drinking and taking drugs. They are told that these substances are forbidden because they are bad for them—in any quantities—and that is that. "For kids under twenty-one," states the federal Office for Substance Abuse Prevention, "there is no difference between alcohol and other drug use and abuse." But eighteen-, nineteen-, and twenty-year-olds do drink, and the majority of them who drink in moderation find it a very pleasant experience, without any adverse side effects. They realize that their elders have been lying to them when they have told them that all alcohol is dangerous. As a result, they are less inclined to believe what their elders say about other substances they ought not to consume or other things they ought not to do, some of which really are harmful.

They might, moreover, express their disapproval at what they regard as oppressive, unnecessary, and hypocritical legislation not merely by ignoring it or evading it covertly but by open resistance. This happened in the nineteenth century in those states that attempted to prevent their citizens from buying liquor; it was for fear of such an eventuality that national Prohibition was repealed; and this is now starting to occur on those campuses where police and university officials have attempted to enforce the minimum-drinking-age legislation. In May 1998 a ban on drinking at a favorite site before football games led to a protest by a crowd of 3,000 students at Michigan State University in East Lansing, who overturned cars and lit bonfires, while attempts to suppress the consumption of alcohol at fraternities and other off-campus housing led students at Washington State University in Pullmann, at Plymouth State College in New Hampshire, and at Ohio University at Athens into violent confrontations with the police. University officials have sought to play down the significance of these riots, suggesting that they are one-time incidents that are unlikely to recur. They should be so lucky.

The consequences of national Prohibition from 1920 to 1933, and of the age prohibition that has long survived its repeal, both give support to the argument that legal controls on a substance that people want to consume, and see nothing morally wrong in consuming, do not work as effectively in preventing abuse of that substance as do social controls backed up by education. There can be little doubt that American children would grow up with a healthier attitude toward alcoholic drink, and learn to consume it a more responsible manner, if they were allowed to drink under the supervision of their parents. If they were allowed to drink at home they could learn informal controls; if they were allowed to drink in bars, they would be under the supervision of formal ones.

The unhealthy drinking habits of many American teenagers should be blamed not only on the law that prohibits people under the age of twenty-one from consuming alcoholic beverages but also on the attitudes of their parents. In a number of states children are allowed by law to drink at home, but their parents forbid them. The prohibition on teenage drinking accurately reflects the prevailing mood within society at large. Most American adults simply do not want their offspring to drink. They want to be able to continue to regard them as children rather than as young adults who do the sort of things adults do. In particular, they disapprove of drinking by adolescents because it so often leads to sex—especially when they have been drinking heavily.

In reality, of course, the sexual activity is not unplanned, nor is it caused by the drinking. Rather, their desire to indulge in sex has led the young people to drink in the belief that this will provide an excuse for their misbehavior.[26] Nevertheless, one of the main reasons adolescents drink is as a prelude to sexual adventure. And the idea of their children drinking and engaging in sexual activity is something that strikes many parents with horror; they have been used to thinking of them as children and now they find that they have grown up and do all the things adults believe should be reserved for their own enjoyment.

And there is more to it than that. Many adults have moral qualms about their own attitudes to alcohol and to sex. They worry whether they are drinking too much, and wonder if they should really drink at all. They worry whether they are having too little sex, or too much, and have not made up their minds whether they approve or disapprove of casual sexual liaisons. One way in which they can resolve these moral ambiguities is by allowing themselves to drink and to indulge in sex while preventing their children from doing so. After all, their children are more vulnerable, are they not? They are less able to control their behavior or to resist temptation—or so adults seem prepared to believe. As Males points out, "Postulating a vast gulf between 'immature adolescents' and 'mature adults' is a crucial element in the formation of misguided youth policy. Sometimes the results of maximizing adult freedoms, 'balanced' by maximizing youth restrictions, are ludicrous. For example, most states' statutory rape laws allow an adult to have sexual intercourse with a sixteen-year-old girl while ob-

---

[26]This is discussed in the Introduction and in Chapter 3.

scenity distribution laws protect her from being corrupted by seeing a photograph of it."

It appears as though alcohol, like sex, is regarded as a contaminant, from the existence of which children should be shielded. In 1990 an award-winning adaptation of *Little Red Riding Hood* was withdrawn from a children's recommended reading list by the school board in Culver City, California, because the heroine had included a bottle of wine in the basket of goodies she brought to her ailing grandmother.

It is thought improper to introduce alcohol into an environment where children are likely to be present. What are described as "family restaurants," for example, tend not to serve alcoholic drinks. There are nearly 900 branches of Shoney's, mostly but not exclusively in the South, serving reliable, inexpensive, all-American food. None of them serves any alcohol. A spokeswoman explained that "we don't serve alcohol because Shoney's is a family restaurant . . . we wouldn't consider it proper to sit at a table and have a drink in front of children." The same policy is adopted in many American homes. Parents tend not to drink in front of their children and, if they do, their children may well do their best to dissuade them. The children are taught at school that alcohol is a drug, just like heroin and cocaine, and are encouraged to believe that a family that enjoys wine with dinner has a substance abuse problem that requires confrontation and treatment. This is quite the opposite of what happens in European countries such as France and Italy, where it is considered to be part of children's social education to go out to dinner with their parents, to see them drinking wine with their meals, and maybe even try a small glass—perhaps diluted with water—for themselves.

The gulf between American and European attitudes is demonstrated by the experience of Shawn Colleary, principal of the Cherry Creek Challenge School in the suburbs of Denver, Colorado. In the spring of 1998, Colleary took a group of seventh- and eighth-graders on a trip to Paris, France. As part of their experience of French culture, they enjoyed a three-hour meal at which they ate snails and duck, washed down with a very small glass of wine. For having allowed his charges to consume an alcoholic beverage, contrary to the rules of the district, Colleary was demoted from principal and assigned to another school. It may have been the custom in France to give children small quantities of wine with their meals, but, as far as school superintendent Robert

Tschirski was concerned, this was irrelevant. "The laws of that country mean nothing to me," he declared. "This was a district program."[27]

Well, maybe Cherry Creek, Colorado, could learn something from Europe. The "Mediterranean diet" has become very fashionable in America recently because it appears to protect middle-aged men and women from heart disease. People have adopted it only in a partial form, however. They eat the food and drink the wine that the diet stipulates. But they do not sit down together as a family, the children eating the same food and drinking the same wine as the adults, thus learning how to drink sensibly and pleasurably from an early age—as happens in European countries. Yet, if such a policy were adopted, it would save the health and even the lives of many young adults who have been led to drink alcohol in an unhealthy and irresponsible way.

As has frequently been pointed out by those who campaign to have it reduced, setting the minimum drinking age at twenty-one amounts to an unfair form of discrimination against young people, who in almost all other respects are regarded as having attained adulthood at the age of eighteen—at which point they are permitted not only to be drafted into the army and compelled to die for their country[28] but also to vote, serve on a jury, drive a car, purchase a gun, buy tobacco, gamble, start a family, engage in financial contracts, and be sent to adult prison. In some states, seventeen-year-old prisoners can be executed.

Surely it requires more responsibility to vote, serve on a jury, use a gun, start a family, and engage in financial contracts than it does to take a drink. By allowing people to select a president and decide to send someone else to prison and to bring up their own children while still teenagers yet prohibit them from drinking until they are twenty-one, legislators are effectively telling them the opposite. After President Reagan had signed the National Minimum Drinking Age Act, Ted Galen Carpenter, a public policy analyst, argued in *The Nation* that "the drinking-age bill is a hoax, a cynical attempt to use young adults as

---

[27]After Colleary acknowledged his "poor judgment" and praised Tschirski for demoting him, he was given his job back.

[28]Not that adult soldiers on active service are allowed to drink either. Of all the armies stationed in Bosnia in the mid-1990s, only the United States forbade its men from drinking. One army sergeant told the forces newspaper *Stars and Stripes* that "I drink here—I admit it. I'm insulted by the rules that allow me to die for my country but won't allow me to have a beer. The military treats us like five-year-olds."

scapegoats for a complex national problem. The significance of the law lies not in its potential impact on statistics for drunk-driving (which many experts believe will be largely unaffected, given the probability of mass disobedience) but in the willingness of Congress to sacrifice the rights of young people. Unfortunately, this episode is merely the latest sortie in a campaign to restrict the rights of adults under twenty-one years of age and adolescents—a counterrevolution, in effect, which threatens important gains young people made during the late 1960s and the 1970s."

Maybe the unhealthy and repressive minimum drinking age of twenty-one could be justified if it had succeeded in its aim of reducing deaths and injuries in drink-driving accidents. When President Reagan signed the National Minimum Drinking Age Act in 1984, he appealed for cooperation in ending the "crazy quilt of different states' drinking laws," explaining that the aim of the new law was to end the existence of "blood borders"—borders between states with differing minimum drinking ages—where teenagers "drink and then careen home and all too often cause crippling fatal accidents."

But has the removal of the differences between the states reduced the number of deaths and injuries in drink-related traffic accidents? MADD claims that it has been a great success. "Perhaps MADD's biggest legislative accomplishment . . . was the passage of the federal twenty-one drinking age law in 1984," argued Rebecca Brown, its president, eleven years later. By removing "blood borders," she said, the establishment of a national minimum drinking age of twenty-one had saved 1,000 lives, prevented 25,000 injuries, and saved an estimated $2 billion in health care costs every year.

Naturally, these statistics have been exaggerated. What group would not seek to magnify the danger against which it is campaigning, nor to maximize the degree to which that danger had been reduced as a result of the implementation of measures that it had recommended? MADD's dramatic figures are based on the fact that the number of deaths and injuries in drink-driving accidents involving teenagers has fallen sharply since the minimum drinking age standard was introduced, allied with the assumption that the reduction in deaths and injuries should be attributed to the age reduction rather than to other factors.

It is true that deaths and injuries in drink-driving accidents involving teenagers have fallen substantially; no one would deny that this has been a considerable achievement. But deaths and injuries in alcohol-related traffic accidents have also fallen significantly in the population as a whole. More strict law enforcement, an increased emphasis on the liability of bartenders, and the introduction of designated driver schemes—as well as the campaigns of MADD itself—have led to a reduction in drink-driving accidents among all age groups. There has been a transformation in social attitudes. Most people used to think nothing of driving after they had consumed several drinks. Today it is generally regarded as unacceptable.

The minimum drinking age has not been raised in Canada, where it varies from eighteen to nineteen, depending on the province. Yet Canada has been no less successful than the United States in reducing deaths and injuries in drink-driving accidents, especially among young drivers. Roadside breath-test surveys have found that the proportion of young people between sixteen and nineteen who drove after drinking fell from 16.7 percent in 1981 to 7.1 percent in 1993, a larger reduction than among the population at large. In Canada, even MADD does not campaign for the introduction of a minimum drinking age; it is perfectly well aware that such a proposal would not meet with popular support.

In the United States the number of people under the age of twenty-one who have been killed or injured in drink-driving accidents has fallen faster than among the population as a whole since the introduction of a standard minimum drinking age. According to the National Highway Traffic Safety Administration (NHTSA), the proportion of teenagers killed in what it defines as "alcohol-related" traffic accidents has fallen from 63.2 percent of all teenage car crash deaths in 1982 to 36.6 percent in 1996, while the proportion of adult deaths has fallen from 58.4 to 43.3 percent over the same time period. This disparity, however, may have nothing to do with the imposition of a minimum drinking age of twenty-one but may simply be explained by the fact that the age has been standardized across the country. No longer are there "blood borders" across which young people might travel in order to be able legally to obtain alcoholic drink, only to have to drive a long way home afterward, having consumed quite a lot of it. To reduce drink-related accidents among young people, it would have been just as effective to standardize the age at eighteen as at twenty-one.

Furthermore, some "blood borders" still do exist. One of the arguments offered in the early twentieth century for expanding state into national prohibition had been that this would eliminate the problem of smuggling drinks from out of state, because the drinks trade would be banned right across the country; yet the introduction of national Prohibition simply expanded the problem, as smugglers imported liquor by land from Canada and by sea from the Caribbean. In the same way, establishing a national minimum drinking age has not eliminated "blood borders" but expanded them. There is nothing to prevent people who are younger than the national United States minimum drinking age from driving north across the border to drink in Canada or south across the border to drink in Mexico, where the minimum drinking age is eighteen.

Every weekend, thousands of young Americans drive from California to the Mexican border city of Tijuana, fifteen miles south of San Diego, in order to drink in bars that stay open until dawn. In all, Tijuana is visited by 15 million American citizens each year. Not all of them are eighteen-, nineteen-, and twenty-year-olds in search of legal refreshment, but the behavior of these young drinkers does dissuade many older people from coming. "Sometimes when I'm walking home at night, it looks terrible," Carlos Rubio, a bartender at Tijuana's Hard Rock Cafe, told a reporter from the *Washington Post*. He explained that on his walk home he had to make frequent detours around people lying dead drunk on the sidewalks and groups of young people involved in drunken brawls. "When the tourists see it, they get really scared." The city has been trying to clean up its image and become more family oriented, but it does not want to discourage the partygoers who bring in $300 million a year. So young Americans continue to spend the night drinking in Tijuana, only to be involved the following morning in alcohol-related traffic accidents in the San Diego area.

It is possible that the proportion of people under the age of twenty-one who have been killed or injured in drink-related accidents has fallen faster than among the population as a whole, not because of the removal of "blood borders" but because the deaths and injuries have been shifted to another age group. One effect of banning eighteen- to twenty-year-olds from drinking has been to increase deaths and injuries in drink-related accidents of drivers aged between twenty-one and twenty-four. The age at which people are in most danger of being involved in drink-driving accidents is the period immediately after they have taken up drinking, before they have learned how best to handle the effects of alcohol. The first year of legal drinking is hazardous— whenever it occurs. According to two researchers at Rutgers University, Peter Asch and David Levy, who were given a grant to investigate this topic by the NIAAA, "It does not appear that the high fatality risk presented by new drinkers can be ameliorated by raising the legal drinking age . . . The problem arises not because we permit people to drink when they are 'too young,' but rather because we permit them to experience the novelty of 'new drinking' at a time when they are legally able to drive. If drinking experience preceded legal driving, a potentially important lifesaving gain may follow."

If legislators are seriously interested in reducing the number of deaths and injuries among young people, they should see to it that these people are able legally to accustom themselves to the effects of alcoholic drink some time before they are allowed to drive. This could be achieved by allowing young people to drink at home and in bars and restaurants under parental supervision from the age of fourteen or fifteen onward, or by raising the minimum driving age from sixteen to nineteen at the same time as lowering the minimum drinking age from twenty-one to eighteen. Neither of these measures might be regarded as politically acceptable; yet they might well save more lives than has been achieved by raising the minimum drinking age to twenty-one.[29]

Imposing a minimum drinking age is a ridiculous way of trying to stop people from drinking and driving. It does not even begin to address the problem, which is not to prevent young people from drinking but to stop them from driving after they have done so. If people in this age group have not been persuaded by all the propaganda about the dangers of drinking and driving that they are best advised to stay sober when behind the wheel of a car, then telling them that they are forbidden to drink alcohol at all is not going to make any difference. Since the crime of drink-driving carries much heavier penalties than the misdemeanor of drinking underage, people who are prepared to risk driving while under the influence of alcohol are unlikely to care whether they are also breaking the minimum drinking age law.

Regardless of their age, drink-drivers do cause a worryingly large number of deaths and injuries in the United States. According to the NHTSA, 17,126 people were killed in alcohol-related accidents in

---

[29]Another lifesaving measure would be to impose different minimum drinking ages for men and women. As it is young men under twenty-five who are the most likely to be involved in drink-related automobile accidents, it would be logical to impose a minimum drinking age for men of twenty-five, while allowing women to drink at eighteen. Were such a distinction to be introduced, however, it would be knocked down under anti–sex-discrimination legislation. One might reasonably wonder why discrimination by age is legal whereas discrimination by sex is not.

1996, amounting to 40.9 percent of all people killed in traffic accidents in that year. This total, however, includes anyone involved in an accident who is found to have any alcohol in his system. A more representative statistic is the number of deaths in traffic accidents in which one or more people involved had a blood alcohol content (BAC) above the legal limit of 0.1 percent that applies in the majority of states: this figure is 13,395, accounting for 32 percent of all fatal crashes.

In comparison, in Britain approximately 540 people die in alcohol-related accidents each year. Obviously, the United States is a much bigger country than Britain, with more than four times the population. People use their cars more often in the United States than in Britain, and drive farther. Even so, the contrast is extraordinary. In Britain, approximately 15 percent of total road deaths occur in accidents in which one or more people involved is over the BAC limit (which is lower than in the majority of the American states, at 0.08 percent).

Current discussion as to how the number of deaths (and injuries) in drink-driving accidents in the United States might be reduced focuses principally on the suggestion that the maximum permitted BAC be lowered. At present, thirty-four states allow people to drive with a BAC of up to 0.1 percent. MADD, which remains the most influential campaign group, has argued that people's driving skills are significantly impaired at this level, and that reducing the permitted limit to 0.08 percent would prevent several hundred deaths per year. It has also been suggested that the limit should be reduced in tribute to Diana, the Princess of Wales, who was killed in a drink-driving accident in France in the summer of 1997. After her death, supporters of a proposal by the New York State government to lower the BAC to 0.08 percent called it the "Diana bill" in her memory, and MADD produced an advertisement listing the names of 120 girls and women under the title "We've Seen Too Many Princesses Die." Katherine Prescott, the president of MADD, pointed out that "it sounds bizarre, but it takes a tragedy to get people's attention again. Hopefully, people will focus on the severity in drunk driving and reunite in an effort to stop it."

So far, however, only a minority of states has been persuaded to reduce the maximum permitted BAC to 0.08 percent. MADD has tried to persuade Congress to introduce legislation to force the recalcitrant states to lower their BAC limits to 0.08 percent by similar means to those used to compel them to raise their minimum drinking ages— threatening to withhold federal highway construction funds. "If you're clinically drunk, driving across a state line shouldn't make you legally sober," explained Frank Lautenberg, Democrat senator from New Jersey and the chief Senate sponsor of this measure. In the spring of 1998, the Senate voted in favor of adding Lautenberg's proposal as an amendment to a transportation bill that was passing through Congress. But the Rules Committee of the House of Representatives voted to prevent the amendment from being added to the bill. MADD issued a press release in which it stated that the beverage alcohol and hospitality industries had defeated this amendment by "spreading the myth that 0.08 would criminalize social drinking and reduce alcohol sales." Karolyn Nunnallee, the new president of MADD, declared that "We are outraged at the obvious special interest cave-in by the Rules Committee. The danger imposed by drunk drivers does not end at state lines and neither should the standards that define drunk driving. The states' right argument touted by opponents of 0.08 legislation is a smoke screen that hides what is really going on behind the scenes: alcohol and hospitality interests peddling big money to prevent lifesaving public policy. . . . We are terribly disappointed to find out that money—not safety—talks in the House of Representatives."

It is hard to argue against MADD, which holds the moral high ground because many of its members are parents of children who have been killed or injured by drink-drivers. This does not mean, however, that the measures it suggests are necessarily appropriate—any more than it would be right for the relatives of victims of violent crime to be allowed to determine the sentences that are passed on the criminals who have harmed members of their family.

MADD refers to "conclusive research, including a study published [in 1996] in the *American Journal of Public Health* which showed that lowering the limit to 0.08 BAC in all states would reduce alcohol-related traffic deaths by 500 to 600 deaths per year." The lead author of this study was a Boston University sociologist named Ralph Hingson, who also sat on the board of MADD. Hingson and his colleagues compared alcohol-related deaths in the first five states to reduce the BAC limit to 0.08 percent with five "nearby" states that retained the higher 0.1 percent limit. They found that the proportion of crashes in which drivers over 0.08 percent BAC were killed declined by 16 percent, and that the proportion of crashes in which drivers over 0.15 percent BAC were killed declined by 18 percent. From this they concluded that if all states adopted 0.08 percent laws, at least 500 to 600 fewer deaths would occur on the nation's roadways each year.

To jump from the research findings to the conclusion required a large leap of logic. Given that deaths among drivers over 0.15 percent BAC declined in the same proportion as deaths among drivers over the new 0.08 percent limit, it would be logical to conclude that factors other than the reduction in the maximum permitted BAC explain the reduction in the deaths. After all, drivers over 0.15 percent BAC were as guilty of drink-driving under the old as under the new legislation, so there is no reason why reducing the limit to 0.08 percent should have reduced the number of them who were killed. As Hingson and his colleagues admit, the first states to introduce the new 0.08 limits were the ones that were most interested in all kinds of legislative initiatives against drink-driving, not just lowering the maximum permitted BAC; among other measures, all of them introduced administrative license revocation laws, which permitted roadside police officers to confiscate the license of any driver who failed a breath test or refused to take one. These laws might well have been more significant than the reduction in the limit in decreasing the number of alcohol-related deaths.

If reducing the maximum permitted BAC to 0.08 percent does significantly reduce deaths in drink-driving accidents, then logically the states with 0.08 percent limits should have the lowest rates of alcohol-related fatalities in the country. But they do not. Of the ten states with the lowest rates, only two, Utah and New Hampshire, have adopted a 0.08 percent limit. New Mexico has the highest rate of alcohol-related deaths despite its 0.08 percent limit.

Reducing the maximum permitted BAC does not work because it does nothing to affect the vast majority of drivers that are causing the problem. According to data from the NHTSA, the average BAC among fatally injured drinking drivers is 0.18 percent, approximately double the legal limit. Nearly two thirds of what the NHTSA describes as alcohol-related fatalities involve drivers with a BAC of 0.14 percent and above. Reducing the limit will not stop people who drive after consuming large amounts of alcohol from continuing to do so. Henri Paul, who was driving the car in which the Princess of Wales was killed, had a BAC of 0.18 percent. Yet the legal limit in France is already much lower than in the United States, at 0.05 percent. The lesson of Diana's death may well be that princesses should beware of consorting with aging playboy sons of paranoid and fantasist fathers who allow them to be driven through the streets of Paris in a defective vehicle at excessive speed by an untrained driver with inadequate security support, or, more simply, that the existing French drink-driving laws should be better enforced, but it is certainly not—whatever campaigners might say—that the permitted maximum BAC should be reduced.

Not only would lowering the BAC limit do nothing to stop the drivers who already drink far more than they are permitted before driving, it would make them less likely to get caught because it would stretch police resources more thinly. H. Laurence Ross, professor of sociology at the University of New Mexico and the author of several studies on drink-driving, has estimated that reducing the limit to 0.08 percent would increase the number of law violators by about 60 percent. As he has pointed out, those states that have so far adopted a BAC of 0.08 percent have not accompanied this measure by investing in new police resources, "thus diluting an already inadequate control system. The effect may well be to reduce the chances of any impaired drivers being arrested."

If drivers find that they are less likely to be arrested, then the whole panoply of drink-driving laws will lose credibility. In this respect, lowering the maximum permitted BAC to 0.08 percent in the hope that this will reduce the number of deaths and injuries can be compared to prohibiting people under twenty-one from drinking in order to decrease the number of deaths and injuries in drink-related accidents involving young people. Neither measure deals directly with the problem; in both cases many innocent people suffer in order that a few guilty ones may be controlled; both reduce respect for the law. Even Candy Lightner, the founder of MADD, has argued against lowering the maximum permitted BAC to 0.08 percent, on the grounds that it would not help to catch drunk drivers. "If we really want to save lives, let's go after the most dangerous drivers on the road," she has written. "Putting our trust in new laws and regulations that attack only the tip of the iceberg will not make our highways safer." Lightner has been branded a traitor by MADD, but she knows what she is saying. The man who ran down her thirteen-year-old daughter in 1980 has been arrested several times for drink-driving, each time with a BAC of 0.2 percent or higher. And each time he is released from jail he does it again.

Why, then, is MADD pushing to have the maximum permitted BAC reduced? Might its opponents be right when they suggest that it needs to create a new fear in order to raise money and stay in business? There is a public perception that MADD has succeeded in changing attitudes toward drink-driving to such an extent that the problem has been "dealt with." Media interest in drink-driving had declined and MADD needed to do something to stimulate it. The argument over whether the limit should be reduced to 0.08 percent has done that. But what will happen if MADD succeeds in having a national standard of 0.08 percent established? According to Rick Berman, general counsel for the American Beverage Institute, which represents the interests of hoteliers, restaurateurs, and bar owners, such a reduction would be the equivalent of allowing the proverbial camel to push its nose under the tent. As he points out, the arguments that are used in favor of reducing the maximum permitted BAC from 0.1 to 0.08 percent are not specific to this reduction, and could be used to argue for lowering it further. "The organization that is most interested in all of this is MADD," he explains. "Today they say they want to be at 0.08 percent but, if they achieve it, what will their goal be next year? MADD generates income of more than $40 million. What are they going to do?"

The arguments that are currently being employed in the United States in favor of reducing the limit from 0.1 to 0.08 percent are the same as those being applied in Britain in support of a reduction from 0.08 percent to 0.05 percent; the lower limit is already in place in many European countries. The American Medical Association has argued for a maximum of 0.05 percent and the Department of Health and Human Services for one of 0.04 percent—the figure that was proposed in 1988 by the then surgeon general, Dr. C. Everett Koop, who expressed the view that "our goal must be the *total unacceptability* of driving after using alcohol or other drugs."

Koop also recommended that the permissible BAC for drivers under the age of twenty-one be reduced to zero. This latter recommendation has been adopted by a large number of states which have established zero-tolerance laws for drivers under the legal minimum drinking age, by imposing a maximum BAC of 0.02 percent or less, thus effectively forbidding them from driving after consuming even one drink. If people under twenty-one are forbidden from drinking, then it is logical that they should not be allowed to drive after drinking anything at all. But it is also logical that if the driving skills of young people are impaired at this level, then so are the abilities of adults, and zero-tolerance laws should apply to them also.

It is not fanciful to conceive of a future in which American citizens will not be allowed to drive after drinking, period. Maybe a majority of drivers would not object to such a restriction on their liberties, and be prepared to accept that they could not drink at a social event, in a bar, or in a restaurant if they were going to drive home afterward. But they should not be deluded into thinking that they would be sacrificing their social lives for the noble cause of reducing the number of people killed and injured in alcohol-related accidents.

In the first case, there are much better means of decreasing the number of drink-driving accidents. Britain has far fewer drink-driving accidents by any measure than the United States, and has reduced the number of deaths in these accidents by a much greater margin, by two thirds between 1982 and 1996, compared with a one-third reduction in the United States. Although the BAC limit has not changed since the Breathalyzer was introduced more than thirty years ago, the system of punishing people who have broken that limit has become more sophisticated. A graduated system of punishment has been introduced, variable according to the judge's discretion; in general, someone who is found to have been only slightly over the limit will be fined for a first offense, whereas someone who has significantly exceeded it may well be sent to prison. Thus, dangerously drunken drivers cannot go out and reoffend immediately. In the United States, on the other hand, everyone who is found to be over the limit prevailing in his state (whether 0.1 or 0.08 percent) is treated the same; there is no system of graduated punishments. Dangerously drunk drivers are punished no more harshly than people who have drunk two or three glasses of wine at a social event and are only marginally incapacitated. First offenders are hardly ever sent to prison, however much they may have drunk before getting into their cars.

They do have their licenses suspended. But only for ninety days, compared with a year in Britain. And suspension of a license is not such an effective means of preventing a convicted drink-driver from reoffending as locking him up in prison. Many still continue to drive after having had their licenses confiscated. There are, however, effective means of preventing them—or at least of ensuring that if they continue to drive, they do so very carefully. If states were generally to introduce laws specifying that people caught driving while their licenses were suspended would have their vehicle impounded, they might think twice before doing it. So why has this not been done? Would it be regarded as politically unacceptable forcibly to part people from their cars, however much damage they have caused when driving in them?

Furthermore, the campaigns of MADD and other groups, by focusing on drink-driving as a cause of accidents, has led people to ignore other factors that are no less significant.

According to the NHTSA, a fatal traffic crash is alcohol-related if anyone involved has a BAC of 0.01 percent, in other words any measurable amount of alcohol in his body at all. Involvement is defined in the widest terms, to include not only drivers of vehicles but also pedestrians. Thus, a pedestrian walking home after having consumed one drink in a bar who is run over and killed on the sidewalk by a sober driver is defined as an alcohol-related fatality. This said, the vast majority of those killed in drink-driving accidents are drivers who have been drinking and their passengers. If one takes accidents in which the driver has a BAC of more than 0.1 percent, at which level he is legally regarded as being intoxicated, then only four percent of those killed (531 out of 13,395 in 1996) are nonintoxicated nonoccupants, the innocent victims of drunk drivers of whom so much is made in anti–drink-driving propaganda. Obviously these are several hundred too many, but it is a long way from 17,126 to 531.

If, for a moment, one accepts the NHTSA's definition of "alcohol-related" crashes, then these represented a little over 40 percent of all traffic fatalities in 1996—a considerable reduction from more than 50 percent a decade earlier. These 40 and 50 percent figures have been much cited by anti–drink-driving campaigners. The Presidential Commission on Drunk Driving that was set up by President Reagan in 1982 under pressure from MADD stated on the first page of its report that "at least fifty percent of all highway deaths involve the irresponsible use of alcohol." This led the president to declare in his introduction to the report that "over the past ten years, 250,000 Americans have died in accidents caused by drunk driving, and millions have been maimed or crippled."

These figures have exerted a major impact on the perception of the public, legislators, government officials and lobbyists, but they do not withstand serious examination. Forty percent of traffic fatalities have not been *caused* by alcohol; rather, they are alcohol *related* according to the very broad definition of that term offered by the NHTSA. Furthermore, even to say that 40 percent of road traffic deaths are alcohol related is a true statistic only in the sense that 80 percent of road traffic deaths are coffee related because that is the approximate proportion of fatal accidents involving a driver, passenger, pedestrian, or cyclist with coffee in his bloodstream. Defining a drink-related accident as one in which someone involved has been drinking does not mean that the alcohol has caused the accident. The biggest problem with statistics for drink-related accidents and deaths and injuries resulting from them is that no one knows in how many cases the alcohol was the principal factor, or indeed a contributory factor at all.

How many of these notional "drunk-driving" accidents were actually caused by the slowed reactions and impaired judgment of a driver who was tired or ill or was under the influence of prescription or illegal drugs? What proportion of drink-related accidents should be ascribed primarily not to alcohol but to driving too fast or too aggressively? The more that campaigners go on about the 40 percent of fatal accidents that are supposedly "caused" by alcohol, the less likely are drivers to consider whether they are endangering themselves and others by driving while talking on a mobile telephone or while eating or while putting on makeup or while reading a newspaper. The more campaigners focus exclusively on the dangers of driving after drinking, the less likely are drivers to think twice before setting out in a car after taking tranquilizers or antidepressants, or when they have a cold or the flu, or when they are so tired that they may well fall asleep at the wheel. The obsession with the dangers of drink-driving means that efforts to reduce other bad driving practices are largely ignored and thus opportunities to save lives on the road are missed.

If the alcohol has been singled out, it is partly because it is more easily measurable. Much more might have been made of drugged driving, for example, were there an easy and quick roadside system comparable to the Breathalyzer to test for the presence of drugs in a driver's system. Instead, it is necessary to analyze urine samples. In the summer of 1993 the Memphis police carried out an experimental investigation into the prevalence of drugged driving, having fitted out an old ambulance with a lavatory, interview area, and videotaping equipment. This enabled them to give roadside drug tests to any reckless drivers who were not obviously drunk. The officers took urine samples from 150 drivers, and found that 89 of them tested positive for either cocaine or marijuana. "The reality is," said Dr. Daniel Brookoff of the Methodist Hospital in Memphis, who compiled and published the results, "we think it's as big a problem as drunk driving, or maybe bigger."

Another problem in detecting drugged driving is that it is not always possible to tell from looking at and conversing with a driver whether he or she is under the influence of drugs—unlike alcohol, the effect of which is often obvious to police before they give a driver a breath test. Whereas marijuana affects drivers in a similar manner to alcohol, cocaine can actually improve coordination and concentration. It does, however, affect judgment, making them wildly overconfident of their abilities and thus leading them to drive recklessly.

· Detection is even more difficult in the case of another form of impairment that is believed to be a major cause of accidents—fatigue. Indeed, it is impossible. There is no means of testing for tiredness. As a result, there are no reliable statistics on sleep-related accidents. Yet these are often fatal because they tend to involve lone drivers traveling at high speeds along interstates and other main roads. In one study of accident patterns on the New York State Thruway, drivers who fell asleep accounted for only 3 percent of crashes but for 50 percent of fatalities. Studies such as this one have led to the suggestion that as many as 30 percent of all fatal crashes, or approximately 12,000 per year, are sleep related, but, in the absence of reliable figures, this is only a guess. There is no doubt, however, of the pervasiveness of drowsy driving. A survey conducted in 1995 by Gallup on behalf of the National Sleep Foundation, a public-awareness organization in Washington, D.C., found that in the previous year 52 percent of those interviewed had driven while feeling drowsy, 30 percent had fallen asleep at the wheel, and 12 percent of the latter group had crashed as a result. The real figures may be higher than this, not only because people who had been killed as a result of falling asleep at the wheel were obviously unable to take part in the survey but also because people often do not realize they have dropped off for a very brief period while driving. "Fall-asleep crashes are an underrecognized 'silent killer' that is reaching epidemic proportions in our sleep-deprived society," says the president of the foundation, Lorraine L. Wearley.

Two groups campaign for better recognition of the dangers posed by drowsy drivers: PATT (Parents Against Tired Truckers) and VOIDD (Victims of Irresponsible Drowsy Drivers). So far, however, they have achieved little, especially by comparison with MADD. In an editorial in *The New England Journal of Medicine* in 1997, William C. Dement, director of the Sleep Disorders Clinic and Laboratory at the Stanford University School of Medicine, compared attitudes to drowsy driving today with the way that drink-driving was considered as recently as a generation ago. Then, the dangers of driving under the influence of alcohol were poorly understood, and most people were casual about driving after they had been drinking. The same, he argued, is true today of driving when short of sleep. Like intoxication with alcohol, this is a voluntary, self-imposed condition; the difference is that the dangers it poses are not appreciated by drivers, who rarely think twice before setting off on long trips when already tired.

Some persuasive steps are now being taken to compel drivers to notice the dangers of fatigue. In a recent case in Prince William County, Virginia, Neal Semich was sentenced to five years in prison for having fallen asleep briefly when driving his car, causing it to cross to the other side of the road, resulting in the death of two people. It is unlikely, however, that even sentences such as this one will lead to driving while tired being regarded with the same public opprobrium as drink-driving. As Dement explained in his editorial, "In many circles, being sleep deprived is described with pride as a badge of honor, indicating hard work on an important job. Furthermore, 26 percent of Americans believe that you cannot be successful in a career and get enough sleep." The United States is a country founded upon hard work, in which people work long hours and travel great distances between home and the workplace. To blame sleep deprivation for traffic accidents would be tantamount to saying that the American way of life is wrong.

The same is true of mobile telephones, which people use so that they can work even when they are driving. Yet these are dangerous. A study in Toronto of 699 drivers who had cellular telephones and had been involved in car collisions resulting in substantial property damage (but no personal injury) found that people were four times as likely to be involved in a crash when they were using their telephones as when they were not. The authors of the study pointed out that this relative risk was similar to the hazard associated with driving with a blood alcohol level at the legal limit. This research was published in *The New England Journal of Medicine* early in 1997. A few months later, in Britain, a businessman who caused the death of another driver in a crash seconds after making a call on his mobile telephone was convicted of causing death by dangerous driving and sent to prison for six months. The British Royal Society for the Prevention of Accidents responded to this sentence by saying that using a telephone while driving should become as unacceptable as drinking and driving. Yet there has been no conspicuous public campaign to publicize the dangers of the use of mobile telephones by drivers in America, let alone to have the practice criminalized. Mobile telephones are regarded as an essential element of the modern American way of life. Even if they are dangerous, people will insist on their perceived "right" to continue to use them.

The same is true even of road rage. The United States was founded not only on hard work but also on aggressive competition, and nowhere is that manifested more nakedly than in aggressive driving. A survey by the American Automobile Association (AAA) revealed that more than half of those interviewed confessed to having engaged in such hostile driving procedures as tailgating other drivers, cutting them off, and changing lanes suddenly, without warning. Sometimes these aggressive acts are countered with even more aggressive ones. The AAA found that instances of an angry or impatient driver trying to injure or kill another driver after a traffic dispute had risen by 51 percent between 1990 and 1996; that 37 percent of the people involved in these incidents had used firearms against other drivers, 28 percent had used other weapons, and 35 percent had used their cars. The AAA has no doubt that "personal frustration, anger, and testosterone are the most dangerous drugs on the highway."

Indeed, they probably kill more people than any other drug, including alcohol. The NHTSA has estimated that about two thirds of the deaths on America's roads each year "can be attributed to behavior associated with aggressive driving." This equates to 28,000 deaths in 1996, 60 percent more than the NHTSA figure for alcohol-related deaths.[30] Yet there are no groups dedicated to campaigning against road rage, no major legislative initiatives to try to do something to reduce the problem. It would appear that road rage is so closely associated with the competitiveness inherent in American life that no one dares to attack the former for fear of questioning the virtues of the latter.[31]

For all this, a majority of people still appear to think that most road accidents are caused by alcohol. According to a poll carried out by Allstate Insurance Company on behalf of MADD in November 1997, 52.9 percent of Americans consider drink-driving to be the number one highway safety problem; number two is excessive speeding, down at 18.6 percent. These beliefs are encouraged not only by MADD and

---

[30]Added together they come to more than the total number of deaths. And that is without taking into account other factors such as fatigue, which is believed to be involved in 12,000 road deaths a year, and speeding, which the NHTSA has calculated played a part in 13,000 fatalities in 1996. Most fatal accidents are caused by a combination of factors.

[31]Driving gives people a feeling of power; the center of power in America is to be found in Washington, D.C. It is no coincidence that this is also probably the worst place in the country for road rage. As Stephanie Faul of AAA explains, in Washington, D.C. "there is an overall climate of self-importance. They come here because of power, and the car is power. When the power is taken away, you feel frustrated."

other campaign groups and the government but also by the liquor industry. On the face of it, it might have appeared sensible for the industry to defend itself against those who accuse it of contributing to the problem of drink-driving by arguing that the statistics have been inflated and that other causes of crashes have been ignored. In fact, such an approach would be counterproductive; on those occasions when liquor producers have mentioned other causes of crashes, they have been charged by anti–drink–driving groups with trying to deflect resources away from measures that would stop people from being killed as a result of consuming their products.

The liquor industry likes to talk about drink-driving. This is a subject on which it can show itself to be responsible, by spending money on advertisements that tell people not to drink and drive while at the same time encouraging them to buy as many of its products as they can afford. As long as legislators and campaigning groups are talking about drink-driving, they are not talking about introducing measures that really would worry liquor companies, such as bans on alcohol advertisements or increases in taxation. Also, campaigns against drink-driving, by focusing on individual behavior, counter the arguments of supporters of the Ledermann hypothesis that more controls should be placed on the many in order to reduce drinking problems among the few. The appearance of MADD at a time when the Ledermann hypothesis had been exerting an increasing amount of influence on the government was greeted with great enthusiasm by the liquor industry. Unlike other campaigning groups, MADD did not argue that alcohol itself caused death or injury, but rather the abuse of alcohol. It therefore had no difficulty in accepting financial contributions from liquor producers. The two groups made common cause in asserting the obligations of individuals over the responsibility of society as a whole. The liquor industry has become less well disposed toward MADD in recent years, as it has expanded its range to include issues such as advertising, but it remains very happy about all the attention that MADD continues to draw to the issue of drink-driving.

Thus, vested interests conspire to exaggerate the number of deaths and injuries caused by drinking drivers and to play down other causes of traffic accidents. This is a conspiracy in which the public appears content to participate. "Americans feel good about driving cars because they are in control," explains Morris Chafetz, former director of NIAAA and now head of his own Health Education Foundation. "They are scared of alcohol because they risk losing control." Popular attitudes toward drink-driving manifest the tension that arises out of combining the American fear of alcohol with the American love of the motor car. As Henry Ford pointed out during Prohibition, "We can't have liquor and automobiles too." For him, this served as justification for maintaining Prohibition—so that people could keep on buying his cars. He even threatened to give up making them if Prohibition were to be repealed. "If booze ever comes back to the United States," he declared in 1929, "I am through with manufacturing . . . I wouldn't be interested in putting automobiles into the hands of a generation soggy with drink."

Ford did not, of course, carry out his threat. But the attitudes that he embodied remain true today. Banning alcohol in the belief that this would enable people to drive more safely did not work.[32] Everyone accepts that. Yet now increasingly people are required to choose between their cars and their drink. Either drive a car or drink alcohol, they are told, but not both. The primary role of the car in American society is asserted at the same time as the primal fear of alcohol is exposed. Drink-driving is not caused by drinking, but by driving after doing so. So why is it the drinking that is always blamed, rather than the driving? The best long-term solutions to the dangers posed by drunken drivers are not to be found in devising new ways of trying to stop people from drinking before driving but in encouraging them to look upon motor vehicles in a different light. There would be far fewer traffic accidents of any kind if people stopped believing that they had the right to use motor vehicles whenever and wherever they wished, and started to think of driving as more of a privilege. The United States has created huge problems for itself by designing cities for the convenience of users of private motor cars rather than for people traveling on foot, by bicycle, and on public transportation, as is done in Europe.[33] Cars are so cheap to run in America that few people think of saving money by taking public transportation. Gasoline costs only one fifth of what it does in France or Italy. If it were made more expensive for people to drive, and if better and safer public transportation were pro-

---

[32]Being the chief means of transportation employed by bootleggers, the car played a major part in the failure of Prohibition. So intimately did motoring come to be associated with bootlegging that in a number of unfortunate incidents innocent drivers were shot by Prohibition agents in pursuit of bootleggers. In Michigan, drivers had wanted to put stickers on their windshield saying "Don't Shoot, I'm Not a Bootlegger," but the attorney general stopped them.

[33]The consequential decline in social life is discussed in the Conclusion.

vided, especially at night, then fewer people would drink and drive. But the political will to address these issues does not exist. So a scapegoat is sought, and it is found in alcohol. Certainly it is part of the problem, but it is not the root cause.

In the summer of 1997 the Ohio police arrested Dennis Cayse for driving under the influence of alcohol for the twenty-fourth time in twenty-five years. Conventional punishments had not worked. His license had been permanently revoked a long time before, and he had spent two spells in prison. So when he was sentenced at Hillsboro Municipal Court at the end of the year, Judge John Hapner, who had already dealt with Cayse on several occasions, tried something new. He told him that he had to move within "easy walking distance" of a liquor store. "He doesn't deny he's an alcoholic; he just doesn't see that as a problem," the judge explained afterward. "It's my hope that he'll walk to get his beer and wine. Whether it will work or not, I don't know." The sentence was condemned by substance abuse groups and by MADD. Sharon Mason, a MADD member whose son had been killed in a drink-driving accident more than a decade earlier, commented that "it's like making it easier for someone with a gun to get bullets." But, as the judge had explained, what concerned him was not to stop Cayse from drinking himself to death if he so wanted, but to prevent him from harming other people. Cayse did as the judge had told him, and moved to within the Hillsboro city limits, within easy walking distance of not only a convenience store but also a bar, where his wife worked as a waitress. In one case at least, it appeared that the solution to the problem of drink-driving may have been found in telling the driver to walk.

The prohibition of drugs was introduced at much the same time as that of alcohol, in the early years of the twentieth century.[34] The exception was marijuana, which was ignored. No one paid it any serious attention until the 1930s, when authorities in western states noticed that consumption was increasing among Mexicans working in the fields and worried that it would spread to white youths who had heard of its reputation for producing "thrills" and "kicks." As a result, marijuana was banned in 1937.

Marijuana did not become popular among young white people until the 1960s, when they tried it in increasing numbers as part of a general

---

[34]This is discussed in the Introduction.

mood of experimentation and as an expression of rebellion against the prevailing values of American society.[35] They also took it because it was a natural substance, which did not appear to cause anyone any harm. Why, then, they wondered, was it banned—when alcohol and tobacco, which many doctors considered to be more dangerous, were legally available? Even the director of the National Institute on Drug Abuse accepted that marijuana posed a less serious health hazard than alcohol or tobacco. Even Mary Tyler Moore, then regarded as the epitome of wholesomeness, admitted to using marijuana, which she said she considered no more harmful than her pre-dinner martini.

At this period, far too many young people were using marijuana for the police to arrest them all. Several surveys at the beginning of the 1970s found that between 40 and 50 percent of college students had tried marijuana at least once. As a result, the police were enforcing the law selectively. In general, they distinguished between private and public use, and did not arrest otherwise respectable people who smoked marijuana at home.[36]

In order to determine whether such practice should become official policy, the National Commission on Marijuana and Drug Abuse was established (largely as a result of the initiative of Ed Koch, then a Democratic representative living among the potheads of Greenwich Village and a firm supporter of marijuana law reform). Most of the members of the commission were white, middle-aged, and conservative, so they were not expected to support reform. However, when they reported in the spring of 1972, they declared that they had come to the conclusion that marijuana, smoked in moderation, was harmless. They recommended that possession or use of marijuana in private should be permitted; that possession of up to an ounce of marijuana in public should not be punished (although the drug might be confiscated); and that possession of more than one ounce in public, or its public use, should be punishable by a fine of no more than $100, but that its production or sale for profit should remain a criminal felony offense. This approach, which was new to the public, was described as "decriminalization"—a sort of halfway house to legalization, in which the drug itself remained contraband but the people who consumed it were no longer regarded as criminals.

---

[35]This is also discussed in the Introduction.
[36]As one observer noted at the period, "In California, it is illegal to smoke marijuana unless you have your hair cut at least once a month."

The conclusions of the Marijuana Commission surprised almost everyone, including the commissioners themselves. As one of the more liberal members later explained in an interview, "We operated under unusual circumstances. Law-enforcement people were very cooperative with us, because we were perceived as conservative. They were very candid about how they practiced selective enforcement. . . . We talked to federal officials who admitted they'd lied about marijuana for years—it had been official policy to lie."

Not that the recommendations of the commission were officially accepted. The president, Richard Nixon, had ridden to power on a law-and-order platform, and had already expressed his opposition to drug use by instituting a "war on drugs." Even before the commission had reported, he had stated that he was not going to accept its recommendations if these were going to include the legalization of marijuana. Two days after the commission issued its report, Nixon told a news conference: "I oppose the legalization of marijuana and that includes sale, possession, and use. I do not believe you can have effective criminal justice based on a philosophy that something is half-legal and half-illegal." He refused to receive the report in public from the chairman of the commission, former Pennsylvania governor Raymond Shafer, and made it clear that marijuana would not be decriminalized as long as he remained in office.

Within a couple of years Nixon had been forced to resign as a result of his failure to respect the law and order he had advocated for the public at large. Prospects for the decriminalization of marijuana grew brighter. President Gerald Ford was not as virulently hostile to drug use as Nixon had been, while President Jimmy Carter actively favored implementing the recommendations of the Marijuana Commission. After Carter took office at the beginning of 1977, Dr. Peter Bourne, who had been a major figure in Carter's election campaign and had headed the state drug program in Georgia (where Carter had been governor), was appointed his special assistant for health issues and became his chief drug adviser. In March, less than two months after Carter's inauguration, Bourne and high officials from the Drug Enforcement Administration, the State Department, the National Institute on Drug Abuse, the National Institute of Mental Health, the Customs Service, and the Justice Department appeared before the House Select Committee on Narcotics Abuse and Control to argue for the decriminalization of marijuana. Bourne recommended that the federal law be amended to give the states the option to determine the penalty to be applied in the case of possession of small amounts of marijuana, pointing out that federal law was rarely enforced with regard to simple possession. He did not, however, recommend full legalization. Later the same year President Carter told Congress that "penalties against possession of a drug should not be more damaging to an individual than the use of the drug itself, and where they are, they should be changed. Nowhere is this more clear in the laws against the possession of marijuana in private for personal use." He called for decriminalization and asked that the conclusions of the Marijuana Commission be implemented.

But then, in July 1978, Bourne wrote a prescription for fifteen Quaalude tablets for an aide who complained of nervousness and difficulty in sleeping. He wrote the prescription in a fictitious name, which he justified on the grounds that the aide would have nothing in her record to indicate an emotional problem. This, however, grew into a scandal. Then it was reported that Bourne had been snorting cocaine at a party marking the annual meeting of the National Organization for the Reform of Marijuana Laws the previous December. Bourne had no choice but to resign. The Carter administration could no longer appear to be soft on drugs. The president ceased to urge Congress to decriminalize marijuana. Governmental and popular toleration of marijuana use had peaked.

By this time several states had adopted the recommendations of the Marijuana Commission and had decriminalized marijuana. The first to do so was Oregon, which in 1973 changed the penalty for possession of the drug from a felony prison sentence to a $100 civil misdemeanor fine, making it no more serious an offense than a parking ticket. By 1978 eleven states had adopted similar laws.[37] Then, however, the mood in the country changed, and after Carter lost the presidential election in 1980 the Republican administration reinstituted Nixon's "war on drugs." Ronald Reagan had won this election with the support of conservative parents' groups who believed not only that marijuana symbolized the weakness and permissiveness of liberal society

[37] Oregon recriminalized marijuana in 1997. Decriminalization laws remain in California, Colorado, Maine, Minnesota, Mississippi, Nebraska, New York, North Carolina, and Ohio. In theory, this means that someone caught in possession of small quantities of marijuana in one of these nine states will simply have to pay a small fine. But only if he is charged under state laws. If he is charged under federal law, he may well end up in prison. See the case of Joel Proyect, later in this chapter.

but also that it was responsible for the slovenly appearance and apparent lack of motivation of their teenage children. Reagan appointed a "drug czar," Carlton Turner, to direct his "war"; in Turner's opinion, the use of marijuana was inextricably linked to "the present young-adult generation's involvement in anti-military, anti–nuclear-power, anti-business, anti-authority demonstrations."

In these circumstances, no one talked about decriminalization. The issue was not revived until 1988, when Kurt L. Schmoke, the mayor of Baltimore, shocked a meeting of the United States Conference of Mayors by saying that the consumption of illegal drugs should be treated as a health concern rather than as a criminal justice problem, and calling for congressional hearings to examine the possibility of legalization. "Have we failed to consider the lessons of the Prohibition era?" he asked. "Now is the time to fight on the only terms the drug underground empire respects—money. Let's take the profit out of drug trafficking."

The *New York Times* ran a front-page story on Schmoke's statement, under the headline: "The Unspeakable Is Debated: Should Drugs Be Legalized?" As the newspaper pointed out, not only had Schmoke, together with two other big-city mayors[38] and several congressmen, declared in the previous few weeks that the "war on drugs" had failed and that the federal government should consider whether legalization might not prove a better course, but detailed arguments to this effect had recently appeared in a number of highbrow public-policy and medical journals. These had argued that the drug laws caused more damage to society than the drugs themselves, principally because the prohibition bred violence, both by drug gangsters and by addicts who committed street crimes in order to obtain money to pay the inflated prices charged by dealers, and because enforcement cost a great deal of money that could better be spent on treating addicts and educating people about the dangers of drugs. These arguments—that prohibition bred violence and was a waste of money—were precisely those that had been used so successfully a little more than half a century earlier by campaigners for the repeal of alcohol Prohibition. As Ethan A. Nadelmann, assistant professor at the Woodrow Wilson School of Public and International Affairs at Princeton, argued in an article in *Foreign Policy,* drug legalization would not only save federal, state, and local

---

[38]One of them being Marion S. Barry of Washington, D.C., who may have had a personal interest in drug legalization.

governments more than $8 billion a year from the cost of police, courts, and prisons, but would produce billions in tax revenue. "Legalization of the drug market, just like legalization of the alcohol market in the early 1930s, would drive drug-dealing business off the streets . . . and into legal government-regulated tax paying stores," he wrote.

Ever since this *New York Times* article revived the issue of drug legalization, it has refused to go away. At the end of 1993 the surgeon general, Jocelyn Elders, joined the debate. Appearing before the National Press Club to speak about violence in the streets and in the home, she was asked whether crime might be reduced if drugs were made legal. "I do feel that we would markedly reduce our crime rate if drugs were legalized," she replied. "But I don't know all the ramifications of this. I do feel that we need some studies." Although Dr. Elders did no more than suggest that the government should study the idea of legalizing drugs, rather than overtly recommend that it legalize them, she was immediately rebuked for her remarks by President Clinton, and was obliged to issue a statement later the same day saying that she had been expressing her personal views and not those of the administration. According to the White House press secretary DeeDee Myers, when President Clinton had been told about Dr. Elders's suggestion, he had replied, "Basically, it's not going to happen." The Clinton administration was going out of its way to look tough on crime, and part of that agenda involved waging the "war on drugs" and rejecting out of hand any suggestion that an alternative should even be examined.[39]

President Clinton, who claims that he managed to smoke marijuana without inhaling when he was a young man, has not simply perpetuated the "war on drugs" but has intensified it. Between 1990 and 1996 the number of people arrested for marijuana offenses increased by 80 percent to 642,000, of which 545,700 were for simple possession. These people are not merely fined, nor sent for treatment; many of them are sent to prison for long periods. There are mandatory minimum sentences for many marijuana offenses, ranging from five to

---

[39]Instead of listening to Dr. Elders's suggestion, her opponents tried to sabotage not only her proposal but also her career. Two weeks later, her son Kevin was arrested and charged with selling one eighth of an ounce of cocaine to an undercover police officer. Kevin suggested that the charge was a politically motivated response to his mother's comments. This suggestion was supported by the fact that the offense had occurred in July yet the warrant was not issued until just after his mother had made her remarks in December.

twenty years, or life for a repeat offender, on the "three strikes, you're out" provision. As a result, there are now far more people in federal prisons for marijuana crimes than for violent crimes. Prison cells across the country are filled with nonviolent drug offenders whose mandatory minimum sentences do not allow for parole. This exacerbates the problem of prison overcrowding, which can be ameliorated only by releasing violent offenders earlier than had been intended. In 1992 the average punishment for a violent offender in the United States was 43 months in prison. The average punishment, under federal law, for a marijuana offender was 50 months in prison. "In an era when fear of violence pervades the United States, small-time pot dealers are being given life sentences while violent offenders are being released early, only to commit more crimes," writes Eric Schlosser in one of a series of articles in *The Atlantic Monthly* on the subject. "A society that punishes marijuana crimes more seriously than violent crimes is caught in the grip of a deep psychosis."

In 1991, Joel Proyect, a middle-aged lawyer in Sullivan County, New York, was arrested for growing marijuana for his own use in a greenhouse beside his house. Proyect, an ex-hippie who had spent much of his life defending the weak and poor, often for free, was charged with the federal felony of manufacturing marijuana. The judge who tried his case declared that he was "very unhappy" about having to do so, but that under the Controlled Substance Act he was given no option but to sentence Proyect to five years in prison. His house, which he had spent nine years building himself, was seized by the government.[40]

Except for his being a well-known lawyer, there was nothing particularly unusual about Proyect's case. Since the passage of the Comprehensive Crime Control Act of 1984, the federal government has had the right to seize any property connected to a marijuana offense. The government need not prove that the property was bought with the proceeds of illegal drug sales, only that it was used, or intended to be used in the furtherance of a crime. A farm can be taken if a single marijuana plant is growing there; a house can be confiscated if it contains books on marijuana cultivation. The Supreme Court has ruled that the government can appropriate property even if its owner had no involvement in, or even knowledge of the crime that was commit-

---

[40]Having proved a model prisoner, Proyect was released early, after serving only three years and four months. Friends bought back his house from the government for $180,000.

ted. When property is seized, the legal title passes instantly to the government, and the burden of proving innocence falls upon the original owner. In 1994, assets worth roughly $1.5 billion were forfeited under state and federal laws; in 80 percent of these cases the owner was never charged with a crime.

"The more you think about it," says Proyect, "the less sense it makes. It's Kafkaesque. I can prove that I didn't sell pot, but I am not allowed to under the law. The crime is 'manufacturing' marijuana. They could take my house away for one seedling. If you want to understand the 'war on drugs,' look at McCarthy and the Red scare. They'd say: 'He went to a Communist Party meeting twenty years ago; he can't teach school.' Today, it's: 'He grew pot for his own use; lock him up for five years, take everything he owns, ruin the guy.' "

And to what end? The forfeiture laws do not so much prevent crime as create it. Because the proceeds are divided among the law enforcement agencies involved in the case, they are tempted to abuse their powers. A report by the *Sun Sentinel* in Orlando, Florida, revealed that one county sheriff's department seized $5 million in cash by randomly stopping motorists on Interstate 95. Former Justice Department officials have admitted in newspaper interviews that many forfeitures are driven by the need to meet budget projections. Furthermore, the only way a defendant can be sure of avoiding a mandatory minimum sentence under federal law is to plead guilty and give "substantial assistance" in the prosecution of someone else. Many defendants, who simply do not have this kind of information to offer, end up framing innocent people. They are encouraged to do so by a system that rewards them with up to 25 percent of the assets seized as a result of their testimony.

The government tries to justify its persecution of harmless dope-smokers by claiming that marijuana is a dangerous drug. Well, not compared to alcohol, it isn't. No one has ever died of an overdose of marijuana. It would simply not be possible. Someone would have to take many thousand times a normal dose in order for this to happen. Yet people are killed by overdosing on alcohol quite frequently. Several thousand die this way each year.

At the end of 1997 the World Health Organization published a report on the effects of marijuana, its first for fifteen years. The experts who had drafted the report had originally included a comparison between the effects of marijuana and those of legal drugs such as alcohol and tobacco, which demonstrated that on many health grounds marijuana was less harmful than either. As the report had originally stated, the comparison had been made "not to promote one drug over another but rather to minimize the double standards that have operated in appraising the health effects of [marijuana]." This comparison was removed at the last minute on the instruction of WHO officials, ostensibly on the grounds that "the reliability and public health significance of such comparisons are doubtful," but actually as a result of political pressure from representatives of the United States National Institute on Drug Abuse, who told the WHO officials that if they allowed the comparison to be published, they would be playing into the hands of groups campaigning to legalize marijuana.

Not only does the government spread deliberate misinformation about the harmful effects of marijuana, and seek to suppress any information that might show it to be less damaging than it says it is, it also persists with the unsubstantiated claim that marijuana is a "gateway" drug: that even if marijuana itself is relatively harmless, once someone starts smoking it, he or she is led inexorably to the consumption of "harder" and more dangerous drugs such as heroin, cocaine, and crack, and that on these grounds the legalization or decriminalization of marijuana cannot be contemplated.

This has not been the experience of the towns and cities in the Netherlands, notably Amsterdam, that have decriminalized the possession of marijuana. Although the possession of the drug technically remains forbidden, the Amsterdam city authorities not only ignore people who use it on a small scale but have licensed "coffee bars"[41] where people over the age of eighteen can buy and smoke small amounts of marijuana, or take them away to smoke at home, without fear of being harassed by the police. Local opponents of this system claimed that this would cause more people to move from marijuana to "hard drugs." But it has not. Very few Dutch users of marijuana consume cocaine, and hardly any of them take heroin, while crack is virtually unknown. The Netherlands has fewer addicts per capita than many other European countries, and far fewer than the United States.

In a 1997 review of the Dutch experiment with decriminalization, the Netherlands Institute of Mental Health and Addiction pointed out that the coffee shop system helped to *prevent* users of marijuana from trying "hard" drugs. It explained that there was no pharmacological reason why people should move on from marijuana to heroin or co-

---

[41]Not to be confused with "cafés," which sell coffee.

caine, but there were social reasons. "The more users become integrated in an environment where, apart from [marijuana], hard drugs can also be obtained, the greater the chance that they may switch to hard drugs. Separation of the drug markets is therefore essential and forms the basis of the current [marijuana] policy." Contrary to the claims of America's "drug warriors," it is not the legalization or decriminalization of marijuana that leads people to try "hard" drugs, but its prohibition. Where marijuana is forbidden, people who want to buy it have to go to black-market dealers, who will try to sell them other drugs at the same time. These users of marijuana will have heard their government tell them that marijuana is a dangerous and addictive drug, and have found this message to be untrue; this leads them to wonder whether official warnings about the dangers of other drugs might not be equally unfounded. Why not try them and see? Furthermore, the "war on drugs" has proved more successful in repressing the trade in marijuana than in preventing the traffic in heroin or cocaine because marijuana is bulkier and thus easier to detect. This has made marijuana scarcer and more expensive, encouraging both dealers and users to abandon marijuana for more dangerous drugs, in much the same way as prohibition of alcohol encouraged people to drink spirits in preference to wine and beer.

So why does the American government persist in its prohibition of marijuana, and lie to its people in an attempt to justify its position?

When Dr. Elders suggested in 1993 that the issue of drug legalization should be examined, government officials and antidrug campaigners rejected her proposal out of hand, refusing even to contemplate consideration of the issue, on the grounds that this would send out the wrong message. Joseph A. Califano Jr. who had been secretary of health, education and welfare in the Carter administration and was now president of the Center on Addiction and Substance Abuse at Columbia University, replied that legalization would "sabotage" efforts to deal with drug problems "by removing the stigma of criminality."

This symbolic aspect is one of the reasons the idea of "decriminalization" has been put forward. Although it is unclear what precisely decriminalization should mean—whether the private possession and consumption of marijuana should be permitted, or whether they should be regarded as no more than misdemeanors, punishable only by a small fine—the principle behind it remains evident: that small-scale users should not be punished excessively yet the drug itself should remain contraband and subject to seizure wherever found, thus demonstrating continuing social disapproval. But for antidrug campaigners, this won't do. As Richard Bonnie, one of the members of the Marijuana Commission, has explained, marijuana has not been decriminalized "simply because the act of repealing criminal penalties, however inappropriate they are, is thought to communicate an unintended message—that marijuana use is acceptable and that the government condones or even approves it even though the drug remains illegal and its distribution remains punishable as a felony. In short, it is thought that the law must prescribe punishment for the user so that the government can register its disapproval."

For the fear of sending the wrong message, the government persists not only with the prohibition of marijuana but with the whole farrago of the "war on drugs," even though it is not working and will never do so. "Had drugs been decriminalized," argues the eminent economist Professor Milton Friedman, "crack would never have been invented and there would today be fewer addicts. . . . The ghettos would not be drug-and-crime-infested no-man's lands. . . . Colombia, Bolivia, and Peru would not be suffering from narco-terror, and we would not be distorting our foreign policy because of [it]." Yet the drug war goes on. It continues because it suits politicians to blame drug abusers for many of the social problems that currently beset America; by sounding tough on drugs they can sound tough on crime and caring about the causes of crime without having to address the real problems confronting the urban poor. As one writer on the subject, Richard Miller, has explained, the drug war "conveniently diverts attention from problems that people want to ignore. . . . Drugs are a powerful symbol for things that upset us: changing standards of morality; changing concepts of parenting; changing job markets; a whole world changing. People are afraid. In some cultures, people respond by sacrificing goats. In some, people bloody their foreheads. In some, people attack neighbors who use drugs. Each of these responses is different in action, but all are futile in effect."

The drug war is a failure, but people continue to imagine that it can work. According to Jack Lawn, the former head of the Drug Enforcement Administration, "The public still believes in the possibility of a simple solution; it thinks that better law enforcement will solve the problem. Americans believe in the 'quick fix.' " This is a feature of an optimistic society, which considers that problems can be solved by action, and is not prepared to accept such wishy-washy European notions as "harm reduction"—which would mean abandoning the "war on drugs," giving up punishing users and addicts and focusing instead on trying to get them into treatment and on reducing the harm that drugs cause.

People still believe that prohibiting drugs and punishing their users will put an end to drug-related crime, just as they believed in the middle of the nineteenth century that prohibiting alcohol would eliminate alcohol-related crime; just as they believed in the early twentieth century that forbidding drink to blacks in the South would stop them from attacking white women while drunk; just as they believed that banning cocaine in 1914 would stop blacks from committing crimes while high on the drug, and that outlawing heroin in 1924 would prevent young white men stealing and robbing to finance their addiction.

Although the national prohibition of alcohol has long since been abandoned, it remains in place today on a local basis in many counties in the South, as well as being applied nationally to everyone under the age of twenty-one. And the prohibition of drugs not only remains in force, but is continually reinforced. These bans may not work, but that does not seem to matter. They continue to receive both official and popular support because they serve symbolically to demonstrate the extent of public disapproval of the substance that is supposedly forbidden—regardless of the harm that the prohibitions cause.

For the sake of laws that do not and cannot work, the United States government not only contemplates the deaths of thousands of its citizens but actually conspires to cause them. Virtually every civilized country includes a system of needle exchange in its drug policy, under which clean needles are provided by drug centers to heroin addicts who bring in dirty ones, as a means of preventing the spread of AIDS. One country that refuses to introduce such a system is the United States,[42] where HIV infection among heroin users who have shared contaminated needles has reached epidemic proportions. Needle exchange is rejected on the grounds that this would somehow appear to "encourage" or "condone" the use of illegal drugs. So people die of AIDS instead. Are they to be regarded as "deliberate suicides," as prohibitionists in the 1920s referred to people who died after drinking industrial alcohol that had deliberately been poisoned in an attempt to prevent them from drinking it? or might someone in the government someday admit that its drug laws are perversely dangerous, and wickedly wrong?

---

[42]Some cities do have needle-exchange schemes, but the federal government disapproves of them.

CHAPTER 6

"The True Friends of Liberty"

T he four main communities that emigrated from the British Isles to America in the seventeenth and eighteenth centuries shared little in common. Puritans from East Anglia colonized New England, Quakers from the North Midlands established themselves in the Delaware Valley, Anglicans from the south and west of England made their home in Virginia, and Scotch-Irish from the north of Ireland settled the back country on the western side of the Appalachian Mountains. "Fire and water are not more heterogeneous than the different colonies in North America," wrote Andrew Burnaby, a British clergyman who visited them in the middle of the eighteenth century. "Nothing can exceed the jealously and emulation which they possess in regard to each other. . . . Such is the difference of character, of manners, of religion, of interest of the different colonies that I think . . . were they left to themselves, there would soon be a civil war from one end of the continent to the other."

Fighting did break out on occasion between the different groups, but never with any serious consequences, because America offered enough open space for them to avoid each other.[1] They would not have joined together, however, had the British government not forced them to do so. Whereas the American settlers clung to the old ways that seemed

---

[1]Except in the seaports.

to offer them security in a strange new country, the manners of the Britons who had stayed at home on the other side of the Atlantic changed substantially in the century between 1660 and 1760. The ruling classes developed a new accent, distinguished by a broad A, which Americans though pretentious and which remains today characteristic of the British upper class. With new manners came new attitudes and new legal and political institutions, notably the concept of joint sovereignty between the king and Parliament. New relationships were established between Church and state, and between the executive and the judiciary. By the middle of the eighteenth century, it appeared to the ruling classes in Britain that the American colonists were hopelessly out of touch. They sought to bring them into line with new British ways of thinking and governing. But the settlers regarded this attempt to modernize their behavior as a threat to their hard-won independence. In response to what they perceived as a common danger, they forgot their differences and joined together in the movement that led to the American Revolution.

The colonists shared few experiences in the first century and a half of settlement. They lived in different climates, grew different plants and suffered from different diseases.[2] They practiced different forms of Protestantism, established different institutions, and socialized in different ways. But they did import the same goods from abroad—even when they lived in the remotest regions of the interior. By buying the same things, they came to participate in the same experiences. They had not been able to express commonly held feelings about their relationship with Britain through religious or political bodies because they did not share any institutions in common. Only their collective consumption of consumer goods offered them a medium through which to express their political attitudes. It was imported merchandise rather than representative organizations that enabled ordinary Americans to become politicized in the quarter century preceding the revolution. They were encouraged to join together to resist the attempts of the British government to control their consumption of rum, Madeira, and tea.

---

[2]It is not fanciful to attribute the characteristics of the inhabitants—and the historically divergent economic performances—of different regions of America to the differences in their climates. Certainly, in colonial times, the bracing climate of New England encouraged activity, whereas the heat and endemic diseases in the South led to indolence and irritability (but better hospitality). There is actually a branch of science devoted to this subject, called biometeorology.

The most popular alcoholic drink in colonial America was rum, distilled in New England from West Indian molasses, a by-product of the process of refining sugar. New England rum was purchased at a low price by laborers who believed it helped them to perform their work.[3] It was sold so cheaply that even common laborers could afford to get drunk every day. This was true not only in New England but also in the southern colonies. Although James Oglethorpe, the founder of Georgia, had tried to forbid the sale of rum in his new colony, it could be obtained so cheaply from neighboring South Carolina that workers could buy sufficient rum from the proceeds of one day's work to spend the rest of the week in a drunken stupor.[4]

One reason for the cheapness of New England rum was that the molasses from which it had been distilled had been imported at a low price, and free of excise duty, from French colonies in the West Indies. This annoyed the planters in the British West Indies, who wanted to be able to go on making money without having to work for a living. So they brought their influence to bear in the British Parliament, which in 1733 passed the Molasses Act. This imposed heavy import duties on molasses brought into the American colonies from French or other foreign-controlled islands. At first the New England distillers were able to evade the provisions of the new act and to carry on buying from the French colonies as before, but from the middle of the century the British government began effectively to enforce the Molasses Act. Boston merchants feared ruin: Some of them went out of business; they claimed that the trade of the province had come to an end and that every prudent man should resort to farming and homespun.

A number of groups forswore imported produce. The students of Yale unanimously agreed to abstain from the use of foreign liquors; Philadelphia firemen pledged not to drink imported beer. But the protests against the attempt by the British government to extract the duties on molasses were limited to the northern provinces, where the molasses were traded and the rum distilled. Common cause was not made with the southern provinces until 1765, when in the Stamp Act the British government imposed stamp duties on commercial papers, newspapers, and the like. This led Patrick Henry and his followers to push a series of resolutions through the Virginia assembly asserting the principle of no taxation without representation. Now the northern and southern

---

[3]This is discussed in Chapter 1.
[4]See Chapter 1 for this also.

provinces had a cause on which they could unite against the British government. Mobs began to attack the symbols of imperial authority: In Boston they hanged the distributor of stamps in effigy under what came to be known as the "liberty tree" and sacked the home of the chief justice. In October representatives of nine of the colonies met at the Stamp Act Congress in New York and resolved to cut off all trade with Britain. In the face of this resistance, the British government backed down: The Stamp Act was repealed, and the duty on all molasses, whether imported from British or from foreign possessions in the West Indies, was reduced to one penny per gallon. "I know not why we should blush to confess that molasses was an essential ingredient in American independence," John Adams later observed. "Many great events have proceeded from much smaller causes."

Whereas British efforts to impose a duty on the molasses from which rum was distilled had caused particular concern to the workingmen who were the biggest consumers of rum, a similar attempt to tax Madeira inspired resistance among precisely those groups that the British government should have been going out of its way *not* to alienate—the well-read, politically aware middle and upper classes, the colonial intelligentsia and quasi-aristocracy. These were the men who drank Madeira, and theirs was the class that provided the leaders of the revolution.

The immense popularity of Madeira in colonial America had a great deal to do with its ability to withstand the rigors of the voyage across the Atlantic and to thrive in the unusual conditions in which it was stored, especially in the southern provinces.[5] But it could also be explained by its import free of duty. Whereas European wines were permitted by the British government to be brought into America only in "British bottoms," after payment of the requisite taxes to British customs, there was no such restriction on the carriage of wine from Madeira, which was not part of Europe, but an island off the coast of Africa. Madeira wine could be carried directly to the colonies by ships of any country.

In 1764, however, the British government imposed a prohibitive excise duty on wines imported from Madeira, in an attempt to persuade the colonists to convert to port, which had been imported via Britain, but on which a much lower rate of duty had been charged. The col-

---

[5]These are described in Chapter 1.

onists might still have their wine, but the British government wanted to make some money from it.

The colonists would have none of this. Some of them boycotted both port and Madeira, declaring that they would "think themselves better entertained with a good glass of beer or cider." Others drank smuggled Madeira instead. On May 9, 1768, the *Liberty*, a ship belonging to the wealthy Boston merchant John Hancock, docked in Boston harbor. The crew unloaded it surreptitiously the same night.[6] A tidesman, who had been employed to await the arrival of ships in order to ensure that they observed customs regulations, did come on board but was shoved into a cabin and detained because he refused to cooperate with the illegal removal of the cargo. "I heard a noise as of many people upon deck at work hoisting out goods," he later explained. When the noise ceased, the captain "came down to me in the cabin, and threatened that if I made any discovery of what had passed there that night, my life would be in danger, and my property destroyed." The next morning, customs officials boarded the vessel in order to tax its cargo. They found that 100 of its 125 pipes[7] of Madeira had disappeared.

So the ship was seized and Hancock charged with smuggling. The news of the seizure traveled fast. A crowd of two or three thousand local rowdies assembled on the dockside and attacked the customs officers, who were forced to flee for protection to the British frigate *Romney*, anchored in the harbor. At the beginning of November a warrant was issued for Hancock to appear in court; in order to retain his liberty he was required to pay a bail of £3,000 (the equivalent of more than $150,000 today). The trial lasted all winter. Eventually, in the spring, the crown withdrew. But Hancock was not placated. His ship was never returned to him but was retained on the grounds that the cargo had been illegally unloaded. This episode did a great deal to dispose Hancock toward revolution.

By this time, twelve warships full of British troops had arrived in Boston, in response to the mob action against the customs officers. Far from quieting the colonists, this measure made them more determined to resist. John Adams wrote in his diary that "their very appearance in Boston was strong proof to me that the determination in Great Britain to subjugate us was too deep and inveterate ever to be altered by us."

---

[6]The work was so strenuous that it killed the ship's captain.
[7]Each containing 126 gallons.

Considering its role in the events leading up to the revolution, it is not surprising that Madeira was used to inspire and celebrate some of the principal stages by which America acquired its independence. Thomas Jefferson wrote the first draft of the Declaration of Independence in the Indian Queen Tavern in Philadelphia while sipping a glass of Madeira; George Washington's inauguration in April 1789 at Fraunces Tavern in New York was toasted with Madeira; Jefferson drank Madeira in July 1792 to commemorate the decision to locate the capital in Washington, D.C. There also survives a letter written in 1776, during the Revolutionary War, by Colonel Lambert Cadwalader to Jasper Yeates at Lancaster, in which he sends news of Washington's victory at Trenton but only after he has asked "that you would be kind enough to let the two quarter-casks of Madeira . . . be deposited in some safe place under lock and key in your cellar . . . as I value them more than silver and gold in these times of misfortune and distress."

This said, tea played a much greater part in developing the American independence movement than either molasses or Madeira. Whereas only the laborers who drank rum and the merchants who traded in it had been disturbed by the attempt to raise a duty on molasses, and only the gentlemen who drank Madeira had been concerned about the efforts of the British government to convert them to port, everyone drank tea; by imposing a duty on this staple drink the British government succeeded in uniting the colonies as no measure taken against any other product could have.

By the middle of the eighteenth century, tea had become popular among all classes throughout the colonies. According to Israel Acrelius, a pastor who lived in what was then called New Sweden (in Pennsylvania), "Tea is a drink very generally used. No one is so high as to despise it, nor anyone so low as not to think himself worthy of it." Even the inhabitants of isolated country villages insisted on making tea, despite their ignorance of how to do so. Toward the end of the century a historian living in East Hampton, New York, interviewed a seventy-eight-year-old woman, Mrs. Miller, who "remembers well when they first began to drink tea on the east end of Long Island." She explained that none of the farmers knew what to do with the dry leaves. "One family boiled it in a pot and ate it like samp-porridge. Another spread tea-leaves on his bread and butter, and bragged of his having ate half a pound at a meal, to his neighbor, who was informing him how long a pound of tea lasted him." According to Mrs. Miller, the arrival of the first teakettle was a particularly memorable day in the community: "It came ashore at Montauk in a ship. The farmers came down there on business with their cattle, and could not find out how to use the teakettle. . . . Some said it was for one thing, and some said it was for another. At length one, the more knowing than his neighbors, affirmed it to be a ship's lamp, to which they all assented."

The consumption of tea was first transformed into a political symbol in 1767. When repealing the Stamp Act the previous year the British government had sought to save face by declaring at the same time that its Parliament still retained the right to do whatever it wanted with the colonies whenever it wanted to do it. In order to reassert this supposed right, the British Parliament passed an act placing duties on tea, paper, lead, and paint imported into the colonies. This provoked many of the colonists into boycotting a whole range of British goods, not just those that had been taxed by the new act. The argument was put forward that anyone who bought any British imports was effectively threatening the liberties of other Americans. Everything from clocks to carriages and hats to house furniture was declared contraband. This nonconsumption campaign encouraged people who had previously been excluded from colonial politics to resist the British government. By converting even the most mundane items of the household economy into symbols of oppression, the boycott politicized American women. The ladies who attended one wedding in Connecticut appeared in garments of their own making and insisted upon having "Labrador tea," a concoction brewed from indigenous herbs; other women in New England participated in spinning and weaving competitions. At a time when women had few other pleasures, it was a great sacrifice that was being asked of them to abandon their tea. Yet they did so willingly. In 1770 three hundred ladies of Boston agreed to abstain from the use of tea, stating that "we think it our duty perfectly to concur with the true friends of liberty in all measures they have taken to save this abused country from ruin and slavery."[8]

The boycott worked: The act was repealed. People went back to buying British goods. Radical leaders such as Samuel Adams warned Americans that the threat to their political liberties had not been removed. He begged them to maintain the boycott. But few listened: Adams complained that in the southern colonies "we hardly see anything in their public papers but advertisements for the baubles of Britain for sale."

---

[8] The importance of tea in female culture is discussed in Chapter 3.

The threat to American political liberties remained in place because the British Parliament, while abandoning the other duties, had retained the three-pence duty on tea. The prime minister, Lord North, was concerned that the British government should retain its claim to levy taxes upon the colonies, and was convinced that Americans would drink tea if the price were right, regardless of their principles.

During this period, between 1770 and 1773, many patriotically minded Americans demonstrated an ambivalent attitude to tea drinking. Some continued to consume tea in the hope that it had been smuggled across the Atlantic free of British excise duty. In the spring of 1771 John Adams recorded in his diary that he "dined at Mr. Hancock's . . . and spent the whole afternoon, and drank green tea, from Holland, I hope, but don't know." Adams could not be sure of its source because during this period a number of Boston merchants, including Hancock, did import tea on which British excise duty had been paid, as well as tea from Holland. The Boston merchants did not extend their patriotism to reject tea imported via Britain until they had been confronted with the prospect of losing their dominance of the trade in both legally imported and smuggled tea to the British East India Company.

This possibility was raised by the Tea Act of 1773. In theory, the East India Company was supposed to enjoy a monopoly of tea imports into Britain but in fact an equivalent amount of tea was brought into the country by smugglers. Finding itself unable to dispose of its produce on the British market, the company piled up millions of pounds of unsold tea in its warehouses. Why not dump the surplus on the American colonies? Hitherto American consumers had been reluctant to buy the company's tea, not only on grounds of principle but also because it cost them much more than the smuggled version. The company had been obliged to land all its tea in Britain, where a duty was paid before it was bought by British and American merchants for marketing in America. But now the Tea Act gave the company the right to import tea directly into America in its own ships and sell it through its own agents. By eliminating British duty the cost to the American consumer would have been halved; the company would have been able to undercut even Dutch smugglers. But for Americans, more than money was at stake. The British government, declared Benjamin Franklin, "can have no idea that any people can act from any principle but that of interest. They believe that three pence on a pound of tea . . . is sufficient to overcome the patriotism of an American."

News of the Tea Act reached the colonies in October 1773. A meeting in Philadelphia warned that the tea tax had "a direct tendency to render assemblies useless, and to introduce arbitrary government and slavery." Anyone who aided or abetted the sale of tea while it remained subject to this duty was "an enemy to his country." American patriots campaigned against British East India Company tea not only on ideological but also on medical grounds. The Philadelphia physician Benjamin Rush condemned it as "a slow poison in a political as well as physical sense." Dr. Thomas Young of Boston claimed that tea drinking in Europe caused "spasms, vapors, hypochondrias, apoplexies of the serious kind, palsies, dropsies, rheumatisms, consumptions [and] low nervous, miliary, and petechial[9] fevers."

The first tea ships appeared in Boston at the end of November. Notices posted all over the city read:

Friends! Brethren! Countrymen!
That worst of plagues, the detestable tea, shipped for this port by the East India Company, is now arrived in this harbour. The hour of destruction or manly opposition to the machinations of tyranny stares you in the face.

On the night of December 16, three tea ships were boarded by colonists disguised as Mohawk Indians. They spilled the contents of 342 chests of tea (worth about £10,000) into the water and triumphantly marched through the town accompanied by pipes and drums.[10] "Last night three cargoes of Bohea tea were emptied into the sea," wrote John Adams in his diary. "This is the most magnificent moment of all. There is a dignity, a majesty, a sublimity in this last effort of the patriots that I greatly admire. The people should never rise without doing something to be remembered—something notable and striking. This destruction of the tea is so bold, so daring, so firm, intrepid, and inflexible, and it must have so important consequences, and so lasting, that I cannot but consider it as an epocha in history. . . ."

The news was carried to New York by Paul Revere on the first of his famous rides. It soon spread throughout the colonies, rousing and

---

[9]The victim of a miliary fever suffers from a rash resembling millet seed; someone suffering from petechial fever shows small spots of blood on his skin.
[10]Sam Adams and John Hancock helped organize the tea party, but it is unlikely that they boarded the ships themselves.

uniting patriot Americans. Sam Adams wrote that "the ministry could not have devised a more effectual measure to unite the colonies. . . . Old jealousies are removed and perfect harmony subsists between them." Over the course of the next year, tea parties were held also at Greenwich, New Jersey; New York; Annapolis, Maryland; and Charleston, South Carolina. Throughout America the ceremonial destruction of tea strengthened the bonds of political solidarity. Towns called for their citizens to surrender all their tea to a central committee, which then arranged for its destruction in a public bonfire. Everyone was expected to contribute some leaves, purchased long before the hated Tea Act had been passed, so that they could be destroyed in flames that purged the town of ideological sin. The seizure and destruction of tea became an instrument of political indoctrination, forcing all members of the community, regardless of their personal views, publicly to commit themselves to the cause of liberty.

Within a few years, however, tea drinking had regained not only its acceptability but also its popularity. The French cleric Claude Robin, who traveled to the States in 1781 and followed the campaign of his country's army during the Revolutionary War, observed that Americans "drink a lot of tea; this insipid beverage is their principal source of pleasure; there is no one who does not drink it out of china; the greatest sign of courtesy among them is to offer it to a visitor."

This sudden reversal of popular attitudes may seem strange, but as soon as the first shots of the American Revolution had been fired at Lexington and Concord in the spring of 1775, the need for a tea boycott had ended. Once the rejection of tea had ceased to symbolize the repudiation of British rule, once the American colonies had declared themselves to be free, there was nothing to stop them from drinking tea again. Physicians, who in 1773 and 1774 had condemned tea on health grounds, complained during the Revolutionary War that the hospitals were suffering for want of adequate supplies of tea. Benjamin Rush had signed the Declaration of Independence and served as surgeon general to the Continental Army. Yet before long he was recommending that professional men who habitually turned to spirits for relief from mental fatigue should try tea instead. It was, he stated, "a much better remedy for that purpose. By its grateful and gentle stimulus, it removes fatigue, restores the excitement of the mind, and invigorates the whole system."

It has become an article of popular belief that ever since the Boston Tea Party, Americans have preferred coffee to tea. This conviction has been encouraged by various authorities on the subject, including William H. Ukers, author of *All About Tea,* a hefty two-volume book which, although published three quarters of a century ago, remains the standard work on the subject. The Boston Tea Party, he wrote, "cast the die for coffee; for there and then originated a subtle prejudice against the 'cup that cheers,' which 160 years have failed entirely to overcome."

This popular belief must, however, be consigned to mythology. Most Americans did eventually give up tea for coffee, but not until well into the nineteenth century, by which time residual anti-British feelings would no longer have been strong enough to account for such a change in taste. The consumption of coffee increased from the 1830s onward, when the duty was lowered and therefore the price reduced. But still tea remained popular. Its consumption gradually declined during the course of the century for the simple reason that the source of immigration to America altered from the British Isles to countries without any tradition of tea drinking, many of which enjoyed an equally long-standing custom of drinking coffee.

By the time of the Civil War, coffee was as well established as the national hot beverage as tea had ever been before the revolution. Southerners were so wedded to their coffee that if one were to take contemporary accounts at face value, one would assume that its absence was the greatest hardship they endured in the war. The northern blockade prevented the importation of coffee from Brazil. All kinds of substitutes were tried. One traveler in Texas recorded that "peanuts, sweet potatoes, rye, beans, peas, and corn meal were used; the latter was the favorite of taverns, all of them wretched imitations, though gulped down, when chilly and tired, for want of anything better—a hot sickening drink, entirely devoid of the stimulating effects of the genuine article."[11]

Before the war, coffee had been a staple of all classes of society, consumed morning, noon, and night. As soon as the war ended, it became a staple once again. Unlike in Europe, where it was taken as a short drink after meals, or in the intervals between them, in America coffee became the main mealtime beverage, the equivalent of tea in Britain or beer in Germany or wine in France. Within a generation of

---

[11]The small quantity of real coffee that found its way through the blockade sold for such a high price that it was not drunk neat but used as a flavoring for the imitations.

the ending of the war, it could confidently be declared that "Americans are the greatest coffee consumers in the world." Per capita consumption was now more than twice that of Germany, nearly three times that of France, twelve times that of Britain, and more than twenty times that of Italy.

Not only had it become the national hot beverage, coffee had acquired a legendary status of its own—as one of the symbols of the Old West, of a way of life that was fast disappearing now that the western and eastern borders of the United States had been joined in the middle. "The insatiable appetite acquired by travelers upon the prairies is almost incredible, and the quantity of coffee drunk is still more so," wrote Josiah Gregg in his account of life on the Santa Fe Trail in the 1830s. "It is an unfailing and apparently indispensable beverage, served at every meal—even under the broiling noonday sun, the waggoner will rarely fail to replenish a second time his huge tin cup." So much coffee was drunk on cattle drives in the West, so pervasive was the image of large steaming pots of coffee boiling on an open stove, that it became a symbol of the West in much the same way as the six-shooter[12] or the covered wagon.

Yet, despite having become part of the legend of the opening up of the West, and despite having become a national beverage, coffee never acquired the same status as tea had among its opponents in the late eighteenth century. Tea could be hated because it was a foreign product bearing foreign taxes, a symbol of foreign oppression; coffee could not be loved as a national symbol because it, too, was a foreign product: It had to be imported from abroad. It could be an American drink, but not an all-American one. If Americans wanted to have drinks that symbolized their way of life, they had to look elsewhere.[13]

---

[12]The term "six-shooter" was sometimes used to describe the coffee, which was claimed to be so strong that a pistol could be floated on top of it.

[13]The alien origins of coffee help to account for the popularity of Coca-Cola, another stimulant containing caffeine that helped people to work harder and keep going for longer. Although it contained imported ingredients, including extract of coca leaf and kola nut, and oil of nutmeg and cinnamon, Coca-Cola, manufactured in Atlanta, became such a powerful symbol of the American way of life that during the Second World War the men who installed soda fountains to serve it behind the front lines were regarded as no less important than the civilians who repaired tanks and airplanes. One soldier wrote home, "If anyone were to ask us what we were fighting for, we think half of us would answer, the right to buy Coca-Cola again." According to the veteran Kansas newspaper editor William Allen White, then regarded as the voice of middle America, Coca-Cola was "a

* * *

The revolution may not have persuaded Americans to abandon tea for coffee, but it did lead them to give up rum for whiskey. During the Revolutionary War the British blockaded imports of the molasses that American distillers had been accustomed to turn into rum. So the distillers switched to making whiskey. But they could not produce enough to meet wartime demand. Prices rose sharply, and whiskey was often unobtainable. Patrick Henry, wartime governor of Virginia, embarrassed his friends by serving home-brewed beer to important guests.

After the war, rum distilling resumed. But it was no longer as easy for the distillers to obtain molasses as it had been before the revolution. French and other European colonies in the West Indies had followed the British example and started to turn their molasses into rum themselves. Furthermore, the French, like the British, had closed their colonies to American trade. Faced with erratic supplies, the American rum industry fell into decline.

This process was hastened by the rise of American nationalism. Imported molasses and rum served to remind Americans of their colonial past. The colonists of the earlier part of the eighteenth century might have been happy to import these products from the British Empire, but independent Americans now believed that importing consumer goods from foreign countries demonstrated an economic weakness that might lead them to lose control over their own destiny.

So they turned to whiskey instead. But not until whiskey had itself served as a symbol of a schismatic movement within the new union. At the First and Second Congresses of 1789–93, representatives of the separate interests of New England, of the Middle Atlantic states, and of the South managed to reach agreement on the essential issues of establishing a national capital, a fiscal policy, a foreign policy, and a means for regulating foreign trade. But the Scotch-Irish would not agree.

These formed the largest group of immigrants into America in the eighteenth century; roughly a quarter of a million had arrived in the half-century or so before the revolution. As their name indicated, they had come originally from Scotland but had moved during the seventeenth century to Ireland, where they had settled largely in rough country in the North.[14] When they emigrated to America they chose to settle

---

sublimated essence of all that America stands for, a decent thing honestly made, universally distributed, conscientiously improved with the years."

[14]The Scotch-Irish, Protestants who had lived in northern Ireland, should not be

as far as possible from existing settlements, in many cases in what was then regarded as the West, on the far side of the Appalachians, where they sought to live according to their belief in "natural liberty." They entertained no respect for law and order, considering that they had the right to do as they pleased in their portion of wilderness. As the concept was explained by George Harrison, a native of Kendal in the northwest of England, "Every man at nature's table has a right to elbow room."

The impossibility of incorporating the Scotch-Irish notion of "natural liberty" within the federal system was demonstrated when, at the instigation of Alexander Hamilton, the secretary of the treasury, Congress voted in 1791 to impose an excise duty on domestically produced spirits. The following year, a group of western Pennsylvanians petitioned Congress to repeal the tax. "To us," they argued, "that act appears unequal in its operation and immoral in its effects. Unequal in its operation, as a duty laid on the common drink of a nation, instead of taxing the citizens in proportion to their property, falls as heavy on the poorest class as on the rich; immoral in its effect, because the amount of duty resting on the oath of the payer, offers, at the expense of the honest part of the community, a premium to perjury and fraud.

"Your Petitioners also consider this law as dangerous to liberty, because the powers necessarily vested in the officers for the collection of

---

confused with the Catholics from southern Ireland who emigrated to the United States in large numbers in the nineteenth century. There was no love lost between the two groups. When they were forced to emigrate together, Irish Protestant passengers condemned their "papist" companions as lice-ridden, "barbarous dirty scum." "The most ignorant and most degraded mass of human beings with whom I had ever been brought into contact," complained one Ulster Presbyterian. Whereas the Scotch-Irish generally settled in the backwoods, where they encountered conditions similar to those of northern Ireland and southern Scotland, the Irish Catholics settled mostly in the cities. A certain amount of assimilation has taken place between the two groups in America. President Ronald Reagan, for example, was the son of an Irish Catholic father and a Scotch-Irish Protestant mother who met in the store where his mother worked in Fulton, Illinois, at the turn of the century. Her father strongly disapproved of the liaison. The groups remain mostly separate, however, in Ireland. Confusion between them has largely arisen as a result of the recent tendency of all Americans of Irish origin to associate themselves with the Catholics of southern Ireland, which has led to such absurd historical anomalies as American descendants of Scotch-Irish immigrants sending back money to finance the Irish Catholic terrorist group the Irish Republican Army.

so odious a revenue are not only unusual but incompatible with the free enjoyment of domestic peace and private property, . . . and because we are apprehensive that this excise will by degrees be extended to other articles of consumption, until everything we eat, drink, or wear be, as in England and other European countries, subjected to heavy duties and the obnoxious inspection of a host of officers."[15]

Many of the distillers were persuaded to pay the duty, but a small number refused. They were encouraged in their resistance by militant members of radical "democratic-republican" societies, who appear genuinely to have believed that they were being threatened by a plutocratic conspiracy: that Hamilton sought to oppress the populace with taxes for the benefit of the rich, that he had chosen to levy an excise because this was the favorite tax of tyrants, and that preparations for national defense masked a design to crush the people under a military despotism. These democratic-republicans called for the Scotch-Irish to rise in rebellion.

In 1794 the government made an effort to bring the delinquent distillers into line by serving subpoenas requiring them to appear in the federal district court in Philadelphia. In response, a group calling themselves the "whiskey boys" attacked and burned down the home of the inspector of excise, destroyed his crops, and drank his stock of liquor. Armed bands began to roam the countryside, beating and tarring and feathering excise officers, and destroying the property of distillers who had complied with the law. They formed an army, several thousand strong, marched on Pittsburgh, and took it. They approached the governments of Britain and Spain with plans for a separate republic. George Washington saw no alternative but to call out the militia. This display of strength by the federal government caused the insurrection to collapse. The rebels fled. A few were arrested, taken to Philadelphia, and tried for treason; two were convicted, but Washington pardoned them both.

---

[15]Historians have tended to sympathize with the Scotch-Irish, arguing that their livelihood was threatened by the excise duty, because they depended on sales of their whiskey to consumers on the eastern side of the Appalachians. Supposedly, because it was impractical for the backwoodsmen to haul bulky consignments of grain over the mountains to sell it in eastern markets, they distilled the grain into whiskey and sent that over the mountains instead. This, however, was a myth created by their descendants. There is no evidence of whiskey being sold in eastern Pennsylvania in the eighteenth century. Far from hauling their whiskey over the mountains, the backwoodsmen drank it all themselves.

Despite the ease with which their uprising was suppressed, the "whiskey rebels" (as they came to be known) really did threaten the existence of the American republic. Contemporaries feared not only that the Scotch-Irish would secede from the union but that the separatist spirit would spread throughout North America, and that every region would become a nation. From a modern perspective, this might seem fanciful, but a comparison with the history of Latin America shows how readily North America might have been divided into a large number of small countries.

After the failure of the Whiskey Rebellion, an increasing number of independent-minded Scotch-Irish moved even farther away from the influence of the federal government, into the newly formed state of Kentucky. Here they developed a new kind of whiskey of superior quality.

Back in western Pennsylvania they had distilled their whiskey from rye, which produced a full-flavored but relatively harsh drink; now in Kentucky they made whiskey from a mixture of rye and corn, the latter contributing sweetness to the blend. Why they began to use corn is not known, but it was certainly easier to grow among the stumps of newly cleared land than other cereals. To this sweetness were added vanilla and caramel flavors, extracted from the charred interior of the wooden barrels in which the spirit was matured. It is not known who introduced the process of maturing whiskey, nor when nor why he did so; it may well have begun as a result of the opening of a trade route down the Ohio and Mississippi rivers to New Orleans following a treaty of 1794 with Spain, which then owned Louisiana. Whiskey could not be sent downriver at any time of year, but had to wait for the waters to rise in spring; even then the journey to New Orleans was a long and slow one. The whiskey would certainly have improved as a result of the rocking motion of the boat and the time that it spent on the journey;[16] the distillers and whiskey merchants would presumably have been informed of this improvement, or have noticed it for themselves, and have begun deliberately to mature their whiskeys. It is possible—although this is pure speculation—that they did not have enough new barrels available, so had to use old ones as well, which they would have burned on the inside in order to sterilize them and prevent the new whiskey from picking up unwanted flavors from the old wood. Clearly they liked the effect of the charring on the whiskey,

---

[16]Just as Madeira had been on its voyage to America. See Chapter 1.

because before long they began to burn the insides of new barrels as well. By the early nineteenth century, Kentucky whiskey was beginning to resemble the deep-colored, smooth-tasting bourbon that we know today.[17]

There is no doubting the superior quality of this product. As Ebenezer Hiram Stedman, a papermaker in Georgetown, Kentucky, recorded in letters to his daughter: "In the early days of Kentucky one small drink would stimulate the whole system. One could feel it in their feet, hands, in every part. There was a warm glow of feeling, a stimulus of strength, of buoyancy, of feeling, a something of reaction of joy in place of sorrow. It brought out kind feelings of the heart, made men sociable. And in them days everybody invited everybody that came to their house to partake of this hosesome [sic] beverage." Bourbon rapidly became popular among discerning consumers throughout the country.

The other reason that whiskey supplanted rum during the first half of the nineteenth century was price. Even after the Whiskey Rebellion had been crushed, resistance to the excise had continued, rendering it uneconomical to collect.[18] In 1802 it was repealed by the federal government. This meant that not only Kentucky and Pennsylvania whiskey but also New England rum could be sold free of duty. But the whiskey was made from native cereals, whereas the rum was distilled from foreign molasses, on which import duties were imposed. Hamilton had intended his tax on domestic spirits to maintain the ratio that had previously existed between the prices of rum and whiskey. But now

---

[17] The law today requires that any product sold as bourbon must have been matured for at least two years in charred new oak casks. The term "bourbon" became current only in the second half of the nineteenth century. This referred to the name of a county in which was situated the port of Maysville on the Ohio, then an important entrepôt for the whiskey trade. The name of the whiskey thus commemorates the place from which it was traded rather than the place in which it was made, in the same way as Bordeaux wine and port (from Oporto). Bourbon is a much smaller county today; it does not reach the Ohio River; it does not produce any bourbon; and it is dry, so no one is allowed to sell any bourbon within it.

[18] The Kentucky distillers had not joined those of Pennsylvania in rebelling against the 1791 excise tax, but many of them had refused to pay. By 1793 resistance against federal tax collectors had reached such a point that the inspector of revenue in Kentucky was burned in effigy in Lexington and his deputies were abused and assaulted; their horses' ears were cropped; their manes and tails shaved, and their saddles cut to pieces. The Kentucky distillers eventually agreed in 1798 to pay half the tax they owed.

the tax had been adandoned, whiskey was much cheaper than rum, and it rapidly became much more popular.

Unlike rum, whiskey could be produced anywhere in the country where cereals were grown. It could be obtained almost everywhere, even in the Far West, where other provisions were often scarce.[19] It sold at a price that everyone could afford. "Rye and Indian corn," observed the Kentucky doctor Daniel Drake, "furnish us sturdy republicans with whiskey at so cheap a rate that the poorest man in the community can get drunk as often as his wealthiest neighbor—so that our boasted equality does not entirely rest on the basis of our political institutions." Unlike wine, whiskey was a democratic drink; unlike rum and brandy, unlike tea and coffee, it was an American one, because it was made from native ingredients. As the distiller Harrison Hall put it, "The French sip brandy; the Hollanders swallow gin; the Irish glory in their whiskey; surely John Bull finds 'meat and drink' in his porter—and why should not our countrymen have a national beverage?"

As the national drink, whiskey complemented the national diet, which was dominated by fried and salt food. Whiskey was strong enough to cut through the grease, and sweet enough to counteract the salt.[20] This made it popular even in vine-growing regions such as California. "Even now, it is a source of surprise to visitors that, while the state produces the finest of wines,[21] the national beverage of California is whiskey," wrote the journalist and author John Beadle in the early 1870s. "This is a remnant of the tastes of the early settlers, who worked hard and lived hard, on beef, pork, and . . . flour, and never tasted milk, wine, or vegetables for years together."

People drank whiskey rather than wine with their meals, and they drank whiskey in the bars to which they rushed after they had finished them.[22] If they did not have enough food, at least they had sufficient whiskey. On his lecture tour of the States in 1882, Oscar Wilde spoke to an audience of silver miners at Leadville in Colorado. The miners asked him to dine with them. "Having accepted," Wilde recorded, "I had to descend a mine in a rickety bucket. . . . At the bottom of the mine we sat down to a banquet, the first course being whiskey, the second whiskey, and the third whiskey."

---

[19] The lack of provisions in the West is described in Chapter 2.
[20] Also discussed in Chapter 2.
[21] California wine is discussed later in this chapter.
[22] See Chapter 2 again.

Miners drank whiskey in vast quantities. One newspaper editor in Virginia City, Montana, reported having seen some of them down seventeen tumblers of whiskey a day with no adverse effects. Soldiers drank a great deal of whiskey too. This created problems during the Civil War, when supplies ran short, especially in the South. In some states the distillation of corn into whiskey was forbidden in an effort to safeguard essential food supplies, but this prohibition was largely ignored. Faced with a choice between whiskey and food, most people seem to have chosen the former.

Not only was whiskey the favorite drink of soldiers on both sides, it also became a symbol of the war through its association with the man who played the largest part in winning it, General Ulysses S. Grant. It has since become a commonplace of American history that Grant drank prodigious quantities of whiskey. Whether this helped or hindered his military efforts was debated at the time, and has been discussed ever since. Rumors that Grant drank to excess arose periodically during the war, and newspapers claimed that drinking was the cause of his mismanagement of the Battle of Shiloh in April 1862. Certainly he got drunk on a number of occasions during the siege of Vicksburg in the spring of 1863. At that point, according to the account of B. F. Carpenter, an artist who spent six months the next year painting Abraham Lincoln declaiming his Proclamation of Freedom (and would have heard the story from Lincoln himself), "A self-constituted committee, solicitous for the morale of our armies, took it upon themselves to visit the President and urge the removal of General Grant. In some surprise Mr. Lincoln inquired, 'For what reason?' 'Why,' replied the spokesman, 'he drinks too much whiskey.' 'Ah!' rejoined Mr. Lincoln, dropping his lower lip. 'By the way, gentlemen, can either of you tell me where General Grant procures his whiskey? because, if I can find out, I will send every general in the field a barrel of it.'" Vicksburg fell soon after, and Grant's reputation as a great general, and a great drinker of whiskey, was forever established.

Seventy years since it had served as a symbol of backwoods resistance to American union, whiskey had become a symbol of that union through its association with the man who had ensured that the country would remain united.

This marked the high point of its popularity. The consumption of whiskey and other spirits now began to decline in favor of beer. From colonial times until the middle of the nineteenth century, relatively little beer had been drunk in America compared with England, where it was regarded (alongside tea) as the national drink. Beer was more difficult to make in America, because the top-fermenting yeasts that had been introduced by English brewers tended to pick up wild yeasts from the air, which turned the beer bitter. The failure of English yeasts to perform in America was attributed either to some difference in the climate or to the fact that the huge London breweries made their beer in much larger quantities, thus exposing a smaller proportion of their contents to the atmosphere. Beer was also more difficult to transport and store in America, which had a similar population but was a far larger country. The brewing scientists of the eighteenth and early nineteenth centuries could not render beer sufficiently stable to be sent long distances across extremes of climate; whiskey and rum, on the other, hand, could be sent anywhere, under any conditions, without any risk of spoilage.[23]

In the 1840s, German-style lager was introduced. This was made with a bottom-fermenting yeast, so problems of spoilage did not arise provided it could be kept cool. It was a more refreshing drink than its English-style predecessor. And it had a captive audience among German immigrants.[24] Before long, native-born Americans were drinking it too. By the mid-1850s the *New York Times* was expressing its concern that lager was "getting a good deal too fashionable." In the mid-1860s, a spokesman for the Cincinnati chamber of commerce attributed the growth in consumption of beer "in no little degree to the taste which has been acquired for 'lager' as a beverage, not only among the native German population, but all classes. Beer gardens, where this beverage is swallowed by old and young in incredible quantities, have become institutions of great magnitude in this and all the large cities of the Union."[25]

By the end of the century, most of the beer drunk in America was lager, and half of the alcoholic drinks consumed in America were beer. Americans converted in large numbers from whiskey to beer not only because the latter had become a more reliable and refreshing beverage but because it was significantly cheaper than its rival. The heyday of cheap, untaxed whiskey had come to an end in 1862, when an excise duty was imposed on domestically produced spirits in order to help pay for the Civil War. A tax was also imposed on beer, but at a much lower level. Just as rum had lost out to whiskey in the early years of

---

[23]See Chapter 1.
[24]See Chapter 1 again.
[25]Beer gardens are discussed in the next chapter.

the century because import duties made it more expensive, so it now made economic sense for workingmen to stop drinking highly taxed whiskey and start drinking more lightly taxed beer.

The new excise regime not only increased the price of whiskey but caused its quality to improve. In 1868 Congress created a bonded period, which permitted the distiller to store his whiskey without payment of duty while seeking a purchaser. Only when the whiskey was sold and removed from bonded storage did the distiller become liable to the tax. This regulation encouraged whiskey distillers to mature their whiskey for long periods and thus to improve their quality to a level that justified their higher price. Whiskey became a middle-class drink and was largely supplanted by beer as the beverage of the ordinary workingman. By the end of the century, spirits consumption had fallen to half of what it had been during the Civil War, while sales of beer had increased fourfold.

This did not mean, however, that beer had replaced whiskey as the American national drink. Another effect of the introduction of taxation was to concentrate the brewing (and distilling) industries. The introduction of the tax made it difficult for small manufacturers with limited capital to stay in business. Many had to give up. Others survived by enlarging their business, by investing more capital, which required them to generate more income. These factors led to increased competition.

The brewers reacted to this competition by taking over the saloons. Evidently, a saloon that was owned by a brewery would stock only the brands produced by the brewery in question. By owning saloons, breweries could exclude a competitor's products and guarantee sales of their own beer. Instead of expending their energies on selling their produce to independent saloon keepers, as in the past, brewers now pressured the men whom they employed to manage their saloons to sell as much of their beer as possible. If a manager did not sell a sufficient quantity of beer, he would be dismissed. So he had to devise means of attracting as many customers, and of selling as much beer as possible.

In order to bring in customers, a lot of money was spent on making the saloons appear imposing. They were equipped with large mirrors and grand-looking paintings, which usually displayed women in various stages of undress.[26] Some sought ostentatiously to display the

---

[26]See Chapter 3.

wealth of the brewery that owned them by paving the floor with silver dollars. By measures such as these, the saloons sought to apply a veneer of respectability to their trade.

In general, however, the marketing methods were rather less respectable. Saloon keepers attracted male customers in search of other forms of entertainment by encouraging prostitutes to tout for business on their premises. In many saloons in the big cities prostitutes were paid a commission on the sale of drinks.[27] Many customers were also enticed into saloons by the offer of a "free lunch." This was not a charitable gesture intended to provide nourishment for the poor, but a marketing device calculated to excite thirst. Only dry or salty food was provided, such as pretzels, pickles, smoked sausage, and salt fish. If a customer ate too much food, or failed to purchase a sufficient number of drinks to wash it down, he would be thrown out by a bouncer.[28]

Bartenders also sought to persuade their customers to drink more than they had intended by encouraging them to treat one another to drinks; often the bartender would start the process going by buying drinks for everyone on the premises, which the individual patrons then felt obliged to follow.[29] Bartenders also gave free drinks to new customers, including children. As one member of the liquor trade told a meeting of the Retail Liquor Dealers Association of Ohio in 1912, "We must create an appetite for liquor in the growing boys. Men who drink . . . will die, and if there is no new appetite created, our counters will be empty as well as our coffers. The open field for the creation of appetite is among the boys. Nickels expended in treats now will return in dollars to your tills after the appetite has been formed."

These remarks were given wide publicity by the Anti-Saloon League, a campaigning organization that believed the abuses associated with the saloon could be eliminated by abolishing it. The league published pamphlets in which it described the saloon as a training school for crime and immorality. "The saloon," it declared, "produces eighty percent of the criminals in this country. The saloon is responsible for most of the 60,000 girls who go astray into immoral lives every year. The saloon and the brothel are twin evils, and every man who votes for the liquor traffic is indirectly voting to create conditions which feed

---

[27] This is also discussed in Chapter 3.
[28] Hence the phrase "To give someone the bum's rush," referring to bouncers expelling vagrants who tried to help themselves to the free lunch.
[29] See the Conclusion for more on treating.

the social evil. . . . The saloon is responsible for more vice, degradation, sorrow, misery, tears, heartaches, and deaths than any other cause tolerated by Government."

The more the league publicized the excesses of the saloons, the less they came to be regarded as places that respectable people might enter. By the end of the century many of the customers who patronized saloons did so furtively, entering by a side door down a back alley and spending their time in premises hidden from the outside world by curtains and blinds. On leaving, they chewed coffee or sucked cloves in order to conceal the smell of alcohol and hide from their relatives or business associates what they felt was a dirty little secret.

The saloons gave public drinking such a bad name that respectable people generally gave up drinking in public altogether. Middle-class men who dined in restaurants might leave the table to drink in the bar, where their wives would not see them,[30] those people who could afford to do so might order champagne in restaurants, or serve a profusion of wines when entertaining guests at home, in both cases as gestures of ostentatious wealth rather than demonstrations of their habits,[31] but, for the most part, those native-born Americans who continued to drink alcoholic beverages no longer did so openly and proudly. In restaurants, at banquets, at all public occasions, the predominant drink was now iced water. This served to symbolize the public rejection of alcohol and the adoption of temperance principles by the leaders of American society.[32]

Likewise, at ordinary family meals in the home, water, milk, tea, and coffee would have been served, but not alcoholic beverages. The woman of the household would not have permitted any alcohol in her home. To have done otherwise would have compromised the very moral standards that the woman herself was supposed to set.[33]

George Sala, returning in 1879–80 to a country he had previously visited as a war reporter during the Civil War, was struck by the dramatic change in drinking habits. Where previously there had been "a terrible consumption of cocktails," now most of the population drank

---

[30]See Chapters 2 and 3.
[31]These are also discussed in Chapter 2.
[32]For more on the popularity of water, see Chapter 2 again.
[33]These moral standards have been discussed in Chapter 3. Women did, however, take highly alcoholic patent medicines, for which also see Chapter 3.

nothing stronger than tea or coffee. " 'Tis only the Germans and Irish, I am told, who drink lager beer and whiskey in the America of today."

This may have been something of an exaggeration, but it did show how the image of the two drinks had altered. Whiskey had ceased to be regarded as the American national drink and was now associated primarily with immigrants from Ireland;[34] beer, which had appeared to be on the way to replacing whiskey as the national beverage, was now connected principally with immigrants from Germany.

In Worcester, Massachusetts, the Irish and Germans accounted between them for only one sixth of the population but for two thirds of the saloon keepers and perhaps an even large proportion of their customers. Among the rest of the population this nativist rhyme became popular:

> The Irish and the Dutch, they don't amount to much,
> For the Micks have their whiskey and the Germans guzzle
>   the beer,
> And all we Americans wish they had never come here.

Not only were whiskey and beer now associated with the immigrants who had become their most conspicuous consumers, but they had come to symbolize the behavior of the immigrants and in particular the manner in which they appeared to refuse to integrate into American society.[35]

Not only did the Irish drink whiskey, they identified themselves with it: They drank it as a means of asserting their Irishness. They had long enjoyed a reputation for heavy drinking back in their own country, but the circumstances in which they found themselves in America encouraged them to lay the foundations of a reputation with which Irish-Americans remain tarnished to this day. Suffering from discrimination as Catholics in a Protestant country, Irish immigrants in America turned to drink as a symbol of ethnic loyalty, as a form of self-

---

[34]This helps to explain why so little is known about the early history of bourbon: why it is not known who distilled the first whiskey in Kentucky, or who first made use of corn as well as rye, or who first thought of maturing the whiskey in charred barrels. The records of early distilling were expunged by descendants of the distillers, under the influence of the temperance movement; such a family history would have been regarded as shameful.

[35]The link between Irish (and German) immigration and temperance and prohibition campaigns is discussed in Chapter 3.

identification. "We are known," declared two Irish-American bishops, "as a religion of saloon keepers, of men who drink and men who provide the means of drinking."

Instead of becoming the American national drink, beer was associated in the public mind with the un-American behavior of Germans, who liked to spend their time drinking lager in large groups in beer gardens, especially on Sunday afternoons. One such gathering was described by a *New York Times* journalist: "The object is to drink just as much beer as you can hold, smoke just as many cigars as you can bite the ends off of, and see who can sit in his chair the longest. . . . And, bless us, how the beer pours down! . . . The man who can drink the most . . . is the best man. There is nothing to eat—and who would eat when he can blow off the foam and have her filled up again. . . . The bill of fare was varied and extensive. Following is a translation: Beer, Cigars, Beer, More Beer, Cigars, Beer, Beer, Beer, Beer, Beer, Beer, Beer, Beer, Beer, Beer, Beer Beer, Beer, Beer, Beer."

The consumption of German-style lager beer came to appear even more unpatriotic after the formation of the National German-American Alliance in 1901. This was a perfectly legitimate organization, intended to encourage the appreciation of German culture, which was increasingly being ignored by the children and grandchildren of German immigrants. By 1914 it claimed a membership of two million. Unfortunately, by this time many of its cultural aims had been forgotten because it was being subsidized by the brewers, who were using it as an instrument to fight the campaign for prohibition. An article in the alliance's *Bulletin* declared that the antidrink campaign was directed primarily against "German manners and customs, the joviality of the German people. . . . In order to gain for the Germans of America that place in the sun which has hitherto always been denied them, it is absolutely necessary that they enjoy personal liberty, and that this should not be whittled away by the attacks of the prohibitionists and the persecutors of the foreign born."

The alliance continued to support German interests after war broke out in Europe in the summer of 1914. It sought to link German patriotism with the right to drink and the rejection of prohibition. John Schwaab, head of the Ohio branch of the alliance, stated that "the drink question is forced upon us by the same hypocritical Puritans as over there [in England] are endeavoring to exterminate the German nation."

At the same time, the opponents of the brewing industry sought to connect German aggression in Europe with the unhealthy effects of drinking too much beer. "The Junker, the Kaiser, the murderer of the Archduke Ferdinand and his wife, in fact the very house of Hohenzollern," claimed the prohibitionist campaigner Purley A. Baker, "are but the merest incidents in bringing on this world holocaust. The primary and secondary and all-compelling cause is that a race of people have arisen who eat like gluttons and drink like swine—a race whose 'God is their belly' and whose inevitable end is destruction. Their sodden habits of life have driven them constantly toward brutality and cruelty until they were prepared to strike for universal conquest, though millions of lives and oceans of blood were to be the price of reaching that unholy ambition. Beer will do for a nation exactly what it will do for an individual. . . . We seek a saloonless and drunkless world."

For the first three years of the war in Europe, America remained steadfastly neutral and German-Americans were free to side with Germany—as many of them did. This did not mean they were popular. In May 1915 the British liner *Lusitania* was torpedoed by a German submarine when sailing for Liverpool with 1,900 passengers and crew on board; more than half were killed, including 128 American citizens. The American public was appalled that an apparently civilized nation should have stooped to such a barbarous act as the sinking of an unarmed passenger vessel. From this point on, the German-Americans and their alliance were regarded with great hostility by the majority of the population.

Some of the activities of the alliance, moreover, proved inconsistent with American neutrality. Reports were circulated that the German flag was displayed and *Deutschland über Alles* sung at some meetings. In spring 1916 the *New York World* published letters and documents showing that the alliance had been engaging in pro-German activities ever since the outbreak of war in 1914. These revelations, wrote the *New York Times,* came as an "astounding chapter in the continued story of German conspiracy against the United States. They prove that a secret campaign has been carried on by a nationwide German organization, the National German-American Alliance, to prevent legislation unfavorable to the designs and interests of Germany and to promote legislation favorable to those designs and interests."

In April 1917 America joined the war, unleashing a huge wave of popular hostility toward Germans and German culture. German books were removed from public libraries. German music was scorned. Many place names of German origin were replaced by those of French and Belgian towns that the Germans had destroyed. In Bismarck, North Dakota, the name of the town on the Northern Pacific Railroad station was blotted out with yellow paint, and a six-foot sign erected in its place with the inscription "To hell with this stupid Hun. What did he ever do for us?" Many families of German origin turned their names into more American-sounding ones: Strauss was changed to Stratford, Schmitt to Smith, Fritz to Fox and Rosenstein to Rose. Hamburg steak was renamed "liberty steak," and sauerkraut became "liberty cabbage."

In various parts of the country, attempts were made to prohibit the use of the German language and fines were imposed on people who persisted in speaking German in public. Street fights occurred when people were heard talking in German; the windows of their homes were smeared with yellow paint or else covered with notices that they spoke German or read a German paper.

Crowds broke into high schools in cities with large German-born populations and burned all the German books they could find. In Hawley, Minnesota, a bonfire of German texts ended with citizens suspected of pro-German leanings being forced to kiss the American flag. In Los Angeles, a German youth was beaten severely by his schoolmates for refusing to stand during the singing of *America*. A pastor in Cincinnati who was regarded as an active pacifist and an opponent of conscription was carried in an automobile into the Kentucky hills, tied to a tree, stripped, and whipped "in the name of the women and children of Belgium." Many suspected German sympathizers were flogged, or tarred and feathered, but only one was murdered: Robert Prager, a German coal miner and active socialist, was hanged by a mob in Collinsville, Illinois, supposedly because he had spoken disparagingly of the president. Prager was in fact a patriot who had three American flags in his home; the leaders of the mob were charged with his lynching but found not guilty.

The National German-American Alliance could not survive such hostility. The Senate passed a resolution stating that "the organized liquor traffic is a vicious interest . . . because it has been pro-German in its sympathies and conduct. Around these great brewery organizations owned by rich men, almost all of them of German birth and sympathy, have grown up the societies, all the organizations in this country intended to keep young German immigrants from becoming real American citizens. It is around these *Sangerfests* [choral festivals] and *Sangerbunds* [choral societies] . . . generally financed by the rich brewers, that the young Germans who come to America are taught to remember, first the Fatherland, and second America."

The activities of the alliance were investigated by a subcommittee of the Senate's Judiciary Committee. Although it did not succeed in establishing any direct connection between the National German-American alliance and the German propaganda machine, it managed to prove that the brewers had spent $1.7 million to buy the *New York Daily Mail and Express,* which had become a mouthpiece for pro-German material, and that the alliance controlled many smaller societies, some of them secretive groups with dubious motives. This Senate investigation forced the alliance to disband.

The brewers had been compelled to abandon their alliance, and their cause had been discredited. Prohibitionist campaigners took advantage of the war to argue that the part played by brewers of German origin in supporting German national interests demonstrated the necessity of putting them out of business. As John Strange, a leading prohibitionist and former lieutenant-governor of Wisconsin, stated at the beginning of 1918, "We have German enemies across the water. We have German enemies in this country too. And the worst of all our German enemies, the most treacherous, the most menacing, are [the brewers] Pabst, Schlitz, Blatz, and Miller. They are the worst Germans who inflicted themselves upon a long-suffering people."

Prohibitionists rode the wave of popular hostility to the German brewers, and took advantage of a national mood of patriotism and self-sacrifice. They argued that the consumption of alcohol lessened the efficiency of workers in munitions factories and the precision of soldiers who were shooting at the enemy. They referred to the need to conserve food materials rather than waste them on the production of alcohol. One dry economist claimed that the grain used in liquor manufacture would produce eleven million loaves of bread a day for America's starving allies on the other side of the Atlantic.

The beginnings of national Prohibition are to be found in the legislation that was passed in the fervent atmosphere of the war. In order to ensure the efficiency of the forces, dry zones were established in May 1917 around military camps throughout the United States, and civilians were prohibited from selling or serving alcoholic beverages to members of the armed forces, even in private homes. In order to preserve grain supplies, spirits production was stopped in September 1917, and the maximum strength of beer was reduced to 2.75 percent by weight (3.5 percent by volume) in December.[36] In the same month, Congress passed the Eighteenth Amendment to the Constitution, prohibiting the manufacture, sale, or transportation of "intoxicating liquors" within the United States. This was to come into effect one year after it had been ratified by a three-quarters majority of the states (thus giving the liquor companies sufficient time to dispose of their businesses). By January 1919 thirty-six of the forty-eight states had ratified the Eighteenth Amendment, which meant that national Prohibition came into force in January 1920.

The effect of the war upon German-Americans was dramatic. Until then they had managed to remain both Germans and Americans. Once America had joined the war, they could no longer remain Germans as well as loyal American citizens. Some of them found the prospect of fighting against their fatherland so painful to bear that they committed suicide while waiting in the draft camps. Others performed their patriotic duty and fought against the country of their birth. As a result, they broke decisively with their German origins and became fully integrated into American society.

By the time America fought in another war, a generation later, the brewers, who had been careful to distance themselves from events in Germany in the intervening period, no longer attracted any anti-German sentiment.[37] This time ethnic hostility was directed at Americans of Japanese rather than German origin. And it was the prohibitionists rather than brewers who found themselves associated with enemy propaganda. They sought to exploit the raid on Pearl Harbor for their own ends. The Reverend Samuel Morris claimed that the attack was timed for a Sunday morning because a typical Saturday night of "strong drink rendered the island helpless, befuddled, off guard, and at the mercy of the heartless Japs." In fact, when a presidential commission under Supreme Court justice Owen Roberts investigated the raid, it found no evidence of excess drunkenness among the defending forces. By persisting with their allegation that the troops defending Oahu had been drunk, the prohibitionists ended up in bed with enemy propagandists, who were seeking to spread the same rumor. The claims of the prohibitionists appeared all the more foolish in

---

[36]This is discussed in Chapter 4.
[37]Since the late 1970s there have been persistent rumors about the supposed "Nazi" connections of the Coors brewery; these do not in fact relate to its wartime activities but to its more recent support for extreme right-wing causes.

the light of their enthusiastic commendation before the war of Hitler's personal rejection of alcohol, of his policy of "racial hygiene,"[38] and of his promotion of temperance among his people. No wonder their demands for restrictions on the supply of alcohol during the war were ignored.

Far from acceding to the request of prohibitionist campaigners that they should forbid the sale of 3.2 percent (by weight) beer on domestic and overseas military bases, the War Department declared that the presence of beer in controlled surroundings encouraged temperate drinking. During the war, beer was officially regarded as patriotic rather than as a threat to military progress. Government agencies did their best to ensure that the supply to the troops did not run out. A Food Distribution Administration Order of 1943 required brewers to set aside 15 percent of total beer production for use by the armed forces. In January 1945 the War Labor Board ordered the Teamsters Union to end a strike against Minneapolis breweries because beer manufacturing was considered an essential industry.

Before the war, beer consumption had been lower than before Prohibition. Brewers blamed poor sales on the Depression, on high taxes, and on the lingering effects of Prohibition. During the war, as a result of military procurement policies and increased consumer spending, beer consumption grew sharply, passing its pre-Prohibition level in 1943. The Brewers Digest described the army camps as "a chance for brewers to cultivate a taste for beer in millions of young men who will eventually constitute the largest beer-consuming section of our population."

During the war, the brewing industry spent a lot of money on advertising and public relations campaigns designed to show that the consumption of beer was part of American culture and essential to good morale. By claiming in its advertisements that "Morale Is a Lot of the Little Things," the Brewing Industry Foundation sought to ensure that beer drinking was regarded as a normal part of wartime life.

This process continued after the war had ended. The brewers used advertisements in order to make beer drinking seem like an ordinary everyday activity. While the distillers remained preoccupied in their public relations with taxation and other political issues, the brewers sought to create through their publicity a perception of their product as fundamental to American society—showing it being drunk in a fam-

---

[38]The connection between Prohibition and eugenics is discussed in Chapter 3.

ily gathering or by a group of middle-class people "in this friendly, freedom-loving land of ours." Television, too, played its part in normalizing the consumption of beer by showing people drinking it without any apparent ill effects. In an early television advertisement the Pabst brewery declared, "It's beer, Mama, and TV . . . three ingredients of a recipe for successful living."

In order to achieve their aim of having beer regarded as an integral part of American life, the brewers needed it to be drunk in as many families as possible. This requirement gives the lie to the argument currently put forward by the liquor industry, in response to demands from temperance campaigners that advertisements for alcoholic beverages be restricted or banned, that it does not advertise in order to enlarge the total consumption of alcoholic drink but only in order to increase the relative sales of individual brands. In fact, brewers have for many years used advertisements specifically for the purpose of increasing the consumption of alcoholic drinks, not so much in terms of quantity per head as in respect to the number of people who drink them. One of the prime purposes behind the advertising of beer has been to extend the consumer base and thus make it a more normal part of American life.

This is demonstrated by the impact of Philip Morris on the American beer market. Philip Morris, previously a producer of cigarettes, entered the beer industry when it purchased a controlling stake in the Miller brewery, the seventh largest in America, in 1969. Using its experience of selling tobacco in a hostile market, Philip Morris introduced a new approach to beer advertising, focusing not on the product itself but on the occasion on which it was drunk. "It's Miller time!" it proclaimed—and it soon transpired that almost any time was "Miller time," anywhere. It did take a few years for Miller's sales to respond to the massive investment in advertising, but this did not matter to Philip Morris, which was able to subsidize its initial losses on beer from the profits it made from tobacco. Between 1972 and 1979 Miller's expenditure on publicity increased from $11 to $75 million per annum and its share of the beer market from 4 to 22 percent, making it the second biggest brewer in the country after Anheuser-Busch, the producer of Budweiser. Having pushed aside all its other rivals, Miller indulged in an advertising war with Anheuser-Busch that continues to this day.

Not only has the entry of Philip Morris into the beer market greatly increased the overall consumption of beer—which grew by 50 percent during the 1970s alone—it has compressed the brewing industry into two principal brands. One in every four beers drunk in America is a Budweiser, and one in ten a Miller Lite. On average, every adult in the country drinks six gallons of Budweiser a year. All over America, at any one time, a significant proportion of the population is drinking the same beer.[39] Many consumers appear to believe that drinking a national brand of beer is part of being American—that it serves to demonstrate one's patriotism in much the same way as planting the national flag in one's front yard. The fact that Budweiser commemorates the German name of a Czech city is evidently lost on most of the people who drink it.[40]

Another effect of the consolidation of the American brewing industry has been to move its principal brands farther away from their German models.[41] American lagers have become increasingly tasteless in order to satisfy the basic principle of mass marketing that the blander a product is made, the more easily it can be sold to very large numbers of people. And in an attempt to widen their market still further, the brewers have developed yet blander variants of their major brands in order to appeal to consumers who find even mainstream lager too demanding for their palates. First, in the 1970s, came "light" beer, in which more of the sugar was fermented into alcohol, producing a lager with fewer calories and less body; next in the 1980s came "dry" beer, actually the same thing, but marketed as a new product, with less aftertaste; then in the 1990s came "clear" beer, from which all the color had been removed by filtration along with most of the taste. No wonder many committed beer drinkers abandoned mainstream brands for micro-

[39]This has been made possible by improvements in brewery hygiene and by the introduction of refrigerated transportation, which allow beer to be transported long distances, and by the development of chemical treatments that enable different sources of water to be made to resemble each other, so that identical beers can be brewed in several different places at the same time.

[40]This connection, and the battle over the Budweiser brand name, are discussed in Chapter 1.

[41]The origins of this process are also discussed in Chapter 1. It is possible to appreciate the extent to which American lager has changed by comparing Budweiser with Samuel Adams Lager, created in 1985 by Boston businessman Jim Koch, using the recipe of his great-great-grandfather Louis, a brewer in St. Louis. This is a fuller-flavored and more bitter beer, made entirely from malted barley. It was named after the eighteenth-century revolutionary Samuel Adams because of his involvement in the brewing industry in Boston—not (as Koch claims) as a brewer, but as a maltster of barley. Only a tiny proportion of this beer is actually brewed in Boston.

brews, which promised them a return to the characterful beers of pre-Prohibition America,[42] while others turned to imported lagers, which might not have been as fresh as their American counterparts but offered more flavor.

The major brewers have responded by buying microbreweries and bringing out their own versions of microbrewery beers. Anheuser-Busch has bought shares in the Red Hook brewery in Seattle; Miller brews a brand called Red Dog that does not reveal its true origins on the label but claims to have been made somewhere called the Plank Road Brewery. They have also, on occasion, sought to pass off their own products as imported beers. In 1979 Anheuser-Busch complained to the Federal Trade Commission that Miller was seeking to conceal from consumers the fact that it had converted from importing Löwenbräu from Germany to brewing it in America. The domestically brewed Löwenbräu was packaged in the same bottle and with the same label as the German version; advertisements featured the European brewing awards that had been won by the German product; many bars and restaurants continued to list it under the heading of "imported beers." Anheuser-Busch argued that not only were the two versions of Löwenbräu brewed in different continents, they followed different recipes: that Miller was using a cheaper form of malted barley, to which it was adding a substantial quantity of corn, and that it was maturing the beer for only nine days compared with the traditional six weeks. The Federal Trade Commission passed the complaint to the Treasury Department, where it attracted the attention of assistant secretary Richard Davis, a former Watergate prosecutor and a disgruntled ex–Löwenbräu drinker who had stopped buying the brand when it had become a domestically produced beer. Offended that Miller was blatantly misleading consumers about its current origin, Davis put pressure on the company to admit the truth. The label was altered to carry the words "product of the USA" and the television advertisements added the phrase, "a fine American beer."

Why did Miller go to such lengths to pass off a domestic beer as an import? American beers may enjoy a reputation for being less flavorsome than European ones, but there is no reason that should necessarily be the case. As a number of microbreweries have proved in the last generation, American-produced beers can be just as good as their European models, even, in some instances, superior to them; Miller

---

[42]The microbreweries are also discussed in Chapter 1.

could perfectly well have produced a version of Löwenbräu that accurately replicated the original. The significance of this episode is that it demonstrates the survival of what in Australia is called the "cultural cringe"—the notion that nothing that comes out of Australia (or America) can be as good as the original version made in Europe because Australia (or America) is a new country that lacks the history, tradition, and culture of Europe.

The survival of the "cultural cringe" in America is demonstrated by the popular preference for imported over domestic beers, by the development of a "fusion" cuisine that is not an integral style of American cookery but a haphazard combination of ingredients and techniques from all over the world,[43] and by the history of California wine.

In the middle of the nineteenth century, the main vine-growing area of California was situated around Los Angeles. This was too warm a region for the successful production of table wine; the grapes over-ripened in the hot sun. Two Englishmen named Rivington and Harris, who visited America in 1869, commented that "the native wines of America are not very palatable. . . . The California port and sherry are far too sweet; and the difficulty in making wines in California is how to get rid of the large excess of alcohol which they contain."

Gradually, as more vines were planted in relatively cool areas around San Francisco, the quality of the wines coming from California improved, but, from the point of view of marketing, it was already too late. Wine merchants had gotten in the habit of bottling the better California wines with foreign labels in order to command higher retail prices, and of bottling cheap foreign wine with California labels, thus encouraging the popular belief that California could at best product only inferior imitations of European wines. The vine grower Arpad Haraszthy complained in 1872 that "the reputation of California wines in the Eastern States is at this moment undergoing one of the severest trials that can be put upon the product of any country: that of palming off upon the confiding public spurious, inferior, and barefaced imitations of the same, which never saw the soil of the state, nor resemble wines in any particular. This unscrupulous traffic is carried on openly throughout the Eastern States, and millions of gallons of these compounds over and above the actual product of this are probably sold."

---

[43]Fusion cuisine is described in Chapter 2.

These fake wines, Haraszthy said, were usually made from cider, flavored and colored with chemicals.

In 1879, Pierre Klein, an emigrant to California from Alsace,[44] opened the Occidental Restaurant in San Francisco. So shocked was he to learn that California wine had to pass under phony French labels in order to be accepted by American wine drinkers that he planted his own vineyard in the Santa Cruz Mountains. He hoped that by making his own wine he would encourage the notion that California could produce wine good enough to sell under its own name. His Mira Valle, made from the same blend of grapes as the best red wines in Bordeaux, won a gold medal at the Paris Exposition of 1900, and gave the produce of the Santa Cruz Mountains a reputation for excellence that they carried through Prohibition and down to the present time.

Despite the development of Mira Valle and other high-quality vineyards such as Inglenook[45] in the later years of the nineteenth century, California wines did not feature prominently on the lists of the snobbish, Eurocentric restaurants in the cities on the East Coast. "The native wine of California is still fighting against the unfavorable reputation it acquired from the ignorance and impatience of its early manufacturers," explained James Fullarton Muirhead. "The art of wine-growing, however, is now followed with more brains, more experience, and more capital, and the result is in many instances excellent. . . . It is a thousand pities that the hotels and restaurants of the United States do not do more to push the sales of these native wines, which are at least better than most of the wine sold in America at extravagant charges."

A generation later, the fine-wine industry that had developed in California was destroyed by Prohibition. Many of the leading wineries were forced to close, and other vineyards were converted to grapes best suited for sale to home winemakers, notably the deep-colored and strong-flavored but poor quality alicante bouschet.[46] In the book on American wines they wrote at the beginning of the 1940s, in which they sought to persuade consumers to renew their interest in domestic produce, Frank Schoonmaker and Tom Marvel stated that "Americans have turned to table wines since Prohibition much more slowly than most of us expected. For this, our national attitude is largely to blame:

---

[44]France had just ceded Alsace to Prussia after losing the Franco-Prussian War.
[45]This is described in Chapter 1.
[46]This is discussed in Chapter 2.

The trouble has been that we have all thought of such wine in terms of Europe, as the equivalent of French lessons or a course in Gothic architecture or a trip abroad. . . . Morally, practically, and economically, the damage of Prohibition in California is not likely to be repaired for another fifteen or twenty years. It may never be repaired. With a few notable exceptions, those who had created the traditions of wine producing in California, and had maintained its standards, did not survive Prohibition. The industry fell inevitably into far less scrupulous hands."

It did not help that wineries that opened after Repeal reverted to the bad old practice of selling California wine under French names. It is true that they no longer, on the whole, attempted to pass off their wines as French, but they nevertheless appropriated the names of the finest of French wines, notably champagne, Chablis, and burgundy, to add a touch of class to their own lesser produce. Their pretension was immortalized in the famous cartoon by James Thurber in which a host owned up to his guests about the wine he had served them, "It's a naïve domestic burgundy without any breeding, but I think you'll be amused by its presumption."

When representatives of the French wine industry complained to the United States government, Congress passed an act that prohibited American wine producers from using French or other European regional names on their labels unless the wine was of the same type. Congress did not, however, determine how narrowly or widely a type should be defined. Since wine produced in Chablis in France is always dry, white, and still, one would have thought that a "California Chablis" should at the very least conform to the original in one or two if not all three of these respects. In 1965, however, Gallo introduced a Chablis from California that was sweet, pink, and sparkling.[47]

To this day, supermarket shelves are filled with California wines labeled "burgundy" or "Chablis."[48] This is morally indefensible. It is

---

[47]Although they had appropriated French wine names, in 1986 Ernest and Julio Gallo sued their brother Joseph when he attempted to use the family name to market a brand of cheese.

[48]The only French wine name that Californian producers have been persuaded to abandon is "Gamay Beaujolais"; not only does this come from many thousands of miles west of the Beaujolais region of France, it is not even made from the gamay grape, but from a clone of the pinot noir. American vintners will be permitted to continue to use the name "Gamay Beaujolais" until 2007 as long as they specify the true origin and grape variety from which the wine has been made.

also unwise. Maybe it is understandable that producers of lesser-quality California wines should have appropriated the names of fine French ones in order to suggest a degree of sophistication that they otherwise lack, but it is foolish for companies who are striving to produce wines of high quality to have done the same. Although most serious wineries in California now label their products with the names of the grapes from which they have been made, significant exceptions remain.

Schramsberg, which was established on the site of a pre-Prohibition vineyard in the Napa Valley in 1965, has enjoyed an international reputation for its sparkling wines ever since President Nixon had thirteen cases flown over to Peking to serve at his historic banquet for the Chinese prime minister Chou En-lai. Since the 1987 vintage it has produced a prestige *cuvée* called "J. Schram" (after Jacob Schram, the founder of the original estate) which sells for $50 a bottle. Yet the company persists in taking advantage of the reputation established by French sparkling wines from the Champagne region by selling its California sparkling wines as "champagne." Its owner, Jack Davies, sought to justify this practice by explaining that consumers would not expect a bottle labeled simply "sparkling wine" to be of high quality. True, but no justification. Why does Schramsberg exploit the prestige of Champagne rather than further the reputation of California?

The use of French names for the marketing of California wines has done nothing to improve the image of California wines among sophisticated or snobbish American consumers. Despite his insistence on serving Schramsberg when in China, Richard Nixon was unenthusiastic about offering California wines in the White House. Although a native of California and a former senator from the state, he instructed that California wine should not be served at official dinners, especially if foreigners were present.

Not until the 1970s did the image of California wines improve sufficiently to permit them to be served at official functions, and to be listed alongside clarets and burgundies in the most prestigious restaurants in cities on the East Coast. A major factor in this change of image was a comparative tasting of California and French wines held in France in 1976 by the English wine merchant Steven Spurrier in order to gain publicity for his Paris wine shop, Caves de la Madeleine. The wines were tasted "blind," which meant that the participants did not know what they were tasting, but Spurrier had tried to rig the competition so that the French wines would win. Against California cabernet sauvignons and chardonnays he pitted first-growth Bordeaux and *premier cru* and *grand cru* white burgundies, all from good or very good vintages; and all the tasters were French.

In fact, Stag's Leap 1973 Cabernet Sauvignon from California came before the red wines, ahead of Château Mouton-Rothschild 1970, and Château Montelena 1973 Chardonnay from California came first among the white wines, ahead of the 1973 Meursault *premier cru* Les Charmes from Guy Roulot. These results gave American wine merchants and restaurants the confidence to purchase American wines. Before the tasting, one buyer had told Warren Winiarski, the owner of Stag's Leap, that he could not see why he should purchase any of Winiarski's wine when he could obtain good red Bordeaux. After the tasting, he telephoned Winiarski to tell him that his California wine was better.

Not only did this event give California wines a new status among the American wine trade and the American public, it encouraged their producers to promote them by means of comparative tastings against French wines. In 1985 William Hill, the owner of an eponymous winery in the Napa Valley, held tastings around the country in which he pitted his Cabernet Sauvignon against first-growth Bordeaux. In an event billed as "the showdown in Texas," 150 consumers were given the opportunity to compare four of Hill's recent vintages with wines from Châteaux Latour, Margaux, and Mouton-Rothschild. The tasters judged the 1978, 1979, and 1980 vintages of Hill's Cabernet Sauvignons to be superior to the wines from Bordeaux; only in the case of the 1981 vintage did they place Châteaux Margaux first, William Hill Cabernet Sauvignon second, and Château Mouton-Rothschild third. Hill wisely did not seek to argue that this tasting proved that his wines were better than the first-growth Bordeaux, only that, at one third the price, they offered superior value for money. As Frank Prial, the veteran wine correspondent of the *New York Times,* explained, this was not really a comparative tasting but a positioning exercise: The purpose was not to see whether people preferred California cabernet sauvignon to classed-growth Bordeaux, but to ensure that they came to associate the two. "It's like those automobile commercials that say 'More trunk space than the legendary BMW!' Even if the car in question is powered by squirrels on a treadmill, the association has been made."

Another California wine company that promotes its wines principally by means of tastings, many of them comparative, is the celebrated family firm of Mondavi. In September 1990 Michael Mondavi traveled to London to present a blind tasting of four vintages of Robert Mondavi Reserve Cabernet Sauvignon and first-growth Bordeaux. The purpose, he said, was to see whether the Mondavi wines were "worthy of being served at the same table as the great wines of France." Most of the wine writers who attended (including the author of this book) identified the Château Lafite 1986 as having come from California and the Robert Mondavi Reserve Cabernet Sauvignon 1985 as coming from France. Michael Mondavi seemed pleased with the result. But he may not have been wise to be so. At the time, only one percent of the wine imported into Britain came from California, and the British were unlikely to want to buy more of it if they were encouraged to think of it simply as a Doppelgänger of French wine.

Now that fine California wine has become popular throughout the United States, now that American sophisticates no longer look down snobbishly upon their domestic produce, now that many self-conscious wine drinkers in restaurants in New York and other East Coast cities have decided that their image is better served by ordering California than by insisting on French wines, now that the demand for some California wines has enabled them to be marketed at a sufficiently high price to satisfy those consumers who equate cost with status, American wine producers and many American wine experts have turned their attention to what they regard as the unfair denigration of their national produce by an arrogant and reactionary British wine trade.

In the summer of 1997 the British wine magazine *Decanter* published the results of a tasting of California chardonnays, mostly from the 1995 vintage. This was summed up as "disappointing." Out of 106 wines tasted, none was given the highest rating of five stars and only six were given four stars out of five ("highly recommended"). Many of the wines were censured as dilute, overoaked or overacidified. In general, they were described as overpriced for their quality.

Matt Kramer, the wine correspondent for the *Los Angeles Times*, responded by criticizing the *Decanter* tasters for their "unspoken premise that California wines should be cheap. In other words, how dare California wines cost as much as French?" A few weeks later, the American wine magazine the *Wine Spectator* published its annual tasting report on California chardonnay, looking at the 1995 vintage, which it described as "another blockbuster. . . . Chardonnay lovers have never had it this good. . . . There's a strong case to be made for California chardonnay being the most consistently excellent wine in the world today." The Mendocino County Barrel Select Chardonnay from Fetzer, to which *Decanter* had given only one star out of five ("acceptable"), was marked by the *Wine Spectator* at 88 out of 100 ("very good"). Red Shoulder Ranch Chardonnay from Shafer, Central Coast Chardonnay from Calera, and Stefani Vineyard Chardonnay from Gallo, to each of which *Decanter* had given only two stars out of five ("quite good"), were all rated at 91 out of 100 ("outstanding"). And so on.

Sensing more than a difference of opinion between two groups of tasters, William Cash, a British journalist based in Los Angeles working for the London magazine *The Spectator,* published an article on the *Decanter* tasting entitled "Sour Grapes About California." He interviewed various wine merchants and winemakers, including British-born Richard Crichton, a producer of fine California chardonnay at his Crichton Hall vineyard, who suggested that "there is jealousy in England over the success of American wine that most people can't even afford." As Cash pointed out, "Whereas the British are a nation of serious cheap wine drinkers, Americans are increasingly a nation of ultra-serious wine connoisseurs and collectors. . . . What really makes wine snobs in Europe spit into their glasses is the galling sense that after just twenty years of really being in business Americans are now strutting around with an almost smug superiority about wine." He was supported by a correspondent to the magazine, an Englishman who had emigrated to California, who claimed that "there certainly are a lot of snobs in Europe who regularly pontificate on the subject of wine and dismiss Yank vintners. . . . The unpleasant truth is that many California wines are infinitely superior to most European wines."

A difference of professional opinion between two panels of experts with different tastes, operating on opposite sides of the Atlantic, had been blown up into a full-scale defense of the honor of American wine against the supposed prejudices of British wine-tasters. If this dispute showed anything, it showed that the chip has not yet been removed from the shoulder of many in the California wine business. The British are not the colonial masters any longer, nor are they the enemy; they are supposed to be the customers. France is no longer the source of all that is fine in food and drink, but a medium-sized European country, obsessed with its past, frightened of its future, rapidly falling victim to the attractions of American fast food and soft drinks. So why should California winemakers take umbrage at the comments of British tasters, or keep on comparing their produce to that of France?

* * *

It is not surprising that wine has provided a focus for the expression of tension between America and Europe, because it possesses great symbolic power. Wine is a prestigious product that captures within a bottle the essence of a particular place and time. That is why it has often been used as a pawn in negotiations over trade. For example, in a dispute in 1992 between the United States and the European Community during the Uruguay round of the General Agreement on Tariffs and Trade, the United States government threatened to increase the federal tax on imported French white wines[49] by $10 a bottle. Not only would this have damaged significantly an export trade then worth $133 million a year to the French economy, it struck at a product in which the French had invested considerable national pride and prestige.

The symbolic status of wine explains why the French government has ensured that its most prestigious vineyards do not fall into foreign ownership. When Château Margaux was put on the market during the slump of the early 1970s, the American conglomerate National Distillers offered 82 million francs for the property, but this bid was vetoed by the government; instead the château was sold for the lower price of 72 million francs to a French supermarket chain. In the late 1980s, it was reported that the Japanese were trying to buy the most celebrated estate in Burgundy, the Domaine de la Romanée-Conti. In fact, a Japanese company had offered to buy a one-third share of the French company that had the rights to distribute the wines of the Domaine all over the world (except in the United States and Britain). But even this was enough for the French minister of agriculture, Henri Nallet, to swear that he would block the sale. "Romanée-Conti is like a cathedral," he declared.

Wine is symbolic of French culture, but not of American. Partly, no doubt, it is a matter of history: Château Margaux, the Domaine de la Romanée-Conti, and the other leading estates in Bordeaux and Burgundy have established their status over centuries, whereas the reputation of the vast majority of today's most prestigious Californian wineries goes back no more than a generation or two. Only a very few, such as Schramsberg and Niebaum-Coppola (the old Inglenook estate), can trace their heritage back to vineyards that were well known in the late nineteenth century; and these ceased production during Prohibition.

But it is also that wine is thought to represent the hierarchy and

---

[49]At this time white wines were much more popular in America than red.

formality of the Old World and not the democratic culture of the New. Although fine wine can certainly be enjoyed by a novice, it requires a certain amount of knowledge fully to appreciate its qualities. Beer, on the other hand, can be drunk and appreciated without any effort. Beer fits into the national myth of a classless society, the fruits of which can be enjoyed by anyone, whatever his background; wine is still perceived by many as elitist and un-American.[50]

Yet beer remains relatively anonymous: It can be made anywhere, usually to a standard recipe; only wine expresses the character of the specific place where the grapes were grown. Pinot noir from California does not taste like pinot noir from Oregon; merlot from Washington State tastes different from merlot from New York. There are regional differences between California cabernet sauvignon from the Napa Valley and California cabernet sauvignon from the Sonoma Valley. And there are local differences between the Stag's Leap, Rutherford, and Spring Mountain districts within the Napa Valley.

These individual characteristics are fundamental to the appreciation of fine wine. Such a wine specifies its origin precisely and proudly on its label because this matters to the people who made it, and to the people who drink it. By consuming the produce of a specific vineyard in a particular region in a single harvest, a city dweller can travel to the countryside: He can experience its changes of climate and sense its aromas without leaving the comfort of his air-conditioned apartment. "People drink wine," explains Paul Draper, winemaker at Ridge Vineyards, a prestigious estate in the Santa Cruz Mountains, "as a corrective to the high technology of today, as a link with the seasons and the soil. Wine naturally made is the foremost symbol of transubstantiation: That is why it has been part of so many religions. . . . It is an essential truth which human beings need to keep themselves in touch with nature, in touch with art, in touch with magic, in touch with God."

---

[50]This is discussed, in connection with fast-food culture, in Chapter 2.

"The lips that
touch Welch's
are all that
touch mine"

Social Drinking

n Greek mythology, the secret of turning grapes into wine was revealed by the god Dionysus to the peasant Icarios and his daughter Erigone, with whom he had stayed as a guest. Having disclosed his mysteries to them in return for their hospitality, Dionysus told them to teach the art to other people. So Icarios shared his wine with a group of shepherds. At first they enjoyed the delicious new drink, but as they became intoxicated they began to suspect Icarios of having poisoned them. So they turned on him and battered him to death with their clubs. At first his body could not be found, but then his faithful dog Moera led Erigone to the spot where it lay. The sight of her dead father caused Erigone to hang herself in despair. However, in death they received their due rewards: Icarios became the star Boötes and his daughter the constellation Virgo. Boötes, also known in Greek as "the grape gatherer," rises in the autumn, at the time of the vintage; and in Greece the harvest took place under the sign of Virgo.

Another myth about Dionysus, the god of wine, has him dying along with the crushed grapes and being resurrected in the spring, when then vines sprouted again. In his last play,[1] written at the end of the fifth

---

[1]Euripides called his play *The Bacchae*, Bacchus being the name by which Dionysus was known across the Aegean Sea in Lydia (now Turkey).

century B.C., the Greek playwright Euripides described Dionysus as the son of a divine father and a mortal mother, and told of his arrival in Thebes to bring a gift of wine to its citizens, and their refusal to believe in his divinity. The play showed him working miracles and being persecuted.

Four centuries later, the man through whom the myths of Dionysus were to be revived and transformed was born in Bethlehem in the Roman province of Judaea.[2] Jesus Christ appears to have been well aware of the competition from the cult of Dionysus: That explains why St. John in his Gospel cites him as saying that "I am the true vine." He was dissociating himself from the false vine, the vine that led people astray because it concealed a false god and a false religion. At his Last Supper, Jesus offered himself as an alternative symbol of death and rebirth to Dionysus. Here, in the words of the Gospel according to St. Matthew, he "took the cup, and gave thanks, and gave it to them, saying 'Drink ye of it; for this is my blood of the new testament, which is shed for many for the remission of sins.' "

In telling his disciples to drink the wine he had blessed as a symbol of his blood, Jesus was associating himself with wine as the product of an apparently miraculous transubstantiation, as the followers of Dionysus had done. Jesus had himself demonstrated the wondrous nature of this process when he had solved the problem of a wedding feast without any wine by turning water into wine. We understand today that grapes are converted into wine by a natural fermentation. But we have known this for only a little over a century, since the French scientist Louis Pasteur demonstrated that grape juice was transformed into wine by the action of yeasts. In ancient Greece, in the time of Jesus, and for more than eighteen hundred years afterward, fermentation was regarded as miraculous—as a no less inexplicable transubstantiation than turning water into wine, or wine into blood.

"My blood is drink indeed," Jesus told the Jews. "He that . . . drinketh my blood, dwelleth in me, and I in him." Jesus derived his imagery not only from the cult of Dionysus but also from the concept of the "blood taboo." Among ancient civilizations, it was thought that plants such as vines were animate because they bled when cut. It was also believed that the souls of animate beings lived in their blood because

---

[2]Bethlehem is situated today in a Palestinian autonomous area within the geographical boundaries of Israel.

they died when it was spilled. Therefore, by drinking their blood, it was possible to take in their souls.[3]

Since his death, the life and deeds and symbolic significance of Jesus Christ have been commemorated by his followers just as he directed them at his Last Supper, by drinking wine as a symbol of his blood.[4] The consumption of wine in the Eucharist, the ceremony of Thanksgiving that forms part of Holy Communion, has formed the central ceremony of the Christian faith.

The need to ensure that wine was provided for the celebration of Holy Communion even in places where it was not commercially available explains why founders of churches and abbeys and monasteries planted vines at the same time as they laid the foundation. The importance of having wine for the performance of religious ceremonies helps to explain where and why vineyards have been planted. In particular, it accounts for the origin of the wine industry in the New World.

The Spanish adventurers who conquered large portions of Central and South America in the sixteenth century were no less convinced of the importance of having wine for Mass than the missionaries who accompanied them. In 1540 Pedro de Valdivia marched with his men the best part of two thousand miles from Cuzco in Peru to central Chile, crossing the Atacama Desert, and founding Santiago in February 1541. They had trouble obtaining enough food and water on their journey, and had to do without wine. So they could not celebrate Mass on their arrival; devout as they were, they were not prepared to hold Holy Communion without wine. Valdivia sent some of his men back to Peru to fetch supplies; a consignment of wine finally arrived in May 1543, and they could hold their Mass.

Once the Spanish had established their new colonies, it would have been possible for them to have had wine sent out from Europe, but this would have been expensive and taken a long time, especially in the case of the more remote countries such as Chile and Peru. Moreover, vines grew wild in America, so it was clear to the Spaniards that

---

[3]The idea that souls lived in the blood explains the biblical insistence that flesh be drained of its blood before eating, a practice still observed by Orthodox Jews today.

[4]The fact that blood and wine are of a similar color is irrelevant. In order to avoid giving any such impression, the Lutheran Church in California prefers to use white wine in the Eucharist. In England, many Anglican clerics also choose white wine, because it reduces cleaning expenses.

if they brought their own vines from home and grafted them onto American rootstock, they would grow too. So this is what they did. Hernando Cortés, the conqueror of Mexico, first sent out to Spain for cuttings in 1522, not long after he had landed in the New World. Vineyards were planted in Chile and Peru somewhat later, mostly in the 1550s and 1560s. In Chile, the vineyard area grew to such a size that militant natives appear to have regarded the vines as a symbol of the religion that the white men had brought with them. It is possible that having noted the religious importance of wine, the Chilean Indians thought that by striking at the sacred plant they would be making war on that Christian God in whose name they were being enslaved and massacred. When the people of Concepción rose under their *cacique* Antecul, they destroyed every vineyard they could reach.

Farther north the expansion, of the vineyards at least, was achieved more peacefully. Vines were taken from central Mexico by Jesuit missionaries to the Baja California peninsula, where the first Jesuit mission was established among the Indians in the 1680s. Father Eusebius Kino planted vine cuttings as soon as he arrived, declaring that "we have planted [vines] in the hope that in time this land of California will produce wine for the Mass."

While Baja (Lower) California remains part of Mexico to this day, what used to be called Alta (Upper) California was incorporated in the 1840s into the United States. By this time its wine industry had already been established for more than sixty years, thanks primarily to missions set up by Franciscan friars. The Franciscans had taken over from the Jesuits, whose activities, both in the New World and back in Europe, had aroused hostility, and whose order had been suppressed. The Jesuit missions in Lower California were handed over to the Franciscans; it was a Franciscan friar, Father Junípero Serra, who led the first mission into Upper California in 1769. At first the missionaries had to obtain their wine from Lower California; as he moved up and down the coast, Serra regularly complained of the difficulty of obtaining a supply of wine for the celebration of Mass.

The first vines were planted in Upper California at the mission of San Juan Capistrano in 1779. It was soon followed by others. By the early nineteenth century the region had a thriving wine industry, producing sweet, syrupy wines for both Mass and table from the appropriately named mission grape. In 1833, however, the Franciscan wine industry was brought forcibly to an end when the missions were secularized by the Mexican government, causing most of them to be abandoned.

The Franciscans had demonstrated that vines could be grown successfully in California, although only a few of their vineyards remain in cultivation today. The best known is Buena Vista, originally planted in 1832. It was made famous by "Count" Agoston Haraszthy,[5] a political exile from Hungary who bought the estate twenty-five years later and put in vines that he had brought from Europe. Haraszthy, a brilliant publicist, wrote pamphlets extolling California's climate and sold cuttings of his vines to farmers throughout the state. He may not have deserved the title "Father of California Viticulture" that he was subsequently awarded, but he played a significant part in its growth. His efforts came to an end in 1869, when, in Nicaragua to set up a rum factory, he fell into a stream and was eaten by an alligator.

It had taken European immigrants to North America several centuries to establish a successful wine industry. Long before they planted the first settlements on the East Coast they had been aware of its potential. In 1524 the Italian explorer Giovanni da Verrazano found vines growing around trees on the shore of what is now North Carolina, a region he thought so lovely that he called it Arcadia. The English who settled Virginia early in the next century made wine from wild grapes almost as soon as they landed. In 1622 some Virginia wine that had been made from native grapes was sent to London it is not known how it tasted initially, but it was spoiled by a musty cask and a long voyage, and by the time it arrived it did not taste pleasant at all. From London, the Virginia Company wrote to the colonists to say that the wine "hath been rather of scandal than credit unto us."

Rather than persevering with native vines, the colonists attempted to introduce European vines into America. Already, in 1619, the Virginia Company had sent out a consignment of European vines, together with French vine growers to tend them. But these plants did not grow successfully. Nor did the vines that were sent to New England in the 1640s, nor those shipped to Maryland in the 1670s, nor those brought by French Protestant refugees to South Carolina in 1680, nor those transported from Bordeaux to Pennsylvania by William Penn in 1682, nor those that were taken to Georgia in the 1740s and 1750s. According to Thomas Pinney in his *History of Wine in America,* the stan-

---

[5] The father of Arpad Haraszthy, cited in the previous chapter and later in this one.

dard work on the subject, the colonists' efforts to grow European vines failed because vines already grew in America, and therefore there were already pests that preyed upon them—pests to which the native vines had developed resistance but against which the European vines proved powerless.[6]

No doubt the presence of pests and disease made vine growing difficult. But it did not make it impossible. Rather, it contributed to making it unprofitable. The efforts of James Oglethorpe, the founder of Georgia, to prohibit the consumption of rum and encourage the production of wine have been mentioned earlier.[7] So, too, have the reasons that these efforts were not continued for much more than a decade after the colony's foundation: Oglethorpe having outlawed slavery, it proved impossible to obtain sufficient labor to develop a commercial wine industry.[8]

Similar problems confronted efforts to establish wine industries in other colonies. Some good wines (as well as bad ones) were made by self-indulgent gentleman farmers in Virginia in the colonial period, but commercial growers concentrated on more remunerative crops, such as tobacco.[9] It was possible to produce wines in New England and the Middle Atlantic colonies in the seventeenth and eighteenth centuries, but there did not seem much point in doing so, when it involved a great deal of time and effort, and there was far more money to be made from distilling molasses into rum.

The English crown went out of its way to encourage commercial wine production in North and South Carolina. Huguenots—French Protestants who had been persecuted in their own country—were carried to the New World free of charge in the hope that they would be able to apply their winemaking skills to the creation of a local wine industry. They planted vineyards with European varieties that had been sent over with them and experimentally made a little wine from native grapes that was described as "very good in color and taste." By the end of the century, however, these efforts had come to naught. The

---

[6] The most famous of these pests was the phylloxera louse; when, in the late nineteenth century, it attacked the vineyards of California, a solution was found in the grafting of European vines onto resistant American ones. Phylloxera has reappeared in California recently because vines have been grafted onto insufficiently resistant rootstocks.

[7] In Chapter 1.

[8] This is discussed in Chapter 4.

[9] The success of tobacco in Virginia is described in the Introduction.

colonists had found that they could obtain higher and more immediate returns on their investment in labor and capital by producing pitch, tar, and rice. The English writer John Oldmixon had never been to South Carolina but that did not prevent him from commenting in his *History of the British Empire in America* on the claims that had been made for the potential of viticulture in the colony by those who had sought to encourage emigration. "Since the climate is so proper, since grapes are so plentiful, and the wine they make so good, why is there not more of it?" he wondered. "Why do we not see some of it?" The explanation, he suggested, was "that the inhabitants either think they can turn their hands to a more profitable culture, or impose on us in their reports; for I would not think them so weak as to neglect making good wine, and enough of it, if they could, and thought it worth their while."

If they had needed to provide their own wine for use in religious services, then doubtless Americans in the colonial period would have persevered with their efforts to produce it, just as the Spanish had done in South America and Mexico. But, on the eastern seaboard of America, imported European wines could readily be obtained, at a reasonable price, certainly less than it would have cost them to make the wine for themselves. Only on the West Coast did there exist a geographical justification for the production rather than importation of wine.

The suggestion has also been made that English colonists in North America did not experience as pressing a need to make wine as their Spanish counterparts because many of them were Puritans who did not use wine to celebrate Mass. It is true that the Puritans migrated across the Atlantic in the first half of the seventeenth century because they had been alienated and in some cases persecuted by the Church of England, which did not allow them to worship in the simple manner they desired but insisted that they follow its own formal and highly ritualized services. They were called "Puritans" because they sought to purify the Church of England: to remove the "outer trappings" associated with Roman Catholicism; to abandon much of the ritual and ceremony, and to focus on plain Bible reading and Bible preaching.[10]

---

[10] The small group who emigrated to New England on the *Mayflower* in 1620 should not properly be called Puritans, but Separatists, because they did not want to purify the Church of England but to leave it; the thousands who left in the Great Migration of the 1630s were indeed Puritans who expressed the desire to

Like other Protestants, the Puritans rejected the rule of the Catholic Church that only its ordained priests and not the congregation might drink wine in the Eucharist, and abandoned the Catholic doctrine that through the agency of the priest the wine was magically transformed into the actual blood of Christ. This did not mean, however, that they stopped using wine in the celebration of Holy Communion. Rather, they all shared in the experience, as they believed it helped to bring them in touch with Christ's redemptive power.

Attitudes toward the consumption of wine as an essential part of Christian ritual began to change only after the revolution. Independent Americans, especially those who lived on the western frontier, remote from the influence of traditional social groupings, started to listen to traveling preachers who told them that they needed to cleanse themselves of sin in order to prepare for the Second Coming of Christ. Methodist and other preachers organized camp meetings where large groups of people pitched their tents and spent several days listening to the ministers who told them that they should prepare for judgment and that they would be saved if they opened up their hearts to the Lord. Many of the audience, overcome by the power of the Holy Spirit, starting twitching their bodies spasmodically, or laughing uncontrollably, or barking at the foot of a tree in pursuit of the devil. Huge numbers were converted.

The promise of salvation may have proved attractive to the pioneers and farmers who led precarious and lonely lives and who lived in the hope of future security, whether in this life or in the next, but it did create problems for the preachers who propounded it. In particular, it was impossible to tell whether someone who claimed to have renounced sin and accepted the Lord had actually done so. Preachers could only look at a man's behavior for some visible proof of conversion. One such proof was abstinence from alcoholic drinks. A man reborn of God had no need to drink liquor, since his love of the Lord would fully satisfy him. On the other hand, a man who drank liquor could not give himself to God, because his drinking confirmed his hardness of heart.

Almost from their foundation in the early eighteenth century the Methodists had rejected the consumption of distilled spirits. In 1743 their founder, John Wesley, had made it a rule that all Methodists were

---

reform the Church of England from the inside, although by leaving for America they made this task more difficult.

"expected to evidence their desire of salvation . . . by avoiding evil of every kind, especially that which is most generally practised, such as . . . drunkenness, buying, or selling spirituous liquors, or drinking them, except in cases of extreme necessity." Wesley and his followers regarded the drinking of spirits as a obstacle to religious reform. As a new movement they needed to assert themselves by rejecting tradition; their refusal of spirits was a radical act that demonstrated their determination to eradicate what they regarded as the bad habits of old. By the early 1830s the Methodists had made it their policy to abstain completely from alcoholic drinks.

At this point, another Evangelical group was founded in Manchester, New York, by a young man named Joseph Smith. Originally he had been "somewhat inclined to the Methodist sect" but angelic messengers directed him otherwise. With their assistance (so the story goes) he found buried in the local hillside a volume called *The Book of Mormon* in which the long-lost teachings of Jesus had been recorded. From these beginnings Smith created a faith that focused on the imminent return of Christ, the importance of moral purity, and the potential of every believer to enjoy an intense personal experience of the Holy Spirit.

Those who adhered to traditional Protestant theology regarded Smith and his followers as heretics. The Mormons were persecuted and (in conformity with American tradition) fled westward in search of a home where they could practice their beliefs unmolested. They escaped to Illinois, where they built the city of Nauvoo on the Mississippi River, but here, too, they attracted hostility, and in 1844 Smith was shot and killed by a crowd of angry citizens. The Mormons' new leader, Brigham Young, then led them to freedom in the Great Salt Lake Valley, in what was then part of Mexico.

Throughout their travels, the Mormons had relied upon the consumption of wine to help them to combine into a community of "glad hearts" that had the strength to withstand persecution. In so doing, they were following the precepts of Jesus in *The Book of Mormon,* in which he commanded his North American followers, the Nephites, to "take of the wine of the cup and drink of it" in honor of their Lord. Many Mormons enjoyed wine during the early years of the faith, maybe on occasion to excess. It has been alleged that Joseph Smith drank intemperately at home and in the barroom in the back of his store in Nauvoo, although he was seldom seen intoxicated in public. After the Mormons had settled in Salt Lake City, Young sent some colonists to the region then known as "Dixie" in the southwest of the territory,[11] where they were directed to cultivate a number of "useful articles," among them grapes for making wine. To this end, mission vines were brought from California. For a period of thirty years, wine was made for sacramental and medicinal purposes, and sold to non-Mormons as a source of revenue. The Dixie Mormons also drank a great deal themselves. In 1900, however, church officials ordered the winemaking to cease. By this time, wine was no longer used in the celebration of the Sacrament and Mormons were expected to practice total abstinence.

It is not known for certain why the Mormon church banned alcoholic beverages, but one factor was its belief in the imminence of Christ's return and its insistence that its followers should be morally pure before their Lord. All evangelical churches emphasized the importance of faith rather than religious or moral works in securing salvation. This applied equally to Methodists, Baptists, and Seventh-Day Adventists. They spread their creed through the American population principally by appealing to people's emotions, but they also insisted that emotions would not bring the believer to salvation, which could be achieved only by faith. Evangelical groups were wary of alcohol because it appeared to release the wrong emotions or to prevent the emotions from being centered on their true object.

In order to persuade their followers to forswear alcohol, they needed to remove wine from the celebration of the Sacrament. As Edward C. Delavan, a wealthy businessman from Albany who had retired in his thirties in order to devote himself to temperance reform, explained in a letter to the dean of Carlisle in England: "So long as the Savior of the world is held up as a maker and dispenser of intoxicating wine—wine, the mocker—the cause you advocate will make but slow progress."

The movement toward abandoning the use of wine in the Eucharist began in the 1820s, when some churches converted from Madeira to unfortified wine. The biblical scholar Moses Stuart pointed out that Madeira, like most of the wines consumed in the United States, had been fortified by the addition of distilled spirits; he referred to the recent revelation by the chemist William Brande that nearly one quarter of the volume of Madeira was made up of alcohol; such a beverage,

---

[11]Near St. George. Utah had been transferred from Mexico to the United States in 1848, a year after the first Mormon settlement, but was refused statehood until 1896, because of the Mormons' polygamy.

he insisted, should be regarded as intoxicating. Yet "the simple wine of Palestine," as had been drunk in biblical times, "was the mere juice of the grape, fermented and purified. This of itself could never have been a very strong liquor. . . . Indeed, it cannot properly be ranked under the denomination of an intoxicating liquor, in the usual sense of this appellation."

Others went further than this. The radical temperance campaigner Gerritt Smith accepted that Jesus Christ had drunk wine and that the Bible had sanctioned its use by his followers, but this did not mean that in the bright modern world of the 1830s Americans had to do the same. Christ, explained Smith, lacked the "better knowledge of our times" that discoveries in chemistry and physiology had provided. At this period, however, few people were prepared to accept that Scripture might be wrong. Campaigners were compelled instead to pursue a casuistical argument: that the Bible had hitherto been misinterpreted; that Christ had not, in fact, turned water into wine; that he had not served wine at his Last Supper; that wine had not been recommended as a source of health and goodness. After a further eighteen years' study of the Bible, Moses Stuart came up with an explanation of why the Bible appeared to contradict itself, describing wine in some places as a blessing and in others as a curse. The answer, he said, was that the Jews used two different kinds of wine, a fermented and an unfermented version. The fermented wine was intoxicating: It led to drunkenness and an unhealthy appetite for alcohol, and injured the bodies of the people who drank it. The unfermented wine, by which he meant grape juice, was "a delicious, nutritive, healthful beverage. . . . Wherever the Scriptures speak of wine as a comfort, a blessing, or a libation to God, and rank it with such articles as corn or oil, they mean only such wine as contained no alcohol . . . ; Wherever they denounce it, prohibit it, and connect it with drunkenness and reveling, they can mean only alcoholic or intoxicating wine. . . . I regard it as all but absolutely certain that unfermented wine was used at the original celebration of the Lord's Supper."

This attempt to reinterpret Scripture according to the needs of the temperance movement was received with the scorn it deserved. In the opinion of many communicants, such an attack on the plain words of the Bible was tantamount to blasphemy. Although a few individual congregations of Baptists, Presbyterians, and Congregationalists did convert to grape juice in the 1840s and 1850s, general church conferences refused to consider the issue. Even the Methodist Church, a pioneer of both temperance and evangelical campaigns, refused to endorse the use of grape juice to celebrate Holy Communion.

Before the Civil War, churches also generally refused to adopt grape juice for practical reasons. The scientific knowledge did not yet exist to prevent grapes from fermenting if crushed and converted into juice; grape juice could be made available for Communion only if fresh grapes were readily at hand. In a country where vine growing had failed to prosper, these were a scarce commodity. Not until Pasteur discovered the role of yeasts and a means of counteracting them— pasteurization—did it become possible to produce stable juice that would not ferment. Thomas Welch, a Methodist minister turned dentist, and an ardent prohibitionist who needed money to care for his wife and seven children, applied Pasteur's methods in 1869 to the grapes he had grown on a trellis in front of his home in Vineland, New Jersey. He brought the grapes into his kitchen, cooked them for a few minutes, squeezed them through cloth bags, and filtered them into bottles, which he immersed in boiling water. He sought to market the result as "Dr. Welch's Unfermented Wine." But the churches rejected his product, saying that they preferred to stick with their fermented version. Not until a generation had passed, and Thomas's son Charles had taken control of the company and launched a major advertising campaign for the product, now renamed "Welch's Grape Juice," were the churches persuaded to reconsider their position. Some of Charles Welch's most persuasive advertisements featured his father's arguments that the use of alcoholic wine to celebrate Holy Communion was "an offense to those whose taste is unperverted," as well as "dangerous to the reformed inebriate"; that it made "intoxicating wine respectable" and crippled "the influence of the church in the temperance cause"; that it was "inconsistent with the character of the occasion," and "unnecessary" now that Welch's Grape Juice was available.

Among these arguments, the suggestion that the use of sacramental wine was "dangerous to the reformed inebriate" may have been the most persuasive. The churches were being pressured by the Women's Christian Temperance Union (WCTU) to abandon their fermented wine on pragmatic grounds. As was explained by Mrs. S. M. M. Woodman, state superintendent of the WCTU's Viticultural Department in California, by converting to grape juice the churches were able to save the souls of numberless reformed drinkers who might otherwise have been overcome by the mere smell of wine and have gone directly from Communion to the nearest saloon.

By the time that national Prohibition was introduced, the Presbyterian, Congregationalist, Methodist, and Baptist churches had abandoned the use of wine in the celebration of Holy Communion. But the Episcopal, Lutheran, and Roman Catholic churches persisted in their traditional practice (as did the synagogues). Since sacramental wines were still required, they were exempted from the prohibitory laws, which provided a loophole through which bootleggers might pass. Some went to the length of turning themselves into false rabbis, and manufactured wine for fictitious congregations, while others simply hijacked wine on its way to church.

Another factor that persuaded many Protestant denominations to abandon their Communion wine in the early twentieth century was hostility to Roman Catholics. The majority of the immigrants who had arrived in America in large numbers in the late nineteenth and early twentieth century were devout Catholics from southern and eastern Europe who insisted on practicing what many Protestants regarded as an un-American style of worship, full of reverence and ritual. By rejecting the use of wine in the Eucharist, and by ceasing to drink wine with their meals, native-born American Protestants demonstrated their disapproval of Catholic immigrants and their old-country practices.[12]

After Prohibition was repealed in 1933, the survival of this anti-Catholic sentiment helped to keep much of the country dry. Writing in the 1940s, John Gunther suggested that prohibitionist feeling endured in the South, which remained the driest area of the country, in part, at least, because of the association between wine and Catholicism. "Catholics use wine in celebration of the Mass," he explained; "the backwoodsmen hate Catholicism, and hence hate wine too, which they associate with Catholic ritual."

To this day, much of the South remains devoutly Protestant, and determinedly dry. And many Protestant churches still do their best to ensure that it stays that way. In Kentucky, preachers have condemned from the pulpit people who have proposed holding votes on whether dry counties should go wet, helping to ensure that Kentucky retains more dry counties than any other state.[13] "I remember listening to a preacher who told his congregation that everything that was wrong in the world was because they had allowed liquor into their town," says

---

[12]The hostility of native-born Americans to wine drinking by new immigrants from southern Europe is discussed in Chapter 2.

[13]See Chapter 5.

Chris Morris of United Distillers. The preacher told them that "they ain't going to go to heaven. They ain't going to see the Lord."

In Alabama in 1983, a plebiscite was proposed on whether Decatur, then the largest dry city in the nation, should go wet. Local churches expressed their opposition. Ron Lambe, assistant pastor at the Central Baptist Church, said that "we cannot continue to maintain the quality and Christian atmosphere of life that we cherish . . . if we permit the rampant and legal sale of alcoholic beverages. And I think that the majority of folks who live here feel just that way." In South Carolina in 1991, hoteliers and restaurateurs proposed that the minibottle law should be abandoned and that they should be allowed to serve spirits from the same size bottle as their counterparts in every other state.[14] Again, local Protestant churches resisted the proposal. Bob Jones III, head of the evangelical Bob Jones University in Greenville, said, "I don't see how anyone who loves his fellow man and believes in the sacredness of life and fears God could not oppose any effort to make liquor more easily obtainable and plentiful." The minibottles remained—as they do to this day.

Many southern Protestant churches go out of their way to prevent the spread of alcohol in their locality; many of their members not only abstain from drinking themselves but refuse to stock alcoholic beverages in their homes and even to eat in a restaurant where they are served. The largest Protestant group in the United States is the Southern Baptist Convention, with 38,700 churches and 15.4 million members, the great majority of whom reject all alcoholic drinks because they are taught that the human body is the "temple of God" and that alcohol would pollute it.[15]

Of the one third of Americans who abstain from alcohol, half do so on religious grounds. Many equate it with alcoholism: They have no sense of moderation. Like those who supported Prohibition in the past, and those who attend meetings of Alcoholics Anonymous[16] today, they have been taught to regard the consumption of one single drink as the first step on a slippery slope to dependency and degradation. "There is no such thing as responsible drinking," writes David Wilkerson, the founder of the Christian Teen Challenge organization, in a book designed to discourage Christians from drinking. "It is always irrespon-

---

[14]The minibottle law is described in Chapter 4.
[15]This belief does not, however, prevent them from consuming fast food.
[16]The philosophy of Alcoholics Anonymous is discussed in the Introduction.

sible and dangerous. . . . The very thought of drinking alcoholic beverages is evil. . . . Name any of the sins Jesus listed as defiling to a man, and you can trace every one of them to alcohol."

The United States remains a highly religious country. One recent Gallup poll found that 71 percent of the population are members of a church or synagogue; 41 percent attend that church or synagogue on a weekly basis; 88 percent say that religion is "very important" or "fairly important" in their lives; 59 percent describe themselves as Protestants and 46 percent as "born-again" or "evangelical" Christians. Yet it is precisely the most religious elements of American society who reject the most potent symbol of the Christian religion, in the form of wine. The association of Christian religious institutions with wine, which began with the European monasteries that helped the knowledge of viticulture and winemaking to survive the Dark Ages, and continued with the development of fine wines in the Middle Ages by the monasteries of Burgundy, Champagne,[17] and Germany, and with the transplantation of vines to the New World by Spanish conquistadors and missionaries, came to an end in the United States in 1989, when the Christian Brothers sold their winery to the British Grand Metropolitan corporation. An international Catholic teaching order, they had established the winery in the Napa Valley in California in the late nineteenth century; it had survived Prohibition by making sacramental and medicinal wine; its cellarmaster since the 1930s, Brother Timothy, had responded to critics, who had argued that the manufacture of wine was an inappropriate activity for a religious order, by pointing out that both the grapes and the yeast from which the wine was made had been given to man by God. The Christian Brothers sold their winery ostensibly because they wanted to devote their money to educational programs rather than wine production; in reality, many industry observers suggested, they abandoned the enterprise because they were concerned about the publicity being given to alcohol abuse and feared that by continuing in the wine business they might come to be associated with the consequences of excessive alcohol consumption.

Today the American religious institutions that pride themselves on their production of wine are not traditional Christian but New Age concerns, such as the Renaissance vineyard in California, cultivated by

---

[17]Contrary to popular belief, the Benedictine monk Dom Pérignon did not invent sparkling champagne, although he did a great deal to improve the quality of what was then a still wine.

the Fellowship of Friends, who believe that they benefit therapeutically from working on the soil, and point to the allegorical connection between viticulture and human personal development; and Summum, based in Salt Lake City, which seeks to "rediscover" the liquids supposedly used by ancient peoples to convey spiritual power and information, and attempts to imbue its wines with spiritual energy by placing them in a pyramid and subjecting them to meditation.

Outside institutions such as these, the role of wine in American society has become secularized. Those people who are most interested in wine, who attend wine classes, buy wine magazines, stock their cellars, and organize tastings, tend to be among the least religious elements of the population. In his book *Religion and Wine,* a history of the relationship between wine and religion in the United States, Robert C. Fuller, professor of religious studies at Bradley University in Peoria, Illinois, has suggested that many wine lovers have elevated their interest in the subject to the status of a secular religion, with its own rituals and beliefs: that they seek through the object of their devotion to attain some form of inner beauty or harmony in a manner comparable to that of Christians in search of their God. Wine does plays a huge role in the lives of some Americans today, but not of those Protestants whose religion originally placed it at the center of its ritualized commemoration of its beliefs.

Unlike many of today's Protestant groups, the settlers of the seventeenth century had not been opposed to the consumption of wine or other alcoholic drinks in moderation. As in the case of sex,[18] so-called "puritan" attitudes to drink did not in fact originate with the Puritans who colonized New England but with the evangelical Protestant reformers of the nineteenth century. The Puritans did not have any problems about people drinking as long as it did not lead to drunkenness. "Drink is in itself a good creature of God," stated the Puritan preacher Increase Mather, "and is to be received with thankfulness, but the abuse of drink is from Satan; the wine is from God, but the drunkard is from the devil."

The Quakers who settled in Pennsylvania later in the century held similar attitudes. In his advice to his children William Penn told them to drink only when they were thirsty, and to avoid drinking between meals; that "small" drink, such as beer, was preferable to strong drink

---

[18]See Chapter 3.

in the form of spirits, because "the smaller the drink, the clearer the head and the cooler the blood, which are great benefits in temper and business. . . . Strong liquors are good in some times and in small proportions, being better for physic than food, for cordials than common use." Penn had a brewhouse built at his estate in Pennsbury, twenty miles upriver from Philadelphia, and in describing the progress the colony had made during its first years of settlement wrote approvingly of the beer that the settlers had begun to produce. By the end of the seventeenth century, it was being claimed by Gabriel Thomas, one of the original emigrants, that beer brewed in Philadelphia had a "better name, that is, is in more esteem than English beer in Barbados and is sold for a higher price there." In making this claim, Thomas may have been overcome by his enthusiasm for the progress of the city and colony, but there is no doubt that Philadelphia beer became well known in the other colonies, especially in the South.

In New England, too, a lot of beer was brewed in the seventeenth century, but by the eighteenth century the most popular drink was cider; and it is this that has come to symbolize the domestic drink production of the colonial period. All the colonists, old and young, drank cider, at all times and in all places. It was served at home on the table three times a day, and was automatically offered to every visitor; it was carried by farmers in jugs into the fields in summer and into the woods in winter; it was given mulled to babies to help them sleep; it was served at funerals and weddings, at vestry meetings and church raisings. When the French exile Brillat-Savarin visited a Connecticut farmhouse toward the end of the century, he saw at each end of the dining table "two huge jugs of a cider so excellent that I could have gone on drinking it for ever."

Americans of the colonial period looked favorably upon cider and beer because they remembered how they had been forced in the early years to make do with water, which in England had been scorned as a poor man's drink.[19] To the Puritans of New England and the Quakers of Pennsylvania, the production of fermented beverages served as a symbol of successful settlement, of overcoming the obstacles that had confronted them. No wonder the Puritan preacher Samuel Parris described alcohol as "the principal drink that is given to mortal man, being profitable not only to moderate thirst but also to strengthen the heart, and revive the drooping spirits."

---

[19]See Chapter 1.

In the 1770s the consumption of homemade beer and cider also acquired political importance, as a result of the nonimportation campaign against British produce.[20] Brewers in Philadelphia now began to make their own version of the most prestigious imported English beer, porter. A strong, dark, dense beer, it had acquired its name on account of its popularity among the porters who worked in the London markets. A certain amount had been imported into America in the middle of the century, but the size of the trade had been restricted by its expense. By brewing porter in Philadelphia, the price could be reduced and the need for a high-quality domestic beer could be satisfied. The first porter brewery was established in the city in 1774 by Robert Hare, an immigrant from England, and the son of a porter brewer in London. One of Hare's customers was George Washington, who had previously imported his porter from England, but had now embarked on a policy of buying American produce whenever possible. As he explained in 1789, the year in which he became president, in a letter to the Marquis de Lafayette (his former companion in arms, now embroiled in French politics), "We have already been too long subject to British prejudices. I use no porter or cheese in my family but such as is made in America: Both these articles may now be purchased of an excellent quality." This good opinion of American porter was shared not only by Washington's new compatriots but also by French and even English observers. The French politician and journalist Brissot de Warville described how Americans had previously drunk English porter, "but it has now been replaced by an excellent porter brewed near Philadelphia, which is so similar to the English that even British palates have been deceived." The popularity that porter enjoyed at this period continues to be commemorated today in the term "porterhouse steak," which refers to the cuts of meat served in taverns that sold porter.

Americans after the revolution looked favorably upon homemade alcoholic beverages because these symbolized their success in freeing themselves from their dependence on their former colonial masters.[21] But alcoholic drinks were also regarded generally as an important symbol of independence because of the part they had played in the revolution. Not only had resistance against attempts by the British government to tax molasses and Madeira helped to impel Americans

---

[20]See Chapter 6.
[21]See Chapter 6 again.

toward rebellion,[22] it had been in the public drinking places—the taverns—that independent-minded Americans had met in the 1760s and 1770s to plot their resistance to the crown. Inside them they had organized the formation of militia; outside they had planted liberty poles. In return the British authorities regarded the taverns with hostility, believing that they helped to spread dissent.

The taverns of New England performed a similar role in the American Revolution to that played by the coffeehouses of Paris in the French Revolution a few years later. These, too, were described by observers as "hotbeds of sedition and revolt," where revolutionary orators inspired the crowds within them to take up arms and overthrow the monarchy.

It is hardly surprising that public meeting places should play a part in popular movements to overthrow authoritarian governments. What is unusual, maybe unique, about the American experience is that it was the taverns that filled this role rather than coffeehouses. Ever since they had first opened in the cities of the Near East in the sixteenth century, coffeehouses had been regarded with great suspicion by the authorities, who believed they offered the opportunity for people disloyal to the regime to meet and plot against it in an atmosphere of perfect sobriety. In Istanbul, the capital of the Ottoman Empire, the coffeehouses were ordered for this reason to be closed on several occasions, notably by the grand vizier, Mehmed Köprülü in 1656. Köprülü is supposed to have imposed harsh punishments upon those who disobeyed his order: For a first violation, the offender was to be cudgeled; for a second, he was to be sewn into a leather bag and thrown into the Bosporus;[23] there would consequently be no likelihood of a third violation. Although Köprülü shut the coffeehouses, he left the taverns alone, since these were frequented by people who "enjoyed themselves, who sang, and who talked of their loves or of their exploits in battle" rather than by men who discussed politics and plotted against the government. It is ironic that in a Muslim country, where alcoholic drinks were forbidden by religion, the coffeehouses should have been closed and the taverns allowed to stay open. But the government placed the maintenance of good order above the strict observance of religious law.

In America, rebellion was not plotted in coffeehouses because they did not exist. Certainly there were places that called themselves "cof-

---

[22]See Chapter 6 for these too.
[23]The strait of water that runs through the city, separating Europe from Asia.

feehouses," but, unlike the London institutions on which they were supposedly modeled, they all served a range of intoxicating beverages as well as coffee. They were no more than glorified taverns. Such was the regard with which alcoholic drinks were held in colonial America that no meeting place could have survived in business for long had it refused to sell them. Even in the so-called coffeehouses men were exposed to the temptation of intoxication. Wherever they met to plot against the government, they risked assuaging their resentment with the cheering effects of alcohol.

In America, unlike France or the Ottoman Empire, it was the taverns that were associated with revolution and were therefore regarded with increased respect by a generation of newly independent Americans.[24] Many of the latter, moreover, associated the freedom to drink with freedom from English rule. They made a connection between their newfound political liberty and their perceived right to drink what they wanted when they wanted, without hindrance from the government. The new republican authorities found it difficult to impose controls on the taverns, many of whose customers equated any attempt to place restrictions on the drinking place with the efforts previously made by the British authorities to restrict the autonomy of Americans.

The taverns embodied the egalitarian spirit of independent America. All men were equal before the bottle, and no man was allowed to refuse to drink. This was true both within the taverns and without. Custom required Americans who met at social gatherings to demonstrate their equality, not only by drinking but by drinking the same amount. A guest who attended an evening party was expected to consume just as much as the other participants. If he drank more slowly than they, or sought to abstain altogether, he would be dragged to the sideboard and required to catch up. Were he to refuse, he would be ostracized on the grounds that he appeared to think himself better than other people. Not only would he not be invited to another party, he would be excluded from society altogether. After one English-born schoolmaster offended Americans by declining to drink with them, they ignored him to such an extent that it was not noticed when he fell ill and died, and several days passed before his body was discovered. To refuse to drink with other men was a social offense, indicating a lack of respect. It could even be dangerous. One group of men in Kentucky,

---

[24]It was appropriate that Thomas Jefferson wrote the first draft of the Declaration of Independence in a tavern in Philadelphia: See Chapter 6.

insulted by the refusal of one of their comrades to drink with them, was reported to have roasted him to death.

"From my earliest recollection," wrote the Methodist preacher Peter Cartwright, who spent the first half of the nineteenth century traveling the backwoods of Kentucky, Tennessee, Indiana, and Ohio, "drinking drams, in family and social circles, was considered harmless and allowable socialities. It was almost universally the custom for preachers, in common with all others, to take drams; and if a man would not have it in his family, his harvest, his house raisings, log rollings, weddings, and so on, he was considered parsimonious and unsociable; and many, even professors of Christianity, would not help a man if he did not have spirits and treat the company." One man whom Cartwright was seeking to convert to Methodism was so angered by the preacher's refusal to drink cherry bounce (cherries macerated in whiskey) with him that he told him that "I was no friend of his, or his family, and he would never hear me preach again."

In Kentucky, wrote Daniel Drake, most people "regarded it as a duty to their families and visitors, not less than themselves, to keep the whiskey bottle well replenished. For a friend to call and find it empty was a real mortification to one party, and quite a disappointment to the other, who was apt to revenge himself by speaking of the matter to some other neighbor as an instance of meanness."

At this time the majority of American men drank more or less constantly, but rarely to excess. Basil Hall, a retired British naval captain who visited the United States in the late 1820s, encountered "very little drunkenness, properly so called. . . . I was perfectly astonished at the extent of intemperance, and the limited amount of absolute intoxication. To get so drunk as to kick up a row, or tumble about the streets, or disturb a peaceable household all night long, are feats that require a man to sit down to his bottle, and swill away till inebriety is produced. To what extent this practice is followed as a habit in America, I cannot say. I certainly never saw any of it. But what I did see, at every corner into which I travelled, north or south, east or west, was the universal practice of sipping a little at a time, but frequently. In many places, it was the custom to take a dram before breakfast, and in some parts of the country another was taken immediately after that meal; and so on at intervals, which varied from half an hour to a couple of hours, during the whole day."

Drinking habits changed as a result of the opening up of the West between the late eighteenth and late nineteenth centuries. As each new group moved westward, it found itself cut off from the stabilizing influences of traditional society, and abandoned regular, social sipping in favor of drinking alone, in binges.

The growth in the population of the eastern seaboard in the late eighteenth century made it necessary to bring a lot of new land into production. Farmers crossed the Appalachian Mountains and began to cultivate the land on the western side. They may not have enjoyed their isolation but they reveled in their independence: Like the Scotch-Irish who had settled in the same areas earlier in the century, they sought to assuage the former and demonstrate the latter by drinking large quantities of whiskey.[25]

As more migrants moved westward, towns were established and social gatherings held. The reestablishment of society did not, however, persuade the settlers to return to civilized habits. "A striking feature of the intemperance of that period," Drake recalled, "was its clamorous and unblushing display. It was no disgrace, and scarcely any discredit, to be seen reeling and boisterous in the public streets; and drinking at the close of dinner parties, balls, and even weddings was sometimes carried through all the successive stages of gaiety, mirth, and uproar, to a comfortable state of dead drunkenness."

This was nothing, however, compared with the behavior of the miners who rushed to the newly Americanized state of California when gold was discovered in the middle of the nineteenth century. Most of them arrived without their families, hoping to find gold quickly: to make their fortune and return home. Because they regarded themselves as transient workers, they made no effort to conform to the social patterns they had followed back east. "Dame Shirley" was a doctor's wife who recorded her impressions of life in a California mining community. During the winter of 1851–52 a spell of heavy and constant rain rendered mining impossible, and prevented the men from traveling anywhere, even if there had been anywhere to go. So they drank. They started on Christmas evening and kept on going for three days, "growing wilder every hour." On the fourth day, lying in drunken heaps about the barroom, the miners "commenced a most unearthly howling; some barked like dogs, some roared like bulls, and others hissed like serpents and geese. Many were too far gone to imitate anything but their own animalized selves. . . . Some of these bacchanals were among

---

[25]The behavior of the Scotch-Irish, and their rebellion when the government tried to tax their whiskey, are discussed in the previous chapter.

the most respectable and respected men upon the river. Many of them had resided here for more than a year, and had never been seen intoxicated before. It seemed as if they were seized with a reckless mania for pouring down liquor, which . . . everything conspired to foster and increase." After a lull, on New Year's Day they started drinking again.

Cowboys did not behave any better. They spent on average four months guiding herds of longhorn cattle from the Texas plains to railroad towns in Kansas, for transport to eastern markets. While on the trail they consumed large quantities of coffee[26] but no alcohol. It would have been too dangerous to drink: Unless the cowboys remained constantly alert, they risked losing their cattle to stampedes or to Indians. After they arrived at the cow towns and loaded their cattle onto the railroad wagons, they often tried to catch up with four months worth of drinking in a few days. Since they were rarely married, they did not even have thoughts of dependents back home to temper their conduct.

There were also the fur trappers, who imagined that they lived lives of perfect freedom but were actually controlled by the fur companies. They would come to a rendezvous in the summer in the Rocky Mountains and trade their skins for whiskey, which they would then consume in a single binge, drinking away all their profits. They drank in the society—but not the company—of others as a means of assuaging their loneliness. They drank to escape from the reality that the liberty in which they believed was no more than a myth.

Thus, as the United States expanded westward during the course of the nineteenth century, the old tradition of frequent, sociable, generally moderate drinking, established in the relatively stable communities of colonial America, was for many people replaced by a new pattern of drinking in which periods of abstinence were interspersed with ones of intoxication. This change in behavior helps to explain the origin of the temperance movement in the first half of the century as an attempt to eliminate solitary bouts of drinking, which campaigners considered to be harmful both to the drinker and to society. Unfortunately all that they succeeded in doing was to persuade moderate social drinkers to give up. In the face of growing public disapproval, those people who continued to drink now started to hide their actions from their family and colleagues, and thus to become precisely the kind of solitary and sporadic drinkers against whom the temperance movement had been directed. At the same time, heavy binge drinkers became increasingly

---

[26]See Chapter 6.

alienated from society and even less receptive to temperance appeals. So, in the middle of the nineteenth century, some states introduced prohibition, but this merely encouraged drinking practices to become even more secretive and less sociable than before. No doubt temperance advocates had honestly believed that they could arrest the tendency away from moderate sociable drinking and toward drinking alone and to excess, but the effect of their campaigns was to achieve precisely the opposite.[27]

Temperance campaigners numbered among the abuses of alcohol the custom of treating other people to drinks, which they equated with drunkenness.

It was certainly widespread. When Laurence Oliphant, superintendent of Indian affairs in Canada, went into a general store in Superior, Wisconsin, to obtain the food he needed for a western trip, he bought nothing unusual: flour, ham, bacon, tea, sugar, biscuits, and brandy. Yet "the purchase of these articles involved an immense amount of liquoring up. . . . Conflicting advice was tendered in every direction by people who knew nothing whatever of the matter, but who all expected a drink for their trouble. . . . It is one of the most ancient and sacred institutions of the country, whenever you are introduced to a man at the bar of a hotel, to 'liquor him right away'; a compliment which, according to the strict rules of American etiquette, he ought to return before parting with you."

There is also no doubt that, as temperance campaigners asserted, the practice of buying drinks for other people led many to drink to excess. When men gathered in a tavern on a Saturday night, they would each buy half a pint of whiskey, which was passed around the room. Since everyone was expected to treat in turn, by the end of the evening each man had drunk half a pint.[28]

---

[27]Most admonitory campaigns succeed only in influencing those people who do not need to change their behavior and fail to affect those who do, as is demonstrated by the current campaigns to persuade pregnant women not to drink, which is discussed in Chapter 3, and to persuade people not to drink before they drive, which is covered in Chapter 5. And prohibitory laws have generally proved counterproductive: Both national Prohibition and the present prohibition on drinking under the age of twenty-one have caused people to drink in a less healthy manner, for which also see Chapter 5.

[28]This would have been considerably stronger than present-day whiskey, which is diluted with water before bottling.

But treating was more than a means to drunkenness: It was an important social ritual, and a medium of exchange. This was particularly true on the western frontier, where money was scarce: In this barter economy, labor and services were exchanged rather than paid for, and the provision of alcoholic drinks formed an integral part of the system. Even where money was available, many pioneers chose to reward the friends and neighbors who helped them with their house raising or log rolling by giving them alcohol. This was not supposed to replace monetary payment; as a form of remuneration it was deliberately inexact. People rewarded their neighbors with alcohol to demonstrate the reciprocal nature of local society: that everyone was involved in a continual state of mutual obligation.

The exchange of drinks lubricated all kinds of social occasions. "To drink with a friend when you meet him is good fellowship, to drink with a stranger is politeness and a proof of wishing to be better acquainted," explained the visiting English novelist Frederick Marryat. "They say that the English cannot settle anything properly without a dinner. I am sure Americans can fix nothing without a drink. . . . So much has it become the habit to cement all friendship, and commence acquaintance by drinking, that it is a cause of serious offence to refuse."

In the West, Marryat added, "it is literally, 'Stranger, will you drink or fight?' " This is confirmed by an account of Houston in the pioneering days of the 1830s from a local periodical, which described how "drinking was reduced to a system, and had its own laws and regulations. Nothing was regarded as a greater violation of established etiquette than for one who was going to drink not to invite all within a reasonable distance to partake; so that the Texians [sic], being entirely a military people, not only fought but drank in platoons."

The exchange of drinks also performed an important function in the workplace. In the eighteenth and early nineteenth centuries, this was as much a social as an economic community, in which the symbolic acts that established social ties took precedence over productive activity. The most important of these acts was the consumption of alcoholic drink. Laboring men drank together in order to demonstrate that they belonged to a group; it was through drink that their equality was affirmed. If a man refused to drink, or refused to contribute to the drinking expenses of his companions, he was ostracized: He had effectively chosen to withdraw from society. It was also through drink that the loyalty of an apprentice to the group he had joined was ensured. Apprentices were expected to pay a footing in the form of alcohol when they began their service and when they completed one of various stages in their learning process. Jacob Carter of Philadelphia recalled in his autobiography, *My Drunken Life,* that he had gotten into the habit of drinking when employed as a brushmaker's apprentice at the age of fifteen. "The first day that I entered upon my duties, I was surrounded by both men and boys, workmen who exclaimed, 'Come, my boy, we suppose you are aware that 'tis the rule of this shop that each boy when entering upon his apprenticeship, as well as each new journeyman, shall pay their footing: one gallon of whiskey.' Why, nothing could have pleased me better, said I to myself; this is the place for me. I can get as much rum here as I want."

Carter and his colleagues had to smuggle their liquor into the workshop, a pint at a time, because their boss would have disapproved of their drinking at work. Other employers were more tolerant, however; many were former journeymen themselves and accepted drinking as a natural part of workplace culture. The quantity of work in preindustrial workshops fluctuated according to demand and the time of year, and as long as the orders were filled, most employers did not worry too much about their employees' behavior.

But when the workplace was industrialized, it became dangerous for men to drink at work. Operators of power-driven machinery had to remain sober and alert, or else risk losing limbs to the machines. The employers, moreover, needed to operate their expensive equipment for as many hours as possible. The timetable was set by the machines, not by the men. Drinking was no longer acceptable.

The purpose of the workplace now lay solely in maximizing production; it had lost its social function. The social values of the workplace, and the drinking customs that had affirmed them, were transferred to the saloon. Here, the traditions of providing alcoholic drinks for one's colleagues, and of sharing them at certain times of day, were continued in the form of treating: Every man was required to buy drinks for his fellow drinkers. The convention was reinforced by the influx of emigrants from rural Ireland,[29] where social and economic relations had been based on a system of mutual obligations, and where alcohol had been exchanged rather than money paid in return for services, just as on the American frontier.

There is no doubt that the practice of buying drinks for other men

---

[29]See Chapter 6.

in saloons did lead to abuse, as temperance campaigners claimed. It was exploited by saloon keepers to persuade their customers to consume more than they had intended. In an editorial in which it described the practice of treating as "the curse of this age in the U.S.," a Catholic temperance newspaper in Worcester, Massachusetts, described how "if two men not previously acquainted . . . come into his barroom together . . . [the barkeeper] introduces them and sets the ball rolling. Two or three rounds of drinks are not enough for him. He is getting the money. So he produces the dice box and proposes 'to shake' for the drinks. He never lets up as long as his customers can stand on their feet and there is any money in sight."

The abuses associated with treating help to explain why reformers directed their hostility against saloons and why they sought to close them down. For temperance campaigners, they presented a convenient target. By focusing on the perceived evils of drinking in saloons, campaigners deprived their enemies of the argument that they were advocating sumptuary legislation and interfering with personal liberty. They did not tell people how to behave in their own homes; they did not argue that private drinking should be banned. Sam W. Small, an associate editor of the *Atlanta Constitution* and a lecturer for the prohibitionist Anti-Saloon League, later testified that in his thousands of speeches favoring the introduction of Prohibition he had "strenuously combated the charge that we sought to deny an individual citizen his right to have and drink what he pleased; we only denied that a man had an inalienable right to run a barroom and conduct a commercial manufactory of drunkards." It was not by accident that the legislators who introduced national Prohibition permitted the consumption of alcoholic drinks in private while forbidding their public sale.[30]

Reformers objected to the saloons not only for practical reasons but also for symbolic ones. The saloon served as a home away from home for recent immigrants to the United States, who felt excluded by the increasingly acquisitive and self-centered character of American culture. Within the saloon there was real democracy. Everyone was regarded as an equal, as was demonstrated by the practice of treating. The saloon had become a refuge for the reciprocal values that had been rejected by the marketplace society that now prevailed outside its doors. In retaliation, this new capitalist society sought to have the

---

[30]See Chapter 4.

saloons closed down, because they seemed to represent a rebellion against its principles and a threat to its survival.

Many native-born Americans objected to the saloon because they believed it prevented immigrants from becoming naturalized. "The saloon fosters an un-American spirit among the foreign-born population of our country," argued John M. Barker in *The Saloon Problem and Social Reform.* "The influx of foreigners into our urban centers, many of whom have liquor habits, is a menace to good government. . . . The foreign-born population is largely under the social and political control of the saloon. . . . The hope of perpetuating our liberties is to help the foreigners correct any demoralizing custom, and through self-restraint assimilate American ideas."

The saloon symbolized the tension between native-born Americans and immigrants that culminated in the imposition of Prohibition. In the saloon, foreign-born workers were free from native middle-class interference. They could live in their own world, in an alternative society. For immigrant workers, the saloon served many purposes: It was to the saloon keeper they turned if they were looking for a job, or needed to borrow some money, or intended to participate in politics. The middle classes sought to close down the saloons because they wanted to be able to control these aspects of immigrant life for themselves, to mold them to what they considered an American model of behavior. Reformers perceived the model of society that the saloons provided to be a threat to their own; they did not understand that the existence of this alternative community might help to make it easier for workers to cope with the society that existed outside the doors of the drinking place. "The saloon exists in our town," insisted one worker, "because it supplies a want—a need. It offers a common meeting place. It dispenses good cheer. It ministers to the craving for fellowship. To the exhausted, worn-out body, to the strained nerves, the relaxation brings rest."

The saloon was much more than a drinking place; it was the church of the poor. One enlightened reformer even suggested that the church could learn a lot from the saloon. The saloon had glitter; the church was drab. The saloon was easy to enter; the church was locked. The saloon was active 140 hours a week, the church four. No one bothered about a man's business at a saloon. In the saloon every man was equal; ragged clothes were not a mark of shame. The saloon provided newspapers, billiards, card tables, bowling alleys, lavatories, and washing facilities. It offered a free lunch in return for a five-cent glass of beer;

if the saloons of New York were closed, 25,000 men would declare that the food had been taken out of their mouths. The saloon provided information and company. "For many," he concluded, "the saloon is the most precious thing in life—why destroy it?"

But destroyed it was. The passage of Prohibition rendered the sale of drink illegal: The saloons had to close, and the drinking place moved underground. During Prohibition, facilities for public drinking were provided by speakeasies, which sold bootleg beverages at high prices, too high for most working-class people to afford. As a result, they drew most of their customers from the middle classes. Treating disappeared. Not only were drinks in speakeasies sold much too expensively to permit such an indulgence, but the middle classes had never taken up the practice.

For the most part, Prohibition proved a failure: Contrary to what had been intended, it increased the popularity of alcohol among women and young people; it caused beer drinkers to convert to spirits; it made drinking synonymous with drunkenness; it engendered disrespect of the law.[31] The one significant respect in which the intentions of Prohibition were fulfilled was in effecting a conversion from public to private drinking. By closing down the saloons and preventing law-abiding restaurants from serving wine, while permitting people to drink at home, Prohibition moved drinking from the public to the private sphere. Dinner parties became very popular, cocktail parties even more so.[32]

At the same time as it was imposed in the United States, prohibition was also introduced in Canada. During the 1920s, however, it was abandoned by the majority of the provinces[33] and replaced by controls on the basis that the problems associated with drinking had been caused principally by the saloons and could be prevented if it were confined to people's houses. It was made illegal for anyone to drink in a public place or have an opened bottle of liquor in his possession anywhere except in a private dwelling. In Canada, even more than in the United States, drinking was converted from the public to the private sphere. The consequences of this change were far from beneficial. A

---

[31]See Chapters 3 and 5.
[32]See Chapters 2 and 3.
[33]The reasons why prohibition was abandoned in Canada are given in Chapter 4.

law that required people to do their drinking in private made it secretive and more likely to lead to abuse. In several provinces, the law forbade guests in hotels from drinking in the public dining room and permitted them to do so only in their own rooms, which hardly encouraged the civilized habit of drinking with meals. "There is a tendency," explained George Catlin, a British authority on liquor legislation, "to regard the consumption of liquor rather as a tolerated but somewhat furtive vice than as a reputable conduct."

An attempt was made to mitigate the severity of Canadian alcohol-control laws by introducing beer parlours. Or, rather, laws were passed permitting beer parlours to open, but, in order to discourage people from using them, they were made uncomfortable. Because prostitutes had frequented the old-time saloons, women were excluded from beer parlours altogether, or else required to sit in separate rooms. The parlours sold only beer, no spirits, no wine, no soft drinks, no food, no cigarettes. No entertainment of any kind was permitted, not even board games. There was little to do in a beer parlour but drink.

In other Anglo-Saxon countries, the drinking places were never required to close but were instead made unattractive and difficult to patronize in the belief that this would lessen abusive drinking. In much of Australia and all of New Zealand, prohibition was avoided by means of a compromise, in which laws were passed requiring pubs to close for the night at six P.M. This left most workingmen only one hour in which to drink between leaving work and closing time. This did not mean, however, that they drank less than they would ordinarily have done, merely that they tried to squeeze a whole evening's drinking into one hour. Hence the antipodean tradition of the "six o'clock swill." The old notion of the pub as a social center in which men conversed and played games was abandoned. Anything that interfered with the fast dispensing of drink, such as dartboards or billiard tables, was removed. The walls of many bars were tiled so that spilt beer and vomit could be cleaned off more easily. In New Zealand, W. H. Woodward, a magistrate and a chairman of two licensing committees, described the six o'clock closing time, and the licensing laws in general, as "the results of a battle between greed and fanaticism, in which the interests of ordinary sensible citizens have been ignored. The outcome is a system in which said citizens drink, jowl by jowl like pigs at a trough, what they are given instead of what they want, and, like pigs, gulp down more than they need of it while they can get it; and, for the privilege of doing so, pay many times the cost of the hogwash they swallow."

In England the pubs were prohibited from opening until late in the morning and required to close during the afternoon and at ten or eleven at night, in an attempt to reduce drunkenness among workers. However, as Arthur Reade told the Royal Commission on Licensing that sat in 1929 and 1930, during the last few minutes before closing time "customers may be seen clamoring at the bar to gulp down two or three drinks where, in a free country across the Channel [on the Continent], they would have been perfectly content to sit at their leisure over one." Even at a relatively civilized hour, early closing proved counterproductive.[34]

Despite the evidence from Canada, Australia, New Zealand, and England that restrictions on public drinking, even of a limited nature, did not reduce drunkenness and alcohol-related problems but increased them, the laws that were introduced in the United States after Repeal sought to limit public drinking. Fifteen states continued to prohibit the sale of spirits "by the drink" in bars and restaurants, and most of the others restricted such sale to hotels, restaurants, and clubs where meals were served. Many states prohibited the use of the word "saloon," while others also banned the term "bar" and some even forbade the use of any words to indicate a drinking place.[35] It was many years before drinking establishments in California were allowed to display anything more than their name and the symbol of a tilted glass with a stirrer.

Before Prohibition, people had gone to saloons not only in order to drink on the premises but also to buy beverages to take home.[36] Neither wine nor beer was sold in grocery stores, while package stores for the retail sale of spirits did not yet exist. These were introduced as part of the liquor licensing system that replaced Prohibition after 1933. The sale of packaged alcoholic drinks was separated from the drinking place; and, with the encouragement of brewers who wanted to normalize the consumption of their product, drinking increasingly became

---

[34]Afternoon closing remained in force until 1988, while eleven P.M. closing is still the law today, even in major cities such as London.

[35]Some bar owners took pleasure in poking fun at the restrictions. When Michael O'Neal opened O'Neal's Saloon in New York in 1967, only to be informed by the state liquor authority that he was breaking the law, he changed the "S" into a "B" and traded, with a deliberate misspelling, as "O'Neal's Baloon."

[36]"Rushing the growler" is described in Chapter 3.

something that people did in their own homes.[37] The beer can had been introduced soon after Repeal. Whereas bottled beer had cost more to make and to transport than draft beer, the canned version did not. So the brewers could now concentrate on selling their product in grocery stores. In the twenty years after 1935 the proportion of beer sold in packaged form for home consumption increased from 30 to 78 percent. This development was completed after the Second World War, when grocery stores ceased stocking beer in a special liquor section and placed it alongside soft drinks instead.

In recent years, people have been pressured to drink in private rather than in public by the publicity given to drink-driving and the increased penalties imposed for so doing; by the enforcement of "dram shop laws" that make bartenders responsible for the subsequent behavior of customers to whom they have sold alcoholic drink; by public disapproval of drinking by pregnant women and of drinking in front of children.[38] Whereas, in the period immediately following Repeal, about nine tenths of the consumption of alcoholic drinks took place in bars and restaurants, today that figure has fallen to approximately one quarter.

The decline in public drinking is symptomatic of the general decline in public life in America. At the end of the 1980s the sociologist Ray Oldenburg argued in *The Great Good Place* that modern American society was suffering for lack of a "third place," an alternative to the twin worlds of home and work, an informal public meeting place where people could go to escape from the demands of the one and the pressures of the other, where they would find company and conversation, where they could enjoy themselves.

As Oldenburg explained, Americans have substituted the vision of the ideal home for that of the ideal city. By purchasing large homes on large lots in lifeless neighborhoods, people have not so much

---

[37] The normalization of beer consumption is described in Chapter 6.

[38] These have led many people to adopt one position in their private and another in their public lives. Their attitudes to alcohol can be seen as an example of political correctness. They have shrunk away from a public display of natural social behavior, such as drinking, smoking, and the pursuit of members of the opposite sex, and from the public expression of legitimate but controversial opinions, such as disapproval of homosexuality and approval of abortion, because they have learned that they must restrict these ideas to the private arena. The effect of political correctness has not been to change their attitudes but to turn them into hypocrites.

joined communities as retreated from them. They have rejected the public or shared environment in favor of their private home. "They proceed," says Oldenburg, "as though a house can substitute for a community if only it is spacious enough, entertaining enough, comfortable enough, splendid enough—and suitably isolated from [the] common horde."

As a consequence of its retreat to isolated suburban communities accessible only by car, contemporary American society is far from the "convenience culture" of popular conception. If Americans really lived in a convenience culture, Oldenburg argues, they would have the necessities of life close at hand, within walking distance, as in European cities. There are plenty of trivial conveniences in American life, such as plastic credit cards, vending-machine coffee and prepackaged frozen dinners. But these are insignificant beside the fundamental problems created by an inconvenient society in which an automobile must be used to perform even the most mundane errands.

Because of their inconvenient culture, Oldenburg continues, Americans are largely denied those means of relieving stress that serve other cultures so effectively, such as sharing a drink in a local meeting place. This source of relief used to exist in America, before Prohibition. In the nineteenth and early twentieth centuries, saloons did a very good job of easing the worries of immigrants and the working class. The destruction of the saloons and the transference of drinking from the public to the private arena have deprived people of a means of restoring equilibrium through social interaction. Instead, they have developed such solitary consolations as meditation and jogging or have simply devoted their energies to improving the environment of their private sanctuary in which they seek to isolate themselves from the outside world.

When temperance campaigners closed down the saloon in the early twentieth century, they also terminated the beer garden, which Oldenburg describes as "the model, par excellence, of the third place." Whereas saloons tended to be run and patronized by Irish immigrants, the beer garden was a German institution. It was not necessarily a garden, although it derived from the Continental custom of spending Sunday afternoon outdoors with the family. Some were indeed gardens, while others were situated indoors, with only a few plants in tubs to pay obeisance to their horticultural origins, but they all had tables and chairs rather than a bar, and the food they served was as important as the beer in attracting customers. So, too, was music. Many beer gardens charged an admission fee in order to recoup money from people who came to listen to the music but did not order any beer.

Temperance advocates objected to the beer gardens because they exposed young people to what the campaigners regarded as the evils of drink, because the presence of attractive young women in a place where alcohol was served supposedly aroused irresistible temptations among men, and because the gardens offered a spectacle of people enjoying themselves in a public place on a Sunday when they should properly have been devoting their time to prayer and good works.

Few of these advocates visited the gardens. To do so might bring them too closely into contact with sin. It might also have persuaded them that in campaigning to close down the gardens along with the saloons, they were making a big mistake. Toward the end of the nineteenth century a group of sociologists called the Committee of Fifty investigated the public drinking place as part of a thorough examination of the "liquor problem" in the United States. They focused on Chicago, in the suburbs of which were situated a large number of beer gardens. In their report the committee described a "typical" beer garden, which they said was frequented by an average of three thousand people daily in summer, "principally for the music. . . . The waiters, most of them fine-appearing elderly gentlemen, dressed in black, serve beer, wines, and soft drinks to the people out in the open, while at tables beneath the roof, dinners are being served. The garden is brilliantly lighted with Japanese lanterns hanging from the trees. The lights, the trees, the starry heavens above, the moon gliding now and then behind the clouds, soul-stirring music, now strong and full, now soft and sweet, make this a charming spot where lovers delight to come, where the businessman, returned from the crowded centers of the city, comes with wife and child, and the business cares float gradually away, borne on the lighter strains of music. Old men with their pipes find in this place a never-ending source of pleasure, and will sit by the hour philosophizing and reminiscing over a single glass of beer. . . . A young woman of strong temperance views exclaimed, after spending an hour in this garden for the first time, 'Isn't it beautiful? Can it be, is it possible, that after all our ideas are wrong and these people are right?' "

No such gardens exist today. Many modern bars are hostile, exclusive places in which the appearance of outsiders is resented. They do not offer the companionship of strangers; men rarely attend with their wives; children are forbidden. Other establishments are more sociable.

The last few years have seen the opening of a number of "martini" and "cigar" bars in major cities. This development has been given considerable attention by the media, as it appears to manifest not only a reaction against the trend away from public drinking but also a rejection of the healthy ways of living that people were supposed to have adopted in the 1980s.

There is no doubt that many people have returned to cocktails in response to the demands of neotemperance campaigners that they should drink less. Having been told that drinking is bad for them and that they should abstain as far as possible, they have naturally reacted by turning to the most alcoholic and potentially most harmful drinks they can find. In further demonstration of their spirit of rebellion, many have also taken to smoking cigars in public. In New York, cigar bars owe much of their popularity to the ruling of the state government in 1995 that restaurants should either exclude smokers or seat them in a separately ventilated area. "This country is rebellious by nature," explains Danny Thames of Maloney & Porcelli, a steakhouse with a separate smoking room. "Tell us we can't smoke and we'll just light up the biggest, nastiest cigar we can find."[39]

Thus, the cocktail bar revival cannot primarily be regarded as an attempt to reassert the social values of drinking. The bars do, however, seek to associate themselves with the behavior of times past: to evoke the glamour with which the consumption of cocktails was supposedly once connected. That is why their customers generally demand classic cocktails, notably the martini.[40] Cocktail bars look backward, but it is not clear precisely to what point in American history they refer. Or, rather, they deliberately do not seek to evoke a specific period but suggest vaguely some time between the 1930s and the 1960s. They are unspecific in their imagery because they are seeking to evoke a legendary past, not a real one, a time when people did not live isolated in suburbs but close to each other, both in cities and in small towns, where they enjoyed some kind of communal life. The cocktail bars

---

[39]Cigar smoking has also become popular among young women, for much the same reason as drinking in the 1920s, to demonstrate their emancipation.

[40]At the same time, however, they insist on contemporary flavors, which explains the recent invention of "martinis" that include all kinds of flavorings, not just gin or vodka and vermouth but ingredients such as Cointreau, cranberry juice, and chocolate. Today "martini" is well on its way to becoming a generic term for a cocktail, just as happened to "cocktail" itself at the end of the nineteenth century, as is discussed in Chapter 1.

represent a symbolic revolt against the sterility of society in modern America.

With their old-world appeal, most martini and cigar bars are civilized places, where people can meet and talk. Some even impose a dress code, requiring male customers to wear jackets. They also pride themselves on serving high-quality drinks, at high prices. They are the descendants of the Prohibition-period speakeasies that were patronized by the middle and upper classes rather than of the old-time working-class saloons where drinks were cheap and treating was expected. The customers of cocktail bars may buy drinks for each other, but there are no social requirements for them to do so, and each customer chooses the drink he prefers; people may drink together, but they do not share the same beverage.

Although the working-class practice of treating other customers to drinks in public drinking places has been abandoned,[41] its middle- and upper-class equivalent, of drinking to one's fellow guests at private social gatherings, still survives.

This practice predates treating by many centuries. According to the medieval chronicler Geoffrey of Monmouth, the custom of drinking to the health of another person was brought to Britain by the ancestors of the English—Angles, Saxons, and Jutes from what is now Denmark and northern Germany—during the Dark Ages. Geoffrey told in his *History of the Kings of Britain* how the first of the English to settle in Britain were the Saxon leaders Hengist and Horsa, who had been asked by Vortigern, king of South Britain, to come over to help him fight the Picts of the North in A.D. 449. Sensing an opportunity to acquire some land as well as booty, Hengist invited Vortigern to a feast, at which he plied him with large quantities of drink. At the end of the meal, Hengist's daughter, Rowena, "one of the most accomplished beauties of that age," appeared, bearing a golden goblet filled with wine. She approached Vortigern, curtseyed, and offered to drink to his health. The king, who was struck by her beauty, and filled with desire, bade her do so. After Rowena had drunk from the goblet, Vortigern took it from her, kissed her, and drank in his turn. He then asked her father for her hand in marriage; the price that Hengist demanded and obtained for this union was the whole of the county of Kent.

This story, it must be said, is more of a parable with reference to

---

[41]It survives in Britain, where people who go to a pub in a group are expected to buy "rounds" of drinks for each other.

historical figures than an accurate historical account: Although it suggests the manner in which the practice of drinking to someone's health might well have been introduced into Britain, it is simply not known when or where this custom originated.

Like so many of the "historical" accounts written in the Middle Ages, the story about Hengist, Vortigern, and Rowena tells us more about the period in which it was written than about the time to which it is supposed to refer. The fact that Geoffrey of Monmouth chose to embroider history in order to include an explanation for the origin of health drinking showed how important this had become by the early Middle Ages. In the Anglo-Saxon and medieval periods, when England was less of a country than a conglomeration of tribal loyalties, it served the practical purpose of demonstrating one man's loyalty to another and willingness to fight on his behalf.

Also, by having Vortigern and Rowena drink out of one goblet, Geoffrey of Monmouth showed that in the Middle Ages it was common practice for everyone at a ceremonial gathering to drink from the same vessel. There was often only one glass or goblet for the whole table, which was why a man of good breeding would wipe his mouth with a napkin before drinking, and would empty the entire contents of the container in one draft.

This practice of drinking from the same vessel survived in colonial and early republican America. In 1780 the Marquis de Barbé-Marbois attended a Quaker betrothal in Philadelphia at which everybody drank punch from the same glass, which he explained was "a very common custom, especially among the Quakers." At this period, when a father brought his son for his first drink at a tavern, they would drink from the same glass, in order to show that they were now equals.

The practice of drinking healths survived in America too, despite the attempt of the Puritans to ban it. They regarded it as a profane and pagan custom that should not be allowed to survive in the new Christian world they were seeking to create. In 1639 the General Court in Boston declared that "the common custom of drinking one to another is a mere useless ceremony . . . and is also an occasion of much waste of the good creatures, and of many other sins, as drunkenness, quarreling, bloodshed, uncleanness, mispense of precious time, etc., which . . . ought in all places and times to be prevented. . . ." It announced that the practice was forbidden, and that anyone who drank to the health of someone else would be subject to a fine of twelve pence for each offense. The prohibition was disregarded, however, and was repealed in 1645.

It had proved impossible to ban the custom of drinking healths, because it helped to give English migrants in America a sense of commonalty, of community in a strange land. It also reminded them of how they had behaved at what they still regarded as home. The colonists considered themselves to be "English";[42] many of them felt homesick, which encouraged feelings of nostalgia, and a tendency to conservatism. In the early colonial records, the adjectives "new" and "novel" were employed as pejorative terms.[43]

The colonists of the seventeenth and eighteenth centuries stuck as far as possible to their traditional attitudes and behavior, which included the practice of drinking to the health of other people. The custom also served some social function. The Marquis de Chastellux, a major-general in the French Expeditionary Force that fought in the Revolutionary War, reported on a dinner at General Washington's quarters in the autumn of 1780 where "I accommodated myself very well to the English 'toast.'[44] You have very small glasses, you pour out the quantity of wine you choose, without being pressed to take more, and the 'toast' is only a sort of refrain punctuating the conversation, as a reminder that each individual is part of the company and that the whole forms but one society."

---

[42]This explains why Paul Revere could not possibly have exclaimed, "The British are coming!" when rousing the minutemen of Massachusetts on his famous ride on the night of April 18–19, 1775. At this time the people of Massachusetts still considered themselves to be British. What Revere actually said was, "The Regulars are coming out!"

[43]This conservatism helps to account for the revolution, as has been explained in the previous chapter. While the American settlers clung to their old ways, the British in Britain developed new forms of behavior, and new legal and political institutions. When the British authorities tried to bring the colonists into line with their new ways of doing things, the settlers felt that their way of life was being threatened, and revolted.

[44]In England, "toast" originally referred to a piece of toasted bread that was placed in a cup of wine or beer, supposedly to improve the flavor. The word came to be transformed from an object that was put into a drink into the object of the act of drinking following an incident that occurred in the then fashionable spa town of Bath in the west of England in the second half of the seventeenth century. As the story goes, a celebrated beauty was bathing under the gaze of a large number of admirers, one of whom took a cup of water from her bath and drank her health to the assembled company. Another admirer responded that he would prefer to jump into the water and carry off the lady: that he did not like the liquor, but he would have the toast.

After America had established its independence, toasting took on new connotations. Many post-revolutionary banquets were political. Each diner was expected to deliver at least one toast, in which he either lauded his own party and predicted great victories, or condemned the opposition and foretold its defeat. After each toast the diners would shout, "Hip, hip, hooray!" Long lists of these toasts were printed in the newspapers, so that those who had made them might publicize the vigor with which they had supported their party.

By the 1820s, however, the practice of toasting, both for political and for social purposes, was in decline. The toasts that had previously been made at political dinners were replaced by postprandial addresses, while at private dinner parties toasting was now regarded as an antiquated ceremony that progress had left behind. "Drinking of healths is now growing out of fashion, and is now very unpolite in good company," explained the author of The American Chesterfield in the 1820s. "Custom once had made it universal, but the improved manners of the age now render it vulgar. What can be more rude or ridiculous than to interrupt persons at their meals with unnecessary compliments? Abstain, then, from this silly custom. . . ."

The growing influence of the temperance movement in the 1830s and 1840s also discouraged toasting, which was considered by campaigners to lead people to consume more alcohol than they would otherwise have done. The practice did not disappear, however. The more ridiculous, ceremonial aspects of toasting rituals had been abandoned; so, too, in many temperate households, was the practice of drinking deeply from a glass each time one made or responded to a toast; but the symbolic elements of the ritual remained. "If either a lady or gentleman is invited to take wine at table, they must never refuse," stated the author of The Perfect Gentleman in 1860. "If they do not drink, they need only to touch the wine to their lips." At the very least, diners were expected literally to pay lip service to the custom, to demonstrate their involvement in a shared experience.

Toasting not only survived throughout the nineteenth century but has lasted to this day. It remains as an international language that can be spoken by people who dine together for business or other reasons yet do not share a spoken language: People who are unable otherwise to communicate directly can clink their glasses, say "Cheers!" or its equivalent in the language of the hosts or the guests,[45] and drink to

---

[45]"Skol," which is sometimes used in English, has been said to commemorate the

the health of each other. Toasting remains a symbol of conviviality and commonalty, and of good faith, just as it was in Britain in the Middle Ages, just as it was in America two hundred years ago.

It is not only the drinking of the health that is important, but also the clinking of glasses, which demonstrates that although the diners will no longer be drinking out of the same vessel, they are still about to share the same substance. People who dine together, who wish to demonstrate the shared nature of the experience, drink the same wine. People who have not shared the same liquid as their fellow diners have often, consciously or unconsciously, been making a point. Not long before the end of his presidency, Richard Nixon entertained ten congressmen at dinner on the presidential yacht. There was beef tenderloin on the menu, and what Nixon liked to drink with his beef was Château Margaux 1966—a great vintage from one of the finest estates in Bordeaux, which even then retailed for $30 a bottle. While the congressmen enjoyed a rather more humble wine with their dinner, the stewards refilled Nixon's glass from a bottle of his favorite wine, discreetly wrapped in a tea towel.

Doubtless Nixon considered himself guilty of no more than selfishness, but his insistence on setting aside a special wine for himself was worse than that: It was antisocial. It is one thing to share the same food as one's guests, but food does not serve as such an effective symbol of fellowship as wine. The food on one man's plate is never the same as his neighbor's. Especially when roast meats are served—and these have tended to provide the central feature of ceremonial meals—some people are given better pieces than others. With drink, everyone shares, or should share the same liquid.

Not only does drink provide a better symbol of association than food, an alcoholic drink serves this purpose far better than a nonalcoholic one. It would be just as inappropriate and ahistorical to toast other people with a nonalcoholic drink as it is to celebrate the Holy Sacrament with grape juice. Only alcoholic drinks can symbolize an apparently miraculous transubstantiation and embody the achievement of human civilization in harnessing nature to its own ends. The link between blood and wine means not only that a religious celebrant is metaphorically taking into his body the soul of a god but also that

---

old custom of drinking out of the skull of a fallen enemy. This is incorrect: The Scandinavian *skål*, the origin of "skol," is not the same word as *skal*, meaning a shell or skull. But the Vikings did use the skulls of their enemies as drinking vessels.

two people who share a glass of wine are entering symbolically into a blood covenant—an affirmation of friendship and fidelity. This explains why, even today, Orthodox Jews will not accept wine from Gentiles, because it is a small step from establishing such a social bond to diluting the race by intermarriage. Orthodox Jews are permitted to drink only kosher wine, the production of which is controlled in such a manner as to ensure that no Gentile (or even unobservant Jew) has tampered with it. Not only must every stage in the vinification process be undertaken by a Sabbath-observant Jew, under rabbinical supervision, but, when they are drunk in a restaurant, the wines remain kosher only if they have been opened and poured by an orthodox Jew.[46]

It would also be inappropriate to employ nonalcoholic drinks as a symbol of association because, when people drink together, they are sharing not only the substance but also the effect—the gradual, gentle process of inebriation that helps people to lose their reserve and become more sociable and communicative. Wine connoisseurs may try to deny it, but one of the pleasurable aspects of fine wine is that it contains alcohol.

Alcohol provides the pleasure, but also causes the problem. There used to be a time when wine was not thought to contain any alcohol, and was exempt from any condemnation of the social and personal problems with which the consumption of alcohol was connected. The temperance movement was originally directed at spirits, not wine. In 1784, in his *Inquiry into the Effects of Ardent Spirits upon the Human Body and Mind,* the pamphlet that is generally regarded as the origin of this movement, Benjamin Rush sought to persuade Americans to abandon spirits in favor of more healthy types of drink such as wine. "Unlike ardent spirits, which render the temper irritable," he advised, "wines generally inspire cheerfulness and good humor." Until the early nineteenth century, middle-class wine drinkers persevered in their habits while telling working-class spirit drinkers that they should reform.

---

[46]Victor Schoenfield, winemaker at the Golan Heights Winery in Israel, which produces arguably the world's finest kosher wines under its Yarden label, is not permitted to touch the wine himself; although a Jew, he is not an observant one. He may taste the wine, but only if someone else has drawn the sample from the vat. Lesser-quality kosher wine is often pasteurized (*mevushal*) in the belief that the bottles can then be transported and served by Gentiles or nonobservant Jews yet remain kosher; some rabbis argue, however, that the pasteurization, by altering the wine, deprives it of its spiritual power.

Then the chemist William Brande succeeded in measuring the alcohol in wine.[47] The number of people who advocated wine as a temperance beverage declined. The celebrated showman P. T. Barnum had drunk a lot of wine, especially champagne, and had been proud of the contents of his cellar. In 1848 he heard a sermon in which the Universalist clergyman Edwin Chapin told wine drinkers to abandon their beverage in order to set an example to others. "I warn you," he added, "that you are in danger and should give it up for your own sake." The next day Barnum went down to his cellar and smashed his bottles of champagne. He became an advocate of teetotalism and lectured in favor of the cause. There was no such thing as moderation in drinking, he declared, any more than in horse stealing: "A moderate drinker generally commits suicide moderately."

Temperance campaigners now put pressure on the churches to remove wine from the celebration of Holy Communion. Not only did this set a bad example, it might lead to backsliding among reformed drunkards. Thomas Welch was inspired to create his grape juice after a visiting Methodist minister, supposedly as a consequence of sipping the Communion wine, became seized by an uncontrollable urge for strong drink.

More than a century later, many of the same arguments are repeated. Reformed alcoholics are told that they should stay away from drink for the rest of their lives: that they cannot ever become moderate drinkers because alcohol is an addictive drug that creates dependency in the user and cannot be consumed in moderation; that addiction to alcohol is a disease from which it is possible to recover only by abstaining permanently; that the ingestion of alcohol, in however small a quantity, triggers an irresistible craving for the substance.[48]

The prevalence of these beliefs can partly be explained by what has been described as "pharmacological Calvinism": the notion that any substance that makes a person feel good is regarded by the majority of the population as morally bad, since it contradicts the popular belief in moral superiority through self-discipline and violates theological views of salvation through faith and good works. Many people are still waiting patiently for the Second Coming of Christ, and keeping themselves pure in expectation of his imminent arrival.

Many Americans find themselves unable to distinguish between

---

[47]See Chapter 4.
[48]See the Introduction.

moderate and immoderate consumption of alcohol. The true temperance argument that people should convert from distilled spirits to less alcoholic, fermented drinks such as wine and beer has largely been abandoned. The term "temperance" properly means moderation: It refers to the argument that people should consume alcoholic drinks only of moderate strength or in moderate quantities, but its meaning has been perverted to designate campaigners who have advocated abstention from all forms of alcohol. The temperance argument has been turned on its head: It has been suggested that fermented drinks are more noxious than distilled ones, because they encourage people, especially young people, to acquire a taste for alcohol, which will inevitably lead them to consume alcoholic beverages in greater quantities and in stronger form. This was the very argument that led to the prohibition of the manufacture and sale of all alcoholic drinks in the 1850s and 1920s.

Precisely the same argument is also propounded today in order to justify the prohibition of "soft" drugs such as marijuana; it is declared, without the benefit of any supporting evidence, that marijuana is a "gateway" drug that inevitably leads the user to take and become dependent upon "hard" drugs such as heroin and crack cocaine. In fact, by including soft drugs along with hard ones, and by condemning fermented beverages as well as distilled spirits, the prohibition is rendered less effective: The result of banning substances that many people regard as legitimate has been to discredit the whole prohibition and to engender disrespect for the law.[49]

Had the manufacture of beer and the importation and sale of wine been permitted during national Prohibition, it would not have aroused such resistance, and would probably have survived for two generations or more, rather than a little over a decade. People were allowed to drink wine during Prohibition, but only if they were wealthy enough to have laid down supplies to last them through the thirteen years during which the trade was banned, or sufficiently adept to make their own wine at home. Beer was banned, despite strenuous attempts by labor leaders to have the legal definition of "intoxicating" modified so as to permit the manufacture of low-alcohol beer. In the opinion of the federal government even beer containing only 2.75 percent alcohol by weight (3.5 percent by volume) was dangerously intoxicating.[50]

---

[49]See Chapter 5.
[50]See Chapter 4.

During Prohibition, the manufacture and sale of all alcoholic beverages were banned, because they were all regarded as equally harmful.

Since the repeal of Prohibition, most states have imposed more stringent restrictions on spirits than on wine and beer. This has led the distillers to promote the notion of "equivalency": to argue that "a drink is a drink is a drink."[51] The distillers believe that by pointing out that a shot of spirits contains no more alcohol than a standard serving of beer or wine, they will succeed in persuading the regulatory authorities to treat them in the same way as the brewers and winemakers. But their argument also reinforces the popular misconception that there is no difference between different types of drink or the manner in which they are consumed or their effects on the drinker and that therefore if drink can be harmful—as it undoubtedly can be—then the only safe course is to steer clear of it altogether.

This attitude also appears to be shared by the government bodies that have tried to prevent the promulgation of medical evidence showing the health benefits associated with moderate alcohol consumption, on the grounds that this would encourage people to drink: that, being unable to distinguish moderate from heavy drinking, people would regard any suggestion that alcohol might be beneficial as a licence to drink to excess.[52] A similar motivation underlies the advice given to pregnant women that they should not drink at all, which contradicts the findings of scientific research that the risk of damage to the fetus is not increased if the mother drinks moderately but only if she drinks to excess or in binges.[53] Telling pregnant women that they should abstain suggests that they cannot be trusted to drink in moderation, that once they start drinking, they will not stop.

Similarly, the law prohibiting people under the age of twenty-one from drinking in public places (or even, in many states, in private homes) encourages the notion that alcohol, in any form, is a harmful influence from which children should be protected. It is true that many young people, when they start drinking, frequently do so in an unhealthy manner, in binges, often with unfortunate consequences, but this does not prove that the legislators and their parents were right to have stopped them from drinking and to have kept them away from places where alcohol was served. Rather, it is the prohibition of juve-

---

[51]See Chapter 4 again.
[52]See Chapter 4 once more.
[53]See Chapter 3.

nile drinking that leads young people to drink to excess. If children were taught how to drink responsibly and moderately by their parents, they would not start drinking in secret, and fewer of them would indulge in binges.[54]

Bingeing is not merely antisocial; it does not just lead to arguments and hangovers, to the trashing of property and to unplanned sex. It can cause long-term harm to young people by suppressing growth hormones vital to the development of muscles and bones. It can also kill people, especially older ones. About eighteen hours after a heavy drinking session, the platelets, the blood cells that can cling to fatty deposits and clog the arteries, become more adhesive, increasing the risk of thrombosis or stroke.[55]

Yet binge drinking remains a common feature of American alcohol consumption. It provides a modern manifestation of a long tradition of unhealthy drinking practices in the United States.

For many centuries before the first emigrants left for America, the English had been reputed as heavy drinkers. In the twelfth century the intellectual and ecclesiastic John of Salisbury, who had been born in England but had spent much of his life on the Continent, wrote in a letter to a friend that "the constant habit of drinking has made the English famous among all foreign nations." Four centuries later, drinking increased because men started to patronize alehouses. In his *Anatomy of Abuses* the Puritan pamphleteer Philip Stubbes described how the alehouses were "haunted with malt-worms" who sat drinking "all day long, yea, all the night, peradventure the week together, so long as any money is left, swilling, gulling[56] and carousing from one to another, till never a one can speak a ready word. . . . How they stutter and stammer, stagger and reel to and fro, like madmen, some vomiting, spewing, and disgorging their filthy stomachs, othersome pissing under the board as they sit."

English emigrants took their habits with them to America. John Winthrop, who had been appointed governor of Massachusetts, reported in his journal that on the voyage across the Atlantic in the *Arbella* in 1630, a maid-servant "drank so much strong water[57] that she was senseless, and had near killed herself. We observed it a common fault

---

[54]See Chapter 5.
[55]See Chapter 4 for more on platelets.
[56]Guzzling.
[57]Spirits.

in all our young people that they gave themselves to drink hot waters very immoderately." In 1647 the government of Connecticut, concerned about the "great abuse which is creeping in by excess in wine and strong waters," passed a measure forbidding any man from spending more than half an hour at one time drinking in an alehouse in the town in which he lived. But this did not solve the problem. Indeed, it increased in the second half of the century, as a result of the growth in popularity of rum.[58] In a sermon to the General Assembly of Massachusetts in 1709, Cotton Mather[59] inveighed against the consumption of "prodigious quantities" of rum. "One of the sorest punishments which ever did or ever can befall this poor country is the great esteem which this liquor has among us," he declared. "It makes us poor; it keeps us poor; whole families may curse the day that ever the bottle came into them."

In colonial America, men offered various reasons for their consumption of large quantities of rum which would not have applied back in England. They drank spirits, they said, because these gave them the strength to perform their labors; because they counteracted the effects of hot weather by warming stomachs made cold by sweating, as well as of cold weather, by producing a feeling of warmth;[60] because they helped to ward off tropical disease and to purify bad water, or at least to render poor-tasting water potable.[61]

After the revolution, rum was replaced in popularity by whiskey, which, being made in America from local ingredients, served as a symbol of independence, and, since it was cheap, came to be regarded as a token of democracy.[62] Whiskey was available almost everywhere and was consumed in large quantities. Anne Royall, who spent much of her life traveling across the country in stagecoaches, wrote that "when I was in Virginia, it was too much whiskey—in Ohio, too much whiskey—in Tennessee, it is too, too much whiskey!"

This period also saw the development of solitary binge drinking on the western frontier, a new form of behavior that inspired temperance campaigns. Thus began a cycle that has recurred throughout American history, in which alcoholic drinks have tended to fall into and out of

---

[58]See Chapter 1.
[59]The son of Increase Mather.
[60]See Chapter 1 for all of these.
[61]See Chapter 4.
[62]See Chapter 6.

fashion as each generation has reacted against the habits of its predecessor. The temperance campaigns of the 1830s and 1840s, which persuaded many people to give up alcohol, culminated in the introduction of prohibition in many states. From this point, however, drinking increased, provoking renewed temperance concerns in the late nineteenth century, leading to the imposition of national Prohibition in 1920. Drinking then became popular again, and consumption increased steadily, inspiring a third temperance movement and new legislative controls on drinking in the 1980s. The current fashion for cocktails may represent the beginnings of a reaction against this third temperance movement and a return to a period of heavy drinking. Thus, American drinking habits have been moving constantly from one extreme to another, without settling in the middle.

Maybe people might have acquired the habit of drinking in moderation if they had ever learned how to enjoy wine. But this has long been regarded as a pretentious foreign product, inappropriate for the simple tastes of democratic Americans. Patrick Henry attempted to denigrate Thomas Jefferson for having brought back from France an effete taste for wine; President Van Buren lost his reelection campaign of 1840 because his opponents succeeded in portraying him as a man who luxuriated in fine wine, unlike his rival, William Henry Harrison, who supposedly lived in a log cabin and contented himself with hard cider.[63]

Advocates who sought to persuade Americans to drink California wine later in the century could make little headway in the face of such attitudes. "The great obstacle to our success," complained Arpad Haraszthy, "is that the average American is a whiskey-drinking, water-drinking, coffee-drinking, tea-drinking, and consequently a dyspepsia-inviting subject, who does not know the use or value of pure light wine taken at the proper time and in moderate quantities. The task before us lies in teaching our people how to drink wine, when to drink it, and how much of it to drink."

Wine has never become an integral element of the American diet because it has long been a national habit to rush through one's meals and to regard the enjoyment of leisurely meals accompanied by wine as an elitist and un-American activity, as a waste of time that could be better spent working.[64]

---

[63]See Chapter 2 for both of these.
[64]See Chapter 2 for these as well.

There is no denying that wine has become increasingly popular in the past thirty or forty years. But many of the people who took up drinking wine in the 1970s and 1980s chose white wine as an alternative to cocktails, which had fallen out of fashion, rather than as an adjunct to food. And many of the people who have started to drink red wine in the last few years have done so because they think it is good for their health, not because they actually like it.[65]

The majority of people who order wine in restaurants make their choice on the basis of price, rejecting anything inexpensive in the belief that it cannot be good. Many plump for wine in its most ostentatious form, that of champagne. For all the advances that civilization has made in the last century or more, diners continue to behave in this respect exactly as they did in Haraszthy's time.[66] If they felt more comfortable about their knowledge of wine, then they would hardly be so ready to order Dom Pérignon champagne. This is marketed as a "prestige *cuvée*"; everywhere it is stocked it is claimed to be an exclusive product, in short supply. In fact, nearly a million bottles are sold in the United States every year—at a cost of $250 in a restaurant (or $120 in a wine store). The marketing manager of a major champagne company (who has asked not to be identified) has admitted how the price of Dom Pérignon and other prestige *cuvées* is calculated. "The consumer knows nothing," he says. "The more a champagne costs, the better he thinks it is. A high price makes him feel secure." For all its popularity, the style of Dom Pérignon is not one that the majority of consumers enjoy: It is an elegant champagne whose qualities are not obvious to the uninitiated, and which needs to be matured for several years to show of its best. The popular preference is for richer, riper wines that are immediately enjoyable.[67]

Even people who are enthusiastic about wine often know very little about the products they are purchasing. Many of them slavishly follow the advice of wine writers even if this contradicts the evidence of their own taste buds. In 1985 a customer came into Wally's Liquors in Westwood in Los Angeles and bought a case of Chardonnay from Chalone Vineyards in California. A few days later he returned eleven of the twelve bottles, saying he did not like the wine. Steven Wallace, the

---

[65]See Chapter 2, as well as Chapter 4 for people taking up red wine on health grounds.
[66]See Chapter 2 again.
[67]This preference is described in Chapter 1.

owner, gave him his money back. Two weeks later he returned and bought another case of the same wine. Wallace asked him why he had changed his mind. He said that he had just read a rave review of the wine by Robert Parker.[68]

Some of the people who buy expensive wines not only know nothing about them but do not even drink them. In an edition of *The Wine Advocate* in 1990 Parker described having been invited to dinner a few years earlier by one of his readers. The reader showed Parker around his huge, temperature-controlled cellar, which was filled with rare vintages of Bordeaux and top burgundies. At dinner he opened a bottle of Bordeaux from his collection—Château Croizet-Bages 1969, the produce of a mediocre château in a poor vintage. Parker tasted it, and found it unpleasant. The reader explained that he did not actually drink wine himself. "But it sure smells good," he added. This story led Parker to launch a blistering attack on what he called the nondrinking collector. "To him, wine is like a collection of crystal, art, sculpture, or china—to be admired, to be shown off, but never, ever, to be used."

For all that is written about the "Mediterranean diet" nowadays,[69] Americans have never really taken to drinking wine with their dinner. The inhabitants of Louisiana had drunk wine with their meals when they had lived under French rule in the eighteenth century, and had persevered with this custom after Louisiana was incorporated into the United States.[70] Not only did many families drink wine with all their meals, including breakfast, but they gave it to their children, diluted with water. Timothy Flint, an emigrant from Massachusetts, found it remarkable that "every family is provided with [Bordeaux], as we at the North are with cider. I have scarcely seen an instance of intoxication among the respectable planters."

In time, however, the majority of the inhabitants of Louisiana abandoned wine and came to behave more like other Americans. When large numbers of immigrants from wine-producing countries in southern and eastern Europe arrived in America at the end of the nineteenth century, their dietary habits were criticized by public health workers, and their liking for wine was condemned.[71] Prohibition was imposed

---

[68]It is possible that the customer had been right to return the wine in the first place, since Chalone's wines had been spoiled in a number of vintages by a corky taste.

[69]This discussed in Chapter 4.

[70]See Chapter 2.

[71]See Chapter 2 again.

partly in order to demonstrate official disapproval of their consumption of wine with meals.

In retrospect, white Anglo-Saxon Protestant Americans should have been able to learn from these immigrants and their relative lack of alcohol-related problems, and should have freed themselves from their tendency to oscillate between drunkenness and abstinence by adopting the habit of drinking wine in regular and moderate quantities with their meals. But it has been an American tendency to regard the consumption of wine, like other alcoholic drinks, as a secretive vice rather than sociable conduct; to see drinking only in terms of the problems that have been associated with it, while ignoring its social values—as a means of sharing, of cementing friendship, of defining status, of establishing loyalty, of entering adulthood, of declaring freedom. Yet alcoholic drink has itself rarely been the cause of the offenses that have been attributed to it. Instead, it has liquefied tensions inherent in society, such as between Indians and white men in the eighteenth century,[72] between native-born Americans and immigrants from Europe in the nineteenth century, and between young people and adults today. Those people who have attacked, and who continue to attack alcoholic drink, have been aiming at a symptom of social problems, at a means of canalizing and even alleviating them—but not at their cause.[73] If they were capable of learning from their own history, they would not make this mistake. But, as the German philosopher Georg Hegel famously wrote, the only thing we learn from history is that we do not learn from history.

---

[72]See the Introduction.
[73]Attempts to attribute wrongdoings to alcohol are also discussed in the Introduction.

References

INTRODUCTION

History of tobacco: Jordan Goodman, *Tobacco in History: The Cultures of Dependence* (London, 1993). Tobacco and shamanism: Alexander von Gernet, "Nicotian Dreams: The Prehistory and Early History of Tobacco in Eastern North America" in *Consuming Habits: Drugs in History and Anthropology* (ed. Jordan Goodman et al., London, 1995) pp. 67–87; Johannes Wilbert, "Does Pharmacology Corroborate the Nicotine Therapy and Practices of South American Shamanism?" *Journal of Ethnopharmacology*, Vol. 32 (1991) pp. 179–86. Tobacco as medicine: Nicholas Monardes, *Joyfull Newes out of the New Founde Worlde* (tr. John Frampton, London, 1925) pp. 75–91. King James I: "Counterblast to Tobacco" in *Two Broadsides Against Tobacco* (London, 1672) pp. 1–12. Tobacco in Britain: Jerome E. Brooks, *The Mighty Leaf* (London, 1953) pp. 55–57, 85–89; Brian Inglis, *The Forbidden Game: A Social History of Drugs* (London, 1975) pp. 37–48; Larry Harrison, "Tobacco Battered and the Pipes Shattered: A Note on the Fate of the First British Campaign Against Tobacco Smoking," *British Journal of Addiction*, Vol. 81 (1986) pp. 553–58. Tobacco in Europe: Joel Best, "Economic Interests and the Vindication of Deviance: Tobacco in Seventeenth-Century Europe," *Sociological Quarterly*, Vol. 20 (1979) pp. 171–82. Biphasic effect of alcohol: Alan Marlatt, "Alcohol, the Magic Elixir," Permission for Pleasure Conference, New York, June 28–July 1, 1998.

First Indian encounter with spirits: John Heckewelder, *History, Manners and Customs of the Indian Nations* (Philadelphia, 1876) pp. 71–75; *Henry Hudson the Navigator: The Original Documents* (ed. G. M. Asher, London, 1860) pp. 85–86. First English-language description of New York: Daniel Denton, *A Brief Description of New York* (Cleveland, 1902), p. 46. Treaty of Easton: Mark E. Lender and James K. Martin, *Drinking in America* (2nd ed., New York, 1987) p. 26. Governor Thomas: Hugh Brogan, *The Penguin History of the United States of America* (London, 1990) p. 59. Conversion of Europe from smoking to drinking culture: Andrew Sherratt, "Alcohol and Its Alternatives: Symbol and Substance in Pre-industrial Cultures" in *Consuming Habits* pp. 11–46. Mohammed's Meccan and Medinite followers: Hugh Johnson, *The Story of Wine* (London, 1989) pp. 98–101. New desert tribes: Sherratt, loc. cit. Christianity at risk from shamanism: Inglis, op. cit. pp. 25–39. Peyote ceremony: Weston La Barre, *The Peyote Cult* (5th ed., Norman, Oklahoma, 1989); Richard E. Schultes and Albert Hofmann, *The Plants of the Gods* (Rochester, Vermont, 1992) pp. 132–43. Witchcraft not a survival of old pagan religions: Ronald Hutton, *The Pagan Religions of the British Isles: Their Nature and Legacy* (Oxford, 1991). Flight in shamanistic ritual: Mircea Eliade, *Shamanism: Archaic Techniques of Ecstasy* (tr. Willard R. Trask, London, 1989) pp. 487–92. Broomsticks: Michael J. Harmer, "The Use of Hallucinogenic Plants in European Witchcraft" in *Hallucinogens and Shamanism* (ed. Michael J. Harmer, New York, 1973) pp. 125–50; Schultes and Hofmann, op. cit. pp. 86–91; John Mann, *Murder, Magic and Medicine* (Oxford, 1992) pp. 76–82. "Sabbath": Norman Cohn, *Europe's Inner Demons* (rev. ed., London, 1993) pp. 145–47. Witches mostly women: Keith Thomas, *Religion and the Decline of Magic* (London, 1971) pp. 620–22, 678–79.

History of drugs in America: H. Wayne Morgan, *Drugs in America: A Social History 1800–1980* (Syracuse, New York, 1982). Benjamin Franklin: David F. Musto, "Opium, Cocaine and Marijuana in American History," *Scientific American*, July 1991, pp. 40–47. Alexander Hamilton: William Coleman, *A Collection of the Facts and Documents Relative to the Death of Major-General Alexander Hamilton* (New York, 1804) pp. 18–22. Literary drug users: Virginia Berridge and Griffith Edwards, *Opium and the People: Opiate Use in Nineteenth-Century England* (London, 1981) pp. 49–61; Alethea Hayter, *Opium and the Romantic Imagination* (London, 1968). Poe: Kenneth Silverman, *Edgar A. Poe* (London, 1992) pp. 183–84, 481n. Use of morphine to alleviate pain leads to addiction: Edward Parrish, *A Treatise on Pharmacy* (3rd ed., Philadelphia, 1864) pp. 172–73. Upper classes take opium in order to dissociate themselves from lower-class drunkenness: *The New York Times*, December 30, 1877; Norman H. Clark, *Deliver Us from Evil* (New York, 1976) pp. 217–24. Older people took drugs: *Report of the International*

Opium Commission (Shanghai, 1909) Vol. 2 pp. 19–20. "Odorless and occupies but little space": *Catholic World* 1881, on http://www.druglibrary.org. Morphine "less inimical to healthy life than alcohol": Dr. J. R. Black, "Advantages of Substituting the Morphia Habit for the Incurably Alcoholic," *Cincinnati Lancet-Clinic* 1889, on http://www.druglibrary.org.

Alcohol consumption during Prohibition: Jeffrey A. Miron and Jeffrey Zweibel, "Papers and Proceedings of the 103rd Annual Meeting of the American Economic Association," Washington, D.C., December 28–30, 1990; *The American Economic Review*, Vol. 81 (1991) pp. 242–47; Clark Warburton, *The Economic Results of Prohibition* (New York, 1932). President Harding: Alice Roosevelt Longworth, *Crowded Hours* (New York, 1933) p. 324. Drug use during Prohibition: Morgan, op. cit., pp. 30, 127; David Courtwright, *Dark Paradise: Opiate Use in America Before 1940* (Cambridge, Massachusetts, 1982) p. 179 n. 60; David F. Musto, *The American Disease: Origins of Narcotics Control* (New Haven, Connecticut, 1973) pp. 138, 140, 219–20, 302; contra Louis Lewin, *Phantastica: Narcotic and Stimulating Drugs* (tr. P.H.A. Wirth, London, 1931) p. 253. Senator Reed: Andrew Sinclair, *Prohibition* (London, 1962) pp. 374–75. Drugs symbolic of deviancy: John C. Burnham, *Bad Habits* (New York, 1993) pp. 113, 119. "Polypharmacy": Ibid. p. 123. Moves to legalize marijuana intended to deprive hippies of the pleasure of rebellion: Timothy Miller, *The Hippies and American Values* (Knoxville, Tennessee, 1991) p. 31, in Burnham, op. cit., p. 122. "Many see the drug as fostering a counterculture": National Commission on Marijuana and Drug Abuse, *Marijuana: A Signal of Misunderstanding* (Washington, D.C., 1972) pp. 8–9, in Morgan, op. cit., p. 159. Poll about parental attitudes: Mike A. Males, *The Scapegoat Generation* (Monroe, Maine, 1996) pp. 159–60. *Daru* and *bhang*: G. M. Carstairs, "*Daru* and *Bhang*: Cultural Factors in the Choice of Intoxicant" in *Beliefs, Behaviors and Alcoholic Beverages: A Cross-cultural Survey* (ed. Mac Marshall, Ann Arbor, Michigan, 1979) pp. 297–312. Robert Louis Stevenson: Myron G. Schultz, "The 'Strange Case' of Robert Louis Stevenson," *Journal of the American Medical Association*, Vol. 216 (1971) pp. 90–94.

Alcohol an "addictive drug": Dr. C. Everett Koop, *Koop: The Memoirs of America's Family Doctor* (New York, 1991) pp. 289–99; *The New York Times*, March 26, 1991. Caffeine addictive: Eric C. Strain et al., "Caffeine Dependence Syndrome: Evidence from Case Histories and Experimental Evaluations," *Journal of the American Medical Association*, Vol. 272 (1984) pp. 1043–48. Antidrug campaigners: David Wagner, *The New Temperance: The American Obsession with Sin and Vice* (Boulder, Colorado, 1997) pp. 73–78. Dependency: Herbert Fingarette, *Heavy Drinking: The Myth of Alcoholism as a Disease* (Berkeley, California, 1988) pp. 48–69; Royal College of Psychiatrists, *Alcohol: Our Favourite Drug* (London, 1986) pp. 52–65.

Origins of AA: Barry Leach and John L. Norris, "Factors in the Development of Alcoholics Anonymous" in *Treatment and Rehabilitation of the Chronic Alcoholic* (ed. Benjamin Kissin and Henri Begleiter, New York, 1977, Vol. 5 of *The Biology of Alcoholism*) pp. 441–543; Jack S. Blocker Jr., *American Temperance Movements: Cycles of Reform* (Boston, 1989) pp. 139–44. Nineteenth-century origin of disease theory of alcoholism: Mark Keller, "The Disease Concept of Alcoholism Revisited," *Journal of Studies on Alcohol*, Vol. 37 (1976) pp. 1694–717. Public acceptance of disease theory: Robin Room, "Sociological Aspects of the Disease Concept of Alcoholism" in *Research Advances in Alcohol and Drug Problems*, Vol. 7 (1983) pp. 47–91. Hospitals had not wanted to admit drunkards: Blocker, op. cit., p. 150. Disease theory gets alcoholics into treatment: Fingarette, op. cit., pp. 22–26; George E. Vaillant, *The Natural History of Alcoholism Revisited* (Cambridge, Massachusetts, 1995) p. 22. Attitude of the military: Robert Bray et al., "Progress Toward Eliminating Drug and Alcohol Abuse Among U.S. Military Personnel," *Armed Forces and Society*, June 1, 1992.

AA treatment ineffective: Fingarette, op. cit., pp. 88–90; Morris Chafetz, *The Tyranny of Experts: Blowing the Whistle on the Cult of Expertise* (Lanham, Maryland, 1996) pp. 23–45. AA members transfer their fixation: *The Los Angeles Times*, July 1, 1995; James Milam and Katherine Ketcham, *Under the Influence: A Guide to the Myths and Realities of Alcoholism* (New York, 1983) p. 157. Controlled drinking therapy: Room, loc. cit.; Stanton Peele, "The New Prohibitionists," *The Sciences*, Vol. 24 (1984) pp. 14–19; Alexander W. Logue, *The Psychology of Eating and Drinking* (New York, 1986) pp. 211–13; Fingarette, op. cit., pp. 124–28; Stanton Peele, "Alcoholism, Politics and Bureaucracy: The Consensus Against Controlled-Drinking Therapy in America," *Addictive Behaviours*, Vol. 17 (1992) pp. 49–62; Stanton Peele, "Recovering from an All or Nothing Approach to Alcohol," *Psychology Today*, September/October 1996, pp. 35–43, 68–70. British research showing that disease theory makes it hard for recovering alcoholics to drink moderately: Nick Heather, Maurice Winton, and Stephen Rollnick, "An Empirical Test of 'A Cultural Delusion of Alcoholics,' " *Psychological Reports*, Vol. 50 (1982) pp. 379–82. "Fulfilling our own prophecy": Peele, "The New Prohibitionists." No foundation for disease theory of alcoholism: Enoch Gordis, "Accessible and Affordable Health Care for Alcoholism and Related Problems: Strategy for Cost Containment," *Journal of Studies on Alcohol*, Vol. 48 (1987) pp. 579–85; Stanton Peele, "Ain't Misbehavin': Addiction Has Become an All-Purpose Excuse," *The Sciences*, July/August 1989, pp. 14–21. Alcohol and tuberculosis: Gene Ford, *The Benefits of Moderate Drinking* (San Francisco, 1988) p. 139. Most doctors do not believe that alcoholism is a disease: Ibid. p. 140. Misuse of alcohol no more an illness than misuse of nuclear energy: Thomas Szasz, "Bad Habits Are Not Diseases," *The Lancet*, July 8, 1972, pp. 83–84. Alcoholics still retain control: Fingarette, op. cit., pp. 34–39.

Placebo tests: G. Alan Marlatt and Damaris J. Rohsenow, "The Think-Drink Effect," *Psychology Today*, December 1981, pp. 60–69, 93; Barbara Critchlow, "The Powers of John Barleycorn: Beliefs About the Effects of Alcohol on Social Behavior," *American Psychologist*, Vol. 41 (1986) pp. 751–64. Response to alcohol is a learned reaction: Craig McAndrew and Robert Edgerton, *Drunken Comportment* (Chicago, 1969) pp. 87–88. Indians, alcohol, and violence: Peter C. Mancall, *Deadly Medicine* (Ithaca, New York, 1995) pp. 79–82, 94–96. Brown University study: *USA Today*, April 17, 1995. Spousal abuse: Glenda Kaufman Kantor and Murray A. Straus, "The 'Drunken Bum' Theory of Wife-Beating," *Social Problems*, Vol. 34 (1987) pp. 213–30; Richard Gelles and Murray Straus, *Intimate Violence: The Definitive Study of the Causes and Consequences of Abuse in the American Family* (New York, 1988) pp. 44–46; Stanton Peele, *Diseasing of America* (New York, 1995) pp. 207–10. Denial: Peele, op. cit., pp. 106–11. People forced into treatment: Szasz, loc. cit.; Peele, op. cit., pp. 221–24. "A citizen of a totalitarian regime": Stanton Peele, "AA Abuse," *Reason*, November 1991, pp. 34–39. Jules Masserman: Peele, *Diseasing of America*, p. 117. All kinds of "addictions": Ibid. pp. 26–28, 134–43. Crimes blamed on addiction: Charles J. Sykes, *A Nation of Victims* (New York, 1992) pp. 147–49. "A completely self-gratifying universe": Peele, *Diseasing of America*, pp. 219–21. Salem witch trials: Richard Godbeer, *The Devil's Dominion: Magic and Religion in Early New England* (Cambridge, 1992).

CHAPTER 1

Indian drinks: Arthur Barlowe, "The First Voyage Made to the Coasts of America" in Richard Hakluyt, *The Principal Navigations, Voyages and Discoveries of the English Nation* (Cambridge, 1965) p. 731; Adriaen van Donck, "A Description of the New Netherlands" (tr. Jeremiah Johnson), *Collections of the New York Historical Society*, 2nd Series, Vol. 1 (1841) pp. 192–94; Howard S. Russell, *Indian New England Before "The Mayflower"* (Hanover, New Hampshire, 1980) pp. 85–86. Water unsafe: Andrew Boorde, *A Dietary of Health* (ed. F. J. Furnivall, London, 1870) pp. 252–58. Water unfashionable: Sir John Fortescue, *De Laudibus Legum Angliae* (London, 1737) p. 83 (ch. 36); César de Saussure, *A Foreign View of England in the Reigns of George I and George II* (tr. and ed. Madame van Muyden, London, 1902) pp. 157–65. Suffering of Virginia settlers: Stanley Baron, *Brewed in America*

(Boston, 1962) pp. 4–6; Richard Ffrethorne, "Letter to His Father and Mother" in *The Records of the Virginia Company of London* (ed. Susan H. Kingsbury, Washington, D.C., 1906–35) Vol. 4, pp. 58–60; Karen Ordahl Kupperman, "Fear of Hot Climates in the Anglo-American Colonial Experience," *The William and Mary Quarterly*, 3rd series, Vol. 41 (1984) pp. 213–40. First Virginia beer: Thomas Hariot, "A Brief and True Report" in *The Roanoke Voyages 1584–90* (ed. David B. Quinn, London, 1955) Vol. 1, pp. 337–38. "Mr. Russell's Project Touching Artificial Wine in Virginia" in *Records of the Virginia Company*, Vol. 3, pp. 365–67.

Concerns of Pilgrims: William Bradford, *Of Plymouth Plantation* (Boston, 1898) p. 33 (ch. 4). Settled for lack of beer: *A Relation or Journal of the Beginning and Proceedings of the English Plantation Settled at Plymouth in New England* (New York, 1848) p. 49. Water pleasant: Bradford, op. cit., p. 99 (ch. 10). Water good: William Wood, *New England's Prospect* (Boston, 1865) part 1, p. 16 (ch. 5). Higginson of Salem: John Hull Brown, *Early American Beverages* (New York, 1966) p. 35. Improved health of the Virginia settlers: Carville Earle, "Environment, Disease and Mortality in Early Virginia" in *The Chesapeake in the Seventeenth Century* (ed. Thad W. Tate and David L. Ammerman, Chapel Hill, North Carolina, 1979) pp. 92–125. Roger Clap: *Chronicles of the First Planters of the Colony of Massachusetts Bay* (ed. Alexander Young, Boston, 1846) p. 353. Filippo Mazzei: Charles H. Sherrill, *French Memories of Eighteenth-Century America* (New York, 1915) pp. 78–79.

Rumbullion: Hugh Barty-King and Anton Massel, *Rum Yesterday and Today* (London, 1983) pp. 10–14. Americans adore rum: Edward Ward, "A Trip to New England" (London, 1699) p. 10 in *Five Travel Scripts* (ed. Howard W. Troyer, New York, 1933). "Triangular trade": Gilman M. Ostrander, "The Making of the Triangular Trade Myth," *The William and Mary Quarterly*, 3rd series, Vol. 30 (1973) pp. 635–44. Beer for strength: Benjamin Franklin, *Autobiography* (ed. William N. Otto, Boston, 1928) pp. 55–65. Reason for elbow: Benjamin Franklin, Letter to Abbé Morellet in *Works* (ed. Jared Sparks, London, 1836–40) Vol. 2, pp. 226–27; Claude-Ann Lopez, *Mon Cher Papa: Franklin and the Ladies of Paris* (2nd ed., New Haven, Connecticut, 1990) pp. 290–96.

Spirits for labor: John Melish, *Travels in the USA in the years 1806 and 1807, and 1809, 1810 and 1811* (Philadelphia, 1812) Vol. 2, pp. 51–52; Israel Acrelius, *A History of New Sweden* (tr. and ed. William Reynolds, Philadelphia, 1874) pp. 160–64; Benjamin Rush, *An Inquiry into the Effects of Ardent Spirits* (6th ed., New York, 1811) p. 16. Dangers of drinking cold water:

Moreau de Saint Méry's American Journey (ed. Kenneth and Anna M. Roberts, New York, 1947) p. 323; James Flint, *Letters from America* (Edinburgh, 1822) pp. 8–9; Joseph Pickering, *Emigration or No Emigration* (London, 1830) pp. 22–24; Charles Haswell, *Reminiscences of an Octogenarian of the City of New York, 1816–1860* (New York, 1897) pp. 112–13. Spirits for inner warmth: Richard Ligon, *A True and Exact History of the Island of Barbados* (London, 1673) pp. 27, 93; Johann D. Schoepf, *Travels in the Confederation* (tr. and ed. Alfred J. Morrison, New York, 1968) Vol. 2, pp. 217–20.

Deaths in Georgia from drinking rum: *An Impartial Enquiry into the State and Utility of the Province of Georgia* (London, 1741) p. 9. English weakened by spirits: Dr. Stephen Hales, *A Friendly Admonition to the Drinkers of Brandy and Other Distilled Spirituous Liquors* (2nd ed., London, 1734) p. 9; Henry Fielding, *Enquiry into the Causes of the Late Increase of Robbers* (London, 1751) p. 18; Andrew Barr, *Drink: An Informal Social History* (London, 1995) pp. 9–10, 189–93. Tybee lighthouse: Francis Moore, *A Voyage to Georgia* (London, 1744) pp. 17–18. Sporadic supply of beer: William Stephens, "A Journal of the Proceedings in Georgia" in *The Colonial Records of the State of Georgia* (ed. Allen D. Candler et al., Atlanta, 1904–16) Vol. 4, p. 211. Oglethorpe's vineyard: Hugh Barty King, *A Tradition of English Wine* (Oxford, 1977) pp. 87–93. Vine growing in Georgia: Thomas Pinney, *A History of Wine in America* (Berkeley, California, 1989) pp. 40–54. Savannah wine: *Colonial Records of Georgia*, Vol. 4, p. 653 (September 1, 1740) and Vol. 5, p. 500 (April 22, 1741). Sir John Mordaunt: Henry A. Scomp, *King Alcohol in the Realm of King Cotton* (Chicago, 1888) pp. 59–68; John Perceval, Earl of Egmont, *A Journal of the Transactions of the Trustees* (Wormsloe, 1886) p. 200.

Winds and Madeira: Hugh Johnson, *The Story of Wine* (London, 1989) pp. 245–51. Healthfulness of Madeira: Christopher Jeaffreson, *A Young Squire of the Seventeenth Century* (ed. John C. Jeaffreson, London, 1878) Vol. 1, pp. 189–92; Hugh Jones, *The Present State of Virginia* (New York, 1865) p. 52. Fortification of Madeira: Noël Cossart, *Madeira* (London, 1984) pp. 102–03. Steam engine: Cyrus Redding, *History and Description of Modern Wines* (3rd ed., London, 1860) p. 266. Madeira stored in attics: Jean-Pierre Pury, "Proposals" in *Historical Collections of South Carolina* (ed. B. R. Carroll, New York, 1836) Vol. 2, p. 131. American connoisseurship of Madeira: Captain Thomas Hamilton, *Men and Manners in America* (London, 1833) Vol. 1, pp. 118–21; Margaret Hunter (Mrs. Basil Hall), *The Aristocratic Journey* (ed. Una Pope-Hennessy, New York, 1931) pp. 89–90; Alfred Bunn, *Old England and New England* (London, 1853) Vol. 2, pp. 205–06.

Sangaree: *Journal of a Lady of Quality* (ed. Evangeline W. Andrews, 2nd ed., New Haven, 1934) pp. 78–79; *Gentleman's Magazine*, Vol. 6 (September 1736) pp. 550–51; Gobblieb Mittelberger, *Journey to Pennsylvania* (ed. and tr. Oscar Handlin and John Clive, Cambridge, Massachusetts, 1960) pp. 50–51. Refreshing light punch: Saussure, loc. cit. Flip: Alice Morse Earle, *Stage-Coach and Tavern Days* (New York, 1900) pp. 108–14. Principled bartender: Herbet Asbury, introduction to Jerry Thomas, *How to Mix Drinks* (New York, 1928) p. xlvi.

Mint julep: Frederick Marryat, *A Diary in America, with Remarks on Its Institutions* (New York, 1962) pp. 386–87; William Howard Russell, *My Diary North and South* (ed. Fletcher Pratt, New York, 1954) p. 149 (June 6, 1861); Lyle Saxon, *Old Louisiana* (New York, 1929) p. 119. Bitters: John E. Wright and Doris S. Corbett, *Pioneer Life in Western Pennsylvania* (Pittsburgh, 1940) pp. 60–61; Bell Irvin Wiley, *The Life of Johnny Reb* (Indianapolis, 1943) p. 259. Origin of term "cocktail": William Grimes, *Straight Up or On the Rocks* (New York, 1993) pp. 60–63. *The Balance and Colombian Repository*; ibid. p. 59. Definition of cocktail: James Alexander, *Transatlantic Sketches* (London, 1833) Vol. 2, p. 51; Jerry Thomas, *How to Mix Drinks* (New York, 1862) pp. 49–51; David Embury, *The Fine Art of Mixing Drinks* (London, 1953) pp. 23–28. Cubanola: Johnny Brooks, *My Thirty-five Years Behind Bars* (New York, 1954) in Grimes, op. cit., pp. 102–03. "Short and snappy": Charles Browne, *The Gun Club Drink Book* (New York, 1939) in Grimes, op. cit., p. 107. Patrick Gavin Duffy, *The Official Mixer's Manual* (New York, 1934) pp. xvii–xviii. Franklin D. Roosevelt: Lowell Edmunds, *The Silver Bullet* (Westport, Connecticut, 1981) pp. 31, 43–44 (n. 63). Frederic Henry: Ernest Hemingway, *A Farewell to Arms* (New York, 1969) p. 245 in Edmunds, op cit., p. 7.

Variety of potations and drinking before dinner: Frederick Marryat, *A Diary in America* (London, 1839) Vol. 1, p. 105; Marryat, *A Diary in America, with Remarks on Its Institutions* (New York, 1962) pp. 381, 389. Disapproval of cocktails: Thomas Colley Grattan, *Civilized America* (London, 1859) Vol. 1, p. 62; Henry Porter and George Roberts, *Cups and Their Customs* (2nd ed., London, 1869) p. 35. Cocktails popularized in Britain in 1920s: Robin McDouall, "Convivial in Clubs" in *The Compleat Imbiber* No. 3 (ed. Cyril Ray, London, 1960) pp. 33–34; Kenneth P. Kirkwood, *The Diplomat at Table* (Metuchen, New Jersey, 1974) pp. 251–53; Robert Graves and Alan Hodge, *The Long Weekend* (London, 1940) p. 38.

Sipping through a straw: Charles Francatelli, *The Cook's Guide* (London, 1861) p. 431. King Henry III: Barbara K. Wheaton, *Savoring the Past* (New York, 1983) pp. 52–55. King Charles II: Sylvia P. Beamon and Susan Roaf,

The Ice Houses of Britain (London, 1990) pp. 18–19. Streams diverted: Pehr Kalm, *Travels into North America* (tr. John R. Forster, Warrington, 1770 and London, 1771) Vol. 1, p. 307. Mount Vernon icehouse: George Washington, *Diary* (ed. John C. Fitzpatrick, Boston, 1925) Vol. 2, p. 381; Beamon and Roaf, op. cit., pp. 35–38, 159–61. Ice in farmhouses: Isaac Weld, *Travels through the States of North America* (London, 1799) p. 145. Iceboxes: *The New York Mirror*, Vol. 16 (July 14, 1838) p. 23. Ice democratic: "Ice—How Much of It Is Used and Where It Comes From," *De Bow's Review*, Vol. 19 (1855) pp. 709–12; "Ice and the Ice Trade," *Hunt's Merchants' Magazine and Commercial Review*, Vol. 33 (1855) pp. 169–79. Ubiquity of ice: Thomas L. Nichols, *Forty Years of American Life* (London, 1864) Vol. 1, pp. 16, 247; George M. Towle, *American Society* (London, 1870) Vol. 1, pp. 267–69. Wenham Lake ice: Henry Coleman, *European Life and Manners* (Boston, 1850) Vol. 1, p. 372; "The Ice Trade," *The Leisure Hour*, June 27, 1863, pp. 413–15; Beamon and Roaf, op. cit., pp. 41–46. "Marsupial claret jugs": George Saintsbury, *Notes on a Cellar Book* (London, 1920) pp. 67–68, 75–76.

Origin of iced tea: Marion Harland, *Breakfast, Luncheon and Tea* (New York, 1875) pp. 360–61; Mary Stuart Smith, *Virginia Cookery Book* (New York, 1885) pp. 41–42; Robert Somers, *The Southern States Since the War* (London, 1871) p. 235. Rarity of iced tea in the South: Rupert P. Vance, *Human Geography of the South* (Chapel Hill, North Carolina, 1935) pp. 428–29; contra Joe Gray Taylor, *Eating, Drinking and Visiting in the South* (Baton Rouge, Louisiana, 1982) p. 128. Cost of refrigerators: Siegfried Giedion, *Mechanization Takes Command* (New York, 1948) pp. 596–606. Primitive air-conditioning: Sarah Mytton Maury, *An Englishwoman in America* (London, 1848) pp. 200–01. Belated spread of domestic air-conditioning: Oscar E. Anderson Jr., *Refrigeration in America* (Princeton, New Jersey, 1953) pp. 309–12. American "addiction" to air-conditioning: "On Condis and Coolth," *Energy and Buildings*, Vol. 18 (1992) pp. 251–66. Nikita Khrushchev: Gary and Mardee Regan, *The Book of Bourbon and Other Fine American Whiskeys* (Buffalo, New York, 1995). Cryonics: *The National Review*, September 2, 1996.

"Brown, thick and unpalatable": Acrelius, loc. cit. American brewers backward: Baron, op. cit., pp. 158–61. John Wagner: Ibid., pp. 175–90. Pabst's "Pilsner": Thomas C. Cochran, *The Pabst Brewing Company* (New York, 1948) pp. 114–23. Josef Tolar: Andrew Barr, *Wine Snobbery* (New York, 1992) p. 286. Pabst's manager asks for a different beer: Cochran, loc. cit. Why Americans wanted a lighter beer: Ibid. Chamber of Commerce in Cincinnati: William L. Downard, *The Cincinnati Brewing Industry* (Cincinnati, 1973) pp. 30–31. Importance of artificial refrigeration: Professor J. E. Siebel,

"Refrigeration and the Fermenting (Brewing) Industry of the United States" in *Premier Congrès International du Froid* (Paris, n. d.) Vol. 3, pp. 71–77; John P. Arnold and Frank Penman, *History of the Brewing Industry and Brewing Science in America* (Chicago, 1933) p. 93; H. S. Corran, *A History of Brewing* (Newton Abbot, Devon, 1975) pp. 274–76. Mark Garvey: *The Independent*, August 2, 1995.

Revue Viticole: Leon D. Adams, *The Wines of America* (4th ed., New York, 1990) p. 19. *San Francisco Merchant and Viticulturalist*: James Conway, *Napa: The Story of an American Eden* (Boston, 1990) p. 73. Improper fermentations: George Husmann, *American Grape-Growing and Wine-Making* (4th ed., New York, 1896) p. 236. Cooling recommended: *The University of California/Sotheby Book of California Wine* (ed. David Muscatine, Maynard A. Amerine, and Bob Thompson, Berkeley, California, 1984) pp. 41–42, 181–82. Niebaum: Frona Wait, *Wines and Vines of California* (San Francisco, 1889) pp. 42–43, 112–13; Adams, op. cit., pp. 270–72. John Daniel's problems: Conway, op. cit., pp. 50–51. Fear of taint in Australia: Alexander C. Kelly, *The Vine in Australia* (Melbourne, 1861) pp. 116–20. Tchelistcheff's secrecy: Johnson, op. cit., p. 451; Cheryll Barron, *Dreamers of the Valley of Plenty* (New York, 1995) pp. 80–82. Tchelistcheff appalled by American conditions: Barron, op. cit., pp. 109–10; Dan Berger, "The Wine Doctor," *Los Angeles Times*, October 31, 1991; Conway, op. cit., pp. 103–10.

"Squeaky clean wines": Robert Parker, *The Wine Advocate*, No. 45 (June 1986). Taste for heavy wines: Husmann, op. cit., p. 240. Aversion to claret: Wait, op. cit., p. 26. English working classes take up wine: William Winch Hughes, the founder of Victoria Wine, in *Report of the Select Committee on Wine Duties* (London, 1879) pp. 180–83 (questions 3732–3854). English middle classes turn to claret: Charles Tovey, *Wine and Wine Countries* (2nd ed., London, 1877) p. 87; James L. Denman, *The Vine and its Fruit* (2nd ed., London, 1875) pp. 481–84.

CHAPTER 2

John Adams on the French: *Letters of John Adams, Addressed to His Wife* (ed. Charles Francis Adams, Boston, 1841) p. 51, letter from Passy, February 21, 1779. Elkanah Watson on the French: Elkanah Watson, *Men and Times of the Revolution* (ed. Winslow C. Watson, New York, 1856) pp. 137–38. Frogs in the soup: *Recollections of Samuel Breck* (ed. H. E. Scudder, Philadelphia, 1877) pp. 24–27. Comte de Moustier on America: John Tebbel, *George Washington's America* (New York, 1954) p. 269 n. Talleyrand on America: Giles MacDonogh, *Brillat-Savarin: The Judge and His Stomach*

(London, 1992) pp. 110–29. French chefs in America: Jefferson Williamson, *American Hotel: An Anecdotal History* (New York, 1930) pp. 192–223. New Orleans: *Historical Sketch Book and Guide to New Orleans and Environs* (New York, 1885) pp. 84–91; John Egerton, *Southern Food* (Chapel Hill, North Carolina, 1993) pp. 110–15. Julien's Restorator: Samuel Adams Drake, *Old Boston Taverns* (Boston, 1917) pp. 65–66. Ice cream: Jean-Anthelme Brillat-Savarin, *Physiologie du Goût*, tr. as *The Philosopher in the Kitchen* (tr. Anne Drayton, Harmondsworth, Middlesex, England, 1960) pp. 335–37, "Gastronomical Industry of the Emigrés."

Wine consumption in the eighteenth century: Harold E. Davis, *The Fledgling Province* (Chapel Hill, North Carolina, 1976) pp. 72–73. "Very strong and fiery:" Pehr Kalm, *Travels in North America* (tr. John R. Forster, Warrington, 1770 and London, 1771) Vol. 1, p. 257. John Rutledge: Richard Barry, *Mr. Rutledge of South Carolina* (New York, 1942) pp. 74–75. Exports of French wines to America: Julia P. Mitchell, *St. Jean de Crèvecoeur* (New York, 1916) pp. 211, 233–35; James Swan, *Causes que se sont Opposées aux Progrès du Commerce entre la France et les États-Unis de l'Amérique* (Paris, 1790) pp. 128–30; Brillat-Savarin, op. cit., pp. 305–09, "National Victory"; George G. Raddin, *The New York of Hocquet Caritat and His Associates, 1797–1817* (Dover, New Jersey, 1953); George T. Curtis, *Life of James Buchanan* (New York, 1883) Vol. 1, p. 235n.; Frederick Marryat, *A Diary in America* (London, 1960) p. 76; *The Perfect Gentleman* (New York, 1860) pp. 193–94. Disappearance of Madeira: *The Perfect Gentleman*, p. 196, Noël Cossart, *Madeira: The Island Vineyard* (London, 1984) pp. 85–93. Problems in transporting claret: *Jefferson and Wine* (ed. R. de Treville Lawrence Sr., The Plains, Virginia, 1976) p. 63.

Not dogmatic: Douglas S. Freeman, *George Washington* (London, 1948–57) Vol. 1, p. 107. Madeira in Jamaica: *A Complete System of Geography* (London, 1747) Vol. 2, p. 709. Madeira in India: David Burton, *The Raj at Table* (London, 1993) pp. 207–08. French water their wine: Philip Thicknesse, *Useful Hints to Those Who Make the Tour of France* (London, 1768) p. 191 and *A Year's Journey Through France and Part of Spain* (3rd ed., London, 1789) Vol. 2, pp. 98–100. Adding water to Madeira: Henry Wansey, *An Excursion to the United States of North America in the Summer of 1794* (2nd ed., Salisbury, 1798) pp. 20, 88, 200. Gave Madeira their full attention: Thomas Hamilton, *Men and Manners in America* (London, 1833) Vol. 1, pp. 118–21. Americans follow English tradition: Jacques Pierre Brissot de Warville, *New Travels in the United States of America, 1788* (tr. Mara S. Vamos and Durand Echeverria, Cambridge, Massachusetts, 1964) p. 91; Marquis de Chastellux, *Travels in North America* (tr. and ed. Howard C. Rice Jr., Chapel Hill, North

Carolina, 1963) pp. 109–10. Louisiana: Frederick Law Olmstead, *A Journey in the Seaboard Slave States* (New York, 1856) pp. 624–25.

Jefferson and wine: "Jefferson and Wine," *The Wine Spectator*, March 15, 1991 pp. 24–33; James M. Gabler, *Passions: The Wines and Travels of Thomas Jefferson* (Baltimore, 1995). "Jefferson wines": Andrew Barr, *Wine Snobbery* (New York, 1992) pp. 205–06. Entertaining in White House: Jack McLoughlin, *Jefferson and Monticello* (New York, 1988) pp. 220–34. "Delicacy and innocence": *Wine Spectator*, loc. cit.

Patrick Henry: James Schouler, *Americans of 1776* (New York, 1906) p. 100. Prejudice against French cooking: Thurlow Weed, *Autobiography* (ed. Harriet A. Weed, Boston, 1883) Vol. 1, pp. 52–55. Comte de Moustier: Michael and Ariane Batterberry, *On the Town in New York* (New York, 1973) p. 24. Marie Antoinette: Gabler, op. cit., p. 199. Delmonico's: Robert Shaplen, "That Was New York," *The New Yorker*, November 10, 1956, pp. 172–95 and November 17, 1956, pp. 99–131; Lately Thomas, *Delmonico's: A Century of Splendor* (Boston, 1967). "Rich new gravy faith": Abram C. Dayton, *Last Days of Knickerbocker Life in New York* (New York, 1882) pp. 96–97, 109–18. French chefs: Williamson, loc. cit. Garlic and offal: Richard J. Hooker, *A History of Food and Drink in America* (Indianapolis, 1981) pp. 104–05. "Every broken-down barber": Thomas Colley Grattan, *Civilized America* (London, 1859) Vol. 1, pp. 106–08. "*Vol-au-vent*." Owen Wister, *The Virginian* (New York, 1902) in Williamson, loc. cit.

Log-cabin-and-hard-cider campaign: Robert G. Gunderson, *The Log-Cabin Campaign* (Westport, Connecticut, 1977). Sneering article: *The Baltimore Republican*, in Dorothy Goebel, *William Henry Harrison* (Indianapolis, 1926) p. 347. Ridiculing of Van Buren: Charles Ogle, *Speech of Mr. Charles Ogle of Pennsylvania on the Regal Splendors of the President's Palace. Delivered in the House of Representatives, April 14, 1840* (Washington, 1840). Opposite of the truth: John Niven, *Martin Van Buren* (New York, 1983) pp. 461–62. "Gastronomic know-nothingism": Waverley Root and Richard de Rochemont, *Eating in America: A History* (New York, 1981) pp. 112–14.

Samuel Ward: *Evening Post*, May 14, 1869, in Shaplen. loc. cit. Delmonico's black list: Williamson, loc. cit. Nat P. Willis, *New York Weekly Mirror*, Vol. 1 (1844–45) p. 131. American plan: Williamson, loc. cit.; James Fullarton Muirhead, *The Land of Contrasts* (Boston, 1898) pp. 251–52. Food wasted: Léon Paul Blouet (writing as "Max O'Rell"), "Reminiscences of American Hotels," *North American Review*, Vol. 15 (1891) pp. 85–90. Quantity rather than quality: Emily Faithfull, *Three Visits to America* (Edinburgh, 1884) p. 49. Food all brought at once: Jacques Offenbach, *Offenbach en Amérique*

(Paris, 1877) p. 28; Paul de Rousiers, *American Life* (tr. A. J. Herbertson, Paris, 1892) pp. 313–18.

Poor, monotonous diet: William J. Rorabaugh, *The Alcoholic Republic* (New York, 1979) pp. 113–18. Jefferson City: Prince Maximilian of Wied, *Travels in the Interior of North America* (ed. R. G. Thwaites, Cleveland, 1906) Vol. 24, p. 123. Food swimming in grease: Constantin François de Chasseboeuf, Comte de Volney, *A View of the Soil and Climate of the United States of America* (tr. C. B. Brown, Philadelphia, 1804) pp. 257–59; Hamilton, op. cit., Vol. 1, pp. 41–45; Anthony Trollope, *North America* (London, 1862) pp. 405–07; Thomas L. Nichols, *Forty Years of American Life* (London, 1864) p. 369. Good things wasted: James Fenimore Cooper, *The American Democrat* (Harmondsworth, Middlesex, England, 1969) p. 213 ("On Civilization"). Speed of eating: James Boardman, *America and the Americans* (London, 1833) pp. 24–26; Washington *National Intelligencer*, November 20, 1836, in Charles Augustus Murray, *Travels in North America* (3rd ed., London, 1854) Vol. 1, pp. 55–56; Basil Hall, *Travels in North America* (Philadelphia, 1829) Vol. 1, pp. 9–10; Colonel Archibald Maxwell, *A Run Through the United States During the Autumn of 1840* (London, 1841) Vol. 1, pp. 67–70; William Baxter, *America and the Americans* (London, 1855) pp. 92–93; "Concerning Restaurants," *Harper's New Monthly Magazine*, Vol. 32 (1865–66) pp. 591–93. Requirements of business: Michel Chevalier, *Society, Manners and Politics in the United States* (Boston, 1839) pp. 283–84; Grattan, op. cit., Vol. 1, p. 43; Henry Sienkiewicz, *Portrait of America* (tr. and ed. Charles Morley, New York, 1959) p. 4. Saratoga Springs: James Silk Buckingham, *America, Historical, Statistic and Descriptive* (London, 1841) Vol. 2, pp. 441–44. "Not at all fastidiou": Ibid., Vol. 1, pp. 348–50. Accelerated pace of life: David Macrae, *The Americans at Home* (Edinburgh, 1870) Vol. 1, pp. 15–19.

Food favored whiskey: Rorabaugh, loc. cit.; Arthur M. Schlesinger Sr., "A Dietary Interpretation of American History," *Proceedings of the Massachusetts Historical Society*, Vol. 68 (1944–47) p. 210. Drinking in the bar after dinner: Henry Bradshaw Fearon, *Sketches of America* (3rd ed., London, 1819) p. 249; Hamilton, op. cit., Vol. 1, pp. 41–45; Anthony Trollope, op. cit., Vol. 1, pp. 60–61; Macrae, op. cit., Vol. 2, pp. 304–11; Muirhead, op. cit., pp. 268–72. Spirits served for free: John Lambert, *Travels Through Lower Canada and the United States of North America in the Years 1806, 1807 and 1808* (London, 1810) Vol. 2, pp. 132–33; James Stuart, *Three Years in North America* (London, 1833) Vol. 1, pp. 42, 67–68, 118, 401–03.

Cheapness of American plan: Williamson, loc. cit. Water not wine: William Chambers, *Things as They Are in America* (London, 1854) p. 184; Isabella

Bird, *The Englishwoman in America* (London, 1856) p. 152; George Augustus Sala, *America Revisited* (London, 1882) Vol. 1, pp. 277–78. Drinking regarded as sinful: Evelyn Leighton Fanshawe, *Liquor Legislation in the United States and Canada* (London, 1893) pp. 5–11. Expense of wine in hotels: Adlard Welby, *A Visit to North America* (London, 1821) pp. 26, 34; Stuart, op. cit., Vol. 2, p. 491; James Boardman, op. cit., p. 156; J. W. Hengiston, "New York—Its Hotels, Waterworks and Things in General," *New Monthly Magazine* (ed. William Harrison Ainsworth, London, 1853) pp. 80–94; Anthony Trollope, op. cit., Vol. 2, pp. 390–409. High markup: Alfred Bunn, *Old England and New England* (London, 1853) Vol. 2, pp. 251–55.

Wine rare in private houses: George M. Towle, *American Society* (London, 1870) Vol. 1, pp. 327–82; *Reminiscences of America in 1869* by Two Englishmen (London, 1870) pp. 55, 67–68; contra Sala, loc. cit. Profusion of wine at dinner parties: Grattan, op. cit., Vol. 1, pp. 106–08; Maxwell, op. cit., Vol. 2, pp. 231–32; *The Perfect Gentleman*, pp. 198–99; Russell Lynes, *The Domesticated Americans* (New York, 1963) pp. 197–99. Cultural differences: Stuart, op. cit., Vol. 1, pp. 401–03. Changes in English taste: Andrew Barr, *Drink: An Informal Social History* (London, 1995) pp. 34–35, 45–46. Americans not drinking light wines: Faithfull, op. cit., pp. 92, 354; Frona Eustace Wait, *Wines and Vines of California* (San Francisco, 1889) pp. 24, 26.

Taste for champagne: Nichols, op. cit., pp. 400–01; *The Perfect Gentleman*, pp. 190–93; Anthony Trollope, loc. cit.; De Rousiers, loc. cit.; A. Maurice Low, *America at Home* (London, 1908) pp. 135–36. Banquet for General Grant: John Egerton, *Southern Food* (Chapel Hill, North Carolina, 1993) p. 81. Champagne with the roast: *The Perfect Gentleman*, pp. 198–99. Corruption of fine dining: Shaplen, loc. cit. Artificial champagne: Marryat, op. cit. pp. 381–82; Asa Greene, *A Glance at New York* (1837) in *A Mirror for Americans* (ed. Warren S. Tryon, Chicago, 1952) p. 179; *The Perfect Gentleman*, pp. 190–93; Cad McBallastir, *Society as I Have Foundered It* (Mobile, Alabama, 1890) pp. 54–8.

Conspicuous consumption: John Mariani, *America Eats Out* (New York, 1991) pp. 49–57. Lillian Russell: Harvey Levenstein, *Revolution at the Table* (New York, 1988) pp. 12–13. French cuisine: Ibid., pp. 14–15. Praise of Delmonico's: Walter Gore Marshall, *Through America* (London, 1881) pp. 35–36; Faithfull, op. cit., pp. 49–51; G. Sauvin, *Autour de Chicago* (Paris, 1893) pp. 16–17; contra Muirhead, op. cit., pp. 268–72. Extravagances: De Rousiers, loc. cit.; Félix Urbain Dubois, *Cuisine Artistique* (Paris, 1978) p. vi. Lavish dinner parties: Williamson, loc. cit. *Service à la russe*: Louise C. Belden, *The Festive Tradition* (New York, 1983) pp. 33–37; Levenstein, op. cit., pp. 16–17; John F. Kasson, *Rudeness and Civility* (New York, 1990) pp. 205–

07. Middle-class efforts: Levenstein, op. cit., pp. 18–21, 60–64; Harvey Levenstein, "Two Hundred Years of French Food in America," *Journal of Gastronomy*, Vol. 5 (1989) pp. 72–73.

Prohibition destroys fine dining: Collinson Owen, *The American Illusion* (London, 1929) pp. 151–54; Julian Street, "What's the Matter with Food?" *Saturday Evening Post*, March 21, 1931, in Levenstein, *Revolution at the Table*, pp. 183–85. Good food in speakeasies: John Chapman Hilder, "New York Speakeasy: A Study of a Social Institution," *Harper's Monthly Magazine*, April 1932, p. 598; Mary Agnes Hamilton, *In America Today* (London, 1932) pp. 135–37. Drinking permitted in the home: Henry Johnston, *What Rights Are Left?* (New York, 1930) pp. 44–48. Prohibition saves dinner parties: Owen, op. cit., pp. 251–54. Hurried drinking of cocktails: Sir Charles Igglesden, *A Mere Englishman in America* (Ashford, Kent, 1929) pp. 153–60; C.R.V. Thompson, *I Lost My English Accent* (London, 1939) pp. 31–32. John Bland: Upton Sinclair, *The Cup of Fury* (Great Neck, New York, 1956) pp. 93–94. "The line of least resistance": Alice-Leone Moats, *No Nice Girl Swears* (London, 1933) pp. 171–76. Cocktail parties in the Depression: Kenneth P. Kirkwood, *The Diplomat at Table* (Metuchen, New Jersey, 1974) p. 251. Cocktail parties afterward: Stephen Birmingham, *The Right People: A Portrait of the American Social Establishment* (Boston, 1958) p. 243.

Sources of immigration: Maldwyn Allen Jones, *American Immigration* (2nd ed., Chicago, 1992) pp. 152 ff. Immigration Restriction League: Ibid, p. 222. Not drinking with meals: Low, loc. cit. Ella Boole: *The Union Signal*, December 15, 1928, p. 12, in Joseph R. Gusfield, *Symbolic Crusade* (Urbana, Illinois, 1963) pp. 123–24. Attitude of immigrants: Constantine Panunzio, "The Foreign-Born and Prohibition," *Annals of the American Academy of Political and Social Science*, Vol. 163 (1932), pp. 147–54. Bootlegger writes to parents: Angelo M. Pellegrini, *Americans by Choice* (New York, 1956) pp. 104–05. Reports from social workers: Martha Bruère, *Does Prohibition Work?* (New York, 1927) pp. 169–71, 186, 257. "Paroxysms of fury": Andrew Sinclair, *Prohibition* (London, 1962) pp. 228, 460 (n. 99).

Alicante bouschet: Ruth Teiser and Catherine Harroun, "The Volstead Act, Rebirth and Boom" in *The University of California/Sotheby Book of California Wine* (ed. Doris Muscatine, Maynard A. Amerine, and Bob Thompson, Berkeley, California, 1984) pp. 50–81. No well-aged wine: Frank Schoonmaker and Tom Marvel, *American Wines* (New York, 1941) pp. 50–55, 79–80. Ignorance of New Yorkers: Thompson, op. cit., pp. 97–102. More sweet than dry wine: Teiser and Harroun, loc. cit. Le Pavillon: Joseph Wechsberg, *Dining at the Pavillon* (London, 1963) pp. 56–58; Mariani, op. cit., pp. 145–53. Market research survey: Jay Stuller and Glen Martin, *Through the Grape-*

vine (New York, 1989) p. 68. Wine boom: Barr, *Wine Snobbery*, pp. 17–18. *Wine Spectator survey: The Wine Spectator*, February 28, 1991, pp. 23–28. Extent of vine growing in America: Leon D. Adams, *The Wines of America* (4th ed., New York, 1990).

Immigrant dishes "unhealthy": Levenstein, *Revolution at the Table*, pp. 103–04. Italian American food: Harvey Levenstein, "The American Response to Italian Food, 1880–1939," *Food and Foodways*, Vol. 1 (1985), pp. 1–24; Harvey Levenstein, *Paradox of Plenty* (New York, 1993) pp. 28–30, 51; Luis Buñuel, *My Last Breath* (tr. Abigail Israel, London, 1984) p. 135. Second World War: Levenstein, *Paradox of Plenty*, pp. 90–92. Pizza: Ibid., p. 230. "Center of an empire:" Ibid., p. 217. Eos: *Decanter* Guide to California (7th ed., 1996) pp. 54–61. Beverly Prescott Hotel: *The Los Angeles Times*, May 19, 1996. Tradition of mixing: Frances Trollope, *Domestic Manners of the Americans* (London, 1832) pp. 238–39; Grattan, loc. cit. John Sedlar: *The Wine Spectator*, December 15, 1993, p. 27.

Popularity of chardonnay and cabernet sauvignon: *Wine & Spirits* magazine annual surveys. Kendall-Jackson Vintner's Reserve Chardonnay: Barr, *Wine Snobbery*, pp. 30–31, 66–67; *Wine & Spirits*, March 1989, p. 39; *The Wine Spectator*, July 31, 1997, p. 75; *Decanter*, January 1998 p. 22. "Trade secret": *The Wine Spectator*, August 31, 1992. Joshua Greene: *USA Today*, March 15, 1996. Frank Prial: *The New York Times*, August 22 and 29, 1984. Nelson Durante: *The Wine Spectator*, May 15, 1990, p. 38. Returning corked wines: Barr, *Wine Snobbery*, pp. 43–45. Survey of wine service in restaurants: *The Wine Spectator*, September 30, 1991, pp. 29–37. America not a wine-drinking nation: *The New York Times*, March 6, 1985. Merlot: *The Wine Spectator*, August 31, 1998, pp. 5, 45–53; *Decanter*, August 1998, pp. 28–31. Ed Moose: Barnaby Conrad III, *The Martini* (San Francisco, 1995) pp. 90–91. Warren Belasco: *The Wine Spectator*, August 31, 1996, p. 29. Mona Doyle: *The Independent*, December 7, 1989. People rarely socialize at meals: *The New York Times*, December 6, 1989; Grattan, loc. cit. "Refueling:" *The Independent*, December 7, 1989.

CHAPTER 3

"Wonderful courtesy": George A. Sala, *America Revisited* (London, 1882) Vol. 1, pp. 277–78. Sorosis Club: Ishbel Ross, *Crusades and Crinolines: The Life and Times of Ellen Curtis and William Jennings Demorest* (New York, 1963) pp. 37–38, 94–100. Ritz and Escoffier: Marie-Louise Ritz, *César Ritz* (London, 1938) pp. 100–01. "The exhibiting of magnificent dresses": Auguste Escoffier, *A Guide to Modern Cookery* (London, 1907) pp. v–vi.

"Fast, if not disreputable": Clement Scott, *How They Dined Us in 1860 and How They Dine Us Now* (London, n.d.) pp. 8–9. "Puritan custom": Jefferson Williamson, *The American Hotel: An Anecdotal History* (New York, 1930) pp. 192–223. Separation of sexes in Puritan New England: Lyle Koehler, *A Search for Power: The "Weaker Sex" in Seventeenth-Century New England* (Urbana, Illinois, 1980) p. 41; Alice Morse Earle, *The Sabbath in Puritan New England* (London, 1892) p. 47. Recreation in Puritan New England: Bruce C. Daniels, *Puritans at Play: Leisure and Recreation in Colonial New England* (London, 1995) pp. 107–59. Only men at dinner parties: William N. Blane, *An Excursion Through the United States and Canada During the Years 1822–1823* (London, 1824) pp. 30–31. Not conducive to refinement: Frances Trollope, *Domestic Manners of the Americans* (London, 1832) p. 270. Different in France: Elkanah Watson, *Men and Times of the Revolution* (ed. Winslow C. Watson, New York, 1856) pp. 87–88, 146–47. Men drinking after dinner: *The American Chesterfield*, by a Member of the Philadelphia Bar (Philadelphia, 1828) p. 245; *Our Revolutionary Forefathers: The Letters of François, Marquis de Barbé-Marbois* (tr. and ed. Eugene Parker Chase, New York, 1929) pp. 66–68; "The Journal of Josiah Quincy, Jr.," *Proceedings of the Massachusetts Historical Society*, Vol. 49 (1915–16), p. 443; Gaillard Hunt, *Life in America One Hundred Years Ago* (New York, 1914) pp. 222–24.

Tea a woman's drink: Mary Caroline Crawford, *Social Life in Old New England* (New York, 1914) pp. 251–52; Pehr Kalm, *Travels into North America* (tr. John R. Forster, Warrington, 1770 and London, 1771) Vol. 1, pp. 360–63. Tea ceremony: Woodruff D. Smith, "From Coffeehouse to Parlour: The Consumption of Coffee, Tea and Sugar in North-western Europe in the Seventeenth and Eighteenth Centuries" in *Consuming Habits: Drugs in History and Anthropology* (ed. Jordan Goodman et al., London, 1995) pp. 148–61. Male ignorance of tea: Esther Singleton, *Social New York Under the Georges* (New York, 1902) pp. 380–81. Extravagant expenditure on tea drinking: Ibid., p. 375. Tea not coffee after dinner: Count of Volney, *A View of the Soil and Climate of the United States of America* (Philadelphia, 1804) pp. 257–59; Asa Greene, *A Glance at New York* (1837) in *A Mirror for Americans* (ed. Warren S. Tryon, Chicago, 1952) p. 179; *The Perfect Gentleman*, by a Gentleman (New York, 1860) p. 177. Exclusion of women regarded as a provincial practice: Russell Lynes, *The Domesticated Americans* (New York, 1963) p. 190. Coffee after Madeira "injurious": Thomas McMullen, *Handbook of Wines* (New York, 1852) p. 227. *Illustrated Manners Book*: Lynes, op. cit., p. 196. Ladies served by the gentleman next to them: *The American Chesterfield*, pp. 242, 245; *The Perfect Gentleman*, pp. 182–87. "Delicate" wines: George A. Gaskell, *Compendium of Forms* (1881) in Lynes, op. cit., p. 197.

Men flock to the bar: James Fullarton Muirhead, *The Land of Contrasts* (Boston, 1898) pp. 268–72. "Lemonade Lucy": Emily A. Geer, *First Lady: The Life of Lucy Webb Hayes* (Kent, Ohio, 1984). Dinner without wine acceptable: "The Wine Question," *The Christian Herald*, 1895, in Lynes, op. cit., p. 199.

Women avoid spirits: Peter Neilson, *Recollections of a Six Years' Residence in the United States of America* (Glasgow, 1830) pp. 66–70; contra *Pennsylvania Gazette*, March 15, 1733, in Carl Bridenbaugh, *Cities in the Wilderness: The First Century of Urban Life in America, 1625–1742* (2nd ed., London, 1971) p. 388. Women drink cordials: George Combe, *Notes on the United States of America* (Philadelphia, 1841) Vol. 2, p. 138. Patent medicines: E. Bok, "The 'Patent Medicine' Curse" and "A Few Words to the WCTU," *Ladies' Home Journal*, May and September 1904, in Andrew Sinclair, *Prohibition* (London, 1962) pp. 426–27. Popular remedies of the period: Martha M. Allen, *Alcohol: A Dangerous and Unnecessary Medicine* (Norwich, Connecticut, 1900) pp. 312–13. Lydia Pinkham: Robert C. Washburn, *The Life and Times of Lydia Pinkham* (New York, 1931) pp. 135, 214–15. Coca-Cola: Mark Pendergrast, *For God, Country and Coca-Cola* (London, 1993) pp. 9, 23–25, 89–91. Cologne drunkards: Cheryl K. Walsh, " 'O Lord, Pour a Cordial into Her Wounded Heart': The Drinking Woman in Victorian and Edwardian Canada" in *Drink in Canada: Historical Essays* (ed. Cheryl K. Walsh, Montreal, 1993) pp. 70–91.

Drug taking by women: Hector St. John de Crèvecoeur, *Letters from an American Farmer* (London, 1962) Letter No. 8, pp. 149–50. Women prefer opiates to alcohol: H.P.C. Wilson, "The Indiscriminate Use of Opiates in the Pelvic Diseases of Women," *North American Practitioner*, January 1891, pp. 9–13, in H. Wayne Morgan, *Drugs in America: A Social History 1800–1980* (Syracuse, New York, 1981) p. 40. Fashionable vice: *Rocky Mountain News*, March 30, 1880, in Thomas J. Noel, *The City and the Saloon: Denver 1858–1916* (Lincoln, Nebraska, 1982) pp. 88–89. Hypodermic medication: *Chicago Medical Journal and Examiner*, 1882, pp. 668–69, in Morgan, op. cit., p. 27.

Drinking by Irish women: Roy Rosenzweig, *Eight Hours for What We Will: Workers and Leisure in an Industrial City, 1870–1920* (Cambridge, 1983) pp. 41–45, 63; Hasia R. Diner, *Erin's Daughters in America: Irish Immigrant Women in the Nineteenth Century* (Baltimore, 1983) pp. 112–14. Mothers "who won't vote for prohibition": Mary Murphy, "Bootlegging Mothers and Drinking Daughters: Gender and Prohibition in Butte, Montana," *American Quarterly*, Vol. 46 (1994), pp. 174–94. Growlers and can rackets: Madelon Powers, "Women and Public Drinking, 1890–1920," *History Today*, February 1995, pp. 48–50. The saloon a male refuge: Leslie Fielder, *Love and Death in the American Novel* (New York, 1969) p. 259. Bouguereau: William H. Gerdts, *The Great American Nude: A History in Art* (New York, 1974) pp. 103–04.

Prostitution in saloons: Vice Commission of Chicago, *The Social Evil in Chicago* (Chicago, 1911) pp. 109–10, 127. Laundry workers: Dorothy Richardson, "The Long Day: The Story of a New York Working Girl" in *Women at Work* (ed. William L. O'Neill, Chicago, 1972) pp. 257–59. Emmons rule: Perry R. Duis, *The Saloon: Public Drinking in Chicago and Boston 1880–1920* (Urbana, Illinois, 1983) pp. 252–53. Taunting of women in Denver: Robert L. Brown, "Saloons of the American West," *Denver Westerners Roundup*, No. 29 (March/April 1973), pp. 3–19, in Noel, op. cit., p. 112. Barmaids rarely seen: Evelyn Leighton Fanshawe, *Liquor Legislation in the United States and Canada* (London, 1893) pp. 6–7. Attractiveness of waitresses: Dr. Alexander Hamilton, *Gentleman's Progress: The Itinerarium of Dr. Alexander Hamilton, 1744* (ed. Carl Bridenbaugh, Chapel Hill, North Carolina, 1948) pp. 90–91, 153. "An objectionable occupation for women:" Emily Faithfull, *Three Visits to America* (Edinburgh, 1884) p. 304. Barmaids beneficial in England: George E. Caitlin, *Liquor Control* (London, 1931) p. 209.

Puritans not puritanical about sex: Edmund Morgan, "The Puritans and Sex," *New England Quarterly*, Vol. 15 (1942), pp. 591–607; David Fischer, *Albion's Seed: Four British Folkways in America* (New York, 1989) pp. 87–93, 162–63. Respectable women not interested in sex: William Acton, *The Functions and Disorders of the Reproductive Organs* (4th ed., London, 1865) pp. 112–13; William W. Sanger, *The History of Prostitution* (New York, 1859) p. 489. New ideal of female "passionlessness": Nancy F. Cott, "Passionlessness: An Interpretation of Victorian Sexual Ideology, 1790–1850," *Signs*, Vol. 4 (1978), pp. 219–36; Carl N. Degler, *At Odds: Women and the Family in America from the Revolution to the Present* (New York, 1980) p. 258. Sex only for procreation: Walter Lippmann, *A Preface to Morals* (New York, 1929) p. 286. Professor Meigs: *Godey's Lady's Book*, March 1852, in Ruth E. Finley, *The Lady of Godey's: Sarah Josepha Hale* (Philadelphia, 1931) pp. 102–03.

Women in colonial taverns: Sarah Knight, *The Private Journal of a Journey from Boston to New York in the Year 1704* (Albany, New York, 1865); Daniels, op. cit., pp. 153–54. "Animal gratification": Cornelia Holroyd Richards, *At Home and Abroad, or How to Behave* (New York, 1853) p. 26, in John F. Kasson, "Rituals of Dining: Table Manners in Victorian America" in *Dining in America 1850–1900* (ed. Kathryn Grover, Amhurst, Massachusetts, 1987) pp. 125–26. "These food talkers": Timothy Edward Howard, *Excelsior, or Essays on Politeness, Education and the Means of Attaining Success in Life* (New York, 1890) pp. 97, 99. Not filling her plate too full: *The American Chesterfield*, p. 243. Purity of breath: Hilary and Mary Evans, *The Party that Lasted 100 Days. The Late Victorian Season: A Social Study* (London, 1976) p. 75. Gloves: Lynes, op. cit., p. 183. Dining *à la russe*: Kasson, op. cit., p. 135. Not eating in public: Louise Fiske Bryson, *Every-Day Etiquette: A Manual of Good Manners* (New York, 1890) p. 97.

Margaret Davis and sex strike: Ian R. Tyrrell, "Women and Temperance in Antebellum America," *Civil War History*, Vol. 28 (1982), pp. 128–52. Causes of German immigration: Maldwyn Allen Jones, *American Immigration* (2nd ed., Chicago, 1992), pp. 93–94. War of women against whiskey: *Woman's Advocate*, March 1869, p. 167, in Mary Earhart, *Frances Willard: From Prayers to Politics* (Chicago, 1944) p. 140. Hatchetation: Jed Dannenbaum, "The Origins of Temperance Activism and Militancy among American Women," *Journal of Social History*, Vol. 15 (1981–82), pp. 235–52; Richard Hamm, "American Prohibitionists and Violence, 1865–1920," http://www.cohums.ohio-state.edu/history/athgroup. Moral suasion "worse than useless": *Kansas City Star*, January 30, 1901, in Robert Bader, *Prohibition in Kansas* (Lawrence, Kansas, 1986) p. 140. "Home is where the heart is": Carry Nation, *The Use and Need of the Life of Carry A. Nation* (rev. ed., Topeka, Kansas, 1908) p. 188. *Scribner's* magazine: Mrs. F. F. Victor, *The Women's War with Whiskey* (Portland, Oregon, 1874) p. 5, in Harry Gene Levine, "Temperance and Women in Nineteenth-Century United States" in *Research Advances in Alcohol and Drug Problems*, Vol. 5 (1980) pp. 25–67.

Temperance and feminism: Andrew Sinclair, *The Better Half* (London, 1966) pp. 220–29; Eleanor Flexner, *Century of Struggle* (2nd ed., Cambridge, Massachusetts, 1975) pp. 185–89; Barbara L. Epstein, *The Politics of Domesticity* (Middletown, Connecticut, 1981) pp. 115–46. Jack London votes for female suffrage: Jack London, *John Barleycorn* (London, 1913) pp. 298–99 (ch. 38). Women "show that they are as good as men": Correa Moylan Walsh, *Feminism* (New York, 1917) pp. 139–40. New freedoms in the 1920s: Frederick Lewis Allen, *Only Yesterday: An Informal History of the 1920s* (New York, 1931) pp. 88–122. Life "one cocktail party after another": *The Times* (London) June 20, 1923. Women in speakeasies: John Chapman Hilder, "New York Speakeasy: A Study of a Social Institution," *Harper's Monthly Magazine*, April 1932, pp. 591–601; Alice-Leone Moats, *No Nice Girl Swears* (London, 1933) pp. 171–76. Heywood Broun: Sinclair, *Prohibition* p. 252. Women's Organization for National Prohibition Reform: David Kyvig, "Women Against Prohibition," *American Quarterly*, Vol. 28 (1976), pp. 465–82. Women drink less during the Depression: Marian Sandmaier, *The Invisible Alcoholics: Women and Alcohol Abuse in America* (New York, 1980) pp. 55–56.

Raspberry daiquiri: *New York Times*, March 30, 1991. Alcohol and women in Biblical times: Ernest L. Abel, "Was the Fetal Alcohol Syndrome Recognized in the Ancient Near East?" *Alcohol and Alcoholism*, Vol. 32 (1997), pp. 3–7. London magistrates: Thomas Wilson, *Distilled Spirituous Liquors the Bane of the Nation* (2nd ed., London, 1736) Appendix pp. xi–xii. History of attitudes to maternal drinking: Rebecca H. Warner and Henry L. Rosett, "The Effects of Drinking on Offspring: An Historical Survey of the American and British Literature," *Journal of Studies on Alcohol*, Vol. 36 (1975), pp. 1395–1420. Children of mothers who drank were less healthy: Justin Edwards, *The Temperance Manual* (London, n.d.) pp. 40–44. "No evidence" of dangers of maternal drinking: H. W. Haggard and E. M Jellinek, *Alcohol Explored* (Garden City, 1942) in Warner and Rosett, loc. cit. Rediscovery of fetal alcohol syndrome: Kenneth L. Jones and David W. Smith, "Recognition of the Foetal Alcohol Syndrome in Early Infancy," *The Lancet*, 1973, Vol. 2, pp. 999–1001. Erroneous advice that moderate drinking is dangerous: Genevieve Knupfer, "Abstaining for Fetal Health: The Fiction That Even Light Drinking Is Dangerous," *British Journal of Addiction*, Vol. 86 (1991), pp. 1063–73; Lee Ann Kaskutas, "Interpretations of Risk: The Use of Scientific Information in the Development of the Alcohol Warning Label Policy," *The International Journal of the Addictions*, Vol. 30 (1995), pp. 1519–48. Report relied upon by the surgeon general: Ruth E. Little, "Moderate Alcohol Use During Pregnancy and Decreased Infant Birth Weight," *American Journal of Public Health*, Vol. 67 (1977), pp. 1154–56. Kenneth Jones and Al Gore: U.S. Congress Senate Committee on Commerce, Science and Transportation, *Alcohol Warning Labels Hearing* (Washington, D.C., 1988) pp. 56–57, in Kaskutas, loc. cit. Eleven percent figure: James W. Hanson et al., "The Effects of Moderate Alcohol Consumption During Pregnancy on Fetal Growth and Morphogenesis," *The Journal of Pediatrics*, Vol. 92 (1978), pp. 457–60. Dundee University study: F. Forrest et al., "Reported Social Alcohol Consumption During Pregnancy and Infants' Development at Eighteen Months," *The British Medical Journal*, Vol. 303 (1991), pp. 22–26. Jancis Robinson: *The Wine Spectator*, September 15, 1991. Breathing city air: Henry L. Rosett and Lyn Weiner, *Alcohol and the Fetus: A Clinical Perspective* (New York, 1984) p. 174. Wine-vinegar dressing: Stanton Peele, *Diseasing of America* (New York, 1995) p. 241.

Pregnancy police: Katha Pollitt, "Foetal Rights, Women's Wrongs" in *Reasonable Creatures: Essays on Women and Feminism* (London, 1995); Morris E. Chafetz, *The Tyranny of Experts: Blowing the Whistle on the Cult of Expertise* (Lanham, Maryland, 1996) pp. 63–79. Diane Pfannensteil: *New York Times*, January 22, February 3 and 5, and June 4, 1990. Deborah Zimmerman: *People*, September 9, 1996; *The Independent*, September 20, 1996. Barb Everist: *The Columbian*, May 24, 1998. Alcohol not the root cause of fetal alcohol syndrome: R. Hingson et al., "Effects of Maternal Drinking and Marijuana Use on Fetal Growth and Development," *Pediatrics*, Vol. 70 (1982), pp. 539–46. Elevating the rights of the fetus: George J. Annas, "Fetal Neglect: Pregnant Women as Ambulatory Chalices" in *Judging Medicine* (Clifton, New Jersey, 1988) pp. 91–96.

Need for children in eighteenth-century Britain: "The Trial of the Spirits" in *A Collection of All the Pamphlets that Were Written Pro and Con on the British Distillery* (2nd ed., London, 1736); Henry Fielding, *An Enquiry into the Causes of the Late Increase of Robbers* (London, 1751). Alcohol a "race poison": Lyman Beecher, *Six Sermons on the Nature, Occasions, Signs, Evils and Remedy of Intemperance* (10th ed., Boston, 1829) p. 49; Caleb W. Saleeby, "Alcoholism and Eugenics," *British Journal of Inebriety*, Vol. 7 (1909), pp. 7–20, in Warner and Rosett, loc. cit. Sterilization: Donald Pickens, *Eugenics and the Progressives* (Nashville, 1968) pp. 86–101. Emma Transeau: *Scientific Temperance Journal*, December 1913, in Sinclair, *Prohibition*, pp. 69–70. William Jennings Bryan: *Proceedings of the Citizenship Conference on October 14, 1923* (Washington, D.C.) p. 115, in Sinclair, *Prohibition*, p. 115. Individual poisoning preferable to racial poisoning: Clarence True Wilson and Deets Pickett, *The Case for Prohibition* (New York, 1923) pp. 79–80. Eugenics and Prohibition: Bartlett C. Jones, "Prohibition and Eugenics, 1920–1933," *Journal of the History of Medicine and Allied Sciences*, Vol. 18 (1963), pp. 158–72; Philip J. Pauly, "How Did the Effects of Alcohol on Reproduction Become Scientifically Uninteresting?" *Journal of the History of Biology*, Vol. 29 (1996), pp. 1–28.

Women forbidden to drink wine in ancient Rome: Dionysius of Halicarnassus, *The Roman Antiquities* (tr. Ernest Cary, London, 1887) Vol. 1, p. 385 (book 2, ch. 25); Valerius Maximus, *Facta e Dicta Memorabilia* (tr. into French by T.C.E. Baudemont, Paris, 1850) p. 274 (book 6, ch. 3); Pliny (the Elder), *The Natural History* (tr. John Bostock and H. T. Riley, London, 1855) Vol. 3, p. 252 (book 14, ch. 14); Maguelonne Toussaint-Saint, *A History of Food* (tr. Anthea Bell, Oxford, 1992) pp. 266–67; Jacques André, *L'Alimentation et la Cuisine à Rome* (2nd ed., Paris, 1981) pp. 170–72; Jessica Warner, "The Sanctuary of Sobriety: The Emergence of Temperance as a Feminine Virtue in Tudor and Stuart England," *Addiction*, Vol. 92 (1997), pp. 97–111. Sermon: Thomas Thompson, *A Diet for a Drunkard* (London, 1608) p. 24. Revival of the old disapproval of female drinking: Warner, loc. cit. Janet Schaw: *Journal of a Lady of Quality* (ed. Evangeline W. Andrews, 2nd ed., New Haven, 1934) pp. 80–81. Association between drinking and whoring: Margaret Sargeant, *Drinking and Alcoholism in Australia* (Melbourne, 1979) pp. 116–27. "A thing so fallen, and so vile": Sydney *Temperance Advocate*, April 24, 1841, in E. Windschuttle, "Women, Class and Temperance: Moral Reform in Eastern Australia, 1832–1857," *The Push from the Bush*, May 1979, p. 18. Male need to control female sexuality: Sandmaier, op. cit., p. 16. Alcohol increases the level of testosterone: C. J. Peter Eriksson, Tatsushige Fukunaga, and Raif Lindman, "Sex Hormone Response to Alcohol," *Nature*, Vol. 369 (June 30, 1994) p. 11. Alcohol and sex: Ernest L. Abel, *Psychoactive Drugs and Sex* (New York, 1985) pp. 40–42; Linda J. Beckman and Kimberly T. Ackerman, "Women, Alcohol and Sexuality" in *Recent Development in Alcoholism*, Vol. 12 (ed. Marc Galanter, New York, 1995) pp. 267–85; Moira Plant, *Women and Alcohol* (London, 1997) pp. 108–11. "Solicits an ass in the street": *The Talmud* (Ketuboth, 65a), in Abel, op. cit., p. 36. Effect of alcohol on men: William Shakespeare, *Macbeth*, Act 2, Scene 3. College in Pacific Northwest: L. H. Bowker, "The Relationship Between Sex, Drugs, and Sexual Behaviour on a College Campus,"*Drug Forum*, Vol. 7, no. 1 (1978–79), pp. 69–80.

CHAPTER 4

Joe and Mike Gallo: Ellen Hawkes, *Blood and Wine* (New York, 1993) pp. 42, 52–53, 56–57, 78–82, 97–98, 105, 107–18. Ernest and Julio Gallo: Ibid, pp. 60, 67. Section 29 of the Volstead Act: Gilman Ostrander, *The Prohibition Movement in California 1848–1933* (Berkeley, California, 1957) pp. 178–79; Henry Johnston, *What Rights Are Left?* (New York, 1930) pp. 32–34. Wine consumption during Prohibition: Andrew Sinclair, *Prohibition* (London, 1962) p. 227. Wine bricks: Leon D. Adams, *The Wines of America* (4th ed., New York, 1990) p. 26. Legal to serve wine: Johnson, op. cit., pp. 44–48.

Letter from Georgia settlers: *The Colonial Records of the State of Georgia* (ed. Allen D. Candler et al., Atlanta, 1904–16) Vol. 3, p. 422–46 (December 9, 1738). Wine in Louisiana: David J. Mishkin, *The American Colonial Wine Industry: An Economic Interpretation* (Ph.D. dissertation, University of Illinois, 1966). pp. 150–73. American farmers accustomed to easy work: Johann D. Schoepf, *Travels in the Confederation* (tr. and ed. Alfred J. Morrison, New York, 1968) Vol. 2, pp. 183–89. Alexander Hamilton: *The Federalist* No. 12 (November 27, 1787) in *The Federalist* (ed. Jacob E. Cooke, Middletown, Connecticut, 1961) p. 78. James Jackson: Thomas H. Benton, *Abridgement of the Debates of Congress from 1789 to 1856* (New York, 1857–61) Vol. 1, pp. 262–67. Cheapness of spirits: Peter Neilson, *Recollections of a Six Years' Residence in the United States of America* (Glasgow, 1830) pp. 66–70; Thomas L. Nichols, *Forty Years of American Life* (London, 1864) pp. 86–89. Expense of wine: William J. Rorabaugh, *The Alcoholic Republic* (New York, 1979) p. 100. Per capita consumption: Ibid., p. 232. Thomas Jefferson: Letter to Monsieur de Neuville, December 13, 1818, in *Jefferson and Wine* (ed. R.

de Treville Lawrence, The Plains, Virginia, 1976) p. 185. Reduction in wine duties: Rorabaugh, op. cit., p. 106. Adulteration: Ibid.; Benjamin Waterhouse, *Cautions to Young Persons Concerning Health* (5th ed., Cambridge, Massachusetts, 1822) pp. 27–28n; Moses Stuart, *Essay on the Prize Question* (New York, 1830) pp. 23–27; Thurlow Weed, *Autobiography* (ed. Harriet A. Weed, Boston, 1883) Vol. 2, pp. 153–55.

Wine not believed to contain alcohol: John Adlum, *A Memoir on the Cultivation of the Vine in America and the Best Mode of Making Wine* (Washington, 1823) pp. 70–71. Wine found to contain alcohol: William Brande, *A Manual of Chemistry* (London, 1819) p. 400–04; Justin Edwards, *Letter to the Friends of Temperance in Massachusetts* (3rd ed., Boston, 1836) pp. 12–13; Rev. J. S. Smart, *Funeral Sermon of the Maine Law and Its Offspring in Michigan* (New York, 1858) pp. 52–56. Elisha Taylor: Edwards, op. cit., pp. 27–30. "Minding everybody's business but their own": Ebenezer S. Thomas, *Reminiscences of the Last Sixty-five Years* (Hartford, 1840) Vol. 2, pp. 116–17, 119. "Virtually a denial of equal rights": *The Springfield Republican*, September 1838 in Robert Hampel, *Temperance and Prohibition in Massachusetts 1813–1852* (Ann Arbor, Michigan, 1982) p. 81. Dram shop "oppresses the poor": John S. C. Abbot, *Lecture on the Licence Law* (Boston, 1836) p. 18 in Hampel, loc. cit.

Maine Law: A. Farewell and G. P. Ure, *The Maine Law Illustrated* (Toronto, 1855); Henry S. Clubb, *Maine Liquor Law: Its Origin, History and Results* (New York, 1856). Wine drinkers support the Maine Law: William E. Baxter, *American and the Americans* (London, 1855) pp. 117–22. Exemption for cider: Evelyn L. Fanshawe, *Liquor Legislation in the United States and Canada* (London, 1893) pp. 100–01, 116, and n. Ohio: Daniel J. Ryan, "History of Liquor Legislation in Ohio" in *History of Ohio* (ed. Emilius O. Randall and Daniel J. Ryan, New York, 1912) Vol. 4, pp. 507–41. Pennsylvania: Asa Earl Martin, "The Temperance Movement in Pennsylvania Prior to the Civil War," *The Pennsylvania Magazine of History and Biography* Vol. 49 (1925), pp. 195–230. Michigan: Smart, op. cit., pp. 44–46. Iowa: Fanshawe, op. cit., p. 149; Frederic H. Wines and John Koren, *The Liquor Problem in Its Legislative Aspects* (Boston, 1898) pp. 97–99.

Wine drinking promoted temperance: Weed, op. cit., Vol. 2, pp. 153–55; Arpad Haraszthy in Vincent P. Carosso, *The California Wine Industry 1830–1895* (Berkeley, California, 1951) p. 132; Emily Faithfull, *Three Visits to America* (Edinburgh, 1884) pp. 92–93; Frona Eunice Wait, *Wines and Vines of California* (San Francisco, 1889) pp. 81–83; Paul de Rousiers, *American Life* (tr. A. J. Herbertson, Paris, 1892) pp. 318–21. Cheapness of wine in California: George Husmann, *American Grape-Growing and Wine-Making* (4th ed., New York, 1896) pp. 254–56; Martha Bruère, *Does Prohibition Work?* (New York, 1927) pp. 57–61. California bill: Ostrander, op. cit., pp. 135–41.

Beer and whiskey consumption: Yandell Henderson, *A New Deal in Liquor: A Plea for Dilution* (Garden City, New Jersey, 1935) p. 50. "Whiskey makes a man ugly": *The Western Brewer*, March 15, 1880, in Perry R. Duis, *The Saloon: Public Drinking in Chicago and Boston, 1880–1920* (Urbana, Illinois, 1983) p. 79. Beer in Chicago: Royal L. Melendy, "The Saloon in Chicago," *The American Journal of Sociology*, Vol. 6 (1900–1) pp. 289–306, 433–64. Division between brewers and distillers: K. Austin Kerr, *Organized for Prohibition: A New History of the Anti-Saloon League* (New Haven, 1985) pp. 28–29, 32, 161–62. Food Control Bill: Peter H. Odegard, *Pressure Politics: The Story of the Anti-Saloon League* (New York, 1928) pp. 166–71. Meaning of "intoxicating": Norman H. Clark, *Deliver Us from Evil* (New York, 1976) pp. 130–33; Philip J. Pauly, "Is Liquor Intoxicating? Scientists, Prohibition and the Normalization of Drinking," *American Journal of Public Health*, Vol. 84 (1994), pp. 305–13. Brewers fight back: Stanley Baron, *Brewed in America* (Boston, 1962) pp. 312–13; Pauly, loc. cit. Gangsters and "near beer": Sinclair, op. cit., pp. 225–26. Association Against the Prohibition Amendment: David E. Kyvig, *Repealing National Prohibition* (Chicago, 1979) pp. 57–58. Public opinion survey: *Literary Digest*, September 9, 1922, in Kyvig, op. cit., pp. 67–68. Prohibition a class law: Samuel Gompers, Letter to President Wilson, October 20, 1919 in Fletcher Dobyns, *The Amazing Story of Repeal* (New York, 1940) p. 253. Abolition of beer would lead to Bolshevism: *The New York Times*, June 15 and July 4, 1919, in Sinclair, op. cit., p. 359. Senate hearings: Kyvig, op. cit., pp. 61–62. Workers losing faith in the government: Harry Gene Levine, "The Birth of American Alcohol Control: Prohibition, the Power Elite and the Problem of Lawlessness," *Contemporary Drug Problems*, Vol. 12 (1985), pp. 63–115. Robert Clancy: House Committee on the Judiciary, *The Prohibition Amendment* (Washington, D.C., 1930) pp. 72–73 in Larry Englemann, "Organized Thirst: The Story of Repeal in Michigan" in *Alcohol, Reform and Society: The Liquor Issue in Social Context* (ed. Jack S. Blocker, Westport, Connecticut, 1979) p. 186. Beer would make workers feel better: Ernest Gordon, *The Wrecking of the Eighteenth Amendment* (Francestown, New Hampshire, 1943) p. 107. Growth of radicalism blamed on Prohibition: Senate Subcommittee of the Committee on the Judiciary, *Modification or Repeal of National Prohibition* (Washington, D.C., 1932) p. 62, in Engelmann, loc. cit. Survival of American government depended on immediate repeal: Fred Green to Henry B. Joy, June 27, 1932, in Engelmann, loc. cit. Yandell Henderson: Pauly, loc. cit. Arrival of legal beer: *The New York Times*, April 8 and 17, 1933.

Rockefeller Report: Raymond B. Fosdick and Albert L. Scott, *Toward Liquor Control* (New York, 1933); Harry G. Levine and Craig Reinarman, "From

Prohibition to Regulation: Lessons from Alcohol Policy for Drug Policy" in *Confronting Drug Policy: Illicit Drugs in a Free Society* (ed. Ronald Beyer and Gerald M. Oppenheim, Cambridge, 1993) pp. 160–93. South Carolina dispensary system: Fosdick and Scott, op. cit., pp. 75–77, 90; Guy Hayler, *Prohibition Advance in All Lands* (London, 1913) pp. 289–90. Alcohol in Sweden: Walter Thompson, *The Control of Liquor in Sweden* (New York, 1935); George E. Catlin, *Liquor Control* (London, 1931) pp. 219–29; Per Frånberg, "The Swedish Snaps: A History of Booze, Bratt and Bureaucracy," *Contemporary Drug Problems*, Vol. 14 (1987), pp. 557–93. Alcohol in Canada: Reginald E. Hose, *Prohibition or Control? Canada's Experience with the Liquor Problem 1921– 27* (London, 1928); Catlin, op. cit., pp. 202–14; Reginald G. Smart and Alan C. Ogborne, *Northern Spirits: Drinking in Canada Then and Now* (Toronto, 1986) pp. 51–61. New state alcohol laws: Leonard V. Harrison and Elizabeth Lane, *After Repeal: A Study of Liquor Control Administration* (New York, 1936) pp. 107, 111; Kyvig, op. cit., pp. 187–89; Levine and Reinarman, loc. cit. Liquor permits in Iowa: Harold A. Mulford, *Alcohol and Alcoholics in Iowa* (Iowa City, 1965); *The New York Times*, December 1, 1986. Oklahoma: *The New York Times*, September 18, 1984 and September 2, 1985. Utah: *The New York Times* July 13, 1969; *Chicago Tribune* February 11, 1990; *The Independent* February 1, 1996. Rules regarding spirits sales: Distilled Spirits Council of the United States, *Summary of State Laws and Regulations Relating to Distilled Spirits* (28th ed., December 1993).

Seagram's prohibition violations: Mark H. Haller, "Bootleggers as Businessmen" in *Law, Alcohol and Order* (ed. David E. Kyvig, Westport, Connecticut, 1985) p. 144. Five Crown whiskey: Peter C. Newman, *King of the Castle* (New York, 1979) pp. 128–30. Edgar Bronfman Jr. and Gallup poll: *The Wall Street Journal*, February 25, 1985. Networks refuse to air advertising campaign: Philip Van Munching, *Beer Blast* (New York, 1997) pp. 103–04. Survey of bars in Atlanta: *The New York Times* April 23, 1991. Gallup poll (1994): *The Los Angeles Times* December 16, 1995. President Clinton: U.S. Newswire, June 15, 1996. Marc Sherman: *Alcoholism and Drug Abuse Weekly*, November 18 1996. Brewers ridicule equivalency argument: Ibid. John De Luca: *Wine & Spirits*, July 1997, p. 13.

French belief in healthfulness of wine: Patricia E. Prestwich, *Drink and the Politics of Social Reform: Anti-Alcoholism in France Since 1870* (Palo Alto, California, 1988) pp. 54–55, 91–92. Postwar attitudes: Roland Sadoun, Giorgio Lolli, and Milton Silverman, *Drinking in French Culture* (New Brunswick, New Jersey, 1965) pp. 50–65; Prestwich, op. cit., p. 261. School blotters: Barbara Gallatin Anderson, "How French Children Learn to Drink" in *Beliefs, Behaviors and Alcoholic Beverages: A Cross-Cultural Survey* (ed. Mac Marshall, Ann Arbor, Michigan, 1979) pp. 429–32. Henry Brougham: *Hansard*,

2nd series, Vol. 24, columns 419–22 (May 4, 1830). "Thee mustn't, Richard, the'll die": Norman Longmate, *The Waterdrinkers* (London, 1968) p. 55. Energy value of beer: H. J. Bunker, "The nutritive value of yeast, beer, wines and spirits," *Chemistry and Industry*, 1947, pp. 203–04. Spirits not necessary to bring in harvest: Anthony Benezet, *The Potent Enemies of America Laid Open* (Philadelphia, 1774) pp. 18–20, 26–27; Job Roberts, *The Pennsylvania Farmer* (Philadelphia, 1804) pp. 61–62; Benjamin Rush, *An Inquiry into the Effects of Ardent Spirits upon the Human Body and Mind* (6th ed., New York, 1811) p. 16. Spirits and slavery: Benezet, op. cit., p. 8; Rorabaugh, op. cit., pp. 36–38. Samuel Gompers: *The New York Times*, April 22, 1924. "Liquid bread:" Sinclair, op. cit., pp. 60–62.

Early history of spirits: Robert J. Forbes, *Short History of the Art of Distillation* (Leiden, 1948); Constance A. Wilson, "Burnt Wine and Cordial Waters: The Early Days of Distilling," *Folk Life*, Vol. 13 (1975), pp. 54–65; Constance A. Wilson, "Water of Life: Its Beginnings and Early History" in *"Liquid Nourishment": Potable Foods and Stimulating Drinks* (ed. Constance A. Wilson, Edinburgh, 1993) pp. 142–64. King Charles II of Navarre: Henri Martin, *Histoire de France* (4th ed., Paris, 1878) Vol. 5, p. 408. Benedictine in the Far East: Peter A. Hallgarten, *Spirits and Liqueurs* (2nd ed., London, 1983) pp. 17–27. Sir Walter Raleigh: A. C. Wootton, *Chronicles of Pharmacy* (London, 1910) Vol. 2, pp. 310–15. "Juniper water": Samuel Pepys, *Diary* (ed. Robert Latham and William Matthews, London, 1971) Vol. 4, p. 329 (October 10, 1663). Spirits should only be sold in apothecaries' shops: George Cheyne, *An Essay of Health and Long Life* (London, 1724) p. 43; Benezet, op. cit., p. 47.

"Brandy has killed most of the Indians": Pehr Kalm, *Travels into North America* (tr. John R. Forster, Warrington, 1770 and London, 1771) Vol. 2, pp. 94–95. Danger of drinking spirits in cold weather: Dr. Thomas Stuttaford, *To Your Good Health! The Wise Drinker's Guide* (London, 1997) pp. 58–59, 191. Spirits not necessary in hot weather: Rush, op. cit., p. 10; Benezet, op. cit., pp. 6–7. Use of bitters: Constantin François de Chasseboeuf, Count of Volney, *A View of the Soil and Climate of the United States of America* (tr. C. B. Brown, Philadelphia, 1804) p. 231. Mint julep "a kind of liquid medicine": *Webster's Dictionary*, 1806, in William Grimes, *Straight Up or On the Rocks* (New York, 1993) p. 54. Quinine better than bitters: Rush, op. cit., pp. 18–19.

Medicinal use of alcohol: Sarah E. Williams, "The Use of Beverage Alcohol as Medicine 1790–1860," *Journal of Studies on Alcohol*, Vol. 41 (1980), pp. 543–66. Alcohol a stimulant: John B. Beck, *Lectures on Materia Medica and Therapeutics* (New York, 1851) p. 440. Robert Bentley Todd: John H.

Warner, "Physiological Theory and Therapeutic Explanation in the 1860s: The British Debate on the Medical Use of Alcohol," *Bulletin of the History of Medicine*, Vol. 54 (1980), pp. 235–57. Prince Albert: Frederic R. Lees, *An Inquiry into the Reasons and Results of the Prescription of Intoxicating Liquors in the Practice of Medicine* (London, 1866) pp. 36, 96. Medicinal use of alcohol in the Civil War: George W. Adams, *Doctors in Blue: The Medical History of the Union Army in the Civil War* (New York, 1952) pp. 140–41. Snakebites: Berton Roueché, *The Neutral Spirit* (Boston, 1960) pp. 92–94.

Whiskey "absolutely indispensable to man and boy": Mark E. Lender and James K. Martin, *Drinking in America: A History* (2nd ed., New York, 1987) p. 47. Rum needed for adding to water: Thomas Penn to Oglethorpe, 4th August 1734, in Phinizy Spalding, *Oglethorpe in America* (Chicago, 1977) p. 51. Petition of inhabitants of Savannah: Henry A. Scomp, *King Alcohol in the Realm of King Cotton* (Chicago, 1888). Spirits do not improve bad water: Benezet, op. cit., pp. 27–30. Addition of wine to water: Henry Sienkiewicz, *Portrait of America* (tr. C. Morley, New York, 1959) p. 233; Andrew Barr, *Drink: An Informal Social History* (London, 1995) pp. 252–53. South Carolina: Neilson, op. cit., pp. 307–08; François A. Michaux, *Travels to the West* (ed. R. G. Thwaites, Cleveland, 1904) p. 122. Bad water in New York: Asa Greene, *A Glance at New York* (1837) in *A Mirror for Americans* (ed. Warren S. Tryon, Chicago, 1952) pp. 176–78; Neilson, op. cit., pp. 66–70. Croton water: E. Porter Belden, *New York: Past, Present, and Future* (2nd ed., New York, 1849) pp. 36–42; Philip Hone, *Diary* (New York, 1889) Vol. 2, pp. 150–52 (October 12 and 14, 1842); Rorabaugh, op. cit., pp. 95–98. Danger of drinking cold water when hot: Neilson, op. cit., pp. 66–70, 198–99; James Stuart, *Three Years in North America* (London, 1833) Vol. 2, pp. 499–503; Charles Haswell, *Reminiscences of an Octogenarian of the City of New York, 1816–1860* (New York, 1897) pp. 112–13. Ice water and the temperance movement: Isabella Bird, *The Englishwoman in America* (London, 1856) p. 152; "Ice and the Ice Trade," *Hunt's Merchants' Magazine and Commercial Review*, Vol. 33 (1855), pp. 169–79. Water purification: Harvey W. Wiley, *Beverages and Their Adulteration* (London, 1919) pp. 33–35; George C. Whipple, "Fifty Years of Water Purification" in *A Half-Century of Public Health* (ed. Mazÿck P. Ravenel, New York, 1921) pp. 161–67; Richard O. Cummings, *The American and his Food* (2nd ed., Chicago, 1941) p. 91. Filtration: Benezet, op. cit., pp. 27–30. Muddiness of American water: Max O'Rell and Jack Allyn, *Jonathan and His Continent* (tr. Mme Paul Blouët, Bristol, 1889) p. 268; Rorabaugh, loc. cit.

Increased use of spirits as medicines: Williams, loc. cit. Overenthusiastic prescription of alcohol: James Samuelson, *History of Drink* (London, 1878) p. 231; Thomas D. Mitchell, *Materia Medica and Therapeutics* (Philadelphia,

1857) p. 104; Rev. William R. Baker, *The Curse of Britain* (London, 1838) p. 144. Alcohol a necessary medicine: Beck. Debunking of beliefs about alcohol: James H. Timberlake, *Prohibition and the Progressive Movement 1900–1920* (Cambridge, Massachusetts, 1963) pp. 40–47. Alcohol does not stimulate the muscles: John J. Abel, "A Critical Review of the Pharmacological Action of Ethyl Alcohol," *Physiological Aspects of the Liquor Problem* (Boston, 1903) Vol. 2, p. 165. Marathon runners: *The Financial Times*, April 20, 1996. Alcohol not a food but a poison: *Physiological Aspects of the Liquor Problem*, Vol. 1, pp. 3–8. Physicians abandon the prescription of alcohol: Sir Victor Horsley and Mary D. Sturge, *Alcohol and the Human Body* (London, 1907) pp. 7–10; Oliver T. Osborne, *The Principles of Therapeutics* (Philadelphia, 1921) pp. 238–44; Timberlake, loc. cit. Medical prescription and Prohibition: Bartlett C. Jones, "A Prohibition Problem: Liquor as Medicine 1920–1933," *Journal of the History of Medicine and Allied Sciences*, Vol. 18 (1963), pp. 353–69; Steven Goldberg, "Putting Science in the Constitution: The Prohibition Experience" in *Law, Alcohol, and Order* (ed. David E. Kyvig, Westport, Connecticut, 1985) pp. 21–34. George Remus: Sinclair, op. cit., p. 428. Colds: Sheldon Cohen et al., "Smoking, Alcohol Consumption, and Susceptibility to the Common Cold," *American Journal of Public Health*, Vol. 83 (1993), pp. 1277–83. Asthma: Stuttaford, op. cit., pp. 171–80.

Robert Warner: George B. Wilson, *Alcohol and the Nation* (London, 1940) p. 262. Emil Kraepelin: Timberlake, loc. cit. Total abstinence the only course: Sir Victor Horsley, *The Effect of Alcohol on the Human Brain* (London, 1900) p. 16. Life insurance companies: Eugene Lyman Fisk, "Alcohol and Life Insurance," *The Atlantic Monthly*, Vol. 118 (1916), pp. 624–34; Timberlake, op. cit., pp. 53–55; Raymond Pearl, "The Experimental Modification of Germ Cells," *Journal of Experimental Zoology*, Vol. 22 (1917), p. 169, in Raymond Pearl, "Alcohol and Mortality" in Ernest H. Starling, *The Action of Alcohol on Man* (London, 1923) pp. 269–78. Pearl's research in Baltimore: Pearl, "Alcohol and Mortality," pp. 237–57; Raymond Pearl, *Alcohol and Longevity* (New York) 1926. Reviews of Pearl's book: *The American Mercury*, Vol. 9 (December 1926) p. 508; *International Review Against Alcoholism*, May–June 1927, in "Longevity and Alcohol" in *The Standard Encyclopaedia of the Alcohol Problem* (ed. Ernest H. Cherrington, Westerville, Ohio, 1925–30) Vol. 4, pp. 1596–600.

Belief of French doctors in healthfulness of wine: Prestwich, op. cit., pp. 224–25. Longevity of wine-drinking Frenchmen: Célestin Cambiare, *The Black Horse of the Apocalypse* (Paris, 1932) pp. 265–76; Blake Ozias, *How the Modern Hostess Serves Wine* (New York, 1934) p. 26. Study of heart attack patients in Rome: Claudia Balboni, "Alcohol in Relation to Dietary Patterns" in *Alcohol and Civilization* (ed. Salvatore P. Lucia, New York, 1963) pp. 61–

74. Healthy inhabitants of Roseto: Clarke Stout et al., "Unusually Low Incidence of Death from Myocardial Infarction: Study of an Italian-American Community in Pennsylvania," *Journal of the American Medical Association*, Vol. 188 (1964), pp. 845–49. Alcohol helps prevent heart attacks: Arthur Klatsky, "Alcohol Consumption Before Myocardial Infarction: Results from the Kaiser-Permanente Epidemiologic Study of Myocardial Infarction," *Annals of Internal Medicine*, Vol. 81 (1974), pp. 294–301; Michael Marmot et al., "Alcohol and Mortality: A U-Shaped Curve," *The Lancet*, March 14, 1981, pp. 580–83. Shaper's argument about nondrinkers: Gerald Shaper, "Alcohol and Mortality in British Men: Explaining the U-shaped Curve," *The Lancet*, 1988, Vol. 2, pp. 1267–73; Gerald Shaper, "Alcohol and Mortality: A Review of Prospective Studies," *British Journal of Addiction*, Vol. 85 (1990), pp. 837–47, 859–61. Shaper wrong: Michael Marmot, "Alcohol and Cardiovascular Disease: The Status of the U-Shaped Curve," *The British Medical Journal*, Vol. 303 (1991), pp. 565–68.

Doctors discuss only the harmful effects of alcohol: Stanton Peele, "The Conflict between Public Health Goals and the Temperance Mentality," *American Journal of Public Health*, Vol. 83 (1993), pp. 805–10; Peter Skrabanek, *The Death of Humane Medicine and the Rise of Coercive Healthism* (Bury St. Edmunds, Suffolk, 1994) p. 118. Neil Stone: *The Wine Spectator*, August 31, 1995, p. 57. Ledermann hypothesis: Sully Ledermann, *Alcohol, Alcoolisme, Alcoolisation* (Paris, 1956). Hans Emblad: *Alcohol in Moderation*, Vol. 3, No. 4 (February/March 1995). American adoption of WHO policy: Department of Health and Human Services, *Healthy People 2000* (Washington, D.C., 1990) pp. 170–71 (section 4.8); Doug Bandlow, *The Politics of Science: The Federal Bureaucracy's War on Social Drinking* (Raleigh, North Carolina, 1995). No such thing as "responsible use" of alcohol: Morris Chafetz, *The Tyranny of Experts* (Lanham, Maryland, 1996) pp. 47–61. Seltzer prevented from publishing his paper: Carl C. Seltzer, " 'Conflicts of Interest' and 'Political Science,' " *Journal of Clinical Epidemiology*, Vol. 50 (1997), pp. 627–29. Kermit Lynch silenced: *The Wine Spectator*, April 15, 1990. Robert Mondavi label: *The New York Times*, March 6, 1991; Andrew Barr, *Wine Snobbery* (New York, 1992) p. 24.

Morley Safer: *The Wine Enthusiast*, May/June 1992, p. 30. Transcript of *60 Minutes* program: *The Quarterly Review of Wines*, Spring 1992, pp. 44–46. Leeward Winery silenced: *The Wine Spectator*, May 31, 1992. Distribution of article from *Alcohol Abuse: Wine & Spirit*, October 1993, p. 61. New guidelines not expected to make news: Marion Nestle, "Alcohol Guidelines for Chronic Disease Prevention: From Prohibition to Moderation," *Social History of Alcohol Review*, No. 32–3 (1996) pp. 45–58. They do make news: *The New York Times*, January 3, 1996; *The Daily Telegraph*, January 4,

1996. Wine Institute labels: Stanton Peele, "Alcoholic Denial: The Government's Prejudice Against Alcohol Is a Hangover from Prohibition," *National Review*, August 11, 1997; *The Los Angeles Times*, March 5, 1998; Gannett News Service, March 20, 1988.

Red wine sales may have overtaken those of white: *Rocky Mountain News*, August 10, 1997. Copenhagen study: Morten Grønbæk et al., "Mortality Associated with Moderate Intakes of Wine, Beer, or Spirits," *The British Medical Journal*, Vol. 310 (1995), pp. 1165–66. Free radicals, antioxidants, and flavonoids: Stuttaford, op. cit., pp. 31–43; Frank Jones, *Save Your Heart Wine Guide* (London, 1995); *The Independent on Sunday*, June 9, 1996. Resveratrol content of Finger Lakes wines: *The Wine Spectator*, September 30, 1997. Resveratrol and cancer: Meishiang Jang et al., "Cancer Chemopreventive Activity of Resveratrol, a Natural Product Derived from Grapes," *Science*, Vol. 275 (1997), pp. 218–20. Alcohol and breast cancer: Moira Plant, *Women and Alcohol* (London, 1997) pp. 89–100; *Health Issues Related to Alcohol Consumption* (ed. Paulus M. Verschuren, Washington, D.C., 1993) pp. 221–44. Benefit of drinking with meals: Serge Renaud, "Wine, Alcohol, Platelets and the French Paradox for Coronary Heart Disease," *The Lancet*, Vol. 339 (1992), pp. 1523–26; *New Scientist*, November 25, 1995.

CHAPTER 5

Women drinking: Alice-Leone Moats, *No Nice Girl Swears* (London, 1933) pp. 171–76. Young people drinking: Paula S. Fass, *The Damned and the Beautiful: American Youth in the 1920s* (New York, 1977) pp. 310–24. "Our reverence for strong drink": A. J. Liebling, *Between Meals: An Appetite for Paris* (London, 1990) pp. 175–76. Drink in the movies: Edgar Dale, *The Content of Motion Pictures* (New York, 1935) pp. 167–70. Cost of alcohol: Norman H. Clark, *Deliver Us from Evil* (New York, 1976) pp. 146–53, 158–65. Speakeasies: Andrew Sinclair, *Prohibition: The Era of Excess* (London, 1962) pp. 249–52. Comparison of beer and spirits consumption: William J. Rorabaugh, *The Alcoholic Republic* (New York, 1979) pp. 232–33; Mark E. Lender and James K. Martin, *Drinking in America: A History* (2nd ed., New York, 1987) pp. 145–46. Heywood Broun: Sinclair, op. cit., p. 255. Hearst changes his mind: William Randolph Hearst, preface to *Temperance or Prohibition?* (ed. Francis Tietsort, New York, 1929) pp. xiv–xv. People drink only for the effect: Moats, loc. cit.

Moonshine: John McGuffin, *In Praise of Poteen* (2nd ed., Belfast, 1988) pp. 71–80. Smuggling: Roy Haynes, *Prohibition Inside Out* (London, 1923) p. 87; Sinclair, op. cit., pp. 219–29. "Prohibition has sure been a godsend":

Ring Lardner, *The Love Nest and Other Stories* (London, 1928) p. 246. The Prohibition Bureau and the Borgias: *The New York World*, August 9–16, 1926, in Sinclair, op. cit., pp. 221–22. Jake: Joseph Earl Dabney, *Mountain Spirits* (Asheville, North Carolina, 1974) p. 108. Methanol and "deliberate suicides:" *The New York Times*, December 30, 1926. Moonshine: Dabney, op. cit., pp. 110–11. Jones Act: Clark, op. cit., pp. 181–208. Prohibition and the courts: Sinclair, op. cit., pp. 230–35. Jury put on trial: *The New York Times*, January 7, 1928. Public competition: *Temperance or Prohibition?* pp. 251–63.

Massachusetts striped pig: B. F. Clark, *Prohibition of the Sale of Intoxicating Liquors Impracticable: The Maine Law a Failure: A Stringent Licence Law the True Policy* (Lowell, Massachusetts, 1864) pp. 9–10. Violent opposition to the Fifteen-Gallon Law: Robert L. Hampel, *Temperance and Prohibition in Massachusetts, 1813–1852* (Ann Arbor, Michigan, 1982) pp. 79–94. Drink and crime in Ohio: Jed Dannenbaum, *Drink and Disorder* (Chicago, 1984) pp. 79–80. Neal Dow and the Portland riot: J. C. Furnas, *The Life and Times of the Late Demon Rum* (London, 1965) pp. 168–73; Ian R. Tyrrell, *Sobering Up: From Temperance to Prohibition in Antebellum America, 1800–1860* (Westport, Connecticut, 1979) pp. 272, 294–96. Kansas prisons: Evelyn Fanshawe, *Liquor Legislation in the United States and Canada* (London, 1893) pp. 144–46. Failure of Maine Law in Portland: Justin McCarthy, "Prohibitory Legislation in the United States," *The Fortnightly Review*, Vol. 10 (1871), pp. 166–79; Fanshawe, op. cit., pp. 103–12; Frederic H. Wines and John Koren, *The Liquor Problem in Its Legislative Aspects* (2nd ed., Boston, 1898) pp. 34–63; Furnas, op. cit., pp. 168–73. Failure of Maine Law generally: Thomas L. Nichols, *Forty Years of American Life* (London, 1864) pp. 86–89; Fanshawe, op. cit., pp. 40–41. "Jug" trade in Atlanta: Ibid., pp. 323–24.

Symbolic value of Maine Law: Clark, op. cit., pp. 45–48; McCarthy, loc. cit.; Fanshawe, op. cit., pp. 14, 141–43, 178–79, 409–15. Symbolic value of Prohibition: Joseph R. Gusfield, *Symbolic Crusade: Status Politics and the American Temperance Movement* (Urbana, Illinois, 1963) pp. 100–06, 123–24. William S. Kenyon: National Commission on Law Observance and Enforcement, *Report on the Enforcement of the Prohibition Laws of the United States* (Washington, D.C., 1931) p. 132, in Harry Gene Levine, "The Birth of American Alcohol Control: Prohibition, the Power Elite, and the Problem of Lawlessness," *Contemporary Drug Problems*, Vol. 12 (1985), pp. 63–115. The Depression, disorder, and Repeal: Levine, loc. cit. Rockefeller: Ibid.; Introduction to Raymond B. Fosdick and Albert L. Scott, *Toward Liquor Control* (New York, 1933) pp. vii–xi. Law redesigned to suit drinkers: W. E. Garrison, "Fitting the Law to the Lawless," *Christian Century*, November 11, 1933 (Vol. 50, pp. 1505–06), in Levine, loc. cit.

Prohibition in Mississippi: Randolph W. Childs, *Making Repeal Work* (Philadelphia, 1947) pp. 202–04; *The New York Times*, February 3 and 6, April 9, May 22, July 23, and August 14, 1966. "A po' man here don't have to drink rotgut": David L. Cohn, "A Little Prohibition in Mississippi," *The Atlantic Monthly*, Vol. 203 (1959), pp. 57–59. Failure of local option: Childs, op. cit., pp. 208–15. Moonshining since Prohibition: *The New York Times*, December 1, 1970, June 3, 1973, and August 29, 1982; *The Economist*, April 4, 1998. Southern attitudes to drink: John Gunther, *Inside U.S.A.* (London, 1947) pp. 669–70. Blacks and Prohibition: Sinclair, op. cit., pp. 48–52; Hanes Walton, Jr., and James E. Taylor, "Blacks and the Southern Prohibition Movement," *Phylon*, Vol. 32 (1971), pp. 247–59. Jimmy Russell and Bud Denman: *The Sunday Telegraph*, September 3, 1995. Roger Brashears: *The Independent*, January 31, 1998. Dustbin survey: *The Times* (London) April 28, 1986.

Drinking by children in colonial and republican America: Johann D. Schoepf, *Travels in the Confederation* (tr. and ed. Alfred J. Morrison, New York, 1968) Vol. 1, pp. 362–63; Charles William Janson, *The Stranger in America* (London, 1807) pp. 297–300; Isaac Holmes, *An Account of the United States of America* (London, 1823) pp. 352–53; Peter Neilson, *Recollections of a Six Years' Residence in the United States of America* (Glasgow, 1830) pp. 66–70; Rorabaugh, op. cit., pp. 14, 180–81. North Carolina court and legislation in California: James F. Mosher, "The History of Youthful-Drinking Laws: Implications for Current Policy" in *Minimum-Drinking-Age Laws: An Evaluation* (ed. Henry Wechsler, Lexington, Massachusetts, 1980) pp. 11–38. "Today's anti–teen-drinking crusade": Mike A. Males, *The Scapegoat Generation: America's War on Adolescents* (Monroe, Maine, 1996) pp. 190, 197. NIAAA: Robert L. Chauncey, "New Careers for Moral Entrepreneurs: Teenage Drinking," *Journal of Drug Issues*, Vol. 10 (1980), pp. 45–70. Candy Lightner and MADD: Craig Reinarman, "The Social Construction of an Alcohol Problem: The Case of Mothers Against Drunk Drivers and Social Control in the 1980s," *Theory and Society*, Vol. 17 (1988), pp. 91–120. National Minimum Drinking Age Act: *The New York Times*, July 18, 1984. South Dakota: *The New York Times*, February 10, and June 24, 1987. Wyoming: *The Economist*, March 26, 1988.

Antonia C. Novello: *The Washington Post*, September 12, 1991. Montgomery County crackdown: *The Washington Post*, October 25, and November 21, 1993 and October 1, 1995. Field parties: *The Washington Post*, July 20, 1995. Thomas Petri: *The Oshkosh Northwestern*, January 18, 1995. Lynn Zimmer: "All Things Considered," National Public Radio, October 16, 1997. Richard Cullen: *USA Today*, December 26, 1997. Peter Coors: *USA Today*, September 10 and October 17, 1997. Kenneth Clarke: *The Times* (London) March 20,

1993. Student drinking: Henry Wechsler and Nancy Isaac, " 'Binge' Drinkers at Massachusetts Colleges," *Journal of the American Medical Association*, Vol. 267 (1992), pp. 2929–31; *The New York Times*, June 23, 1991; Henry Wechsler et al., "Binge Drinking on Campus: Results of a National Survey," http://www.edc.org. Roderic Park: *The Washington Post*, December 9, 1996. Ron Tupa: *Rocky Mountain News*, September 19, 1997. Student riots: *The Columbus Dispatch* (Ohio), May 16, 1998.

Adult freedoms and youth restrictions: Males, op. cit., p. 70. Shawn Colleary: *The Washington Post*, June 5, 1998. Soldiers in Bosnia: *Alcohol in Moderation*, Vol. 5, No. 3 (November/December 1996). "The drinking-age bill is a hoax": Ted Galen Carpenter, "The New Anti-Youth Movement," *The Nation*, January 19, 1985, pp. 39–42. "Crazy quilt of different states' drinking laws": *The New York Times*, July 18, 1984. "MADD's biggest legislative accomplishment:" Rebecca Brown, "MADD: An Example of Unconventional Work for Road Safety in the USA" (Irving, Texas, 1995) p. 3. Decline in teenage drink-driving in Canada: D. J. Beirness et al., "Roadside Surveys in Canada 1974–1993" (Traffic Injury Research Foundation of Canada, Ottawa, Ontario). Tijuana: *The Washington Post*, August 16, 1996. First year of legal drinking is hazardous: Peter Asch and David Levy, "The Minimum Legal Drinking Age and Traffic Fatalities," in Gene Ford, *The Benefits of Moderate Drinking* (San Francisco, 1988) p. 261; Mike Males, "The Minimum Purchase Age for Alcohol and Young-Driver Fatal Crashes: A Long-term View," *Journal of Legal Studies*, Vol. 40 (1986), in Males, *The Scapegoat Generation*, p. 210.

NHTSA: http://www.nhtsa.dot.gov. "Diana bill": Rick Berman, "Is the Drunk-Driving Law Too Soft?" *Newsday*, November 30, 1997. Frank Lautenberg: Gannett News Service, December 17, 1997. Research favoring reduction in BAC limit: Ralph Hingson, Timothy Heeren, and Michael Winter, "Lowering State Legal Blood-Alcohol Limits to 0.08 Percent: The Effect on Fatal Motor Vehicle Crashes," *American Journal of Public Health*, Vol. 86 (1996), pp. 1297–99. Death of Diana: "Dispatches," Channel 4 (London), June 4, 1998; *The Sunday Telegraph*, June 7, 1998. H. Laurence Ross: Michael Fumento, "Catch Drunks, Don't Harass Drivers," http://www.motorists.com; Preface to Terry M. Klein, "DWI—Are We Off Track?" (Washington, D.C., 1991). Candy Lightner: Fumento, loc. cit. Proposed BAC of 0.04 percent: Dr. C. Everett Koop, *Koop: The Memoirs of America's Family Doctor* (New York, 1991) pp. 298–99. Report of Presidential Commission on Drunk Driving: H. Lawrence Ross, *Confronting Drunk Driving: Social Policy for Saving Lives* (New Haven, 1992) pp. 35–36.

Memphis police experiment: *The New York Times*, August 28, 1994. National Sleep Foundation: http://www.sleepfoundation.org. Current attitudes to drowsy driving: William C. Dement, "The Perils of Drowsy Driving," *The New England Journal of Medicine*, September 11, 1997. Dangers of mobile telephones: Donald A. Redelmeier and Robert J. Tibshirani, "Association Between Cellular Telephone Calls and Motor Vehicle Collisions," *The New England Journal of Medicine*, Vol. 336 (1997), pp. 453–58. Royal Society for the Prevention of Accidents: *The Independent* and *The Times* (London), May 24, 1997. Road rage: *The Washington Times*, May 11, 1997; *U.S. News and World Report,* June 2, 1997. Stephanie Faul: Reuters, November 26, 1996. Henry Ford: *Christian Herald*, July 20, 1929, in *The Standard Encylopaedia of the Alcohol Problem* (ed. E. H. Cherrington, Westerville, Ohio, 1925–30) Vol. 6, p. 2661–64; *Pictorial Review*, September 1929, in Grace C. Root, *Women and Repeal* (New York, 1934) p. 17. "Don't Shoot, I'm Not a Bootlegger": *Milwaukee Journal*, August 3, 1929, in Sinclair, op. cit., pp. 338–41. Dennis Cayse: *The Independent*, January 6, 1998; *USA Today*, February 16, 1998.

Prohibition of marijuana: H. Wayne Morgan, *Drugs in America: A Social History 1800–1980* (Syracuse, New York, 1981) pp. 137–43. Director of the National Institute on Drug Abuse: Lester Grinspoon, *Marihuana Reconsidered* (Cambridge, Massachusetts, 1977) pp. 373–74. Mary Tyler Moore: Patrick Anderson, *High in America: The True Story Behind NORML and the Politics of Marijuana* (New York, 1981) p. 181. Surveys of marijuana use: National Commission on Marihuana and Drug Abuse, *Marihuana: A Signal of Misunderstanding* (Washington, D.C., 1972) Appendix pp. 250–53. "Illegal to smoke marijuana unless you have your hair cut": Edward M. Brecher, *Licit and Illicit Drugs* (Boston, 1972) p. 421, in Morgan, op. cit., pp. 161–62. Marijuana Commission: Anderson, op. cit., pp. 63–64, 91–95. Nixon's "war on drugs": David F. Musto, *The American Disease: Origins of Narcotic Control* (2nd ed., New York, 1987) pp. 254–56. Nixon refuses to accept commission's report: Ibid., p. 262. President Carter and Peter Bourne: Ibid. pp. 266–96; Anderson, op. cit. Carlton Turner: Eric Schlosser, "More Reefer Madness," *The Atlantic Monthly*, April 1997, pp. 90–102. Revival of legalization debate: *The New York Times*, May 15, 1988; Ethan A. Nadelman, "Drug Prohibition in the United States: Costs, Consequences and Alternatives," *Science*, Vol. 245 (1989), pp. 939–47. Jocelyn Elders: *The New York Times*, December 8, 1993. Kevin Elders: *The New York Times*, December 19 and 31, 1993.

Oppressive marijuana laws: Eric Schlosser, "Marijuana and the Law," *The Atlantic Monthly*, September 1994, pp. 84–94; "Caught in the grip of a deep psychosis:" Schlosser, "More Reefer Madness." Joel Proyect: *The Independent on Sunday*, June 20, 1993. World Health Organization report: *The New Scientist*, February 21, 1998, p. 4. Review of Dutch experiment: "Cannabis Policy: An Update," http://www.trimbos.nl. Joseph A. Califano, Jr.: *The New*

York Times, December 19, 1993. Symbolic value of marijuana laws: Richard J. Bonnie, "Discouraging Unhealthy Personal Choices Through Government Regulation: Some Thoughts About the Minimum Drinking Age" in *Minimum-Drinking-Age Laws: An Evaluation*, pp. 39–58; Jerome L. Himmelstein, *The Strange Career of Marihuana: Politics and Ideology of Drug Control in America* (Westport, Connecticut, 1983) pp. 32–33, 108, 122, 132–33, 144. Milton Friedman: *The Sunday Times*, February 20, 1994. Drug war is convenient: Harry G. Levine and Craig Reinarman, "When Science and Medicine Are Ignored: The Case of U.S. Drug Policy," *Addiction*, Vol. 89 (1994), pp. 535–36; Richard Lawrence Miller, "The Drug War's Dirty Secrets: What Warriors Won't Tell You," *Kansas City's News and Arts Weekly*. Ann Dally, "Anomalies and Mysteries in the 'War on Drugs' " in *Drugs and Narcotics in History* (ed. Roy Porter and Mikuláš Teich, Cambridge, 1995) pp. 199–215. Origin of cocaine and heroin prohibitions: Morgan, op. cit., pp. 91–96.

CHAPTER 6

Hostility between British emigrant communities in America: Andrew Burnaby, *Travels Through the Middle Settlements of North America in the Years 1759 and 1760* (New York, 1904) pp. 152–53; David Fischer, *Albion's Seed: Four British Folkways in America* (New York, 1989) pp. 821–22. Common consumption of consumer goods: T. H. Breen, " 'Baubles of Britain': The American and Consumer Revolutions of the Eighteenth Century," *Past and Present*, No. 119 (1988), pp. 73–104. Every prudent man should resort to farming and homespun: Francis Bernard, Letter of January 7, 1764, in *Select Letters* (2nd ed., London, 1774) pp. 9–11. Rejection of imported produce: Edmund S. and Helen M. Morgan, *The Stamp Act Crisis* (Chapel Hill, North Carolina, 1953) p. 32; Arthur M. Schlesinger, *The Colonial Merchants and the American Revolution, 1763–1776* (New York, 1917) pp. 63–64. "Many great events have proceeded from much smaller causes": John Adams, Letter to William Tudor, August 11, 1818 in *Works* (ed. Charles F. Adams, Boston, 1850–56) Vol. 10, pp. 343–46.

Free trade in Madeira: Adam Smith, *An Inquiry into the Nature and Causes of the Wealth of Nations* (11th ed., London, 1805) Vol. 2, p. 267 (book 4, ch. 4). "A good glass of beer or cider": Waverley Root and Richard de Rochemont, *Eating in America: A History* (New York, 1976) p. 90. The *Liberty* incident: Paul D. Brandes, *John Hancock's Life and Speeches: A Personalized View of the American Revolution, 1763–1793* (Lanham, Maryland, 1996) pp. 62–72. "The determination in Great Britain to subjugate us": John Adams, Diary for 1768 in *Works*, Vol. 2, p. 214. Jefferson and the Declaration of Independence: *The Wine Spectator*, March 15, 1991, p. 26. George Washington's inauguration and Jefferson's commemoration: Noël Cossart, *Madeira: The Island Vineyard* (London, 1984) p. 58. Colonel Lambert Cadwalader: S. Weir Mitchell, *A Madeira Party* (New York, 1895) pp. 24–25.

Popularity of tea in America: Israel Acrelius, *A History of New Sweden* (tr. and ed. William Reynolds, Philadelphia, 1874) p. 164; Pehr Kalm, *Travels into North America* (tr. John R. Forster, Warrington, 1770 and London, 1771) Vol. 2, pp. 267–68. Arrival of tea in East Hampton: Henry P. Hedges, *A History of the Town of East-Hampton* (Sag Harbor, 1987) p. 142, in Breen, loc. cit. Nonconsumption campaign: Breen, loc. cit. Three hundred ladies of Boston: Mary Caroline Crawford, *Social Life in Old New England* (New York, 1914) pp. 252–56. "Advertisements for the baubles of Britain": Samuel Adams to Arthur Lee, October 31, 1771, in *The Writings of Samuel Adams* (ed. Harry A. Cushing, New York, 1904–08) Vol. 2, pp. 264–67. John Adams dines with John Hancock: John Adams, Diary for April 14, 1771 in *Works*, Vol. 2, p. 255. Patriotism of Boston merchants: Lawrence Henry Gipson, *The British Empire Before the American Revolution* (New York, 1965) Vol. 12, pp. 74–75; Benjamin Woods Labaree, *The Boston Tea Party* (New York, 1964) pp. 50–51. Benjamin Franklin: Hugh Brogan, *The Penguin History of the United States of America* (London, 1990) p. 163. "Arbitrary government and slavery": *Pennsylvania Gazette*, October 20, 1773, in Gipson, op. cit., Vol. 12, pp. 75–76. Tea "a slow poison": Benjamin Rush, "To His Fellow Countrymen: On Patriotism," *Pennsylvania Journal*, October 20, 1773, in *Letters* (ed. Lyman H. Butterfield, Princeton, New Jersey, 1951) pp. 83–85. Thomas Young: *Boston Evening Post*, October 25, 1773, in Theodore Draper, *A Struggle for Power: The American Revolution* (Boston, 1996) p. 393. "That worst of plagues": *Letters and Diaries of John Rowe*, p. 255, in Draper, op. cit., p. 394. Sam Adams and John Hancock did not take part in the tea party: Brandes, op. cit., pp. 117–21. "An epocha in history": John Adams, Diary for December 17, 1773 in *Works*, Vol. 2, pp. 323–24. "Old jealousies are removed": Sam Adams to James Warren, December 28, 1773, in *Warren-Adams Letters* (Boston, 1917) Vol. 1, pp. 19–21. Other tea parties: William H. Ukers, *All About Tea* (2nd ed., New York, 1935) Vol. 1, pp. 58–65. Symbolic destruction of tea: Breen, loc. cit.

"This insipid beverage": Abbé Claude C. Robin, *Nouveau Voyage dans l'Amérique Septentrionale* (Philadelphia, 1782) p. 39. Rush changes his mind: Benjamin Rush, *An Inquiry into the Effects of Ardent Spirits upon the Human Body and Mind* (6th ed., New York, 1811) pp. 19–20; John F. Greden, "The Tea Controversy in Colonial America," *Journal of the American Medical Association*, Vol. 236 (1976), pp. 63–66. Ukers in error: William H. Ukers, *All*

About Coffee (2nd ed., New York, 1935) pp. 102–03. Change in source of immigration: Agnes Repplier, *To Think of Tea* (London, 1933) p. 134.

Coffee during the Civil War: Eliza McHatton-Ripley, *From Flag to Flag* (New York, 1889) p. 101; Joe Gray Taylor, *Eating, Drinking and Visiting in the South* (Baton Rouge, Louisiana, 1982) pp. 96–97; Francis Butler Simkins and James Welch Patton, *The Women of the Confederacy* (Richmond, Virginia, 1936) p. 140. "The greatest coffee consumers in the world": Francis B. Thurber, *Coffee: From Plantation to Cup* (New York, 1881) pp. 44–45. Per capita consumption: P. L. Simmonds, *Popular Beverages* (London, 1888) pp. 178–217. Coffee in the West: Josiah Gregg, *Commerce of the Prairies* (ed. Milo M. Quaife, Chicago, 1926) p. 44; Wayne Gard, *The Chisholm Trail* (Norman, Oklahoma, 1954) p. 122. Coca-Cola: Mark Pendergrast, *For God, Country, and Coca-Cola* (London, 1993) pp. 198–217.

Patrick Henry serves home-brewed beer: George F. Willison, *Patrick Henry and His World* (Garden City, New York, 1969) p. 35, in William J. Rorabaugh, *The Alcoholic Republic: An American Tradition* (New York, 1979) pp. 63–69. Decline of rum industry: Rorabaugh, loc. cit. "Natural liberty": George Harrison to David Holt, October 18, 1819, in "Every Man at Nature's Table has Has a Right to Elbow Room," *Friends Historical Society Journal*, Vol. 21 (1924), pp. 27–30; Fisher, op. cit., pp. 777–82. Hostility of Protestant to Catholic Irish: Kerby A. Miller, *Emigrants and Exiles: Ireland and the Irish Exodus to North America* (New York, 1985) p. 255. Ronald Reagan's ancestry: Anne Edwards, *Early Reagan: The Rise of an American Hero* (London, 1987) pp. 24–34.

Petition of western Pennsylvanians: Albert Gallatin, *Writings* (ed. Henry Adams, Philadelphia, 1879) Vol. 1, pp. 3–4. Scotch-Irish myths and Whiskey Rebellion: Jacob E. Cooke, "The Whiskey Insurrection: A Re-evaluation," *Pennsylvania History*, Vol. 30 (July 1963), pp. 316–46; Forrest McDonald, *Alexander Hamilton: A Biography* (New York, 1979) pp. 297–303. History of bourbon: Henry G. Crowgey, *Kentucky Bourbon: The Early Years of Whiskey Making* (Lexington, Kentucky, 1971); Gerald Carson, *The Social History of Bourbon* (New York, 1963). "This hosesome beverage": *Bluegrass Craftsman, Being the Reminiscences of Ebenezer Hiram Stedman, Paper Maker, 1808–1885* (ed. Francis L. S. Dugan and Jacqueline P. Bull, Lexington, Kentucky, 1959) pp. 181–82. Resistance by Kentucky distillers against excise tax: Willard R. Jillson, *Early Kentucky Distillers 1783–1800* (Louisville, Kentucky, 1940). Cheapness of whiskey: Daniel Drake, *A Discourse on Intemperance.* (Cincinnati, 1828) p. 23. National beverage: Harrison Hall, *The Distiller* (2nd ed., Philadelphia, 1818) p. 17, in Rorabaugh, op. cit., pp. 90–91. "The national beverage of California is whiskey": John H. Beadle, *The*

Undeveloped West (Philadelphia, 1873) pp. 747–48. Silver miners' dinner: Hesketh Pearson, *The Life of Oscar Wilde* (London, 1946) p. 73. Heavy drinking by miners: Allan M. Winkler, "Drinking on the American Frontier," *Quarterly Journal of Studies on Alcohol*, Vol. 29 (1968), pp. 413–45. Popularity of whiskey during the Civil War: William Howard Russell, *My Diary North and South* (ed. Fletcher Pratt, New York, 1954) pp. 170–71; Taylor, op. cit., pp. 102–03. Grant's whiskey drinking: F. B. Carpenter, *Six Months of the White House with Abraham Lincoln* (New York, 1867) p. 247; William S. McFeely, *Grant: A Biography* (1982) pp. 132–35.

Failure of English yeasts in America: Benjamin Silliman, *A Journal of Travels in England, Holland, and Scotland* (3rd ed., New Haven, 1820) Vol. 3, pp. 84–89. Lager "getting a good deal too fashionable": *The New York Times*, October 15, 1856, in Rorabaugh, op. cit., p. 109. Spokesman for the Cincinnati chamber of commerce: William L. Downard, *The Cincinnati Brewing Industry: A Social and Economic History* (Cincinnati, 1973) pp. 30–31. Effect of taxation: William J. Rorabaugh, "Beer, Lemonade and Propriety in the Gilded Age" in *Dining in America 1850–1900* (ed. Kathryn Grover, Amhurst, Massachusetts, 1987) pp. 24–46. Effect of bonding: Carson, op. cit., pp. 95–101. Consumption statistics: Rorabaugh, *The Alcoholic Republic*, pp. 232–33.

Increased competition among brewers: August F. Fehlandt, *A Century of Drink Reform in the United States* (Cincinnati, 1904) pp. 172–78. The "free lunch": George Ade, *The Old-Time Saloon* (New York, 1931) pp. 34–48; Andrew Sinclair, *Prohibition: The Era of Excess* (London, 1962) pp. 94–95. Bum's rush: Michael and Ariane Batterberry, *On the Town in New York* (New York, 1973) p. 147. Treating: Mark E. Lender and James K. Martin, *Drinking in America: A History* (2nd ed., New York, 1987) pp. 105–06. Creating an appetite among children: Peter H. Odegard, *Pressure Politics: The Story of the Anti-Saloon League* (New York, 1928) pp. 40–41. Evils of the saloon: *American Issue* (national edition), November 1912, in Odegard, op. cit., pp. 43–44.

Only Germans and Irish drink lager and whiskey: George A. Sala, *America Revisited* (London, 1882) Vol. 1, pp. 100–01. Nativist rhyme: Roy Rosenzweig, *Eight Hours for What We Will: Workers and Leisure in an Industrial City, 1870–1920* (Cambridge, 1983) pp. 49–50. "A religion of saloon keepers": Joan Bland, *Hibernian Crusade: The Story of the Catholic Total Abstinence Union of America* (Washington, D.C., 1951) p. 127. Symbolism of Irish drinking: Richard Stivers, *Hair of the Dog: Irish Drinking and the American Stereotype* (University Park, Pennsylvania, 1977) pp. 125–31; Lender and Martin, op. cit., p. 60. German gathering: Ibid., p. 62.

National German-American Alliance: Richard O'Connor, *The German-Americans: An Informal History* (Boston, 1968) pp. 386–87. John Schwaab: Sinclair, op. cit., p. 139. "Eat like gluttons and drink like swine": *The Worldwide Prohibition Program, Plans Inaugurated by the Conference of the Anti-Saloon League of America*, Columbus, Ohio, November 19–22, 1918, in Sinclair, op. cit., p. 134. "*Deutschland über Alles*": Sinclair, op. cit., p. 139. Revelations of *New York World* and comments of *New York Times*: James H. Timberlake, *Prohibition and the Progressive Movement 1900–1920* (Cambridge, Massachusetts, 1963) pp. 164–65. Popular hostility toward Germans and German culture: Carl Wittke, *German-Americans and the World War* (Columbus, Ohio, 1936) pp. 179–96. Senate resolution and investigation: O'Connor, op. cit., pp. 386–87. John Strange: *Milwaukee Journal*, February 13, 1918, in Thomas C. Cochran, *The Pabst Brewing Company: The History of an American Business* (New York, 1948) p. 320. Effect of the war upon German-Americans: John A. Hawgood, *The Tragedy of German-America* (New York, 1940) pp. 290–301; Stanley Baron, *Brewed in America: The History of Beer and Ale in the United States* (Boston, 1962) p. 305.

Beer during the Second World War: Jay L. Rubin, "The Wet War: American Liquor Control 1941–1945" in *Alcohol, Reform, and Society: The Liquor Issue in Social Context* (ed. Jack S. Blocker, Jr., Westport, Connecticut, 1979) pp. 235–58. Coors's support for extreme right-wing causes: Russ Bellant, *The Coors Connection* (Boston, 1990). Prohibitionists' claims about Pearl Harbor: Sam Morris, *Booze and the War* (Grand Rapids, Michigan, 1944) p. 9; Dan Gilbert, *What Really Happened at Pearl Harbor?* (Grand Rapids, Michigan, 1943) pp. 9–12; "Baptists Ask Ban on War Liquor," *Christian Century*, June 10, 1942, in Rubin, loc. cit. Enemy propagandists: "John Carlson," *Under Cover: My Four Years in the Nazi Underworld of America* (New York, 1943) pp. 516–17.

Advertisements designed to normalize beer consumption: John C. Burnham, *Bad Habits: Drinking, Smoking, Taking Drugs, Gambling, Sexual Misbehavior, and Swearing in American History* (New York, 1993) pp. 73–76, 78–80. Advertisements intended not only to influence brand preference but to increase total demand: Robert McBride, "Industry Structure, Marketing, and Public Health: A Case Study of the U.S. Beer Industry," *Contemporary Drug Problems*, Winter 1985, pp. 593–620; James D. Norris, *Advertising and the Transformation of American Society, 1865–1920* (Westport, Connecticut, 1990) n. 81 on p. 185; *USA Today*, January 31, 1997. Purchase of Miller by Philip Morris: John F. Cavanagh and Frederick F. Clairmonte, *Alcoholic Beverages: Dimensions of Corporate Power* (London, 1985) pp. 56–59; McBride, loc. cit.; Philip Van Munching, *Beer Blast* (New York, 1997) pp. 27–28, 64.

Samuel Adams: Baron, op. cit., pp. 75–76. *Ersatz* Löwenbräu: Van Munching, op. cit., pp. 51–54. Rivington and Harris: *Reminiscences of America in 1869 by Two Englishmen* (London, 1870) pp. 67–68. Better California wines passed off as foreign and inferior foreign wines as Californian: Vincent P. Carosso, *The California Wine Industry, 1830–1895* (Berkeley, California, 1951) pp. 25, 153–55; Thomas Pinney, *A History of Wine in America* (Berkeley, California, 1988) pp. 360, 493. Arpad Haraszthy: John N. Hutchison, "Northern California from Haraszthy to the Beginnings of Prohibition" in *The University of California/Sotheby Book of California Wine* (ed. Doris Muscatine, Maynard A. Amerine, and Bob Thompson, Berkeley, California, 1984) pp. 38–39. Pierre Klein: Charles L. Sullivan, *Like Modern Edens: Wine growing in the Santa Clara Valley and Santa Cruz Mountains 1798–1981* (Cupertino, California, 1982) pp. 54–55. Restaurants should do more to promote native wines: James Fullarton Muirhead, *The Land of Contrasts* (Boston, 1898) pp. 268–72.

Wine like a course in Gothic architecture: Frank Schoonmaker and Tom Marvel, *American Wines* (New York, 1941) pp. 4, 71–73. Thurber cartoon: James Thurber, *Vintage Thurber* (London, 1963) Vol. 1, p. 252. Gallo Pink Chablis: Andrew Barr, *Wine Snobbery* (New York, 1992) pp. 161–62, 216; Ellen Hawkes, *Blood and Wine* (New York, 1993) pp. 243–44. Joseph Gallo cheese: Ibid., pp. 300–96. Jack Davies: *The Wine Spectator* June 15, 1991, p. 25. Richard Nixon: H. R. Haldeman to Lucy Winchester, August 19, 1969, in *From the President: Richard Nixon's Secret Files* (ed. Bruce Oudes, London, 1989) p. 40.

Steven Spurrier tries to rig his tasting: Simon Loftus, *Anatomy of the Wine Trade: Abe's Sardines and Other Stories* (London, 1985) p. 120. Warren Winiarski: *Decanter*, February 1991, p. 32. William Hill and Frank Prial: *The New York Times* February 5, 1986. *Decanter* tasting of California chardonnays: *Decanter*, June 1997, pp. 70–74. Matt Kramer: *The Los Angeles Times* June 18, 1997. *Wine Spectator* tasting of California chardonnays: *The Wine Spectator*, July 31, 1997, pp. 38–60, 118–34. William Cash: *The Spectator*, August 2 and 23, 1997. Paul Draper: *The Vine*, No. 87 (April 1992) p. 46.

CONCLUSION

Dionysus: C. Kerényi, *Dionysos* (tr. Ralph Mannheim, London, 1977); Hanneke Wirtjes, "Dionysus" in *The Oxford Companion to Wine* (ed. Jancis Robinson, Oxford, 1994) pp. 325–26. "I am the true vine:" St. John's Gospel, 15: 1. "My blood of the new testament:" St. Matthew's Gospel, 26: 26–29. Jesus turns water into wine: St. John's Gospel, 2: 3–10. "My blood is drink indeed":

Ibid. 6: 51–58. Blood taboo: Salvatore P. Lucia, *A History of Wine as Therapy* (Philadelphia, 1963) p. 5. Communion wine: Thomas D. Terry, "Altar Wines" in *The University of California/Sotheby Book of California Wine* (ed. Doris Muscatine, Maynard A. Amerine, and Bob Thompson, Berkeley, California, 1984) pp. 297–301.

Pedro de Valdivia: R. B. Cunningham Graham, *Pedro de Valdivia, Conqueror of Chile* (London, 1925) p. 136; Ida W. Vernon, *Pedro de Valdivia, Conquistador of Chile* (Austin, Texas, 1946) pp. 64–65, 99. Vineyards in Chile: Edward Hyams, *Dionysus: A Social History of the Wine Vine* (London, 1965) pp. 255–59, 293–95. Eusebius Kino: *Kino Reports to Headquarters* (ed. and tr. Ernest J. Burrus, Rome, 1954) pp. 56–57 (November 21, 1683). Introduction of vines into California: Roy Brady, "Alta California's First Vintage" in *The University of California/Sotheby Book of California Wine*, pp. 10–15; Thomas Pinney, *A History of Wine in America from the Beginnings to Prohibition* (Berkeley, California, 1989) pp. 237–43; Desmond Seward, *Monks and Wine* (London, 1979) pp. 144–50. Agoston Haraszthy: Pinney, op. cit., pp. 269–84.

Giovanni da Verrazano: Ibid., p. 11. "Rather of scandal than credit": *The Records of the Virginia Company of London* (ed. S. M. Kingsbury, Washington, D.C., 1906–35) Vol. 3, pp. 646–67 June 10, 1622). Failure of efforts to grow European vines in America: Pinney, op. cit., pp. 25–29. Attempts to establish vine growing in South Carolina: Samuel Wilson, "An Account of the Province of Carolina" (1682) in *Narratives of Early Carolina 1650–1708* (ed. Alexander S. Salley, Jr., New York, 1911) pp. 174–75; John Oldmixon, "History of the British Empire in America" (1708) in *Narratives of Early Carolina* p. 371; David J. Mishkin, *The American Colonial Wine Industry: An Economic Interpretation* (Ph. D. dissertation, University of Illinois, 1966) pp. 275–78; Pinney, op. cit., pp. 33–38.

Revivalist preachers: Bernard A. Weisberger, *They Gathered at the River* (Boston, 1958). Connection between revivalism and temperance: Ian Tyrrell, *Sobering Up: From Temperance to Prohibition in Antebellum America* (Westport, Connecticut, 1979) pp. 58–63; William J. Rorabaugh, *The Alcoholic Republic* (New York, 1979) pp. 205–09. Methodist rules: Henry Wheeler, *Methodism and the Temperance Reformation* (Cincinnati, 1882) pp. 46, 81–94; "Methodist Episcopal Church," *Standard Encyclopaedia of the Alcohol Problem* (ed. Ernest H. Cherrington, Westerville, Ohio, 1925–30) Vol. 4, pp. 1748–50. Mormons and wine: Robert C. Fuller, *Religion and Wine* (Knoxville, Tennessee, 1996) pp. 60–66; "Church of Jesus Christ of Latter-Day Saints," *Standard Encyclopaedia of the Alcohol Problem* Vol. 2, pp. 611–14. Joseph Smith drank intemperately: LaMar Petersen, *Hearts Make Glad: The Charges of Intemperance Against Joseph Smith the Mormon Prophet* (Salt

Lake City, 1975), in Fuller, loc. cit. Wine no longer used in Mormon Sacrament: Walter Gore Marshall, *Through America* (London, 1881) p. 199. Evangelical churches wary of alcohol: Fuller, op. cit., pp. 56, 65.

Edward C. Delavan: P. T. Winskill, *The Comprehensive History of the Rise and Fall of the Temperance Reformation* (Crewe, 1881) pp. 204–07. Churches convert from Maderia to unfortified wine: James Boardman, *America and the Americans* (London, 1833) p. 360. "The simple wine of Palestine": Moses Stuart, *Essay on the Prize Question, Whether the Use of Distilled Liquors, or Traffic in Them, Is Compatible, at the Present Time, with Making a Profession of Christianity* (New York, 1830) pp. 23–27. Gerritt Smith: Tyrrell, op. cit., pp. 145–48. Two different kinds of wine: Moses Stuart, *Scriptural View of the Wine Question* (New York, 1848) pp. 48–49, 56.

Refusal of churches to convert to grape juice: Tyrrell, loc. cit. Thomas Welch: William Chazanof, *Welch's Grape Juice: From Corporation to Co-operative* (Syracuse, New York, 1977) pp. 76–77. Mrs. S. M. M. Woodman: Gilman Ostrander, *The Prohibition Movement in California 1848–1933* (Berkeley, California, 1957) pp. 36–37, 61. Churches abandon use of wine: "Communion Wine," *Standard Encyclopaedia of the Alcohol Problem* Vol. 2, pp. 665–71. Loophole for bootleggers: Roy Haynes, *Prohibition Inside Out* (London, 1923) pp. 210–12; Andrew Sinclair, *Prohibition* (London, 1962) pp. 212–13, 311.

Anti-Catholicism in the South: John Gunther, *Inside USA* (London, 1947) pp. 669–70. Chris Morris: *The Sunday Telegraph*, September 3, 1995. Decatur, Alabama: *The New York Times*, October 16, 1983. Attempt to change South Carolina minibottle law: *The New York Times*, April 23, 1991. Proportion of people who abstain on religious grounds: *Wine & Spirits*, March 1993, pp. 38–39. "There is no such thing as responsible drinking": David Wilkerson, *Sipping Saints* (Old Tappan, New Jersey, 1978) pp. 38, 74. America a highly religious country: *The Gallup Poll: Public Opinion 1993* (Wilmington, Delaware, 1994) pp. 71–83. Christian Brothers: Fuller, op. cit., pp. 28–30. Monastic wine and Dom Pérignon: Andrew Barr, *Drink: An Informal Social History* (London, 1995) pp. 120–23, 334. Fellowship of Friends: *The Evening Standard* October 6, 1992. Summum: Fuller, op. cit., pp. 70–73. Interest in wine a secular religion: Fuller, op. cit., pp. 96–109.

"A good creature of God": Increase Mather, *Wo to Drunkards* (2nd ed., Boston, 1712) p. 7. Small preferable to strong drink: William Penn, *Some Fruits of Solitude* (11th ed., Philadelphia, 1794) paragraphs 59–72 on pp. 29–30. Penn's brewhouse: Stanley Baron, *Brewed in America* (Boston, 1962)

p. 44. Progress of colony: William Penn, "A Further Account of the Province of Pennsylvania and Its Improvements" (October 12, 1685), *The Pennsylvania Magazine of History and Biography*, Vol. 9 (1885), pp. 63–81. Philadelphia beer exported: Gabriel Thomas, "An Historical and Geographical Account of Pennsylvania and West New Jersey" (1698) in *Narratives of Early Pennsylvania, West New Jersey and Delaware, 1630–1707* (ed. Albert C. Myers, New York, 1912) p. 327; Baron, op. cit., p. 73.

Cider takes over from beer: Sarah McMahon, "A Comfortable Subsistence: The Changing Composition of Diet in Rural New England, 1620–1840," *The William and Mary Quarterly*, 3rd series, Vol. 42 (1985), pp. 26–65. Popularity of cider: Jean-Anthelme Brillat-Savarin, *The Philosopher in the Kitchen* (tr. Anne Drayton, Harmondsworth, Middlesex, England, 1970) pp. 77–78 (part 1, ch. 6); Alice Morse Earle, *Stage-Coach and Tavern Days* (New York, 1900) pp. 125–30; Rorabaugh, op. cit., pp. 110–12. Samuel Parris: Stephen Nissenbaum, *Sex, Diet, and Debility in Jacksonian America: Sylvester Graham and Health Reform* (Westport, Connecticut, 1980) pp. 70, 83. London porter: Barr, op. cit., pp. 31–33, 61. Robert Hare: Baron, op. cit., pp. 114–15. George Washington: Letter to the Marquis de Lafayette, January 29, 1789, in *The Writings of George Washington* (ed. John C. Fitzpatrick, Washington, D.C., 1931–44) Vol. 30, pp. 184–87; Baron, op. cit., p. 59. "Even British palates have been deceived": Jacques Pierre Brissot de Warville, *New Travels in the United States of America, 1788* (tr. Mara S. Vamos and Durand Echeverria, Cambridge, Massachusetts, 1964) p. 91.

Revolution plotted in the taverns: Rorabaugh, op. cit., p. 35. Coffeehouses in the French Revolution: Arthur Young, *Travels in France* (ed. M. Betham-Edwards, 2nd ed., London, 1889) pp. 153–54. Coffeehouses in Istanbul: Antoine Galland, *De l'Origine et du Progrès du Café* (Caen, 1699) pp. 59–61; William H. Ukers, *All About Coffee* (2nd ed., New York, 1935) pp. 16–17; Ralph S. Hattox, *Coffee and Coffee Houses: The Origins of a Social Beverage in the Medieval Near East* (Seattle, 1988); Barr, op. cit., pp. 1–4. Coffeehouses in America: Ukers, op. cit., pp. 101–26.

All men were equal before the bottle: Rorabaugh, op. cit., p. 151. People expected to offer alcohol: Peter Cartwright, *Autobiography* (London, 1858) pp. 196–98; Daniel Drake, *Pioneer Life in Kentucky* (ed. Charles B. Drake, Cincinnati, 1870) p. 83; Daniel Drake, *A Discourse on Intemperance* (Cincinnati, 1828) p. 26. Constant tippling: Basil Hall, *Travels in North America in the Years 1827 and 1828* (Philadelphia, 1829) Vol. 1, p. 264; James Stuart, *Three Years in North America* (London, 1833) Vol. 1, pp. 401–03. Heavy drinking in West: Drake, *A Discourse on Intemperance*, pp. 35–38. Miners in California: Allan M. Winkler, "Drinking on the American Frontier," *Quarterly Journal of*

Studies on Alcohol, Vol. 29 (1968), pp. 413–45. "Dame Shirley": Louise Amelia Knapp Smith Clappe, *The Shirley Letters from the California Mines, 1851–52* (New York, 1949) pp. 102–06. Cowboys: Winkler, loc. cit. Fur trappers: Rorabaugh, op. cit., pp. 156–63. New pattern of drinking: Ibid.

Superior, Wisconsin: Laurence Oliphant, *Minnesota and the Far West* (Edinburgh, 1855) p. 165. Whiskey in taverns: Rorabaugh, op. cit., p. 16. Significance of treating: Roy Rosenzweig, *Eight Hours for What We Will: Workers and Leisure in an Industrial City, 1870–1920* (Cambridge, 1983) p. 59. "Will you drink or fight?" Frederick Marryat, *A Diary in America, with Remarks on Its Institutions* (New York, 1962) pp. 381–90. Houston in the 1830s: "Notes on Texas," *Hesperian, or Western Monthly Magazine*, Vol. 1, No. 6 (October 1838), p. 431, in William Ransom Hogan, *The Texas Republic: A Social and Economic History* (Norma, Oklahoma, 1946) p. 40.

Workplace drinking: Marianna Adler, "From Symbolic Exchange to Commodity Consumption: Anthropological Notes on Drinking as a Symbolic Practice" in *Drinking Behavior and Belief in Modern History* (ed. Susanna Barrows and Robin Room, Berkeley, California, 1991) pp. 376–98; Bruce Laurie, " 'Nothing on Compulsion': Life Styles of Philadelphia Artisans, 1820–1850," *Labor History*, Vol. 15 (1974), pp. 337–66. Brushmaker's apprentice: Jacob Carter, *My Drunken Life* (Boston, 1848) pp. 13–14. Treating in rural Ireland: Robert F. Bales, "Attitudes Toward Drinking in Irish Culture" in *Society, Culture, and Drinking Patterns* (ed. David J. Pittman and Charles R. Snyder, New York, 1962) pp. 157–87. Worcester Catholic temperance newspaper: *Catholic Messenger*, May 17, 1907, in Rosenzweig, op. cit., p. 60. Sam W. Small: Norman H. Clark, *Deliver Us from Evil* (New York, 1976) pp. 130–33. "The saloon fosters an un-American spirit": John M. Barker, *The Saloon Problem and Social Reform* (Boston, 1905) pp. 49–50, in James H. Timberlake, *Prohibition and the Progressive Movement 1900–1920* (Cambridge, Massachusetts, 1963) pp. 118–19. Importance of saloons to immigrant workers: William J. Rorabaugh, "Beer, Lemonade, and Propriety in the Gilded Age" in *Dining in America 1850–1900* (ed. Kathryn Grover, Amhurst, Massachusetts, 1987) pp. 25–46. "The relaxation brings rest:" *The Miners Magazine*, June 20, 1912, in Timberlake, op. cit., p. 94. The saloon and the church: F. Laubach, "What the Church May Learn from the Saloon," *Survey*, September 27, 1913, in Sinclair, op. cit., pp. 91–92.

Controls in Canada: James H. Gray, *Booze: The Impact of Whisky on the Prairie West* (Toronto, 1972) pp. 211–20. "A tolerated but somewhat furtive vice": George E. Catlin, *Liquor Control* (London, 1931) pp. 202–14. Beer parlours: Robert A. Campbell, " 'Profit Was Just a Circumstance': The Evolution of Government Liquor Control in British Columbia, 1920–1988" in

Drink in Canada: Historical Essays (ed. Cheryl K. Walsh, Montreal, 1993) pp. 177–78. Six o'clock swill: John M. Freeland, *The Australian Pub* (Carlton, Victoria, 1966) pp. 170–76; Barr, op. cit., pp. 141–44. W. H. Woodward: Conrad Bollinger, *Grog's Own Country* (Wellington, 1959). Arthur Reade: Central Board of the Licensed Victuallers' Central Protection Society of London, *An Examination of the Evidence before the Royal Commission on Licensing (England and Wales) 1929–1930* (London, 1931) p. 36. Opening hours in England: Barr, op. cit., pp. 136–63.

Packaged beer sales: David Fogarty, "From Saloon to Supermarket: Packaged Beer and the Reshaping of the U.S. Brewing Industry," *Contemporary Drug Problems*, Winter 1985, pp. 541–92. Lack of a "third place": Ray Oldenburg, *The Great Good Place* (New York, 1989). Beer gardens: Junius Henri Browne, *The Great Metropolis: A Mirror of New York* (Hartford, Connecticut, 1970) p. 159, in Oldenburg, op. cit., p. 98; Perry R. Duis, *The Saloon: Public Drinking in Chicago and Boston 1880–1920* (Urbana, Illinois, 1983) pp. 153–55. Committee of Fifty: Royal L. Melendy, "The Saloon in Chicago," *The American Journal of Sociology*, Vol. 6 (1900–01), pp. 289–306, 433–64. Danny Thames: *Decanter*, May 1997, p. 111.

Geoffrey of Monmouth: *Old English Chronicles* (ed. John A. Giles, London, 1908) pp. 186–87. Quaker betrothal: *Our Revolutionary Forefathers: The Letters of François, Marquis de Barbé-Marbois* (tr. and ed. Eugene Parker Chase, New York, 1929) pp. 154–55. Father and son drink from same glass: Rorabaugh, *The Alcoholic Republic*, p. 14. Puritans regard toasting as profane: William Hinde, *A Faithful Remonstrance of the Holy Life and Happy Death of John Bruen* (London, 1641) pp. 192–93; Increase Mather, *A Testimony Against Several Profane and Superstitious Customs Now Practised by Some in New England* (London, 1687) pp. 19–30. General Court in Boston: *Records of the Governor and Company of the Massachusetts Bay in New England* (ed. Nathaniel B. Shurtleff, Boston, 1853) Vol. 1, p. 271 (September 9, 1639) and Vol. 2, p. 121 (May 14, 1645). Conservatism of colonists: David Fischer, *Albion's Seed: Four British Folkways in America* (New York, 1989) pp. 55–57, 253–55, 468–69. What Paul Revere actually said: David Fischer, *Paul Revere's Ride* (New York, 1994) pp. 109–10.

Social function of toasting: François-Jean, Marquis de Chastellux, *Travels in North America in the Years 1780, 1781, and 1782* (tr. and ed. Howard C. Rice, Jr., Chapel Hill, North Carolina, 1963) pp. 109–10. Origin of "toast": *The Tatler*, No. 24 (June 2, 1709). Political toasts: John Lambert, *Travels Through Lower Canada and the United States of North America in the Years 1806, 1807, and 1808* (London, 1810) Vol. 2, p. 218; Jefferson Williamson, *The American Hotel: An Anecdotal History* (New York, 1930) pp. 192–223.

More ridiculous aspects of toasting: Elkanah Watson, *Men and Times of the Revolution* (ed. Winslow C. Watson, New York, 1856) pp. 137–38; Marquis de Chastellux, op. cit., pp. 132–33. Decline of toasting: *The American Chesterfield*, by a member of the Philadelphia Bar (Philadelphia, 1828) p. 247. Lip service: *The Perfect Gentleman*, by a Gentleman (New York, 1860) pp. 182–87. Toasting in the late nineteenth century: Florence Howe Hall, *Social Customs* (Boston, 1887) p. 82. Drinking from a skull: Richard Valpy French, *The History of Toasting* (London, 1882) p. 46. Richard Nixon: Bob Woodward and Carl Bernstein, *The Final Days* (London, 1976) p. 238.

"Cheerfulness and good humor": Benjamin Rush, *An Inquiry into the Effects of Ardent Spirits upon the Human Body and Mind* (6th ed., New York, 1811) p. 13. P. T. Barnum: Arthur H. Saxon, *P. T. Barnum: The Legend and the Man* (New York, 1989) pp. 62–65; Philip B. Kunhardt, Jr., et al., *P. T. Barnum: America's Greatest Showman* (New York, 1995) pp. 82–83. Thomas Welch: Chazanof, op. cit., pp. 7–9. "Pharmacological Calvinism": Gerald L. Klerman, "Psychotropic Hedonism v. Pharmacological Calvinism," *Hastings Center Report*, Vol. 2, No. 4 (1972), pp. 1–3, in Peter D. Kramer, *Listening to Prozac* (London, 1994) pp. 274. Dangers of binge drinking: Serge Renaud, "Wine, Alcohol, Platelets, and the French Paradox for Coronary Heart Disease," *The Lancet*, Vol. 339 (1992), pp. 1523–26.

John of Salisbury: Richard Valpy French, *Nineteen Centuries of Drink* (London, 1884) pp. 68–69. "Malt-worms": Philip Stubbes, *The Anatomy of Abuses* (London, 1583) folio 62. Maid on the *Arbella*: *Winthrop's Journal, "The History of New England," 1630–1649* (ed. James K. Hosmer, New York, 1908) Vol. 1, p. 38 (May 3, 1630). Government of Connecticut: *The Public Records of the Colony of Connecticut* (ed. J. Hammond Trumbull, Hartford, 1850) Vol. 1, p. 154 (May 25, 1647). Harm caused by rum: Cotton Mather, *Theopolis Americana* (Boston, 1710) pp. 31–36. "Too much whiskey": Anne N. Royall, Letter No. 8 from Nashville, December 18, 1817 in *Letters from Alabama 1817–1822* (ed. Lucille Griffith, University, Alabama, 1969) pp. 92–95. Temperance cycles: *The New York Times*, January 1, 1991. Arpad Haraszthy: Vincent P. Carosso, *The California Wine Industry, 1830–1895* (Berkeley, California, 1951) p. 132. Wally's Liquors: *The Los Angeles Times* August 24, 1987. Nondrinking collectors: *The Wine Advocate*, No. 70 (August 1990) p. 35. Wine in Louisiana: Timothy Flint, *Recollections of the Last Ten Years, Passed in Occasional Residences and Journeyings in the Valley of the Mississippi . . . in a Series of Letters to the Rev. James Flint of Salem, Massachusetts* (Boston, 1826) p. 336; *Gumbo Ya-Ya: Folk Tales of Louisiana* (ed. Lyle Saxon et al., Gretna, Louisiana, 1987) p. 172. The only thing we learn from history: George Hegel, *Lectures on the Philosophy of History* (tr. J. Sibree, London, 1857), Introduction, p. 6.

Further Reading

It has been the intention of this book to interest the general reader as well as the professional historian. Unfortunately, the same cannot be said for the majority of books written on the history of drink in America. These have tended to concentrate, moreover, on the problems caused by excessive consumption of alcoholic beverages and on campaigns to have them banned, rather than on the pleasurable and social aspects of drinking.

A good but uninspiring overview of the history of the "drink problem" is Mark E. Lender and James K. Martin, *Drinking in America: A History* (2nd ed., New York, 1987). More entertaining, although more academic, is William J. Rorabaugh, *The Alcoholic Republic: An American Tradition* (New York, 1979), which concentrates on the period between 1790 and 1840, when the unhealthy drinking practices that created the "drink problem" were established. The best book on Prohibition remains Andrew Sinclair, *Prohibition: The Era of Excess* (Boston and London, 1962), which has been criticized for its cynicism but provides the most informative and amusing account of the period. For a more sociological approach, see Norman H. Clark, *Deliver Us from Evil: An Interpretation of American Prohibition* (New York, 1976). Unusual perspectives are offered by John C. Burnham, *Bad*

Habits: Drinking, Smoking, Taking Drugs, Gambling, Sexual Misbehavior, and Swearing in American History (New York, 1993) and Robert C. Fuller, *Religion and Wine: A Cultural History of Wine Drinking in the United States* (Knoxville, Tennessee, 1996). A necessary debunking of the prevailing modern interpretation of the "drink problem" is provided by Stanton Peele, *Diseasing of America: How We Allowed Recovery Zealots and the Treatment Industry to Convince Us We Are Out of Control* (New York, 1995).

Whereas a lot has been written about the politics of drink, relatively little has been published on the drinks themselves. The need exists for up-to-date histories of beer and whiskey, and for a secular history of wine drinking in America. Vine growing, however, has been well covered in Thomas Pinney, *A History of Wine in America from the Beginnings to Prohibition* (Berkeley, California, 1989), Leon D. Adams, *The Wines of America* (4th ed., New York, 1990) and *The University of California/Sotheby Book of California Wine* (ed. Doris Muscatine, Maynard A. Amerine, and Bob Thompson, Berkeley, California, 1984). On imported wines, Hugh Johnson, *The Story of Wine* (London, 1989) is magisterial but oddly old-fashioned in its narrative approach. There is also a great deal of useful information on all kinds of drinks in Richard J. Hooker, *A History of Food and Drink in America* (Indianapolis, 1981). William Grimes, *Straight Up or On the Rocks: A Cultural History of American Drink* (New York, 1993) is more limited in its scope than its subtitle pretends; it provides a short history of the cocktail. Of the books devoted to the martini, Lowell Edmunds, *The Silver Bullet: The Martini in American Civilization* (Westport, Connecticut, 1981) is the most erudite, and Barnaby Conrad, III, *The Martini: An Illustrated History of an American Classic* (San Francisco, 1995) the best looking. The most enlightening book on a soft drink is Mark Pendergrast's exhaustive *For God, Country, and Coca-Cola: The Unauthorized History of the Great American Soft Drink and the Company That Makes It* (New York, 1993).

The most authoritative history of food in America is to be found in two sequential volumes by Harvey Levenstein, *Revolution at the Table: The Transformation of the American Diet* (New York, 1988) and *Paradox of Plenty: A Social History of Eating in Modern America* (New York, 1993) but unfortunately they cover only the last century or so. A wider span is encompassed by Waverley Root and Richard de Rochemont in their entertaining but unreliable *Eating in America: A His-*

tory (New York, 1976), and an ever wider one by Reay Tannahill in her classic *Food in History* (New York, 1988).

On the social history of America, the three volumes by Daniel Boorstin, *The Americans: The Colonial Experience* (New York, 1958), *The Americans: The National Experience* (New York, 1965), and *The Americans: The Democratic Experience* (New York, 1973), remain unsurpassed.